CHICAGO'S HISTORIC HYDE PARK

CHICAGO'S HISTORIC HYDE PARK

SUSAN O'CONNOR DAVIS

THE UNIVERSITY OF CHICAGO PRESS ❧ CHICAGO AND LONDON

Susan O'Connor Davis is an
independent scholar and a
founding member of the Kenwood
Improvement Association. After
working in the design industry for
nearly twenty years, Davis now
serves on the board of governors
at the Smart Museum of Art at the
University of Chicago.

The University of Chicago Press, Chicago 60637
The University of Chicago Press, Ltd., London
© 2013 by The University of Chicago
All rights reserved. Published 2013.
Printed in the United States of America
22 21 20 19 18 17 16 15 14 13   1 2 3 4 5

ISBN-13: 978-0-226-13814-5 (cloth)
ISBN-10: 0-226-13814-3 (cloth)

Library of Congress Cataloging-in-Publication Data
Davis, Susan O'Connor, author.
    Chicago's historic Hyde Park / Susan O'Connor Davis.
        pages cm
    Foreword by John Vinci.
    Includes index.
    ISBN 978-0-226-13814-5 (cloth : alk. paper) 1. Hyde Park (Chicago, Ill.)—History. 2. Hyde Park (Chicago, Ill.)—
    Buildings, structures, etc. 3. Dwellings—Illinois—Chicago—History. 4. Architecture—Illinois—Chicago—History.
    I. Vinci, John, writer of added commentary. II. Title.
        F548.68.H9D38 2013
        977.3'1—dc23
                                                                    2012048349

Frontispiece: from *Picturesque Kenwood*, c. 1890, courtesy of University of Chicago Library, Special Collections
Research Center

♾ This paper meets the requirements of ANSI/NISO Z39.48–1992 (Permanence of Paper).

For Jordan and Allison

Contents

Foreword

JOHN VINCI

Throughout my career as a Chicago architect, I have been an admirer and a participant in the Hyde Park community. Over the years, the perception of Hyde Park as a center of leadership in the arts and in politics has led me to study its history. In 1890, two events altered its role as a satellite community to a major urban center. That year planning for the World's Columbian Exhibition of 1893 began, and the University of Chicago was founded, adding an intellectual component to an already enlightened community. The school became known for promoting liberal values and for hiring progressive scholars.

Among its initial faculty members were professors such as John Dewey, Thorstein Veblen, Charles Richmond Henderson, and Oscar Lovell Triggs. Each contributed to expanding the vision of the socialist and art reformer William Morris and the Arts and Crafts Movement begun in England in the 1850s. Besides writing the 1906 essay "Culture and Industry in Education," John Dewey was instrumental in founding the University of Chicago Laboratory Schools. Veblen's 1899 book *The Theory of the Leisure Class* combined sociology with economic production, and in his 1902 essay "Arts and Crafts," published in the *Journal of Political Economy*, he acknowledged "the necessity of the machine" as a factor to be considered in the creative process, a sentiment espoused by Frank Lloyd Wright in his 1901 Hull-House lecture "The Arts and Crafts of the Machine." In Triggs's 1903 essay "A School of Industrial Art," published in the *Craftsman Magazine*, he reinforced that idea. "The new school brings art and labor into necessary association," he wrote. An amusing quote from Henderson's 1908 book, *The Social Spirit in America*, illustrates the condition of taste and the presumed role of members of the new social class:

> We make our houses and they turn upon us the image of our own taste and permanently fix it in our very nature. Our works and our surroundings corrupt or refine our souls. The dwelling, the walls, the windows, the roof, the furniture, the pictures, the ornaments, the dress, the fence or hedge—all act constantly upon the imagination and determine its contents. If a family realizes this truth it will seek to beautify the objects which are silently and unceasingly writing their

nature upon the man within the breast. When the families of a community give no heed to this truth there is missionary ground. . . .

Every county fair might furnish a school of artistic arrangement of the household, from kitchen to parlor. Furniture dealers from cities would be willing to send artists to present a model of desirable interiors. Architects would supply plans and views of charming homes. But the managers must be very careful in selecting the tradesmen who are to make the exhibit and the judges who are made to assign the awards. At this point it would be wise to secure the advice of teachers of art in responsible schools.

One has to believe that these reformers laid the groundwork that influenced the temperament and the tastes of their neighbors. Their presence and that of other faculty members in the community promoted liberal social values and created an intellectual climate.

Architects such as Frank Lloyd Wright, Allen and Irving Pond, Thomas Tallmadge and Vernon Watson, Hugh Garden, George Maher, and Howard Van Doren Shaw found this area of Chicago fertile ground for their trade. Professors and graduates of the university and affluent businessmen gravitated to Hyde Park–Kenwood.

The liberal climate drew figures such as the noted lawyer Clarence Darrow. US senator Paul Douglas, a graduate of the university, was a founder of the Hyde Park Art Center in 1940 and later became known as "the People's Senator." Another famous resident, Leon Mathis Despres, grew up in Hyde Park, attended the University of Chicago, and in 1957, as the alderman of the city's Fifth Ward, initiated landmark designation in Chicago. Despres's wife, Marian, was the daughter of the architect Alfred S. Alschuler and was a leader in the preservation movement.

The promotion of the visual arts was in evidence in the community as early as 1915. The Renaissance Society was founded at the University of Chicago to propagate the arts and gradually began to exhibit modern and avant-garde works. In 1958, Joseph Shapiro, a trustee and benefactor of the university, initiated lending art to students for their dormitories and homes. Many of Chicago's great twentieth-century art patrons, whom I had the privilege to know, began their collections while living in Hyde Park–Kenwood. These included Rose and Morton Neumann, Eleanor and Barnet Hodes, Lindy and Edwin Bergman (both graduates of the university), Adele and Arnold Maremont, and Ruth and Leonard Horwich. The Neumanns and the Hodeses lived next door to each other in Jackson Towers, an apartment building on East 56th Street. According to the Hodeses' daughter, Kay Kamin, her father, the committeeman for the city's Fifth Ward, and Morton Neumann, the owner of Valmor hair-care products, took an art history course at the University of Chicago with the professor Whitney Halstead. Edwin Bergman later became the chairman of the board of the university.

As a young architect I had the opportunity to work for Dan Brenner, a principal of the firm Brenner Danforth Rockwell, who lived in Hyde Park. Among the clients whom I worked with on the design of their homes were the psychiatrists

Charles Kligerman, George Pollock, and Zane Parzen. They were among those who invested in the revitalization of Hyde Park in the midsixties.

But it was the native Hyde Parker Jean F. Block, the president of Midway Editorial Research, who decided to write a book about Hyde Park's history and its architecture. She was a founder of the Hyde Park Historical Society and instrumental in saving South Lake Park's old Cable Car Building, which I was then restoring. Along with her son, Samuel W. Block Jr., who was the photographer for the book, she canvassed the neighborhood, wrote a comprehensive history, and in 1978 produced *Hyde Park Houses: An Informal History, 1856–1910*, a book that is admired and emulated but is now out of print. Jean Block was a consummate researcher and a volunteer at the Joseph Regenstein Library at the university. She was also the author of *The Uses of Gothic: Planning and Building the Campus of the University of Chicago 1892–1932*.

I met Susan and Allison Davis in 1998, when I was commissioned to design their house on South Greenwood Avenue in Kenwood. Our friendship grew as we continued to learn more about one another. Allison's father and mother were both educators. His father, William Boyd Allison Davis, was an anthropologist and in 1942 was the first African American to be given a full faculty position at the University of Chicago.

Both Susan and I are native Chicagoans and have long admired Hyde Park. Our paths had crossed earlier when Susan was the regional manager for Knoll International. As a resident of Hyde Park–Kenwood, Susan came to know and love the architecture of the neighborhood. Her initial idea was to continue where Jean Block left off, beginning in 1910 with Frank Lloyd Wright's Robie House and updating the book to the present. Susan asked that I assist her. Susan moved ahead, collecting data from Hyde Park's beginnings to 2012. Allison, a lawyer and a developer who was a trustee of the University of Chicago Hospitals, was enthusiastic and supportive.

Soon Susan decided to add demolished structures of historical importance, as well as notable structures of architectural interest, to present a clearer picture of the evolving environment. As the project grew, we realized that in order to make a comprehensive and useful guide, Hyde Park and South Kenwood should be included in one volume from its inception to the present day. Delving into the historical underpinnings of the neighborhood produced a trove of engaging facts that only enlivened the book's content.

The pages that follow are the results of Susan's efforts. Arranged first according to "eras," and then roughly geographically, you will find the houses, homes, and history of Hyde Park–Kenwood.

Introduction

As the forty-fourth president-elect of the United States left home for Washington, DC, his motorcade proceeded under a cold and clear sky so typical of a Chicago winter morning. Beneath a vault of intermingled limbs, tinted windows opened to reveal black-capped figures armed with automatic weapons that demonstrated the power of the occupant. The entourage whisked by in stark contrast to the snow-covered lawns of gracious houses, where neighbors stood waving their good-byes.

On January 20, 2009, before a crowd of millions, amid the hopes of a nation and the attention of the world, this unlikely candidate became the most powerful person on Earth.

Three weeks later the First Family came home.

What is the significance of this simple act of coming home—a moment repeated day after day, in cities and towns across the country? What kind of neighborhood and what kind of house have the power to draw us with their comfort? An enduring sense of community has long distinguished the president's chosen neighborhood, and those who built it. Put simply there's something distinctive about this place and the sensibility of those who choose to live here—a feeling of attachment and belonging that goes deep, and lasts a long time. To fully understand Barack Obama's community we have look to the very foundations of the place this multicultural, urbane president chose to call home, Chicago's Hyde Park neighborhood and the adjacent historic district of Kenwood.

On the eve of the Civil War, a lawyer and real estate speculator named Paul Cornell opened a fashionable hotel on a sandy lakeside landscape, naming it Hyde Park House. His foresight in developing an area to the south of Chicago, in assessing the importance of transportation and the subsequent escalating values of real estate, brought to him a fortune and to the city a unique neighborhood that became, for a time, the city's social and political epicenter. Chicago was then becoming known worldwide for railroads, stockyards, and first-class architecture. Almost as soon as Cornell opened his hotel, the surrounding communities experienced a rapid growth that paralleled that of the larger city. But it was in 1893, when Hyde Park served as the location for the Columbian Exposition and witnessed the founding of the University of Chicago, that the area and its population began to grow even more dramatically, bringing with that growth the complex issues that are an inevitable aspect of urban life. Hyde Park was not to escape those concerns, although the future held great promise.

Ringed by a series of parks and boulevards conceived by noted landscape architect Frederick Law Olmsted, Hyde Park and Kenwood became among the most fashionable neighborhoods in the Midwest. The tree-lined streets were gracious, and genteel hotels built to accommodate visitors to the Columbian Exposition offered Chicagoans wide verandahs and ready access to the lakeshore. The advent of motion pictures brought new cinema palaces; the "horseless carriage" meant easier access to the business district in the Loop; and the growing prominence of the University of Chicago made the area attractive to individuals with intellectual and cultural interests.

Amid this atmosphere of high-toned prosperity, business and civic leaders employed the best the architectural profession had to offer. The Ryersons, whose wealth came from the steel industry; the Swift and Morris families, whose fortunes derived from the meatpacking industry; and the faculty and administrators of the university sought the most outstanding designers of the time for their residences. Among the many architects who worked in Hyde Park–Kenwood were Howard van Doren Shaw, George Maher, and Frank Lloyd Wright. The works they created represented the aspirations of a newly emerging and culturally ambitious society.

However, the greatest challenges for the neighborhood were just beginning. Urban decay set in after a depression and two world wars, compounded with a broad shift in demographics that occurred as a result of the great migration of blacks from the Deep South to the industrialized North. In the face of a dramatic shift, Hyde Park and Kenwood represent the success of a plan conceived to achieve racial integration at a time when such a community was unheard of. It is a remarkable neighborhood that came to grips with some of the city's and the nation's most difficult problems during its transformation from bucolic suburb to urban neighborhood.

The community endured as a result of negotiation and difficult compromise. Today restored mansions stand beside low-income housing. Against what seemed to be irreversible decline just three decades ago, home values have increased dramatically in recent years. Rather than pulling up stakes in the 1950s as they had contemplated, the University of Chicago remained and anchors the area both economically and architecturally, combining the neo-Gothic style of its early buildings with new structures by Cesar Pelli, Harry Weese, Ricardo Legorreta, and other distinguished designers.

The Hyde Park–Kenwood neighborhood provides a rich context for a thought-provoking examination not only of architectural styles, but also of the area's social history and the divergent needs of the changing population. There were many dark chapters in the process, from racially restrictive housing covenants to wholesale clearance of undesirable areas, but in the end, Hyde Park and Kenwood are noteworthy examples of what can be achieved both in society and in architecture.

Stunning in its architectural beauty, the urban landscape here developed as the result of a long series of decisions by individual landowners asserting their place within a larger social framework. The unifying environment was not the result of urban renewal, or University of Chicago policies, or city government, although all of those affected the community. Rather, those who chose to reside in the community created and nurtured from its outset what is today one of the best places in America to view the rich complexity and evolution of residential architecture whose history reflects the spirit of ever-changing eras.

The concept for this project began as a continuation of Jean Block's popular and beloved 1978 book, entitled simply *Hyde Park Houses*. The manuscript grew over time to encompass not only the hundred years subsequent to the period covered in her work, but also to revisit the community's earliest days. The goal was to provide the reader with a compelling visual account of the evolution of the neighborhood and the residences that define it, lushly illustrated with current and archival images. Broadly defined to include single-family houses, apartments, and hotels, the "family residence" is woven into the book's eight chapters, which reconstruct chronologically the historical context in which the structures were created. Maps, anecdotes, and scholarly sources provide a deep history of the rich tradition and vitality of one of Chicago's oldest neighborhoods.

The manuscript developed as a narrative that encourages readers to think about the built world that surrounds them, presents multiple viewpoints, and suggests an open-ended view of the laboratory of life. It is a study of the residential structure, wrapped in the historic sensibilities we use to view an object, as well as a study of those who built and occupied those structures. Thus architecture is not reduced to a single theme; rather, it is a multifaceted experience, allowing readers to develop and appreciate a critical awareness of their surroundings.

There are many to thank for their guidance and assistance in this project. Noted architect and preservationist John Vinci has been a stalwart supporter of the project, offering guidance and perspective. From his initial comment, "That's a great idea," through countless suggestions, he never waivered in his enthusiasm for and belief in the book. Historian Neil Harris provided wise counsel and direction in my times of uncertainty. Readers Ann Durkin Keating and Robert Bruegmann offered diligent, thoughtful, and concise commentary on the manuscript. The Graham Foundation and Driehaus Foundation each generously awarded grants in support of research and publication. Kevin Eatinger responded to requests for additional photography with a ready smile and able camera. Robert Devens has been a stalwart editor, offering patience and assurance, while the team at the Press thoroughly organized the vast array of details. Bruce Sagan shared his experiences and demonstrated an enduring love for this community. Leslie Coburn offered thorough fact checking and research, and Joseph Biggott historical perspective, while Sam Guard enthralled with stories that brought neighbors long-gone back to life. Tom Willcockson created an array of maps, edited time and again. Gwenda Blair, Linda Rahm, and Ann Kowalski read and edited the initial text. And to others who shared their maps, stories, images, insight, and advice, my thanks.

And lastly, my profound gratitude for the love and support of my husband Allison and daughter Jordan, for they made the long, lonely days of writing worth all the effort.

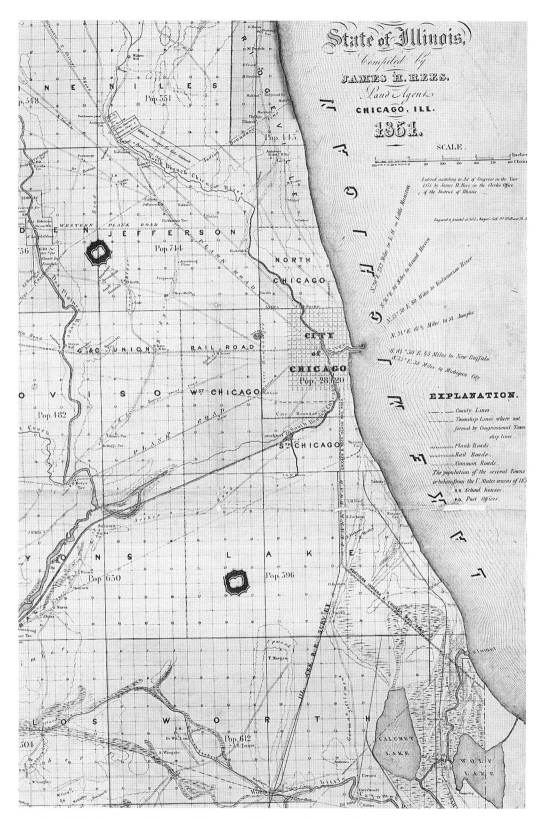

1.01. James H. Rees's 1851 map of the city of Chicago and the surrounding region demonstrates development prior to the extensive growth of the railroad network. The map shows the plank road adjacent to the Chicago, Rock Island Railway line, and the "road to the east" that began at 12th Street, where travelers leaving the city navigated the sandy ridges and low-lying swamps along lakeshore as the route passed Watson's Tavern and the present site of Hyde Park. Rees was a land agent who negotiated real estate transactions and provided valuable information— including locations of rivers and swampy areas, schools and post offices, and roads and taverns—to potential investors.

CHAPTER ONE

A Tapestry Unfolds, 1847–1870

Leaving the city pavements at Twelfth Street, we struck across the prairie, with its velvety turf roads, and following the curve of the shore of Lake Michigan came to the enchanting ground of gravel ridges with deep loam hollows between which tell of receding waters. All of the ridges were decorated with oak trees and wild fruit trees and vines, with wild roses and hazel shrubbery beneath. . . . All the low land had a variety of willows, and every kind of flower that loves to have its feet in water, while the grass fields that stretched between the ridges were blue with violets.

—Annie McClure Hitchcock, "Reminiscences of Kenwood in 1859"

Located just eight miles to the south of the bustling central business district of Chicago, Hyde Park and the adjacent historic district of Kenwood have a long, storied, and sometimes contentious history. Nestled along the sandy shores of Lake Michigan and along the stage route from the east, the area was relatively quiet in its earliest days. Defined topographically by sandy ridges and low-lying swamps, the shoreline was several blocks west of its current location. Then, marshes and sand gave way to prairies—filled with bluestem, switchgrass, cone-flower, and blazing star—stretching westward for hundreds of miles. Home to several Potawatomie settlements, these lands passed into the control of the United States after the Black Hawk War ended in 1832. One of the earliest recorded white residents was a homesteader named Obadiah Hooper; he settled eighty acres in Lake Township when the federal government opened the land around Chicago for settlement in 1835.[1]

That same year Nathan Watson settled his large family south of the Hooper land and opened a tavern in a small log cabin in present-day Hyde Park on 53rd Street at the lakefront, catering to travelers coming to and from the city.[2] In 1836, Thomas Leeds Morgan spent the night at the tavern while riding by horseback from Chicago around the south end of the lake to Michigan City. When Watson explained that he intended to raise fruit in "these sand piles," Morgan regarded the terrain and politely suggested "he have his friends put him in an asylum."[3]

Disregarding this advice, in 1844 Watson purchased a large tract of 75.4 acres adjacent to his tavern.[4] As an ever-increasing stream of newcomers passed Watson's door, Chicago was quickly becoming a "city on the make."[5] With origins as a small trading center, Chicago soon witnessed a period of intense real estate speculation, becoming home to over 4,000 by the time the city was incorporated in 1837.[6] Although the real estate bubble burst and an economic downturn followed, within a decade the outlook improved and the population increased five-fold.

This was a pivotal time in Chicago's history, as developments in the city's infrastructure permitted its future growth as the "leading metropolis of the Midwest."[7] The Illinois & Michigan Canal opened in April 1848 and the telegraph line between Chicago and Milwaukee was extended, linking the midwestern cities with the East Coast. That same year inventor Cyrus McCormick moved his reaper manufacturing plant to Chicago, the Board of Trade was founded, and the fledgling railroad lines embarked upon an expansion that would make Chicago the railroad hub of the nation within a decade.[8]

As the scale of commerce and industry began to change dramatically, many were drawn by the promise the developing city offered, including an ambitious twenty-five-year-old lawyer named Paul Cornell. When he arrived in the city on a Frink & Walker stagecoach, his sole belongings were the suit he was wearing, a package of law cards on which was written *Paul Cornell, Attorney at Law, Chicago*, a package of clothing, and $1.50 in cash. When he checked into the Lake House, a three-story hotel on the southeast corner of Hubbard and Rush Streets, a thief promptly took his belongings and left him with a rather discouraging situation.[9]

Endowed with a "serviceable quality which the Yankee calls pluck,"[10] Cornell was undeterred and joined the law office of Wilson & Freer. Although he soon won his first case, he earned the sum of only one dollar.[11] In a letter written to his uncle, Heman K. Hopkins, in 1848, Cornell betrayed a lack of confidence in his abilities as a lawyer, yet was optimistic about Chicago's future:

> Dear Uncle, . . . I have been in this place since the 1st of June/47 endeavoring to work my way into the practice of Law and tho not *wholly* without success, yet, I find I lack a considerable of being a good Lawyer or eaven one that mite pass readily in our own back woods. . . . I am now a little more than paying my way and our young City offends tolerable fair opportunities for learning and I am in hopes before long to be able to do something for myself—Our Garden City (as it is termed) is quite a thrifty place,—it contains about 20,000 inhabitants and the canal which is now in full opperation together with the Plank Roads and the Rail Road which is now being constructed from it, seems to attract the attention of many Capitalist and tradesmen and this year it appears to be improving more rapidly than usual.[12]

Cornell moved to the firm of Skinner & Hoyne, and through Judge Mark Skinner he met Stephen A. Douglas, whose advice inspired his future. Douglas, a powerful Democratic senator from Illinois, purchased seventy acres of land along Lake

Michigan in 1852 that extended from what is now 31st Street south to 35th Street.[13] He envisioned a southward expansion of the city and encouraged Cornell to put all the money he could save into the land "between the Chicago River and the Calumet."[14]

Lake Calumet was far outside the city, the limits of which stretched south only as far as 12th Street. From there further transportation required crossing the prairie along a "single buggy track" running south from the corner of State and 12th Streets toward the "oak woods," as the area near 35th Street was then called.[15] Along the way the stage road passed a beautiful grove south of 28th Street on the lake, the site of a resort house called "the cottage," and at 31st Street, the property of Stephen Douglas.[16]

Heeding Douglas's advice, as well as the recommendation of his physician, Cornell further familiarized himself with the area. The clean air found outside the crowded city was thought a common remedy for various ailments, and when Cornell's doctor advised the slender, dark-haired young man to "take exercise and fresh air" during a spell of poor health, he purchased a horse and rode out past the Douglas property to the farm owned by the widow of Nathan Watson.[17] Although she had remarried, Electa Watson Garnsey continued to run the tavern as a boardinghouse on the lakeshore, where Cornell would rest and drink a glass of milk before riding back to the city.

Through a new partnership with William T. Barron, Cornell accumulated sufficient funds to follow Douglas's counsel, and hired John Boyd to make a topographical survey made of the Watson/Garnsey farm and surrounding area. His initial purchase of sixty acres from Electa and Chester Garnsey in August 1853 became the center of the community he intended to develop.[18] On May 26, 1855, Cornell added another piece of the Watson property, paying $11,750 for the section between 52nd and 53rd Streets.[19] Through a series of subsequent purchases, Paul Cornell eventually accumulated three hundred acres along the lakeshore.[20]

Cornell's land was defined by a series of sandy ridges that ran diagonally across the prairie, and the lower ground between was often covered with muddy water. In dry weather the most efficient route for travel to the south and east from the growing city was the Stage Road (later Lake and Stony Island Avenues) that ran through his property, around the lake, and on to Detroit. During inclement weather, travelers were forced to venture further westward to a ridge on Vincennes Avenue, a road predominantly used by farmers transporting livestock and grain. However, improvements in transportation beyond the stage line were progressing steadily as the development of the nation's railway system was underway.

Understanding that transportation was key to the success of his development, Cornell negotiated a strategic alliance with the Illinois Central Railroad in order to guarantee convenient transportation and attract future residents. In 1851 the railroad was chartered to build a line from Cairo in southern Illinois to Galena, with a branch from Centralia to Chicago. Initially, the Chicago Branch Line route was planned to pass west of Hyde Park along Halsted Street and near the Chicago River. The Chicago City Council, however, insisted the right of way be near the lakefront and that the railway absorb the cost of building a breakwater

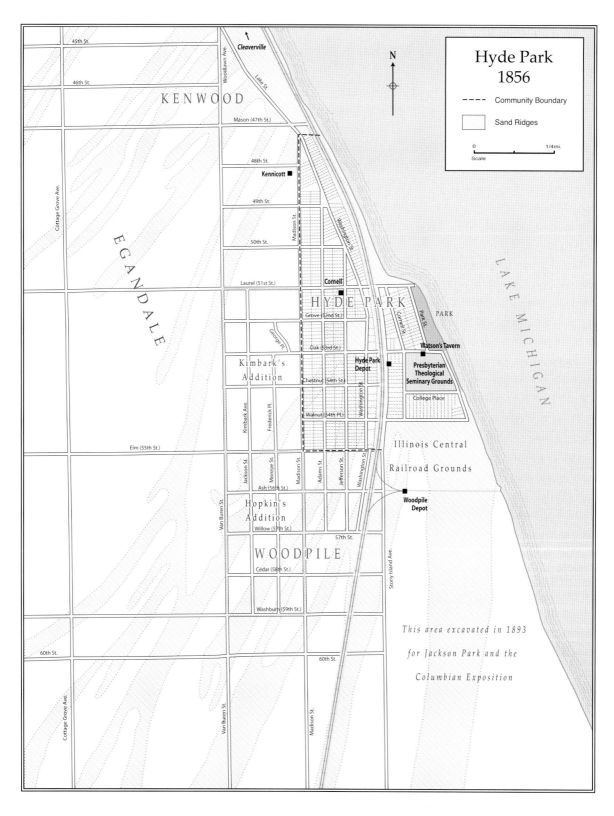

1.02. A prominent feature planned for the Hyde Park area was the twenty-acre tract along the lakeshore marked "Presbyterian Theological Seminary Grounds." The map was based upon one found in the attic of one of Cornell's buildings, prepared for Cyrus McCormick, who was interested in funding an institution of higher learning. The day he rode to view the property, a cold storm blew in from the north and over Lake Michigan. The shore was flooded by waves and McCormick declared the ground too low for a seminary. He subsequently donated funding for the institution, provided it was located on the north side of the city.

from 51st Street north in order to protect the shoreline from erosion.[21] The surveyors then ran the line through the "virgin prairie and woodland" to the site of Watson's tavern northward to the city.[22] The Illinois Central needed to make a deal with Cornell, and he was no doubt elated at the prospect—the railroad would greatly increase the value of his land. In return for his deeding sixty acres to the railroad, the Illinois Central agreed to open a station at 53rd Street and run daily passenger trains between the city and his holdings.[23] The inaugural train ran on June 1, 1856, reportedly without a single paying passenger.[24] "The Hyde Park train made its first trip today," telegraphed railroad agent John B. Calhoun; "nary a passenger up or down."[25] Regular service on the new suburban service began on July 21, 1856, with four trains running daily (except Sunday) at a fare of seven and a half cents.[26]

Paul Cornell's plan for his lakeside holdings mimicked other developments of the time, for suburbia was not a new concept. In fact, a form of the suburb came into being almost as early as the city itself, for the life-sustaining elements of farming and gardening were found in the surrounding countryside.[27] Recreation and health retreats were also located in suburbia, according to urban historian Lewis Mumford; it was believed the further away from the congested city, the better for one's health.[28] A haven away from the industrialized city offered other advantages, and was often considered a symbol of success. For those with the financial means, the suburb offered the opportunity to pursue life "on one's own terms."[29] Situated near the railroad lines that permitted development at ever-increasing distances, a number of suburbs rose on the outskirts of the young city at approximately the same time, including Oak Park, Hinsdale, Evanston, and Cornell's enclave of Hyde Park.

Cornell christened his holdings "Hyde Park," a name presumably chosen because it called to mind images of the sophisticated city of London or the verdant banks of New York's Hudson River and conferred a sense of elegance and gracious living to a relatively swampy site. In the spring of 1856 Cornell platted his tract of land, and although he intended the suburban development to reflect a pastoral setting, he subdivided the property according to the regular rectangular street pattern of the larger city. However, individual lots were large by city standards, laid out with only eighteen per block, a minimum 50' frontage with a standard depth of 125' and no service alleys. Cornell maintained a suburban feel through a required 20' setback from the street for residences.[30] Open green areas provided a sharp contrast to the more densely packed streets and houses of the city.

Cornell's relatives and business associates were the initial purchasers of property within the fledgling community, building houses near the Illinois Central station.[31] Sensing opportunity, several buyers purchased large tracts of land with the intention of opening their own suburban developments. Cornell's uncle, Hassan Artez Hopkins, and his wife Sarah arrived in the area during the winter of 1856 to support his nephew's real estate undertaking. He purchased eighty acres of the original Obadiah Hooper land for development and built a house near the station at 5211 South Cornell. Brother-in-law George Kimbark bought a large tract between what are today 51st and 55th Streets, stretching from Dorchester and Woodlawn. Cornell later purchased both the Hopkins and Kimbark additions and subdivided the properties for development. For his own family, Cornell erected a handsome country house at what is today the southwest corner of 51st and Harper Streets.

Naturally, these initial purchasers found little in the way of improvements—no water, no gas, and only a few streets were laid out—however they were inspired to invest in Cornell's vision.[32] The original settlement consisted of eight houses[33] and grew slowly—the residents valued not only the country atmosphere, but also the "congenial company" fostered by Cornell's enclave.[34] From the beginning, Hyde Park was intended to be a residential community; the busier commercial and dirtier industrial enterprises were to be kept at a safe distance.[35] The only businesses permitted were those that, as described by Jean Block, provided "amenities and necessities" for the residents, clustered west of the intersection of the railroad tracks and Oak (53rd) Street. Hassan Hopkins opened a small store for the sale of groceries and general merchandise in a one-story structure that also housed the post office.[36] Here men congregated at the wood stove "debating the issues of the day," most important among them was the subject of slavery.[37]

Before the Civil War "cast a pall over everything"[38] within the growing community, Cornell built a summer resort to provide Chicagoans with a retreat from the hectic pace of city life. On July 4, 1859, the Hyde Park House opened near the Oak (53rd) Street train depot. The barn-like, five-story, clapboard-covered hotel, measuring 62' × 160' with eighty "neatly furnished"[39] chambers, was designed by one of the city's earliest architects, Gurdon P. Randall.[40] Cornell's selection of a widely known architect set the precedent for his community; well-designed buildings became a hallmark of Hyde Park from the earliest days, reflecting the aspirations of the residents.

Although Cornell's enclave began to grow, and the hotel offered Chicagoans an attractive respite, his development did not proceed without problems. Initial ridership was so low on the Illinois Central that the railroad raised the fare, ran only three trains a day, and threatened to discontinue the local service. During the winter of 1861 Cornell wrote a confidential, impassioned plea to William H. Osborn, the president of the Illinois Central, giving reasons why the railroad was "duty bound" to keep running the trains. Cornell wrote that at the time he "exhibited the plans of the Hyde Park House" he would not "build it unless you would agree that the train should be permanent + should afford all the accommodations that it then did + at the same rate of fair. . . . You said you had no doubt the train would be permanent and that you would agree if the House was built as per plans, the Hyde Park train should run full as often as it then did + probably oftener." Cornell offered a subsidy to cover a portion of the losses, and continued: "I have not a doubt that by adopting the enclosed plan [not found in the archives] it would double the value of the Co. land at Hyde Park and excite an increasing demand for actual use."[41] Cornell proved persuasive and succeeded in saving the link to the city center. Over the years transportation offered to Hyde Parkers grew astonishingly to a high of 542 daily trains in 1929.

Meanwhile Hyde Park's residents were displeased with representation by the township of Lake and demanded the right to govern themselves.[42] They organized and petitioned the Illinois General Assembly to create a separate township, and on February 20, 1861, the township of Hyde Park was incorporated. The breakaway township encompassed a huge forty-eight-square-mile area, stretching from 39th Street south to 138th Street. The first town meeting was held in the depot with seventy-one voters casting ballots for town officers. Hopkins was unanimously elected the town clerk, and all but one vote was cast in favor of Cornell as supervisor, the most important of the offices.[43] Officials of the new town quickly made plans to improve the infrastructure—special assessments and taxes provided the revenue for streets and sidewalks, sewers and drains.

Paul Cornell's settlement was but one of several that took shape along the Illinois Central tracks, providing Chicagoans seeking to leave the city with several South Side alternatives. Included within the boundary lines of the newly incorporated township of Hyde Park were a variety of enclaves that grew as other stations were added; Cleaverville (Oakwood) and Kenwood developed just north Cornell's Hyde Park, while Woodville (South Park), Woodlawn Park and Oak Woods developed to the south.

While Cornell was occupied with plans for his development, during the spring of 1856 another settler arrived on the scene. Dr. Jonathan Asa Kennicott moved out of Chicago, as it was in his view, becoming "too citified."[44] Kennicott, a graduate of Rush Medical College and practicing dentist,[45] and his wife Marie Antoinette Fiske, a well-known painter and educator, purchased eight acres south of the city. He christened the land "Kenwood" after his mother's birthplace near Edinburgh, Scotland, and the family lived in a house on Cornell near 53rd Street while constructing their residence at 4802 Madison (Dorchester) Avenue.[46] The new, solidly constructed house had one of the most magnificent gardens and vineyards in the area, set above the surrounding wooded pastures on a high ridge that is visible to this day.[47]

For the first few years, there were few neighbors near the Kennicotts, and not surprisingly, the next settlers to appear were two representatives of the Illinois Central Railroad, William Waters and John Remmer.[48] Kennicott made no secret of his displeasure at having to walk the several blocks to the Hyde Park station, especially in inclement weather, to get to his downtown office. Cornell, however, vigorously objected to any establishment of stations between the city and Hyde Park. The vice president of the railroad, General George B. McClellan, paid a visit to the Kennicott home in the summer of 1859 during a downpour. There were no sidewalks, and mud filled the roads. McClellan ordered the train to stop opposite Dr. Kennicott's property so the guests could forgo the trek from the Hyde Park station. The following day McClellan issued an order establishing a station at Mason Street (47th Street), calling it Kenwood Station, and eventually the name extended to the entire vicinity.[49]

In contrast to Cornell's planned development, Kenwood developed differently from Hyde Park. Properties purchased by individuals were large—up to ten acres—with houses well set back from the street and shaded by stands of trees. Wealthy lawyer Pennoyer L. Sherman was typical of the early Kenwood residents. He came to Chicago in 1853 and six years later moved just north of the Mason Street station, to seven acres of gardens and woods at 4624 South Lake Street.[50]

The size and use of the Sherman property were common in Kenwood; two acres were set aside for a garden, and Sherman's son John[51] later reminisced about the homegrown melons, cherries, raspberries, carrots, and turnips that were often stolen by the "Stock-yards micks."[52] Their large red barn became a "Saturday rendezvous for the boys who came on their ponies from Oakland to Woodlawn."[53] The Sherman property reflected the idea that a home outside the city provided a better environment for raising children. The open expanses of wooded fields provided play space and established its value as an essential element of the suburban environment.

When Charles Norton settled at the extended southern end of the Illinois Central line in 1863, the station was housed in an old log building. The swampy area became known as "Woodpile," aptly named as here the trains refueled with a fresh supply of oak. Houses built here were large, but in contrast to Kenwood, lots had shallow lawns and residences were not widely spaced. Early residents of this area near 57th Street included William Hoyt, a real estate broker; Samuel Fassett, a pioneer in the field of photography; and composer George Root, who had a house at 5540 Washington Street (Blackstone).[54] These residents renamed the locale with the slightly more prestigious title of Woodville, an area that eventually became known as South Park when Hoyt opened the South Park Hotel in 1874.

At the western boundary of Kenwood and removed from the railroad line, Dr. William B. Egan envisioned a development of a completely different type. He purchased large tracts from the canal commissioners at prices ranging between ten and $100 per acre.[55] With dreams of creating a baronial country estate, he began to drain the marshy land that extended from 47th south to 55th Street and east from Cottage Grove to Woodlawn. Described as a "jovial Irishman," Egan selected a high ridge as the site for his country house and gardens and laid out the grounds in a "stately fashion."[56] An imposing rustic gate and lodge were erected at 47th Street, serving as the formal entrance for visitors to the tract he named Egandale.[57]

"Let us enter his grounds and enjoy them," proclaimed the newspapers.

Egandale is some five miles south of the city, perhaps less than that from its southern limit. At the south-west [incorrectly identified, the location was the northwest] corner of his grounds, an enclosure of some four hundred acres, we enter by a rustic gate, besides which stands a tasteful "lodge" surrounded by beautiful evergreens. A splendid avenue for nearly a mile, widening amid beautiful groves and rich prairie on either side branching to the left brings us to a vine clad farmhouse, and to the right a large mound with two terraces on the top of which stands a rustic summer house. The view from the top of this unique building is truly enchanting.

Clearly smitten with Egan's endeavor the *Tribune* continued:

On either side of the avenue is a wide border filled with forest trees and evergreens of almost every variety, which need but a few years growth to make it one of the most enchanting "drives" that it is possible for the pleasure seeker or the man to enjoy. Dr. Egan has beautified his grounds with sixty thousand trees—a fact that seems hardly credible til one rides through them and sees for himself the richness and extent of their adorning. The useful also has all the necessary attention. Here are acres of asparagus and other vegetables in great variety; an extensive nursery, orchards, and fruit gardens, fields of clover and luxuriant meadow, each attesting to the taste and the skill of this enterprising proprietor.[58]

Dr. Egan, remembered as one who "never failed to bring down the house," died at his city residence on West Division Street in 1860 at the age of fifty-two.[59] Egan was overextended and underfinanced, and after his death the land passed to his banker, George C. Smith of Drexel & Smith. Eight years later the scope of Egandale had been reduced to a tract of one hundred acres. The bank held on to the northwest corner of Egan's property as efforts to create a park system were beginning to take shape. In 1869 James Runnion described this land in his book on Chicago's suburbs as "the most valuable, and will be made to take a leading place among the most beautiful and attractive of all our suburban property." He foresaw a day when a planned boulevard 200 feet wide, would be "made into a splendid roadway, with such beauties of trees," lined with "suburban residences and magnificent gardens along both sides of it, that could scarcely be comprehended now."[60]

Paul Cornell continued to be a leading visionary, organizing a group of local well-to-do landowners in an effort to create a park system that became the major achievement of the period. Conceptually the parks began as early as 1849 when developer John S. Wright proposed a network of urban parks, at a time when there were very few, with the hopes of stimulating development. It took more than a decade for his idea to garner support. In 1866 Cornell, George Kimbark, Jonathan Scammon, and others investigated other parks that provided open pleasure grounds and would give "lungs to the city."[61] In planning, the group found the concept attractive for several reasons, not the least of which was that the money for buying and maintaining the land would come from the public domain, rather than from themselves.[62]

Cornell, like Wright, Smith, and Runnion, believed surrounding land values would increase as a result of the park improvements, as the adjoining communities would be viewed as increasingly attractive places in which to live. He traveled to the state capitol in Springfield during the winters of 1867 and 1868, fighting for a bill that would raise funds through bonds sales and taxes. While voters in the northern part of Hyde Park Township supported the state referendum, they were outnumbered by those residing further south and the bill was defeated. Cornell astutely joined forces with pro-park residents representing the North and West Sides of the Chicago area. The alliance petitioned the Illinois Assembly for the creation of three separate commissions that would create a citywide system of parks and boulevards. The revised bill was passed by the Illinois legislature, and on February 24, 1869, the South Parks Commission was officially created to spearhead the project.

Five commissioners appointed by the governor were directed to survey and acquire over 1,000 acres for parkland.[63] Meanwhile, the South Parks commissioners hired Frederick Law Olmsted and Calvert Vaux, the nation's most influential and admired landscape firm of the time, responsible for the design of New York City's Central Park.[64] Olmsted and Vaux believed in the power of urban parks to offer relief from the congestion of the city, as well as to provide open space where people of all social classes could interact. The elaborate plan they developed for the South Parks was but one element of a vast park and boulevard system that encircled the city. In their design, the natural features of prairie, marshes, and sand dunes were transformed into a recreational sanctuary, featuring equestrian paths, shaded walkways, broad open fields and large reflective ponds. Work began and progressed rapidly—a five-acre nursery with 60,000 trees was planted; roads and sewers were laid out; and preliminary grading of planting areas began.

Cornell's assessment was correct, and adjacent property values began to escalate as soon as the plans for improvement of the parks and boulevards were announced. Property that sold for $15 an acre by frontage foot in 1867 had doubled, even tripled, in value, selling for $30 to $50 a front foot two years later.[65] The enthusiasm was evident: "When the boulevards have been thoroughly inaugurated and parks are not merely bounded on the maps, but rendered beautiful by the most celebrated landscape architects in the world; when the number of residences shall be doubled and quadrupled," mused James Runnion in his 1869 book on Chicago's suburbs, "who shall foretell of the property values at that time?"[66]

Whether on the large estates of Kenwood or the more closely spaced lots of South Park, residences constructed in the area were, from the outset, unique expressions of the owner. Following the lead of Cornell and the design of Hyde Park House, residents invested heavily in their real estate, and the stage was set for the role housing would take in developing the character of the neighborhood. From the suburb came the beginnings of a search for new forms of domestic architecture, wrote Lewis Mumford, "organically one both in function and image, with the life within and the landscape without."[67] The nineteenth-century English picturesque movement influenced houses built during this period, as landscape designers sought to create a relaxed, natural environment for residences.

Breaking from the use of classical styles in residential architecture, Americans sought a fresh approach to housing design. A number of styles became popular, ranging from the elegant Italianate to the highly expressive Gothic Revival. The majority were built of wood, and the very earliest would have been laboriously constructed. Hardwood beams, with mortise-and-tenon joints, had to be attached with hand-made dowels and nails. However, this work-intensive building technique could not be used to produce housing quickly enough to accommodate the flood of new residents.[68]

Balloon framing, an innovative building technique that evolved from early forms of post-and-beam construction, first appeared in Chicago during the 1830s. Made possible by the introduction of inexpensive machine-made nails and the availability of precut lumber, the method revolutionized the construction process. The new method of construction positioned two-by-four-inch studs sixteen inches apart, producing a lightweight yet durable frame that was adaptable to an infinite number of building types. By eliminating the need for heavy timber, builders could quickly and easily frame out a house, meeting the needs of the increasing

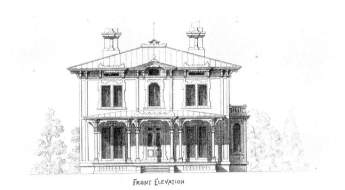

FRONT ELEVATION

1.03. For masons and carpenters, building guides such as *Woodward's National Architect* of 1869 supplemented their own knowledge and skill. This document offered 1,000 plans and details for houses, including the popular Italianate style house, essentially an embellished box with a rigid, formal floor plan.

SIDE ELEVATION.

population. "Born out of necessity," this versatile invention set the stage for larger accomplishments, commented architecture critic Paul Gapp. "Much of Chicago's architectural greatness . . . springs from ingenious engineering, not simply an urge to create beauty."[69]

By the 1860s the Italianate style was the most popular in the country, apparent locally by the number of regal Italianate houses constructed as Hyde Park and the adjacent communities began to flourish. Houses were for the most part constructed on large lots, resulting in a lower population density than that found in the city, and each was placed on the land with the intention of making its best presentation toward the street. Porches were oriented to catch summer breezes and bay windows were positioned to take advantage of the southern light in houses relying on the warmth of fireplaces during Chicago's notorious bitterly cold winter months. Carpenters and builders essentially functioned as architects, designing and planning within their client's financial constraints. But unlike architects, they were responsible for building the house as well.

As houses rose throughout the area and the population began to flourish, problems associated with city life slowly made their appearance in the suburb. In 1860 an organized band of thieves preyed upon cows and horses.[70] Building supplies and carpenters' tools were taken from sites where houses were going up, and groceries were stolen from the Hyde Park depot building. Services were also lacking,

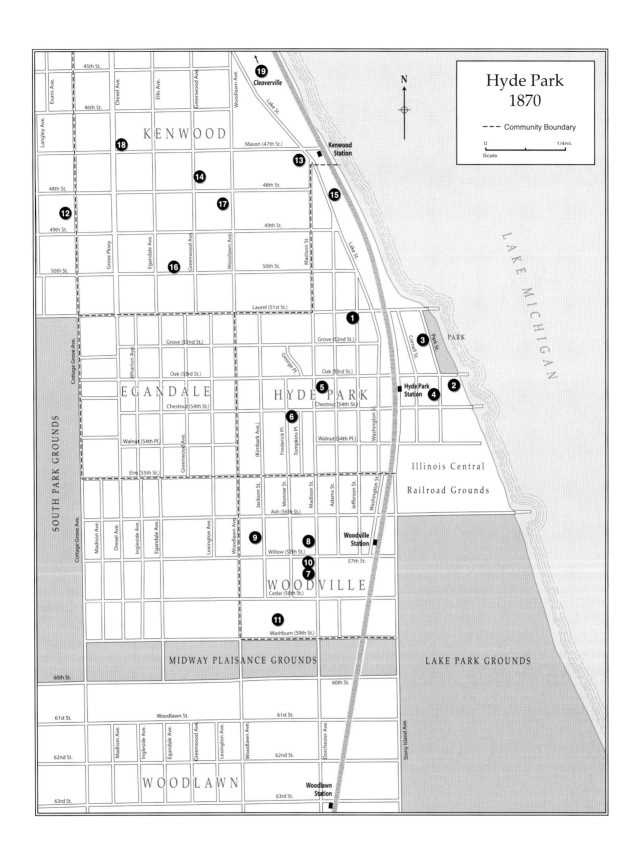

Hyde Park
1870

- - - Community Boundary

0   1/4mi.
Scale

N

LAKE MICHIGAN

LAKE PARK GROUNDS

Illinois Central

Railroad Grounds

SOUTH PARK GROUNDS

MIDWAY PLAISANCE GROUNDS

KENWOOD

EGANDALE

HYDE PARK

WOODVILLE

WOODLAWN

Cleaverville

Kenwood
Station

Hyde Park
Station

Woodville
Station

Woodlawn
Station

PARK

45th St.
46th St.
48th St.
49th St.
50th St.
Mason (47th St.)
48th St.
49th St.
50th St.
Laurel (51st St.)
Grove (52nd St.)
Oak (53rd St.)
Chestnut (54th St.)
Walnut (54th Pl.)
Elm (55th St.)
Ash (56th St.)
Willow (57th St.)
Cedar (58th St.)
Washburn (59th St.)
60th St.
61st St.
62nd St.
63rd St.
60th St.
61st St.
62nd St.
63rd St.
Grove (52nd St.)
Oak (53rd St.)
Chestnut (54th St.)
Walnut (54th Pl.)
57th St.

Evans Ave.
Langley Ave.
Drexel Ave.
Ellis Ave.
Greenwood Ave.
Woodlawn Ave.
Lake St.
Lake St.
Cornell St.
Park St.
Cottage Grove Ave.
Cottage Grove Ave.
Grove Pkwy.
Egandale Ave.
Greenwood Ave.
Woodlawn Ave.
Madison St.
Wharton Ave.
George Pl.
(Kimbark Ave.)
Frederick Pl.
Tompkins Pl.
Washington St.
Greenwood Ave.
Jackson St.
Monroe St.
Madison St.
Adams St.
Jefferson St.
Washington St.
Madison Ave.
Drexel Ave.
Ingleside Ave.
Egandale Ave.
Lexington Ave.
Woodlawn Ave.
Madison Ave.
Ingleside Ave.
Egandale Ave.
Greenwood Ave.
Lexington Ave.
Woodlawn Ave.
Dorchester Ave.
Stony Island Ave.
Woodlawn St.

especially in regard to the often called-for fire-fighting brigade. During the summer of 1868 the "fine residence" of Dr. Theodore Saxchi (or Sachse) burned to the ground.[71] An alarm was sounded when flames were noticed coming from the house, but there was no fire engine in the town of Hyde Park, so it was left to the neighbors to try to extinguish the fire. Unfortunately they were unsuccessful, and the cause of the blaze was blamed upon careless servants.[72]

The small communities of Hyde Park, Kenwood, Egandale, and Woodville had their distinct characteristics at this early stage, and each continued to be influenced by the growth of the greater city. Each boasted any number of handsome houses, and hotel and shops gave the center of Hyde Park a typical town appearance. By virtue of living in a retreat, Hyde Park residents were identified by a number of related social characteristics. The men commuted daily to the city center to work, and women centered their lives on the family home. As lawyers, physicians, bankers, clergymen, real estate agents, and railroad employees and their families arrived, Hyde Park and Kenwood were predominantly identified by upper-class, well-educated, Eastern-born, Republican voting, church-going whites.

However the 1870 census shows that among wealthier families living in the area, there were also many who provided the most basic and necessary services: carpenters, masons, common laborers, and of course, domestic servants. Overall, the environment remained rural, as cows grazed in the fields of houses large and small. However the residents—the saloon keeper John Green, the clergyman Davis Johnson, the architect George Garnsey, the post office clerk Douglas Danforth, the real estate agent W. B. Prescott, and all of the Irish, English, and Swedish servants who lived and worked among those far more privileged and prosperous—were on the cusp of great change. Hyde Park was conceived as a respite from the city, yet the city was its future.

Hyde Park

1 Cornell Residence, 1857. Demolished.
5100 South Jefferson Street (Harper Avenue). Architect/builder unknown.

Known as the "Father of Hyde Park," Paul Cornell (1822–1904) was born in White Creek, New York, to a notable New England family that traced its lineage back to Essex, England, from which Thomas Cornell emigrated to Boston in 1638. Cornell was not yet one when his father, Hiram King Cornell, accidentally drowned in Bennington Vermont. His mother, Eliza (Betsy) Hopkins, remarried in the winter of 1825, to Dr. Jonathan Berry. The family then moved west from upstate New York to the small enclave of Beardstown along the Illinois River. Although Berry was a physician, the family was not wealthy, and Cornell financed his own education by working as a summer laborer at neighboring farms. In 1843 Cornell began to study law in the office of William A. Richardson in nearby Rushville, and later in Joliet, some forty miles west of Chicago. He ventured to the larger city to practice law in 1847.

The summer the Illinois Central made its inaugural trip to Hyde Park, Cornell wed Helen Maria Gray, eleven years his junior, at the home of her brother-in-law Orrington Lunt (a founder of Northwestern University).[73] Cornell acknowledged that he owed much to the "devoted efforts and self-sacrificing spirit" of his wife, who shared with him "a faith and enthusiasm in the great future of Chicago."[74]

One of their children, John E. Cornell, remembered his father as a "most wonderful man" who persevered through any number of trials, yet was "like a sponge that nothing could keep down."[75] In addition to developing Hyde Park and the industrial Grand Crossing area, he established the Cornell Watch Company, the

1.04. The house of Helen and Paul Cornell was typical of many of the larger dwellings built during the early years of the community. Constructed in the Italianate style that first became popular during the 1840s, the exterior of their two-story frame structure featured wide cornices with brackets and elongated, paned windows. A large porch welcomed guests, while overhead a square cupola enhanced the gently sloping roofline.

Republic Life Insurance Company, and the American Bronze Company. Cornell was also a founder of Oak Woods Cemetery, where he and many of Hyde Park's early citizens are buried.[76]

② Hyde Park House, 1859. Destroyed by fire in September 1877.
Oak (53rd) Street at Lake Michigan. Gurdon P. Randall.

Proprietors Tabor, Hawk & Company watched over the Hyde Park House, as it quickly became the center of the small community's social life. In just a short stroll from the train station, one could find a dining room that offered fine delicacies and a wide view of the lake, an elegant parlor, and numerous activities, including bowling and billiards. The property was improved with a landing pier for excursion boats and a pavilion where a band would play on warm summer nights.

Over the years, the Hyde Park House guest register included many prominent names. Not only was this was a first-class summer hotel, but it also promoted an advantage in the era before the establishment of the germ theory of disease: "The purity of the lake breeze and the absence of city air will ensure immunity from the dread cholera," extolled the *Tribune*, "while the beauty of the surrounding scenery and the quiet of the neighborhood constitute, now as ever, undying attractions."[77]

Mary Todd Lincoln and her sons Robert and Tad stayed for two and a half months, seeking solace and a place of refuge after the assassination of President Lincoln.[78] "It almost appears to me that I am at the seashore," Mrs. Lincoln wrote from her suite of three rooms. "Land cannot be discerned across the lake. My friends thought I would be more quiet here during the summer months than in the city."[79] Robert Lincoln quickly became a typical Hyde Park commuter, taking the train for the half-hour ride to his office at Scammon, McCagg & Fuller.[80] Their stay was short-lived, for ten weeks after checking into the Hyde Park House there

1.05. The view from the top of Hyde Park House was "truly splendid," from the spires of the city on the north peering up through the haze that enveloped them, to the broad expanse of the lake on the east. According an article the *Tribune* ran on July 20, 1859, the scenery was always "sublime, whether lashed to fury by the merciless storm or sleeping in quiet dignity in the evening sunlight."

was an outbreak, not of cholera but of scarlet fever, and the former first family departed.

In 1865 J. Irving Pearce and Benjamin Schuyler purchased Cornell's hotel, eventually enlarging and renovating it into a brick structure. In the early morning hours of September 12, 1877, a fire broke out. Hose Company Number 2 appeared on the scene after the fire bell was rung, but they were ill equipped to deal with the flames. By the time water was taken from the lake, the fire had engulfed much of the structure, and by noon the hotel was destroyed. The ruins remained along the lakefront for many years.

③ Bockée Residence, 1857. Demolished.
5152 and 5200 South Park Street (Hyde Park Boulevard). Architect/builder unknown.

Most of Hyde Park's original houses are gone today, although many did last well into the twentieth century. One of the very earliest was the residence of Dr. Jacob Bockée, who built on a desolate parcel at Cornell and 50th Streets. The frame house was constructed on a site east of the railroad tracks described as "sand waste."[81]

The physician and his wife Catherine left New York, coming west to settle on the city's South Side; Bockée operated a wholesale drug store between 1855 and 1861.[82] After he served as a surgeon for the Union forces during the Civil War,[83] the Bockée family later returned to Poughkeepsie.

1.06. Later owners enlarged the Bockée house after it was moved several blocks to the south.

By 1873, when James and Rebecca Morgan acquired the two-story gabled house, it was moved to a new location overlooking the park today known as Harold Washington Park. Morgan enlarged the original house, building an addition in the rear for a kitchen and a verandah on the south to catch the warm sunlight. When their daughter Clara married Dr. Herbert H. Frothingham in 1891, the north section was added for the young couple. With a new roof put over all, the house became known as the "twin house" and had two addresses on Hyde Park Boulevard.

Although Bockée would not have recognized his house in its later years, it remained standing for decades as the neighborhood around grew. The house had seen better days by 1943 when twenty-three young men and women formed a housing cooperative to deal with the scarcity of housing and high living expenses during the Second World War. Renamed the "Concord House," the structure was modified to contain twenty-three rooms and twelve baths, but the Bockées' original walnut staircase, "one of the most beautiful pieces of work in the home," remained intact.[84]

④ Field–Pullman–Heyworth Residence, 1858.

5336 South Park Street (Hyde Park Boulevard). Architect/builder unknown.
Relocated to 7716 South Lake Street, 1912, then 7651 South Shore Drive, 1918.

The books published by American landscape gardener Andrew Jackson Downing provided the country's growing population with visions of the ideal home. These early books often featured the work of architect Alexander Jackson Davis and had an enormous effect on American taste. Carpenters used these inexpensive guides to construct wood-frame houses, set harmoniously on the landscape, that often featured Gothic details such as the elongated, pointed windows, and intricately cut detailing.[85] The primary contribution of the style to the development of the American house was a loosening of the rigid and symmetrical plans of more classical styles.

Although this Gothic-style house had prominent owners before Lawrence Heyworth purchased the home, for much of its existence it was apparently used as rental property. First owned by the Presbyterian Seminary of the Northwest, by 1881 the house and land were sold to a partnership between Marshall Field, of the department store fame, and railroad magnate George Pullman. They held the property until 1909.[86] The house was then sold and moved from Hyde Park to the South Shore neighborhood for J. B. and Mary Watson. During the summer of 1912, a barge took the house several miles south to 7716 South Lake, where it was set on a new foundation facing the blue waters over which it had just traveled. After passing through the hands of several owners the property was sold to the city for the establishment of a public park in 1917.[87]

For decades that followed, Lawrence Heyworth and his second wife, Marguerite, occupied the house. While renting the house in its lakefront location, Heyworth purchased property on nearby South Shore Drive. A foundation permit was issued in May 1918, and the charming house was presumably purchased from the city and then moved to 7651 South Shore Drive.

1.07. Although the Field-Pullman-Heyworth house was considerably altered, the steep roofline of the residence was clearly recognizable in 2010 at its location in Chicago's South Shore neighborhood.

1.08. Characterized by pointed gables, this highly expressive house represented refinement as well the enjoyment of the country. Recreational pursuits were an advantage of suburban life, here demonstrated by women proudly displaying their archery equipment. This early, undated image of the Field-Pullman-Heyworth house was featured in the *Chicago Daily News* on September 9, 1939.

A son of an affluent real estate developer, Heyworth was raised on one of Chicago's most fashionable streets, Prairie Avenue. After studying engineering at Yale University, he returned to Chicago to work for contractor George A. Fuller, whose company oversaw the construction of the famous Monadnock and Rookery buildings, and locally, the Hyde Park Hotel.

In February 1897 Heyworth, a "delightful raconteur,"[88] married Cecile Young, the daughter of wealthy wholesale jeweler and financier Otto Young, also a resident of the Prairie Avenue district. Heyworth soon went into business with his father-in-law, supervising the construction of Young's building at 29 East Madison Street, designed by Burnham & Root. Obviously fond of his son-in-law, Young christened the building "the Heyworth," a title it still holds today.

In 1906, while enduring a divorce that played out in public, Heyworth founded the South Shore Country Club, located just a few miles south of Hyde Park on the lakefront. Benjamin Marshall was hired to design the lavish Mediterranean-inspired clubhouse, which functions today as the South Shore Cultural Center.

While a number of alterations over the years have changed the character of the two-story frame house, its steeply peaked roofline and stately columned porch provide an indication of its former grandeur. An early plan of the house, dating from 1890, shows the simple massing and cruciform plan typical of the style. The house had an addition by this time, a flat-roofed one-story wing, and before it was moved, the porch was added. Despite the additions and moves, the house remained in a picturesque setting. Sheep grazed on the Heyworths' lakefront lawn in 1917, as Americans were encouraged to raise sheep to avert a shortage of wool in the nation.[89] In 1937 the house was altered to enclose the front porch and add a bay window.[90] The Heyworths sold their house in 1944.

⑤ Work Residence, 1859.

5317 South Madison Street (Dorchester Avenue). Architect/builder unknown.

Clearly not all of Hyde Park's houses from this period were large or elaborate residences; however, the owners of smaller houses also possessed aspirations for their surroundings. Henry C. Work built a small peaked-roof cottage in the center of Hyde Park. Work was born in Connecticut and brought west by his father, a passionate abolitionist who operated a station on the underground railroad at Quincy, Illinois. At one time his father was imprisoned in Missouri for allowing thousands of slaves to escape through the family home.[91] Work came to Chicago, married, and purchased a small lot in 1859. The land was typical of the subdivided lots

1.09. Believing that improving the appearance of houses would generally benefit all classes of Americans, Andrew Jackson Downing encouraged the building of picturesque cottages through his books. He defined modest dwellings such as the Work cottage as "so small that the household duties may all be performed by the family."

1.10. *Village and farm cottages*, written by Henry W. Cleaveland and William Samuel Backus in 1856, was aimed toward providing tasteful housing designs to tradesmen and others of moderate means. The preface reads, "A modest home, which he may call his own, is beyond the reach of no capable and industrious man." Chapters included advice on interior decoration and suggestions on how to improve landscaping and garden designs, and even which fruits and vegetables to grow.

in this section of Hyde Park, mimicking the city lot size of 125' depth with a 25' frontage.

After paying $175 for the land,[92] Work built a Carpenter Gothic–style cottage. Although erected at a modest cost, this vertically sided house presents a romanticized view of the family home. The simple floor plan did not permit a hall or large staircase, elements that would considerably reduce the available living space for Work, his wife Sarah, and their two-year-old son. Within the confines of this humble structure Work, a self-taught musician, composed many songs during the Civil War years. He found success in 1853 when Edwin Christy, of the black-faced Christy Minstrels, performed one of Work's songs, "We Are Coming, Sister Mary."[93] When war broke out Work began the most prolific and successful period in his career and, ironically, slaves in the Confederate south sang his music.[94]

Work was elected town clerk of the village in 1864 and continued to reside in the modest structure as his financial circumstances improved. He sold the cottage and the land in 1867 to Guy Sampson, who built a house nearer to the street and used the attached cottage as a dining room.[95]

⑥ Lyman Bridges Residence, c. 1860. Demolished 1961.
1325 East Chestnut (54th) Street. Architect/builder unknown.

Lyman Bridges was civil engineer known as Colonel Bridges after serving in the Civil War.[96] Bridges' business was in supplying "ready made houses and building materials," and he became well known for "two distinctly American structures," a balloon frame cottage and a schoolhouse shipped to Paris for the Exposition Universelle of 1867.[97] Designed by Otis Wheelock, the "Western Farmer's House" was fabricated in pieces and provided as a complete package by Bridges' company.

1.11. The ready-made Bridges house, abandoned when this image was taken about 1960, was built on a typically compact lot prevalent in the area near 55th Street.

The ready-made building attracted the European audience with its simplicity: "decidedly American in its construction—plain, substantial, and convenient—representing thrift and comfort without display."[98] The straightforward structure was awarded one of seventy-six silver medals awarded to the United States exhibitors.[99] Lyman Bridges' company prospered in Chicago between 1866 and 1875; Bridges died in California in 1919.[100]

7 Botsford Residence, 1860.

5714 South Madison Street (Dorchester Avenue). Architect/builder unknown.

Although the grounds were long ago subdivided, the Botsford house remains as a gracious reminder of Hyde Park's earliest years. Charles H. Botsford built the earliest of the Italianate-style houses, constructed when this area was known as Woodpile, so named because the wood-burning Illinois Central trains refueled here. Typically square in plan, the interior of an Italianate-style house was centered on a steep staircase and featured high ceilings.

The house was constructed with a storage cellar below, providing open space that kept the wood of the first floor high, and therefore dry above the marshy ground. Indoor plumbing was still a luxury when these early houses were built; chamber pots, pitcher stands, and chambermaids were the norm. Sanitary facili-

ties were located outdoors, away from the main house until water and sewage systems were introduced.

Botsford lived in the enclave he renamed Woodville until 1863, when he sold the house to the Fassetts. Samuel Montague Fassett came to Chicago in 1854 from New York. He was a pioneer photographer working for the government during the Civil War. Mary Todd Lincoln considered an early image taken by Fassett to be "the best likeness she had seen of her husband."[101] Cornelia Strong Fassett was an "artist with a good deal of ability," known for her presidential portraits.[102] The couple raised their seven children in the house, which at the time had grounds extending one block to the west. The property featured a "grape arbor, strawberry patch and flower bed," recalled neighbor Mrs. C. van Inwegan. "There were stables at the west end of the grounds."[103]

Originally the verandah of the house extended fully across the façade and was connected to a small conservatory. From here one would have had a clear view of the lake. The symmetrical façade features the typical long, narrow, arched windows, heavy brackets under the cornice, and a flat cupola rising from the roof. On the interior, fireplaces adorned with tiles and wooden mantels warmed spacious parlors on either side of the central staircase.[104]

The Fassetts occupied this house until 1875, when they moved to Washington DC. Claudius B. Nelson, a partner in the firm of William Blair & Company, purchased the property that still included all of the west side of Dorchester and the east side of Kenwood south to 58th Street. By 1889 Nelson and his son Walter, a building contractor, developed much of Dorchester Avenue. The circa 1882 flat-roofed town houses constructed on the west side of the street demonstrated the blurring distinction between the suburb and the larger city.[105]

⑧ Residence, c. 1865.

5642 South Madison Street (Dorchester Avenue). Architect/builder unknown.

The original occupants of this frame house on Dorchester are not known. It is believed to have been constructed about 1865, and while considerably enlarged over the years, demonstrates the suburban nature of the Woodville community at the time. The original portion of the house was constructed in a simple rectangular shape; the ell and a wide front porch were added after 1890.

In the rear is the only remaining example of a board-and-batten barn in Hyde Park; although altered long ago for automobiles, it still has its hayloft. "Board and batten" describes a type of siding that has alternating wide boards and narrow wooden strips, called battens. The boards are typically one foot wide and placed vertically. The narrow battens are placed over the seams between the boards. The size of the vertically sided barn suggests this was intended for a horse and carriage, unlike larger structures that were also intended for farm animals.[106]

1.14. At the rear of the house at 5642 Dorchester is the original barn, now converted for use as a garage.

⑨ Residence, by 1868.

5630 South Kimbark Avenue. Architect/builder unknown.

Builders mimicked the larger Italianate residences on a various scales. Examples of the once common house are now rare in Hyde Park; however, one remains at 5630 South Kimbark. This house once occupied a much larger piece of land along a willow-lined stream that once ran behind it. The façade displays a movement toward the use of factory-made millwork. Homebuilders adapted to what the machine was able to produce in batches and in volume, although precision-cut components did not appear until 1880, according to historian Joseph Bigott. Thus the house still required the handwork of a carpenter.

1.15. When built, the house at 5630 South Kimbark occupied a much larger piece of property. The barn, according to Jean Block, was near the corner of 56th and Woodlawn.

The floor plan of this house featured a front hall with a formal stairway and a parlor anchored by a fireplace. The introduction of the cast iron stove in the 1830s eliminated the need for a large, centrally located fireplace and allowed the kitchen to be placed away from the other rooms, at the rear of the house.[107]

10 Hoyt Residence, 1869.
5704 South Madison Street (Dorchester Avenue). Architect/builder unknown.

Although this Italianate-style house was erected a few years after the end of the Civil War, many of its occupants were connected with the bloodiest chapter in America's history. The house was built for successful realtor William H. Hoyt (Bogue & Hoyt) who led a supply expedition taking much-needed blankets to the

1.16. The Hoyt residence was one of the very few early houses constructed of brick.

Union troops.[108] Hoyt and his wife Mary Betteley came west to Illinois from New York in 1854, and moved to Hyde Park ten years later.[109]

After purchasing the land on Dorchester from Paul Cornell's uncle, Hassan Hopkins, Hoyt constructed this elegant two-story brick house in the Italianate style so popular at the time. Although there have been modernizations over the years, much of the interior remains intact. "Here may be seen the fine marble fireplaces, ornamented ceilings and mahogany trim of the days when this house, shaded by elms and flowering bushes was a show place of old Hyde Park," wrote John Drury in his 1941 book on Chicago's oldest houses.

The Hoyts lived in the house until 1888, when the property was sold to two sisters who purchased it jointly as a surprise for their husbands. The Civil War association then continued with the new occupants, for Clarence G. Sholes was General Sherman's personal telegrapher on his famous march to the sea.[110] His brother-in-law William Campbell was one of the first three clerks of the Railway Mail Service, founded at the outbreak of the war.[111]

Today the interior does not much differ from the description written by Drury over sixty years earlier. While the floor plan has been altered to accommodate bathrooms and a first-floor kitchen in the rear, the front parlors with heavy pairs of paneled double doors remain, as do the floor-to-ceiling pocket shutters. A graceful balustrade with a massive mahogany newel post anchors the center, as the stairs rise steeply to the second level. Three original fireplaces remain on the first floor, and on the second level, two grace the front bedrooms.

Originally constructed with a cellar to elevate the house above the muddy

1.17. The floor plans of Italianate-style residences are remarkably consistent, typically centered on an elegant, steep stairway rising to bedrooms on the second level. The double doors lead to a rear deck; these were later additions to the Hoyt residence.

ground, the house was raised on a foundation. The exterior windows have been replaced, although a double-hung paned window remains in the north parlor. In the attic one can glimpse the massive boards of the hip roof, and a stair remains, indicating there may have been a cupola at one time.

The Hoyt house in many ways reflects the changing nature of residential properties in the Hyde Park neighborhood. The Campbell and Sholes families shared the house with their in-laws, the Ten Eycks, as late as 1917.[112] After 1892, the house and its spacious lawn were shaded by a six-story women's dormitory built for the university and erected on the lot adjacent on the north. The property changed hands as the years passed, becoming a rooming house in the thirties. For a time the house hosted a tearoom named the "Gargoyle," frequented by university professors and their wives. Today, the structure has been lovingly restored; rooms were returned to their original dimensions and the fire escapes that marred the rear elevation have been removed.[113]

⑪ Scammon Residence. Before 1870. Demolished.
5810 South Monroe Street (Kenwood Avenue). Architect/builder unknown.

Groves of trees and winding paths marked Horace William Shaler Cleveland landscape plan for Fernwood, the estate of Jonathan Young Scammon. Cleveland (1814–1900) was an important force in landscape architecture, although Frederick Law Olmsted often overshadowed him. Cleveland was not only "a visionary and a skilled and practical designer" known for his writing and landscape design, but also a "pioneering critic" in the subject of city planning.[114] The development of his organic aesthetic was related to ideas about landscape that were explored in literature of the time. The writing of Henry Wadsworth and Ralph Waldo Emerson influenced Cleveland's thinking; Emerson in particular maintained that the landscape should be true to the place in which it was located.[115]

Aware of the opportunities offered by Chicago, Cleveland came to the city in 1869. He advocated a departure from the rectangular system of planning that dominated the landscape. Within Chicago's city limits were hundreds of miles of streets that ran due north-south and east-west, intersected by a few diagonal streets that follow old country roads and Indian trails. "No fact is better established," wrote Cleveland, "than the necessity of sunlight to the highest degree of animal health." Urban houses planned under the rigid grid system did not allow for an abundance of sunlight to permeate the structure. "But every house on the south side of a street running east and west must have its front rooms, which are generally its living rooms, entirely secluded from the sun during the Winter, and for most of the day during the Summer. This fact, coupled with that of the indoor life of American, and particularly Western, women, is enough to account for a very large share of the nervous debility, which so generally prevails."[116]

Cleveland saw Chicago as "simply a vast collection of square blocks of buildings, divided by straight streets, whose weary lengths become fearfully monotonous to one who is under frequent necessity of traversing them." He questioned the city's layout, concerned with how streets could "be best adapted to the natural shape of the ground, so as to economize cost of construction, and attain ease of grade and facility of drainage, by taking advantage of the opportunities offered by nature to save expense of cutting and filling, while preserving the most desirable building sites in the best positions relative to the roads."[117]

Cleveland tackled these issues as he began his professional practice and received several commissions in the Hyde Park area. Cleveland received commissions for two large projects—for Drexel Boulevard and for the reconceived plan for the South Parks. However, his first local project was for pioneer Chicagoan Jonathan Young Scammon, for a time one of the richest men in America. Scammon arrived in the city at the age of twenty-three, in 1835 when the population numbered only 1,500. He was the founder of the Swedenborgian Church and

1.18. Cleveland's hand-colored site plan for "Fernwood" included a vegetable garden, laundry yard, and croquet grounds.

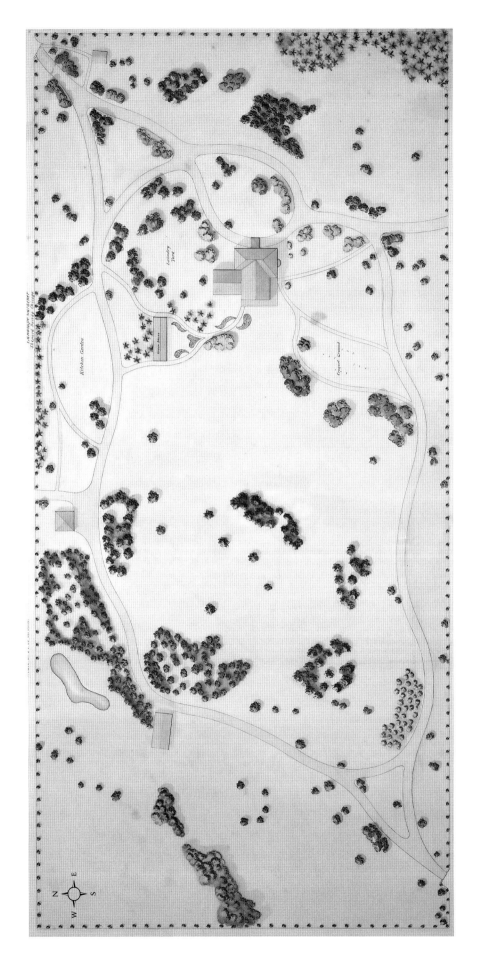

the *Inter-Ocean* newspaper, a lawyer, and a partner of Norman Judd, a successful banker, and friend of Abraham Lincoln. It was rumored that he was active in the underground railroad, offering sanctuary to escaping slaves.[118] During the summer Mary Todd Lincoln stayed at the Hyde Park House, it was Scammon who offered her son Robert employment with his firm.

Scammon and his second wife, Mrs. Maria Sheldon Wright, owned a wooded stretch of twenty acres that they called Fernwood. The property fronted directly on the boulevard (Midway Plaisance) that linked the planned south parks between Woodlawn and Madison (Dorchester) avenues. In 1870 Scammon commissioned Cleveland to develop a plan for his property, on which stood a small gardener's cottage. Cleveland's natural plan for the terrain included groves of trees, vegetable gardens, a laundry yard, and croquet grounds.

After the Chicago Fire, the family left the city to make Fernwood their permanent residence. Their cottage slowly grew into a country house with a number of additions over the years, but whether Cleveland's lush plan was ever fully conceived is doubtful. Scammon had invested large sums of his own money in development projects prior to the fire. In order to rebuild his holdings after the fire, Scammon borrowed heavily, in amounts to be repaid in gold. The financial panic of 1873 and a subsequent fire in 1874 devastated him financially. Scammon staggered under immense debt until his death in 1890. "The man who commanded millions and gave away many thousands," said a lifelong friend, "told me that at this time he knew not where he could raise $5."[119]

When the Scammon family moved to Fernwood it was "like going into a wilderness."[120] However, the rectangular streetscape of the city slowly grew around the property, and by the time of Scammon's death, the land had increased in value enough to provide for the needs of his widow. In May 1901, Mrs. Scammon deeded the tract to the University of Chicago to serve as the site of the Laboratory Schools' Blaine Hall. The university paid half of its financial value to Mrs. Scammon.[121] She decreed that the Scammon Garden should always remain an open space for the students, for school gardening, and as a location of outdoor play. Two bronze tablets later installed at the school read:

SCAMMON COURT
This Enclosure Is Named in Memory of
A Public Spirited Citizen of Chicago
And a Liberal Friend of Education
JONATHAN YOUNG SCAMMON
1812–1890
And in recognition of the Generosity
Of His Widow
MARIA SHELDON SCAMMON[122]

Just two days after her donation was finalized, Mrs. Scammon died in the parlor of her home at 5810 Kenwood Avenue. As for Cleveland, who had planned the magnificent grounds—his wife suffered poor health, his books and records were destroyed in the Chicago Fire of 1871, he endured legal battles over his work for the South Parks, and he suffered the death of a son—all of which combined to make Chicago far less appealing than it once had been.[123] In 1886, at the age of seventy-two, Cleveland moved to Minneapolis, where he worked to create the city's park and recreation system.

Kenwood

⑫ Sheehan Residence, "The Bailey," c. 1855. Demolished.
Cottage Grove Avenue between 48th and 49th Streets. Builder unknown.

But you must see Kenwood as I saw it when we came here in 1861. As we approached, we passed Dr. Eagen's [Egan's] Lodge on the corner of Cottage Grove and Forty-seventh, where Mr. Liston and his five children managed to live in the only one-roomed thatched cottage any where near Chicago.

—Annie McClure Hitchcock, "Reminiscences of Kenwood in 1859"

When Peggy Sheehan died in 1897, few of her aristocratic neighbors mourned her passing. Sheehan had for years occupied a slice of their prestigious neighborhood, living in a small lean-to, a thatched shanty at the edge of the community. As Kenwood transformed into the "Lake Forest of the South Side," this Irish immigrant fought to keep a simple home for her family.[124] Like many other pre-development families, they were squatters on the land. Unlike other squatters, the Sheehans remained.

Sheehan and her husband Thomas came to Chicago at the recommendation of a relative, James Liston, who had arrived fifteen years earlier.[125] A lease of a nine-by-twelve lean-to on land in an area then known as the "Bailey" awaited their arrival.

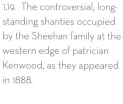

1.19. The controversial, long-standing shanties occupied by the Sheehan family at the western edge of patrician Kenwood, as they appeared in 1888.

The area was named for Elisha Bailey, who in the summer of 1858 purchased property between 48th and 50th Streets along Cottage Grove Avenue.[126] A former squatter named Parker claimed to have built the lean-to, and although Liston said he had purchased rights to the house, there were other claimants to the homestead.

Lively legal battles followed, but the Sheehans kept the place as their family grew. For nearly fifty years, the shanty, with its unwelcome tenants, proved unmovable by the due process of law.

After Thomas' death in 1889 his wife continued the fight, although confronted with numerous attempts to remove her. She held her own until 1895, when she capitulated and for the two years prior to her death paid an annual rental of $40. Peggy Sheehan was known as the oldest surviving pioneer of Egandale "squatting" at the southwest corner of 48th Street, until death finally dislodged her.[127]

13 Judd Residence, c. 1857. Demolished.
Lake Street near Mason (47th) Street. Architect/builder unknown.

Kenwood's political ties can be traced to the earliest citizens of the area. A New York native, Norman Buel Judd, came to Chicago in November 1836 and was attorney for the newly incorporated city from 1837 to 1839. Judd was involved in politics on the state and national level. During his years as a member of the Illinois senate, from 1844 to 1860, he maintained a large legal practice and specialized

1.20. On the wide verandah of the Judd residence, President Lincoln once spent a relaxing summer evening during the fall of 1857. Later purchased by the Kenwood Club, the structure was enlarged with a 40' · 75' addition in 1886 and moved to a 47th Street location, as seen in this photograph taken about 1890 for *Picturesque Kenwood, Hyde Park, Illinois: Its Artistic Homes, Boulevards, Drives, Scenery, and Surroundings.*

in railroad law, becoming attorney for the Illinois Central Railroad. Judd was a loyal supporter of his fellow South Side resident Lyman Trumbull for the United States Senate in 1855. And it was Judd who arranged for the "celebrated debates" between Stephen Douglas and Abraham Lincoln and helped to bring Illinois into the antislavery fight.[128]

Late in the 1850s, Judd purchased ten pastoral acres of land that stretched from 47th to 48th Street and east from Woodlawn to Lake. Set well back on the land was his large frame house, "quite the most stately home in the neighborhood."[129] A three-story central tower distinguished the façade and the broad porch caught the summer breezes off Lake Michigan. The property was improved with a lake of fish, walks, drives, and "a sensible garden," and the although the house was, according to James Runnion, "without any decided architectural beauty," it afforded "great room and comfort."[130]

Judd's wife Adeline, "tall and very slender, with dark hair, and a clear delicate skin," and "a beautiful face that expressed her lovely character,"[131] recalled a visit by Mr. Lincoln to their Kenwood home.

> Mr. Judd had invited Mr. Lincoln to spend the evening at our pleasant home on the shore of Lake Michigan. After tea, and until quite late, we sat on the broad piazza, looking out upon as lovely a scene as that which had made the Bay of Naples so celebrated. A number of vessels were availing themselves of a fine breeze to leave the harbor, and the lake was studded with many a white sail. I remember that a flock of sea-gulls were flying along the beach, and dipping their beaks and white-lined wings in the foam that capped the short waves as they fell upon the shore. Whilst we sat there the great white moon appeared on the rim of the eastern horizon, and slowly crept above the water, throwing a perfect flood of silver light upon the dancing waves. The stars shone with the soft light of a midsummer night, and the breaking of the low waves upon the shore, repeating the old rhythm of the song which they have sung for ages, added the charm of pleasant sound to the beauty of the night. Mr. Lincoln, whose home was far inland from the great lakes, seemed greatly impressed with the wondrous beauty of the scene, and carried by its impressiveness away from all thought of the jars and turmoil of earth.[132]

Evidently Mrs. Lincoln did not share her husband's affection for Judd. She never forgave him for supporting Trumbull, not Lincoln, in the 1855 US Senate election. Judd did back Lincoln at the 1860 Republican presidential convention. However, when it appeared he would receive a position in her husband's cabinet Mrs. Lincoln interceded, writing to David Davis in January 1861,

> Perhaps you will think it is no affair of *mine*, yet I see it, almost daily mentioned in the Herald, that *Judd* & some *few* Northern friends, are *urging* the *former's* claims to a cabinet appointment. *Judd* would cause trouble & dissatisfaction, & if Wall Street testifies correctly, his business transactions, have not always borne inspection. I heard the report, discussed at the table this morning, by persons who did not know, who was near, a party of gentlemen, evidently strong Republicans, they were

laughing at the idea of *Judd*, being any way, connected with the Cabinet in *these times*, when honesty in high places is so important. Mr. Lincoln's great attachment for you, is my present reason for writing. I know, a word from you, will have much effect, for the good of the country, and Mr. Lincoln's future reputation, I believe you will speak to him on this subject & urge him not to give him so responsible a place. It is strange, how little delicacy those Chicago men have.[133]

Judd's consolation prize was an appointment as the administration's minister to Prussia, where "his good hearted and courteous demeanor endeared him to the people of that city [Berlin] as well as to American travelers."[134] Judd remained in Berlin until 1865; however, when he returned to Kenwood he did not resume his legal practice. Judd was twice elected to Congress, and in his private affairs invested heavily in Colorado silver mines, eventually putting most of his fortune in establishing a silver-reduction company. The panic of 1873 and subsequent depression resulted in the "ruin of his schemes and he was hopelessly impoverished, even his homestead being swept away."[135] He withdrew from active political life when the loss crippled him financially, and his friends believed the losses affected his health as well. Judd suffered a severe illness, never fully recovered, and died in their home on North Dearborn Avenue on November 11, 1878.

Judd's house and grounds were sold to developers who opened Kimbark Avenue and put a portion of the land on the market in subdivided lots. In June 1884 the Kenwood Club leased the house for five years and reworked the interior to serve the needs of their 130 members. The structure was eventually purchased by the club, moved to a location facing 47th Street, and was for many years the second home of Kenwood's wealthy residents.

14 Hitchcock Residence, 1859. Demolished 1964.
4741 South Greenwood Avenue. Architect/builder unknown.

In 1922, Annie McClure Hitchcock was buried alongside her husband in Oak Woods Cemetery. As she left her flower-filled home for the last time, the neighborhood bid a final goodbye to a woman, who for sixty years had been "a force for good in the community."[136] She was one of the last of the old pioneers of the area, and her homestead was one of the few early residences that remained relatively unchanged.

Born north of the city in Waukegan in 1839, Annie McClure wed one of Chicago's early lawyers of note, Charles Hitchcock, on the eve of the Civil War. It was in the company of Charles and her childhood friend Marion Heald (and Marion's future husband, attorney Marland Leslie Perkins) that Hitchcock first laid eyes upon the land she would occupy until her death. It was a glorious afternoon in 1859 when Annie McClure's close friends, all busily planning their futures, rode out of the city. Charles pointed out to Annie "in a most casual and modest way, the roof of a wooden house, rising above a thick grove of oaks as the only house and land he *owned*, but it was too far from business."[137]

Not long after their wedding, the Hitchcocks gave up their city residence and came

1.21. Annie Hitchcock named the street on which this house stood, an area she recalled was a "green wood," where children visited to gather wildflowers, nuts, and plums.

to live in Kenwood, on three acres of land south of 47th Street at Greenwood. Just to the north were an additional five acres for raising cabbage and potatoes. Their country home, with riding and carriage horses, two cows, and a chicken house "afforded Mr. Hitchcock all of the joys of a farmer in his leisure hours." Hitchcock "trimmed the oaks so that the finest trees would have room to grow," Annie reminisced, and "laid out a walk with such substantial asphalt that it has not been repaired to this day," and they constructed a barn and gardener's house.[138] "At the corner of Greenwood and Forty-seventh was another swamp, and for the first few years we drove out of our backyard at Forty-seventh and Woodlawn Avenue," she continued, confirming the marshy conditions of the area. "I had the honor of naming Greenwood Avenue; indeed it was a green wood, much frequented by city children, bent on uprooting the wild flowers, and gathering the hazelnuts and wild plums."[139]

There were few neighbors near to the Hitchcocks, as each house was set on many acres. Kenwood's very first settler, Dr. Jonathan Kennicott, divided his time between dentistry and his beautiful gardens. Judge Williams had a house similar to the Hitchcocks on "eight or ten" acres on 46th Street between Woodlawn and Lake. Two other early settlers, lawyer Pennoyer Sherman and his wife Louisa, had "undisputed sway over the corner of Lake and Forty-seventh, and possessed clear right to old Lake Michigan with its sunrises and sunsets, its bathing and fishing, only hindered by the two Illinois Central Railroad tracks and its infrequent trains."[140]

The early years of the Hitchcock's marriage were at times filled with illness and sorrow; the war and "years of bereavement"[141] took their toll and Kenwood mourned a local tragedy. Like many of the men in the neighborhood, Charles would catch the early morning train to his office in the city. On a cold, snow-covered Thursday in January 1862, he boarded the 7:50 as usual, heading for the downtown offices of Hitchcock & Dupee. The small Illinois Central train, consisting of a passenger car and a baggage car drawn by a locomotive, was just leaving the Kenwood station when another train came up behind it.

The Cincinnati Express was running at a high speed when the engineer rounded a curve and saw the Illinois Central train just leaving the station. Alarms were sounded and gears thrown into reverse, but that was not enough to prevent a collision. Passengers on the IC heard the alarm and tried to get back to the platform before the train hit. Fortunately most managed to escape alive before the passenger car was torn apart. The list of the injured was a who's who of Kenwood and included the bruised Charles Hitchcock. But it was the sight of Judge Barron's head "hurled through the air . . . still quivering in some of its lineaments" that provided the greatest shock to all.[142]

Several years later, after the end of the war and the assassination of Lincoln, General Ulysses Grant came to Kenwood. The neighborhood greeted the triumphant Grant with "the finest event ever of such a magnitude,"[143] welcoming him at the home of Norman Judd. Mrs. Hitchcock recalled being of great assistance to Judd on the receiving line that day, providing the name, occupation, and place of residence of each unfamiliar guest.

Annie Hitchcock broadened her involvement in many neighborhood activities well beyond the political spectrum. A forceful, childless woman with a lifelong passion for the printed word, she started a reading room in a Hyde Park storefront. Her early work culminated in the establishment of the present branch system of the Chicago Public Library.

"The years passed on and changes with them," she wistfully recalled. The Hitchcocks added a library wing to the house where, she recalled, the details and the maps for the Park System of Chicago were drawn up. Outdoors they decided to have only lawn and trees and a fountain on the homestead. In spite of the abundance of groundwater, there was not enough spring water on the land, so the fountain was supplied via pipes from an iron spring in Washington Park, several blocks west. A "pretty house" by the French architect Lemonier was built across the street. The five-acre cabbage patch was divided and sold, but Charles left his mark in the "stately row of elms" along the entire front of 47th Street between Greenwood and Woodlawn.[144]

In 1871, when the great fire destroyed a major part of the city, Annie worked diligently to help alleviate the suffering it had brought to many. Unhappy that many of the funds were not reaching the needy, she undertook her own relief efforts. The story is told that she went to the destroyed Crosby's Opera House and rescued allegorical statues that had once graced the Washington Street façade—these could be seen on the grounds well into the 1950s. The fire brought other changes locally, with an influx of people moving away from the city center. Annie recalled that "each new neighbor who came to Kenwood was welcomed as a family friend."[145]

After Charles became ill with heart disease, his death at their home on May 6, 1881 did not come as a great surprise to his friends and family. He was remembered as a "lawyer of great ability and a gentleman of culture and dignity."[146] After his death, Annie expanded her humanitarian and philanthropic work. She was one of the founders of the Chicago Women's Club and a charter member of the Fortnightly Club. Continuing many of these activities for the rest of her life, she remarked that they "made less lonesome the advancing years."[147]

Always forceful, Hitchcock saw the city swallow her homestead and was quite clear on her feelings about the 1889 annexation. She later spoke of "the disastrous day when Hyde Park Village voted itself part of Chicago, so selling its birthright." She saw firsthand the transformation of the prairie into a small town, witnessing the Columbian Exposition, the founding of the university, and the effects of the First World War. As apartments and hotels surrounded her homestead, and as the larger city encroached on the beautiful landscape she had first seen on that sunny Saturday afternoon in 1859, Hitchcock always relied on her home as the center of influence.

Today it is hard to imagine the gracious estate that once occupied the land.[148] Here were held many social events, at all times of the year. One cold winter morning Annie Hitchcock had more than one hundred guests for a musicale and breakfast, bringing spring to Kenwood a bit early. "At the table in the dining room she served coffee and chocolate. The ice cream she had blocked into guitars, mandolins, violins and music books. The mantel in the reception hall was banked with primrose, hyacinth and ferns, while tulips, daffodils, and roses were used in profusion in all the rooms."[149]

As a strong supporter of the University of Chicago, Hitchcock may have given the trustees more than they anticipated. In 1899, she pledged a substantial donation for the construction of the residence hall in memory of her late husband.[150] When the university selected the Boston firm of Shepley, Rutan & Coolidge, she let her feelings be known to president William Rainey Harper. "I am not content," Hitchcock wrote, "that the building should be put up as my expression of an adequate memorial to my husband, and as my ideal of what a boy's dormitory should be, when I have not been consulted at all."[151] She lobbied for the commission to be awarded to rising young architect Dwight Heald Perkins, the son of her good friend Marion Perkins.

Hitchcock prevailed and donated her one-half interest in the building located downtown at the northwest corner of Madison and LaSalle Streets to the university.[152] When Hitchcock Hall was completed in 1902 its Gothic design blended elements of the Arts and Crafts movement and the Prairie School, with a focus on "craftsmanship, simplicity and a geometric rectilinear style."[153] Hitchcock personally selected and donated the furnishings, many of them designed by Gustav Stickley. Perkins and sculptor Richard Bock collaborated on an elaborate frieze for the library.[154] Mrs. Hitchcock would no doubt be pleased to know that Hitchcock Hall is listed on the National Register of Historic Places.

In the summer prior to the dedication of the residence hall, a tea was held on the Greenwood house lawn. "With the wide lawns that surround the stately Kenwood homes, the lawn tea is one of the most successful ways of entertaining on the midsummer days in town," noted the society pages. "Mrs. Charles Hitchcock of 4741 Greenwood avenue, who has one of the most beautiful lawns in the city, entertained yesterday for Miss Mary Willard of Berlin, Germany, who had been her guest last week."[155]

Those gracious summer days did not last forever, and in 1916, after fifty-five years, Hitchcock sold what remained of her Kenwood property, although she continued to live in the house until her death, alone except for a cook and housekeeper and an Irish groundskeeper. "The old frame residence at the northeast corner of Greenwood Avenue and 48th Street, west front 145 × 298 feet on the north and 208 feet on the south, has been transferred by Annie Hitchcock to the First Trust and Savings bank."[156]

Annie McClure Hitchcock died on June 29, 1922, in Berea, Kentucky.

⑮ Remmer Residence, 1861. Demolished.
4833 South Lake Street. Architect/builder unknown.

Englishman John Remmer was one of the earliest residents of Kenwood. Remmer began as a clerk in the Illinois Central superintendent's office and occupied the house at 4833 Lake Avenue from 1861 until 1878, which may have been the year of his death. The house was very near the Kenwood station, and Remmer was one of those seriously injured in the train accident that occurred in the early morning

1.22. Remmer, an employee of the Illinois Central, constructed his house adjacent to the railroad tracks. He was one of those listed as seriously injured in a deadly railroad accident during the winter of 1862.

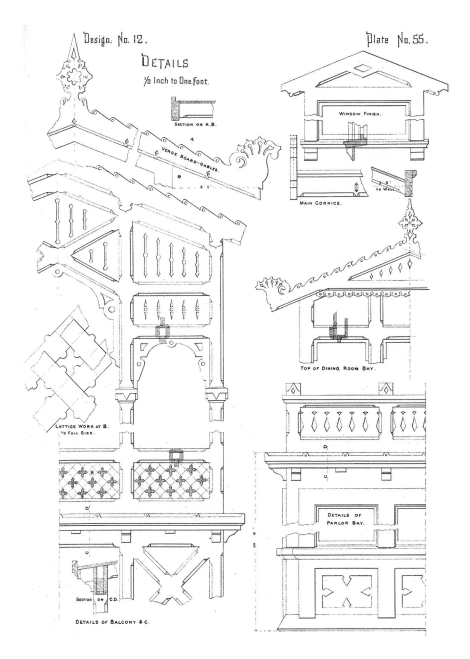

1.23. Charles D. Lakey's pattern book, *Lakey's Village and Country Houses, or Cheap Homes for All Classes* provided suggestions for elegant Greek-inspired detailing, including the distinctive verge board used on the Remmer house.

of January 9, 1862. Remmer became the secretary of the Illinois Central Railroad, and later worked as the general accountant for the Pullman Palace Car Company. In the census of 1880 his wife Elizabeth is listed as a widow, and it appears she and the children then moved to a house at 4827 Lake Avenue.

There are photographs of the two Remmer houses, quite unlike one another and located on adjacent lots, in the Chicago History Museum archives.[157] The more interesting of the two is this small two-story frame. The image is clearly labeled with a location on the east side of Lake Avenue; however, the sunlight apparent on the north side of the house calls into question its exact location on the property. The exterior is richly decorated—detailed with verge board and palmettes, a derivation of the acanthus leaf that has a long classical history.

16 Brainerd Residence, c. 1862.

1030 East 50th Street. Architect/builder unknown.

One of the few residences that remain in Kenwood from this early period is the home of Ezra Leander Brainerd. The two-story frame house was set well back on the large 72' × 297' lot, typical of the Kenwood neighborhood. After graduating from Yale Law School, Brainerd came to Chicago in October 1859. When the Civil War broke out, he served as a lieutenant in the 51st Illinois Volunteers. Jean Block wrote that Brainerd built the house for his fiancée in 1867, with his mustering-out pay. Brainerd was severely injured, however, mustered out under "Hallock's famous order" and returned to Kenwood, marrying Hattie Moorehouse in 1862.[158] Their first child was born the following year; therefore, the house most likely dates from 1862.

Although the house has been considerably altered over the years, the original frame structure can still be easily discerned when viewed from Greenwood Avenue. Even so, the home bears little resemblance to a description of its appearance in 1869: "Mr. Brainerd has a queer, antique-looking establishment," author James Runnion critiqued, "which might have been transported from the town of old Leipsic."[159] The couple resided here for only a few years before moving to a house at Woodlawn and 48th Streets (demolished) that may have been the subject of Runnion's critique.[160]

1.24. Today the porch and main entrance of the Brainerd house face the fifty-foot frontage of 49th Street.

⑰ Bouton Residence, 1873.
4812 South Woodlawn Avenue. Architect/builder unknown.

1.25. The Bouton house features the tight, symmetrical floor plan typical of the Italianate Style. Its frame construction is relatively simple; the decorative bracketed cornices and rounded window shapes provide ornamentation to an uncomplicated box.

Newspaper accounts indicate that this house may have been constructed as late as 1873. It is included in this section because of its similarity with other houses built at the time and to demonstrate by comparison that house styles do not fall neatly into timeframe categories. The house was built for Christopher Bouton, who married Eleanora (Nellie) Hoyt in December 1869. Nellie was a daughter of realtor and Woodville resident William Hoyt. Within several years, the Boutons moved into a house constructed in rural Kenwood on a large parcel of land.

Christopher's brother Nathaniel Sherman Bouton settled in Chicago in 1852 and cofounded the firm of Stone, Boomer & Bouton, Bridge and Car Builders and Railroad Building. Their foundry, located at Clark Street near 15th Street, built many bridges, including the first to cross the Mississippi River at Rock Island, Illinois.[161] Christopher joined his brother in 1863, and in 1871 they incorporated the business under the name of the Union Foundry Company, suppliers of wheels and other materials for the manufacturing of railroad cars, with Nathaniel as president and Christopher as secretary and treasurer.[162] By 1881 the firm reorganized with the Pullman Car Company and built a plant on eleven acres in the town of Pullman.[163] Nathaniel and his wife Ellen were also Kenwood residents—their house at 1122 East 47th Street was demolished long ago.

Although of frame construction, Christopher's Italianate-style house is reminiscent on both the exterior and the interior, of the brick Italianate house at 5704 Dorchester occupied by Nellie's parents William and Mary Hoyt from 1869 to 1888.[164] The similarities are not surprising, given the family relationship and the availability of pattern books that supplied many variations on the theme. The house has been raised on a brick foundation to accommodate a basement, and the large addition at the rear was completed in 2003. Like the Hoyts' front porch, the Boutons' porch initially spanned the entire front of the house.

As land values increased and the neighborhood shed its suburban character, the Boutons sold their land north of 48th Street. The final portion of their once large Kenwood lot was given to their daughter as a wedding gift. Persis Bouton and her husband Robert McDougal erected the large Tudor-style house directly to the north, visible in the photograph.

Drexel Boulevard

18 Clarke Residence, 1870. Demolished 1917.
4651 Drexel Boulevard. Architect/builder unknown.

In 1869 the Western News Company published a "Descriptive Historical and Statistical Account of the Suburban Towns and Residences of Chicago." Written by James B. Runnion, the series originally appeared in the Sunday edition of the *Chicago Sun-Times* under the name *Out of Town*. Runnion noted that it could

1.26. Although constructed as a single-family residence for the Clarke family, for a time the Harvard School for Boys occupied this wood-frame structure. Graduates of the school included author Edgar Rice Burroughs and architects Benjamin Marshall and Bertrand Goldberg.

only be after "acquiring a familiarity with the number, the extent, the growth, the enterprise, and the character of these suburban settlements, that the vigor, the immensity," of Chicago that its possibilities could be understood.

Runnion described the rapid improvement of an avenue that would become home to many of Chicago's elite, noting structures contemplated and nearing construction. On the northeast corner of Drexel at 47th Street, Col. George R. Clarke began construction of a "fine brick residence, " while grain dealer James A. Davol and his wife Annie began construction of a frame house on the west side of the boulevard. Lawyer and real estate backer George C. Walker began construction near this intersection in the fall of 1869.[165]

Clarke joined the volunteer Illinois Infantry in August 1862 and finished the Civil War as a lieutenant colonel. After the war he dealt in real estate until, influenced by his wife Sarah Dunn Clarke, he opened a ministry in Chicago in 1877. The rescue mission moved to the former location of the disreputable Pacific Beer Garden in 1880, taking the name but leaving the "Beer" behind.[166] The Pacific Garden Mission continues to operate as a homeless shelter in the South Loop neighborhood.

Tragedy marked this residence during the years Warren Leland and his family lived on the boulevard. Leland came from a family of hotel managers that were known across the country. In addition to the Leland Hotel on Michigan Avenue in Chicago and the Chicago Beach Hotel in Hyde Park, he was the proprietor of the Windsor Hotel, at 575 Fifth Avenue in New York City. His family was staying at the Windsor in March 1899, and had gathered to watch the St. Patrick's Day parade passing below when fire rapidly spread through the building. The seven-story structure was destroyed within ninety minutes, killing both his wife Isabella and his daughter Helen, who jumped from the roof of the hotel.[167] Leland came back to Chicago for the funerals that took place from the house, and then returned to New York. It was reported that he was in a state of shock from the deaths of his wife and daughter, and from the terrible loss of life and property.[168] Death soon followed: Leland lived only until the fifth of April.

The house was one of the landmarks of Kenwood when it was demolished in 1917 to make way for a large apartment hotel.[169]

Cleaverville

⑲ Trumbull Residence, c. 1855. Demolished.
4008 South Lake Street. Architect/builder unknown.

Several residents of the small town of Cleaverville, just to the north of Kenwood, had associations with the community.[170] It was there that the distinguished senator Lyman Trumbull settled. "A rather tall and spare gentleman with a sandy complexion and gold spectacles,"[171] Trumbull became a friend of then attorney Abraham Lincoln during his travels with the Circuit Court. At this

time they shared similar fundamental beliefs and became early members of the Republican Party.

Earlier in his career, Trumbull was appointed to succeed Stephen Douglas as secretary of state for Illinois in 1840, but he lost a number of subsequent elections as a Democratic candidate for governor, and twice for Congress. By 1848 he was elected a justice of the Supreme Court of Illinois, and although a "retiring" and "unassertive" person, his opinions were thought to be "among the soundest handed down by the court."[172] Trumbull was then elected to the United States Senate in 1855 when Lincoln yielded in order to break a deadlock, and served for eighteen years.

Although a senatorial opponent, Trumbull returned the favor and loyally supported Lincoln's candidacy for president in 1860. Lincoln relied on Trumbull as one of his representatives in Washington for a period after the election, but they drifted apart once the president was inaugurated. The level of their disaffection is reflected in a letter written by Mary Lincoln's cousin, Elizabeth Grimsley. "I have not seen Mrs. Trumbull—she sent me word she expected me to call, as that is etiquette," Grimsley wrote from the White House in March 1861, "but I concluded in the present state of affairs . . . that Mrs. Trumbull might waive ceremony also, if she wished to see me. Trumbull is exceedingly unpopular here and particularly so with the conservative portion of the Republican Party."[173]

Trumbull's brother-in-law wrote a friend that Trumbull had become alienated from the president: "Mr. Lincoln has not treated Mr. Trumbull as he should and Mr. T. said this morning, that he should not step inside the White House again during Mr. Lincoln's four years, unless he changed his course."[174] For men of such

1.27. An "old Negro servant of the Trumbulls" claimed that President Lincoln visited this house. However in *Old Chicago Houses* John Drury wrote that Trumbull did not live here until after Lincoln left Chicago for the last time. Notables who did visit this unpretentious residence included president Ulysses S. Grant, and three-time Democratic presidential aspirant and secretary of state William Jennings Bryan. This image was taken in 1913.

power some of the matters seem petty; other matters, relating to cabinet selections, proved much more serious.

The connections between the Lincoln and Trumbull families ran deep. Julia Jane, Trumbull's first wife, was a bridesmaid for Mary Todd at her wedding; however, their friendship could not withstand the pressures of politics.[175] The "struggle over appointments during the early weeks of the Lincoln administration seems to have completed the break in the friendship between Julia Trumbull and Mary Lincoln," wrote biographer William Miller. "Each wife only saw her husband's side of the imbroglio."[176]

Robert Lincoln once questioned his father about his differences with Trumbull. "We agree perfectly, but we see things from a different point of view," replied the president. "I am in the White House looking down the Avenue, and Trumbull's in the Senate looking up."[177]

By 1864 the Trumbulls returned from Washington, moving to a simple frame dwelling at 4008 Lake Avenue. Constructed sometime in the 1850s, the house was subsequently enlarged and altered. Julia died in this home in 1868, and Trumbull remarried here in 1877. The house, which sat well back on the lot, was the residence of Mary and Lyman Trumbull until his death there in 1896. A bronze marker once placed on the front of the house remembered him as a friend to Lincoln and read, in part:

LYMAN TRUMBULL.

FRIEND OF LINCOLN,

SENATOR FROM ILLINOIS;

SUPPORTED LINCOLN;

SECURED THE PASSAGE OF THE

14TH AMENDMENT.

WAS ONE OF THE REPUBLICANS

WHO VOTED AGAINST

IMPEACHMENT OF

ANDREW JOHNSON.[178]

The 1876 *Lakeside Directory of Chicago* listed Lyman Trumbull at his residence (then 285 Lake), and just to the south at 287 (4016) Lake Street was his extended family—his brother George Trumbull, but also Walter Trumbull and John H. Trumbull. An image of the house they occupied shows it was typical of a suburban house built during the Civil War period. Unlike later construction, the house was positioned on the lot with the length of the structure facing the street.

Senator Trumbull's brother George was considered by some to be "a man of the strictest integrity, modest and retiring, and an accurate and able lawyer."[179] However, when the Illinois Central Railroad employed George Trumbull, it was assumed his powerful brother was responsible for the position, for he possessed a "propensity for family politics," according to the *New York Times*. Senator Trumbull opposed a bill that would have required the Illinois Central Railroad to return $2 million to the US government, paid for carrying soldiers during the Civil War. The bill was defeated, and shortly thereafter a "curious coincidence took place." His brother George, deemed "notoriously inadequate" to fill the position, was made general attorney for the railroad company at an annual salary of $12,000.[180] Ten years later in October 1876 he penned his resignation letter to the president of the railroad, William Ackerman, "I hereby resign my position, as attorney of the Illinois Central Railroad Company. I cannot hold it at the reduced salary."[181]

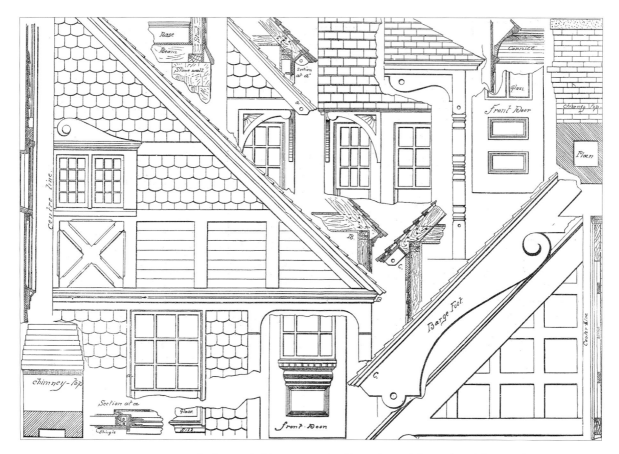

2.01. By the 1870s builders promoted widely read journals for residential design and construction. These pattern books, including Palliser's *New Cottage Homes and Details, Containing Nearly Two Hundred & Fifty New & Original Designs in All the Modern Popular Styles,* claimed to provide a secure and tested alternative to the services of an architect. Palliser offered large-scale drawings of architectural features that builders could use to enrich basic domestic structures.

CHAPTER TWO

Living Patterns, 1871–1891

We struck the home trail now, and in a few hours were in that astonishing Chicago—a city where they are always rubbing a lamp, and fetching up the genii, and contriving and achieving new impossibilities. It is hopeless for the occasional visitor to try to keep up with Chicago—she outgrows her prophecies faster than she can make them. She is always a novelty, for she is never the Chicago you saw when you passed through the last time.

—Mark Twain, *Life on the Mississippi*, 1883

Visitors and residents alike witnessed the astonishing growth of the city and surrounding area. With the vast railroad network in place, Chicago flourished after the end of the Civil War. The population grew to over 300,000 by 1870, within geographic boundaries that stretched to 39th Street on the South Side. The city featured a thriving central business district and neighborhoods formed by immigrants continually pouring into the city. Lured by the brisk economic growth and anticipated prosperity, thousands arrived every year to take advantage of the opportunities Chicago had to offer.

The dreams of success were interrupted on a warm October evening when, after a hot and dry summer, a fire began in Patrick and Catherine O'Leary's barn on the Near South Side. Fueled by densely packed frame houses and wooden sidewalks, and fanned by a strong wind, the fire quickly spread. Despite firefighters' efforts to contain it, the massive blaze moved steadily to the northeast. By the time the fire reached the central business district, it became an inferno and the masonry walls of commercial buildings that were supposed to be fireproof tumbled to the ground. The city's waterworks failed after the blaze crossed the Chicago River, and the fire then destroyed nearly everything in its path. After three days, rain began to fall, and the great fire died out roughly four and a half miles north of the O'Leary barn, leaving the heart of the city in ruins.[1] "As a spectacle, it was beyond a doubt the grandest as well as the most appalling ever offered to our mortal eyes," one eyewitness recalled.[2]

The Great Chicago Fire of 1871 has traditionally been thought of as a turning point in the city's history.[3] While devastating, it was a momentary setback, for in the aftermath the city proved its greatness, and an era of even greater expansion began. Chicago's strategic midwestern location made certain that the city would be rebuilt, and the breadth of devastation provided the opportunity for planning on a massive scale.[4] Architects flocked to the city to participate in the rebuilding. The new business district heralded the future: buildings were taller due to the introduction of the elevator, and within a few years they were lit with electric lights.[5] The potential of Chicago's business district was demonstrated with William LeBaron Jenney's 1884 design of the Home Insurance Building and other innovative buildings that followed: H. H. Richardson's influential design of Marshall Field & Company's wholesale store and Burnham & Root's Rookery Building with its inner courtyard enclosed by a dome of steel and glass. While spared the flames, Hyde Park felt the fire's effect as, in the aftermath, movement of residential settlement away from the commercial center accelerated as the area rebuilt.

Although it did not alter the basic shape of the city, the fire initiated changes that transformed its "social geography."[6] Chicago exhibited "a highly skewed distribution of wealth": 20 percent of the wealthiest families held 90 percent of the total assets of the city.[7] Although differences in their living standards were obvious, people of all economic and social classes lived relatively close together before the fire. However within two years the fire turned an "old fashioned walking city," into a "comparatively modern industrial metropolis."[8] While some affluent Chicagoans chose to rebuild near the city center, for others the residential railroad suburbs outside the city looked especially attractive after the fire. As the outmigration increased, wealthier residents moved with others of their class to the suburbs, particularly those easily accessible and enhanced by parks and boulevards.

Unfortunately, Olmsted and Vaux's grand plans for the South Parks were housed in the offices of the commission in one of the buildings unable to survive the flames, and were destroyed. The loss was a major one—without the original plans, specifications, or contracts, and having lost the atlases of the towns of Hyde Park and Lake showing ownership of land, work on the parks was immediately stopped. The suspension of work continued for nearly a year, until in September landscape architect H. W. S. Cleveland was hired and work on the parks resumed.

The original concept envisioned an eastern park adjacent to the lake (Lake Park) and a western park (South Park), connected by a drive. The plan for these areas combined elements such as shadowy, winding paths with calming and graceful elements such as broad, sunny meadows to create "a sense of mystery."[9] Cleveland supervised the continuation of Olmsted's vision, however there was a "critical difference": Cleveland was to execute a version of the plan under a "rigid economy."[10] By 1875 the commissioners had purchased 1,045 acres, of which 780 had been paid for in full. Nearly four-fifths of the western park had been improved, where 350 acres had been tilled and seeded and planted with trees. One of the first major elements completed was the "South Open Green," a huge pastoral meadow complete with grazing sheep. The connecting drive, the Midway Plaisance, was

constructed between Lake Park and South Park, and the nursery was furnishing several thousand trees each year.[11] In 1881 the commission was asked to officially name the parks, and they were renamed to honor the nation's first and seventh presidents. The park adjacent to the lake became Jackson Park and South Park was renamed Washington Park.

The improvements to the parks and the variety of transportation options enhanced interest in the real estate south of the city, and the result was obvious as the population of Hyde Park and Kenwood expanded rapidly. The population quadrupled from 3,644 in 1870 to 15,724 by the end of the decade.[12] The trend toward urbanization was immediately recognized as requiring more structure, and in 1872 the state legislature granted Hyde Park Township a village form of government. An election followed where 262 votes were cast in favor of the new form of government, with 188 cast against.[13] While the term "village" may imply a cozy settlement, the borders did not change, as the designation applied to the area bordered by 39th Street on the north and 138th Street on the southern boundary. The more comprehensive village form of government combined the leadership of part-time elected officials (six trustees) with the know-how of a manager (the village president). Together they were responsible for setting village policy, determining the annual budget and taxes, and outlining special assessments and condemnations in order to make much needed improvements.[14]

During this period, the residential enclaves of Hyde Park and Kenwood at the northern end of the village developed an identity separate from the greater village of Hyde Park. Demographically, the residents there were on the wealthier end of the spectrum; an average house cost $7,000, in contrast to the southern section, where one cost $2,000.[15] Geographically, the enclaves of Hyde Park and Kenwood

Kenwood Station, Illinois Central Railroad, after 1877. Mason (47th) Street. Architect/builder unknown.

2.02. The Illinois Central Railroad continually upgraded their facilities to enhance the commute between the Hyde Park area and the central business district. Improvements included the structure on the right, next to the older three-room Kenwood station that was designed in November 1877. Both structures in this undated image feature jigsaw lacework and finials on the roof, typical of early railroad architecture.

2.03. Hyde Park petitioned to form a separate township in 1861, and by 1872 adopted a village form of government. However, the boundaries of the area remained constant. This map demonstrates Cornell's settlement of Hyde Park on the north in relation to the larger village. On March 29 of that year, the president of the newly formed village wrote of its appeal in *Hyde Park Herald*: "Hyde Park is to Chicago, not only what Brooklyn is to New York, its natural bed chamber, but also to a great extent its pleasure ground; affording elegant residence sites, charming views, beautiful scenery, pure air, fine drives, and all the other appliances demanded by a refined and luxurious civilization."

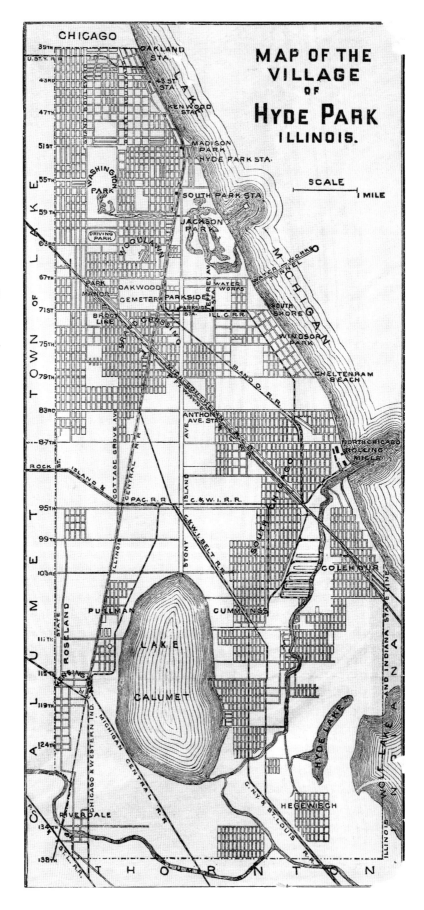

were separated by the South Park system, which provided natural boundaries on both the southern and western borders. Washington Park and the adjacent community served as the boundary between the Union Stockyards further west. Although not yet planted, Jackson Park was to anchor the lakefront, while the Midway provided a narrow boundary line on the south.

The village trustees responsible for this huge area faced a multitude of issues and worked to provide the physical infrastructure needed to sustain the growing population. They gradually provided fire and police protection, sanitation and sewage, and streets and schools, and they outlined a structure to collect revenue to pay for all of these services. The law provided that the cost of any of these improvements was to "be borne by the property which will be benefitted by it."[16] After a petition for a particular improvement was reviewed and approved by the trustees, a department of three commissioners estimated the cost of the project and the amount property owners in the vicinity would have to contribute.

The improvements and expenses were both small and major in scope. Diseases including diphtheria, smallpox, and scarlet fever were common; therefore of prime concern were a pure supply of drinking water and an adequate sewage system. Water initially came from wells and water hawkers, and then from a pumping station at 68th Street.[17] As the lake was used for both drinking water and the disposal of sewage, contamination made the building of the town's waterworks of prime importance. By 1889 a new pumping station had been ambitiously constructed extending one mile into Lake Michigan. However it was still not far enough away to prevent contamination. And although the new waterworks provided high-pressure water service at fire hydrants, at times the high demand depleted pressure and water could not rise above the ground floor of many houses.[18]

Drainage was also a constant problem due to the marshy topography. Streets were ditched on both sides to allow water to run off, wooden sidewalks were built above grade, and houses were constructed on brick or stone foundations to protect them from flooding.[19] In spite of these efforts, the ground remained muddy in the winter and spring and dusty in the summer. Overall, however, the many improvements were soon evident. In 1883 the annual message of the president (of the village of Hyde Park) boasted of 730 street lamps and "a highly efficient telephonic service" that was coordinated with the police and fire departments. By 1887 the village of Hyde Park displayed seventy-two miles of macadamized roads, one hundred fifty miles of wooden sidewalks, and six and a half of stone, seventy-seven miles of water pipes, and thirty-three miles of sewers. Additionally, according to Jean Block, fifteen hundred gas or oil lamps lit the streets. However, none of this happened without considerable cost to village residents.[20]

Although removed from many of the larger urban problems, the small community had other issues to address as it grew. Greater density and prosperity made security a concern. By the mid-1880s the Hyde Park police force included forty men, a number that increased annually. The trustees of the village limited the sale of liquor within the community, yet taverns could be found along the commercial strip on Lake Avenue in the center of Hyde Park. All in all, the small village gov-

2.04. J. B. McClure's *Stories and Sketches* included a romanticized lithograph of the very earliest days of Drexel Boulevard, an avenue intended to be a pleasure drive with no commercial traffic allowed. However, the helter-skelter pattern of carriages indicates a less than serene experience, confirmed by an October 5, 1886, *New York Times* article entitled "A Street Full of Runaways." The boulevard was a scene of great excitement when a "span of powerful horses" attached to an open carriage became unmanageable and tore down the crowded street "at a frightening rate of speed." Unsettling other horse-drawn carriages, the animals continued for a mile, demolishing six carriages, injuring twenty, and scattering occupants all over the drive.

ernment had its hands full as the disparity between the village center and the outer environs of Hyde Park increased.

Sheltered by the lake on the east and the partially completed series of parks, Hyde Park and the adjacent communities were defined by their own unique characteristics that are still visible today. The center of Hyde Park was the commercial hub, and adjacent lot sizes were smaller, resulting in a more urban environment. Trains no longer refueled near 57th Street, and Woodville was renamed South Park. Kenwood featured a series of bucolic estates, and "choice lots" were advertised in the *Chicago Tribune* at any width by two or three hundred feet deep. Meanwhile, the broad avenues on the western border of the community developed as one of Chicago's most fashionable places to live. By 1874 Kenwood competed with the exclusive suburbs north of the city and became known as the "Lake Forest of the south side."[21]

Grove Parkway, one component of Olmsted's concept for the South Parks, was planned to extend north from the eastern edge of Washington Park through land that had been a part of Dr. William Egan's grand estate, Egandale. The Drexel family of Philadelphia developed the parkway and surrounding property after acquiring the land when Egan became overextended and eventually defaulted on the loan held by the Chicago office of Drexel & Smith. Francis Drexel donated a wide strip of the land for a boulevard a mile and a half long, "in the hope of stimulating development" and therefore the value of the newly held property.[22] Grove Parkway became Drexel Boulevard, anchored on its southern end by the Francis Drexel Fountain, the oldest public fountain in the city. Lot sizes on the boulevard varied, but were typically large enough to provide for spacious urban estates.

Drexel Boulevard was just one of many boulevards constructed in cities across

the country during the second half of the nineteenth century. These formal avenues created park-like corridors and were among the city's most fashionable
neighborhoods. Presence upon the boulevard was dictated by one's wealth, which
required an appropriate display of architecture.[23] Drexel was the most exclusive of
the South Side boulevards, and noted architects, including Henry Ives Cobb and
Burnham & Root, designed massive residences, intended to impress. Imitation
castles and châteaus rose, where occupants lived in a world of exclusive clubs, private schools, and reserved church pews. The tree-lined avenue marked the Hyde
Park landscape as a very special place, and by the turn of the century Drexel was a
showpiece that reflected the wealth and status of a prospering society.

   Noting the abundance of private investment in the community, land specu-
lators quickly recognized the profit to be made from South Side properties. As
the early settlers passed away, their large rural estates were sold and subdivided.
For example, after the death of Hon. Norman Judd in 1878, his ten acres were
subdivided and sold as individual lots by Thomas & Putnam. The firm took six
months to complete the initial arrangements, but by June 1881 the first sales on the
4700 block of Kimbark were closed. The first purchase was the northeast corner
of Kimbark at 48th by Walter Coolidge, and others shortly followed, including
prominent Chicagoans Montgomery Ward, George Thorne, and Calvin DeWolfe.
These four houses were erected for a combined value of $100,000, a sum that at
the time "fixed the status of Kimbark Avenue."[24] By 1885 the lots were completely
sold on this block of Kimbark, and the slower-moving lots on Woodlawn were sold
out as well. Today Kimbark remains one of the most delightful and desirable streets
in Kenwood, uniquely representative of life in the community over a century ago.

**Francis M. Drexel Memorial
Fountain, 1882.
Drexel Square. Henry Manager.**
2.05. The Francis M. Drexel
Memorial Fountain and a more
serene flow of carriage traffic
on Drexel Boulevard as seen
in a view from *Picturesque
Kenwood*, c. 1890. The boulevard
was planned as a drive with
traffic lanes on either side of a
median, and was landscaped
with formal plantings set among
winding walks according to plans
developed in 1873-74 by H. W. S.
Cleveland.

2.06. After the Honorable Norman Judd's death in 1878, his ten acres were sold and the property subdivided. Houses quickly rose on Kimbark Avenue, as seen in an image from *Picturesque Kenwood* looking south from 47th Street.

From the estates on Drexel, to the large residences on Kimbark, to the smaller houses in the center of town, a common thread linked the dwellings—the individuality of each structure—as interest in architecture and home decoration grew. After the fire, Hyde Park and Kenwood attracted a wider variety of people, which in turn meant that a wider variety of houses were constructed on varying lot sizes. Residents who could not afford the services of an architect were nonetheless influenced by current ideas about home design. Abundant creativity, made possible by advances in production techniques, was a hallmark of the houses constructed. Pattern books were commonly marketed toward women and utilized for construction, claiming to provide reliable houses for an established price, as opposed to the unknowns presented when working with an architect.

American thought influenced the popularity of the pattern book for housing design. Many of the houses constructed in Hyde Park and Kenwood during this time represented the view of the family as a haven from the industrialized and

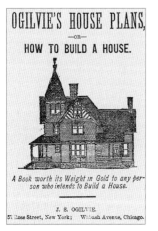

2.07. John Stuart Ogilvie's publication on house building, *Ogilvie's House Plans, Or, How to Build a House,* included plans and specifications for houses and barns. Suggesting the importance of appealing to women, advertisements within the pamphlet offered titles such as "Only a 'Woman's Heart, or, Barbara's Rival" and "What to Eat and How to Cook It: With Rules for Preserving, Canning and Drying Fruits and Vegetables."

commercial world, providing an idealized retreat for men and a refuge for "delicate, nurturing women."[25] Domestic issues took a majority of a woman's time, and while the home was viewed as a sanctuary, it was also isolating. Women began to expand their sphere of influence as the cause of "domestic science" was promoted. "The care of a house, the conduct of a home, and management of children and the government of servants" were in the words of Catherine Beecher "deserving of scientific treatment."[26]

At the same time, the field of architecture was coming into its own. Until the fire, there had been but a few practicing architects in the city, many of whom were former builders who simply hired draftsmen to produce a set of plans. After the fire, architects, masons, and builders flocked to Chicago in order participate in the rebuilding of the city. There were no architectural licensing laws, and the rising complexities of construction led a group of architects from the Midwest and the South to found the Western Association of Architects (WAA). Established in Chicago in 1884, the group merged with the American Institute of Architects (AIA) five years later. The AIA had been organized in 1857 by a group of East Coast architects (including Calvert Vaux and H. W. S. Cleveland) who sought to create an architecture organization to "promote the scientific and practical perfection of its members" as well as to "elevate the standing of the profession."[27]

As the field matured, interest in domestic architecture no longer lagged behind that in commercial buildings, as architects and builders competed for lucrative com-

Aldrich Residence, 1887. Demolished. 321 (1020) 49th Street. Architect/builder unknown.

2.08. The asymmetrical façade, turret, and elaborate woodwork of the residence of J. Franklin and Lulu Aldrich would have been brightly painted, and overall bears a similarity to the cover of Ogilvie's pamphlet. The direction of residential architecture at this time was toward a complex massing of shapes with a rich palette of color not appropriate in the Italianate style. Described as a dignified, forceful, yet considerate United States congressman, Aldrich was active politically for over half a century and served as a Republican in the House of Representatives from 1893 until 1897. The site of the Aldrich home has been subdivided, and is now occupied by three houses designed by Keck & Keck.

missions. America's industrial growth produced large urban upper and middle classes with resources to invest in houses and products for their homes. Residences were increasingly larger and more complicated, reflecting the owner's desires and status. The simplicity and elegance of the Italianate style of the sixties and seventies gave way to other elaborate styles, ranging from the fanciful Queen Anne to the heavy stone of Romanesque Revival. During this era of domestic prosperity, Hyde Park's suburban location offered room for large houses in picturesque surroundings, providing space and comfort while advertising residents' high social aspirations.

Displaying plentiful and varied ornamentation, the Queen Anne style became popular across the country in the latter part of the nineteenth century. At the 1876 Centennial Exposition in Philadelphia, the British government displayed several buildings of varying styles named for earlier English queens. It was noted that the English buildings were "among the handsomest in the Exhibition."[28] The American public was quick to embrace the new forms, viewing the style as representative of the ideal of "home, family and womanhood."[29]

Picturesqueness continued to be the guiding aesthetic principal during this period on residences of varying scale. Throughout Hyde Park are many examples of the intricate wood fretwork, irregular, steeply pitched rooflines, and asymmetrical shapes that characterized Queen Anne houses. Typically of frame construction due to the high cost of brick, the highly decorative structures featured textured shingles that resembled fish scales and an array of elements, including bay windows, rounded towers, and welcoming porches. Industrialization propelled the style's popularity, as mills could mass-produce moldings in elegant beaded or floral designs or spindles in delicate cylindrical shapes. The range of machinery available quickly allowed builders to apply the complexities of the Queen Anne style to the larger residences of Kenwood and South Park, as well as to the relatively less expensive houses in the center of Hyde Park.

Newly available materials were used throughout the area. Stained glass became popular for decoration of windows and doors, and copper replaced tin for roofing.[30] Meanwhile, the availability of pressed brick and quarried stone enhanced the construction of substantial residences. During the latter half of the eighties, the influence of Boston architect Henry Hobson Richardson was widespread. Despite its medieval origins, heavy stone, and arches, "Richardsonian Romanesque" is regarded as an original and highly influential American architectural style. Richardson used natural materials such as rustic stone and implemented Romanesque principles of construction to create picturesque architectural compositions. He believed that outer form should reflect the structure, contrasting with the applied fretwork and other decorative elements of the Queen Anne style. His work, distinguished through the use of thick stone walls, was widely imitated, and his influence can be found throughout the Hyde Park neighborhood in the work of architects Frederick Perkins, Minard Beers, and John Root.

House styles evolved not only on the exterior, as a number of much appreciated interior improvements were introduced. Gas permitted better lighting, although rooms were often dark and cluttered, filled with an array of fabrics, wallpaper, and furnishings. There were improvements in heating; however stoves remained the

norm in smaller residences, supplanting the more meager heat of the fireplace. In larger houses, hot-air furnaces were housed in a new architectural element—the basement—and connected to the upper stories by a maze of flues. During Chicago's long, cold winters these furnaces had to be stoked with coal, which polluted the air. Public concern about sanitation led to new technologies that addressed fears about germs and sewer gas. An 1898 issue of *Architectural Record* stated that after 1880 "true sanitary plumbing began" with the availability of porcelain fixtures and galvanized iron pipes.[31] Hyde Park was on the cutting edge, for in the previous year the village diligently reported that within the 992 residences, there were 376 bathtubs and 384 toilets.[32]

In the broader picture, architects began to consider planning beyond the design of the individual house, and to think about planning groups of residences in a

Charles Friedrich's Family
Resort. Demolished.
5472 Lake Avenue, architect/
builder unknown.

2.10. Among the commercial
enterprises found at Lake
Avenue and 55th Street
were the popular and
sometimes problematic liquor
establishments. Like other forms
of commerce, taverns were
permitted only within a small
area of Hyde Park, clustered
near the Illinois Central Railroad
tracks. The bowler-hatted
gentlemen in this 1892 image
appear in front of a liquor-serving
"family" resort.

suburban setting. Architect Solon Beman specialized in this type of work. Beman
came to Chicago in 1879 at the request of railroad car magnate George Pullman
to design the company's town. Beman was then contracted to design and supervise
the construction of a group of single-family dwellings in South Park that became
known as Rosalie Villas. This suburban development was an attempt to design a
number of houses as a group, rather than to think about each independently, as in
the case of the Kimbark development. However, there was no overriding aesthetic
for the project; some of the houses were heavily adorned, while others featured
graceful arched porches.[33] While Beman designed several of the moderately sized
houses, he contracted and supervised other architects who supplied the variety of
this still charming street.

As these and other new houses rose throughout the area, families gradually became less self-sufficient. Although they grew vegetables in backyard gardens and
kept milk cows and other livestock, for the most part individuals were dependent
on others for the necessities of life. In this increasingly complex society, the center
of Hyde Park accelerated its development as the commercial hub focused on Lake
Avenue between 53rd and 55th Streets. Shopping districts also included a cluster
of stores on 57th Street between Harper and Blackstone. The growing support network was evident as the number of food stores grew to forty from six between 1883
an 1886, and included bakeries, fruit shops, and confectionary stores. There were
cigar and tobacco shops, blacksmiths and livery stables, dressmakers and tailors.

Doctors and dentists opened offices, and five real estate offices opened to serve the needs of prospective buyers.[34] Liquor establishments proliferated; between 1877 and 1878 forty-nine saloon licenses were issued in the village, while just one was refused.[35] There was not a single store to be found in Kenwood, however, and residents had the resources to keep it that way, at least temporarily. In contrast to the industrial southern end of the village of Hyde Park, life in these enclaves remained genteel with many opportunities for relaxation and amusement.

Residents of the area were offered a wide range of social, cultural, intellectual, and recreational pursuits. Lake Michigan was an important attraction in the hot summer months for swimming and boating. The parks and the parkways were in the process of becoming beautifully landscaped for use by all. Private facilities thrived as well—the Kenwood Club was founded, providing members with a social, family-oriented destination that included a dancing hall, reading room, and reception parlors. Four grass tennis courts were installed to meet the mania for the sport, which was introduced from England. There were bicycle clubs, baseball clubs, and facilities for horse racing. Flood's Hall on 53rd near the tracks was a "good sized room above Dow's Drug Store" where public lectures, concerts, political meetings, and dancing classes were held.[36] Rosalie Villas provided a public music hall and a private clubhouse for members. The Kenwood Barge Club was housed in a boathouse at the pier at 53rd Street. Balloons rose to a height of 1,300 feet, accompanied by grand concerts and a ladies orchestra, were offered every afternoon and evening (weather permitting) from the Balloon Park at Cottage Grove and 50th Street. In 1883 Solon Beman designed the elegantly appointed Washington Park Club on eighty acres at 61st Street and Grand Boulevard.[37] With room for 10,000 spectators, the racing club contained parlors, private dining rooms, and a nine-hole golf course believed to be the first within the city limits.

Many of the neighborhood's residents were well versed in politics and cultural endeavors, and organizations including the Mendelssohn Club and the Shakespeare Club flourished. The Hyde Park Lyceum was a community-sponsored library that gradually evolved into the City of Chicago's first branch library.[38] A number of women's associations were also formed as the growing prosperity and availability of domestic servants led to increased leisure time for many of the area's female residents. Kenwood had not only a brick schoolhouse but also a female seminary run by Mrs. Kennicott. For worship, parishioners attended services at new facilities, including an Episcopal church at 4945 Dorchester and a Congregational church on 47th Street.

After the fire the growth of these small communities began to skyrocket. By 1880 the township's population had increased by more then 400 percent over the previous decade, to include nearly 16,000 residents,[39] and then began to grow even more dramatically. In May 1884 the local paper, the *Hyde Park Herald*, noted that ninety building permits were issued the previous month, in contrast to eight permits issued during the corresponding period the previous year.[40] By 1887 the Cottage Grove cable car lines were extended south to 67th Street, with a branch heading east on 55th Street. While the nucleus of Paul Cornell's small village continued to attract Chicago's businessmen who built large residences, builders

Rosalie Clubhouse, 1886.
Demolished. Southeast corner
of 57th Street and Rosalie
Court. Solon S. Beman.

2.11. Known as Rosalie Inn and later as the South Park Club, this elegant establishment rivaled the exclusive Kenwood Club to the north. The club, which offered first-class hotel accommodations and a restaurant, closed in 1906.

began to fill vacant lots along the central streets with small workingmen's cottages, and the once elite suburb slowly came to reflect a broader range of housing and of residents.

Although the economic range of Hyde Park and Kenwood's citizens was expanding, the majority were of the business and professional class, capable of providing greater resources to support the improvement of their community than the geographically separate and predominantly working-class population of the village's southern industrial areas. Dissatisfaction with the village form of government increased year by year due to the growing disparity between northern and southern village residents, and the sheer impossibility that six part-time trustees could administer the needs of a village that had grown to a population of nearly 60,000.[41] Various propositions were put forth to deal with a form of government that was clearly outdated. Ideas ranged from the division of the village into three separate villages where interests would be more fairly addressed, to annexation by the City of Chicago.

Although Hyde Park drifted toward annexation, the issue was a particularly difficult one. Substantial pressure was applied by the city itself, as many dreamed of Chicago as the nation's second-largest city by the time of the 1890 census. The newspapers, particularly the *Chicago Tribune*, took a strong stand for annexation. And the issue was clearly not immune to politics. The *Hyde Park Herald* recognized that Cook County was solidly Republican; however, the city was not so reliable, and often voted Democratic. To annex Hyde Park to Chicago "would make the latter a Republican city for all time to come."[42]

Voters supporting independence from the city, mainly from the northern portion of the village, organized late and lacked the ambition demonstrated by advocates of annexation. Their low level of interest was most likely because the residents of Hyde Park, Kenwood, Oakland, (Cleaverville), and South Park enjoyed a number and quality of services not found in the rest of the village. Residents of the southern end of the village looked forward to the financial advantages of the city services rather than the demands for costly special assessments. There was an unexpectedly small turnout for the vote in June 1889, with the citizens of the Hyde Park and Kenwood enclaves against the measure and the majority of the village favoring annexation.[43] Kenwood resident Annie Hitchcock spoke of "the disastrous day when Hyde Park Village voted itself part of Chicago, so selling its birthright." Her opinion echoed many of those who resided in the northern section of the village. The vote to approve the annexation of Hyde Park and other suburbs made Chicago the second-largest city in the country, adding an area of 126 square miles.[44]

In the twenty-five short years since their founding, the small prairie settlements evolved, and traces of the early days began to disappear. "Maybe lake water, and gas, and paved streets, and electric lights, and taxes had something to do with it. At any rate, the birds . . . , and the rabbits and the flowers are all gone. And so is Hyde Park."[45]

But in spite of the nostalgia for the simplicity and contentment of earlier days, Hyde Park did not disappear. While many thought it may have been swallowed by the greater city, the neighborhoods did not lose their sense of community; in fact the coming years would only serve to strengthen the bond.

2.12. A view of a snow-covered 51st Street looking west toward the house of Paul Cornell on Harper Avenue. The cold winds that blow over the warmer waters of Lake Michigan produce soft, fluffy lake-effect snow, and bring with them the unmistakable scent of winter. This peaceful, very suburban scene was photographed in 1888, the year prior to annexation by the city of Chicago.

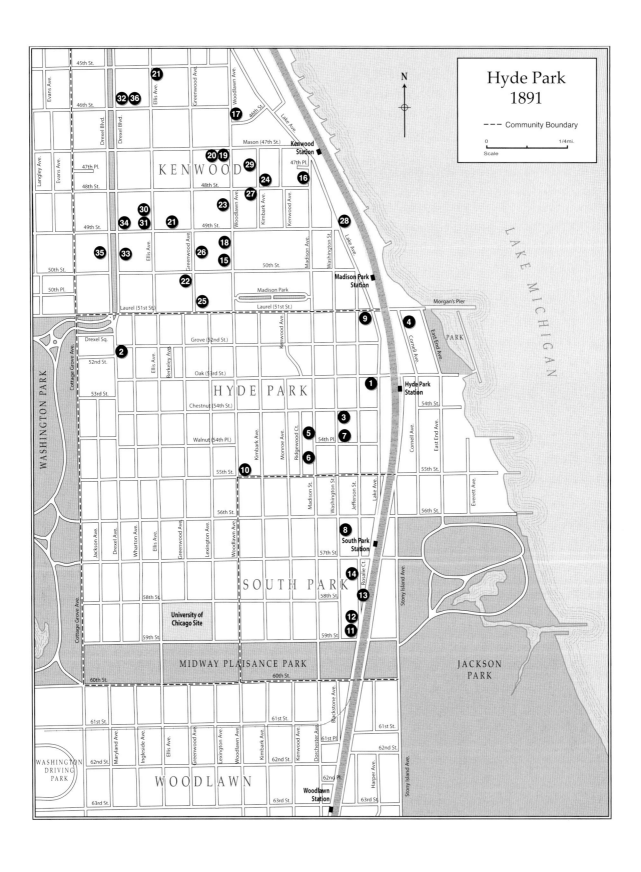

Hyde Park
1891

--- Community Boundary

0   1/4mi.
Scale

N

LAKE MICHIGAN

WASHINGTON PARK

KENWOOD

HYDE PARK

SOUTH PARK

WOODLAWN

JACKSON PARK

WASHINGTON DRIVING PARK

MIDWAY PLAISANCE PARK

University of Chicago Site

Madison Park

Drexel Sq.

Morgan's Pier

PARK

Kenwood Station

Madison Park Station

Hyde Park Station

South Park Station

Woodlawn Station

Streets (labels)

45th St.
46th St.
Mason (47th St.)
47th Pl.
48th St.
49th St.
50th St.
50th Pl.
Laurel (51st St.)
Drexel Sq.
Grove (52nd St.)
52nd St.
Oak (53rd St.)
53rd St.
Chestnut (54th St.)
Walnut (54th Pl.)
54th St.
54th Pl.
55th St.
56th St.
57th St.
58th St.
59th St.
60th St.
61st St.
62nd St.
62nd Pl.
63rd St.

Evans Ave.
Langley Ave.
Evans Ave.
Drexel Blvd.
Drexel Blvd.
Ellis Ave.
Greenwood Ave.
Woodlawn Ave.
46th St.
Greenwood Ave.
Ellis Ave.
Kimbark Ave.
Kenwood Ave.
Madison Ave.
Washington St.
Lake Ave.
Cornell Ave.
East End Ave.
Everett Ave.
Stony Island Ave.
Cottage Grove Ave.
Ellis Ave.
Berkeley Ave.
Kenwood Ave.
Kimbark Ave.
Monroe Ave.
Ridgewood Ct.
Madison St.
Washington St.
Jefferson St.
Lake Ave.
Cornell Ave.
East End Ave.
Rosalie Ct.
Jackson Ave.
Drexel Ave.
Wharton Ave.
Ellis Ave.
Greenwood Ave.
Lexington Ave.
Woodlawn Ave.
Cottage Grove Ave.
Maryland Ave.
Ingleside Ave.
Ellis Ave.
Greenwood Ave.
Lexington Ave.
Woodlawn Ave.
Kimbark Ave.
Kenwood Ave.
Dorchester Ave.
Blackstone Ave.
Harper Ave.
Stony Island Ave.

Hyde Park

1 Hotel Helene, 1874. Demolished 1900.

100–114 East Oak (53rd) Street. Architect/builder unknown.

The center of Hyde Park along Lake Avenue developed into a commercial hub that contrasted with the surrounding suburban environment. In addition to owner-occupied single-family houses, Hyde Park offered housing in apartments constructed over street-level retail establishments. Constructed about 1874 as Flood's Hall, the three-story brick building on the southeast corner of 53rd and Lake Streets was one of the first of the larger structures in Hyde Park and was named for the owner Dr. James Ramsey Flood, the health officer for the village in 1871. Flood was a generous man; he donated his services to the Women's Hospital free of charge for ten years while holding regular office hours in "Flood's Block" from 10:00 a.m. to noon and from 7:00 to 8:00 p.m.[46] Flood, his wife Sarah Douglas, and four children resided nearby, at 5320 Jefferson (Harper) Avenue.

The building later housed the seventy-five-room Hotel Helene. A devastating fire broke out in the early morning hours on May 16, 1900, terrifying the one hundred guests as it spread. While flames lit the entire neighborhood, guests leapt from the second and third stories to escape the ravaging blaze.[47] The fire department quickly concluded that they could do nothing to save the structure and were powerless to help those who jumped, many to their deaths. In spite of lessons learned from the Chicago fire thirty years earlier, neither the police nor the fire department was equipped with safety nets.[48] The fire was blamed on the night watchman, who was arrested nearly a month later in New York City.[49] Additionally, safety conditions at the hotel were in "a deplorable state of affairs," and the verdict read at court stated that "had the laws and ordinances governing exits and fire escapes been enforced" lives would not have been lost.[50] City codes of the time required that buildings over two stories have fire escapes.

② Ayer Residence, c. 1874. Demolished.
5201 South Drexel Avenue. Architect/builder unknown.

Benjamin Franklin Ayer was typical of a new wave of Hyde Park residents who came to Hyde Park after the 1871 fire. "These men bought large tracts of land and established their families in what was then open country," recalled his wife Janet (Jennie) Hopkins. The dense urban streetscape on Drexel south of today's 51st Street was home to only one residence in the early years of the neighborhood.[51] There was no water, gas, or sewer for landowners there; even sprinkling the street "to keep down the dust" was each family's responsibility.[52]

After studying at Dartmouth and Harvard, Ayer came to Chicago in 1857 to practice law and was appointed the corporation council for the city. He was the attorney for the South Parks Commission during the condemnation proceedings for securing the land for Washington and Jackson Parks. "Prominent in the best social circles of the city" the Ayers were long "aligned by marriage with some of Chicago's first families."[53]

In May 1874 Robert Todd Lincoln sought the counsel of the prestigious law firm of Ayer & Kales. In a "locked-door session" at their offices, some of Chicago's best physicians declared Robert's mother, Mary Todd Lincoln, to be insane.[54] When Mrs. Lincoln was committed on the May 19, 1875, the document certifying her insanity was signed B. F. Ayer, on behalf of Robert T. Lincoln.[55] Even under the most trying circumstances Ayer was "in all things cool, keen and contentious."[56]

The following year Ayer became solicitor general of the Illinois Central Railroad after George Trumbull objected to a pay cut and tendered his resignation. The president of the railroad, William K. Ackerman, had suggested his name in a letter dated October 31, 1876. That he "would make in all respects, a satisfactory man, there is little doubt. I know him well as a neighborhood friend and have also inquired concerning him among the lawyers of Chicago. . . . He is one of the highest intellectuals at the Chicago Bar."[57]

Like other residents of this time, Ayer believed in the eventual increase of the value of South Side land and invested in additional tracts. In 1885 he sold one of his holdings, a large, 150' × 297' Kenwood lot on the southwest corner of Greenwood and 49th Streets, for future development.[58]

Life on the outskirts of the city was not always easy, and the Ayer family expe-

2.14. The large and tranquil grounds of the Ayer residence were photographed for *Picturesque Kenwood* about 1890.

rienced their own calamity indicative of the problems the community faced in providing adequate services to its residents. On a cold January evening the stable at the rear of the house caught fire. A fire alarm had to be carried by horse to the Hyde Park "hose-house" a mile away. From there another call was placed to the Oakland community firehouse several miles north. Although the volunteer firemen and their horses went "as speedily on the ground as circumstances would permit," the fire was progressed swiftly.[59] The Hyde Park equipment got stuck in the snow; however, the firemen from Oakland arrived and were able to extinguish the blaze, although the barn was in ruins. However, the frame house, which had broken into flames from the intense heat and burning bits of the barn, was saved from extensive damage. One valuable horse was lost; two cows, a calf, three carriages, and a sleigh were rescued.[60]

Within two weeks, Ayer let a contract to replace the burned structure. Designed by Hyde Park architect James Stephen, the stable was no small structure. Measuring 26' × 56' and rising 52' to the top of a fifteen-foot tower, the "elegant" frame building with two belting courses around it provided four horse and two cow stalls, and a harness and carriage room, while the second level was divided into a loft, coachman's room, store room, and grain bins.[61]

Mrs. Ayer later wrote of her years in Hyde Park in the book, *Chicago Yesterdays*, challenging an old adage: "All of the pleasant things of life are either unwholesome, expensive or wrong—some of them all three." Despite the fire and other difficulties, she wrote in retrospect: "We certainly had lots of wholesome, inexpensive, and harmless fun in old Hyde Park with the group of notable personalities that chance had brought together there."[62]

④ Hutchinson Residence, 1881. Demolished 1961.
5111 South Cornell Avenue. Architect/builder unknown.

Once known locally as the "honeymoon cottage," this house was a wedding gift to Charles Lawrence Hutchinson from his father, Benjamin P. Hutchinson.[63] The earliest records for this property go back to a sheriff's sale in 1870; B. P. Hutchinson purchased the property on August 12, 1872. After Charles's wedding in May 1881, the father presented this "Stick Style" residence to his son and the bride, Frances Kinsley. Hutchinson was a young clerk in his father's bank at the time, and after making his own fortune in banking, he relocated north to the fashionable Prairie Avenue. The younger Hutchinson was a trustee of and donor to the University of Chicago (Hutchinson Commons is currently used as a dining hall at the university), president of the Board of Trade, and a founder of the Chicago Symphony as well as a major fund-raiser for Orchestra Hall.[64]

Hutchinson devoted much of his time to philanthropy, and was passionate about the Art Institute of Chicago. He was only twenty-eight years old when he helped to found the institution in 1882, and later acted as president. Spurred by his father's "single-minded focus on making money" (a drive that eventually led to his commitment in a sanatorium),[65] the younger Hutchinson was motivated by civic duty. He believed art compensated for the "overly materialistic society Chicagoans

were building" and wanted all Chicagoans to feel the Art Institute was for their use, stating, "We have built this institution for the public, not for a few."[66]

The Hutchinson residence was an example of a relatively rare style in American Victorian architecture; the Stick Style was popular between 1860 and 1890.[67] Stick Style houses are noted for a number of unique features united by the use of "sticks," that is, applied flat board banding, in geometric patterns that adorn the exterior. Floor plans are typically asymmetrical in arrangement, and the houses feature steeply pitched slate roofs.[68]

③ Bradley Residence, c. 1880.

5413 South Washington Street (Blackstone Avenue). Architect/builder unknown.

This charming house is noted for its "jerkinhead" roof. The term applies to a distinctive feature of this house; the end of a roof is clipped, forming an intermediate triangular shape that pitches backward.

Although constructed for a Mr. Bradley, for decades this early Hyde Park house was home to the Kilbourn family, from the early 1900s until 1984. Once when the illustrious senator from Illinois, Paul Douglas, failed to show up for a meeting here as promised, Mrs. Frederick H. Kilbourn confronted him. Asked about his absence, the senator replied that he simply could not open her iron gate. Of "pioneer stock," she found this a feeble excuse.[69] Had Kilbourn been confronted by the gate, she "likely would climb it without hesitation, although she is well beyond what is looked upon as romping age."[70]

2.17. An 1873 image and plan for a house from *Hobbs's Architecture, Containing Designs and Ground Plans for Villas, Cottages, and Other Edifices, Both Suburban and Rural, Adapted to the United States* featured the characteristic jerkinhead roof of the Bradley house.

2.16. While pattern books suggested a suburban setting, the Bradley house was located in a more congested area of Hyde Park. Many of the influences on modern life are expressed—the additions at the rear for increased living space, the driveway to provide for the automobile, satellite dish for entertainment convenience, and even the Democratic-leaning tendencies of the community.

Fences have long delineated the line between "mine" and "not mine." Their most valuable function was perhaps expressed most eloquently in Henry Cleaveland's popular 1856 book, *Village and Farm Cottages*. "Though the fence ranks among the minor matters of building, it is not unimportant. Without it no residence is properly protected, or regarded as complete. Its style and condition often indicates, unmistakably, the taste and habits of the owner."[71]

⑤ Bennett Residences, 1882.
5436, 5438, 5440 South Madison Street (Dorchester Avenue).
Architect/builder unknown.

These quaint, solidly built brick bungalows were constructed as investment property for attorney and alderman Frank Ira Bennett. Bennett was from a politically connected family; his father John Bennett (5726 Washington Street) was a popular village president, a post he held from 1878 until 1880. The younger Bennett became the assistant comptroller of the town and ran (successfully) for town assessor in April 1887 on the Republican ticket, after the local newspaper admonished voters to "Be sure to vote BEFORE going to business."[72] Aside from being politically astute, Bennett and his wife, Anna Cartwright were "were well known in social circles." Their 1884 marriage was the social event of the season.[73]

In addition to his legal work with Bennett & Higgins, Bennett built eight houses on Madison Avenue (Dorchester) and twenty-five on Tompkins Place (Ridgewood Court) in the early eighties.[74]

2.18. The maximum use of available land resulted in a tightly woven urban fabric—reflected by the speculative housing constructed by Frank Bennett just north of 55th Street.

Rural Architecture. 9

DESIGN No. 7.

A very Cheap House for small Farm or Village Tenement.

2.19. Although this image for a "rural cottage" from *Ogilvie's House Plans, or How to Build a House* lacks the front porch and features a pair of upper-story windows, the floor plan demonstrates the compact efficiency of the cottage that was especially suitable for the tight lot size prevalent on this street.

6 Residences, c. 1885. 5474, 5476 South Madison Street (Dorchester Avenue). Architect/builder unknown. 2.20. The blocks adjacent to Bennett's brick cottages are lined with frame structures of varying sizes. The lot sizes are compact, smaller than the standard 25′ · 125′ city lot, and are without service alleys. These quaint Chicago cottages are located near St. Thomas the Apostle Church, and the house on the right features some of the original ornamentation.

7 W. I. Beman Residence, 1885.

5425 South Washington Street (Blackstone Avenue). William J. Dodd.

Architect Irving Beman's coworker at the Pullman project, draftsman William J. Dodd, designed this small house in central Hyde Park for Beman and his wife, Iva Ott. Ott's family had resided in Hyde Park since 1879, renting the Field-Pullman-Heyworth house before constructing a residence at 5146 Harper. At the time, the Ott house was the only one on the block other than that of Paul Cornell.[75] Beman and Ott were married in June 1885, and in July work began on the house located in the center of Hyde Park. Not long after it was completed, Dodd left Chicago.

2.21. The Beman house was described by the *Hyde Park Herald* on July 11, 1885 as a "unique and original design and a model for a cozy little home." The automobile-filled setting reflects the dense urbanization of the center of Hyde Park.

2.22. Unfortunately much of the original detailing is gone; however, the Beman house is still recognizable as the "Sketch of a Cottage at Hyde Park" that appeared in an 1885 issue of *Inland Architect*.

8 **Zimmerman Residence, 1887.**
5621 South Washington Street (Blackstone Avenue). Flanders & Zimmerman.

John Flanders and William Carbys Zimmerman's earliest projects in the Hyde Park area include two small Blackstone Avenue residences designed in 1887, the year they founded the firm. These houses, including Zimmerman's own, represent a different trend in architecture at a time when the Queen Anne style was at the height of popularity. Rather than incorporating a number of stylistically different elements and materials, the Shingle Style used simpler forms and a single material for the exterior: wood shingles. The clean, unadorned style became popular along with the rise of the English Arts and Crafts movement that promoted the use of "honest" building materials and a return to hand craftsmanship.

2.23. An iron fence fronts the property of the two picturesque Shingle Style houses at 5611 and 5621; a spare brick house has been constructed between them. The residence of William and Emily Zimmerman looks remarkably like the original drawing, although a few delightful details have disappeared, including the charming dragon downspout.

2.24. *Inland Architect and News Record* featured the residence in 1887. "House for W. Zimmerman, South Park, Ill., by Flanders & Zimmerman, architects, Chicago, two stories high, attic and basement partly finished. Inside woodwork of pine, except hall of oak, all in natural finish. The exterior is shingled all over, stained a Sienna color, with creosote stain, basement of stone, outside walls have a double air space as shown, making a non-conductor against heat and cold, and taking away the look of 'thinness' so common to the wooden house; cost, $3,500."

⑨ Hyde Park Hotel, 1888. Demolished 1962.
1511 East Laurel (51st) Street. Starrett & Fuller.

2.25. The Hyde Park Hotel once commanded the intersection of Hyde Park Boulevard and Lake Avenue, an elegant landmark between two communities. To the north was fashionable Kenwood and to the south, the increasingly commercial area of Hyde Park.

Conceived a decade after Paul Cornell's Hyde Park House was destroyed by fire, this hotel was said to be "the most fashionable on the South Side."[76] Situated on the southwest corner of Lake Avenue and 51st street, the property fronted 216 feet on 51st, 187 feet on Lake and 233 feet on Harper. Cornell chose to locate his hotel on this parcel west of the railroad tracks and across the street from his house; he had sold his lakeside hotel property in 1865. The hotel was constructed in several stages; Theodore Starrett designed the main section of the hotel in 1887–1888. The George A. Fuller Company built the structure; one of Starrett's brothers, Paul, became president of the company. The first section of the hotel was a pressed brick and stone building 80' × 85', rising four stories in height. Always with an eye toward the future, Cornell had the walls built of "sufficient strength" to accommodate additional stories.[77]

An additional three floors were under construction by 1892 in anticipation of the Columbian Exposition. The seven-story hotel was a pioneer in hotel design, for Starrett used innovations that were common to large commercial buildings of the time. The hotel was the first iron-framed construction in the city, and its electric lights, electrically operated elevators, telephone service, and steam heat were all considered revolutionary for hotels of the time.[78]

Other hotels soon followed the example of the Hyde Park. The rounded bays at the corners enlivened the red brick façade, while providing well-lit apartments. On the interior the lobby was paneled in marble, and guests tread upon lush carpets

2.26. North of the Hyde Park Hotel were the elegant residences of Kenwood, still quite rural in nature, as seen in the c. 1890 *Picturesque Kenwood* looking south on muddy Lake Avenue from 49th Street.

2.27. Several blocks south of the Hyde Park Hotel was the bustling business district along Lake Avenue between 53rd and 55th Streets. The three-story structure at the southwest corner of 55th and Lake was built for George F. Busse. In 1886 Busse was awarded a liquor license to operate a saloon at 5464 Lake. Five years later he built this structure, which housed Fahrig's Pavilion as seen in an 1892 photograph. In 1929, a large three-story commercial building known as the Hyde Park Chevrolet Building, designed by Louis Kroman and known for its elaborate Art Deco façade, rose on the site.

and dined under a Tiffany glass ceiling. No one was permitted in the five-hundred-seat dining room without formal attire, enhancing the already elegant setting. When the western wing was added in 1915, the Hyde Park Hotel doubled its size, providing over three hundred guest rooms. The property remained in Cornell's family long after his death, and was sold by his estate in 1947.[79]

From the time it opened until the thirties, the hotel represented fine living, high fashion, and elegance. However, by 1962 the hotel had served its purpose; its luxurious dining room had become a cafeteria; and rooms had been cut into kitchenette apartments. Deemed too costly to restore, the hotel that was for years the ultimate in luxury was slated to be demolished under the Hyde Park Urban Renewal Plan. Residents moved on, and rooms were stripped bare of their furnishings. The Hyde Park–Kenwood Community Conference wistfully collected chandeliers and terra-cotta pieces and even a staircase, memories of an era long past.

⑩ The Stodder Building, 1889. Demolished 1961.
1200–1212 East 55th Street. Architect/builder unknown.

Construction on the four-story wood-framed structure for George F. Stodder began late in the summer of 1889, important to the development of Hyde Park by bringing the commercial development of 55th Street westward. Used as hotel accommodations for the world's fair, the upper three stories later became rental apartments, with shops on the main level. The façade, featuring cast metal bays with ornamental stamping, graced the busy commercial corner of Hyde Park, as seen in this view of 55th Street looking west from the intersection at Woodlawn.

At the corner on the south side of the street was a two-story building that for fifty-

2.28. The Stodder building was one of many commercial structures located on 55th Street that were demolished in the 1960s.

one years was home to Finnegan's Drug Store. The "small, narrow store" was entered through a front door at the corner on 55th Street. The walls were lined with mahogany cases and the space lit by Tiffany fixtures. In the back of the drugstore an exterior window used by patrons to pick up their prescriptions was later used to distribute alcohol during the Prohibition years. After the building fell into disrepair and was slated for demolition, *Hyde Park Herald* owner Bruce Sagan saved the interior. It was donated to the Museum of Science and Industry and operates as an ice cream parlor within the museum.[80]

South Park

⓫ Jackman Residences, 1884.
5832–5834 South Rosalie Court (Harper Avenue). Solon Spencer Beman.

Following his success at Pullman, Solon Beman was contracted to supervise the design of Rosalie Villas, a planned community in South Park. Located on a two-block stretch of Harper Avenue between 57th and 59th Streets, the parcel was developed by Amelia "Rose" Buckingham. In 1890 Buckingham married Harry Gordon Selfridge, the general manager of Marshall Field and Company, and in 1904 they moved to London where he founded Selfridge's department store. Buckingham left her imprint on the neighborhood however, when in 1883 she partnered with her

2.29. These double clapboard houses were designed for John A. Jackman Jr., a manager at the Pullman Company. They share a chimney highlighted with terra-cotta tiles, while decorative wooden cutwork separates the individual porches.

⑫ William Riley Beman
Residence, 1884. 5822 South
Rosalie Court (Harper Avenue).
Solon Beman.

2.30. Most of Beman's family
moved to Chicago when
he was hired to create the
Pullman community. Designed
for his father, this house has
been covered in brown siding
obscuring the original details.
However a few features remain,
including the two-story bay on
the façade.

brother-in-law, F. R. Chandler, a real estate investor, to subdivide the property that
was once the Buckingham farm into lots for forty-two villas and cottages.[81]

Beman's concept for the project included unique and picturesque residences,
many of which were originally used as summer homes, combined with amenities
including a family-run grocery store, a café, a private club, and a public entertainment hall. The terra-cotta arched entrance of Rosalie Music Hall welcomed
those who came to enjoy events at the social center of the community. Erected
in the "old colonial style," the upper story projected over the first level and was
defined by gables and pinnacles. The open-truss construction of the roof allowed
for "eight pretty balcony boxes." Electric bells communicated to the café below, so
refreshments could be easily ordered. The floor of the hall was the most expensive
feature of the building and could be adapted to roller-skating. Safety was of prime
concern, and the plan provided "two ample exits" in case of fire.[82]

Open lots at Rosalie Villas were advertised for sale in 1885 in a community that
touted "pure water, perfect drainage, paved and lighted streets and sidewalks."
The villas offered all the amenities of city living, yet were "free from the dangers
of city life."[83] The majority of the forty-two "villa" sites were to have forty-five to
fifty feet of frontage, with the requirement that every house be detached and no
"blocks of dwellings" were permitted. A uniform building line was established,
and no alleys were planned, since every lot was designed to be wide enough to
reach a stable in the rear.[84]

13 Reynolds Residence, 1884.
**5759 South Rosalie Court
(Harper Avenue). Solon Beman.**
2.31. The house built for
accountant Frederick M.
Reynolds retains many of its
original details. The windows,
brackets, cutouts and spindles
of the porch, and sidelights
around the front door enhance
a charming house that was
originally constructed in a rural
setting. The raised embankment
of the Illinois Central tracks is in
the rear of the lot, obstructing
the once open vista to the east
and Lake Michigan.

14 Cook Residence, 1884.
**5708 South Rosalie Court
(Harper Avenue). Solon Beman.**
2.32. The Shingle-style house
constructed for Dr. John C.
Cook exhibits an arched porch
opening and complex roofline.
Although only a few original
windows remain on the second
level, they are reminiscent of the
multi-paned window detail found
in many Pullman houses.

By 1888 the finished houses had expansive views of the lakefront lagoons and large, deep yards that provided separation from the landscaped railway easement. However, when the Illinois Central train tracks were elevated for the Columbian Exposition, the yards, and views of Lake Michigan disappeared.

Kenwood

⓯ Higgins Residence, c. 1866. Demolished by 1915.
4948 South Woodlawn Avenue. Architect/builder unknown.

2.33. The Higgins house, as it appeared in *Picturesque Kenwood*, was constructed in the Italianate Villa style, which is less symmetrical in plan than the Italianate style, with a complex elevation that features a distinctive tower. According to Samuel Sloan, author of *The Model Architect* (1852), the style represented the owner as "a man of wealth . . . as a person of educated and refined tastes . . . who, accustomed to all the ease and luxury of city life, is now enjoying the more pure and elevating pleasures of the country."

One of the oldest and most respected lawyers in Chicago, Judge Van Hollis Higgins was described in his day as the "greatest case lawyer that ever appeared at the Chicago Bar."[85] "Tall . . . and of a commanding figure,"[86] Higgins and his "beautiful" wife Elisabeth "with her cameo face and white curls"[87] moved from the city to the Kenwood neighborhood in 1866,[88] occupying a two and-a-half-story Italianate house situated on a wooded corner lot. Typical of Kenwood, the 300' × 300' parcel was surrounded by a stone and iron fence and approached by a curving drive. The asymmetrically designed frame house was well known throughout the area. Equally notable was the long-time feud between the occupants of this residence and another of Chicago's early citizens.

By most accounts John Dunham was also an upstanding member of Chicago business and civic life. A contemporary of Higgins, he was born in New York in 1817, and began his career with a small hardware store. He later sold this establishment, married, and came to Chicago. For fourteen years he operated a wholesale

grocery business on South Water Street, which like his earlier enterprise, grew and prospered. Dunham became chairman of the committee to develop a water system for the city; he was also one of the founders of the Illinois Republican Party and one of the first members of the Board of Trade. "He was a stern man, somewhat opinionated . . . but under this forbidding exterior, he was so kind and generous."[89]

Dunham invested heavily in real estate, including a twenty-acre tract of land in Kenwood that he purchased from the Marine Bank when it was in receivership. After acquiring the property in 1868, he designated it as private grounds and named the enclave Madison Park.[90] A short time later Dunham acquired another twenty-acre tract immediately to the north. Although he owned property in Kenwood, Dunham did not reside in the neighborhood; the family residence was at the northwest corner of Michigan and Harrison Streets.[91]

The *Chicago Tribune* provided an animated chronicle of "Hyde Park's Fence War." As the "old inhabitants" of Kenwood remembered, the troubles began when Paul Cornell tried to have an ordinance passed that would extend Kimbark and Hibbard (Kenwood) Streets through Dunham's property.[92] Dunham did not want anything of the sort, because as the Kenwood neighbors said, "it meant assessments and more taxes, and he was only a poor millionaire with a family to support."[93]

Dunham fought his neighbors, Woodlawn Avenue residents Higgins and Albert Spalding, and the village, and although the proposition failed, Dunham was not satisfied with success and began to devise various schemes of revenge. To prevent the extension of streets through his property, he constructed a greenhouse on the north side of the property and rented it out. Next he established a requirement that

18 Spalding Residence, c. 1885. Demolished by 1906. 4926 South Woodlawn Avenue. Architect/builder unknown.

2.34. Higgins's Woodlawn Avenue neighbors were Albert and Josephine Spalding. An entrepreneur in the sporting goods business, Spalding began his career as an athlete. He played for five years for the Boston Red Stockings before joining the Chicago White Stockings, where he managed the team and pitched forty-seven games as the team won the first ever National League Pennant in 1876. He retired from playing the game and opened A. G. Spalding & Bros., a sporting goods store. Spalding obtained the rights to produce the official National League baseball, which was manufactured for the next hundred years. A 1906 house designed by Marshall & Fox now occupies the site of his residence, as seen in this image circa 1890 from *Picturesque Kenwood*.

2.35. In 2001 a collection of images was discovered wrapped in newspapers in the Architecture Library of the University of Melbourne. The photographs, collected by Australian architect Edward George Kilburn during his 1889 tour of the United States and Europe, were examples illustrating architecture that came to influence Australian architects. While Kilburn was an able photographer, he also purchased images, including this attributed to J. W. Taylor. The interior of the Spalding residence echoes the remarkable and intricate woodwork of the exterior.

every house on the oval drive inside Madison Park front on the park, with its rear consequently facing Cornell and others.[94]

These were the years before annexation, and the village levied a special assessment on Dunham's property to provide financing for sidewalks. He believed Judge Higgins to be the force behind this, although the village constantly levied assessments for improvements. Held personally responsible for the cost, Dunham began to retaliate in various ways, the most unusual of which was to erect a row of cheaply constructed cottages directly opposite the entrance to Higgins's gracious house. Threatening to "import a colony of negroes" to live in them, Dunham had the first half dozen "dreadful-looking" rough pine cottages erected at a cost of $500 each. He then took out permits to build twelve more on Woodlawn, and just so everyone would understand, he took out permits for fourteen two-story dwellings to be erected on other parts of his grounds. The feud was "progressing merrily."[95]

In 1891 East 51st Street became a boulevard, and during that summer Dunham began the construction of a number of barns on the south side of Madison Park, abutting the handsome street. The neighbors were upset with this development, and began to knock out boards, eventually pulling down a good portion of five of the barns. Dunham put up notices around the neighborhood offering a $100 reward for information about anyone taking a "whack at his property."[96] Not surprisingly, no one came forward, and toward the end of August he began construction of a nine-foot-tall fence along the boulevard. The neighbors were again up in arms, complaining that "the one absorbing object of Mr. Dunham's life is to resist any attempt to make improvements for the benefit of the neighborhood."[97]

The feud ended only with the deaths of the two main participants, but the story was far from over, as evidence of Dunham's peculiar view of his Kenwood property remains today. John Dunham's will left ten acres of the Kenwood property, his commercial building at the southwest corner of Wacker Drive and State Street, and his residence on Michigan Avenue to his three children with the restriction that none of these parcels could be sold until after their deaths.[98] By the terms of the will Dunham's son-in-law, Kirk Hawes, was able to open only a portion of the Kenwood holdings for development. Recalling the past feud, the *Chicago Tribune* observed, "The old residents of Madison Park are considerably astonished to see preparations made to subdivide the Dunham property."[99] During his lifetime Judge Higgins tried to persuade Dunham to subdivide or sell his property, but he resisted every effort. Residents had even volunteered to fund the expense of platting, "but the old man was obdurate. Now his son-in-law Kirk Hawes is doing the subdividing, but the neighbors are certainly not helping pay for it."[100]

Not all of his property was subdivided—true to Dunham's wish the land known for many years as Farmer's Field was never developed. Cows could be found grazing on the last ten acres of his land into the 1920s, when Dunham's last surviving heir passed away.[101] The property was eventually deeded to the city of Chicago, thanks to the generosity of subsequent owner Albert Harris, and is now a verdant space known as Kenwood Park. Therein lies a great irony, as Dunham, never wishing to provide any improvements for the neighborhood, instead created a spacious respite from the dense urban neighborhood that grew to surround it.

⑯ Bishop Residence, 1874. Demolished c. 1960.
4746 South Madison Avenue (Dorchester Avenue). Architect/builder unknown.

In the years after the Chicago Fire many members of Chicago's business community came to Kenwood to build large, comfortable residences on spacious lots. For years this residence was known as the Faulkner House, as it housed the Faulkner School for Girls. As the community moved from suburban retreat to city neighborhood, the red brick house remained a landmark of the early days of Kenwood.

The house was constructed for Alexander Bishop, a furrier, hatter, and pioneer Chicagoan. Emigrating from Ireland, Bishop first settled in New York before arriving in Chicago in 1860. He founded the firm of A. Bishop & Company, which like so many other enterprises was lost in the fire. He rebuilt on State Street and was quite wealthy when he moved with his wife Carrie and two daughters to fashionable Kenwood.[102]

The Bishop family lived in the house, then numbered as 4736, for over a decade until it was sold in April 1884 to John C. Neemes, the founder of a confectionary company. The Neemes family remained in the house for only six years, when the property again changed hands. Miss Kate B. Martin purchased the property in

2.36. The suburban setting of the Bishop residence in the 1890s was reflected in a photograph for the collection of images published as *Picturesque Kenwood*. In the ensuing years the quiet suburban atmosphere disappeared, although a few of the houses dating from the early era of Kenwood remained.

2.37. The intersection of Dorchester and Lake clearly represents the transition from suburban oasis to congested city neighborhood. Apartment buildings were constructed and gas stations made their appearance to serve the needs of the automobile. However several early residences remained to grace a much-altered landscape. The Bishop house, which became the Faulkner School for Girls, appears in the upper right of this image taken in March 1951.

1889 and established Ascham Hall, a private day and boarding school. After twenty years she sold her school and building to Elizabeth Faulkner, who began a new school, which occupied the lower two floors of the building while Faulkner and her parents lived on the third floor. The interior was well taken care of and featured "white marble fireplaces topped by great mirrors that were the pride of the original owners."[103] The elongated windows and spacious porch remained visible in a dense urban setting as the area near Lake Park evolved from a quiet, unpaved rural road into a congested commercial street. The house has been demolished and an elementary school now occupies the site.

17 Furber Residence, c. 1876. Demolished c. 1906.
Woodlawn Avenue near 46th Street. Architect/builder unknown.

Very few houses from this early period remain in the area of Kenwood that Henry Jewett Furber Sr. called home. His property was a triangular parcel north of 46th Street that extended from Woodlawn east toward Lake Street. Over time this area developed differently from the southern section of the neighborhood, so much so that today it is designated as "North Kenwood."

Furber first came to Chicago in 1865 as the general agent for the Metropolitan Fire Insurance Company of New York. His stay was brief; by the fall he was

2.38. The 1883 *City Directory* lists the Furbers as residing on Woodlawn near 46th Street. However numerous articles from the1884 and 1885 *Hyde Park Herald* mention their residence to be on Woodlawn near 50th Street, calling the exact location of this c. 1890 *Picturesque Kenwood* image into question.

elected vice president of the North America Life Insurance Company and the family moved to New York. In 1874 he was elected president. The firm was merging with Universal Life Insurance Company; his charge was to lead it and the Charter Oak Life Insurance Company out of financial difficulties.[104]

Enjoying his success and displaying a passion for opulence, Furber made a series of major purchases of silver from New York's Gorham Silver Company. Furber's silver service became the largest single commission Gorham ever received, and represented the extravagance of the Victorian era when the collection was displayed at the 1876 Philadelphia Centennial Exposition.[105] The magnificent dinner service for twenty-four, of sterling silver and 24-karat gold, was valued at over $1 million at the time.[106] Within a short time, suits were filed against Furber and other officers of North America Life, accusing them of raiding the company's assets.[107] Although indicted on conspiracy to defraud policyholders and misappropriation of assets, among other crimes, Furber was found not guilty on all counts.

In May 1879 Furber, and his seventeen trunks of silver, returned to Chicago. He became a member of the law firm of Higgins, Furber & Cothran, a law firm that also engaged in real estate speculation. Records indicate Higgins & Furber developed twenty residences just south of 43rd Street, between Lake Avenue and the Illinois Central Railroad in 1884. The "handsome" brick and stone residences were nearly completed that winter and faced onto a paved avenue running south to 45th Street.[108]

Furber's taste was "simply princely" and in addition to silver he built a collection of "art and literature of the rarest and most expensive character in the world."[109] At the Furber residence, the valuable 740-piece silver service was not "restricted to the vault," for the couple entertained in a grand style; a typical menu would include five different wines and fifteen courses.[110] The last occasion on which the family used the silver collection in their Kenwood home was for a dinner honoring the famous actress and singer Lillian Russell.[111] The family history recalls that Furber took a fancy to the beautiful young woman. Soon after, Elvira Irwin Furber left suddenly for Florence, Italy, where she died in 1912.[112]

Meanwhile Furber sold eight acres at 46th Street to a developer who planned to improve the trapezoidal tract with streets and alleys, stone sidewalks, and boulevard lamps, and to erect only "first-class houses." The newspapers noted that this transaction clearly established Kenwood as a "choice residence quarter."[113] Furber was later instrumental in awarding the 1904 Olympic games to Chicago.[114] Despondent after a long illness, he shot himself in 1916.

⑲ Strahorn Residence and Barn, 1884. Demolished.
152 East Mason (47th) Street. Burnham & Root.

The famed partnership of by Daniel Hudson Burnham and John Wellborn Root had humble beginnings. Their first jobs were for small houses; however, their clientele slowly grew to include the large, elaborately detailed residence and barn for Robert and Juliet Strahorn, on the southwest corner of 47th Street and Woodlawn Avenue. Strahorn, an "enterprising and successful merchant," was the head

20 **Griswold Residence, 1884. Demolished. 164 East 47th Street. Burnham & Root.**

2.40. Henry F. Griswold of Spragues, Warner & Griswold (wholesale grocers) lived in this stuccoed, shingled house directly west of the equally architecturally rich Strahorn residence, visible at the left in the *Picturesque Kenwood* image.

of one of the oldest and wealthiest companies at the Chicago Stockyards.[115] He constructed this house at a time when many building permits were issued for construction throughout the neighborhood; no fewer than ninety permits were issued between April 1 and May 10, compared to eight permits for the same period the previous year.[116] An 1884 real estate article in the *Hyde Park Herald* noted "handsome, costly and substantial residences" were appearing in all parts of the village. The paper went to note that the construction of two houses for Robert Strahorn were well underway.[117]

The three-story frame and plaster house, with its steep roofline, leaded glass windows, turrets, and panels of stained glass, contained sixteen rooms. Strahorn lived here until 1895, when the house was sold to Eugene S. Kimball. It was then noted to be "one of the most attractive homes in Kenwood."[118] Kimball held on to the property until 1902, when he sold it to Delonas W. Potter. Kimball also sold Potter another tract at the same time, a vacant lot at the northwest corner of Woodlawn and 47th Street. Signaling the transition of 47th Street, Potter intended to construct an apartment building on the tract.

21 Heckman Residence, 1885.
4505 South Ellis Avenue. Architect/builder unknown.

This single-family house in North Kenwood is one of the few remaining that date to the time when the areas north and south of 47th Street were a unified community. Following the introduction of the streetcar line and subsequent commercialization of 47th, the area to the north gradually came to be known as a separate neighborhood. That was not always the case. The house was constructed in 1885 for lawyer and patron of the arts Wallace Heckman. Serving as the senior member of the firm Heckman, Elsdon, & Shaw from 1885 until 1903, Heckman became the business manager and counsel of the University of Chicago.[119] Under his financial supervision, the university began a period of significant expansion, purchasing

2.41. The Heckman house, as it appeared in *Picturesque Kenwood* c. 1890, demonstrates the rural nature of North Kenwood at the time. The house pictured at the left has been demolished.

2.42. Well before this image was taken in 2008, the Heckman residence had been converted to multifamily housing and was in dire need of repair. Although North Kenwood was designated as a Historic District in 1993, many structures have been demolished and those that remain are in varying states of repair.

lands on either side of the Midway Plaisance and extending from Washington Park east to Dorchester Avenue.[120]

In 1893, Heckman purchased land west of Chicago near the small town of Oregon, which he named Ganymede Farm. Here he built a long, two-story summer house on a beautiful bluff overlooking the hunting grounds of the legendary Sauk Indian warrior, Black Hawk.[121] Five years later he leased fifteen acres of the land to a group for a fee of one dollar per year. Eagle's Nest Artists' Colony, as the group became known, included artists, writers, architects (Irving and Allen Pond), sculptors (Lorado Taft), and musicians who each presented an annual free lecture or demonstration. Taft's famous 50' concrete statue of Black Hawk still stands on the site of the Eagle's Nest Colony.[122] In 1945, the 273-acre plot of Ganymede Farm was purchased by the state and renamed Lowden State Park as a memorial to former Illinois governor Frank O. Lowden.[123]

After Heckman's death in 1927, his widow Tillie continued to reside on Ellis Avenue. She established the Wallace Heckman Memorial Fund, one of the oldest University of Chicago Law Library book funds. Although considerably altered, the Heckman house is easily recognizable as one of the oldest residences in the area.

22 Barker Residence, 1885.
5000 South Greenwood Avenue. Architect unknown.

The Barker residence reflects the rising influence of architect Henry Hobson Richardson and the Romanesque Revival style. His interpretation of the Romanesque was most often found in public buildings constructed of rough stone, with strong arches and deeply set openings. Conveying a sense of strength and power, this massive style was far too expensive for the common homebuilder, and was

2.43. One of the more striking features of the Barker house is the bay window (barely visible on the right), embellished with fleur-de-lis motifs.

reserved for the upper class. In Kenwood, the house built for Attorney Joseph N. Barker and his wife Frances was the first of several in this style to be constructed in the neighborhood. Although the architect is not known, the house is a very early example of steel frame construction used in a residence.

The Barkers were early settlers in Kenwood, first living at 4811 Lake Avenue.[124] Records seem to indicate the family arrived by 1866, and that Joseph Barker organized the Mendelssohn Club that October.[125] Their Greenwood Avenue residence, which they moved into by July 1885, has an interesting oral history. According to the current owners, the house was built with funds inherited from a relative, received as a reward paid for the capture of John Wilkes Booth at Garrett's Farm near Port Royal, Virginia, on April 27, 1865.

Accounts indicate a Luther B. Barker received $3,000 for his role in the capture of Booth, and a David Barker received $1,653.84.[126] The relationship between the two is not known, nor has the flow of the inheritance been traced, yet Joseph Barker was known to possess a strong patriotic streak. On Flag Day, set aside for citizens to pay homage to "Old Glory," flags were draped across the city. Floating over the Barker residence was a historic 1864 flag "bearing the appropriate thirty-three stars."[127]

The Barker's daughter Josephine married George T. Williamson in 1881. Property transfers indicate that in April 1884 Samuel E. Williamson (possibly his father, Judge

Williamson of Cleveland) purchased the 75' × 297' parcel from the Connecticut Mutual Life Insurance Company.[128] In the summer of 1884 George and Josephine constructed the 7,000-square-foot house to the south of the Barkers at 5008 Greenwood. The younger Williamson unfortunately met an untimely death while playing tennis at the nearby Kenwood Country Club in the summer of 1898.[129]

23 Dupee Residence, 1883. Demolished by 1979.
4820 South Woodlawn Avenue. Andrews & Jacques.

In 1868, Horace Dupee bought a 200' × 300' tract of open land in Kenwood on which he intended to construct a house. He lived to see his investment increase tenfold, to a value of $300 per foot, having paid only $30.[130] Dupee came to Chicago from Boston in 1854 and joined his brother Charles in a wholesale provision business. Afterward he founded his own firm, H. M. Dupee & Company, which was located on South Water Street in the central business district. The fire destroyed his company and although suffering heavy losses, he reopened in a shanty on the east side of Michigan Avenue on land temporarily provided by the city. Eventually be purchased a half block on the corner of LaSalle and 25th Street, where he built his warehouses and

2.44. The rambling frame house of Horace Dupee appeared in *Picturesque Kenwood* and stood on Woodlawn Avenue for nearly a century, until damaged by fire in the 1970s.

"cured hams and bacon by the Dupee process." The brand became quite popular, and Dupee enjoyed great success until his retirement in 1892.[131]

Designed by the Boston firm of Andrews & Jacques, the house was remarkable in a number of ways: "The hardwood finish and carvings are among the finest that art can devise, or money can procure—the 'egg and dart' being everywhere present. . . . The spacious mantels show especially beautiful designs in wood carving. By the suggestion of Mr. and Mrs. Dupee" (Dupee married Elizabeth Robinson Buchanan in 1874) "the house was planned especially for home comfort, and presents many peculiar aspects, inasmuch as no parlor exists in it, while the expansive bedchambers and wardrobes suggest comfort, rather than useless luxury or vain show. Antique furniture abounds, and adds not a little to the appearance of solidarity and durability. The British and American architectural journals have embodied a description of the house in their pages, and it has often been visited by artists and has been copied and photographed by architects. It stands as a monument to the good sense and advanced ideas of its owner."[132] Included in these advanced ideas was the use of French plate glass, which added to the attractiveness of the "resplendent" residence.[133]

24 Page Residence, 1886.
4751 South Kimbark Avenue. Jenney & Otis.

For all of his fame, William LeBaron Jenney began with small residential work. Jenney was noted for his role in the development of the steel framed skyscraper— his Leiter Building was completed and the Home Insurance Building underway when plans were drawn for a house and stable for Mrs. Lydia C. Johnson at the corner of 52nd and Woodlawn in January 1884,[134] to be erected "as soon as weather

2.45. The Page house, located on a cul-de-sac of Kimbark Avenue, is a delightful representation of life in Kenwood over a century ago.

permits." The cost of the house rose quickly: estimated at $5,000, the two-story wood house of "English cottage design," was built for $8,000.[135] The house was later demolished for an apartment building. Jenney was commissioned that same year to erect four houses on nearby Oakwood Boulevard.[136] Presumably they were speculative construction, as two were for the McKnoen brothers and two for William Mavor. Rising three stories in height, they were of pressed brick "trimmed with red sandstone and terra-cotta, and finished with all the modern improvements."[137]

After partnering with William Otis in 1886, the firm was commissioned to design a residence on the newly opened stretch of Kimbark Avenue, once part of the ten-acre estate of Hon. Norman Judd, for lawyer William R. Page and his wife Florence.

25 Counselman Residence, 1887. Demolished 1973.
5035 South Greenwood Avenue. Burnham & Root.

Among Burnham & Root's largest and most notable commissions in the neighborhood was the 1887 design for prominent broker and real estate developer Charles Counselman and his wife Jennie E. Otis. The house once stood on a vast expanse of lawn at the corner of Hyde Park Boulevard and Greenwood, the current site of the KAM temple. Counselman came to Chicago in 1869 and two years later became a member of the Board of Trade. He slowly built a fortune, and "Imbued with a profound faith in the future greatness of the city," began to invest in real estate.[138] In 1883–1884 Burnham & Root designed the Counselman Building, a ten-story office building at the northwest corner of LaSalle and Jackson. In 1886

2.46. The Counselman mansion, at it appeared in an 1888 issue of *Inland Architect*, was situated on a corner lot, large even by Kenwood standards of the time.

Counselman commissioned the firm to design this Romanesque-style stone house. Suffering from poor health, Counselman left Chicago in the winter of 1903 for warmer climates. He died in March the following year.[139]

In 1920 the house was sold to Max Goldstine for $85,000. He made a very shrewd purchase, for several months later the site was again sold, this time for $500,000.[140] After Alfred Alschuler designed the temple for the Isaiah Israel congregation in 1924, the house was used as the temple's social hall and youth lounge. When the congregation merged with KAM, they agreed to tear down the old house and replace it with an addition that was completed in 1973. Within the new building is a leaded glass skylight designed by Root. Covered with dirt and discovered just before the wrecker's ball was about to strike, the skylight was saved and is now displayed in the lobby of the addition.[141]

26 Turner Residence, 1888.
4935 South Greenwood Avenue. Solon Spencer Beman.

Several years after the completion of the Rosalie Villas, Beman designed this three-story brick and stone house for dry goods merchant Edward H. Turner. The brick structure combines a number of styles. While the overall effect is Queen Anne (the large, two-story turreted tower and complex elevation), the colonnaded front porch is classical. This residence is sometimes mistakenly identified as that of manufacturing executive Edward A. Turner and his wife Amelia Haigh, whose house once stood at 227 (1044) East 47th Street. Adolphus Green purchased the Turner property in 1899, and commissioned Daniel Burnham & Company to design the barn at the rear of the lot.

2.47

27 Miller Residence, 1888.
4800 South Kimbark Avenue. George O. Garnsey.

George Garnsey was the editor of the *National Builder*, a monthly journal that provided complete sets of plans, specifications, and cost estimates for specially designed homes. The trade journal also kept carpenters and builders familiar with the latest in housing designs, while readers could select from a variety of styles and sizes for anything from small houses to elaborate residences. Garnsey's houses often combined styles from any number of periods; "decorative restraint" was not his motto.[142]

2.48. Garnsey combined half-timbering, shingles and leaded windows with rough stone in his design for the Miller house.

Garnsey certainly followed trends in housing design—he "unabashedly" copied H. H. Richardson's William Watts Sherman house in Newport, Rhode Island, for distilling executive George L. Miller.[143] He designed this house at a time when many residences were constructed on this stretch of Kimbark Avenue. A version of this house also appeared in one of his many publications.

28 Harding Residence, c. 1890 and Museum, 1927.
Demolished 1964.
4853 South Lake (Lake Park) Avenue. Architect unknown.

George F. Harding Jr. was a prominent businessman and political figure in Chicago. He held a number of elected offices—alderman of the Second Ward for ten years, state senator, and city controller—before assuming the powerful role of Cook

2.49. George Harding's house and castle-like museum were among the very last of the structures to be removed on Lake Avenue during the 1960s. The trustees of the museum fought condemnation by the city, unsuccessfully.

Country treasurer in 1926. However his strongest passion was collecting fine art and artifacts.[144] Building upon a collection started by his father, Harding assembled one of the finest collections of arms and armor in the United States and housed it all in a peculiar museum he built in Kenwood. Harding often told his friends, "My father always said that, when the time comes to retire, have something to retire to."[145]

The red brick house was originally constructed for Brenton R. Wells, a member of M. D. Wells & Company, wholesalers of boots and shoes. (Moses D. Wells, whose daughter Frances became the wife of architect Howard van Doren Shaw, had founded the company in 1866.)[146] Harding purchased the property in 1916 and moved his collection not long afterward.

"Short, quite stout, and white-haired," Harding personally conducted tours at the opening of the medieval-style stone castle he built on the property to accommodate his abundant collection. The two-story turreted structure had cannon balls embedded on the exterior stone walls. The museum could be entered from a somewhat secret door on the second floor of the house, where a visitor would find that each room housed a different collection—helmets, coats of armor, swords, guns, rugs, beds, portraits, and paintings. Even a small black sofa once sat upon by Abraham Lincoln was on display.[147]

At Harding's death in 1939, his will endowed the collection as a public trust to protect and display his enormous collection, and for years the museum remained a local landmark known as the "Treasure House." In 1962 the property was condemned by the city in order to complete the widening of Lake Park Avenue as part of a massive urban renewal project.[148] Although legal battles ensued, the house was demolished in 1965. The Art Institute of Chicago salvaged Harding's arms and armor from storage in 1982, and the collection has since become one of the museum's most popular attractions.[149]

29 **Fisher Residence, 1890.**
4734 South Kimbark Avenue. Patton & Fisher.

Normand Patton and Reynolds Fisher were among the foremost of Chicago's Queen Anne designers and several examples of their work can still be found in Kenwood, including Fisher's own residence. The thin clapboards, steeply pitched roof, and asymmetrical façade of Reynolds Fisher's house are typical elements used by the partners in their unrestrained Queen Anne designs. Brightly painted and inviting, these homes stood out for the interplay of light and shadow created by the many textures, projections, and recesses.

2.50 . Patton & Fisher designed a number of houses in the neighborhood and advertised their services in the *House Beautiful Directory of Architects*. Steep gables and thin clapboards appear on the nearly 4,000-square-foot residence designed for Reynolds, where he lived until 1901.

2.51 The front door of the Fisher house opened into a wood-paneled vestibule, detailed with fine spindles of the stair balustrade and warmed by a tiled fireplace, as seen in this 1890 Inland Architect image.

2.52. The family of Alonzo and Charlotte Fuller was aided by the help of a governess, servant, and two gardeners through the early years of the new century, until they relocated to the suburb of Evanston on the city's far north side.

31 Frank Hoyt Fuller Residence, 1891. 4840 South Ellis Avenue. Frederick Perkins.

2.53

30 **Alonzo M. Fuller Residence, 1890.**
4832 South Ellis Avenue. Frederick Perkins.

Prominent society architect Frederick Perkins was heavily influenced by the work of H. H. Richardson, the Boston architect whose Romanesque-inspired stone architecture had already made its effects felt in houses constructed in the Kenwood neighborhood. Walls were thick, and forms were simple and structurally honest, and in that way the work was, "markedly different" from the previous eclectic styles.[150]

Perkins received two commissions for brothers and wholesale grocers Frank and Alonzo Fuller, combining stone and steep rooflines with completely different results. The large Romanesque residence of Alonzo, with its heavy stone and large wraparound porch, contrasts with steeply pitched roof of his brother's charming rustic stone house to the south.

Alonzo M. Fuller came to Chicago from New York about 1860 at the age of seventeen and built a wholesale grocery business. After it was destroyed in the 1871 fire, Fuller joined the firm of William M. Hoyt & Company, where he remained until his retirement.[151]

Drexel Boulevard

32 **Hale Residence, 1885–1886.**
4545 South Drexel Boulevard. Burnham & Root.

By 1885 the improvement of Drexel Boulevard had stimulated construction just as the Drexel family had envisioned. The northern end of the avenue was anchored by a "fine hotel" at Oakwood and Drexel Boulevards, constructed in brick with "all the modern improvements."[152] During an era when wealthy businessmen publicly demonstrated their success, the large lots along the boulevard south of this intersection became favored sites. By 1890, new construction extended south to 47th Street, and few open lots remained in this section. South of 47th Street several new large residences began to appear, predominantly on the east side of the boulevard.

The residences designed by Burnham & Root during this period quickly progressed from the "clutter and fussiness"[153] of the 1884 Strahorn residence to a relatively cleaner aesthetic, dominated by "undecorated expanses and unusually large areas of plate glass."[154] The trend toward greater simplicity had its beginnings in the Romanesque-inspired mansion they designed for William E. Hale.

Architect Louis Sullivan once praised Hale as one of two men "who are responsible for the modern office building."[155] In 1869 Hale, working with his brother George, patented the Hale Water Balance Elevator, and Otis Elevator manufactured the invention. Hale's hydraulic elevator ran quickly and more smoothly than the steam elevators that were in use at the time, making new heights of the sky-

2.54. The exterior of the Hale residence appears as regal today as in this 1888 *Inland Architect* image, in spite of the large institutional addition on the rear designed in 1925 by E. Norman Brydges. However, the interior the space has been altered, cut up into the twenty units of the "Observatory Condominiums and Lofts."

scraper possible. In 1890 Hale branched into construction of the tall office building, commissioning Burnham & Root to design the steel framed Reliance Building, noted for its broad plates of glass and double-hung windows arranged as the "Chicago window."

③⑥ Kenwood Astrophysical Observatory, 1890. Demolished.
4545 South Drexel Boulevard, rear. Burnham & Root.

Hale was supportive, to say the least, of his son George Ellery Hale and his interest in astronomy. While riding a streetcar in Chicago in 1889, an idea came to the younger Hale that made photographing the sun possible. His father commissioned Burnham & Root to design an observatory in the backyard and by 1891 George achieved important results with his new spectroheliograph at the Kenwood Observatory, photographing the solar corona.[156]

The younger Hale was appointed to the newly founded University of Chicago as an associate professor of astrophysics, where he remained until 1905. Hale became a distinguished scientist; as the founder of the Charles T. Yerkes Observatory and the Mount Wilson Solar Observatory, he played a "pioneering role" in astronomy. Although he left the University of Chicago, the institution considered Hale to be a "superb astrophysicist" and a "master creator of institutions within which scientists could work."[157]

255

33 Nolan Residence, 1887.
4941 South Drexel Boulevard. Burnham & Root.

The Drexel Boulevard residence of John H. and Emily Nolan was one of two major residences designed in Kenwood by Burnham & Root after completion of the Hale residence. The Nolan residence, although large, is straightforward in comparison to the many opulent mansions that once lined Drexel Boulevard. The design represents a new, and simpler, aesthetic. Constructed of variegated brick, the house features a prominent gable, a characteristic of Root's later residential work.[158] "The value of a plain surface in every building is not to be overestimated," Root advised. "Strive for them."[159]

Nolan was obviously pleased with the results of Root's work. "You not only can make a good picture of a house," Nolan wrote to him, "but you can also build a good one . . . and in the end, when it comes to delivering up the keys make a man happier . . . than he expected he would be." He continued his praise, "You might, without straining anything, gather the suspicion that I rather like you people. Well, I own up to that I do. Why shouldn't I?"[160]

After serving in the Civil War, Nolan began his career as an agent for the Travelers' Life Insurance Company, first in New Haven and then in Chicago, where he worked for over forty years.[161] His wife Emily became involved with the Chicago Women's Club, an organization that promoted a "higher civilization of humanity."[162] She was one of the founders of the Society for the Promotion of Physical Culture and Correct Dress, whose 150 Chicago members were a "liberal and progressive group."[163] The dress club led the effort to reform clothing and free women from the restraints imposed by stiff, corseted styles.[164]

34 **Ryerson Residence, 1887.**
4851 South Drexel Boulevard. Treat & Foltz.

One of the few remaining lavish estates on the boulevard is the residence of Martin Ryerson. Situated on a large parcel of land surrounded by a wrought-iron fence, the Romanesque Revival–style house is defined by the use of rusticated stone and Bedford limestone. Although Treat & Foltz began their partnership just after the Chicago fire, this mammoth urban estate was their earliest remaining work in the neighborhood. Ryerson was a Harvard Law School graduate who joined his father's lumber business, assuming control when his father died, the year this house was completed. Ryerson was one of the Art Institute's founding trustees and one of the museum's most important donors.[165]

The interior of the house contained many details stunning in their intricacy. From inlaid floors, to stained glass, to custom hardware on cabinetry and doors, the lavish attention to detail is apparent. Formal rooms on the first floor are tightly clustered and separated by pocket doors. With a different design in each room, the flooring demonstrates the family business, a theme echoed in the woodwork, bookshelves, and window shutters of mahogany, cherry, and oak.[166]

On display throughout the rooms was an extraordinary collection of art, ranging

2.58. The interior of the Ryerson house contained many details astonishing in their creativity and craftsmanship, including this Arts and Crafts-style door handle.

2.57. The erection of a tall wrought-iron fence and the relocation of the driveway represent the minimal changes to the Ryerson estate since this image was taken. Note the wide-open vistas east of Drexel Boulevard in the distance.

from Old Master paintings to a breathtaking collection of French Impressionists that included five paintings by Renoir and sixteen by Claude Monet, to works of Winslow Homer and John Singer Sargent.[167] Most of the collection, once considered one of the finest in the country, was given to the Art Institute the year after Ryerson's death in 1932. The property was donated to the university and was sold in 1944 to a religious order seeking a site for a monastery.

35 McGill Residence, 1890.
4938 South Drexel Boulevard. Henry Ives Cobb.

Undoubtedly, prominent architect Henry Ives Cobb's most significant work in the community was the campus for the University of Chicago; however, he also received several residential commissions in the Hyde Park area. Prior to the university project, Cobb designed the massive limestone mansion of Dr. John A. McGill. McGill was an innovator of "patent medicine" that made him a fortune. The term is commonly used to describe various drug remedies sold in the eighteenth and nineteenth centuries. "With colorful names and even more colorful claims," these popular medicines were often amply laced with alcohol.[168]

A sumptuous addition to Drexel Boulevard, McGill's magnificent Chateauesque-style residence was based on sixteenth-century French palaces, which Cobb would have become familiar with on his European tour. The style is characterized by an eclectic array of elements and was favored by America's newly wealthy families. Massive round towers topped with battlement parapets, the steeply pitched

2.59. The spires, towers, turrets, finials, and sculpted chimneys of the Chateauesque style are indicative of the time and expense required to produce an ornate urban mansion. Although condominiums now obscure this 1892 *Inland Architect* view of the McGill mansion, the style, a true relic of the Gilded Age, is one of the most easily recognizable examples of urban residential architecture.

2.60. This 1895 *Architectural Record* image of the McGill mansion's highly crafted main hall and side parlors demonstrates the excesses of an earlier era. Another publication, *Inland Architect and News Record*, highlighted the importance of the entry in establishing the "pedigree of the family." More than any other room, it was recommended the reception room should "be a harmonious whole, a dream of perfection for it is here that we declare our taste and education to the world." Additionally it was recommended that great care be given to the selection of colors for the entry, for it was important that "those selected should be becoming to the mistress of the house, for otherwise she will appear at a disadvantage and out of place with her surroundings just when she should feel and appear at her best."

roof, and ornately carved archways signify the 20,000-square-foot residence as a very special place indeed.[169]

McGill bequeathed his grand limestone mansion and the land to the YWCA in 1928, when it became known as the Carrie McGill Memorial YMCA. A three-story limestone annex was designed by Berlin & Swern that same year. Following decades of decline as a nursing home, the structure was renovated to accommodate thirty-four condominiums. In 2006, the imposing mansion was granted landmark status by Chicago's City Council.

Study for
University of Chicago
founded by
John D. Rockefeller.

Henry Ives Cobb, Architect.   1893

3.01. An early site plan for the University of Chicago campus, prepared by Henry Ives Cobb for John D. Rockefeller, clearly demonstrated an inward focus and separation between the institution and the surrounding neighborhood.

CHAPTER THREE

Threads of Gray, White, and Gold, 1892–1908

Not the least of my agonies was going to dinners and parties in the Drexel Boulevard neighborhood. These were church people who had grown rich on running grist mills, plumbing factories, piano factories; they were managers of drygoods stores and proprietors of elevators and wholesale candy houses. There were no saloon-keepers, owners of breweries, no free-faring men, lovers of sport and horsemen. . . . There were no philosophical anarchists or single-taxers or readers of Herbert Spencer. They were all Republicans.

—Edgar Lee Masters, *Across Spoon River*

Determined businessmen, eager to shed Chicago's image as a "greedy, hog-slaughtering backwater"[1] and to present the city as a place of refinement and culture, undertook two tremendously ambitious projects in the 1890s. Each of these endeavors had significant and lasting effects on the community. Located on adjacent parcels of land in city's newly annexed suburb, the University of Chicago was founded, and Jackson Park was selected as the site for the World's Columbian Exposition.

There the similarities ended, as differences between the two projects were profound.[2] The Columbian Exposition was a dramatic, once-in-a-lifetime event intended to astound and entertain. The plan of the world's fair was based on classical principals, emulating the architecture of ancient Greece and Rome. Buildings were aligned, forming a formal court with a water basin that flowed into Lake Michigan. Dedicated to learning and research, the University of Chicago was to appear timeless and enduring. The university was composed of neo-Gothic structures that created cloistered courtyards, giving the campus an intellectual air akin to European universities.

In 1856, when Chicago was not even twenty years old, Paul Cornell's advisor, Stephen Douglas, founded the first University of Chicago, a small Baptist institution on land west of Cottage Grove at 35th Street. Classes began two years later. However, by 1886 the college experienced financial difficulties and closed.[3] A short time later one of the nation's leading businessmen, oil magnate John D. Rock-

Cobb Hall, 1892, 5811–5827, South Ellis Avenue, Henry Ives Cobb. 3.02. Cobb Hall was not named for the architect but for a benefactor—industrialist Silas Cobb. The first building constructed for the university, Cobb Hall housed classrooms, offices, a large hall, and a chapel and served as a model for all future structures designed by Cobb for the campus. It was, according to Block's *Uses of Gothic*, the most expensive and the largest of his sixteen buildings. The Gothic style building was constructed of blue Bedford limestone, a plentiful, durable material that provided the illusion that the university was a very old one.

efeller, expressed an interest in founding a college either in New York or Chicago. In December 1888, the Education Society supported the founding of a college in the city of Chicago and in May of the following year Rockefeller donated $600,000 toward an endowment fund.[4]

Varying suggestions were made as to a location, but the consensus was that it be within the borders of the city of Chicago and not in a suburban location.[5] The site of Douglas's old institution was considered; however, the cost to obtain the land and the building was "prohibitive."[6] Further south, between Washington and Jackson Parks and north of the Midway Plaisance, was a low-lying, region of open land that featured a mixture of scrub oak trees and marshes. Marshall Field, founder of the department store of the same name, owned a portion of this land. At first glance the property was less than desirable. Nonetheless, Field was approached, and when he offered to donate a portion of his land as a site for the new institution, it was readily accepted.[7] What soon followed was an extended period of extraordinary generosity by Martin Ryerson, Rockefeller, and many others.

On September 10, 1890, John D. Rockefeller, E. Nelson Blake, Marshall Field, Fred T. Gates, Francis E. Hinckley and Thomas W. Goodspeed incorporated the University of Chicago. Professor William Rainey Harper, of Yale University, was chosen president.[8] Harper was a small man physically, but in "character and philosophy a man of . . . towering stature. . ."[9] Prior to accepting the position, Harper proposed that the scope be greatly enlarged to found not a college, but a university. He imagined a world-class institution that would "combine an American-style undergraduate liberal arts college with a German-style graduate research university."[10]

With the founding of the university, Paul Cornell's full vision was realized. He had wanted a lakeside institution of higher learning to anchor his fledgling community. Although he set aside land to establish a Presbyterian theological seminary, the project never came to fruition. Cornell—who had purchased the land, initiated transportation alliances, planned the parks, excluded industry, and encouraged the upper and professional classes to call his Hyde Park home–would now see his dream completed.[11]

The trustees of the newly founded university were responsible for the establishment of a building program. Early sketches indicate that the style initially considered was Romanesque, but the selected architect, Henry Ives Cobb, promoted a style known as late English Gothic, complete with towers, spires, and gargoyles.[12] Although Harper envisioned the institution as a new approach to higher learning, it was housed in the most traditional of buildings. Cobb designed all of the buildings erected prior to 1900, with the exception of Blaine Hall by James Gamble Rogers, Hitchcock Hall by Dwight H. Perkins, and Rosenwald Hall by Holabird & Roche.

The erection of the first university buildings began in November 1891, on the east side of Ellis between 58th and 59th Streets. On September 1, 1892, Cobb Hall was completed, and one month later the first class was held on a Saturday morning at 8:30 after Harper and the other faculty members had pulled a "feverish all-nighter . . . unpacking and arranging desks, chairs, and tables" in the new build-

The Beatrice Hotel, 1891. Demolished 1962. Southwest corner of 57th and Dorchester Avenue. Architect unknown.

3.03. Undated photograph by Al Henderson. The building served dual purposes that reflected the two major developments in the Hyde Park area. It was initially used as the first University of Chicago women's dormitory, until residents were moved to Ida Noyes Hall in 1893. The structure was then used as originally planned, providing accommodations for the World's Columbian Exposition.

ing.[13] When the university opened, the faculty numbered 120 with a student body of 742, on a site that encompassed seventeen acres.[14]

While planning for the new university was underway, the city awaited the announcement of the location selected to host the World's Columbian Exposition. Intended to commemorate the four hundredth anniversary of the discovery of America, the fair would symbolize the nation's growing power and international stature. Competition was fierce; New York, St. Louis, and Washington were all in the running. However, Chicago displayed its might, rebuilding after the fire, and growing to become the Midwest's leading center of commerce, manufacturing, and innovative architecture. As a result of the annexation of enormous areas by the city, Chicago was now the second-largest city in the nation, and in a prime position to be selected as the location for the upcoming fair.

Chicagoans reacted with vigor when the decision was announced and soon were consumed with planning.[15] The World's Columbian Exposition Company was established to finance and to build the fair. Architects Daniel Burnham and John Wellborn Root were selected as consultants for the project, but the location was far from settled.[16] A downtown site was considered and rejected by the business community; a location in the west parks was deemed too far from the city's splendid lakeshore.[17]

First considered for the purpose of accommodating overflow from a central location, Daniel Burnham's favored site was the unimproved acreage of Jackson Park. Frederick Law Olmsted's original plan for the park was to transform the raw landscape into a recreational area unlike any other in the country. He envisioned a parkland of canals, lagoons, and shady groves, all focused on the water. Although his initial plan for Jackson Park was never realized, the unimproved site was large enough to provide the required minimum of four hundred acres and was framed by a stunning backdrop—the deep blue water of Lake Michigan.

By the late fall of 1890, the location for the fair was settled and Burnham & Root prepared a preliminary plan for Jackson Park. Almost immediately, surrounding property values began to escalate. There was great speculative activity and apartment houses rose in adjacent residential sections. Three luxury hotels were under construction in 1892; the Del Prado, located on the north side of the Midway, the Chicago Beach Hotel at the lakefront and 51st Street, and the Windermere situated on 56th Street. These joined the new Hyde Park Hotel, completed several years earlier and enlarged to accommodate the many anticipated visitors as well as permanent residents.

The amenities and technical innovations featured in these apartment hotels became "so common," wrote architectural and urban historian Carl Condit, "that, like all the great basic inventions on which our lives depend, they have come to be regarded as natural things which have always existed." The advancements were varied and numerous, with "hot and cold running water at all times, continuously circulating steam or hot water heat." Electric lighting became standard in hotel construction, as did electric call bells and the telephone. Moveable partitions were developed to vary the size and number of rooms in a suite, which included built-in furniture such as chests, sideboards, and wardrobes. And finally, "in pursuit of their aim to free the resident of the last care of homeownership, the Chicago architects introduced the safe-deposit vault at the central desk."[18]

Not only luxurious hotels rose to accommodate visitors to the fair. In an effort

3.04. The grade level of the Illinois Central Railroad tracks was raised to provide improved service for the crowds anticipated at the fair. In the background is the elegant Chicago Beach Hotel, which opened in 1893. The image is dated September 10, 1894.

to provide clean, safe quarters "for the great army of industrial women, wage earn-ers, and working girls" who would visit the fair, the Women's Dormitory Associa-tion was founded in May 1892 with a goal of raising funds for the construction of six facilities.[19] One of the six structures was planned for a parcel of mostly vacant property between Lexington (University) and Ingleside, 52nd to 53rd streets. The two-story frame building was erected about ten blocks from the fair entrance, in "one of the pleasantest portions of Hyde Park."[20] Although "destitute of ornamen-tation," the building, designed by Paul C. Lantrop, provided secure housing for a thousand women.[21]

In contrast to these large structures, blocks of small cottages appeared to house the workers hired to construct the fair. These were clustered on small lots in the center of Hyde Park, near the St. Thomas the Apostle Catholic Church at 55th and Kimbark. Some of the large houses of the early residents were converted into boardinghouses for fair and railroad workers, and saloons and billiard halls opened nearby. Urban row houses and three-flats quickly rose to accommodate the tre-mendous influx of workers, many of whom were immigrants from Ireland, Ger-many, and Sweden.[22] South Park became increasingly commercial as a shopping area grew along 57th Street. This area was overbuilt, and the subsequent low rent and vacant apartments attracted laborers from across the city. Unlike the rest of the community, the demographics of this area were more like the larger city.[23]

Amid all the construction, the challenge of transporting hundreds of thousands of visitors to the fair each day had to be addressed. The Illinois Central line purchased forty-one new locomotives, raised the grade level of the railroad bed to provide cross streets with a clear flow of traffic, and erected new station facilities.[24] These significant improvements to the rail service had a tremendous physical impact on the com-munity. In particular, the raised grade level divided the community, and over time the section adjacent to the lake would become known as East Hyde Park. In all, the railroad company made substantial improvements that enabled it to transport an estimated four million passengers to and from the world's fair.[25]

The intense flurry of activity paled, however, next to Burnham and Root's charge to build an entire city in a very limited time frame. Burnham was the chief of construction, and Root was to oversee the design and architecture of the exposition. At this time all of Chicago's architectural firms were busy; there were seventeen major buildings in the late planning or construction stages in the Loop, in addition to hundreds of smaller commercial buildings and residential commissions.[26] At first, Burnham chose to ignore the city's architectural firms. Instead, the proposed board of architects was to consist of the five leading architectural firms in the country. Selected from outside the city of Chicago, they were to construct a fair that would be unlike any before—a monument to architecture.[27]

Facing controversy by ignoring local architects, in January 1891 the group was expanded. The initial list of Peabody & Sterns of Boston (Machinery Hall), Richard M. Hunt of New York (Administration Building), George B. Post of New York (Manufacturing Building), Van Brunt & Howe of Kansas City (Electricity Building), and McKim Mead & White (Agriculture Building), was augmented to include five Chicago firms. Added were Burling & Whitehouse (Venetian Village), Henry Ives Cobb (Fisheries Building), Jenney & Mundie (Horticulture Building), Solon S. Beman (Mines and Mining Building), and Adler & Sullivan (Transportation Building).[28] Frederick Olmsted returned to the site he had planned nearly twenty years earlier to supervise the landscape design. In the end, over one hundred architects designed buildings for the fair, and half of them practiced in Chicago.[29]

When the entire board met in Chicago that winter, one architect was notably absent from the group. On hearing of his partner John Wellborn Root's untimely death from pneumonia in January, Burnham is said to have exclaimed, "I have worked, I have schemed and dreamed to make us the greatest architects in the world. I have made him see it and kept him at it—and now he dies—damn! damn! damn!"[30] It was Root who envisioned the design of the fair; the buildings were to be a refinement of the architecture that defined Chicago after the fire, many-hued and human-scaled. The first principle of architecture to Root was truth: "Every building must simply and perfectly express its purpose and the material with which it was constructed."[31] In Root's absence, east coast architect Charles McKim forcefully convinced Burnham that the only approach was to adopt a uniform, classical Beaux Arts style.

In later years architect Louis Sullivan reiterated his objections to the revised aesthetic. He saw the progressive designs fostered by Chicago School architects supplanted by an architecture in which appearance was cynically separated from its structure.[32] In ancient Greece and Rome, the columns and stone walls were the temple's structure; under McKim's vision they were a veneer that concealed the underlying structure. No surface was to be left untouched as they aimed toward magnificence. Figures and ornament covered every surface, later described by Ada Louise Huxtable as if conceived by "a mad pastry chef at work."[33]

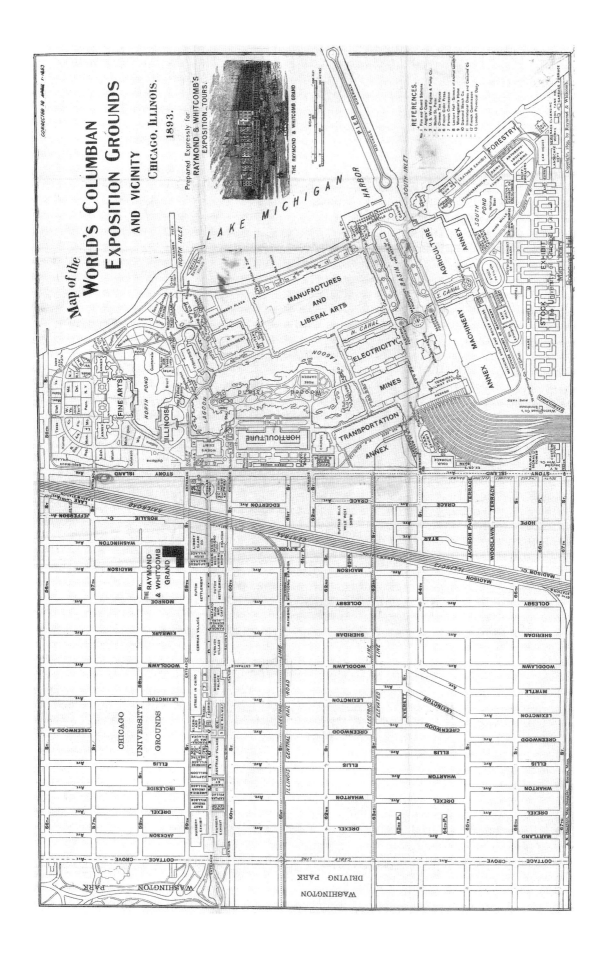

COPYRIGHTED 185 3 BY C.D.ARNOLD.

Despite Root's death, Burnham pushed forward, and the plans developed by the architects were spectacular. Centered on the Court of Honor, an assemblage of colonnaded arcades, peristyles, porticos, and pavilions were constructed. In plan the buildings were essentially huge sheds, designed to exhibit materials. Their impressive exteriors were molded of a plaster-like material called "staff," not designed to last; had the structures not been destroyed, they would have deteriorated within several years.

The Mines Building by Solon Beman was one of the first to be completed and provided a test for color selection. New York painter Francis Millet was hired, and after experimentation he settled on a single color for the entire exposition, an ordinary white lead and oil paint. The regal white buildings provided a dramatic spectacle against the blue backdrop of the lake and the lush greenery of Olmsted's plantings. Thomas Tallmadge, writing in his memoirs forty years later, said of the sight, "Imperial Rome in the third century might have approached but surely did not surpass it."[34]

Although the fair was dedicated in October 1892 with a dazzling program of parades, music, and fireworks, the official opening was on the first of May the following year. A heavy rain fell that morning and although pools of water were everywhere, more than 200,000 people entered the park grounds. Shortly after noon, president Grover Cleveland declared the fair to be open and touched an ivory and gold key that started the machinery humming. The exhibits and inventions were compelling; however, the fair's greatest power lay in the buildings and grounds themselves. The

World's Columbian Exposition Grounds and Vicinity. Chicago, Illinois, 1893.

3.06. (*Opposite*) Prepared for Raymond & Whitcomb's Exposition Tours, the map detailed the Midway Plaisance and grounds of the 1893 World's Columbian Exposition, where an entire classical city was erected within Jackson Park on the city's southern lakeshore.

3.07. The elaborate Beaux Arts structures facing the Grand Basin clearly represented Daniel Burnham's credo: "Make no little plans, they have no magic to stir men's blood." The edifices expressed a confident America and a desire to create a symbol of national unity. The homogeneous, classical façades became influential in the City Beautiful movement, and were emulated in other cities as urban planners shaped America's civic and cultural identity.

majestic Court of Honor was powerfully moving. Emerging poet Edgar Lee Masters
wrote that it was "the most beautiful thing that has ever existed on this earth."[35]

The architecture was powerful, yet everything about the spectacular fair was
intriguing. Electric lights filled the evening sky. Visitors tasted a new snack called
Cracker Jack, a breakfast food called Shredded Wheat, a gum called Juicy Fruit,
and a popular thirst quencher, Pabst Blue Ribbon.[36] Convenience foods were promoted; a box purporting to contain all the ingredients to make a mouthwatering
stack of pancakes appeared under the stereotypical name of Aunt Jemima. There
were new inventions ranging from a simple zipper, to the first moving pictures, to
a miniature version of the house of the future, where the washing, ironing, and
cooking were all powered by electricity.[37]

Just outside the magical city, one could delight in the sights and sounds of the
Midway Plaisance, a mile-long, circus-like area stretching from Jackson Park west
to Washington Park. In contrast to the fair, exhibits here were intented to thrill and
sometimes shock. Whole villages were imported from foreign lands—Egypt, Algeria,
and Arabia—along with their "belly dancing" inhabitants. By midsummer the giant
Ferris wheel, America's alternative to the Eiffel Tower, transported visitors hundreds
of feet in the air, offering panoramic views of the splendor below.

The fair lasted just six months, and when it closed over twenty-seven million

3.09. A hushed crowd watched in awe as the dream city disappeared in flames. Only a few structures were spared, including the Fine Arts Building designed by Charles Atwood of Burnham & Root. Marshall Field later donated $1 million for the conversion of the structure to house the fair's remaining exhibits. In 1926, Kenwood resident Julius Rosenwald donated $3 million more to rebuild the decaying structure in stone. The exterior design of the original building was reconstructed in its entirety, and the Museum of Science and Industry, envisioned as a great industrial museum, anchors Hyde Park's lakefront today.

had visited the grounds, an astonishing attendance given that the population of the country was sixty-five million.[38] The grandeur created by Burnham and his team of architects exceeded what each could have imagined on their own. The dream city occupied over one square mile and was filled with more than two hundred buildings. Just as magically as the fair appeared, it went up in flames. A more dramatic ending could not have been planned, as the classical city disappeared, leaving only charred remains and memories of one glorious summer.

Just as quickly, the optimism of the fair receded to encompass a new reality. Within the confines of the "White City" was a beautiful, well managed, and seemingly incorrupt environment. The streets were clean, transportation reliable, and sanitary facilities up-to-date. The world Burnham created was unlike the rest of the city, where corruption was an accepted reality, filthy streets and poor sanitation were pervasive, and crime and vice increased steadily. There were growing economic problems; by 1894 the country slipped into a deep depression. Locally, the closing of the fair meant thousands were unemployed. Blocks were lined with vacant houses, and apartment buildings were boarded up. There was anxiety about labor unrest, and concern about the poor and the continual waves of immigrants.

The unease, depression, and social strife were addressed as a period of reform swept into the city. Involved were Chicago's wealthiest and most powerful men and women, including many who lived in the Hyde Park and Kenwood neighborhoods.[39] A citywide program emerged to deal with the conditions, and Hyde Park organized its own chapter of the Civic Federation in 1894. The university addressed the issues by opening its Chicago Settlement House in 1894, modeled after Jane Addams's Hull-House.[40] Settlement houses such as this arose in response to "problems created by urbanization, industrialization and immigration."[41] Students and faculty contributed to programs designed to educate workers and improve the living conditions of their families.

Problems were exacerbated when workers at the nearby town of Pullman (part of Hyde Park Township before annexation) became dissatisfied with layoffs and a reduction in wages, while rents in the company town remained firm. Under the leadership of Eugene Debs, workers founded a union and went on strike, essentially crippling railroad service nationwide. For a time the strike went on peacefully; however, President Cleveland saw the boycott as a threat to the nation's mail service and ordered federal troops to Chicago to quell the uprising. When attacks were made against the strikers, riots followed.[42]

For the railroad officials and executives of the meatpacking industry who relied upon the railroads and backed Pullman's position, this was a frightening time. During the hot summer months of 1894 blazing fires at Pullman lit the night skies south of Hyde Park and Kenwood. Thousands of federal and state troops were in the vicinity when Debs and other leaders were arrested. The strike continued until early August when the Pullman works reopened. As to Debs, he was charged with obstructing commerce, and the case worked its way to the nation's highest court. Although defended by Clarence Darrow and the venerable eighty-one-year-old Lyman Trumbull, the Supreme Court ruled against Debs.[43] The Pullman strike demonstrated the vast power of a unified labor union, and the willingness of the federal government to support businessmen against organized labor. As for those workers at Pullman, their rents remained the same.

In the midst of the unease, Hyde Park and Kenwood were at the apex of their development. Wealthy business and civic leaders flocked to the attractive and easily accessible communities to escape the ills of the city. This was the gilded age, particularly in Kenwood, where businessmen amassed fortunes and built palatial, elaborate homes for their families. The Ryersons, whose wealth came from lumber and steel, joined the Swift and Morris families, whose fortunes derived from the meatpacking industry. In Hyde Park, the faculty and administrators of the university were encouraged to live near the institution, and gracious houses rose on the surrounding blocks.

Fashionable social routines continued despite the unfavorable financial climate and labor unrest following the fair. Social calling cards and visiting hours were the norm. Servants pressed and washed and cleaned and cooked, which afforded women leisure time. Clubs opened for boating and tennis during the summer months and in the winter there were ice-skating and toboggan chutes. For horse racing, The Kenwood Club expanded its facilities with the new 1895 clubhouse, and the Quadrangle Club, founded in 1893 as a social club for the faculty of the newly established university, moved into permanent facilities in 1896. The Hyde Park YMCA was constructed, and the new high school, designed by Flanders & Zimmerman, was said to be the finest in the state when it opened in 1894. And it was not long before the site of the fair underwent a transformation, as Olmsted began converting the site back into parkland.[44]

In the midst of this high-toned prosperity, small changes became apparent that eventually altered the character of the neighborhood. Forty-Seventh Street began its evolution as early as the mid-1880s when a township ordinance passed that provided for the widening of the street seven feet on each side from Drexel Boulevard to Lake Avenue. Although fences on most properties had been moved back five feet on either side several years earlier, several property owners refused and created "some little stir" over the requirement.[45] Equally unwelcome was the erection of a line of "immense unsightly telephone poles" on the north side of the street. The village trustees promptly stopped the installation when property owners protested.[46] After annexation the Chicago City Railway electrified trolley made its appearance on 47th Street in 1896, much to the dismay of those who had recently invested heavily in lavish residences.

The Kenwood community gradually accepted progress and convenience—a block of stores that opened at 47th and Lake Avenue stoked indignation for only a brief time. Residents did wage a lively battle over a small fruit stand near the 47th Street station, successfully negotiating with the landowner and removing the "banana stand."[47] Property owners opposed a westward expansion of stores along 47th, fearing a decrease in their property values. Local residents fought against the "invasion" by purchasing all available property.[48] Kenwood was successful for a time in limiting nonresidential structures; however, improvements in transportation gradually shifted the character of 47th street from residential to transit and commercial usage.

Kenwood's residents protested not only commercial development, but also apartment construction. Builders were taken to court over the erection of an apartment on the corner of 44th and Greenwood, but in 1893 the Illinois Supreme Court ruled in favor of the project. In Hyde Park, the combination of high land values and pressure for housing resulted in streets lined with row houses and apartment buildings. A natural extension of hotel living, the construction of apartments and flats was most often undertaken by real estate developers and investors. A range of multifamily dwellings appeared, from block-long buildings to unpretentious three-flats and six-flats.

The railroad ensured that the area at the heart of Hyde Park developed the most rapidly. Centered on Lake Avenue between 55th and 53rd Streets, shops and flats and offices stretched west from the original commercial area near the Illinois Central tracks. Convenient to transit, Lake Avenue was the first of Hyde Park's streets to be developed and became increasingly commercial. Property owners in Hyde Park and

Kenwood opposed an 1897 bill that would improve Lake Avenue, contending that such a boulevard would make the street a natural artery between downtown and South Chicago and throw heavy traffic off into the surrounding residential neighborhood. Residents on Lake Avenue represented the broadest range of incomes and ethnic groups found within the neighborhood, and curiously were not opposed to the bill.[49]

Density on the improved avenue increased significantly as many of the large old dwellings became boarding houses, some accommodating the black cooks and waiters working at nearby hotels. A survey of the area from the 1900 United States Census demonstrates a range of inhabitants, and nearly all rented the properties they occupied. White men worked as pipe welders, ice dealers, floor varnishers, and tailors. A small black population included waiters and a barber, hailing from Kentucky, Tennessee, and Mississippi. An even smaller contingent came from China and owned their own laundry establishments, while single white women (laundresses) performed similar tasks, although they usually worked and boarded at the same location.

Meanwhile, as the community matured, an important movement began to express discontent with the industrialism celebrated by the fair. Many felt manufacturing impoverished workers, destroyed individuality, and eliminated creativity. A new search for human values came to be expressed in literature, education, and art, represented locally by a group of novelists and poets passionately committed to social justice and concerned with individual responsibility. A literary bohemia surrounded Floyd Dell's studio at the Artists Colony on 57th Street, a group of structures conceived as concession stands for the world's fair. Participants in the movement included novelists Edgar Lee Masters ,Theodore Dreiser, and University of Chicago English professor Robert Herrick. Herrick often wrote of Chicago; *The Common Lot* was a thinly disguised adaptation of his own unhappy experiences with architects and builders, set in a fictional version of Hyde Park. Masters wrote much of his 1915 *Spoon River Anthology* while living at 4853 Kenwood, and later reminisced about his time in the neighborhood in his 1936 biography *Across Spoon River.*[50]

Sculptor Lorado Taft founded Midway Studios in 1907, in a converted carriage house where aspiring young artists gathered. The space on the Midway Plaisance at Ellis housed a studio and dormitory where Taft worked until 1929.[51] Architects also expressed dissatisfaction with the emphasis on industrialism and were drawn to the philosophical notion of a return to craftsmanship. Along with the rise of the Arts and Crafts movement emanating from Britain, architects began to experiment with a rejection of the historical styles and precedents so prevalent at the fair.

Frank Lloyd Wright, a member of the Arts and Crafts Society, aptly expressed the threatening aspects of industrialization and architectural mimicry. In a 1901 Hull-House presentation, Wright argued in "The Art and Craft of the Machine" against the handcrafted aesthetic in favor of an architecture that used the machine to create a new aesthetic, not to reproduce designs of the past.[52] Thus, hydraulic presses, saw mills, and steel manufacturing would contribute to a new architecture rather than dominate it.[53]

The Prairie Style grew out of these concerns as Wright moved toward a new form of architecture, and while his designs were clearly influential, he was not the only forward-thinking architect of the time. A movement began that sought a fresh and original architecture as Prairie School architects searched for new forms. Generally speaking, these manifested themselves primarily in residential architecture, where the features were precise and angular, and where ornament was not applied, but dependent on the expression of materials used.

These architects sought a distinctive American style, freed from the constraints of European influences and historic references. Meeting in Steinway Hall, a group of young architects including the Pond brothers, Dwight Perkins, Myron Hunt, and Hugh Garden, among others, produced work that displayed a deep reverence for the concepts of Louis Sullivan. Many received their first commissions in the Hyde Park neighborhood as university professors selected these architects precisely because they represented a new school of thinking.[54]

Although the campus of the University of Chicago cloistered itself from the surrounding city, members of the faculty understood the advantages of living and working within a metropolitan area. A university within the city offered scholars an "ideal laboratory for investigation, experimentation, and discovery."[55] Sociologists, economists, educators, and social workers understood the opportunities for research Chicago provided. The problems of immigration and social class, the complexities of financial markets, the need for new methods of teaching, and the inequities in employment and health care were all evident in the city. And of course, in Chicago political scientists found an ample supply of corruption. As the university grew, a large number of professors chose to live very near to their institution. Faculty members began buying lots, many from Marshall Field on Woodlawn and University Avenues, and the progressive houses they constructed provided a contrast with the Gothic ornamentation of the university.[56]

In the twenty-year period following annexation, this once quiet suburb became a vibrant and bustling neighborhood, changed forever by the establishment of the university and by the fair. The university grew in stature and size, the commercial areas solidified, houses filled nearly all available space, and the apartment building was well on its way to becoming a fixture of the neighborhood. By 1901 nearly a third of city residents were housed in flats or apartment buildings.[57] While Hyde Park clearly exhibited this trend, it also featured works designed by the best the architectural profession had to offer, and the residences they created represented what this culturally ambitious society aspired to be. Hotels and resorts continued to prosper; however, other areas of the city's South Side were declining.

The once exclusive neighborhoods to the north of the community had begun to deteriorate as immigrants, factories, and warehouses pushed the higher-income class out. Fashionable Prairie Avenue was experiencing the difficulties of its location near the Illinois Central tracks and the city's vice district. There the wealthy began an exodus to the North Side of the city. However, protected by the parks and lakefront, and anchored by the university, Hyde Park and Kenwood closed the golden era remaining quite fashionable places to live.

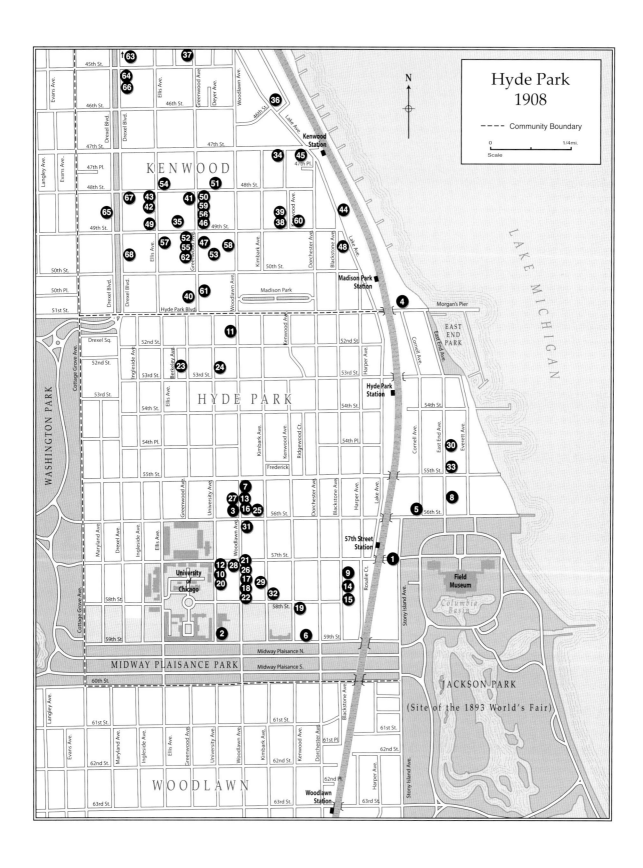

Hyde Park
1908

- - - - Community Boundary

0   1/4mi.
Scale

N

WASHINGTON PARK

LAKE MICHIGAN

KENWOOD

Kenwood Station

HYDE PARK

EAST END PARK

Morgan's Pier

Madison Park

Madison Park Station

Hyde Park Station

University of Chicago

57th Street Station

Field Museum

Columbia Basin

MIDWAY PLAISANCE PARK

Midway Plaisance N.
Midway Plaisance S.

JACKSON PARK

(Site of the 1893 World's Fair)

WOODLAWN

Woodlawn Station

HYDE PARK

1 **Artists Colony, c. 1891. Demolished 1962.**
1500 Block of East 57th Street. George Beaumont.

2 **President's Residence, 1892.**
5855 South University Avenue. Henry Ives Cobb.

3 **Rice Residence, 1891–1892.**
5554 South Woodlawn Avenue. Mifflin E. Bell.

4 **Chicago Beach Hotel, 1892. Demolished 1927.**
Hyde Park Boulevard at Lake Michigan. Possibly Starrett & Fuller.

5 **Windermere Hotel, 1893. Demolished 1959.**
56th Street at Cornell Avenue. Architect/builder unknown.

6 **Hotel Del Prado, 1893. Demolished before 1931.**
59th Street between Blackstone and Kenwood Avenues. W. D. Cowles.

7 **James G. Miller Apartments, 1894.**
5515 South Woodlawn Avenue. Pond & Pond.

8 **Thompson Residence, 1895.**
5533 Hyde Park Boulevard. Howard van Doren Shaw.

9 **Whiton Row Houses, 1896.**
5719–5721–5723 South Blackstone Avenue. Robert Closson Spencer.

10 **Vincent Residence, 1897.**
5737 South University Avenue. Howard van Doren Shaw.

11 **Heller House, 1897.**
5132 South Woodlawn Avenue. Frank Lloyd Wright.

12 **Hale Residence, 1897.**
5727 South University Avenue. Hugh Garden.

13 **Carpenter Residence, 1898.**
5533 South Woodlawn Avenue. Pond & Pond.

14 **Thompson Residence, 1899.**
5747 South Blackstone Avenue. Pond & Pond.

15 **Residences for Katherine Rush, 1899.**
5757–5759 South Blackstone Avenue. Nimmons & Fellows.

16 **Eckels Residence, 1899.**
5537 South Woodlawn Avenue. Henry Holsman.

17 **Howland Residence, 1900.**
5725 South Woodlawn Avenue. Rapp & Rapp.

18 **Roche Residence, 1901.**
5729 South Woodlawn Avenue. Rapp & Rapp.

19 **Lillie House, 1901.**
5801 South Kenwood Avenue. Pond & Pond.

20 **Herrick Residence, 1901.**
5735 South University Avenue. Hugh Garden.

21 **Wiles Residence, 1901.**
5711 South Woodlawn Avenue. Dwight Perkins.

22 **Zeisler Residence, 1903. Demolished 1958.**
5749 South Woodlawn Avenue. Pond & Pond.

23 **Greenwood Avenue Residences, 1903.**
5208, 5210, 5220, and 5224 South Greenwood Avenue. James C. Brompton.

24 **Finch Residence, 1904.**
5235 South University Avenue. James Gamble Rogers.

25 **Professors' Row Houses, 1904.**
1220, 1222, 1226, 1228, and 1232 East 56th Street. Mann, MacNeille & Lindberg.

26 **Mason Residence, 1904.**
5715 South Woodlawn Avenue. Howard van Doren Shaw.

27 **Ingals Residence and Stable, 1905.**
5540 South Woodlawn Avenue. Holabird & Roche.

28 **Goodspeed Residence, 1906.**
5706 South Woodlawn Avenue. Howard van Doren Shaw.

29 **Jackman Residence, 1907.**
5730 South Kimbark Avenue. Howard van Doren Shaw.

30 **Lauten Apartment Building, 1907.**
5451–5455 South Hyde Park Boulevard. Frommann & Jebsen.

31 **Professors' Row Houses, 1907.**
1201 and 1215 East 56th Street; 5605 and 5609 South Woodlawn Avenue. Tallmadge & Watson.

32 **Hale Residence, 1908.**
5757 South Kimbark Avenue. Argyle Robinson.

33 **Apartments, 1908.**
5487–5491 South Hyde Park Boulevard. Doerr & Doerr.

KENWOOD

34 **The Kenwood Hotel, 1892. Demolished c. 1960.**
4700 South Kenwood Avenue. Charles Sumner Frost.

35 **Beman Residence, by 1887.**
1030 East 49th Street. Solon S. Beman. Remodeled 1892.

36 **Sullivan Residence, 1892. Demolished 1970.**
4575 South Lake Park Avenue. Louis Sullivan.

37 **Harlan Residence, 1892. Demolished 1963.**
4414 South Greenwood Avenue. Frank Lloyd Wright.

38 **Blossom Residence, 1892.**
4858 South Kenwood Avenue. Frank Lloyd Wright.

39 **McArthur Residence, 1892.**
4852 South Kenwood Avenue. Frank Lloyd Wright.

40 **Goodman Residence, 1892.**
5026 South Greenwood Avenue. Treat & Foltz.

41 **Morse Residence, 1893. Demolished 1931.**
4800 South Greenwood Avenue. Mifflin E. Bell.

42 **Hutchins Residence, 1894.**
4810 South Ellis Avenue. Charles Sumner Frost.

43 **Potter Residence. By 1896.**
4800 South Ellis Avenue.

44 **Shaw-Atkinson Residence, 1894. Demolished 1961.**
4833–4847 South Lake Park Avenue. Howard van Doren Shaw.

45 **The Kenwood Club, 1895. Demolished c.1960.**
1361 East 47th Street. Patton & Fisher with Charles S. Frost.

46 **Lord Residence, 1896.**
4857 South Greenwood Avenue. Charles Frost.

47 **Carton Residence, 1896.**
4923 South Greenwood Avenue. William Otis.

48 **Residence, 1897.**
4925 South Blackstone Avenue. Howard van Doren Shaw.

49 **Swift Residence, 1897.**
4848 South Ellis Avenue. Flanders & Zimmerman.

50 **Dau Residence. Before 1897.**
4807 South Greenwood Avenue. George Washington Maher.

51 **Wait Residence, 1897.**
1120 East 48th Street. Dwight Heald Perkins.

52 **Vierling Residence, 1899.**
4914 South Greenwood Avenue. Dwight Perkins with H. H. Waterman.

53 **Green Coach House, 1899.**
4935· South Greenwood Avenue. Daniel H. Burnham & Company.

54 **Fenton Residence, 1901.**
1000 East 48th Street. Wilson & Marshall.

55 **Barton Residence, 1901.**
4920 South Greenwood Avenue. Frost & Granger.

56 **Ames Residence, 1902. Demolished c. 1970.**
4835 South Greenwood Avenue. Frost & Granger.

57 **Julius Rosenwald Residence, 1903.**
4901 South Ellis Avenue. Nimmons & Fellows.

58 **Morris Rosenwald Residence, 1903.**
4924 South Woodlawn Avenue. Howard van Doren Shaw.

59 **Schaffner Residence, 1904.**
4819 South Greenwood Avenue. Holabird & Roche.

60 **Waterman Residence, 1905.**
4849 South Kenwood Avenue. Harry Hale Waterman.

61 **Stilwell Residence, 1905.**
5017 South Greenwood Avenue. Jarvis Hunt. Coach house demolished 2010.

62 **Magerstadt Residence, 1908.**
4930 South Greenwood Avenue. George Maher.

DREXEL BOULEVARD

63 **Fuller Residence, c. 1890. Demolished 1963.**
4353 Drexel Boulevard. Charles Sumner Frost.

64 **Smith Residence, 1893. Demolished.**
4501 South Drexel Boulevard. William W. Boyington.

65 **Blair Residence, 1897. Demolished.**
4830 South Drexel Boulevard. Shepley, Rutan & Coolidge.

66 **Shedd Residence, 1898. Demolished.**
4515 South Drexel Boulevard. Frederick Perkins with Edmund Krause.

67 **Born Residence, 1901.**
4801 South Drexel Boulevard. Frost & Granger.

68 **Mandel Residence, 1901. Demolished c. 1970.**
4925 South Drexel Boulevard. Frost & Granger.

Hyde Park

① Artists Colony, c. 1891. Demolished 1962.
1500 Block of East 57th Street. George Beaumont.

3.10. Interest in art and literature increased after the fair, resulting in a greater demand for moderately priced studios and stores. Although these structures were meant to be temporary, the one-story spaces were popular rentals for artists and writers

Constructed for Frederick Gibbs two years prior to the Columbian Exposition, these twenty-six simple one-story frame store buildings were not intended to be large income producers. They began to pay "big returns" however when used as concession stands for the 1893 Columbian Exposition.[58] After the fair there was a growing demand for moderately priced stores and studios for painters, writers, and "lovers of a bohemian life"[59]—these narrow spaces topped with pagoda-like gables were attractive to rent. Although built without heat, electricity, or gas, the spaces gradually filled and eventually attracted national attention.[60] The area became known as a literary bohemia when critic, poet, and novelist Floyd Dell moved into a converted Chinese laundry in 1913. Writers including Sherwood Anderson, Theodore Dreiser, Margaret Anderson, Carl Sandburg, and poet Harriett Monroe gathered at Dell's studio, which he later described. "I have returned to my ice-cold studio," wrote Dell, "where I have built a fire with scraps of linoleum, a piece of wainscoting, and an elaborate filing system of four years creation. I am writing at a desk . . . lighted by four candles."[61] By the twenties, fame came to these once fledgling writers and they moved on to more comfortable quarters.

② President's Residence, 1894.

5855 South University Avenue. Henry Ives Cobb.

Henry Ives Cobb received commissions for several residences near the newly founded University of Chicago, including the residence for the university president, Dr. William Rainey Harper. In contrast to the institutional buildings, here Cobb used pale Roman brick with limestone trim for a simply detailed structure. The president's residence is distinguished by the sharply pitched roof and dormers, and it initially featured an open porch that was enlarged to a broad verandah facing the Midway. The verandah was removed in 1931 for president Robert Maynard Hutchins to allow additional light into the drawing room and to make the exterior appear "less heavy" and the entry "less ornate."[62]

By 1900, Cobb was seeking work nationwide and opened an office in Washington, DC. His relationship with the university became increasingly strained; the trustees believed the institution was not receiving the attention it deserved. And

3.11. The president's residence has been altered numerous times by its various occupants; the main entry has been relocated to the original side entry on University Avenue.

then there were the complaints; classical scholar William Gardner Hale protested that the interiors of the buildings were "cheerless and gloomy."[63] In 1901 the relationship between Cobb and the university was terminated.

④ Chicago Beach Hotel, 1892. Demolished 1927.
Hyde Park Boulevard at Lake Michigan. Possibly Starrett & Fuller.

The impact of the Columbian Exposition on the neighborhood was profound, as luxury hotels rose to accommodate the huge number of expected visitors. During the summer of 1892, excavation began and the concrete foundation was laid for the Chicago Beach Hotel, anticipated to be the finest hotel on the Chicago lakeshore. The L-shaped hotel fronted on 51st Street and was located only five blocks from the entrance to the fair.[64]

The property upon which the hotel was constructed has an unusual history. According to the *Chicago Tribune*, "About the time of the Chicago fire, James Morgan purchased a tract of three acres of land north of 51st Street and east of the Illinois Central tracks. . . . Despite the continual washing away of the shore lands, this particular tract now contains 11.52 acres, or an increase of nearly 8 acres in thirty-nine years."[65] Morgan made this land through a simple method. With a "pile driver, a crew of men, a few boats of lumber," he built a series of piers, the first running east from the north side of 51st Street.[66] Morgan kept a clamshell dredge busy taking sand from the outside of the pier and dumping it on the inside, a quick and inexpensive way of making land that he claimed as his. In 1892 when the world's fair was being planned, Morgan leased a portion of his tract to the Chicago Beach Hotel Company and construction of the luxurious lakefront hotel began.

3.12. The refined Chicago Beach Hotel, erected on the Hyde Park lakeshore, as it appeared in 1905.

Backed by investors, Kenwood resident Warren F. Leland directed the design and construction of the six-story hotel, one of Chicago's largest resorts serving both permanent residents and transient guests. Leland came from a well-known family of hotel proprietors and had a long hotel career. He introduced many new features to hotel life, including serving meals from 5:00 o'clock until late at night. And he was successful: during the four and a half months of the fair, the hotel's large profits eclipsed all previous records.[67]

An interior rotunda of 148' × 52' welcomed visitors to the resort, which was surrounded by a long veranda overlooking the lake and Cornell Park.[68] On the north, the shoreline made a sweeping curve, and the wading beach stretched five hundred feet into the lake, with a view north toward the city. Boardwalks and cabanas were readily available in the summer months on the beach, and Morgan's Pier was used as a boat landing. The "Finest Hotel on the Great Lakes" tempted guests with beautiful surroundings and an abundance of activities: there were "walks, drives, sequestered spots and spacious apartments; for the gay there are sailing, bathing, golf, tennis, walking, driving, tally-ho rides, dancing, live music and town amusements."[69] From the dining room one could look out over miles of open water that stretched into the distance while enjoying regionally themed entrees that were "always tempting and liberally supplied."[70]

Residents of the hotel had exclusive access to the beach until the Chicago City Council Finance Committee approved funding for the construction of a public bathhouse on land the city claimed adjacent to the hotel. The hotel company had for twenty years claimed riparian rights to the choice lakefront property; however, the state held that lands under Lake Michigan belong to the State of Illinois.[71] After 1915 the beach was to be accessible to the general public; however, the hotel retained ownership until 1926.

⑤ Windermere Hotel, 1893. Demolished 1959.
1614 East 56th Street. Architect/builder unknown.

Another of Hyde Park's glamorous apartment hotels, the six-story 235-room Windermere, was situated near the 56th Street entrance to the Columbian Exposition. Although designed for guests attending the 1893 fair, this and other hotels continued to operate for and transient and long-term residents for decades to come. It was considered technologically advanced when the hotel opened—every room was wired for the telephone, although the phone company officials said the owners were "crazy to do it."[72] In 1911 the hotel was expanded to include the structure to the west, connected by an elongated verandah and formal gardens. The hotel added a long, narrow sunroom called the Palm Room, proudly noted as furnished by Marshall Field & Company.[73] During the twenties the hotel expanded its facilities, with a large new structure directly across the street to the east.

One of the more famous residents of the hotel was novelist Edna Ferber,[74] author of *The Girls*, among other titles, in which she describes the changing attitudes toward apartment living through her characters, the Kemps. They lived in "one of the oldest of Hyde Park's apartment houses and one as nearly aristocratic as a

3.13. The original Windermere Hotel was expanded to include the structure to the left in the photograph.

Chicago South Side apartment house can be. It was on Hyde Park Boulevard, near Jackson Park and the Lake. When Belle married she had protested at an apartment. . . . No privacy. Everything huddled together on one floor and everybody underfoot. People upstairs; people downstairs. But houses were scarce in Hyde Park and she and Henry had compromised on an apartment much too large for them and as choice as anything for miles around."[75]

⑥ Hotel Del Prado, 1893. Demolished before 1931.
59th Street between Blackstone and Kenwood Avenues. W. D. Cowles.

Owned by the Barry Brothers and originally called the Raymond and Whitcomb Grand, the Hotel Del Prado was completed in April 1893 to provide accommodations for visitors to the World's Columbian Exposition. Fronting 250' on the Midway Plaisance and constructed of buff brick, the hotel stood four stories tall and contained three hundred and twenty-five sleeping rooms in the main section and an additional sixty-two in an annex. The hotel offered guests a full-length verandah from which to view the excitement of the fair in comfort.

3.14. By 1930, the Del Prado was worn and tired; its long and airy verandah fronting the Midway had been enclosed. The structure was demolished to provide the land for the University of Chicago's International House, designed by Holabird & Root.

On the very day the fair was to close a fire broke out in the servants' quarters. The "bandbox," as the accommodations on the roof were called, was home to one hundred-fifty women. The flames did considerable damage before the firefighters arrived—there was no loss of life but apparently plenty of excitement. Newspaper accounts of the incident claimed that the inhabitants of the Java Village across the street from the hotel "almost burst out in a frenzy of fear." The villagers "had not the slightest doubt that they were to be roasted in the embers of their thatched dwellings."[76]

After the excitement of the fair and the fire passed, the hotel was renamed the Hotel Barry for a short time. By the summer of 1895, the property was sold, the name was changed to the Del Prado, and extensive improvements were undertaken. The structure was used as rental and short-term housing for visitors to the university community until it was razed. International House now stands on the site.

⑦ James G. Miller Apartments, 1894.
5515 South Woodlawn Avenue. Pond & Pond.

At the time this apartment was constructed, there were only two other houses on this block of Woodlawn Avenue; however, before long the street became lined with the residences of faculty and businessmen. Because of increasing land values and a need for housing, a variety of multifamily dwellings began to appear throughout Hyde Park, from three-flats and six-flats to large courtyard apartments.

Although the English Arts and Crafts movement influenced the Ponds' architecture, they were creating a unique style of their own, finding ornament in the way the building material, particularly brick, was used. Their "well-detailed craftsmanship"[77] is apparent in the design of one of the first apartments constructed on Woodlawn Avenue. Setting the building diagonally to the street addressed the problematic issue of permitting light and air into a six-flat while preserving privacy.

3.15. The Pond brothers sited the structure to permit a generous amount of sunshine, as seen in this view from the southwest. Their "diaper pattern" brick detailing is evident on the third level, while the entire structure rests on a base of a darker-hued rock-face brick. The apartments were outfitted with light fixtures of both gas and electricity, and the Ponds are thought to be the first to put electrical wires in conduit.

⑧ Thompson Residence, 1895.

5533 Hyde Park Boulevard. Howard van Doren Shaw.

Howard van Doren Shaw, a most prolific architect, designed everything from small structures such as this to sprawling country houses. It was Shaw's early work in the Hyde Park area that established his prominence as an architect, beginning with his own home and this small brick and limestone house with Tudor detailing. Designed for Henry C. Thompson, a business manager, the house was constructed on a small, 30' × 125' lot. Shaw's wife Frances later recalled the "proud moment" early in his career when he received this commission.[78]

This house, similar in scale to the residences Shaw designed in Kenwood several years later, is now dwarfed by the neighboring flat and high-rise apartment buildings.

3.16. Shaw's use of quoined corner detailing is masked by the half-timbering on the second level.

⑨ Whiton Row Houses, 1896.
5719–5721–5723 South Blackstone Avenue. Robert Closson Spencer.

A prominent architect in the Arts and Crafts movement, Robert Spencer designed this series of three row houses soon after forming an independent practice. Constructed for broker L. K. Whiton, the structure reflects the denser land usage prevalent in this part of Hyde Park. Like Pond & Pond, Spencer found innovative ways of dealing with the issues of light and ventilation in multifamily housing and used brick as ornament on the façade. Spencer's concept is similar to the Ponds' work in the complexity of the façades and the use of brick "diaper pattern" detailing.

3.17. In 1896, the year the Whiton row houses were built, Spencer moved his practice into Steinway Hall where he shared offices with Dwight Perkins and Frank Lloyd Wright.

⑩ Vincent Residence, 1897.
5737 South University Avenue. Howard van Doren Shaw.

The brick and limestone house designed for George Edgar Vincent was the first university-associated commission Howard van Doren Shaw received. Considered "one of Shaw's finest Georgian style houses," the Vincent house features a two-story bay with a side entrance.[79]

Vincent was a "brilliant and influential"[80] professor of the then new science of sociology at the university. "Intellectually eager and able," the Yale graduate came to the University of Chicago in the fall of 1892, earning his doctorate in sociology in 1896. Studying under Albion W. Small, he advanced to become a full professor in 1904.[81] Vincent became the dean of arts, literature, and sciences at the university

3.18. Shaw was at the beginning of a prolific career when he was commissioned to design the house for George Vincent.

between 1907 and 1911, when he resigned to become the president of the University of Minnesota. In 1917 he accepted the post as head of the Rockefeller Foundation.

Earlier in his career, Vincent was deeply involved in the Chautauqua movement, which brought education and culture to rural communities across the country. The movement believed that education, "once the peculiar privilege of the few," must become "the valued possession of the many."[82]

12 Hale Residence, 1897.
5727 South University Avenue. Hugh Garden.

Although architect Hugh Garden worked to free architecture from a reliance on classical forms, at the time he designed the Hale house he was still using a traditional vocabulary. The Hale residence was originally constructed on a south-facing corner lot at 5757 University. In the 1920s the house was moved to the current location, now facing the tennis courts of the Quadrangle Club on the north.[83]

A "noted classics scholar and professor of Latin," William Gardner Hale earned his undergraduate degree at Harvard in 1870.[84] Hale was recruited by William Rainey Harper and joined the University of Chicago faculty in 1892, where he remained until his retirement in 1919. Hale was one of the founders of the American School of Classical Studies at Rome, now the American Academy at Rome. Hale's writing was enormously influential; his most important work was the 1908 publica-

tion of the *Catullus Manuscript*, a series of poems from the first century BC found in the Vatican.[85] Hale, his wife Harriet and their four children lived in this house until moving east to a house at 5757 South Kimbark designed by architect Argyle Robinson in 1908.

The Hale house is now owned by the university, and underwent an extensive renovation in 2010.

13 Carpenter Residence, 1898.
5531 South Woodlawn Avenue. Pond & Pond.

Pond & Pond began to practice at an auspicious time in the development of the university community. The institution's progressive approach was reflected in the choice of young architects such as the Pond brothers, who created a style all their own, designing with simplicity and a respect for the materials themselves. The Ponds continued their experimentation with brick in two houses for university professors located near the campus, inking the details and plans on starched cloth. The symmetrical façade designed for Frederick Ives Carpenter is unusual for the Ponds, who typically used complex and irregular forms. The residence is defined by the use of relieving arches that support the brickwork over the windows—turning what was in the past a structural necessity into a decorative element—and by the repetitive coined corner detailing. The property to the north was originally part

3.20. The façade of the Carpenter house has been altered from the Ponds' initial design; the open-entry porch has been fully enclosed and its triangular pediment replaced by an arch, echoing the forms on the third level.

of the Carpenter property, and a coach house remains but is obscured by a small "Cotswold" cottage constructed in the thirties.

Educated at Harvard, Carpenter joined the university faculty in 1895 and worked "quietly and without ostentation" for many years as a professor of medieval and Renaissance literature in the Department of English.[86] He left the institution to manage the sizeable estate left to him by his father in 1911, but continued to reside in this house.[87]

14 **Thompson Residence, 1899.**
5747 South Blackstone Avenue. Pond & Pond.

The Ponds returned to the use of the diaper-pattern brickwork on the third floor of the house for James Westfall Thompson. Thompson was an internationally known scholar and professor at the University of Chicago, specializing in the history of medieval and early modern Europe. He was an engaging lecturer, speaking with a "dramatic touch" that drew former students back to "once again the see Otto of Wittelsbach's sword flash at Besancon or to hear Louis the Debonaire's wail of contrition at Attigny."[88] Thompson was such a popular professor that the number of graduate students studying under his direction at the time was the largest such group in the country.[89]

3.21. The Ponds' emphasis on brickwork is evident in the detailing of the Thompson residence.

3.22. The entry hall and parlor display the simplicity and strength of the Ponds' work, as seen in this undated photograph of the Thompson residence.

15   Residences for Katherine Rush, 1899.
5757–5759 South Blackstone Avenue. Nimmons & Fellows.

By the turn of the century, substantial multifamily dwellings replaced a number of the original frame houses on Blackstone as land values continued to increase. The firm of Nimmons & Fellows designed several residences in the area between 1898 and 1904, including this elegant brick and limestone duplex on Blackstone. The first residents of these double houses were William T. Beatty (5757) and Weller van Hook (5759). Beatty was the president and general manager of the Austin Manufacturing Company, and van Hook was a prominent surgeon and a professor at Northwestern University Medical School.[90]

The most well known occupant of 5757, however, was the unassuming William E. Dodd, a professor of American history at the university. Appointed by President Roosevelt as US ambassador to Germany in 1933, Dodd moved to Berlin anticipating a quiet post where he could complete his study of the Antebellum South. Instead, for four years, he was forced to finesse the volatile situation and mounting Jewish oppression as Hitler rose to power.[91]

16   Eckels Residence, 1899.
5537 South Woodlawn Avenue. Henry Holsman.

When Henry K. Holsman designed this classically detailed house for corporate attorney George Morris Eckels, many residences were under already construction along Woodlawn near the university. Although that meant many other commissions might be available, Holsman soon left the practice of architecture and began to manufacture automobiles.

Eckels's passion was a collection of books and other materials relating to Oliver Cromwell. His widow, Edith Oberly Eckels, presented the collection, consisting of over five hundred books, pamphlets, and engravings related to a turbulent period in British history, to the university.[92]

The Eckels residence later became the home of physicist Enrico and Laura Fermi during the 1940s. Fermi won the 1938 Nobel Prize in Physics while a faculty member at the University of Rome. An expert on uranium fission, Fermi continued his research at the University of Chicago between 1942 and his death in 1954, working on the Manhattan Project. The atomic age arrived on December 2, 1942, when he produced the first controlled nuclear chain reaction in a laboratory, in a squash court under the west stands of Stagg Field, the university's stadium.[93] That same evening the Fermis held a party where many of the guests were colleagues. Laura Fermi was puzzled when many of the guests offered their congratulations, but could get no answers as to what the "pats on the back" were about, for all were "sworn to secrecy."[94]

Laura Capon Fermi wrote *Atoms in the Family*, chronicling her life married to the father of the atom bomb. She remained a Hyde Park resident until her death in 1977. Although the stadium and squash court have been demolished, a sculpture by Henry Moore commemorates the site.

3.23. Although Nimmons & Fellows were industrial architects, primarily for Sears Roebuck & Co., they were awarded several residential commissions including these elegant speculative residences for Katherine Rush.

3.24. The formal entry of the Eckels house is on the north, leaving the triangular pediment and limestone lintels to define the spare street façade.

3.25. The houses on the east side of Woodlawn were constructed on one of the sand ridges that defined this area of Hyde Park; hence they are raised above the grade of the street.

⑰ Howland Residence, 1900.
5725 South Woodlawn Avenue. Rapp & Rapp.

Theater architects, the Rapp brothers once said that the show starts on the sidewalk, and their residential architecture often follows that credo. The Rapps were responsible for these two exuberant houses near the university campus, constructed side by side on Woodlawn Avenue for the children of a former mayor of Chicago, John A. Roche. Elected on the Republican ticket, Roche was in office briefly, serving as the city's twenty-fifth mayor between 1887 and 1889. He tried with limited success to "upgrade the morals of the city," and cracked down on gambling to spoil "at least for the time being" Chicago's reputation as a "wide open town."[95] However, Roche was more successful with public works; he improved the city's sewage system and recommended the construction of the Ship and Sanitary Canal to take waste away from Lake Michigan.[96]

The house at 5725 Woodlawn was designed for Roche's daughter Cora and her husband George C. Howland, a member of the University of Chicago's original teaching staff. Howland was a lawyer and a professor of Romance languages and literature.[97] He was the author of two textbooks and also an editorial writer for the *Chicago Tribune*. The house next door at 5729 was designed for John A. Roche Jr., secretary of the Elevator Supply Company.

The elder Roche resided at 4605 Drexel Boulevard, and died unexpectedly in 1904, when he was managing director of the Otis Elevator Company.

18 Roche Residence, 1901.
5729 South Woodlawn Avenue.
Rapp & Rapp.
3.26. While narrow in scale, the English Gothic house of John Roche has a forceful personality, echoing the Rapps' belief that the "show starts on the sidewalk."

⑲ Lillie Residence, 1901.
5801 South Kenwood Avenue. Pond & Pond.

The Pond brothers most likely became acquainted with Frank Rattray Lillie and his wife Frances through their mutual commitment to Hull-House. They received this commission after Lillie returned to the University of Chicago, where he had received his doctorate in 1894. Pond & Pond designed a house that seems somewhat stark and disjointed. "But on closer examination it turns out to be an exceptionally complex building," wrote historian Tim Samuelson, "whose subtle features reflect a high degree of craftsmanship and attention to detail."[98] When the Lillie House was designed, the brothers promoted the "builded beauty" of their designs. This was the Ponds' phrase, for they believed that the internal structure of a building should be expressed on the exterior. A prime example of this philosophy, the house is listed on the National Register of Historic Places.[99] Its condition was for years tenuous; owned by the university and featuring a bronze plaque, the house was vacant for several years and in a deteriorating state. Renovation began in 2012.

Lillie was connected with the University of Chicago for most of his life. A prominent academic, he was appointed chairman of the Department of Zoology and in 1931, the dean of the Division of Biological Sciences.[100] Lillie also had a long-standing relationship with the Marine Biological Laboratory at the Massachusetts-based Woods Hole Oceanographic Institute, where he met his future wife, Frances Crane.

Frances was the daughter of Richard Teller Crane, the founder of a huge business empire based on manufactured products such as railroad equipment and plumbing fixtures. Crane's great fortune meant Frances was a very wealthy woman. However her political views and her conversion to Catholicism embarrassed her father and made Frances the "black sheep" of the family.[101] The mother of seven children, she persevered with her progressive causes, including taking an active role at Hull-House, where she was a long-time contributor. After her arrest during a garment workers' strike, she declared herself a socialist, willing "to do all in my power to abolish the wrongs practiced against the working people."[102]

Her friendship with Hull-House cofounder Ellen Gates Starr, and their mutual deep interest in the Catholic Church, led to their involvement with St. Thomas the Apostle's new church, designed by Barry Byrne in 1924. They were instrumental in contracting two artists for the project: Alfonso Iannelli (the sculptor who worked with Frank Lloyd Wright on Midway Gardens) to design the bronze Stations of the Cross, and Alfeo Faggi to design the reredos (decorations behind the altar) in the church.

20 Herrick Residence, 1901.
5735 South University Avenue. Hugh Garden.

Robert and Harriet Herrick wanted a traditional English Tudor design, but were up against new trends rising in Chicago's architecture. The Herrick house is one of the first houses in America to which one could attach the word "modernity." According to historian Tim Samuelson, instead of hiring an architect comfortable with traditional styles, "Herrick for some reason engaged Hugh Garden, an

3.28. The stark simplicity of Garden's design for the Herricks is evident in this 1902 image published in *Inland Architect*.

advocate for Chicago's emerging modern design movement."[103] Garden drew up plans for a "flat, boxy brick" house, with none of the details that Herrick desired. Previous construction relied on ornamentation; here Garden used the absolute simplicity of brick interrupted only by the voids of windows. The house did feature two traditional elements: the brick was from Boston, and shutters framed the upper-story windows, although they have since disappeared. But even those did not soften the austere rectangular form of a house conceived well ahead of its time.[104]

Herrick was an influential but apparently unhappy novelist who left MIT to join the University of Chicago faculty in 1893 and became a professor of English in 1905. Herrick's outspoken novels were often thinly disguised accounts of his life in Chicago, a city of which he grew to have an apparently intense aversion. His book *The Common Lot* (1904) was an account of an architect living in a fictionalized Hyde Park. In this novel, the architects and builders are written of bitterly, as incompetent and eager to exploit the unsuspecting client, at times with disastrous consequences.[105] "So when it came to the structure of the building, the contractor ordered the architect to save expense in every line of the details. The woodwork was cut to the thinnest veneer; partitions, even bearing-walls, were made of the cheapest studding the market offered; the large floors were hung from thin outside walls, without the brick bearing-walls advised by the architect," wrote Herrick. "The architect tried to swallow his disgust at being hired to put together such a flimsy shell of plaster and lath."[106]

By 1915 the house became the imperial consulate of Japan, home of Saburo Kurusu and his American-born wife Alice.[107] Kurusu, described as the "most pro-American of all of the close advisors of the Japanese government," is best remembered for his role the day the Japanese attacked Pearl Harbor.[108] At the time, Kurusu served as a special envoy to Washington in a last-minute attempt by Japan's ambassador to conduct peace negotiations with President Roosevelt and secretary of state Cordell Hull. Some historians view his mission as a tactic to deceive the Americans and to delay while the Japanese navy prepared for an attack. Others suggest his own government deceived Kurusu by instructing him to attempt a peaceful settlement, while never revealing the plans to attack America.

"Saburo Kurusu, special Japanese envoy who has been conducting 'peace' negotiations while Japan was preparing for this attack, and Ambassador Kichisaburo Nomura called at the State Department at 2:05 P.M. after asking for the appointment at 1 P.M.," recorded the *New York Times* the day after Pearl Harbor was attacked. "They arrived shortly before Secretary Hull had received news Japan had started a war without warning. Mrs. Roosevelt revealed in her broadcast last night that the Japanese Ambassador was with the president when word of the attacks was received."[109]

The house now serves as a center of Catholic ministry at the university. Frances Crane Lillie purchased the house for the Newman Center, then commissioned architect Barry Byrne to remodel the interiors to provide a suitable space for the new purpose, including converting the large dining room to a chapel. Today the property is known as Calvert House, which was chartered in 1941.

3.29. Working in Steinway Hall with other Prairie School architects, Perkins contributed to the development of an original form of American architecture through his use of materials and expression of the structure, as seen in the Wiles residence.

21 Wiles Residence, 1901.

5711 South Woodlawn Avenue. Dwight Perkins.

Along with Garden's Herrick house, Perkins's design for patent attorney Russell Wiles and his wife Ethel is representative of a huge step in the search for a modern form of architecture. Perkins was one of the early participants in the Prairie School, the movement toward a new architecture "seeking above all truthfulness in the use of materials and the beauty that comes from the utility of the structure."[110] Relying on the texture of the masonry for ornamentation and the simple use of dentils to accentuate the flat roof, Perkins allows brickwork of the bay and pointed relieving arches to define the façade of this house.

22 Zeisler Residence, 1903. Demolished 1958.
5749 South Woodlawn Avenue. Pond & Pond.

3.30. The Zeisler residence as it appeared in an undated photograph for *Brickbuilder* magazine. This house and the two barely visible in the image were demolished during the 1950s to make way for the expansion of the Chicago Theological Seminary.

Late in the evening of Tuesday, May 4, 1886, at the close of a long day of speeches in support of striking workers, something flew over the heads of those in the audience and fell into the middle of the police stationed there. A terrifying explosion rattled the street and shattered windows in the surrounding Near West Side blocks. A bomb had been thrown; for a brief moment there was nothing but bewildered silence, then other officers drew their guns and fired into the crowd.[111]

Seven police officers and an unknown number of civilians were killed immediately, in what became known as the Haymarket tragedy. Six more policemen died as a result of their wounds. In the well-publicized legal proceedings that followed, eight anarchists were tried for murder. Although the prosecution conceded that none of the defendants had thrown the bomb, four men were executed and one committed suicide while in prison.[112]

The associate defense counsel for the Haymarket anarchists was a twenty-six-year-old lawyer named Sigmund Zeisler. Born in Austria, he immigrated to Chicago in 1883, and the following year earned his law degree at Northwestern University. Zeisler was known locally as a liberal and was a member of many related associations, including the American Anti-Imperialist League and the Civil Service Reform Association. He was also a member of several social clubs, including the Cliff Dwellers, whose members included the Pond brothers.[113]

In 1885 Zeisler married Fannie Bloomfield (Blumenfeld), an internationally known concert pianist whose career spanned four decades. Born near Vienna in 1863, she immigrated to the United States with her family in 1866, finally settling in Chicago in 1870, where her father was a dry-goods merchant. Always "musically precocious," she began to study piano at a young age, and although talented, she suffered from poor health and was unhappy in school.[114]

Fannie returned to Vienna for five years of study and began building her reputation as a concert pianist in 1883 when she returned to the US and toured the country. Two years later she married Zeisler, but did not give up her professional life in spite of motherhood and her continuing poor health. Zeisler made more than forty appearances in the 1901–1902 season, a schedule that eventually took its toll. At the beginning of these extensive concert appearances, the Zeislers moved to their "beautiful home in the immediate neighborhood of the University of Chicago" on Woodlawn Avenue.[115]

Fannie Bloomfield-Zeisler died in 1927, never improving after returning from her European trip in October of the previous year. She died at the Cooper-Carleton Hotel, and is remembered as an important force in the development of music in Chicago.[116]

Sigmund Zeisler married Amelia Spellman in 1930 and died the following year.[117]

㉓ Greenwood Avenue Residences, 1903.

5208, 5210, 5220, and 5224 South Greenwood Avenue. James C. Brompton.

Brompton had a long association with Chicago developer Samuel Eberly Gross. Described by Donald Miller as the "impresario of the suburban quick sell," Gross was the inspiration for Samuel E. Ross, a daring and for a time successful real estate mogul in Theodore Dreiser's novel *Jennie Gerhardt*.[118] Like his fictional coun-

3.31. The developer of these houses, Samuel Gross, was not only the inspiration for a character in literature, he was an author as well. According to the *New York Times*, he accused the French dramatist Edmond Rostand of plagiarizing his work. A Chicago judge found Rostand relied a bit too heavily on Gross's *The Merchant Prince of Cornville* for his play, *Cyrano de Bergerac*.

3.32

terpart, Gross was one of a number of developers who bought land along railroad lines and marketed the affordable properties to working-class families.

Described as "a highly colorful realtor,"[119] Gross constructed more than twenty-one subdivisions. His success was due to a combination of factors, including the use of standardized plans for affordable, mass-produced buildings. Although his subdivisions were often located near transportation lines for easy transit to the city, Gross was foremost a "master marketer."[120] Gross was also prolific, claiming to have built over 7,000 houses in Chicago. His formula worked until the recession of 1907–1909 left him bankrupt.[121]

In 1903 Brompton designed a series of professors' houses for Gross in Hyde Park. The *Tribune* noted that Brompton was "preparing plans for forty two-story brick and stone houses, to be built at once for S. E. Gross, on University Terrace."[122] The Greenwood site was developed by a partnership between Gross and Charles Counselman, who lived nearby at Greenwood and Hyde Park Boulevard. The Greenwood Avenue Row House District was the first major site in Hyde Park to acquire landmark status. The 2004 designation protects the twenty houses from demolition and requires to owner to obtain approval for any changes to the exterior.

24 **Finch Residence, 1904.**
5235 South University Avenue. James Gamble Rogers.

Best known for his work at major American universities, Rogers designed a two-and-a-half-story slate-roofed house for Hunter Woodis Finch, president of the Hunter W. Finch & Company, and of the Powhatan Coal Company. Finch experienced financial difficulties not long after the house was completed and it was sold to banker Harry A. Wheeler in 1907.

The symmetrical brick and limestone façade belies the complicated cruciform

3.35. Construction began on the Finch house in July 1904. Later that year Rogers moved his practice to New York, where he worked until retiring in 1947.

3.36. At the turn of the century, the Art Nouveau style swept into America from European cities. The wall sconces of the Finch residence, with their fluid, flowery design, embody the essence of this elegant, yet short-lived style.

3.37. The main stairway of the Finch residence is placed at the center of the cruciform plan, and rises over an arched passageway that links the hall and a study with the formal dining room.

floor plan of the interior. Rogers placed the main staircase at the center of the cruciform, yet oriented it away from the main entrance. The stairs rise over a striking arched entry to the dining room, which opens onto two porches. The porch in the rear once had a glass ceiling; however, that entire structure has been lost.

The living room features a beamed ceiling and a massive yet clean, forward-thinking paneled fireplace—in contrast to the curved details of window and door transepts, and the fluid elegance of Art Nouveau gas lamps.

25 **Professors' Row Houses, 1904.**

1220, 1222, 1226, 1228, and 1234 East 56th Street. Mann, MacNeille & Lindeberg.

Architect Horace B. Mann's brother, Charles Riborg Mann, was a physics professor at the University of Chicago, which may provide the link to the selection of a New York firm.[123] The firm designed three complexes of row houses built near the university between 1904 and 1905. Mann opened an office here during the construction of these projects, and architect Argyle E. Robinson became the firm's representative in Chicago.

3.38. The steeply pitched roofline and the raised diaper pattern brickwork unify the attached professors' residences.

26 **Mason Residence, 1904.**

5715 South Woodlawn Avenue. Howard van Doren Shaw.

Constructed for Arthur J. Mason, this three-story house features a traditional symmetrical façade defined by Shaw's favored deeply set entry, here elaborately surrounded

3.39. Mason's four-bedroom house features a finely detailed side porch opening from the first-floor library.

by columns and pilasters. Located near the university campus, this house is one of several of solid brick construction and designed for the urban-scale lots. Mason was a contracting engineer in the firm of Hoover & Mason, specialists in machinery for the iron and steel industry, noted for the invention of the clamshell crane.[124]

28 Goodspeed Residence, 1906.
5706 South Woodlawn Avenue. Howard van Doren Shaw.

Well-known biblical scholar Edgar Johnson Goodspeed graduated with the final class of the original University of Chicago. He entered Yale to study Semitic languages under William Rainey Harper, and returned to Chicago to continue his graduate studies at the new institution, where he received a PhD in 1898 and joined the university faculty. In 1923 Goodspeed was appointed chairman of the Department of New Testament and Early Christian Literature.[125] Goodspeed worked with other scholars for fifteen years on a revised standard version of the New Testament and published a guide for beginning Bible readers.[126]

The symmetrical façade exemplifies restraint as well as Shaw's use of historical elements, in this case, the fanlight over the recessed central entry.

3.40 . The Goodspeed house was featured on the cover of Jean Block's *Hyde Park Houses.*

29 Jackman Residence, 1907.
5730 South Kimbark Avenue. Howard van Doren Shaw.

Designed for Mrs. Wilbur S. Jackman (variously attributed to attributed to Mrs. W. D. Jackman),[127] this residence displays a "unique eclecticism," as Shaw combined the style of an English country house with Georgian brick detailing.[128] Its original charm is less evident due to the addition of the dormer on the third story. The plan is compact; the first floor features a living and dining room, with a kitchen

3.41. The Jackman residence features two stairways, common in houses of the time. The main stair is approached from the entry hall, and a utilitarian stair connects the kitchen and the maid's bedroom.

and glazed dining porch in the rear. The second floor has three "chambers" and a maid's quarters, all sharing a single bath.

In 1902 Shaw designed the house at 5724 S. Kimbark for professor Wilbur Samuel Jackman, an "influential leader in education"[129] who came to Chicago to join the Cook County Normal School at the request of Col. Francis Parker. He became dean of the School of Education at the university in 1904, but died unexpectedly in January 1907 at the age of fifty-two.

27 Ingals Residence and Stable, 1905.
5540 South Woodlawn Avenue. Holabird & Roche.

William Holabird and Martin Roche established what was to become an enduring, influential, and prolific architectural firm, pivotal in the development of early skyscrapers. Although Holabird & Roche was noted for large-scale commercial work in the style known as the "Chicago School," five residences remain in the neighborhood, representing their work over a span of over thirty years. One of their earliest commissions was for a two-story frame residence at 5809 South Blackstone for Miss Nellie D. Woods. After her marriage to Frank B. Lines in February 1886, the couple lived in that four-bedroom residence.

3.42. The classically ornamented masonry exterior of the Ingals residence was typical of Holabird & Roche's residential architecture.

The firm's work progressed to include large-scale brick and stone residences including the straightforward yet substantial residence of Dr. Ephraim Fletcher Ingals and his wife Lucy. Dr. Ingals was a professor of laryngology at Rush Medical Center and according to their archives, "a leading advocate for the affiliation of Rush Medical College with the University of Chicago." At the time of his death in 1918, Ingals was head of the Department of Disease of the Chest, Throat, and Nose.[130] The Ingals moved to the Hyde Park neighborhood from 4757 South Grand Boulevard (Martin Luther King Drive). That two-story brick residence, also designed by Holabird & Roche in 1895, has been demolished.

31 Professors' Row Houses, 1907.
1201 and 1215 East 56th Street; 5605 and 5609 South Woodlawn Avenue.
Tallmadge & Watson.

Robert Andrews Millikan, an eminent scientist and Nobel laureate, occupied the heavily timbered gabled residence designed by Prairie School architects Thomas Tallmadge and Vernon Watson at 5605 South Woodlawn. Millikan made many important discoveries, primarily in electricity, optics, and molecular physics.[131] He came to the University of Chicago in 1896 to work with Albert Michelson, and

3.43. Combining elements of the Prairie School with Tudor detailing, this structure houses three attached residences.

became a professor in 1910. Millikan remained at the university until 1921, when astrophysicist and former Kenwood resident George E. Hale persuaded Millikan to join him in Pasadena, California, where they developed the physics research facility known today as Caltech.

32 Hale Residence, 1908.
5757 South Kimbark Avenue. Argyle Robinson.

Encouraged by the university to live near the campus, two professors commissioned Hyde Park architect Argyle Robinson to design houses on adjacent parcels at Kimbark and 58th Streets. William Gardner Hale lived in a house designed by

3.44. Argyle Robinson was no longer associated with Mann, MacNeille & Lindeberg when he was commissioned to design the Hale Residence.

Hugh Garden prior to moving into this elegant three-story residence. Later, the house was for many years the home of Florence Lowden Miller, the daughter of Frank O. Lowden, a governor of Illinois, and his wife Florence Pullman, the daughter of George Pullman and the namesake of the Florence hotel.[132]

Just to the east of the Hale residence, Argyle designed a house for James Parker Hall. Hired by William Rainey Harper in 1902, Hall was an authority on constitutional law and dean of the University of Chicago Law School from 1904 to 1928.[133]

30 Lauten Apartment Building, 1907.
5451–5455 South Hyde Park Boulevard. Frommann & Jebsen.

After the Columbian Exposition, a lull appeared in multifamily construction in Hyde Park, the result of an oversupply of apartments built for the fair and a recession during the mid-1890s. However, by the end of the nineteenth century the financial crisis had passed and apartment buildings rose on every street; some were ordinary three-flats, others exhibited a flair for the dramatic. Frommann & Jebsen's residential work evolved with the changing architectural fashions of the time. After embracing the Prairie Style for other commissions, they designed this exotic six-flat for builder Phelps J. Lauten. Scaled to fit within the context of the surrounding houses present at the time of construction, the sculptured façade was inspired by the aesthetic of French Art Nouveau, and featured stained glass windows and an elaborate stone entrance.

3.45.

33 Apartments, 1908.
5487–5491 South Hyde Park Boulevard. Doerr & Doerr.

Prolific builders, John and Jacob Doerr constructed numerous three-story six-flats in the neighborhood.[134] More luxurious than the typical Hyde Park apartment, this six-flat is defined by the large Corinthian columns that support the open porches of the upper floors. A third brother, William, lived in this building. His influence on Hyde Park was enormous. As an architect and developer, his many buildings transformed city living by providing affordable, convenient apartments.

Hyde Park

34 The Kenwood Hotel, 1892. Demolished c. 1960.
4700 South Kenwood Avenue. Charles Sumner Frost.

Kenwood was a suburban residential area, yet nestled among the single-family houses was a structure built to offer the luxuries of a hotel to a distinctive clientele, supplementing the services offered by the Hyde Park, Del Prado, and Chicago Beach Hotels. Designed by Charles Sumner Frost, the Kenwood Hotel was one of the South Side's oldest and best-known hotels, operating for years after opening for the Columbian Exposition.

Rising seven stories, the hotel was of brick construction with stone trim, and

3.47. A 1907 view of the Kenwood Hotel, photographed from the north side of 47th Street, shows the streetcar tracks and surrounding single-family residences that once lined the street.

housed seventy-three apartments. The property fronted 100' on 47th Street and 150' on Kimbark. In the midthirties the property was sold to buyers who intended to modernize the building and divide the larger apartments into smaller suites, a trend indicative of the changing nature of Kenwood at that time.[135]

35 Beman Residence, by 1887.
1030 East 49th Street. Solon S. Beman. Remodeled 1892.

In the late nineteenth century Solon Beman enjoyed significant success in Chicago, although many of his buildings have been demolished and few of the records of Beman's small firm have survived. Although the Pullman project remained his most significant commission, Beman was widely regarded for his residential designs, including the residence of Robert Todd Lincoln that once stood at 1234 Lake Shore

3.48. Beman's interest in classical architecture is clearly evident, and continued in his work for the Christian Science church.

Drive, designed about 1890. In Hyde Park and Kenwood, however, we have several examples of his work, including the house he occupied at the turn of the century.

The stunning display of the classical architecture at the World's Columbian Exposition heavily influenced Beman's future work. Set well back from 49th Street is the Classical Revival home of Solon and Mary Miller Beman, his second wife. Houses of this style are typically a two-story rectangular block, dominated by imposing columns and a pedimented two-story entrance. The basic structure, built for W. M. Crain, predates the neoclassical porch, which is attributed to Beman.

For a time the structure operated as the John D. Hertz Livery Stable. Hertz partnered with Kenwood resident Walden Shaw, president of Walden W. Shaw Auto Livery Company, to purchase a number of "horseless carriages" and outfit them with meters. The distinctive yellow cab shuttled passengers around the city beginning in 1909 and went on to become the Yellow Cab Company.[136]

36 Sullivan Residence, 1892. Demolished 1970.
4575 South Lake Park Avenue. Louis Sullivan.

Although located in what is now North Kenwood, at the time Louis Sullivan designed this house, the community was still considered to be one cohesive neighborhood. One of the most influential architects of his time, Sullivan was commissioned by his older brother Albert to design this house for their mother Andrienne, and it is generally considered to be one of Sullivan's finest small houses. The property had been purchased from Martha Holden on May 5, 1891, and the project was completed in 1892. Louis Sullivan resided in the house while working on the Transportation Building for the Columbian Exposition, a remarkable building and the only structure not reliant on the fair's overall classic design.

After Sullivan's wife Mary sold the house in 1914, the property had a string of

3.50. Sullivan's two-story house featured an intricate, copper-sheathed bay window, as seen in this image taken by Richard Nickel.

3.51. Sullivan's ornamental designs would evolve from this relatively simple limestone stoop detail to complex organic and geometric forms made of terra-cotta, crafted metal, and mosaics.

owners, and by 1963 when the National Park Service surveyed the structure it had been divided into four small apartments and exhibited serious fire damage. Additionally, in the process of cutting up the house, much of the interior ornament was destroyed. The exterior remained in good condition, featuring smooth-faced limestone, an ornamental copper cornice and bay, and a tripartite first-floor window of columns topped by "basket-shaped, foliated capitals."[137] The house was recognized in 1959 by the Chicago Commission on Architectural Landmarks; however, vandals removed the copper on the façade in 1964 and the house fell into disrepair and was demolished in April 1970.

3.52. The Harlan house as photographed for an 1897 issue of *Inland Architect*.

37 Harlan Residence, 1892. Demolished 1963.
4414 South Greenwood Avenue. Frank Lloyd Wright.

While employed by Adler & Sullivan, Frank Lloyd Wright moonlighted with commissions for seven houses, including that of Dr. Allison W. Harlan. Designed when he was twenty-five, the house showed Wright's early use of organic elements in its series of richly textured fretwork panels on the balcony that extended across the house. Fretted decoration was common to earlier houses, but its use here was innovative because it "expressed the horizontal aspect of the house." Although simpler in detail than most of Sullivan's ornament, the fretwork made ornament an integral part of the design.[138]

Dr. Harlan, a dentist, was clearly a creative fellow—a full decade before the World's Columbian Exposition he drafted a letter to a Chicago newspaper and made the first public proposal to hold a fair in Chicago.[139] During the design phase of his house he demanded several changes to Wright's initial plan. Originally the living room spanned the full width of the façade. To accommodate the doctor's wishes, the fireplace was moved from the central hall into the open living room, which was then divided into two parts.

Around 1904, Harlan traded houses with his neighbors, the Byrnes, who sold Wright's structure in 1912. For a short time it was used as a nursing home and then fell into ruin. Vacant for years, the neglected house became a hangout in the declining neighborhood until a fire caused enough damage to require demolition.[140]

38 **Blossom Residence, 1892.**
4858 South Kenwood Avenue. Frank Lloyd Wright.

Wright was familiar with the Kenwood neighborhood—it was there he courted his first wife, Catherine Tobin. The Tobin family lived at 4721 South Kimbark (demolished), and one evening Wright went with Catherine to see the nearby houses under construction. "That meant to see some curious effects," Wright later recalled, "because Kenwood was in the process of becoming the most fashionable of Chicago's residence districts."[141] Two of Wright's "bootleg" houses are on the very block he walked with Catherine.

Wright designed the residence of George and Carrie Blossom, as well as another on the lot adjacent on the north for Warren McArthur. The exterior of Wright's "bootleg" design for insurance executive George Blossom is one of his more traditionally designed works, as he used classical motifs, including the columns on the semicircular porch, a symmetrical façade, and simplified Palladian-style windows. The symmetry and squareness of the house demonstrate Wright's mastery of classical form; however, the dramatic interior design, the base of Roman brick, the narrow wood cladding, and the depth of the eave hint of his future direction. Fifteen years later Wright returned to design the coach house with the large overhanging eaves that became emblematic of his Prairie Style.

39 McArthur Residence, 1892.
4852 South Kenwood Avenue. Frank Lloyd Wright.

3.55. Wright's design for the McArthur family, primarily in the Dutch Colonial style, situates the main entrance on the south, facing the Blossom house.

On the lot adjacent to the north, Wright again did not "try anything radical,"[142] designing a gambrel-roofed house for Warren and Minnie McArthur. The name on this building permit was that of his friend, Cecil Corwin, used in an attempt to disguise Wright's extracurricular activity. Like the Blossom house, this house sits upon a base of narrow Roman brick. Wright placed the main arched doorway on the south, flanked by octagonal leaded bay windows nestled under the eaves.

This house represents a long association between the owner and architect; how they came to meet is not exactly clear. McArthur was a partner in the Hamilton Lantern Company with Edward Boynton, who later commissioned Wright to design his house in Rochester, New York.[143] McArthur was adventurous, one of the first in the neighborhood to own a car, and ambitious, for he reportedly sold more tubular lanterns than anyone else. Albert Chase McArthur, one of three sons raised in the home, studied architecture at the Armour Institute of Technology and at Harvard. He became one of Frank Lloyd Wright's draftsmen, working with him between 1907 and 1909. Later in his career, Albert was commissioned by his brothers to design a hotel in Phoenix, the Arizona Biltmore. McArthur used Wright's concept of concrete textile blocks on the project, and the building is often credited to Wright.[144] Albert's brother Warren McArthur designed the original furnishings for the hotel, as well as a popular line of tubular aluminum furniture.[145]

3.56. A large wraparound porch was added to the Goodman residence after this image was taken.

40 Goodman Residence, 1892.
5026 South Greenwood Avenue. Treat & Foltz.

Treat & Foltz continued to be sought-after architects as Chicago's business leaders flowed into Kenwood and constructed residences representative of their wealth and stature. The firm was awarded an important commission that produced the ornate, 10,000-square-foot mansion of William Owen Goodman and his wife Eva. In 1878, Goodman and his brother organized the Sawyer-Goodman Lumber Company, of which he later became president.[146] For their son Kenneth, a playwright, the third floor of the new house included a theater. After Kenneth perished in the deadly 1918 outbreak of influenza, Goodman commissioned Howard van Doren Shaw to design a theater as a tribute to him. In 2005 the Art Institute demolished the original 1925 Goodman Theatre to make room for the Modern Wing designed by Renzo Piano.

During the twenties and thirties, Kenwood became less fashionable and many residents moved to the North Side of the city. In 1921 the Goodman's yellow brick house, reminiscent of an Italian palazzo and containing eighteen rooms with fifteen fireplaces, was relegated to an institutional use, serving as the Chicago Normal School of Physical Education. The house was completely restored in 2006.

41 Morse Residence, 1893. Demolished 1931.

4800 South Greenwood Avenue. Mifflin E. Bell.

Mifflin Bell was awarded the commission to design the residence of Charles Hosmer Morse, a nineteenth-century industrialist. His story was a "rags-to-riches tale of American success."[147] In 1850, Morse began his career in Vermont as an apprentice for a manufacturer of scales, essential at that time to many businesses. He moved ahead quickly, and after two years as a salesman in New York, he came to Chicago to establish the first branch of an enterprise that became known as Fairbanks, Morse & Company.

The great fire of 1871 destroyed the firm's offices on Lake Street, but several days afterward, using the "charred books and papers rescued from the safe," the company was back in business.[148] Morse's company prospered in the years after the fire, growing from a small business that produced balance scales into a corporation that manufactured industrial equipment.

Morse had a number of residences in the Chicago area; as he amassed a fortune he upgraded with each move. From a simple two-story town house at Ann and Washington Streets, to a large Victorian frame in Oak Park, Morse finally settled in aristocratic Kenwood. While the family resided at 1031 East 48th Street, Morse commissioned architect Bell to design a residence on the adjacent property.

A luxurious twenty-room mansion rose on a wooded lot that fronted 254' on 48th Street and 207' on Greenwood. The heavy stone of the exterior demon-

3.57. (Oppposite) Morse continued to reside in this house after giving it to his daughter. In 1915 he retired to Winter Park, Florida, a community that he heavily supported.

3 Rice Residence, 1892. 5554 South Woodlawn Avenue. Mifflin E. Bell.

3.58. Designed for Theodore and Edith Rice, this Queen Anne-style house is thought to be the one remaining example of Bell's earlier residential work. Of frame construction with distinctive red slate shingles, the turret was repeated in stone for the Morse house.

3.59. The heavily paneled entry hall of the Morse residence featured a fireplace, upright piano, and a chandelier outfitted with electric lights.

3.60. Morse's elegant dining room was lined with built-in cabinetry custom made by the Diblee Company. Typically, the most important feature of a dining room was considered to be the sideboard. Pictured here is a massive piece, showcasing the best china, glittering glassware, and polished silver. A gas chandelier, or gasolier, hung directly over the table and was supplemented with candles, as well as sconces placed on either side of the sideboard.

strates the dominant influence of architect H. H. Richardson. Charles and Martha Morse filled its rosewood-paneled rooms with custom-made Arts and Crafts style furniture, Tiffany glass, and paintings by American Impressionist artists.[149] As a reminder of Charles Morse's early career, there was a large scale in front of the coach house, where the coal was weighed before being put in the cellar.[150]

The Morses' first child and only daughter, Elizabeth, spent a good deal of time at their Florida and Vermont residences, yet her life was rooted in Chicago.

After graduation from college she returned to the family home and often acted as hostess for her father following her mother's death in 1903. When Elizabeth married Dr. Richard Millard Genius at the Kenwood Evangelical Church at 46th and Greenwood in 1905, five hundred guests attended the reception at this house, which her father gave the young couple as a wedding present. This was Elizabeth's residence until her sudden death in March 1928. Three years later, in November 1931, the house was torn down at the request of a presumably distraught Dr. Genius.

The demolition of the house was a point of contention among the family, some raced to save artifacts from the salvage company before they disappeared. Unfortunately, the storage facility that subsequently housed the heirlooms was broken into and many of the rescued items were lost. The remaining works of art, Tiffany pieces, and period clothing are now housed in the Morse Museum of American Art in Winter Park, Florida. The Morse property lay vacant until purchased and subdivided by developers and construction of three smaller-scale houses began in 1936.

42 Hutchins Residence, 1894.
4810 South Ellis Avenue. Charles Sumner Frost.

On a beautiful September morning in 1884 two hundred guests departed the city on the Chicago, Rock Island Railway, bound for a wedding at the summer villa of millionaire iron manufacturer Orrin W. Potter in Lake Geneva, Wisconsin. Potter's eldest daughter Agnes was marrying James Calhoun Hutchins, an attorney for the railroad that provided a special train for the trip. When the guests arrived,

3.61. The Hutchins and Potter residences were constructed on Ellis Avenue, an area of large suburban lots that were subdivided by Drexel & Smith after William Egan defaulted on his Egandale estate.

steam yachts transported them across the lake to the site of the wedding. After
the lavish ceremony, Mr. and Mrs. Potter presented the newlyweds with a gift—a
completely furnished house situated on 47th Street, and a check for $1,000.[151] An
1890 directory listing Chicago's elite citizens notes that Mr. and Mrs. James C.
Hutchins lived at 231 East 47th Street, next door to Mr. and Mrs. E. C. Potter residing at 227 East 47th Street. Before long, the street was widened, telegraph poles
were installed, and the streetcar began to run—making these addresses far less
exclusive. The Hutchins family relocated to this red brick house on Ellis Avenue.

Designed according to the traditional, yet fashionable, ideals of the time by
Charles Frost, the Hutchins house recently operated as the only bed-and-breakfast
in Kenwood, only possible due to peculiarities in the zoning restrictions. In 1946
the property was purchased for the St. George's School for Girls, zoned as multifamily, and operated as such until the school merged with the Harvard School for
Boys in 1964.

Adjacent on the north is a residence, also designed by Frost, for Edward C.
Potter, an engineer, chemist, and younger brother of Agnes Potter Hutchins.
Potter began his career working for North Chicago Rolling Mills; his father was
president of the firm from 1871 until 1899, which in 1901 became a part of US
Steel Corporation.[152] The design of Edward Potter's house is reminiscent of the
work of East Coast architect Charles McKim, who popularized the double towers
of the façade.

The elder Potter left for New York in 1901 and put all of his "Chicago holdings"
on the market.[153] His house and that built for his daughter on 47th Street have all
been demolished. As to the architect, Frost ended his independent practice in 1898
and partnered with Alfred Hoyt Granger, after each married a daughter of Marvin
Hughitt, the president of North Western Railway.[154]

44 Shaw-Atkinson Residence, 1894. Demolished 1961.
4833–4847 South Lake Park Avenue. Howard van Doren Shaw.

Howard van Doren Shaw's first project in Kenwood was for these attached houses, designed at the request of his father-in-law, wholesale merchant Moses Dwight "Shoe King" Wells. The houses were built for Wells's two daughters: Shaw's wife Francis Wells and her sister Mrs. Charles Atkinson. Connecting by a passageway, and known as Dorencote, this became Shaw's home for the next fifteen years. The Romanesque Revival design featured a brick and limestone façade with slate roofs and copper sheathing on the bays and dormers. Much of the interior detail was imported from England; every room with a fireplace was of a different design; woodwork was of oak, mahogany, and cherry; and arched windows featured leaded glass.[155] The houses were demolished during the relocation of Lake Park Avenue in the early 1960s.

3.63. Connected by a secret passageway on the second floor, the Shaw-Atkinson residences (as they appeared in an 1895 image from Inland Architect) rose on a site fronting 100' on then fashionable Lake Avenue, and stretching two hundred feet east toward the Illinois Central right-of-way.

45 The Kenwood Club, 1895. Demolished c. 1960.
1361 East 47th Street. Patton & Fisher with Charles S. Frost, consulting architect.

Not long after the death of Norman Judd in 1878, a portion of the grounds were sold to the newly formed Kenwood Club, and his house was acquired as the club-house. The residence was enlarged to accommodate the growing membership of this exclusive neighborhood club. For many years the venerable establishment was the second home of Kenwood's residents; on the grass tennis courts national tournaments were held, and members enjoyed dining facilities and card rooms in the clubhouse. Located at the center of the aristocratic community, it continued

3.64. An 1896 image published in *Inland Architect* of the Kenwood Club's elegant new building, with the old Judd residence visible on the right.

to be the oldest and one of the most exclusive social clubs of the city; however, membership declined as the original clubhouse deteriorated. A new facility was planned, intending to "reawaken the dormant enthusiasm" and once again make the Kenwood Club the social center of the South Side.[156]

In the calm before a fierce thunderstorm in March 1895, the cornerstone was laid for the new home of the club. Designed jointly by Charles Frost and Patton & Fisher on the irregular lot at 47th and Lake Park, the two-and-a-half-story colonial building housed the membership of three hundred of Kenwood's most prominent citizens. The architects used "rain-drop" brick, in a dark red color, with Bedford stone trim.[157] Huge fluted pillars dominated the east façade, where a side porch caught the cool breezes off the lake in the summer months. After members entered through an iron gate, with the club's title glowing overhead in a series of electric lights, a solid mahogany door opened to welcome them to an array of amenities.

Inside were four bowling alleys, a shuffleboard court, a large dining room, a library, a ladies' parlor and men's dressing rooms, a billiards room, three card rooms, a gymnasium, and of great importance to the times, the servants' quarters. The telephone room was equipped with the latest invention, "a long-distance instrument,"[158] and electric bells and speaking tubes connected the office with every room. But it was the ballroom, with its 53' × 82' dance floor made of the finest maple, which gave the club its greatest pride, as no expense was spared to make it the best of its kind in the city.

The family-oriented club continued to operate here until 1922, when only 110 active members remained. By then flats and stores surrounded the club, and the grass tennis courts were long gone. Most of the "wealthy old-timers" had passed away, and the younger generation now preferred membership at golf and country clubs rather than at the "more sedate and timeworn" Kenwood Club.[159]

46 Lord Residence, 1896.

4857 South Greenwood Avenue. Charles Frost.

This imposing house was designed for John B. and Annie Lord. Lord was the president of Ayer & Lord Railroad Tie Company, a manufacturer of oak and cypress railroad ties.[160] The Chicago based firm was widely known and perhaps the largest of its type in the country.[161] For the design of this three-story red brick residence situated on a south-facing corner lot, Frost combined the popular Palladian-style central window and dormer, massive bays, and copper, stone, and terra-cotta for the trim details. This house, like Frost's design for Edward Potter, is reminiscent of McKim Mead & White's use of historical styles in the revival mansions of Newport, Rhode Island.[162]

3.65

47 Carton Residence, 1896.
4923 South Greenwood Avenue. William Otis.

After ending his partnership with William LeBaron Jenney, William Otis designed two houses on Greenwood Avenue before the turn of the century—for the treasurer of Swift & Company, Laurence A. Carton, at 4923, and for Charles Gill, an executive with Chicago Law Publishers, at 4917. The residence of Edith and Laurence Carton features a distinctive roofline and a welcoming front porch that proved to be a bit too inviting on a warm evening in 1903. While the Carton family was enjoying dinner, "porch climbers" took advantage of an unlit porch and open second-story window to make away with over $1,000 in valuables. The family maid went upstairs and found everything in disorder. Although bureau drawers were emptied and rugs displaced, "not a sound" was heard during dinner.[163]

3.66. The most striking element of the façade of the Carton house and the coach house is the crow-stepped gable, a design typically found in the European lowlands.

48 **Residence, 1897.**

4925 South Blackstone Avenue. Howard van Doren Shaw.

Howard van Doren Shaw produced a series of five smaller-scale residences on narrow 28' × 100' lots at the eastern edge of Kenwood, each with its own unique personality. This house is the southernmost of four existing residences; the fifth and most northern of the grouping was demolished to make room for the addition to the Blackstone Library.

3.67. This Howard van Doren Shaw house was once nestled behind the Bryson Hotel. When that structure was demolished in 1971, the owners of this property were able to purchase a small section for access to the backyard.

49 Swift Residence, 1897.
4848 South Ellis Avenue. Flanders & Zimmerman.

The major and final achievement of the partnership between John Flanders and William Zimmerman was the elaborate mansion of meatpacking magnate Gustavus Franklin Swift and his wife Ann M. Higgins. Swift was a national figure in the business world, beginning his career as a butcher. He came to Chicago in 1875 as a cattle buyer and in 1878 opened Swift Brothers, a meatpacking company. It was his pioneering use of the refrigerated car that changed Chicago from a cattle-shipping center to a meat processing and distribution center, and revolutionized the industry.[164] The firm's growth was phenomenal, and by 1918 Swift & Company was second in volume among the nation's businesses, exceeded only by United States Steel.[165] Like many of his fellow neighbors, Swift was a philanthropist, a trustee, and a loyal supporter of the university.

The Swift family resided near the stockyards, until moving to the spacious grounds surrounding this ornate yellow brick house. Construction began in the spring of 1898, and Swift was determined to celebrate Thanksgiving in Kenwood. The architects and builders deemed it impossible, yet Ann Swift remarked, "If Gustavus' heart is set upon it, it will be accomplished."[166] The house was com-

3.68. Swift's daughter Helen recalled that her father enjoyed visitors, but not visiting; her parents rarely spent a night away from this house.

3.69. The religious iconography, as seen in the main entry hall, was added to the Swift residence after the property was purchased by a religious order.

3.70. Polished wood balustrades rise three stories in a dramatic stairway that is accentuated by intricate stained glass windows.

pleted by November, and twenty-eight enjoyed a traditional midday meal in the beautiful dining room.

The façade combines any number of historic elements, from the pair of second-story Palladian windows to the ionic columns that support the welcoming porch, and it includes elaborate terra-cotta details such as the third-story corner shields engraved with the letter S. This detail is repeated on the large coach house that at one time featured horse heads mounted on either side of the south facing door. The mansion is now owned by a religious order (the Croatian Franciscan Fathers purchased the property in 1952) and the interior remains magnificent. From the three-story staircase to the embellished ceiling of the dining room, the opulence of Kenwood's golden era is clear. Swift did not enjoy the beauty of his home for long—he died here unexpectedly at the age of sixty-three. The man who began his career as a butcher left a fortune and a company that employed over 22,000.[167]

50 Dau Residence. Before 1897.
4807 South Greenwood Avenue. George Washington Maher.

In contrast to the opulence of the Swift house is the work of George Washington Maher, a significant contributor to the Prairie School movement. His work often combined "traditional American house styles with more progressive European Arts and Crafts–style designs." Maher's work in the neighborhood extends over a twenty-year period, ranging from his earliest commissions, several ornate frame houses, to the design of two apartment buildings on Ellis. The design of many of his later residences possesses "a broad horizontal character," achieved through the use of "overhanging roof eaves, a strong rectilinear massing, and symmetrically placed windows centered on a prominent central entry."[168]

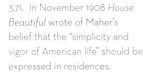
3.71. In November 1908 *House Beautiful* wrote of Maher's belief that the "simplicity and vigor of American life" should be expressed in residences.

For wholesale merchant J. J. Dau, Maher designed a bold, square house in a lustrous deep-hued red brick. He used limestone for the dominant entry, which in his later residences he would alter to encompass the full width of the house. Maher was concerned with the complete structure of his commissions, believing that the interior should "express simplicity, dignity and repose."[169] He used a motif from nature, in this case, leaves and berries, consistently on the exterior and interior of the house.

The Daus were Kenwood residents, moving to Greenwood Avenue from a house at 164 East 47th Street designed by Burnham & Root. A native of Denmark, Dau came to Chicago in 1868 and entered the grocery business. He was successful, becoming vice-president, president, and eventually chairman of Reid Murdoch & Company.[170] The company building is a city landmark; George Nimmons designed a warehouse and the food processing for the company in 1913–1914. Noted for its four-sided clock tower, the seven-story brick building overlooks the Chicago River and is on the National Register of Historic Places.[171]

⑪ Heller House, 1897.
5132 South Woodlawn Avenue. Frank Lloyd Wright.

After his unpleasant departure from Adler & Sullivan, Wright retreated to Oak Park and began an independent practice. He received a number of residential commissions, and with each moved closer to a form of architecture influenced by its physical setting. A National Historic Landmark, the house Wright designed for Isidore and Ida Heller rests near the border between Hyde Park and Kenwood and

3.72. The upper story of the Heller house features a Beaux Arts frieze by Richard W. Bock, a sculptor and important collaborator of many Prairie School architects. Here his design includes figures and elaborate Sullivan-inspired ornament.

3.73. Louis Sullivan's influence on Frank Lloyd Wright is evident in the ornament of the south-facing main entry of the Heller residence.

3.74. The main staircase of the Heller house is forceful in its simplicity, a marked contrast to the elaborate stairway of the Swift mansion designed by Flanders & Zimmerman the same year.

marks a crucial point in his work. It is one of "the most important surviving examples of his quest for a new style of architecture."[172] Starkly modern, this residence sat in complete contrast to the traditionally styled residences of the neighborhood.

Heller was in the meatpacking business (Wolf, Sayer & Heller) when he purchased the narrow lot in 1895 and commissioned Wright to design a house the following year. Wright responded with a plan that blended a modern geometric house of buff-colored Roman brick with rich Sullivanesque detailing.

51 Wait Residence, 1897.

1120 East 48th Street. Dwight Heald Perkins.

The house for Ada and James J. Wait was Dwight Perkins' first commission in Kenwood, and marks the beginning of his success. The house was designed on a $75' \times 175'$ portion of the grounds of the Hitchcock estate. Wait, educated at Hyde Park High School, was the manager of the freight department of two establish-

3.75. Subsequent owners of the
Wait residence made alterations
to Perkins' original design,
enclosing the porch and building
an addition at the rear.

ments; Hibbard, Spencer, Bartlett & Company, wholesalers of hardware, and Reid
Murdoch & Company, wholesale grocers.[173]

For the Wait house Perkins used common brick. Kiln-fired brick is made in
batches and consequently the color varies; architects would have the brick sorted
into like hues. Perkins took a different approach and material, and the result is a
thickly textured façade, appearing almost as if it were woven.

52   Vierling Residence, 1899.
4914 South Greenwood Avenue. Dwight Perkins with H. H. Waterman.

Perkins was awarded the commission for two additional houses, the Greenwood
residence of Robert and Clara Vierling, in association with H. H. Waterman, and
the Hyde Park residence of attorney Russell Wiles. The house designed for Vierling, an iron and steel executive, appears from the exterior to be constructed in the
same manner as other houses along Greenwood Avenue. The stone façade mimics

the Barton house by Frost & Granger to the south, yet "the horizontal masonry lines, and low-pitched roofs carried by a lace of wrought iron are clues that this house is original and modern, a sophisticated and subtle version of the brand new Prairie school style."[174]

Using a steel structural system entirely hidden from view, Perkins adapted the construction techniques of early Chicago skyscrapers such as the Monadnock Building into residential construction. "With masonry walls and a steel interior skeleton there is no weight bearing structural wood in the entire building, as would be almost universal in residential buildings of this era," commented the local historical society.[175] The long-neglected structure, representative of a marriage between structural innovation and the popular aesthetic of the time, was in a serious state of deterioration when purchased by a local developer and restored in 2006.

3.76. Perkins' attention to detail is evident not only in the intricate iron work of the Vierling house. Note also the carved "green men" that adorn the corners of the square columns and pilasters of the front porch.

53 Green Coach House, 1899.

4935½ South Greenwood Avenue. D. H. Burnham & Company.

Eleven years after Solon Beman designed the residence at 4935 South Greenwood for Edward H. Turner, Adolphus and Esther Green purchased the property. Green came to Chicago in 1873, practiced law and was the attorney for

3.77. The structure was originally designed to accommodate the carriages and horses of the Green family. The interior of the first floor was of white glazed brick with a wooden ceiling, with an apartment on the second floor. The coach house was eventually sold as a separate parcel from the main property, and has been remodeled into a single-family house.

the Village of Hyde Park for two years. He became a specialist in corporate law, which led to his association with the National Biscuit Company, today known as Nabisco, where he rose from general counsel to president in 1905. Green conceived the concept of packaging the product in airtight containers, as opposed to selling the product in bulk. This would keep the product crisp and "untouched by human hands."[176]

Green commissioned nationally famous Daniel Hudson Burnham to design a barn at the rear of the house. Green was undoubtedly acquainted with Burnham through his business activities; however, Burnham's staff would have handled a project of this size.

54 Fenton Residence, 1901.
1000 East 48th Street. Wilson & Marshall.

Architect Horatio R. Wilson was comfortable working in a combination of architectural styles and details. His houses ranged from compact, vertically organized town houses designed with his former partner O. W. Marble, to large and lavish mansions designed in partnership with Benjamin Marshall. The dramatic and stately Corinthian columns of the portico that define the red brick mansion for banker William Taylor Fenton indicate it was most likely the work of Marshall, an "enormously gifted" architect with "extravagant tastes."[177]

With a reputation of being one of the "most conservative figures in Chicago's banking world," Fenton moved from his striking Kenwood home to the Streeterville neighborhood. Living along the lakefront can provide a glimpse of nature's fury at all times of the year. Often during Chicago's notoriously long winter months and into spring a cold wind sweeps down from the north, bringing snow, sleet, heavy winds and high waves. While senior vice president of the National Bank of

3.78. Marshall was not a proponent of the Prairie School movement; his lavish work borrowed heavily from classical styles, as demonstrated in the Fenton house.

the Republic, Fenton hailed a cab to drive from his office to the lakeshore. Into a fierce storm and "seething breakers" Fenton leapt and drowned "in a spectacular fashion" before anyone could reach him.[178]

56 ## Ames Residence, 1902. Demolished c. 1970.
4835 South Greenwood Avenue. Frost & Granger.

Frost & Granger were architects sought after by many of Kenwood's elite listed in the *Blue Book*, a register of socially prominent residents. Included in the listing is Franklin L. Ames, a manager for Marshall Field & Company. Ames, his wife Emma, and their two children had the assistance of two Swedish servants in

3.79. *Inland Architect and News Record* featured the Ames house in a 1903 issue.

the three-story red brick house. According to local legend the traditionally embellished structure was demolished in error in the years before the neighborhood was landmarked, and the property lay vacant for many years. Every spring when the ground loosens after a thaw, pieces of the Ames house work their way to the surface, revealing bathroom tiles, bricks, and shards of dinner plates.

55 Barton Residence, 1901.
4920 South Greenwood Avenue. Frost & Granger.

Frost & Granger designed this massive limestone residence for Enos Melancthon Barton, who purchased the property of Albert Bremer and demolished his large frame residence (c. 1885). Barton began work as a telegraph messenger boy in New York during the Civil War. After moving west to Cleveland to find employment as a telegraph operator, he revolted when his salary was cut from $100 a month to $90 and walked out. He founded Gray & Barton, and the "shabby little machine shop" was successful from the start and recognized as an important part of the fledgling electrical business. After relocating to Chicago in 1869, the firm survived the fire of 1871 and was afterward reorganized as the Western Electric Company. At first Bar-

3.80. Barton's house was immense—built no doubt with the thought of accommodating his children. He had five from his first marriage to Katherine Richardson, and four more after remarrying and moving from 143 East 47th Street to this house.

ton was a skeptic of the telephone, recalling his "disgust when someone told me it was possible to send conversation along a wire."[179] His disbelief was suspended when his plant housed research and manufacturing for the Bell Telephone Company. Barton became the president of Western Electric in 1887.[180]

Barton built this residence for his second family after the death of his first wife, Katherine, in 1898. The following year he married Mary C. Rust, twenty-eight years his junior. Described as a "plain, candid and unostentatious man, who loves best the simple life," Barton also had a "beautiful summer house" on a 1,000-acre farm in a rural area near Chicago's suburb of Hinsdale.[181]

57 Julius Rosenwald Residence, 1903.
4901 South Ellis Avenue. Nimmons & Fellows.

A spectacularly successful merchandiser, Julius Rosenwald began his career in New York working as an apprentice in the family clothing business, then opened his own firm in 1884. Sensing promise of a market in the Midwest, Rosenwald and his younger brother Morris moved to Chicago and were joined in business by their cousin, Julius Weil, in Rosenwald & Weil Clothiers, one of the first companies to offer men's suits in standardized sizes.[182]

Ten years later Rosenwald purchased a quarter interest in Sears Roebuck & Company for $37,500 and went on to become president of the company, presiding over a period of tremendous growth while amassing a fortune.[183] He was a generous philanthropist and supporter of the university, and spearheaded efforts to assist African Americans across the country. The Field Museum, founded through his generosity, was housed in the Fine Arts Building, the only building remaining

3.81. After use by the university and a Baptist church, in 1987 the Roman brick Rosenwald mansion was purchased for use as a private family home and renovated.

Morris Rosenwald Residence, 1903. 4924 South Woodlawn Avenue. Howard van Doren Shaw.

3.82

from the Columbian Exposition of 1893. The structure was later rebuilt and renovated to house the Museum of Science and Industry.

Nimmons & Fellows were the architects of many of Sears' buildings, and Rosenwald commissioned them to design his immense residence, constructed on 1.7 acres of land. The Prairie-style, twenty-two-room house has approximately 13,000 square feet of living space and amenities including a grape arbor, pergola, and coach house. Characterized by the strong horizontal lines and taupe-colored roman brick, the spartan exterior displays ornamentation only in the delicate Sullivan-inspired terra-cotta under the eave line. Perhaps because of the house's "industrial feel" the younger Rosenwald children called it "the old pickle factory."[184]

Howard van Doren Shaw was commissioned by Julius Rosenwald's younger brother to design a residence. Situated only a block away, the 8,000-square-foot residence of Morris and Mae Rosenwald once featured plantings, footpaths, and seating areas conceived by noted landscape architect Jens Jensen—they have unfortunately vanished over the years.[185] The house features over twenty rooms, including eight bedrooms as well as five fireplaces, a solarium, two wine vaults and a gracious terrace. An investment banker, Rosenwald died in his home at the age of fifty-nine, leaving a fortune to his widow and three children.[186]

59 Schaffner Residence, 1904.
4819 South Greenwood Avenue. Holabird & Roche.

It was not uncommon for the architects of business enterprises to be commissioned by the owners to design their residences. The garment-manufacturing firm of Hart Schaffner & Marx utilized Holabird & Roche for their office buildings and factories, and Joseph Schaffner and his wife Sarah commissioned the firm to design this red brick Georgian house. Like others designed by Holabird & Roche after the turn of the century, the Schaffner house features a classically ornamented masonry exterior. However the setback of this structure is unusual—it was constructed on the site of an earlier dwelling, which permitted the stand of oak trees to flourish.

Hart Schaffner & Marx rose to become a leader in the clothing industry by producing ready-to-wear clothing of good quality at a price most people could afford. However it was Schaffner's recognition of the Amalgamated Clothing Workers of America that was his most noted achievement. During an era of conflict between business and labor, any dealings with unions were regarded "as little short of treason."[187] In 1910 strikers in clothing trade were demanding a living wage, better working conditions, and recognition of union labor.[188] With a "sharp sense of fairness and a strong social conscience," Schaffner decided to experiment in "industrial democracy," and offered better sanitary conditions for his workers, regular lunch hours, a minimum wage, and time and a half for overtime work.[189] The progressive labor-management relationship between the Amalgamated Clothing Workers and Hart Schaffner & Marx proved to be mutually beneficial.[190] Schaffner died in his home in April 1918.

3.83. The Schaffner house, noted for its brickwork in the Flemish bond pattern, was constructed on the grounds of the Bogue estate. Hamilton Bogue married Emily Hoyt, the daughter of William Hoyt of South Park, in June 1876. The couple moved to Greenwood Avenue in the fall of 1871. Hamilton was active in the real estate firm of Bogue & Hoyt with this father (early settler Warren S. Bogue) and father-in-law.

3.84. The restrained façade of the Waterman house contrasts sharply with the red brick, classically embellished residences on either side.

60 **Waterman Residence, 1905.**
4849 South Kenwood Avenue. Harry Hale Waterman.

Best known for his residential work in the Beverly–Morgan Park area, Harry Hale Waterman received one commission in Hyde Park and two in Kenwood, one in association with Dwight Perkins. On his own, Waterman designed a residence in the progressive modernist vocabulary of the times. Situated on a compact urban lot and surrounded by traditional red brick houses, the structure is defined by its simple detailing, flat roof, pale brick, and spare façade. In the 1900 and 1910 *Chicago City Directories* the Watermans were listed at 8929 South Vincennes, so this house may have been speculative construction.

61 Stilwell Residence, 1905. Coach house demolished 2010.
5017 South Greenwood Avenue. Jarvis Hunt.

It may not be evident by this residence, but Jarvis Hunt was one of the designers influenced by the progressive group of architects at Steinway Hall. In 1905 he received a commission from Homer Allison Stilwell, and designed a massive house of pressed brick and stone laden with heavy detailing.

Stilwell came to Chicago in 1882 and worked in one of the city's major warehousing firms, Butler Brothers, becoming vice president in 1907. Like many other Kenwood residents, he held affiliations with various clubs that played an integral role in his daily life. Stilwell was a member of the Commercial Club, the Chicago Athletic Club, the Mid-Day Club, the Midlothian Club, the Onwentsia Club, the South Shore Country Club, and of course the local Kenwood Club.[191]

3.85. The Stilwell coach house, visible through the archway in this photograph, has been demolished. In 2000 the owners applied for a demolition permit that was denied following significant neighborhood opposition. For ten years the structure was left to deteriorate, until the Landmarks Commission received notice that the Department of Buildings Commissioner determined the building to be imminently dangerous and hazardous. The commission then had no choice but to approve the wrecking application.

3.86. The speculative property was marketed for sale in the *Chicago Tribune* on September 30, 1908. This image had been digitally altered the exclude the location of the house.

Speculative Residence, 1908.
South Greenwood Avenue. Thomas Bishop, with Clark & Trainer.

Not long after moving into the White House, President Obama called the astronauts aboard the space shuttle *Atlantis*. The crew had flown over Illinois earlier in their mission, and Obama asked if they noticed that someone was taking care of his home back in Chicago.[192] "Did you guys see my house?" Obama joked with the crew. "I'm trying to figure out if my lawn is getting mowed there. I haven't been back in a couple months."[193]

The Obamas' Chicago residence was a speculative collaboration between architect Thomas Bishop and real estate developers Clark & Trainer. In 1905 a construction loan was opened for Wallace Grant Clark, who commissioned Bishop to design a speculative house on a 60' × 200' vacant lot in Kenwood. Clark & Trainer advertised the fourteen-room residence in the *Chicago Tribune* beginning in November 1907. By April 1910 the property had failed to sell and it was offered "at a bargain."[194] The house was built with over 6,000 square feet of living space, seven bedrooms, three baths, and hot water heat. Interior details included four fireplaces and glass-door bookcases fashioned from Honduran mahogany.

It was not until 1912 that the house had its first occupants, the family of William Lewis Hodgkins. Hodgkins succeeded his father as the head of the Brownwell Improvement Company, contractors for the construction of public buildings. Hodgkins sold the property in 1919 and moved to the city's Gold Coast neighborhood. During the summer of 1927 he perished in a horrific boating accident on Lake Huron. The motor of his speed yacht *Play Boy* caught fire and the boat was suddenly engulfed in flames. Hodgkins is credited with saving the lives of two crew members and two young socialites aboard at the time, who were able to swim a mile to safety.[195]

In October 1919 Max and Ethel Goldstine became the owners of the house and at the same time purchased the adjacent vacant lot on the northwest corner of East Hyde Park Boulevard and Greenwood Avenue. Goldstine was a "successful Chicago real estate entrepreneur" who came to the community along with many others of the Jewish community during the twenties.[196] The family sold the property in 1926.

During the Depression years of the 1930s, the property foreclosed and was held by the banks until it was acquired by the Hebrew Theological College in 1947. The Orthodox rabbinical seminary wanted to establish a base to serve the large South Side Jewish community. In the late forties the property became the South Side Jewish Day School, now known as the Akiba-Schecter Jewish Day School and located on Hyde Park Boulevard. In the early 1950s Hyde Park's Orthodox population declined, and in 1954 the house and adjacent property were sold to the Hyde Park Lutheran Church.[197]

The Lutheran Church used the house as a chapel, complete with an organ, and remodeled the interior to provide for Sunday school rooms, a nursery, a kitchen, and a pastor's apartment. The congregation contemplated erecting a church on the open lot to the south. During the 1970s the church ran a program designed to bring inner-city black and suburban white teens together without "this militant thing, this hate thing, [and] this prejudice thing getting in the way."[198] The following summer, perhaps in response to the progressive attitude of the church, four firebombs made of plastic and gasoline were hurled at the converted house during the middle of the night. A passer-by noticed the flames and the fire department responded before much damage had been done.[199]

The Obamas moved from a condominium facing East End Park after purchasing the house in 2005. Ironically, for a vast part of Kenwood's history, they would not have been permitted to reside in either location. Restrictive covenants and neighborhood associations worked in concert during the first half of the twentieth century to keep the community segregated.

While other American presidents' residences were often isolated on a ranch or farm, the Obamas are distinctly urban. Secret Service agents and Chicago police officers now guard their tree-lined street. Immediately after Obama accepted the nomination at the Democratic Convention in Denver during the summer of 2008, concrete barriers were set up around the house. When the first family visits, the security perimeter is widely expanded. The armored motorcade zips through red lights and stop signs, hurrying past neighbors waving small American flags that welcome them home.

62 Magerstadt Residence, 1908.
4930 South Greenwood Avenue. George Maher.

The house for city collector Ernest J. Magerstadt is considered to be one of George Maher's finest accomplishments. Defined by strong horizontal lines and constructed of Roman brick, the main entrance faces north on the narrow lot. Maher continued his emphasis on simplicity and natural forms with the use of his "motif-rhythm" theory of design. As in the Dau house, he used a stylized form of

3.87. Magerstadt's wife Hattie lived in the house until her death in 1957; very few alterations were made during this time. Owners who purchased the property in 1998 completed the large family room and kitchen addition.

3.88. The south-facing dining room windows are set above built-in cabinetry, and feature the poppy motif. The light fixtures are original to the Magerstadt house; however, the Maher-designed dining room furniture was sold.

3.89. Defined by a muscular, paneled main staircase, the main entry of the Magerstadt house is situated on the north side of the rather narrow Kenwood lot.

an indigenous plant, in this case the poppy, as the unifying motif for the house. "The leading flower of a neighborhood is nature's symbol of the spirit breathed there," Maher said.[200] For the Magerstadt residence, the poppy appeared on exterior stone carvings and was repeated on the interior in moldings, mosaics, and leaded glass panels.

Drexel Boulevard

⑥⑶ Fuller Residence, c. 1890. Demolished 1963.
4353 Drexel Boulevard. Charles Sumner Frost.

By the 1890s the Drexel Boulevard had become one of Chicago's most exclusive addresses. Many of the city's wealthiest citizens came to live on this formal, park-like corridor. Presence upon the boulevard was dictated by one's wealth, which required an appropriate display of architecture. Chicagoans did not disappoint.

Situated on a relatively narrow lot was the finely detailed house of George Allon Fuller and his wife Emily Channing. Early in his career, Fuller spent four years with architects Peabody & Stearns in both Boston and New York. He came to

3.90. The George A. Fuller house was featured in an 1893 issue of the *Inland Architect and News Record.*

Chicago and entered into partnership with C. Everett Clark in 1880, founding the Clark & Fuller Construction Company. In the years after the fire, architects were encouraging new styles and innovative ways of building.

An ambitious man, Fuller soon left the Clark & Fuller partnership and in 1882 formed the George A. Fuller Company. Fuller understood that in his new city one could experiment, and he had a radical idea: his new company would handle only the construction of a building, and would partner with architects from various firms for the design. It was an innovative and successful concept, and before long the company became the leading builder of skyscrapers in Chicago and in New York.[201]

The *New York Times* said of the Fuller Company, "No other firm in the world played so large a part in revolutionizing the building trade." Fuller had the foresight to coordinate every aspect of construction by hiring a series of smaller contractors, something today taken for granted and known as general contracting.[202]

Fuller was obviously a very successful man when he hired Charles Frost to design a residence and five-car coach house on Drexel Boulevard. The mansion featured thirty rooms; the most spectacular were on the main level, including an oval dining room with wainscoting, hand-painted murals, and an Italian marble floor. The gold-plated lamps were imported, and the woodwork and mosaics were all hand-laid.[203]

John and Alice Williams purchased the property in 1945 for $39,500, an amount that clearly demonstrates the decline in stature of the once grand boulevard. Williams was an African American realtor who owned a number of properties in the Bronzeville and Oakland areas. Although conditions on Drexel Boulevard deteriorated, the house remained in excellent condition well into the 1950s when the *Chicago Daily News* ran an article about the boulevard. The residence was demolished in 1963 to make way for an elementary school.[204]

64 Smith Residence, 1893. Demolished.
4501 South Drexel Boulevard. William W. Boyington.

3.91. (Opposite) In 1897 Smith sold his residence to the colorful gambler and political boss Michael Cassius "Big Mike" McDonald and his third wife, Dora Feldman. In 1907 she was accused of murdering her teenage lover, bringing scandal to the boulevard.

The influence of H. H. Richardson is apparent in the stone house designed for Charles Head Smith. A "legendary and reckless" member of the Board of Trade for fifty years, he was a grain trader who made and lost his fortune many times over. Smith and his wife Alice commissioned William W. Boyington, one of the city's first practicing architects, to design a lavish fifteen-room turreted mansion and stable. The property, on the southeast corner of Drexel and 45th Street, was said to have been a "magnificent showplace";[205] the marble on the floor and in the main staircase was nothing short of extravagant. The house was finished in time for the 1893 Exposition, but Smith kept it for only a few years, selling the property in December 1897 for far less than the reported construction price.

Like other successful financial entrepreneurs and businessmen, Smith was heavily involved with sports. He was a regular at the Washington Park racetrack, and he operated a large racing stable at the turn of the century. His prizewinning thoroughbreds included the celebrated winner of the 1900 Kentucky Derby, "Lieutenant Gibson."[206]

65 Blair Residence, 1897. Demolished 1928.
4830 South Drexel Boulevard. Shepley, Rutan & Coolidge.

Also constructed on the boulevard was the equally fashionable residence of "blue blooded aristocrats" Chauncey and Mary Blair.[207] When influential architect Henry Hobson Richardson died in 1886, three of his employees took over the practice. Charles Coolidge moved to Chicago to oversee Shepley, Rutan & Coolidge's work in the Midwest, including this classically designed residence on Drexel Boulevard.

Constructed in the Italian Renaissance Revival style and distinguished by a Palladian arch set above the main entry, the Blair house was further defined by the two curving bays of the façade. Like so many others on the boulevard, this home was designed to represent the family's wealth; Blair's father came to the city in 1861 and made his fortune shipping midwestern grain prior to founding Merchant's National Bank of Chicago in 1865. Chauncey Blair began in the family banking business and took over as president following his father's death in 1899. Mary Blair collected medieval and Renaissance paintings and sculpture, many of which were given to the Art Institute, and she was said to have purchased the first gold dinner service in the city.[208]

3.92. An image of Chauncey Blair's mansion appeared in the *Chicago Architectural Sketch Club, Illustration Index to Annual Exhibitions.*

The family moved here from 4342 South Drexel—the new house would come to represent the continually changing fortunes of Drexel Boulevard. Blair fought long and hard to prevent the erection of an apartment building next to his home, and was successful until the time of his death. As the boulevard fell out of favor, the house, like so many others, was converted for institutional uses. After housing the offices of the United Bakeries Corporation, it was demolished in February 1928, and the following month construction began on the apartment building designed by Alvin M. Johnson that currently occupies the property.

66 Shedd Residence, 1898. Demolished.
4515 South Drexel Boulevard. Frederick Perkins with Edmund Krause.

The fanciful and massive three-story limestone mansion designed for John and Mary Shedd was one of the most flamboyant of the architectural showpieces on Drexel Boulevard. The luxurious twenty-four-room home mimicked a French chateau of the Loire valley, with medieval-inspired turrets, towers, finials, and balconies. The interior featured fourteen-foot ceilings, mahogany paneled walls, marble fireplaces, and a third-floor ballroom. It was a long, long way from the humble farm in New Hampshire where Shedd was raised.

John Graves Shedd came to Chicago and began as a clerk in the Field, Leiter & Company dry goods store after the fire. Shedd was another of the city's many rags-to-riches stories, working his way up the ladder to become president of Marshall Field & Company when Field died in 1906. He built Field's into the largest department store in the world, and like many of his peers, Shedd was not only a businessman but also a civic-minded philanthropist. He founded the Commercial Club of Chicago, dedicated to promoting the economic development of the city. Burnham's *Plan of Chicago* was commissioned and published by the club. In 1924

Shedd donated $3 million for the establishment of an aquarium, to be housed in a building designed by Graham, Anderson, Probst & White. [209]

By the fall of 1924, Drexel was no longer one of the city's premiere addresses, and the Starrett School for Girls purchased the Shedd property. In 1942 the house once again changed hands, and housed the Martha Washington Home for Dependent Children, an institution dedicated "toward the rehabilitation of crippled boys and girls." [210]

3.93. Shedd was no doubt pleased with the work of Frederick Perkins; in 1915 Perkins was commissioned to design a twenty-seven-room mansion for Shedd's daughter Laura Schweppe in north suburban Lake Forest.

3.94. Situated on a corner and facing Drexel Boulevard, the Born house appeared in a 1904 issue of the *Inland Architect and News Record.*

67 Born Residence, 1901.
4801 South Drexel Boulevard. Frost & Granger.

Frost & Granger continued their use of smooth-faced limestone for the 12,000-square-foot residence of Moses and Isabella Born. Born was a wholesale tailor and opened a retail store on State Street, originating "tailoring the trade."[211] After making a fortune as president of one of the country's largest wholesale clothing businesses, he became a philanthropist. Born's name was one of eight that adorned the 1905 cornerstone of Michael Reese Hospital. The hospital building, designed by Schmidt, Garden & Martin, was to replace a hospital created by the United Hebrew Relief Association destroyed in the Great Chicago Fire. Born helped to raise funds to create a hospital that was to be "free of the kind of prejudice that remained prevalent in other Chicago institutions, serving patients regardless of their race or religion."[212] The structure has been demolished.

68 Mandel Residence, 1902. Demolished c. 1970.
4925 South Drexel Boulevard. Frost & Granger.

The limestone-clad coach house is all that remains of the large Romanesque Revival mansion designed for Simon and Pauline Mandel. Mandel was one of three brothers who opened a dry goods shop in partnership with their uncle. Klein & Mandel operated until the Great Chicago Fire consumed the store. In 1877 Marshall Field convinced them that State Street would become a significant central shopping district, and they opened the Mandel Brothers store, which operated

Mandel Coach House, 1902.
4935 South Drexel Boulevard.
Frost & Granger.

3.96

until 1958.[213] In 1884 they considerably expanded their facilities and made many improvements, including elevators, "handsomely finished furniture and fixtures and one thousand of the Edison electric lights" to make it one of the finest dry goods stores in the city.[214]

4.01. The contrast to the city's congestion is what made Hyde Park such an appealing place in which to live; however, the neighborhood was not immune to the pressures of increased urbanization. Pictured here are the streetcar tracks, telephone lines, and alcohol-serving establishments on Lake Avenue as the street appeared north from 55th Street in 1909.

CHAPTER FOUR

The Urban Fabric, 1909–1919

As he passed down the suburban avenue, now properly paved and quite well filled with detached houses, Clavercin recognized the more settled aspect that a few swift years had brought to this slice of prairie wilderness. In these comfortable, roomy brick houses, with little strips of lawn in front, little yard behind, that peculiar institution so often discussed as the "American home" was developing luxuriantly. Not merely for the few prospective members of the faculty who could afford to live in their own houses, but for professional and business men whose families like the "advantages" and "refinements" of a university neighborhood, as the real estate agents put it. Indeed the latter outnumbered the former and were rapidly filling the empty squares.

—Robert Herrick, *Chimes*

In the years leading up to the outbreak of the First World War, the city of Chicago was in its heyday. As the center of the nation's railroad transportation network and the undeniable meatpacking capital of the world, the city continued to attract newcomers, who flocked to take advantage of the opportunities it offered. The population of Chicago exploded, from 4,000 in 1837 to over 2,000,000 inhabitants after the turn to the twentieth century.[1] The result of this astounding growth, according to Carl Smith, was that the city was "literally choking on its own success." Crucial to the city's economy, the Chicago River had become a "disgraceful cesspool," and the noise level of the surface and elevated train lines was "excruciating."[2] Bridges were insufficient, streets not wide enough, the air quality was miserable and congestion abounded.

The thinking among many powerful Chicagoans was that if the city failed to address these problems, it would be difficult to attract new commerce and existing businesses would move elsewhere.[3] Daniel Burnham, having completed the planning for the Columbian Exposition and a 1901 plan for the nation's Capitol, was commissioned to work with Edward H. Bennett on a master plan for the city. The plan had roots that stretched back to 1895, when Burnham was asked to explore the feasibility of a lakeshore parkway connecting Jackson Park with Lake Park on the shoreline downtown. Burnham published a paper on the topic, and in 1896 the City

Council passed an ordinance that called for a massive landfill project and entrusted the lakefront improvements south of Monroe Street to the South Parks Commission.

Many of Burnham's early ideas were worked into a master plan that was backed by the Commercial Club, whose membership included many of the wealthiest and most powerful men of the city, including many from the neighborhood: Enos Barton, John Shedd, J. J. Dau, John J. Mitchell, H. G. Selfridge, Edwin A. Potter, Homer Stilwell, Bernard Sunny, Edwin A. Turner, and architects Allen Pond and James Gamble Rogers.[4] *The Plan of Chicago* was published in 1909 after thirty months of work. Burnham and Bennett's lavishly presented plan reflected a city with classically designed buildings of uniform height, clearly reminiscent of Burnham's vision for the White City. Anchored by magnificent parkland on the lakefront, the plan projected order as opposed to the chaos created by the city's rapid growth. Highways were envisioned in semicircles radiating from the city center; rapid transit was to be improved; railway terminals were to be relocated at the edge of the business district; and streets were to be widened and supplemented with diagonal avenues to improve transit to and from the downtown area. The development of "centers of intellectual life and of civic administration" would provide consistency and unity. In short, the plan idealized how Chicago could become a visually coherent city, while providing for the "health, prosperity and happiness to all those fortunate enough to dwell there."[5]

Fifty years separated Paul Cornell and Daniel Burnham's plan, yet the two men shared a belief that a solid community was a good foundation for business. Initially Cornell's suburb was conceived as a respite from the very ills *The Plan of Chicago* sought to address; however, the complex issues of urban living had arrived on the community's doorstep. In the now residentially mature neighborhood, the University of Chicago became an increasingly important force within the community. By investing in its campus and continually encouraging faculty and staff to live nearby, the university provided a level of stability. In contrast, improvements in transportation increased the number of transit options to and from the crowded city center, allowing a broader range of Chicagoans to consider the area as a potential home.

The area of the community north of 47th Street was thought of as Kenwood; however, its character changed at a rapid pace when the elevated line from the downtown business district was extended to 42nd Street in 1910, providing an inexpensive, efficient commute that not only appealed to workers employed in the Loop, but also enabled those who worked near the stockyards to consider residing in the area.[6] The demand for housing by both blue- and white-collar workers resulted in the conversion of older structures to rooming houses, and the construction of numerous walk-up apartment buildings accelerated.

Over time, this middle-class neighborhood became increasingly linked with the lower-income Oakland (Cleaverville) community to the north, separated from the more affluent sections by the commercialism of 47th Street. Once lined with gracious houses belonging to the city's civic and business leaders, the street evolved into a bustling thoroughfare. Featuring shops, theaters, and apartments, the commercial district stretched from Cottage Grove east to Lake Park Avenue, bisecting the once tight-knit community.

South of the thriving commercial street, Kenwood retained much of its original suburban character; however, demolition of the large homes of the community's earliest years became a common occurrence. Land became available as the population aged and heirs could not manage or maintain the large estates. Properties were often subdivided into increasingly smaller parcels to meet the demand for more modern houses, or were redeveloped for the now popular form of apartment living. Flats and apartment buildings, cost-effective ways of housing a multiple number of families, appeared on the periphery of the Kenwood neighborhood.

In 1917, construction began on the Cooper-Monotah Apartment Hotel at Drexel Boulevard and 47th Street. Typical of redevelopment sites, the large apartment hotel with suites containing 236 bedrooms and 134 baths rose on land once occupied by single houses. A two-story house constructed by Col. George R. Clarke, one of the first appear on the elegant boulevard, was demolished to provide the land for the seven-story hotel. "One of the landmarks of Kenwood," observed the *Tribune*, "has been wrecked in order to provide space for a new fireproof hotel which is to be built on the same site." At the same time, work began on a garage necessitated by the introduction of the newly introduced automobile. Described as one of the largest in the city, the structure swallowed up the eastern section of the grounds.[7]

A new architectural form was introduced to accommodate the "horseless carriage" after Ford's affordable, reliable, and popular Model T was introduced in

4.02. Grand residences with large lawns lined 47th Street at the time it was photographed for *Picturesque Kenwood*, prior to the introduction of the controversial streetcar.

4.03. This 1922 *Chicago Daily News* photograph demonstrates the sweeping change that occurred during this period as commercial enterprises replaced the older residential structures on the street. Viewed east from Cottage Grove Avenue, the new streetscape divided the Kenwood community into two distinct districts.

1908. For years the residents of Kenwood opposed the development of their local streets, preferring a bad road to the new automobile.[8] "If the street is paved automobiles will use it. Milk wagons will awaken the inhabitants as early as 6 o'clock in the morning. Why not pave Lake Park instead?" questioned residents. "It needs it." In spite of opposition, the streets were paved; the automobile changed traditional transportation patterns and ushered in the now ubiquitous garage.

The construction of the Cooper-Monotah reflected a change in land usage, increasing population density, a decreasing percentage of owner-occupied housing, and the ebbing affluence of Drexel Boulevard. One of many broad avenues constructed during the second half of the nineteenth century, Drexel had for years been a showpiece of the area's prospering society. However, with construction of the last of these grand estates came concerns about the changing character of the aristocratic neighborhood.

A decline in property values on Drexel Boulevard was demonstrated by a 1915 real estate transaction. Undeveloped lots that sold for $325 a foot in 1909 had fallen to a little over $255 a foot when Chauncey Blair purchased property adjacent to his stately three-story residence.[9] His intention was to prevent the construction of an apartment building on the corner next to his elegant residence, which had been designed by the distinguished firm of Shepley Rutan & Coolidge in 1897. After Blair died in 1916, a large, albeit luxurious, six-unit apartment building rose next door to his home.[10]

The ease of commuting to and from the area, the dawn of the automobile age, the high-density apartment construction, and resulting decrease in land values combined to make a Kenwood address less exclusive. The 1914 real estate transaction by Marshall Field signaled the end to an elegant, genteel way of city life. "The vacant block surrounded by Drexel Boulevard, Ellis Avenue, 47th and 48th Streets, the only large vacant tract along the Boulevard and which for twenty years has been the home of the tennis courts of the Kenwood Country Club has been sold by the estate of Marshall Field and will be improved with high-grade apartments."[11]

Nonetheless, the large, well-designed residences south of 47th Street remained highly desirable, and an unusually active demand for these high-end properties was reported. Property values ranged from the 1918 sale of 4816 South Kenwood for $18,000 to $40,000 for the larger twelve-room four-bath house at 4925 South Woodlawn the following year.[12] The increased demand may have been the result of the decline in high land values as the once exclusive residential district evolved. For example, when the John J. Mitchell estate at 50th and Woodlawn was sold, the transaction was for less than $80,000, a significant loss. Designed by Minard Beers, the twenty-two-room residence and the land on which it had been erected twenty-five years earlier had cost about $265,000.[13] Flat buildings replaced the Mitchell's house.

As the Kenwood neighborhood evolved, there continued to be considerable investment in new residential construction. As they had in earlier years, business leaders employed exceptional and innovative firms, engaging Howard van Doren Shaw, Max Dunning, Frost & Granger, Pond & Pond, and other distinguished architects. For the most part, older frame houses were demolished to supply the land needed for the stone and brick mansions of the privileged, as they attempted to dictate and maintain a style of life that would soon disappear from the city proper. Although constructed in 1915, the residence of philanthropist Max Adler reflected the nineteenth-century ideal that home was a sanctuary from the outside world for one's family, since "only men were strong enough to survive daily contact with the dirty world of commerce and industry."[14]

The size and scope of Adler's Kenwood was consistent with those built during the height of the neighborhood's exclusivity—large and well set back from the street with ample room for coach houses, tennis courts, or garages. Maintaining a residence of this size was no easy endeavor, and as in the past, required the help of live-in servants. For those unwilling or unable to support large households, the apartment became a way of life, bringing convenience into everyday living.

Hyde Park had received its first taste of urban redevelopment in the years leading up to the world's fair of 1893. As three-flats, six-flats, and courtyard buildings rose across Hyde Park, they no longer represented a loss of status and privacy, and became acceptable, and even luxurious places in which to live. Residents gravitated toward the freedom the apartment represented, and the desire for ease and affordability that came with apartment living was evident in the number of flats that quickly sprang up. Although a fair number were cheaply constructed, many were elegantly designed as architects continually refined solutions to the inherent problems of multifamily design, including privacy, noise, ventilation, fireproofing, and lot usage.

Permits for apartment construction were issued in abundance prior to the First World War, and as a result these buildings quickly changed the character of entire blocks in Hyde Park. Speculative builders were often criticized, for it was sometimes assumed their only concerns were how quickly and profitably a particular project could be completed. Large multifamily buildings were constructed in the

Apartment Building, 1913. 851–855 Drexel Square. Western Engineering Company.

4.04. Situated on a corner lot and facing onto Drexel Square and the oldest public fountain in the city, this ornate apartment building is just another of the many constructed prior to the outbreak of the First World War. The elegant red brick structure is more elaborately detailed than most, with Sullivan-inspired terra-cotta embellishments on the north and east façades. Terra-cotta became widely used as a cost effective, relatively maintenance-free material that mimicked stone.

midst of single-family houses, altering the suburban appearance of the street and, more importantly, the density of the neighborhood. The popularity of the apartment confirmed another major shift in the community, for as density was increasing, the movement away from owner-occupied dwellings accelerated.

Construction of single-family houses in the more densely populated areas of the neighborhood became unprofitable. When the increasing land values resulted in the construction of yet another apartment building, the newspapers lamented "the loss of another of Hyde Park's pretty residential spots on the west side of Kenwood Avenue between 52nd and 53rd Streets. Three attractive frame dwellings are now on this property, which, combined with the handsome trees, the curving street

4.05. Evidence of Hyde Park's
transformation during the early
years of the last century can
be found on many streets. The
house designed by Treat & Foltz
for Charles S. and Ann Dennis
represents the transition from
a suburban retreat to a densely
occupied urban neighborhood.
Land was at a premium and
apartments were constructed in
place of single-family houses, of
which very few remain in many
areas of Hyde Park.

and its generally attractive character have set this particular spot apart from the conventional character of the streets in this part of the city."[15]

It was evident that the era of Hyde Park as a suburban retreat was over—a wide range of apartment buildings filled block after block, resulting in a dense urban landscape and residents who had little financial investment in the community. In 1889 there were 4,000 dwelling units in the area; between 1900 and 1920 another 6,000 were constructed.[16] Meanwhile in sections of Hyde Park blocks of single-family houses completely disappeared, replaced by a wall of apartments constructed to meet the burgeoning demand for housing. Nowhere is this more evident today than on Woodlawn or Drexel south of 53rd Street, where the three-flats, six-flats, and courtyard apartment buildings completely transformed the streetscape.

However, the design of the new buildings display a uniformity of character, which is not surprising given the brief time frame in which they were constructed. The majority are three-and-a-half stories tall and of brick construction with limestone trim. Floor plans and structures were formulaic, and the apartment became a successful enterprise for owner and renter alike. On any given block, the streetscape has been described as a "dense urbanization composed of different, but not disparate elements."[17]

The center of Hyde Park, a middle and working-class neighborhood with row houses, apartments and flats, and small cottages, was even more densely populated than the surrounding area.[18] As a result, the nearby commercial areas on 53rd and 55th Streets accelerated their growth to meet the burgeoning demand and reflected a mixed-use pattern of walk-up apartments and a variety of commercial spaces. The streets were vibrant, enhanced by new forms of leisure entertainment—vaudeville and the silent motion picture. Theaters, often built in combi-

4.06. An image of the north side of the commercial district on 53rd Street at Lake Street, photographed from the embankment of the Illinois Central tracks in 1915.

nation with apartments and retail space, rose in each of the commercial districts. The Kenwood appeared on 47th Street, the Frolic at 55th and Ellis Avenue, and the Hyde Park on 53rd Street.

While the grand hotels built during the Columbian Exposition, including the Hyde Park and the Chicago Beach, continued to operate, a remarkable number of large hotel projects were announced. In East Hyde Park, as the area between the Illinois Central tracks and the lakeshore came to be known, there were several early additions to an area that changed considerably in the ensuing years. Noted theater designers C. W. and George Rapp planned the Jackson Shore Apartments at 5490 South Shore Drive. The twelve-story structure contained twenty apartments facing east and was then just yards away from the lakeshore.

In addition to the Cooper-Monotah on Drexel Boulevard, Henry Newhouse and Felix Bernham designed the mammoth Cooper-Carleton Hotel, an apartment hotel now known as the Del Prado, on the site of Paul Cornell's first hotel, the Hyde Park House. Originally described in a marketing publication as "the finest residential and transient hotel in the Middle West," the structure contained an astonishing four hundred guest rooms. For the design of these large structures, architects used elements and materials commonly associated with the single-family residence. Constructed of brick with terra-cotta or limestone ornamentation, the new larger structures attempted to take their place in the neighborhood despite their size.

The University of Chicago continued to expand the campus with traditional, Gothic-inspired structures. As the campus grew to play a larger role in community affairs and the South Side began to change, it brought a larger level of stability to the neighborhood. The university surrounded itself not only with members of the faculty who were encouraged to live nearby, but also with businessmen who constructed residences on nearby streets. University professor and novelist Robert Herrick wrote of the community in his fictionalized account of university life, *Chimes.* He noted the broad, paved avenues and the "comfortable, roomy brick houses" with squares of lawn in front and a yard behind. The "American home" was developing splendidly not only for the members of the faculty, but also for businessmen who appreciated the "advantages" and "refinements" of a university community.

The movement that began at the turn of the century seeking a fresh and original architectural expression reached its pinnacle at the outset of this time period. Frank Lloyd Wright's ground-hugging masterpiece for Frederick Robie rose just blocks from the university. While influential, Wright's Prairie Style was relatively short-lived and never achieved the widespread popularity of period revival styles. As the First World War broke out, the public became more concerned with traditional symbols of affluence than the unique philosophy associated with the Prairie Style. Consequently the houses they chose to build tended more and more to be colonial revival or Tudor-style manses.

These classically styled residences near the university created a buffer between the institution and the surrounding city. The university's relationship with the neighborhood was based on control, not collaboration, and as the institution sought to increase the size of the campus, its land purchases were often hidden. This practice became increasingly common during campus expansion toward the south and west, when the university acquired a number of apartment buildings on Drexel and Ellis between 56th and 59th Streets. For example, in a transaction for the acquisition of property on University Avenue, title was placed under the name of architect Allen Pond.[19] The university gradually became the central player in shaping decisions of land use, and these secretive arrangements played a continual role in the community's development. The process served to insulate the university, but kept the area stable by carefully delineating the boundaries of the campus.

Between 1909 and 1919, the city's demographics began to change dramatically as the great migration from the Deep South was underway. The poor fled to the promise of jobs in the industrialized North, and Chicago was the destination for nearly 50,000 black Southerners who arrived between 1916 and 1920. The masses that fled the cotton farms of the South were lured by the promise of high wages in packinghouses and railroad yards, and the sudden influx on the city's South Side influenced the stability of the neighborhood.

A struggle for living space ensued as poor blacks poured into the Near South Side, into a cramped area of "aging, dilapidated housing" that eventually stretched south from 12th Street over thirty blocks along State Street.[20] Known as the "Black Belt," the sliver of the city had already absorbed over 10,000 migrants and by 1914 the saturation point of their community had been reached. With the further influx of migrants, the black community began a gradual expansion southward. In the years prior to the war, conditions in the communities adjoining Kenwood and Hyde Park favored accommodating the overflow from the Black Belt. These areas became less aristocratic, as white homeowners left large houses for the newly constructed apartment buildings, either selling or renting their properties at attractive rates. At this time, the expansion was met with little opposition, demonstrated by a survey that showed of the 3,300 property owners in the district (which included Grand Boulevard), nearly one-third were black.[21]

However, as the war began, building construction ceased, leading to fears about where and how the black population would expand. White residents moved southward into Hyde Park as the black population expanded into the area along Grand Boulevard, and the university became increasingly concerned over the scarcity of housing. Racial hostility increased due to the lack of jobs and good housing when soldiers returned from Europe. African American soldiers came back "expecting to enjoy the full rights of citizenship that they fought to defend overseas,"[22] yet were forced to return to the segregated confines of the Black Belt. There, the overcrowded spaces brought a huge demand for housing, resulting in rents that skyrocketed. Realtors, black and white, realized there were huge profits to be made by those able to provide the much-needed housing.

At its northwestern limit, the Hyde Park-Kenwood community was not separated by any geographical boundaries, and African Americans began to move into the neighborhood in greater numbers. When the last of the white tenants of a building at 545 East 44th Place moved out in 1917, a sign appeared stating that the apartments were available for blacks to rent. "A sprinkling of Negro families had moved into the neighborhood in the past few years," the *Tribune* stated, "but it is only within the past few years that the blacks have been moving into the neighborhood in numbers." A bank informed one property owner attempting to borrow money on his home that it was "not good business" to lend in the Black Belt. The incident was reported, and a "property owners' association" was formed.[23]

Property associations became a way to combat the "infiltration" of a neighborhood by outsiders, particularly blacks. The university increasingly supported these groups, which often began as neighborhood improvement associations. When Hyde Park attorney Frances Harper founded the Hyde Park Improvement Protective Club in 1909, its purpose was not to keep the neighborhood clean, but to "maintain the color line."[24] For the university, these independent property owners associations offered dual benefits, holding the value of real estate near the campus and protecting its borders from "undesirable" elements.

Some associations were notorious, including the Hyde Park–Kenwood Property Owners' Association, as plans were discussed to reestablish an exclusively white neighborhood. Fears of "the alleged depreciation of property by Negroes"[25] fueled this heightening interest in race. By promoting a foreseeable decline in property values through meetings and literature, such groups further stoked racial antagonisms. The *Property Owners Journal*, published by the Hyde Park–Kenwood Property Owners Association with the intention of stopping the influx, promoted the idea with remarkably hostile overtones: "Every colored man who moves into Hyde Park knows that he is damaging his white neighbors' property. Therefore, he is making war on the white man."[26]

While neighborhood groups argued that blacks had to be kept out to prevent "almost certain destruction,"[27] some resorted to violence to achieve their goals. Bombing of black properties occurred throughout the South Side; however, tensions were at their height during the summer of 1919, a watershed year in the history of race relations in America.[28] Brutal race riots erupted in cities and towns across the country. Chicago experienced the most severe of these, when the city was devastated by a series of riots following the death of a young black boy who

4.07. For an all too brief time, the Hyde Park community enjoyed the pleasures of Wright's architectural fantasy and his largest public building in the city, the Midway Gardens. On the south side of the Midway Plaisance guests dined, drank, and danced while surrounded by dazzling architecture, brightly colored murals, and sculpture. When the war erupted, attendance declined and the property was sold to the Edelweiss Brewing Company for use as a beer garden.

ventured into the waters of a "white" beach, north of the Hyde Park community at 31st Street, on a hot July afternoon. Five days of intense racial violence followed, and in the aftermath thirty-eight people lay dead.[29] Young Eugene Williams inadvertently challenged the Chicago's defined racial boundaries, contributing to the city's "rising entrenchment of segregation."[30]

Amid the social problems neighborhood residents were politically active, seeking an honest and efficient government. Despite a gerrymander of the city's ward boundaries in 1911, Hyde Park remained Republican—its wards were the only ones in Chicago where a Democratic candidate lost every major election.[31] Witnessing the excess of some Republicans, including "Bathhouse" John Coughlin and Michael "Hinky Dink" McKenna, Hyde Park's progressive residents explored other options. However, their hopes for reform were dashed by the reelection of Mayor William Hale "Big Bill" Thompson in 1919.[32] Hyde Park's favored Republican candidate was influential University of Chicago political science professor Charles Merriam. His work as alderman earned him a "solid reputation in both Chicago and national political circles for his efforts to root out corruption."[33] Merriam ran on a platform of good government, but lost in the Republican primary.[34]

While Chicago's racial violence escalated and its penchant for cutthroat, give-and-take politics thrived, Hyde Park and Kenwood remained highly desirable places to live. Theaters and entertainment venues grew to include the Midway Gardens, a premiere center for music and fine dining designed by Frank Lloyd Wright. The university provided stability, while the growth of the transit system, the proximity of the lakeshore, and the protective natural barriers of Washington and Jackson Parks, combined to enhance a community that seemed prepared to flourish as the twenties came roaring in.

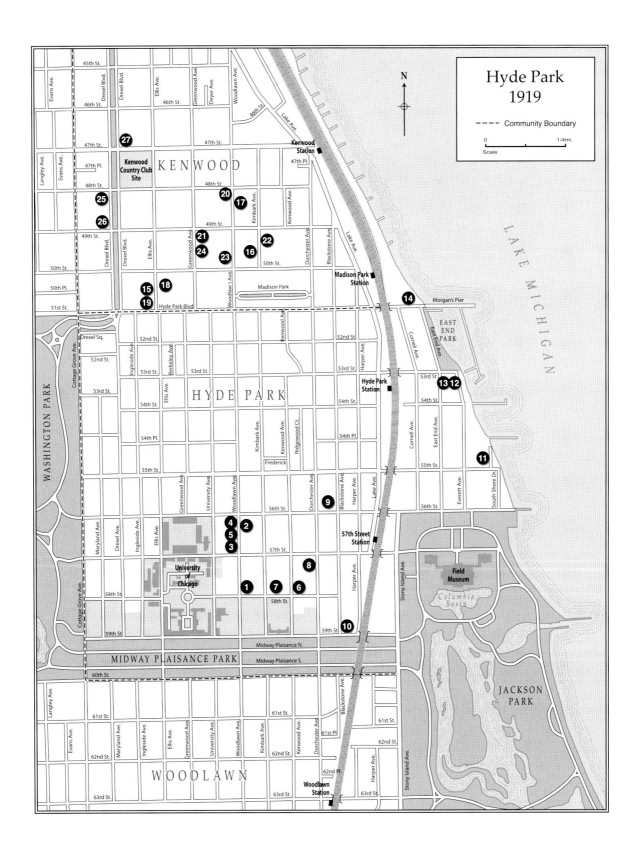

Hyde Park
1919

- - - - Community Boundary

Scale: 0 — 1/4mi.

N

LAKE MICHIGAN

KENWOOD

Kenwood
Station

Kenwood Country Club Site

27

25

26

20

17

21

24

23

16

22

15

18

19

Hyde Park Blvd.

Madison Park

Madison Park Station

14

EAST END PARK

Morgan's Pier

HYDE PARK

WASHINGTON PARK

Hyde Park Station

13 12

11

9

4 2

5

3

8

University of Chicago

1

7

6

57th Street Station

10

Field Museum

Columbia Basin

MIDWAY PLAISANCE PARK

Midway Plaisance N.

Midway Plaisance S.

JACKSON PARK

WOODLAWN

Woodlawn Station

Hyde Park

1 ## Robie House, 1909.
5757 South Woodlawn Avenue. Frank Lloyd Wright.

Nestled on a corner lot adjacent to the university campus is a pivotal work of twentieth-century architecture, created for Frederick and Lora Robie. With gently sloping rooflines, low, ground-hugging proportions, strong horizontal lines, and open interiors, Frank Lloyd Wright's buildings came to define a new aesthetic. Wright was the most famous of the Prairie School architects, and his work reached its pinnacle with the design of this house, which he later declared to be his finest.

Only thirty years old at the time the house was built, Frederick Robie was an executive of his father's company, Excelsior Supply, a firm that manufactured bicycles. Robie brought new ideas to incorporate into Wright's plans, desiring rooms that flowed uninterrupted from one to the next, an abundance of daylight and views of the surrounding open land, without compromising privacy. The strong horizontal lines of the structure, the dramatic cantilevered overhangs, and the open floor plan are elements that sharply challenged the verticality and boxlike organization of period styles.

The backbone of the 9,000-square-foot house was formed of steel beams over a hundred feet long. The use of steel was by then taken well beyond the earlier use in residences, as in Dwight Perkins's design for Robert Vierling. Instead of using steel as an armature within the structure, Wright used the material to create striking cantilevers. For the interior Wright's use of art glass windows and doors was

4.08. Wright's rejection of classicism and the towers and turrets of Victorian styles culminated in his design of the Robie House, an enduring hallmark of the Prairie Style. Ignoring European influences, Wright succeeded in developing a uniquely American style focused on strong horizontality and an emphasis on open and free-flowing interior spaces inspired by the surrounding prairie.

4.09. The 147 art glass panels in the Robie House are of varying designs that combine angular forms with shafts of grain. Made of clear and colored glass, the windows allow a profusion of light into the south-facing rooms, while provided privacy at the same time.

intended to "blur the line between exterior and interior spaces."[35] Wright included built-in cabinets and Prairie-style furnishings for the family, and once stated, "It is quite impossible to consider the building one thing and its furnishings another, its setting and environment still another."[36]

Wright's innovative design was completed just as the affordable automobile was introduced to the public. Although most famous for its large horizontal eaves, the residence was the first in the neighborhood to feature an attached garage, despite fears of housing gas and oil in proximity to the living quarters. The original design

featured a turntable for the car, as automobiles of the time had only a forward, not reverse, gear. However the greatest effect of the garage was on the traditional organization of the single-family house. The logical progression of entering through the front door, proceeding through the hallway flanked by the parlors, with the kitchen at the rear was completely reorganized. Over time, the automobile and the garage made certain that the side door would become of equal importance to the ceremonial front entry, if not greater.[37]

Wright was not present to supervise the construction of the Robie house; he left his family and departed for Europe with Mamah Cheney, the wife of a client, where they remained for several years. The scandal played out in public until her gruesome death at the hands of a deranged employee on the grounds of Taliesin, the Wisconsin residence Wright constructed for them after their return from Berlin.

While highly influential, Wright's Prairie Style was relatively short-lived and never achieved the widespread popularity of period revival styles. Yet the power of his work was profound, particularly in his flexible approach to the treatment of interior space. Swiss art historian Sigfried Giedion wrote of Wright's design bringing "life, movement, freedom into the whole rigid and benumbed body of modern architecture."[38]

4.10. This view of the dining room demonstrates the expansiveness of open space desired by Robie, uncommon in residences of the time. Wright designed a number of pieces for the house—considering the exterior and interior as one, he was able to provide a harmonious aesthetic scheme. He incorporated lighting (also with the stylized wheat motif) and greenery in the formal, handcrafted dining room table. The high-backed chairs provided intimacy at the dinner table, in effect creating a room within a room. The University of Chicago's Smart Museum of Art houses several pieces of the furniture Wright designed specifically for the Robie family, including the restored dining room table.

② Sippy Residence, 1909.
5615 South Woodlawn Avenue. Howard van Doren Shaw.

Although conceived at the same time and situated just up the street from the Robie house, Shaw's design for Bertram Welton Sippy is in complete contrast to Wright's Prairie Style.

This traditional house is built of brick in the Flemish bond pattern, and the joints have been raked to provide texture on the symmetrical façade. Shaw used his favored elements for decoration in the limestone details of the Gothic-inspired entry: fruits and birds. The corner details are decorative, yet also serve to keep everything in its place. Chicago's hot summers and frigid winters play havoc with brick, as it expands and contracts in response to the changing temperature.

Sippy, a doctor and professor of medicine at Rush Medical College, was well known for his work on digestive diseases and built a large fortune through his treatment of ulcers with medicines and diet instead of surgery. He provided "Sippy Powders" along with a bland diet during the day, while his powder was to be given during the evening. This complex dietary regimen was said to have been a "challenge for both the patient and nursing staff."[39]

③ Hilton Residence, 1911.
5638 South Woodlawn Avenue. Howard van Doren Shaw.

Shaw designed this symmetrical Federal-style house for Henry Hoyt Hilton and his wife Charlotte. A graduate of Dartmouth, Hilton came to Chicago in 1890 with the publishing firm of Ginn & Company. Shaw most likely received this commission because he also designed the firm's building in Chicago.[40]

The Hiltons donated the nearby quaint chapel at the Chicago Theological Semi-

nary, 1150 East 58th Street, in the memory of their son, Thorndike Hilton. Architect Herbert Riddle, who also lived on Woodlawn, designed the main buildings of the seminary and the small chapel, dedicated in 1926, featuring stained glass windows modeled on those of Chartres Cathedral.[41] The University of Chicago purchased the complex, which was gutted to house the Milton Friedman Institute. The stained glass windows of this peaceful sanctuary were removed and preserved in other locations.

4 Lewis Riddle Residence, 1911. 5622 South Woodlawn Avenue, Riddle & Riddle.

4.13. Residents on Woodlawn Avenue have felt the increasing presence of the university on the street. The two Riddle-designed houses remain privately owned single-family homes.

5 Herbert Riddle Residence, 1911.
5626 South Woodlawn Avenue. Riddle & Riddle.

Across the street from the Sippy house, architects Lewis and Herbert Riddle designed these two residences for their families. Lewis, his wife Elizabeth, and their three children resided in the three-story Georgian home at 5622 Woodlawn. After the family moved from the neighborhood in 1941, a string of prominent Chicago-

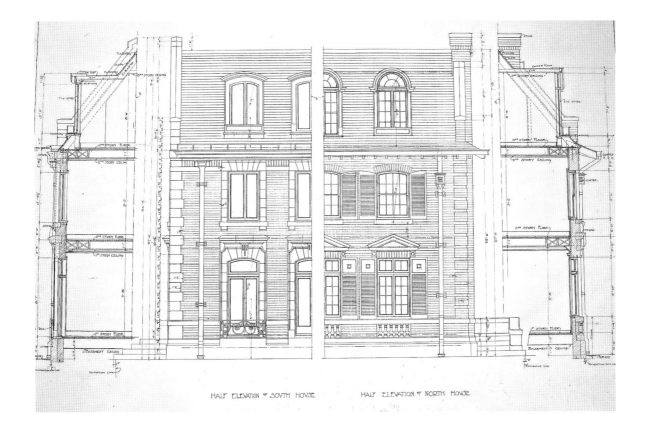

HALF ELEVATION OF SOUTH HOUSE   HALF ELEVATION OF NORTH HOUSE

4.14. The Riddles' drawings included half elevations of both structures, clearly delineating the similarities and differences in the two façades.

ans called this home, including Julian Levi, the executive director of the South East Chicago Commission, who planned and implemented Hyde Park's massive urban renewal project.[42]

Herbert, his mother, and his sister lived just to the south, in a residence with a distinctly French elegance—the entrance ornamentation mimics the metal and glass canopy of the Paris Métro station design of Hector Guimard.[43] While the two structures are detailed differently, they have similar massing and side entrances, hooded dormers, classically proportioned elongated windows, slate roofs, and a common central element labeled "batten door" on the plans. The house to the north is the more masculine of the two compositions, while the one to the south exhibits graceful arched windows and Art Nouveau–inspired iron railings. The Riddle brothers experimented with the interior layout, placing the living room far from its traditional location facing the street, to face onto the expansive rear yard.

⑥ Mosheim Craig Apartments, 1912.
5749–5759 South Kenwood Avenue. Schmidt, Garden & Martin.

4.15. (Opposite) Mosheim Craig, listed as an artist living at 5535 Cornell in the 1910 city directory, commissioned the architects to design the brick and stone building on a 122' · 127' lot.

Although known primarily for their commercial and institutional designs, Schmidt, Garden & Martin designed several residential structures near the university. This four-story sunlit apartment building is set at an angle at the corner of Kenwood and 58th Street and is distinguished by semicircular rooms and traditional detailing. The placement in relation to the street permits an abundance of light and air to enter the apartments and creates a welcome and rare open urban space.

7 **Angell Residence, 1913.**
1314 East 58th Street. Schmidt, Garden & Martin.

Facing south toward Scammon Garden of the Laboratory Schools, this traditional red brick residence was designed for James Rowland Angell, an educator and psychologist who joined the university faculty in 1894. In 1911 Angell became the dean of the faculties and served as acting president in 1918–1919.[44] Although dedicated to the university, Angell was "distressed" that "salaries were small, the costs of living high."[45] As a result he left Chicago in 1920, accepting a position as the president of Carnegie Foundation and then in 1924, he became president of Yale University.

The house was later the residence of Ernest J. Stevens, a hotelier and director of the Illinois Life Insurance Company. Its occupants made history well into the current century. Stevens's youngest son John Paul was seven years old when the Stevens Hotel on Michigan Avenue (now the Chicago Hilton and Towers) opened in 1927. No one had constructed a hotel on this scale before; it was a destination for businessmen and travelers with 3,000 guest rooms, and the largest hotel in the world. It was also "possibly the most opulent"; there were sweeping staircases, elegant restaurants, exclusive shops, and vast ballrooms all decorated with marble and hand-painted frescoes.[46]

It was expensive to build, and costly to operate. Stevens was hard-hit by the Depression, and the family loaned him money, but not nearly enough to save the

hotel. Stevens and his brother Raymond turned to Illinois Life for funds to keep the property afloat. When Illinois Life failed, Stevens was arrested and charged with conspiracy to defraud the insurance company.[47] The newspapers reported that the evening Stevens was arrested, his three children were sent to bed early so that they would not see their father taken away.

Things went from bad to worse for the family. In February 1933 four armed men invaded the house, demanding millions that were supposedly hidden within its walls.[48] Threatened with kidnapping if he reported the robbery to the police, Stevens temporarily moved the family from 58th Street to protect them. In March, Stevens's despondent brother committed suicide over the financial troubles.[49] Then on October 14, 1933, after five hours of deliberation, a jury found Ernest Stevens guilty of embezzlement.[50] Stevens lost the businesses and his fortune was wiped out, but ultimately he did salvage his name. In 1934 the Illinois Supreme Court unanimously ruled that he had been wrongly convicted.

Stevens's son John Paul was appointed a justice of the Supreme Court of the United States in 1975. In 2000 Justice Stevens wrote a scathing dissent on the court's ruling to abandon the recount of votes in Florida during the disputed presidential election between George Bush and Albert Gore. He believed the court to be profoundly mistaken in its judgment, writing "Time will one day heal the wound to the confidence that will be inflicted by today's decision. One thing; however, is certain. Although we may never know with complete certainty the identity of the winner of this year's presidential election, the identity of the loser is perfectly clear. It is the Nation's confidence in the judge as an impartial guardian of the rule of law."[51]

8 Newman, Marsh & Baskerville Flat, 1913.
5712 South Dorchester Avenue. Purcell, Feick & Elmslie.

The only structure in the area by architects William Purcell, George Feick, and George Elmslie is an apartment building located near the university campus. Over the course of their partnership, the firm became one of the most commissioned among the Prairie School architects, second only to Frank Lloyd Wright. While several of the firm's houses were influential, the architects "lacked the single-mindedness that fame seems to require." Ultimately, "their success never met their promise."[52]

George Elmslie joined Purcell and Feick in Minneapolis where the firm was headquartered, and moved to Hyde Park to open an office on 53rd Street in 1913. That year, as the partnership's work had reached its peak in creative and commercial success, three University of Chicago professors commissioned Elmslie to design this

4.17. The large windows of the Newman, Marsh & Baskerville Flat have been replaced with double-hung windows, in contrast to the intended simplicity of the façade evident on the ground floor.

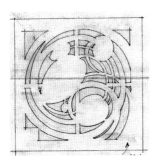

4.18. George Elmslie wrote to his partners in 1912, addressing them as "Citizens" and advising of a possible commission.

4.19. The influence of Louis Sullivan is clearly evident in Elmslie's drawing of a sawed detail for the sideboard.

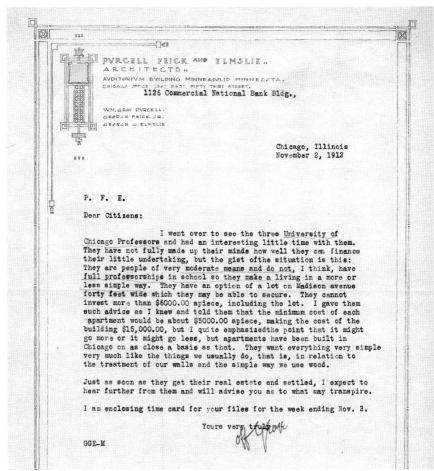

PVRCELL FEICK AND ELMSLIE..
ARCHITECTS..
AVDITORIVM BVILDING MINNEAPOLIS MINNESOTA.
CHICAGO OFFICE 1367 EAST FIFTY THIRD STREET.
1126 Commercial National Bank Bldg.,

WM. GRAY PVRCELL.
GEORGE FEICK JR.
GEORGE G. ELMSLIE

Chicago, Illinois
November 2, 1912

P. F. E.

Dear Citizens:

        I went over to see the three University of Chicago Professors and had an interesting little time with them. They have not fully made up their minds how well they can finance their little undertaking, but the gist of the situation is this: They are people of very moderate means and do not, I think, have full professorships in school so they make a living in a more or less simple way. They have an option of a lot on Madison avenue forty feet wide which they may be able to secure. They cannot invest more than $6000.00 apiece, including the lot. I gave them such advice as I knew and told them that the minimum cost of each apartment would be about $5000.00 apiece, making the cost of the building $15,000.00, but I quite emphasized the point that it might go more or it might go less, but apartments have been built in Chicago on as close a basis as that. They want everything very simple very much like the things we usually do, that is, in relation to the treatment of our walls and the simple way we use wood.

Just as soon as they get their real estate end settled, I expect to hear further from them and will advise you as to what may transpire.

I am enclosing time card for your files for the week ending Nov. 3.

        Yours very truly

GGE-M

three-story flat building. The scholars had an option to purchase this lot; however, were not sure they could afford to develop the property. Undoubtedly aware of the monetary gains of other such ventures, they managed to finance the project.[53]

⑨ Rectory of the Episcopal Church of the Redeemer, 1915.
5550 South Blackstone Avenue. J. E. O. Pridmore.

Rising land values and increasing density encouraged the construction of apartment houses throughout Hyde Park. Institutions too were forced to respond to increased financial pressures by constructing on every inch of available land. The Episcopal Church of the Redeemer provides but one example; its 1915 Tudor Revival rectory was erected on a small portion of the land at 56th Street and Blackstone. The Reverend John Henry Hopkins noted at the time that the congregation "utilized every square foot of our available space in this new house and chapel."[54]

Reverend Hopkins recalled that the rectory was used for many purposes. "We always went to the door ourselves. . . . Our maid simply could not do her work and also answer the doorbell. When the telephone in the workmen's shanty broke down, they would come to the Rectory to use our telephone. When things had to be delivered for the parish housework, they were not infrequently sent to the Rectory. And so the path to the doorbell was worn smooth."[55]

4.20. The main entrance to the house was once hidden behind a church that occupied the now open corner lot.

Episcopal Church of the Redeemer, 1909. Demolished 1968. 1420 East 56th Street. J. E. O. Pridmore.

4.21. A view as the church appeared in 1909.

When the church merged with Kenwood's St. Paul in 1968, the sanctuary closed and the church was unable to keep up with the maintenance. Problems were reported when local teenagers broke into the building, vandalizing the property and causing a great deal of damage. Empty liquor bottles and beer cans were found throughout and obscenities were scrawled on the walls.[56] The rector wrote that he doubted "how long the building will stand, for at this juncture fire is a great danger."[57] The three parcels that made up the property were offered for sale, and the church, also designed by Pridmore, was demolished. The parsonage is now a private residence.[58]

 **The Eleanor Club, 1916.**
1442 East 59th Street. Schmidt, Garden & Martin.

Schmidt, Garden & Martin continued to work in the neighborhood with their design of a boardinghouse for the Eleanor's Women Foundation. Support from the foundation made possible the construction of the Eleanor Clubs, providing an affordable and supportive environment for young workingwomen in Chicago. The boardinghouses were very popular when this building was constructed; the city's six residential clubs housed six hundred young women. Residents paid a "fair price" for their room and board, enabling the clubs to be "self-supporting" and not reliant on charity.[59] The organization occupied the sedate classical structure until 1967 when residents became "increasingly associated with the university and not with the business community."[60]

Schmidt, Garden & Martin was noted nationwide for the design of more than three hundred hospitals, including in 1914 the Illinois Central Hospital that once stood at 5744 South Stony Island, two blocks east of the Eleanor Club. The structure included a number of innovations, such as a departure from the system of housing patients in a large common ward, and the inclusion of a surgical viewing suite. University faculty and Hyde Park residents made up a large part of the clientele before the University of Chicago opened a hospital in 1927.[61]

This building was the basis for a book on hospitals and institutional architecture by Richard Schmidt, and although concerned preservationists attempted to save it, the structure was demolished in 2011 to make way for the University of Chicago Laboratory Schools expansion.

4.22. The three-story Eleanor Club faces the Midway and is conveniently located near the Illinois Central Station.

East Hyde Park

11 **Jackson Shore Apartments, 1916.**
5490 South Shore Drive. Rapp & Rapp.

Although best known for their elaborate cinemas, Rapp & Rapp hardly limited their practice to that field. They designed one of the first tall luxury apartment buildings in East Hyde Park, the Jackson Shore Apartments. The twelve-story, classically detailed building is of cream-colored pressed brick with a ground-story Bedford stone base. Apartments are large and featured the luxuries of a private home; formal living rooms and dining rooms with a butler's pantry, maids quarters, and at the corners of the building, circular sunrooms or "orangeries."[62]

The twenty-unit building, which faces east and was originally much closer to the Lake Michigan shoreline, remains one of Hyde Park's most luxurious apartment buildings. The expansion of the lakefront during the twenties distanced the building from the lake; however, the landfill now provides neighboring park space and an easy walk to Hyde Park's beloved Promontory Point.

4.23. The Jackson Shore Apartments were built by Gustav Gottschalk, who was also responsible for the huge Shoreland Hotel erected just to the north.

12 The Sisson Hotel, 1917.

1725 East 53rd Street. H. R. Wilson & Company, John Armstrong.

The Sisson Hotel was the first of the two large apartment hotels to be built at the lakeshore on the site of Paul Cornell's first hotel, the Hyde Park House. When the hotel opened in 1918, *Hotel Monthly* described the construction of the Sisson as "something different in hotel construction, plan, and operation" than anything that had previously been built in the city.[63] Designed for a prolonged stay, the Sisson was the brainchild of Harry W. Sisson and offered a collection of luxurious furnished units where a family could enjoy the privacy of a single-family residence yet be free of housekeeping chores, including cooking.

Situated directly on the shoreline at the time, the hotel offered expansive views in a structure designed to "permit maximum light, freedom from odors, elimination of noise, and safety in construction."[64] The twelve-story structure was constructed in the shape of two Es, set back to back. The first story is of glazed terra-cotta and the upper floors of red brick with cream terra-cotta trim. Architect John Armstrong, the surviving partner after Horatio Wilson's death in August 1917, was responsible for most of the detailing of the steel-framed building, according to *Hotel Monthly*.

Now known as Hampton House, the Sisson has a checkered history. During the twenties, when it was alleged that the proprietor Harry W. Sisson was a member of the Ku Klux Klan, Catholics and Jews boycotted the hotel, while the KKK newsletter urged Klansmen to stay on the premises.[65] Ironically, a half century later the hotel became the home of Chicago's first African American mayor, Harold Washington.

Washington served fifteen years in the Illinois state legislature and one and a half terms in the United States House of Representatives. As a candidate in Chicago's 1983 mayoral race, he put together a "rainbow coalition" of Chicagoans, uniting blacks, Hispanics, Asians, and liberal whites. As mayor, Washington increased the number of city contracts awarded to minorities and expanded opportunities for women and minorities in public employment. By signing a decree to end patronage hiring, Washington tried to break from "the city's legendary political machine."[66]

4.24. The back of the postcard of the Sisson reads "Sisson: Luxurious Detached Homes, Two to Six Rooms, Beautiful Sun Garden and Terrace atop. Delightful Dining Room at water's edge. Sunlit Kitchen adjoining. Unexcelled cuisine and service— Ten minutes along lakefront to business center. 375 Hyde Park trains daily." The dining room offered "the privacy of a beautiful home with the service of a most luxurious hotel." Note the location of the shoreline at the time.

13 The Cooper-Carleton (Del Prado) Hotel, 1918.
5307 South Hyde Park Boulevard. Newhouse & Bernham.

The Cooper-Carleton was the third of the early large apartment hotels constructed in East Hyde Park. Described in a marketing pamphlet as the "Finest Residential and Transient Hotel in Middle-West," the ten-story red brick and terra-cotta building is listed on the National Register of Historic Places. Built in a neoclassical style, the H-shaped hotel has a hefty terra-cotta base containing large Palladian windows. The ivory terra-cotta trim that frames the edges of the building rises to feathered Native Americans in headdress just below the cornice.

4.25. In a stretch of creative marketing, the image used on one of the hotel's postcards not only erased the Sisson Hotel that separated the Del Prado from the lakeshore, but also indicated a lovely and nonexistent beach in its stead.

4.26. Terra-cotta representations of Native Americans in a feathered headdress adorn the uppermost story of the Cooper-Carleton Hotel and were featured in the original lobby.

These adornments are echoed in the window cornices and also on the interior ornamentation.[67] The Native American theme can reportedly be traced to the owners of the hotel, descendents of James Fenimore Cooper, author of *Last of the Mohicans*.

Originally the hotel featured four hundred guest rooms and an equal number of baths. Nearly every room had two large clothes closets, which were advertised as a novel idea and exclusive to this hotel. The hotel was renamed the Del Prado in 1930 when the original Del Prado on 59th Street was demolished. In 2012 the building underwent a massive restoration.

Both the Sisson and the Del Prado have a long association with the game of baseball, hosting visiting American League teams when they were in town to play the Chicago White Sox; and for a short time the Cooper-Carleton was home to Judge Kenesaw Mountain Landis, the first commissioner of baseball, before he moved to the new annex of the Chicago Beach Hotel.

⑭ Chicago Beach Hotel Annex, 1919. Demolished 1970.
1600 East Hyde Park Boulevard. George C. Nimmons & Company.

With very few exceptions, the city's lakefront properties are not privately held. In the days of the world's fair, however, Chicago Beach Hotel guests enjoyed private access to the lakeshore. In 1915, the city wanted to open the beach to the public and filed a lawsuit on the grounds that submerged lands were the property of the state, that therefore the landfill completed years prior by James Morgan had been illegally done, and that it was the duty of the state to preserve the land for public use.[68] The hotel obtained an injunction retaining the use of the lakefront for their private beach. However after long negotiations with the

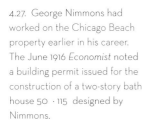

4.27. George Nimmons had worked on the Chicago Beach property earlier in his career. The June 1916 *Economist* noted a building permit issued for the construction of a two-story bath house 50 · 115 designed by Nimmons.

South Park Board, a compromise was finally reached in 1926.[69] The hotel company gave up their riparian rights in exchange for the large piece of land north of the hotel grounds.

During the hotel's battle with the city, the enterprise continued to prosper. In 1919, the construction of a thirteen-story 550-room addition was announced. Morgan surely made a wise business venture with his manufacture of sandy landfill — the proprietors of the hotel purchased twelve acres for the hotel addition from his daughter for $500,000, in cash.[70]

After completion, guests and residents used the indoor and outdoor golf facilities, danced in the open-air pavilion, enjoyed the renowned dining room, and swam in the cool waters of Lake Michigan. Among the residents of the new building was Kenesaw Mountain Landis, a US district court judge who presided over some of the most famous trials of the early years of the twentieth century.[71] Elected in 1920 as baseball's first commissioner, he immediately had to deal with the aftermath of the 1919 Chicago "Black Sox" scandal, and permanently banned eight team members for throwing the World Series to the Cincinnati Reds.[72] While credited with restoring integrity to the game, Landis is also remembered for prolonging racial segregation in the sport.

The old hotel was razed in the summer of 1926, and although plans were contemplated to replace the old wooden structure, the Depression put a halt to any further expansion. East Hyde Park remained fashionable over the ensuing years and the hotel annex operated until the Second World War, when a federal court order authorized the US Army to take possession of the hotel for use as a military hospital in May 1942.[73] The military continued to use the hotel annex as an office building until 1963, when they relocated to Fort Sheridan. The property sat vacant until demolition in September 1970. The two thirty-six-story Chicago Beach Towers (now Regents Park) were constructed between 1972 and 1974. The Algonquin Apartment high-rises and a gas station now occupy the site of the original hotel.

Kenwood

15 **DeLee Apartment, 1909.**
5028–5030 South Ellis Avenue. George Washington Maher.

Maher brought his Prairie School ideals to the design of multifamily housing as land values escalated and space was at a premium, even in Kenwood. The robust façades of two buildings constructed on Ellis offered interesting solutions to the increased demand on land usage. Built with multiple units, the DeLee dwelling and the apartment next door at 5024 for Frank Schoenfeld give the appearance of single-family houses.

The DeLee property was not intended to include a rental unit; the apartment was reserved for members of the family. Dr. Joseph Bolivar DeLee was a prominent obstetrician and the founder of the Chicago Lying-In Hospital, a pioneering institution in the field. The hospital was important to the city as it provided services regardless of race or ability to pay.[74]

4.29. Although designed as multifamily dwellings, the buildings at 5025 and 5028 South Ellis blend in comfortably with the surrounding single-family residences.

Dr. DeLee founded Chicago's Lying-in Dispensary in 1895, a time when Chicago's low-income mothers had little access to good maternity care. A graduate of Chicago Medical College (now part of Northwestern University), DeLee began with donations totaling $500, "a stove, a table, some chairs, and an old carpet. His family supplied linen. From a second-hand store he was able to procure two beds."[75] With these meager supplies, he opened a free clinic on Maxwell Street. Although expenses threatened to close his clinic, the practice grew and Dr. DeLee eventually prospered. The Chicago Lying-In Hospital opened in 1917, and became a key institution in the development of modern obstetrics and gynecology.[76]

The property features the first garage constructed in Kenwood, designed in 1910 by Herman von Holst & James Fyfe. Cars were becoming readily available and were for the most part kept in coach houses or public garages until this time. The simple two-story, flat-roofed garage signaled a basic change in living patterns and introduced a new architectural form. As Jean Block so aptly stated, "The size and shape, not to mention the care and feeding of an automobile, make very different demands on space from those of a horse and carriage."[77]

16 Antoine Residence, 1910.
4940 South Kimbark Avenue. N. Max Dunning.

Architect Max Dunning was commissioned to design two residences in Kenwood for Charles Antoine: an investment property at 4949 Woodlawn and the Kimbark Avenue house where Antoine resided. The Arts and Crafts movement of late nineteenth-century England heavily influenced Dunning's work on this bungalow. Valuing "efficiency and modern conveniences," the bungalow became a practical expression of the craftsman philosophy, focusing on a straightforward way of liv-

4.30. Typically 2-stories in height and square in plan, the classic Craftsman-style residence is defined by the low-hipped roof, the overextended gable, and windows that were proportionally wider and squatter than earlier Victorian designs.

ing.[78] These houses feature simple, informal floor plans, interiors of wood detailing with built-in sideboards and bookcases, and large fireplaces.

Antoine established the partnership of Von Lengerke & Antoine in 1891, a "well known retail hardware and sporting goods firm"[79] that sold guns, holsters and ammunition.[80] He occupied the Kimbark house for only three years, selling this property in 1916. "An interesting transaction in high grade Kenwood residence property closed late in the week was the sale by Charles Antoine to Arthur A. Goes of the Goes Lithography Company," reported the *Tribune*. The property, an "attractive eleven room brick colonial structure erected about three years ago," occupied a lot 33' × 170'.[81]

⑰ Wilson Residence, 1910.

4815 South Woodlawn Avenue. Howard van Doren Shaw.

Prolific architect Howard Van Doren Shaw continued his work in the Hyde Park area, using historical styles—as he attracted a clientele drawn from the city's society and business leaders. Shaw designed this Tudor Revival estate for Thomas E. Wilson, the head of the Wilson Packing Company, one of the leading packing firms of the Union Stockyards at 47th and Halsted Streets. Wilson was also the

4.31. The Wilson family owned the Tudor Revival estate until 1958, when the residence and coach house were sold to the current owners.

founder of Wilson Sporting Goods, which has endured as a familiar name in sporting goods. The family owned the house and coach house until 1958, when it was sold to the current owners.

Many of the period details found in the 8,000-square-foot mansion can be traced to sixteenth-century England, including the elaborate plasterwork of the living room ceiling that mimics the detailing of the Elizabethan country house Haddon Hall in Derbyshire.[82] The largest of Shaw's remaining houses in the neighborhood, it retains nearly all the original features, including the interior lighting fixtures and the first-floor woodwork and ceiling finishes. Leaded glass windows are found throughout, and the dining room has the original silk damask wall covering. Shaw's meticulous attention to detail is evident throughout the home, as found in the elaborate woodwork and sconces that adorn the walls.

Within the leaded glass doors of the living room bookcases are 127 volumes of the *War of the Rebellion: Records of the Union and Confederate Armies* that belonged to the original owner. They been maintained in nearly perfect condition, and each volume is clearly embossed with Thomas Wilson's name on the spine. The living room also features the Wilson's Steinway player piano, manufactured in 1923 and most likely occupying the same corner of the living room ever since.[83]

The exterior of the house features an open sleeping porch, one of Shaw's favorite elements, and is adorned with leaded glass windows and shallow bays with crenellations.[84] The coach house features many of the same exterior details, as well as a hayloft and servants' quarters. It was long ago converted for automobiles.

After Shaw's death in 1926, his office closed and few of the original drawings survived. In this case the current owners have something rare—the complete set of blueprints for this house, including interior and exterior detailing, floor plans, wiring diagrams, and exterior elevations.

18   Loeb Residence, 1910. Demolished 1971.
5017 South Ellis Avenue. Arthur Heun.

Noted architect Arthur Heun designed some of the most distinguished houses and country estates in Chicago and the exclusive suburb of Lake Forest on the city's North Shore. On the South Side, Heun was commissioned by Albert H. Loeb, a lawyer and later the vice president and treasurer of Sears, Roebuck & Company, to design a house in Kenwood.[85]

Anna and Albert Loeb raised four sons in this mansion, which in 1924 figured prominently in "the Crime of the Century." Their son Richard, while brilliant and handsome, had a dark side. Loeb and his friend Nathan Leopold believed their high intellect made them capable of committing the perfect crime. A gruesome plot was conceived in this house, within two blocks of where they kidnapped and brutally murdered their neighbor Bobby Franks.

Albert Loeb suffered from heart disease, and his condition steadily worsened following the verdict of life imprisonment for his "best beloved" son.[86] He died here just six months after the crime, and his magnificent estate stood, albeit in dilapidated condition, until it was demolished in 1971. Like many of the large houses

4.32. The Loeb mansion, with its coach house, tennis courts, and formal rose garden, was for years plagued by lawsuits and confusion. The house had been vacant for over a decade when Richard Loeb's brothers sold the estate in 1947. The property was granted a zoning variance in 1952 permitting use as an orphanage until 1964 when the institution closed. A 1979 *Hyde Park Herald* article recalled that in 1967 the house was used as collateral on a fraudulent loan, and three years later it was severely damaged by fire. After the city condemned the property, scavengers dismantled paneling and other fixtures and sold them as antiques. Following demolition, the Chicago Park District was awarded the property for the construction of a playground, but owing to the peculiarities of title, it was never built. A series of lawsuits continued for years, while the property remained a weed-choked vacant lot.

in Kenwood, it was for a time used for institutional purposes. Today the property has been subdivided and there are two new houses on the property, surrounded by the original brick fence.

⑲ Franks Residence, 1910.
932 East 51st Street. Henry Newhouse.

Best known as the architect of large apartment hotels, Henry Newhouse was awarded several single-family commissions by the German Jewish elite moving into Kenwood, including the yellow brick house for Jacob Franks. Although Franks made his fortune financing Chicago real estate, he earned the title "Honest Jake" because of his reputation for fairness during his early years in the pawnshop business. However, life became anything but fair. On a spring morning in 1924, a special-delivery ransom note was delivered here, and the Franks were distraught to learn their son had been kidnapped. It was later discovered that two University of Chicago students and Kenwood neighbors, Nathan Leopold and Richard Loeb, had murdered their fourteen-year-old son.

The house from which young Bobby Franks's coffin was carried was sold six months after the funeral. His parents moved to the North Side and away from the "unpleasant reminders."[87] The house and coach house remain today, although for years they were in a serious state of deterioration and neglect. Plans to develop the property into two condominiums units that required a zoning variance were met with neighborhood resistance, but received city approval.

4.33. The Franks and Loeb families knew each other well—their sons were second cousins and the houses were within a half block of each other.

4.34. Although in disrepair, the detailing of the second-floor transom of the Franks house repeats the design of the windows and indicates a cohesive approach to the interior and the exterior design.

4.35. The McDougal residence is just one of many examples of the Tudor Revival-style found throughout Hyde Park and Kenwood. The style, an American interpretation of English manor homes of the sixteenth and early seventeenth centuries, was popular in the years leading up to and following the First World War. The style is dominated by the use of half-timbering on the second level and battlements near the eave line.

20 **McDougal Residence, 1909.**
4804 South Woodlawn Avenue. H. R. Wilson & Company.

In the early years of the twentieth century, many of Kenwood's large suburban estates were subdivided when owners were no longer willing to sustain them. Christopher Bouton and his wife Eleanora (Nellie) transferred the 99' × 297' parcel of land north of their residence to their daughter Mary Persis Bouton and her husband Robert McDougal.[88] A grain broker with the firm of Knight & McDougal and a member of the Board of Trade, McDougal was secretary of the Kenwood Country Club at Ellis and 48th Streets and for a time president of the Kenwood Club.[89] The young couple selected Horatio Wilson to design their Tudor Revival-style residence, completed the year Wilson reorganized his firm as H. R. Wilson & Company. Prolific and popular, Wilson was comfortable working in a wide variety of architectural styles and never developed a signature style.

22 **Graff Residence, 1913.**
4907 South Kimbark Avenue. H. R. Wilson & Company.

Wilson was commissioned to design a number of houses on the 4900 block of Kimbark, a stretch that had been prevented from being developed by the peculiarities of John Dunham's will. Eventually the heirs developed the property, selling some of the lots individually with speculative houses, while others were sold as vacant parcels.

Clearly comfortable combining a variety of styles, in this home Wilson used many disparate elements: the façade features woodwork of the Arts and Crafts movement with a classically inspired entry, a feature he used repeatedly.

Edwin Adolphus Graff was a grain merchant, coming to Chicago in 1897. He was the founder and president of the Columbia Malting Company.[90] A widower,

4.36. Described as quiet and
dignified, Edwin Graff is listed as
a member of the Board of Trade
as early as 1894; however, he did
not move to the city until three
years later.

he lived with his second wife, Josephine, directly to the north of this house at 4901
Kimbark (designed by William Pruyn) and they moved here upon the house's
completion in 1914.[91]

23 Grassell Residence, 1916.
4944 South Woodlawn Avenue. H. R. Wilson & Company.

A larger-scale lot became available when the grounds of Judge Van H. Higgins's
estate were subdivided, and his distinctive Italianate villa house was demolished.
John Grassell, president of Wilson Steel Products, purchased a 61' × 197' section

4.37. Grassell was vice president
of Depositors State and Savings
Bank at the time this house was
constructed.

and commissioned Wilson to design the imposing Tudor Revival mansion now on the site.[92] Residents often upgraded to larger houses within the community—John and Janey Grassell moved their family to this new residence from 1344 Madison Park. Although the site of the long, bitter feud between Higgins and John Dunham was long forgotten, the Woodlawn Avenue property was once again in the spotlight when famed boxer Mohammed Ali purchased this property during the 1960s.

21 Gatzert Residence, 1912.
4901 South Greenwood Avenue. Ottenheimer, Stern & Reichert.

Ottenheimer produced many residences with a "charming baroque exuberance," predominantly for German Jewish businessmen on Chicago's Near South Side. Dubbed "the dainty designer of beautiful homes," Ottenheimer received the commission for this residence from August Gatzert, a German-born clothing manufacturer who came to Chicago in 1881. He became the secretary of Rosenwald & Weil, a wholesale manufacturer of clothing that had been founded by his Kenwood neighbors Julius and Morris Rosenwald and Julius Weil (4921 South Ellis). Gatzert and his wife Isabel desired a house influenced by the modernist designs of Germany that they viewed while traveling in Europe. "Traditional in form but elegantly minimalist in its details," commented architectural historian Tim Samuelson, "the Gatzert House blends in comfortably with its neighborhood."[93]

4.38. The architect of the Gatzert house is perhaps best known not for his work, but for stabbing Frank Lloyd Wright during an office disagreement.

24 **Adler Residence, 1916.**
   4939 South Greenwood Avenue. Arthur Heun.

Arthur Heun designed a 12,000-square-foot mansion in the heart of Kenwood for Max Adler, the brother-in-law of the founder of the retail giant Sears, Roebuck & Company, Julius Rosenwald. Adler served as the vice president of Sears until 1928, and was greatly admired for his philanthropic activities. He became interested in planetariums; he traveled to Munich to study the first institution of its kind, the Deutsches Museum, and returned to Chicago to sponsor the building of the planetarium on the city's lakefront.[94]

In 1930, the year Adler dedicated his planetarium, Adler lived here with his wife Sophie and daughter Lois, attended by seven servants: a secretary, a cook, a ladies' maid, a chambermaid, a waitress, a house man, and a butler. Their twenty-room residence reflected the nineteenth-century ideal of the home as a sanctuary from the outside world. The grounds covered nearly one acre, and the elaborate house featured twelve bedrooms and seven baths.

4.39. "Society architect" Arthur Heun had completed the magnificent estate of J. Ogden Armor, Mellody Farm in north suburban Lake Forest, and the Kenwood mansion of Albert Loeb several years prior to receiving the commission for the urban estate of Max Adler.

4.40. An elegant entry rises from street level to the main floor of the Adler house through a dramatic marble foyer, leading to a library with leaded glass windows, a walnut-paneled living room, and a dining room, each enhanced by fireplaces.

4.41. The Adler library features a black granite floor, panel woodwork, leaded glass windows, and a traditionally detailed green marble fireplace.

When the Adlers moved to Beverly Hills, California, in 1950, they donated the house to Michael Reese Hospital as a nurses' residence. After a number of years in that role, the residence was left vacant until it was purchased and partially restored in 1982. In the early 1990's the former Adler mansion was again sold and has been lovingly restored to its former grandeur.

Drexel Boulevard

② Morris Residence, 1910. Demolished 1946.

4800 South Drexel Boulevard. Howard van Doren Shaw.

At the western boundary of Kenwood on stately Drexel Boulevard was one of Howard van Doren Shaw's largest projects, designed for Edward and Helen Morris. Built to impress, the mansion was the last of the great estates to be constructed on the boulevard. Edward was the son of Nelson Morris, the pioneer meatpacker of the Union Stockyards and a central figure there for fifty years. Edward, president and treasurer of the family company, was also a director of the First National Bank and the Livestock Bank.[95] He married Helen Swift in 1890, the daughter of Gustavus Swift, a Kenwood resident and also a founder of one of the major meatpacking companies in Chicago.

In September 1904 Morris purchased the Drexel property, a very large parcel with a frontage of 198' and a depth of 202'.[96] Construction began in 1910, and three years later Helen moved to Drexel from their residence at 4455 Grand Boulevard (now King Drive). Apparently Morris never occupied the house; he became ill and died unexpectedly at their home on Grand Boulevard.[97]

A huge ornate gate on 48th Street welcomed visitors to a spectacular urban estate. In addition to the English Tudor style mansion there was a large coach house and servants' quarters topped by a cupola, a conservatory, vegetable and flower

4.42. The mammoth urban estate of the late Edward Morris was photographed for the *Chicago Daily News* on March 13, 1917; his widow remarried six months later. The massive house marks the end of the opulent era of Drexel Boulevard.

gardens, a tennis court and a even small teahouse on the property.[98] Shaw designed the interior of the house with the motifs of fruit and bounty. Details included ornately plastered ceilings, carved wood trim, and arched French doors, and in the library there was exposed half-timbering. To manage the house and grounds the family employed a staff of seven servants: one housekeeper, three general house workers, one private family servant, a butler, and a coachman.

Four years after Edward's death, Helen Swift Morris married Francis Neilson, an author and former member of the British House of Commons; it was this house they then made their home.[99]

The lavish three-story estate did not last much more than thirty years; it was demolished in April 1946. Ten years later a low-income housing project designed by Bertrand Goldberg was constructed on the property. As a reminder of days long past, when the excavation for the project began, a marble fishpond was discovered under the wreckage of the house.[100]

26 Apartments, 1916.
4856–4858 Drexel Boulevard. Lebenbaum & Marx.

Although primarily known as industrial designers, Fred G. Lebenbaum and Samuel Marx received several commissions in Kenwood. The firm designed this large apartment building on the northwest corner of Drexel Boulevard and 49th Street at a time when values on the stately avenue were declining. Chauncey Blair, whose elegant three-story residence once stood north of this site, purchased the property to prevent the construction of a flat building; however, Blair died in 1916 and shortly afterward this six-unit apartment building rose next door to his home. Lebenbaum & Marx were able to demonstrate a similar kind of elegance in a decidedly urban way; they created a well-appointed building that did not degrade the street in spite of its size.

4.43. Noted for their semicircular bays and adorned by Grecian urns, the six spacious units were altered to accommodate thirty-six small apartments to meet the increased demand for housing during the forties.

27 The Cooper-Monotah (Sutherland) Hotel, 1917.
4659 South Drexel Boulevard. Newhouse & Bernham.

Newhouse & Berman, best known for large commercial buildings and apartments, designed the mammoth Cooper-Monotah Apartment Hotel on a prime corner of elegant Drexel Boulevard on the grounds of one of Kenwood's landmarks, the residence of Col. George R. Clarke, built about 1870.

In January 1918 the large new structure was taken over by the US Government and operated as General Hospital No. 32. The nation had mobilized to go to war, but lacked facilities to treat the injured. The hotel, one of many such structures taken over by the government, had not been completed on the interior, and that permitted the construction of two large wards of sixty and eighty beds.[101] After the war ended, the boulevard fell out of favor with Chicago's elite, and the large hotel completely changed the streetscape.

In 1952 the lounge of the hotel, no longer luxurious and renamed the Sutherland, became the first "whites only" jazz club to admit African Americans. For a time the music was legendary and the hotel was home to many artists, including Louis Armstrong and Miles Davis. Etta James, Marvin Gaye, Curtis Mayfield, and "everyone who mattered in Black music"[102] played in the lounge or stayed in the low-budget hotel. James recalled the early days of her career in an interview for *Rolling Stone* magazine, "We were hungry, starving musicians."[103] The club has long been shuttered, and in 1988 the hotel was remodeled to provide 154 units of low-income housing. In 2012 the building was renovated for market-rate rental apartments.

4.44. Five floors rose above the mezzanine level, which once featured a large porch that opened from the dining room and ran the full length of the building on the boulevard side. The Cooper-Monotah contained 230 bedrooms and 154 baths arranged in suites of varying sizes, and one could shop in eight stores located on the ground floor.

5.01. The developing Hyde Park lakefront, as seen in an aerial view photographed from 57th Street looking north, c. 1929. In the foreground are the new Windermere and Jackson Towers, and in the distance are the Powhatan, the Narragansett, and the Chicago Beach Hotel. To the east the old shoreline is clearly visible, and the construction of the breakwater and landfill well underway.

CHAPTER 5

Blood Stains, 1920–1929

A smell of starch, wet linen and steam mingles with an aromatic mustiness. The day's work is done. Sing Lee sits in his chair behind the counter. Three walls look down upon him. Laundry packages—yellow paper, white string—crowd the wall shelves. Chinese letterings dance gaily on the yellow packages.

Sing Lee, from behind the counter, stares out of the window. The Hyde Park police station is across the way. People pass and glance up:

Sing Lee, Hand Laundry,

5222 Lake Park Avenue.

Come in.

There is something immaculate about Sing Lee. Lee has been ironing out collars and shirts for thirty-five years. And thirty-five years have been ironing Sing Lee out. He is like one of the yellow packages on the shelves. And there is a certain lettering across his face as indecipherable and strange as the dance of the black hieroglyphics on the yellow laundry paper.

—Ben Hecht, *One Thousand One Afternoons in Chicago*, 1922

The Hyde Park community continued to thrive after the war ended; its population grew as the national economy prospered. Improvement of Chicago's infrastructure made jobs plentiful. For Hyde Park the improvements included a vast project on the lakefront, including a scenic shore drive and an extension of the parks planned by Daniel Burnham in 1909. After a series of lengthy lawsuits was settled, and the Illinois Central agreed to give up its riparian rights to the lakefront in exchange for a terminal at 12th Street, work began on Burnham's plan.[1] The South Shore Development was an immense project; with a theme of a playground for the people, this vast swath of land was destined to include beaches, pavilions, and bathing houses, all open to the public.

In February 1920 voters approved a $20 million bond issue to be used to fund construction of Soldier Field near Grant Park on the north end, to create shore infill and breakwaters from 12th Street south to 56th Street, to build Promontory Point at 55th Street, and to develop the four-lane roadway now known as Lake Shore Drive.[2]

By 1924 the breakwater was under construction, but the southern lakefront remained unsightly. The area was used as a dumping ground for all matters of refuse: "Ashes, tin cans, broken brick, and plaster from demolished buildings" were strewn along the shore. Hyde Park's residents were anxious to see the work completed, for in addition to the unsightly and foul-smelling mess, traffic on Lake Avenue had increased dramatically.[3] The country was in the midst of its long love affair with the automobile, and the new road was anticipated to relieve the congestion.

Sing Lee was but one of many who toiled in the shops on heavily traveled Lake Avenue. People representing all walks of life were present on the street—policemen, tailors, laundresses, bartenders, and garage keepers. Their physical setting was a jumble of three-flats and timeworn houses adjacent to fine residences and splendid hotels. Sing Lee's life was one of great contrast to that of nearby wealthy residents, wrote Ben Hecht. "He has never been to a movie or a theater play. He has never ridden in an automobile. He has never looked at the lake."

The popularity of the movies and the theater was representative of a period that witnessed an explosion of mass culture, as society shed the constraints of earlier years. The notion of "celebrity" enthralled the American public; crowds lined 53rd Street to get a glimpse of Amelia Earhart during her visit to Hyde Park.[4] The first radio stations went on the air, bringing entertainment into the living room. The "talkies" became a staple of entertainment, and spectacular movie houses rose in the community. Although Sing Lee never entered a theater, architects believed the movie house to be a great social equalizer—relatively inexpensive entertainment available to all classes. "Watch the bright lights in the eyes of the tired shop girl who hurries noiselessly over carpets and sighs with satisfaction as she walks amid furnishings that once delighted kings and queens," said architect George Rapp, speaking of his theater work. "See the war-torn father whose dreams have never come true, and look inside his heart as he finds strength and rest within the theater. Here is a shrine to democracy where there are no privileged patrons. The wealthy rub elbows with the poor."[5]

Success was redefined to include pleasure and consumption; however, both were dealt a setback on January 17, 1920, when America went "dry." Prior to Prohibition, liquor could not be sold in most of Hyde Park and Kenwood.[6] However, Lake Street came under jurisdiction of the railroad, and saloons were permitted within a "certain radius" of the Illinois Central tracks.[7] After Prohibition took effect alcohol became more popular than ever, and speakeasies developed thriving yet illicit businesses—until some became overly conspicuous and were padlocked. The *Hyde Park Herald* noted that the closing of "the last and most renowned" of Lake Street's seventeen saloons, Adolph's Place at 5492 Lake Street, marked the end of an era as a place for entertainment as it heralded in a new era of business establishments.[8]

In addition to the bootlegging of alcohol and the operation of speakeasies like these, Chicago became known as a city of gangsters and guns during the twenties, a reputation the city would endure for decades. In Hyde Park–Kenwood, two widely publicized murders occurred during the spring of 1924, bringing unwelcome notoriety to the otherwise quiet community. The first occurred on April 24, when a married bookkeeper invited her lover to her apartment in a three-story red brick courtyard building at 817 East 46th Street, just west of Drexel Boulevard.[9] Beulah May Annan and Harry Kalstedt had a drunken argument and struggled for a gun that lay on the bed. Beulah reached the gun first, shot Kalstedt, and watched him slowly die. The sensational trial was followed nationally, with "the most beautiful woman ever tried for murder in Cook County"[10] posing for pictures for reporters covering the story. In the end Annan feigned regret[11] and plied the jury for sympathy by claiming she was pregnant and had fired in self-defense. The trial ended in acquittal,[12] and Annan became the inspiration for the character Roxy Hart, one of the subjects of Maurine Watkins' play *Chicago*, written that same year. The play was adapted into a 1927 silent film, a 1975 stage musical, and in 2002 a movie musical that won the Academy Award for Best Picture. The city's reputation was compelling, and well publicized.

Meanwhile, a dramatic shift in demographics was well underway. Known as "The Great Migration," the mass movement of African Americans from the South to jobs in the industrialized North continued, after crops failed and as oppressive conditions increased. During the period between 1916 and 1930, over 75,000 African Americans arrived on the South Side of the city.[13] The newcomers quickly became part of the already flourishing community known as the Black Belt, bounded by 12th Street on the north and edging south of 39th Street, in two segments, east of Wentworth to State Street and west of Cottage Grove nearly to South Parkway. Initially Chicago's white community was indifferent to the relatively isolated black community; "consequently it gradually evolved a complete, commercial, social, and political base of its own."[14]

However, relationships between white and black communities had been strained, especially due to competition for jobs and housing. For blacks, the jobs that had been plentiful during the war years disappeared, and many were asked to work for very low wages or were let go. By 1925 the tensions temporarily subsided; the economy prospered, the construction of roads, bridges, and airports provided opportunity, and the unemployment levels declined. The second half of the twenties, according to St. Clair Drake, was one of the "most prosperous ones the Negro community in Chicago had ever experienced."[15]

The black population continually expanded its boundaries, purchasing property at often highly inflated prices and transforming white communities into mixed communities, then into solidly black ones. Chicagoans watched the Black Belt expand south along once fashionable South Parkway (Martin Luther King Drive) and Michigan Avenue. The area east of Cottage Grove to the lakeshore, from 39th Street on the north as far south as 47th Street on the south, became black. The center of the black community shifted two miles further south during the twenties, expanding block by block, "taking over stone-front houses and the apartments, buying large church edifices and opening smaller churches in houses . . . and building a political machine as they went."[16]

During this time of prosperity and social upheaval, the Hyde Park area was lively. The mid-1920s witnessed the establishment of the bohemian world of the "Chicago Renaissance." The term applies to a "second wave of Chicago writing" beginning before the war and continuing through the midtwenties. Key figures included Sherwood Anderson, Edgar Lee Masters, and Floyd Dell, and others who lived locally, including reporter Ben Hecht.[17] The wave extended to the stage; Hecht, Anderson, Kenwood resident Kenneth Goodman, and others founded the Little Theater in

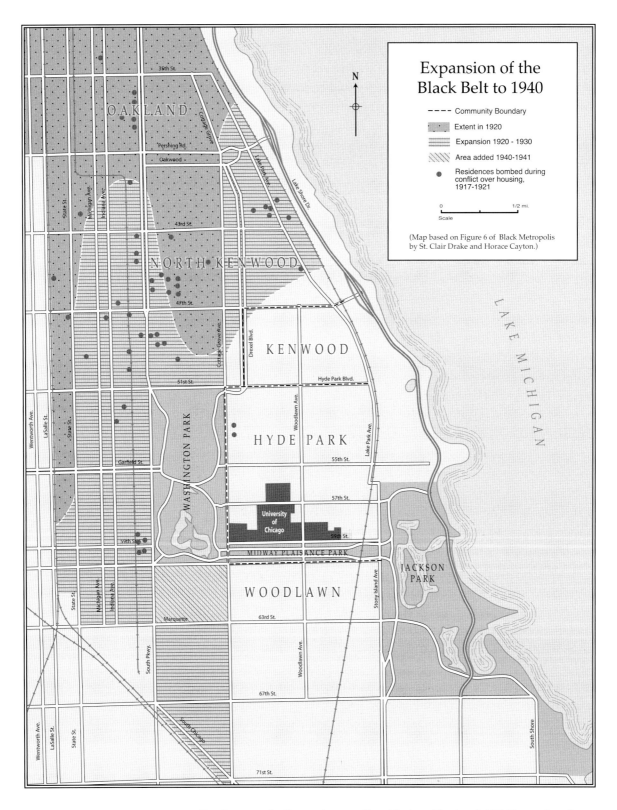

5.02. Already surrounding the area known as Grand Boulevard (centered at Michigan and 43rd), the Black Belt expanded during the twenties and thirties. Residents of this community were predominantly German Jews, who began to move south to Hyde Park and Kenwood as the black population encroached.

Hyde Park. A particularly colorful figure, Hecht began his career as a picture stealer for a newspaper whose standards were "regrettably low," but from this rough world of journalism came "the basis for his craft."[18] Hecht explored the coarser side of the city for the *Chicago Daily News*, profiling Sing Lee and others in his powerful column called "One Thousand and One Afternoons in Chicago."

Hotels and entertainment venues opened catering to those with disposable income and increased leisure time. The 210-room Ritz Hotel on 47th Street, directly across the street from the older Kenwood Hotel, opened in 1925 for visitors who came to enjoy the lakeshore and elaborate entertainment palaces. The Rapp brothers designed the large, ornate Piccadilly Theater on Hyde Park Boulevard, joining the Frolic and the Kenwood movie palaces. With its 2,500 seats, antique furnishings, paintings, and sculptures, the "Pic" served an affluent middle class, a growing population that occupied the large apartment hotels rising to the east of the Illinois Central tracks.

The owners of the Chicago Beach announced a building program intended to make the hotel one of the most imposing and elaborate establishments in the world. Described by the *Chicago Tribune* as the city's first great lakeside hostelry, the original wooden building was to be demolished in order to erect an elegant twelve-story replacement. The *Tribune* described the planned project as a "semicircular two story casino . . . adjoining the east and west sections and containing the main kitchen, main dining room and twenty or more private dining rooms overlooking the main floor." The dining room was to have a seating capacity of at least 2,000. The improvements were to include Turkish baths for both men and women and two "mammoth swimming pools to be open all year."[19] Architects George C. Nimmons & Co. drew plans for an elaborate dancing pavilion on the beach, and a 600-car garage demonstrated the rising importance of the automobile.[20]

Construction along the lakefront profoundly escalated during the twenties. There were three significant milestones that contributed to the development and prestige of East Hyde Park: the massive lakefront project, improvements to the Illinois Central line, and implementation of zoning regulations. The southern extension of Burnham's plan for the lakeshore, which began with the installation of a breakwater and subsequent landfill, finally culminated in 1938 with the landscaping of the new lakefront park. As part of the plan, the much anticipated new shore drive provided relief to the heavy traffic of Lake Avenue when a portion opened in 1929.[21]

Substantial changes were made to the busy Illinois Central commuter train line in 1926 after the Chicago City Council passed a smoke abatement ordinance, forcing the Illinois Central to replace the old coal-burning teakettle type of steam engine with a cleaner, electric-powered car. The improvement helped to decrease the smoke nuisance of the nearly 400 locomotives that passed through the area daily.[22] However, the freight service was not electrified, and most residences continued to use coal furnaces, so the overall air quality did not significantly improve until after World War II. The electrification did improve travel times. As the papers pointed out, "Although about five miles from downtown, the new Illinois Central electric trains whisk one from Hyde Park Boulevard to Van Buren quicker than one ordinarily can get from the original Streeterville to the Loop."[23]

In 1923 Chicago reworked its building codes to define types of land usage and confine those types to specific zones. The comprehensive zoning changes allowed cooperative apartment ventures and permitted large-scale building along the lakefront. Co-ops were the earliest form of apartment ownership in Chicago, predating the now familiar condominium form of ownership. A cooperative building was owned by a legal entity, from which buyers purchased shares of stock. That stock entitled purchasers to occupy their chosen apartments; however, applicants first had to meet admission requirements set by the co-op board.[24] Co-ops were able to discriminate against selective groups of prospective purchasers, typically through the use of informal, unwritten agreements.

An earlier form of multifamily living that was popular during the late nineteenth century reemerged during this period along the lakefront. Apartment hotels for middle- and upper-class residents combined the best elements of apartment and hotel living. Their popularity was a reflection of the rapid growth of East Hyde Park, where the pressure of rising land values and shifting attitudes toward apartment living made these large buildings a popular choice. The apartment hotel offered the services and gracious public spaces found in leading hotels to long-term residents without the responsibility or financial commitment of a house. Often marketing brochures outlined the various benefits of this arrangement, promoting the idea that a family could live as comfortably in an apartment as in one of the large private residences of the neighborhood. The apartment hotel was marketed to appeal to women, who would find their responsibilities simplified, no longer having to deal with "servants, coal bills, janitors, repairs, and a thousand and one other vexing problems."[25]

As the infrastructure was improved and zoning was in place, an ambitious plan was announced for the Hyde Park lakefront based upon the North Side "Streeterville" area and designed to compete with it.[26] Plans were unveiled for the development of twenty-five and a half acres of land, four of which were occupied by the

Chicago Beach Hotel. In 1926 the hotel owners reached a compromise with the city whereby they relinquished riparian rights in exchange for a large tract of land north of the hotel grounds.[27] As part of the plan, this land was to be improved with a mile of new streets linking Hyde Park Boulevard with the new shore drive. Of the five buildings constructed as part of this large project, two were particularly important cooperatives—the Powhatan and the Narragansett. Completed in 1928 and rising twenty stories, the Powhatan was located just to the north of the Chicago Beach Hotel. At the time, the building was "up to the minute of thought in American architecture" and presented "an imposing appearance on the parkland it faces."[28] The following year construction was underway on the Narragansett, also designed in the popular Moderne style, more commonly known as Art Deco.

Meanwhile, significant changes were occurring in other areas of the Hyde Park–Kenwood community. The University of Chicago continued to exert a powerful influence, and it embarked upon a major expansion program for the campus. Between 1926 and 1933 the size of the campus nearly doubled as twenty-one buildings were added.[29] The University adopted the Gothic style of architecture as its own, and now further transformed it to meet their needs, as buildings such as Rockefeller Chapel by Bertram Goodhue and the Quadrangle Club by Howard van Doren Shaw rose on campus. However, as it grew, the institution began to realize the physical limitations of the campus. In but one example, the construction of Rockefeller Chapel required purchasing and demolishing houses on Woodlawn Avenue. This became a controversial and ongoing process as the university developed long-range plans to meet the needs of the student body and faculty.

Hyde Park's population grew steadily during the twenties, rising to over 48,000 residents in 1930, from 37,523 ten years earlier. Over 6,500 dwelling units were constructed between 1920 and 1930, a figure that represented 40 percent of its existing housing stock. Thirty percent of all structures in Hyde Park were apartments, compared with an average of 6 percent citywide.[30] The improvements in East Hyde Park in particular were reflected in the increasing value of real estate—values skyrocketed between 200 and 500 percent for properties near the lake. Overall Hyde Park was in the upper echelon of rent, with half of all apartments renting for fifty dollars at a time when the city average was seventeen dollars per month.[31]

The increasing numbers of residents fostered the need for additional churches, synagogues, schools, banks, and hospitals. In Kenwood and East Hyde Park, Jewish residents comprised an increasingly significant part of the social fabric, and by 1930 they were the largest ethnic group in the neighborhood. Many owned single-family homes in Kenwood; however, the large residential hotels near the lake were also favored by those moving from the Grand Boulevard and Washington Park communities, where in the early years of the twentieth century imposing synagogues and residences lined streets. By 1930 the black population of those neighborhoods was over 90 percent; just ten years earlier it had comprised 15 percent in Washington Park and 32 percent in Grand Boulevard.[32] Following a pattern documented nationwide, the easiest point of entry for blacks into a new community was often a Jewish area, as the Catholic and Protestant working classes offered a "more formal and organized resistance to their presence," while the Jewish population preferred to relocate.[33]

Rockefeller Chapel, 1928.
5850 South Woodlawn Avenue.
Bertram Grosvenor Goodhue.

5.04. Construction of
Rockefeller Chapel required
the demolition of single-family
houses on Woodlawn Avenue,
seen at the lower left in this
photograph looking south toward
the Midway.

Two large synagogues were constructed in Kenwood to replace the temples left behind. In 1923 Henry Newhouse designed the classically styled Kehilath Anshe Ma'ariv Temple on Drexel Boulevard, now the home of Operation PUSH. The following year the synagogue for the Isaiah Israel congregation was constructed on Greenwood Avenue at Hyde Park Boulevard. In order to build the temple, the estate of Charles Counselman was purchased for $85,000. The house, one of the most imposing mansions in Kenwood, had been constructed thirty years earlier at a cost of $150,000.[34]

Hyde Park of the twenties reflected a tightly woven combination of single-family houses, apartments or flats, and rooming houses. The area south of 55th Street continued to be associated most closely with the university, while the northern half was oriented toward the Loop through the affordable and convenient commute provided by the Illinois Central trains. The largest ethnic group at the beginning of the decade was Irish, and facilities rose to accommodate their religious needs, including St. Thomas the Apostle Church by Barry Byrne. Completed in 1924, the church at 5472 South Kimbark broke away from the traditional verticality of church design. Byrne

collaborated with other designers in the creation of the building's ornament; Alfonso Iannelli designed much of the stained glass and created many of the terra-cotta sculp-tures, and Alfeo Faggi, an Italian sculptor, produced a bronze *Pieta*.

In the commercial area two notable buildings were constructed during the twen-ties. The Hyde Park Bank commissioned architect K. M. Vitzhum & Company in 1928 to design a building on 53rd Street. At the time the ten-story Classical Revival structure was completed, it was one of Chicago's largest commercial buildings out-side the Loop.[35] The following year M. Louis Kroman designed the 88,000-square-foot Art Deco/Moderne style Ritz 55th Garage on the busy corner at 55th Street and Lake Avenue. The lavish terra-cotta façade features automotive motifs glamorizing the car, its engines, tires, headlamps, and gearshifts. The completion of the garage marked a transition point of old Lake Avenue, from a street lined with saloons before the days of Prohibition to a street of businesses and garages.[36]

Terra-cotta embellishments were widely used in the construction of large build-ings from the beginning of the twentieth century through the 1930s. The material could be glazed in a variety of colors and made into forms ranging from simple, flat blocks to decorative three-dimensional figures.[37] The material was durable and relatively inexpensive, allowing architects to design structures compatible with the surrounding brick and stone structures, yet in a more cost-effective manner that required little maintenance.

In the design of single-family residences, the twenties were a transition period from the nineteenth-century view of home as a refuge to the more compact and efficient type of single-family houses now commonly constructed. New materials and building methods meant these smaller houses were less costly to build than in years past, and their popularity was reflected in the ubiquitous Chicago bungalow, constructed throughout the city. Residents did not go along with this trend toward repetition; only one bungalow can be found in Kenwood, at 5046 South Ellis. The progressive styles had fallen out of favor before the war; during the twenties archi-

tects used a traditional vocabulary for smaller-scale, efficiently designed residences constructed within the confines of an already dense neighborhood.

Many advances were apparent in the interior of the home—there was an explosion in the availability of consumer goods, as innovations in appliances made housework less time-consuming and meal preparation easier. Women's roles within the home were changing—the women's movement challenged the idea that women were required to dedicate their lives to the home and be judged by their success as good wives and homemakers. Although they were paid less and had fewer opportunities, women were employed in increasing numbers, and, given the right to vote, were now considered a political force within the nation.

Household servants were still common in the neighborhood's wealthier residences, while middle-class women had to balance the management of households and raising a family with new employment opportunities. New appliances were promoted as an efficient way to make housekeeping an easier task. The vacuum cleaner, washing machine, and spin dryer were introduced, and "the icebox gave way to the Frigidaire," as frozen foods became popular.[38]

Despite the considerable investment near the lakefront and by the university, property values declined at the community's western edge. Here the boundary was particularly fragile; the alley between Cottage Grove and Drexel Boulevard became the dividing line between communities. To the east lay the expensive apartment buildings and mansions of Kenwood; to the west, a window shade factory, several garages and auto repair shops, and apartments housing residents of the expanding Black Belt. Although the boundary held, Drexel Boulevard no longer had its once lofty status.

Concerns about the changing demographics and physical condition of Chicago's South Side led to the formation of an increased number of property owner associations. Fearing for their community and their livelihood, the local real estate board recommended that owners in every white block of the neighborhood form a society. The Hyde Park–Kenwood Property Owners' Association continued to be influential as well as divisive, promoting the exclusion of blacks through the "united action of white property owners."[39]

Restrictive covenants became widely used contractual agreements among property owners that "prohibited the lease, purchase or occupation of their premises by a particular group of people, usually African Americans."[40] By 1925 restrictive covenants became, as one realtor commented to the *Hyde Park Herald*, "like marvelous delicately woven chain armor . . . [excluding] any member of a race not Caucasian."[41] The Chicago Real Estate Board provided model contracts and encouraged these racial restrictions.[42] However these contracts were often violated. With an eye on profits, owners of properties began to break the covenants. Blacks were allowed to move into an apartment building and then rents were raised substantially. The borders of the Black Belt expanded as owners saw the economic advantages of renting to blacks. However, while rents may have escalated, property values began a decline, furthering the intensity of the property owners' efforts.

Although cows continued to placidly graze in John Dunham's undeveloped field, and racial covenants kept the Hyde Park community predominantly white, changes in the neighborhood were readily apparent. Forty-Seventh Street divided Kenwood into two distinct communities, with the area to the north the most heavily populated and progressively black. There, over a hundred existing structures were converted from single-family houses into multifamily dwellings, while Drexel Boulevard the wealthy fled for the city's North Shore. Novelist Edna Ferber reflected on the city's changing neighborhoods in her novel, *The Girls*:

> Anyone who has lived in Chicago knows that you don't live on the South Side. You simply do not live on the South Side. And yet Chicago's South Side is a pleasant place of fine houses and neat lawns . . . ; of trees, and magnificent parks and boulevards; of stately (if smoke-blackened) apartment houses; of children, and motor cars; of all that makes for comfortable middle-class American life. More than that, booming its benisons upon the whole is the astounding spectacle of Lake Michigan forming the section's eastern boundary. And yet Fashion had early turned its back on all this as is the way of Fashion with natural beauty.[43]

Cherishing their community and its illustrious past, residents feared for the future. Anxious about the growth of the Black Belt to the north and west, residents hired private watchmen to patrol the nighttime hours.[44] While Beulah May Annan awaited her fate, another highly publicized murder occurred. Once again heartbreak did not come from outsiders, but ironically at the hands of two of the community's own. On May 21, 1924, a young boy failed to return home after school, and before long the neighborhood was horrified to discover fourteen-year-old Bobby Franks had been abducted and murdered.

Nathan Leopold Jr. and Richard Loeb were exceptionally bright University of Chicago students living blocks apart in Kenwood. As young Bobby Franks walked toward his home from the Harvard School on Ellis Avenue, Leopold and Loeb

Francis Drexel Fountain, c. 1930.

5.07. Under the watchful eye of Francis Drexel, exuberant neighborhood children took full advantage of his fountain on one of the city's steamy summer days.

pulled alongside and offered a ride in their car. As they made a left on 50th Street, Bobby was hit over the head with a heavy metal chisel and a piece of cloth was stuffed down his throat. They drove south to Wolf Lake with the body, dumping it in a culvert where it was later found and identified.[45]

Rewards for the capture of the murderer were offered as police and newspaper reporters searched for clues. A pair of glasses found near the body had unusual hinges. Sales records showed that only three had been sold in the Chicago area—one pair to Nathan Leopold. Several days after Bobby Franks was laid to rest, both Leopold and Loeb were detained and questioned separately by authorities under intense media coverage. Though their stories did not match perfectly, police were unable to build a case and they were released.

When the Leopold chauffeur provided a contradictory timeline for the use of the automobile, gradually their alibis began to crumble.[46] Faced with the new evidence, Leopold and Loeb confessed to the murder and kidnapping and told their story. They revealed that the kidnapping and request for a ransom had been planned for months as a challenge to the two bored students. Leopold added that they had no need of the money; it was merely to make the murder "more interesting."[47] The lurid case became a major story in newspapers across the country, and an outraged public demanded swift trials and executions. Albert Loeb went to one of the country's best criminal defense lawyers, sixty-seven-year-old Clarence Darrow.[48]

Leopold Residence, c. 1885.
Demolished 1925.
4754 South Greenwood Avenue.
Architect/builder unknown.
5.08. The Leopolds were
German-Jewish immigrants who
made their fortune in shipping
on the Great Lakes. They did
not construct the house situated
on the northwest corner of 48th
Street and Greenwood Avenue;
it was built about 1885 and had
been altered to remove the
original Victorian detailing.

On June 5, 1924, a grand jury indicted Leopold and Loeb for kidnapping and murder.[49] Darrow, "a passionate opponent of the death penalty," immediately stunned the courtroom by changing their pleas from not guilty to guilty by reason of insanity. Darrow then needed to argue that there was a medical reason, mental illness, in order to save his clients from the death penalty. The psychiatrists for the prosecution, including Kenwood resident Dr. Archibald Church, found neither defendant to display any sign of "mental derangement."[50] On August 22, 1924, Darrow made an impassioned speech against the death penalty. Leopold and Loeb were found guilty, but sentenced to life imprisonment.

The sprawling frame house of the Leopold family disappeared a year after the verdict was handed down. It was demolished on October 2, 1925, and the property was later subdivided to accommodate the construction several smaller houses. The Leopold garage, where the car was cleaned of evidence, was converted into a coach house after the war.[51] The massive Loeb mansion at 5017 Ellis survived into the seventies, but was demolished and the property subdivided. The Franks family moved shortly after the crime; their house exists today, although the structure for many years was in a serious state of disrepair. The residence of Dr. Church, designed by Handy & Cady in 1897, remains at 4858 Dorchester. The Harvard School at 4731 South Ellis, from which Bobby Franks walked was sold in 2006 and the structure renovated to luxury condominiums. Famed attorney Clarence Darrow lived at 1537 East 60th Street, just south of the Midway, for much of his professional life. His ashes were scattered nearby in the Jackson Park lagoon, now the site of an "annual celebration of his life and principles."[52]

Although Hyde Park and Kenwood gained unwelcome notoriety, a more significant impact on the community's future would occur in the fall of 1929, on Black Tuesday, the 29th of October, when the stock market collapsed and the ensuing period known as the Great Depression took a major toll on the neighborhood.

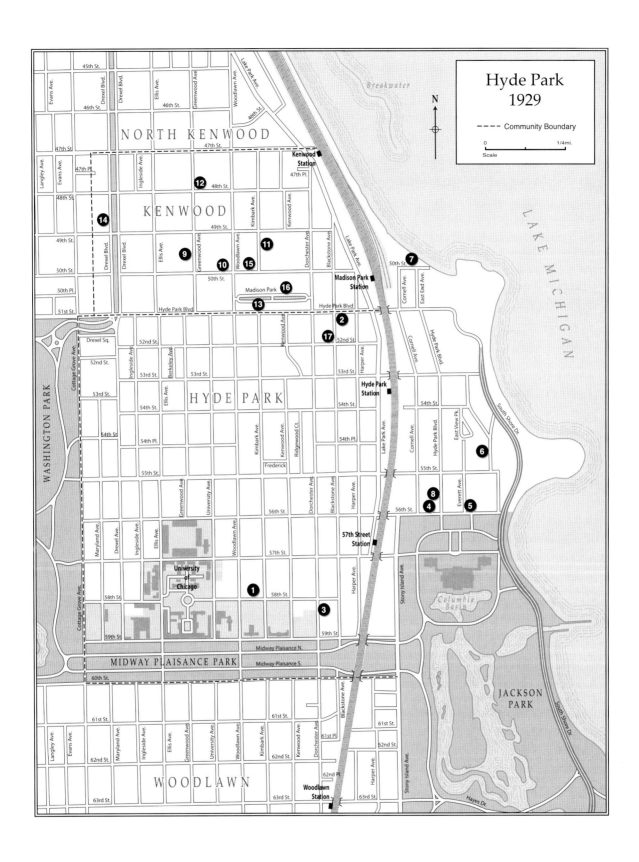

--- Community Boundary

0   1/4mi.
Scale

Breakwater

LAKE MICHIGAN

N

NORTH KENWOOD

45th St.
46th St.
47th St.
Kenwood Station
47th Pl.

Evans Ave.
Drexel Blvd.
Drexel Blvd.
Ellis Ave.
Greenwood Ave.
Woodlawn Ave.
Lake Park Ave.
46th St.

KENWOOD

48th St. ⑫
49th St.
⑭
Drexel Blvd.
47th Pl.
Langley Ave.
Evans Ave.
48th St.

49th St.
50th St.
Drexel Blvd.
Ellis Ave.
⑨
Greenwood Ave.
⑩
Woodlawn Ave.
⑮
⑪
Kimbark Ave.
Kenwood Ave.
Dorchester Ave.
Blackstone Ave.
50th St.
Madison Park Station
Cornell Ave.
East End Ave.
50th St.
⑦

50th Pl.
51st St.
Hyde Park Blvd.
Madison Park ⑯
⑬
Hyde Park Blvd.

Drexel Sq.
②
Kenwood Ave.
⑰
52nd St.
Harper Ave.
Cornell Ave.
Cornell Ave.
Hyde Park Blvd.
South Shore Dr.

WASHINGTON PARK

Cottage Grove Ave.
Drexel Sq.
52nd St.
53rd St.

Ingleside Ave.
Berkeley Ave.
Ellis Ave.
53rd St.
54th St.

HYDE PARK

53rd St.
54th St.
54th Pl.
54th St
55th St.
Kimbark Ave.
Kenwood Ct.
Ridgewood Ct.
54th Pl.
Frederick
54th St.
Hyde Park Station
54th St.
East View Pk.
55th St.
⑥

Maryland Ave.
Drexel Ave.
Ingleside Ave.
Ellis Ave.
Greenwood Ave.
University Ave.
Woodlawn Ave.
56th St.
Dorchester Ave.
Blackstone Ave.
Harper Ave.
56th St.
⑧
④
Everett Ave.
⑤

57th St.
University of Chicago
①
57th St.
58th St.
Harper Ave.
57th Street Station

Cottage Grove Ave.
58th St
59th St.
③
59th St

Columbia Basin

Stony Island Ave.

MIDWAY PLAISANCE PARK
Midway Plaisance N.
Midway Plaisance S.
60th St.

JACKSON PARK

61st St.
61st St.
Blackstone Ave.
61st St.
62nd St.
62nd St.
62nd Pl.
Harper Ave.
Stony Island Ave.

Langley Ave.
Evans Ave.
Maryland Ave.
Ingleside Ave.
Ellis Ave.
Greenwood Ave.
University Ave.
Woodlawn Ave.
Kimbark Ave.
Kenwood Ave.
Dorchester Ave.

WOODLAWN

63rd St.
63rd St.
Woodlawn Station
63rd St.
Hayes Dr.
South Shore Dr.

Hyde Park

1 ## Michelson Residence, 1923.
1220 East 58th Street. Philip Maher.

By the twenties, available land was scarce for construction in Hyde Park. New residences such as this charming house for Albert Michelson, the 1907 Nobel Prize–winning head of the Physics Department at the University of Chicago, were rare. Albert and Edna Michelson and were interested in having a smaller house built in the yard behind the large residence at the 5756 South Kimbark (now demolished). Before departing on an extended trip to Europe they had dinner with their daughter

5.09. The traditional Michelson house is nested just east of Frank Lloyd Wright's striking Robie house.

5.10. Originally constructed as a cooperative, the Cloisters offered apartments with a stone fireplace and from four to nine rooms.

and son-in-law, architect Philip Maher, and suggested he design and build a house while they were away. Maher "sketched out a floor plan on a napkin," which was immediately approved.[53] The traditional French Provincial house was completed by their return and is nestled just east of Wright's groundbreaking Robie house.

Although not as well known as his father, George, Philip Maher is recognized as a "significant architect who combined architectural historicism with his father's more progressive style."[54] In his later works Maher's designs were a combination of both schools of thought, but here on 58th Street he used historic styles and forms. The Michelson's house features steeply sloped slate roofs and a turreted staircase; the pattern of bricks and wood trim on the exterior indicated the location of the interior stairs. The contrast between these time-honored forms and the arresting horizontality of the Robie house, designed fifteen years earlier, provides a striking example of two very different approaches to residential architecture.

③ The Cloisters, 1927.
5801–5811 South Dorchester Avenue. Granger, Lowe & Bollenbacher.

When land was available in this area of Hyde Park, economics often made certain multifamily housing would be constructed, evident by the number of three-flats lining many streets. The twenties witnessed apartments rising to new heights, including the thirteen-story Cloisters apartment building, now owned by the University of Chicago and long favored by professors. Notables who have resided in the building include Nobel Prize winner Saul Bellow; the subject of his novel *Ravelstein*, professor Allan Bloom; and the winner of the 1992 Nobel Prize in Economics, Gary Becker. Traditionally detailed, the eighty-four spacious apartments feature built-in bookcases and carved stone mantels of wood-burning fireplaces. The two sections of the building surround an open courtyard with a central fountain.

② Piccadilly Theater and Apartments, 1926. Theater demolished 1972.
1429–1451 East Hyde Park Boulevard. Rapp & Rapp.

In the early months of 1920 workers demolished several three-flat buildings on the southeast corner of Hyde Park Boulevard and Blackstone Avenue, a site one block to the west of the Hyde Park Hotel. A structure, tentatively named Hotel Marquette, was planned for construction and included a luxurious theater within its L-shaped confines.[55] Seven years later, the Schoenstadt family opened one of the largest theaters on the South Side of Chicago. Designed by the Rapp brothers, the Piccadilly Theater quickly became the flagship of the Schoenstadt theater chain. The theater and ground-floor shops were housed within the fourteen-story apartment building, where Herman Schoenstadt resided in a top-floor luxury suite during the 1930s and 40s.

Cinema palaces of the era typically featured several common elements, including a projecting marquee and large, elaborate main lobby. The Rapps' design for the Piccadilly was slightly different; the marquee was flush with the front wall, with

5.11. The Piccadilly Apartments, as seen in an undated photograph, are now university housing.

5.12. When the Piccadilly Theater opened on January 24, 1927, the *Hyde Park Herald* noted it was the "fulfillment of a dream" for Herman Schoenstadt. In an elaborate stage production entitled *Fan Fantasy*, the opening program featured "dainty costumes . . . , graceful pantomime," and a new composition by the musical director Albert E. Short brought to life by a thirty-piece symphony orchestra. Featured on the screen that week was the popular Reginald Denny in the silent film comedy *The Cheerful Fraud*.

an enormous window above it trimmed in terra-cotta. To compensate for the lack of a vast lobby, the Rapps designed a double-height space with a small mezzanine above, giving the illusion of grandeur.[56] Patrons entered to the sounds of a spotlit grand piano and harp.

The drama was not all on the screen; the auditorium was the "true treasure" of the building, designed in an ornate French Renaissance style to accommodate 2,500 patrons. The luxurious interior was decorated with "antique furniture, oil paintings, and copies of ancient sculpture" the Schoenstadt family brought back from their travels.[57] A Kilgen organ, with decorative scrollwork and bronze trim, was used during vaudeville performances. However five years after the theater's opening, the organ was made obsolete by the advent of the "talkies."

In the ensuing years, as the neighborhood changed, attendance declined, and the theater closed in 1963. The University of Chicago purchased the property, and nine years later the theater was demolished. The apartment building remains, and although the theater is now a parking lot, traces of its former glory remain etched on the south wall of the structure.

East Hyde Park

4 The Windermere East, 1924.
1642 East 56th Street. Rapp & Rapp.

The new Windermere was one of the many high-rise apartment hotels constructed during the twenties in the area that became known as East Hyde Park, In 1922 the owners of the old Windermere Hotel broke ground on a new hotel adjacent to the property, and when the new structure opened it was hailed as the "South Side's

5.13. Various advertisements for the Windermere touted the famous cuisine, refined atmosphere, and high standards of service.

Greatest Hostelry."[58] The classically detailed structure faces Jackson Park and the Museum of Science and Industry, the only building remaining from the Columbian Exposition of 1893.[59]

Noted theater architects George and Cornelius Rapp designed the building primarily for long-term residents, planning six apartments per floor, many with full kitchens to supplement the services of the hotel's dining rooms, the Anchorage and the Classic Room. The Windermere offered apartments with all the services of a regular hotel: dining, maid service, and laundry.

When construction began on this structure, the owner was considering a duplicate structure to replace the old Windermere hotel at the northwest corner of Cornell and 56th. A tunnel connected the two hotels at this time, and while the old Windermere had every room wired for the telephone, the new hotel was wired for radio.[60]

The Windermere was foreclosed upon during the Depression, its twin never built, and the old structure stood just to the west until razed in 1957.

⑤ Jackson Towers, 1924.

5555 South Everett. Walter W. Ahlschlager.

In 1921 *American Builder Magazine* featured an article on the work of architect Walter Ahlschlager. "High-grade residential hotel construction has been a notable feature of 1920 building," the publication noted. "With sky-rocketing prices putting a stop to all other building work, these immense hotel enterprises have gone ahead. The demand for satisfactory living accommodations with freedom from household cares and domestic servant worries has filled all the hotels to capacity. The work, in this hotel field, of Walter W. Ahlschlager, architect of Chicago, has been conspicuously successful."[61]

Ahlschlager designed the Jackson Towers Apartments on a site east of the Windermere and overlooking Jackson Park. Of fireproof construction, the nineteen-story brick building used terra-cotta details of columns and cartouches to mimic a regional look, breaking down the mass of the structure to make it more a part of the neighborhood despite its size. Considered very fashionable in the thirties, the

5.15. Jackson Towers was conceived as rental units in combination with cooperative apartments. The interiors were opulent—many of the apartments featured two-story living rooms with elaborate rounded fireplaces, coffered ceilings, and dramatic curving stairways. In 1967 the building was converted to condominiums.

structure contained seventy-three apartments of three to twelve rooms each, for a total of 438 rooms.[62]

Among Jackson Towers' more famous occupants was Charles A. Comiskey, who lived here for a short time before his death in 1931.[63] A Chicago legend, Comiskey is credited with creating the American Baseball League and founding a lucrative baseball franchise on the city's South Side.[64] Grace Reidy Comiskey, his eldest son's widow, moved from the apartment in 1940 in controversial fashion. According to the *Chicago Tribune*, a lawsuit was filed by the building owners accusing her of trying to "take part of the apartment with her," moving out "eight doors, three walls, and seven chandeliers" that would be difficult to replace. The widow claimed she had purchased the items herself and had them installed in the apartment.[65]

⑥ The Shoreland, 1925–1926.
5454 South Shore Drive. Meyer Fridstein.

Facing east toward open parkland and the waters of Lake Michigan, the once luxurious Shoreland for a time faced an uncertain future; however, the building began an extensive renovation in 2012. When it opened its doors in 1926 the Shoreland was the South Side's largest hotel, built to accommodate full-time residents and visitors to the area. The imposing fourteen-story, U-shaped structure was built of buff-colored pressed brick and Bedford limestone with neoclassical and baroque terra-cotta detailing.[66] Meyer Fridstein designed the Shoreland in partnership with Gustav Gottschalk, a prominent builder of apartment hotels, including the Jackson Shore Apartments (5490 South Shore Drive) in Hyde Park.

The Shoreland was a major center of the social life of Hyde Park for decades, providing extensive services for the residents and guests of its 1,000 rooms, including an array of shops, an indoor miniature golf course, a bowling alley, and a gourmet restaurant. Residents entered through a lobby with soaring thirty-foot ceilings

5.17. Advertisements for the Shoreland noted an atmosphere of refinement and culture—a hotel sure to define the guest as a person of importance.

5.18. The Shoreland's original elaborate black and red Spanish-themed lobby, not considered fashionable ten years later, was remodeled in the streamlined Art Deco style as seen in this image taken in 1937.

and danced in the second floor Crystal Ballroom, where countless lavish wedding receptions were held.[67] Over the years Chicago's elite, and notorious, visited the hotel. Amelia Earhart returned to visit the Hyde Park of her youth; mobster Al Capone was thought to have conducted his "business" here; and labor leader Jimmy Hoffa held raucous union meetings. Legend has it one of Hoffa's minions once strangled a hotel employee who demanded payment of his boss's tab.[68]

7   The Powhatan, 1928.
4950 South Chicago Beach Drive. Robert DeGolyer and Charles L. Morgan.

This mid-rise represents the last of the ornamental-style buildings constructed prior to the influence of the glass box. Developers for the Powhatan mimicked the North Side Streeterville neighborhood, as the cooperative building was part of a larger development intended for an area of Hyde Park long known as "Indian Vil-

5.19. The twenty-two-story Powhatan contains two tiers of cooperative apartments.

5.20. The Powhatan's east entrance on Chicago Beach Drive is adorned with Indian figures standing guard in the grillwork of the doors, flanked by trios of arrows in the light fixtures.

lage." Playing upon this theme, DeGolyer and associate architect Charles Morgan designed the exterior of the Powhatan with a pattern of projecting piers and mullions, panels inserted between windows in the upper elevations, and details such as American Indian figures in full headdress that support the entrance canopy. Lights on either side of the entrance mimic geometric arrows, and warriors stare out from panels on the windows of the first floor, all motifs reflected in a structure named for an Algonquin Indian chief.

On the interior, the octagonal foyer has mosaics featuring ladies of fashion, other exotic figures, and abstractions. The *Tribune* noted the elevators were "marvelous examples of Art Deco, combining etched mirrors, ornately molded white metal trim and highly polished wood." The interior detailing was carefully con-

ceived and constructed, but when the lobby and swimming pool were remodeled in the 1950s, many of Morgan's mosaics were lost. Saved, however, was the twentieth-floor ballroom, "straight out of a French movie set of the period."[69] The fifty-four apartments were designed with luxurious, amenities: wood burning fireplaces, galleries with plaster beam ceilings, "mechanical refrigeration," and incinerator systems in the kitchen.[70]

Today the lobby appears much as it did originally, after restoration by Vinci/Hamp Architects during the 1990s. The curved walls and dropped ceiling of the lobby were removed, and windows facing the lakefront were unblocked. Reinventing the technique of *scraffiti*, sheets of cast plaster were made into mosaic tiles of 430 different hues to restore the murals. The original andirons that resembled skyscrapers were found and are now repositioned on either side of the fireplace.

The Powhatan faces onto the park and the open expanses of Lake Michigan; however, its positioning on the site does not provide for the most sweeping views available. Urban legend provides two possible answers to the location on the property. According to construction engineer and local historian Sam Guard, the building was to be situated ninety degrees from its current position, allowing for views north to the city and east to the lakefront. However, test core drilling indicated that the hardpan clay beneath the soil was not satisfactory to support the caissons and piers of the structure. In order to construct the building as the architect intended, the developers would have to absorb the extra cost and difficulties of digging down to bedrock, an additional forty to sixty feet below. It was determined that rotating the structure provided the proper support, hence the unusual positioning on the property.

The second theory is that the Powhatan was to be one of two buildings on this property. The utilitarian side of the structure would then have been hidden by the utilitarian side of the next building north.

8 **Poinsettia Apartments, 1929.**
5528 South Hyde Park Boulevard. Leon F. Urbain.

The Poinsettia Apartments are listed on the National Register of Historic Places, which notes that the terra-cotta ornamentation is "one of the finest examples in Chicago."[71] The building is designed in the Spanish Colonial Revival style, one of the more eclectic of the historical revival styles that dominated residential architecture in the first decades of the twentieth century. The distinctive features of the building according to the National Register "include arched openings in the lobby and in apartments, a yellow brick façade with colorful ornaments, spiral finials, and balconies."

5.22. The apartments within the twelve-story Poinsettia still have features from earlier days; small portals, formerly used for convenient milk deliveries, are found between the kitchens and hallways.

The twelve-story building contains eleven one-room and thirty-three three-room apartments. "Mechanical refrigeration and ventilation" were among the features of these small apartments at a time when air conditioners and refrigerators were novel amenities.[72] The apartments were as advertised in the *Guide Map to a Century of Progress* as "large, cool and airy, with a convenient location to the World's Fair."

Kenwood

⑨ McCormick Residence, 1922.

4942 South Greenwood Avenue. John A. Armstrong.

Once common, the moving of houses was gradually limited since the elevated train system, overhead electric and telephone lines, and railroad embankments provided serious impediments.[73] However, in 1922 the old frame house of Frank and Maria Spooner was moved from Greenwood Avenue to the northwest corner of 50th Street and Woodlawn Avenue. In its new location, the house stands out as the only frame structure on a block of stone and brick mansions designed by architects such as Howard van Doren Shaw and Horatio R. Wilson. Henry Newhouse made the plans for the relocation and designed the new foundation and garage on a portion of the grounds of the old Van Higgins estate.

John McCormick purchased the Spooner property and hired John Armstrong to design the three-story Tudor Revival house on the vacated land. In a style that closely emulated the idea of Howard van Doren Shaw's English country houses, his design contrasts with the strong horizontal lines of the 1908 Magerstadt house

5.23. The house originally on the McCormick property was built by Frank and Maria Spooner. They lived there until 1909, when the twelve room frame house and 100' · 297' grounds were sold to James P. Hutchinson. In 1922 that house was lifted off the stone foundation and moved around the corner to Woodlawn Avenue.

10 Spooner Residence, 1887. Relocated from 4940 South Greenwood, 1922.
4950 South Woodlawn Avenue. Jenney & Otis.

5.24. Frank E. Spooner's house was described by the May 1, 1909, *Economist* as "one of the most attractive places in Kenwood." Mrs. Spooner was a member of the Daughters of the American Revolution and her husband, a dealer in building materials, was active in the American Bible Society and the Kenwood Evangelical Church.

by Prairie School architect George Maher directly to the north. The McCormick residence features a ballroom on the third floor and an abundance of Gothic detailing on the exterior.

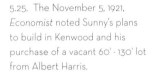 Sunny Residence, 1922.

4913 South Kimbark Avenue. Holabird & Roche.

The last of the five residences designed by the firm of Holabird & Roche that remain in the Hyde Park–Kenwood area is the house of Bernard E. and Ellen Sunny. Sunny served as president of General Electric until 1908, when he became president of the Chicago Telephone Company. A supporter of the University of Chicago, Sunny donated the funds for the gymnasium that bears his name at the Laboratory Schools.[74] As a member of the South Park Board, Sunny negotiated with the Chicago Beach Hotel to release their claim of ri-

5.25. The November 5, 1921, *Economist* noted Sunny's plans to build in Kenwood and his purchase of a vacant 60' · 130' lot from Albert Harris.

parian rights, allowing the outer drive to be constructed along the lakefront.[75] The family had previously lived at 4933 Woodlawn, in a residence designed by George Beaumont and altered by Holabird & Roche several times. In 1921 Sunny purchased the vacant lot on Kimbark from Albert Harris, who lived directly to the south. The house was completed in 1922, although the Holabird & Root designed alterations in 1929.

12 **Zisook Residence, 1927.**
1100 East 48th Street. Bishop & Company.

Thomas Bishop specialized in the design of apartment buildings and worked with Harry Zisook, a "very successful contractor," on many projects throughout the neighborhood. They concentrated on purchasing large old properties and subdividing the lots to construct either smaller-scale, efficiently designed houses with traditional detailing or "perfectly managed" hotels in convenient locations.[76] For Harry and Marian Zisook's residence Bishop employed a number of historical devices, including his favored clay tile roof, terra-cotta embellishments, and an entrance flanked by columns. This house was constructed not long after the death of the property's original owner, Annie McClure Hitchcock, one of the first settlers in Kenwood.

5.26. Bishop favored the use of pale brick and clay tile roofs in his adaptation of the Spanish Colonial Revival for apartment buildings and houses, such as the Zisook residence. The style became popular following the Panama-California Exposition in 1915, where Bertram Goodhue's design for the California Building was widely admired. Although suited for the warmer climates, the style became popular in the Midwest.

13 Zisook Apartment Building, 1924. Demolished. Kimbark Avenue and East Hyde Park Boulevard. Bishop & Company.
5.27. Bishop was the architect of many apartments in the neighborhood. This terra-cotta-embellished courtyard building was typical of the increasingly dense development of the neighborhood.

14 Tudor Gables Apartments, 1928.
4830–4848 South Drexel Boulevard, Alvin M. Johnson.

By the twenties, Drexel Boulevard was no longer one of Chicago's most fashionable streets and was generally considered a part of Kenwood. Densities increased as apartments rose to occupy the land where the turreted heavy stone mansions of the city's elite once graced the street. Chauncey Blair's mansion at 4830 Drexel was demolished in February 1928 in order to make way for the appropriately named Tudor Gables Apartments. Rising three and a half stories, the elaborately detailed brick and terra-cotta building made an attempt to tie the larger structure in with the aesthetics of the boulevard.

15 Cummins Residence, 1928.
1220 East 50th Street. Armstrong, Furst & Tilton.

Land was scarce during the twenties; the last remaining parcels in Kenwood were subdivided lots along the east-west streets. Construction began on this traditionally detailed house for investment banker Albert Cummins and his wife Myrna during the summer of 1927. Details of the façade include the use of a relieving arch above

5.29. Albert and Myrna Cummins did not live in their new house for long. The *Hyde Park Herald* notes they resided in Baltimore in January 1934.

the first-floor windows. Once a structural necessity, the brickwork carries on an old tradition, albeit now as a decorative architectural embellishment. The fifteen-room Cummins residence underwent an extensive remodeling in 1961 to convert the six-servant residence into one for a family with six children. Featured on the Kenwood Open House tour that year, the original cramped spaces of the kitchen butler's pantry and servants' breakfast nook were opened up into one larger space.[77]

17 Residence, c. 1890.
5132–5136 South Blackstone Avenue. Remodeled by Edgar Miller, c. 1928.

5.30. Much of Edgar Miller's work is found in the Old Town neighborhood on the city's near north side; however, these residences are attributed to Miller and provide a flavor of what is found in abundance there.

16 Residence, c. 1890. 1338 East Madison Park. Remodeled by Edgar Miller, c. 1928.

5.31

Chicago artist Edgar Miller created exquisitely crafted hand-made residences during the late 1920s and early 1930s, often liberally embellished with stained glass windows, frescoes, murals, mosaics, and woodcarvings. At the same time, his work could be viewed as spartan, producing an interesting dichotomy between the Victorian age façade and the solids and voids indicative of a new era.

A key figure among the artists and writers of Hyde Park during the twenties, Miller was unconventional, eclectic, even quirky, in his approach to architecture: "I accepted influences from anyplace. Every time I saw something that was of value, I absorbed it. Influence is nothing but nourishment and you grow by it. To be afraid of influence is like being scared to eat."[78] Influenced by Alfonso Iannelli and Barry Byrne, Miller was a success at this point in his multi-faceted career, but grew "weary of renovating old houses" by 1935.[79]

6.01. The rich texture of the University of Chicago campus and the surrounding Hyde Park neighborhood is evident in this view to the southwest, centered on the First Unitarian Church at Woodlawn and 57th Street designed in 1931 by Denison Bingham Hull.

CHAPTER SIX

Frayed Edges, 1930–1948

One day, as result of one of the violent shifts which are a part of the destiny of cities . . . Chicago was cut in two: the east-west axis . . . determined the destiny of two sections of the city. The fashionable quarter was in the south; suddenly it changed to the north. The southern part was abandoned. Who will live in these princely (and dubious) residences on Drexel Avenue? No one. Nevertheless, after a certain amount of time, the Negroes take it over. They settle down behind broken windows covered over by boards; a villa becomes a village; there are weeds in the rubbish-filled gardens, behind rusting iron fences. There is misery there. For whoever says Negro in the USA says pariah.

—Le Corbusier, *When Cathedrals Were White: A Journey to the Country of Timid People*, 1937

In spite of everything that happened on Wall Street in the fall of 1929, the economy did not immediately collapse. Investment was certainly down, when a rolling series of bank panics began late in 1930. Hundreds of banks closed across the country, including the newly housed Hyde Park Bank, as nervous customers lined up and demanded their money. Homelessness, hunger, misery, and fear gripped the nation as prosperity disappeared. The building industry came to a standstill as the apartment boom of the 1920s turned into "an epidemic of receiverships." By 1932, Chicago had suffered the worst drop in property values of any major American city.[1] The effect on the nation's economy lasted for years.

In the midst of this economic crisis, plans were underway for Chicago to host its second world's fair, the Century of Progress Exposition. Initially intended to "commemorate Chicago's past," the fair instead came to "symbolize hope for America's future."[2] The pivotal role of architects exhibited in the planning of the 1893 Columbian Exposition was repeated forty years later for fairgrounds that stretched along the lakefront from 12th to 39th Streets. However for the 1933–1934 exposition, a colorful, forward-thinking American architecture replaced the monochromatic classicism of the earlier fair. A "broad definition of modern architecture" was promoted for the fair, one that was "not relying on purely aesthetic characteristics but instead focusing on new design solutions."[3] Architects used new building materials

Model House, House of Tomorrow, 1933. Century of Progress International Exposition, Keck & Keck.

6.02. America's first glass house, which *House & Garden* magazine's editors described as "revolutionary in design and construction," was showcased at the Chicago world's fair of 1933. Designed for the Century of Progress and known as the "House of Tomorrow," the nearly circular structure was constructed of glass and steel around a spiral staircase that enclosed the electrical, plumbing, and air conditioning systems. "No windows open," explained the editors, "the air-conditioning system keeping the atmosphere as fresh as a day in June." The photograph appeared in the September 1933 issue of *House & Garden* and as the cover of promotional material distributed at the fair.

such as masonite and gypsum board in their designs for the fair's pavilions. A variety of structural innovations were introduced in the construction process, including dramatic suspended roofs and the use of prefabricated elements.[4]

As the fair opened the message portrayed was that "cooperation between science, business and government could pave the way to a better future."[5] This message extended to the evolution of the family residence, as architects George Fred Keck and William Keck designed one of six model houses displayed on Chicago's lakefront. Their "House of Tomorrow" was built on a steel frame with no bearing walls, designed from the center, where the utilities were located, outward.[6] Featuring the use of synthetic building materials, the house "forecast a future" where an all-electric kitchen and air conditioning would become commonly used in domestic architecture. For a country in financial turmoil, the fair represented the power of technology to overcome the hardships of the Depression, and promoted the role that consumers could play in bringing them to an end.[7]

From the Depression through the Second World War, university trustees and neighborhood residents watched the results of the influx of African Americans from the Deep South and the movement of rural whites to the city. While still a stable and desirable neighborhood in 1930, Hyde Park and Kenwood experienced changes that "affected all large cities in the Northeast and Midwest,"[8] as concerns festered about the changes taking place in the neighboring communities. The changing demographics, the growing unemployment and crime, overcrowding that encouraged illegal conversions, and a deteriorating housing stock combined to put Hyde Park and Kenwood on a path toward a tenuous state.

The network of racially restrictive housing covenants sponsored by the Chicago Real Estate Board no longer kept the surrounding neighborhoods white. As these contractual agreements were broken, blacks moved into previously all white areas in numbers. Owners saw the economic advantages of renting or selling to African Americans while property values began a decline. By 1930 the borders of the Black Belt expanded to surround the Hyde Park community, with the exception of two neighborhoods, Washington Park to the southwest and Woodlawn to the south.

Complicating matters was a Chicago Real Estate Board policy, known as redlining, created through the Home Owners Loan Corporation. Through the production of color-coded maps of American cities, racial and economic criteria were used to evaluate risk for banking and insurance companies. Green lines highlighted affluent white neighborhoods, while poor neighborhoods, both black and white, received the red designation. With limited access to loans or insurance the undesirable redlined areas surrounding Hyde Park lacked the funding necessary for maintenance, improvement, and repairs, which only accelerated their decline.[9]

The majority of the Hyde Park and Kenwood neighborhood remained racially stable, and sections of the community were affluent. However, the cumulative effect of shifting demographics and a depression became profound. Hotels built for the world's fair of 1893 continued to operate but were renovated to smaller units and catered to transients. The once elegant Chicago Beach Hotel became Gardiner General Hospital after a federal court order authorized the US army to take possession of the property for use as a military hospital in 1942. At this time the hotel had been a landmark on Chicago's shoreline for fifty years and housed nearly three hundred families, all of whom had to be relocated within thirty days.[10]

Small family-operated stores on the commercial streets saw their more affluent clientele move elsewhere, and many closed their doors. Fourteen years after the Eighteenth Amendment was ratified, it became the only constitutional amendment to ever be repealed. In the demise of Prohibition, the location of liquor serving establishments began to change dramatically, spreading from the initial hub at Lake Park and 55th Street to locations along 47th, 51st, and 55th Streets, filling the empty and often worn commercial space. The number of taverns increased steadily, from twenty-five listed in the 1935 telephone directory to thirty-nine in the 1945 directory.[11] Gambling was concentrated in the bars along Lake Park and at newsstands along 55th Street, an affordable area for lower-class whites who settled there after moving to the city to find jobs during the war. The postponement of general maintenance on many of Kenwood's fine old mansions became obvious as structures declined. During the Second World War, new construction was at an absolute minimum.

Many of the large properties in Kenwood became schools, nursing homes, and other institutions. The trend began in the 1930s with the old mansions that lined Drexel Boulevard and then moved into the heart of the community.[12] Chauncey Blair's boulevard residence housed the office of the United Bakeries Corporation.

Veteran's Housing on the Midway, 1946.

6.03. The university dealt with the housing shortage following the Second World War by erecting 201 prefabricated units of two and three rooms on the Midway. These were available to student veterans at a cost of forty to forty-five dollars per month, which included electricity, fuel for heat and cooking, and garbage disposal.

The Goodman mansion became the Normal School of Physical Education, while other residences were used for religious purposes. Single-family houses were altered to accommodate numerous families. One of Hyde Park's oldest houses, the 1857 Bockée residence on Cornell, was modified in 1943 to provide twenty-three rooms and twelve baths. Walk-up apartments were likewise cut up into smaller units to address the housing shortage brought on not only by this shift in demographics, but also by soldiers returning at the end of the Second World War.

An important element added to this mix was the general aging of the housing stock. A vast majority of buildings both large and small had been erected in the community four decades earlier. Many architect-designed structures used the best available quality of materials and practices known to the time. Others were more shoddily done. In the best possible case an architect would strive for a "40 year service life," meaning for that period of time the building should operate with few expenses other than those for general maintenance. However just as the Depression took hold and war came, houses needed new roofs, major tuckpointing, new heating systems, doors, and windows. Apartments required new boilers and elevators. These costly expenses came just as there was little money, leading to an inevitable decline.

Additionally, the 1939 Land Use Survey found that 10 percent of Hyde Park's residential structures had been converted during the decade, and nearly a third of these were former single-family structures. A substantial portion (37 percent) of these conversions were furnished units, indicating that transiency was increasing throughout the area.[13] Deterioration first appeared in some of the smaller frame structures constructed for the 1893 fair and quickly spread, encouraged by the division of apartment buildings into numerous small units without the addition of new plumbing or electricity. The kitchenette, formerly a staple form of housing in nearby communities, now infiltrated the neighborhood. The term *kitchenette* usually describes one-room units, created by conversions of existing housing into smaller units.[14] They were often rented out by the week with shared facilities, lead-ing to a serious deterioration of the sanitary conditions within the building.

Meanwhile, the University of Chicago had invested heavily in its campus, and the increase in students and faculty was remarkable. The Depression temporarily halted expansion through the end of World War II, when the university resumed its building program. The university was then the largest property owner in Hyde Park, and a majority of the faculty continued to reside on the surrounding streets as they had from its very earliest days. Recognizing the steady deterioration in the surrounding communities as a source of pressing concern, the institution was determined to play a role in shaping their future. University president Robert May-nard Hutchins, considered a progressive and liberal reformer, faced a series of dif-ficult choices. Uncertain about how to best handle the racial issues, the university reacted with "half measures." Supporting the restrictive racial covenants quietly, the university would in time be "forced to face some of its own prejudices."[15]

The university encountered the first of many legal challenges to restrictive covenants in 1933, when African Americans moved into property east of South Park Avenue (Martin Luther King Drive) and west of Cottage Grove, a section adjacent to the Hyde Park community on the southwestern border. The university was a quiet participant in a legal battle, financing a lawsuit filed by the Woodlawn Property Owners Association to prevent blacks from moving into that commu-nity. The defendant's lawyers argued that three previous black tenancies had gone unchallenged, and that the racial covenants should not be enforced.[16] The court ruled against the defendants, and the Washington Park neighborhood remained predominantly white for the next several years.

In 1937 another case arose, leading to the opening of the subdivision to the black population. Carl Hansberry, a successful black businessman, attempted to purchase property in the area. Hansberry engaged in a legal battle that challenged the covenants that prohibited him from purchasing property in the community.[17] In 1940, the U.S. Supreme Court ruled in favor of Hansberry; however, it did not rule that racially restrictive covenants were illegal:[18] "The iron band of restrictive covenants . . . was pierced by a decision handed down by the Supreme Court . . ." read an article in the Chicago Defender; the decision opened nearly three hundred properties to African Americans.[19]

Migrants from the rural South came to Chicago at a slower pace during the thirties; however, the collapse of cotton tenancy and continued widespread dis-crimination led to another wave of arrivals, beginning in the midforties. During this second wave of migration, the promise of opportunity failed as jobs proved difficult to secure. Many were unemployed and became dependent on govern-ment relief, exacerbating the problems in the nearby neighborhoods—overcrowd-ing housing, unsanitary conditions, and a basic lack of public services. Within the Black Belt the poor suffered because they "inherited the technologically obsolete city that the middle and upper class abandoned," wrote Perry Duis in Challenging Chicago. "Deficient heating and lighting systems in their homes resulted in fires. Inadequate water and sewage technologies in their streets contributed to disease."[20]

The Black Belt was racially homogeneous; however, areas were defined by the general economic status of the residents.[21] The poorest blacks lived in the oldest section on the north; the middle class continually moved south into better housing as the boundaries expanded. As housing in the worst areas of the Black Belt was disintegrating and being demolished, the lower classes were continually pushed southward into middle-class areas that had higher-quality apartments, where the trend would then be repeated.

The racial challenges, growing unemployment, overcrowding, illegal conversions, and increased density combined to produce widespread blight. Options for the university were limited and the board of trustees wavered, seeking a solution. Robert Mitchell, in charge of the Special Committee on Community Interests, stated that his job was to maintain a "stable, white population of high character." (At the time the nonwhite population of Hyde Park/Kenwood was a mere 1.5 percent.)[22] Renowned urban sociologist Louis Wirth believed the restrictive covenants to be "morally repulsive," and advised the university to abandon them in support of housing projects.[23] Among the possibilities, the idea of an integrated community was not considered.[24] And although the university was seriously concerned in the midforties, it was not until the early 1950s that it took steps to address the issues presented by the declining neighborhood.

Meanwhile, an African American professor joined the faculty of the University of Chicago. In 1939, William Allison Davis came to the institution and received his PhD in anthropology in 1942. While Davis "earned the admiration and respect" of key figures at the university, his race was an issue in an appointment to the Department of Education. The university trustees approved his position after Julius Rosenwald provided the funding; however, they could not assure his "personal happiness." Although Davis was the first African American to hold full faculty status with teaching duties at any major American university,[25] he was for many years denied faculty membership at the university's Quadrangle Club. The family could not live in either Hyde Park or Kenwood; the newly opened Washington Park community was, for a time, their neighborhood.

While struggling with the issue of race, the institution played a prominent role in the Second World War. Physicist Enrico Fermi's suggestion that the United States could develop atomic weapons led to his work on the Manhattan Project, the code name for America's attempt to split an atom. The atomic age arrived on December 2, 1942, when Fermi produced the first controlled, self-sustaining nuclear chain reaction in a laboratory under the Stagg Field bleachers. His work led to the development of the nuclear bomb as well as to peaceful applications of nuclear power.[26] A 1967 bronze sculpture by Henry Moore now commemorates the Ellis Avenue site of the makeshift laboratory.

Historically a Republican bastion, the neighborhood evolved to develop a strong Democratic constituency. After the Depression, mayor Edward Joseph Kelly lived in Kenwood, occupying the craftsman-style house designed by Horatio R. Wilson at 4821 South Ellis. Elected in 1933 following the assassination of mayor Anton Cermak, Kelly was handpicked by the chairman of the Democratic Party and eventually built a powerful political organization. His term was marked by controversy; gambling and organized crime were prevalent, and Kelly expanded the Democratic Party's base to include African Americans.[27] It was his progressive approach to the issue of race, especially as it related to housing, that eventually led to his downfall. Kelly, a supporter of integration and open housing in the highly segregated city, was mayor until pressure from the party forced him not to run for another term in 1947.[28]

The thirties and forties were a remarkable time in the field of design and architecture. American designers incorporated the speed and efficiency of machine-age technology into their products. Sweeping horizontal lines, rounded corners, and metallic materials were used in everything from Chrysler's Airflow automobile to the *20th Century Limited* streamliner train. Within the family home, a range of appliances from alarm clocks to toasters to refrigerators sported a new streamlined look.[29] Through these products, domestic life became integrated with the rapidly changing technology of the times, and the trend was gradually reflected in new construction in the neighborhood.

In Europe, an extraordinary institution had emerged, the Bauhaus, literally "building house." The roots of the Bauhaus stretched back to the nineteenth century: "one long attempt to reconcile the arts with the machine."[30] "The Bauhaus," wrote founder Walter Gropius for its prospectus in 1919, "strives to bring together all creative effort into one whole, to reunify all of the disciplines of practical art— sculpture, painting, handicraft, and the crafts—as inseparable components of new architecture."[31] After a slow start the Bauhaus began to produce a stream of influential designs for furniture, household appliances, textiles, stained glass, wallpaper, tableware, and experimental houses.

In 1933 the political pressures of Nazi Germany forced the Bauhaus to close. The director of the school, architect Ludwig Mies van der Rohe, left Germany and arrived in Chicago in 1938 to become the director of the School of Architecture of the Armour Institute, now the Illinois Institute of Technology. Mies designed with clarity, stripping all components down to their essential qualities. Prior to his departure from Berlin, he designed the Barcelona Pavilion (1929), a milestone of modern architecture. The single-story structure, consisting of a flat roof resting on steel columns, was set upon a travertine base. Freestanding walls of onyx and green marble separated the free-flowing space, interior indistinguishable from exterior.

Although architects experimented with new forms, most construction during this time relied on traditional concepts, as the American public was slow to embrace the innovative designs. Mies van der Rohe, while renowned, received relatively few contracts. However as the forties closed, a new architectural era began in Chicago with Mies's commission for the Promontory Apartments on the Hyde Park lakefront. The building was a forerunner of his exquisite design for 860–880 North Lake Shore Drive, which features a curtain wall, freed of its role as a supporting structure. The Second Chicago School, as the style became known, eliminated all historical references and relied upon forms that expressed their function.[32] Mies van der Rohe's influence on future architects would be profound.

After the war the American automobile became the most important factor in single-family construction, as low-cost transportation provided the freedom to locate to the suburbs. Levittown, a New York suburb built by Levitt & Sons in the 1940s and 1950s, came to define American home ownership. The cookie-cutter

5012, 5016 South Drexel
Boulevard. Demolished 1970.
6.04. Le Corbusier witnessed
scenes such as this: billboards
along once elegant thoroughfares
and vacant lots strewn with trash
and abandoned cars, as seen in
this photograph of a lot south
of several still attractive stone
mansions.

shapes, designed to look "prosperous and perfect," became a symbol of starter-home communities.[33] Many who sought new houses bypassed the city altogether for the newly burgeoning suburban ring, and as a result, Chicago lost its preeminence in residential design. Few of the houses constructed across the city possessed architectural significance, according to historian Carl Condit, but those that did were, for the most part, located in Hyde Park.[34] The design of these residences reflected European influences and the rise of modernism in America, demonstrated by the early works of Keck & Keck, Bertrand Goldberg, and Ralph Rapson.

In 1935, when Swiss architect Le Corbusier visited the city, "its rich and poor were divided into rigidly demarcated zones."[35] Although Le Corbusier felt directed toward only the city's "handsomest quarters," he saw enough of the South Side to describe the slums as tragic, where lives were "crushed by the horror of the physical setting."[36] Once prosperous, much of the area had been abandoned by the wealthy, and white middle-class families were following their exodus.[37]

The challenge facing the community was to some obvious, and simply a part of the ebb and flow that exists within all cities. For the university, the changes provided the basis for the study of the city's spatial framework, believing that social facts separated from geography were meaningless.[38] Scholars whose work during this period is often referred to as the "Chicago School of Sociology" established the study of urban centers as an important academic field. The result of their work was the production of a group of maps of the city based on census-tract information that captured and quantified city life. These maps focused on "population density, ethnicity, housing, and living standards"[39] and confirmed what Le Corbusier witnessed on his visit to Chicago. During the period from 1920 to 1934 population density in poorer inner-city neighborhoods was high, and immigrant neighborhoods were common. Owner-occupancy was low in these areas, but higher at the periphery of the city as new single-family houses were constructed. The neighbor-

hoods adjacent to the central business district were the least affluent in the city. On the other hand, neighborhoods at the edge of the city, including the South Shore community to the south of Hyde Park, had the highest income levels.[40]

Residents hardly needed a Swiss architect or university-sponsored studies to remind them of the flux of their community, as even the children marked the passage of the earlier era. "There was a funeral in Kenwood the other day," read an article in the city paper.[41] The neighborhood children had come to pay respects to a willow chopped down in the summer of 1932. It was one of the last great drooping trees that once dotted the landscape and gave rise to a local legend of an underground river that flowed through Kenwood and the trail of willows that marked its course, a path the cows once followed from 55th Street north to the old town of Cleaverville.

According to legend, the early settlers lined the boundaries of their land with willow posts, each of which later sprouted and grew into two or three or more graceful trees. The *Tribune* wrote that the "poor cousins of the maple and the oak sent out shoots from long interlacing roots that develop with little or no care." The increasing settlement of the area gradually dried up the stream, but for years enough water remained to allow the willows to thrive.[42]

Kenwood's children played among these water-loving trees behind the homes of Bernard Sunny and Albert Harris, in the ten-acre pasture once owned by John Dunham. The field was enclosed by a wobbly fence and bisected by an unsteady row of wooden rails, "paralleled by a file of fine old trees."[43] Perhaps giving credence to a legend long forgotten, but certainly a clear demonstration of the effect of urbanization on Le Corbusier's "former paradise."

6.05. A reminder of the area's rural days could be found well into the 1920s, where cows continued to graze in the fenced field on land once owned by John Dunham. The wobbly fence and line of trees in Farmer's Field, as Dunham's open pasture was then known, disappeared in the early thirties.

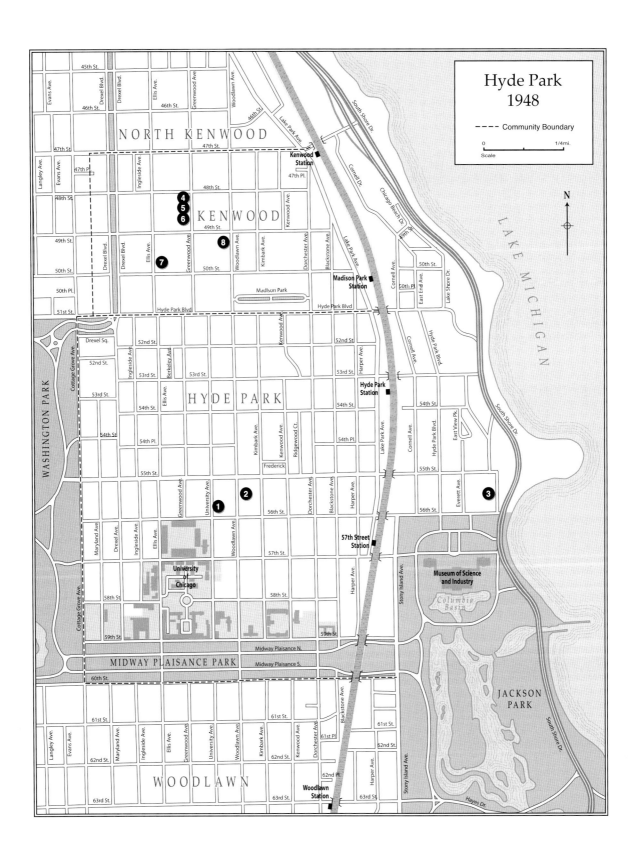

NORTH KENWOOD

KENWOOD

WASHINGTON PARK

HYDE PARK

LAKE MICHIGAN

Madison Park

University of Chicago

Museum of Science and Industry

Columbia Basin

MIDWAY PLAISANCE PARK

JACKSON PARK

WOODLAWN

Kenwood Station

Madison Park Station

Hyde Park Station

57th Street Station

Woodlawn Station

Hyde Park

❶ Keck-Gottschalk-Keck Residences, 1937.

5551 South University Avenue.

In 1937 architects Fred and William Keck teamed with University of Chicago history professor Louis Gottschalk to purchase an old single-family house conveniently located near the university. Previously used as a fraternity house, the property was for sale at a low price as a result of financial difficulties during the Depression. The group founded a cooperative with a ninety-nine-year lease, demolished the existing frame structure, and designed three units within a single, and important, structure.[44]

With this building were the beginnings of an enormous body of work and an

6.06. A rendering of the Keck-Gottschalk-Keck building, dated March 16, 1937.

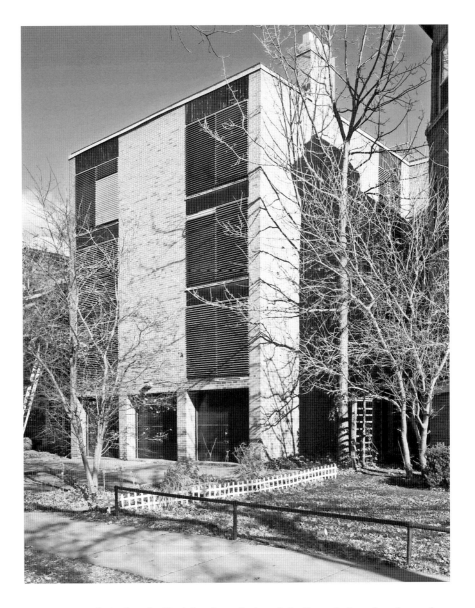

6.07. The Keck-Gottschalk-Keck residences were a clear departure from the more traditional residences in the Hyde Park community.

impact on Hyde Park—the Keck brothers designed, built, and altered no fewer than 120 structures in the community. Following the success of their 1933 House of Tomorrow and the Crystal House the next year, the Kecks became important players in the development of the International Style. The four-story structure they created had load-bearing walls of a "richly colored but inexpensive" brick that complemented the neighboring structures. Two glazed areas rise from the garage, providing a feeling of verticality without any decoration or ornamentation. Originally these glass panes had pockets for aluminum horizontal blinds that could be concealed from view; however, they were replaced with permanently attached exterior jalousies.[45]

After reviewing the Kecks' plans, Chicago's building commissioner doubted the need for the three-car garage and questioned the design. The garage doors were designed to face the street, as there are no alleys in this particular block.[46] Time has proven the wisdom of the plan, for the growth of the university brought increased density, making on-street parking a problem.

In addition to the garages, a laundry room, workshop, and communal recreation room are on the ground floor. The three apartments above have setbacks in the rear to provide space for small garden terraces. The Kecks' signature radiant heat in the floor was used throughout. The structure, one of the city's earliest examples of modern architecture in the International Style and a vast departure from the nearby Gothic buildings, was designated a Chicago landmark in 1994.

② MacNair Residence, 1937.
5527 South Woodlawn Avenue. Holsman & Holsman.

In contrast to the forward-thinking cooperative residence designed by the Keck brothers, Henry Holsman returned to traditional forms in a low-cost "Cotswold Cottage" for Professor Harley Farnsworth MacNair. Although without the characteristic stone walls and thatched roof, the house clearly evokes the image of a style rooted in the pastoral Cotswold area of England. This cozy structure was built with the least expensive of materials, including stock metal windows and cinder block walls, and construction took a mere six months from excavation to occupancy.

Celebrated as "an authority on the history of Far Eastern international relations," MacNair was a professor of history and government in Shanghai until he returned to the United States in 1927.[47] Although he often returned to China, MacNair taught Far Eastern history at the University of Chicago from 1928 until his death in 1947. The year this house was completed, his work entitled *The Real Conflict between China and Japan* was published. Thirteen years older than her husband, Florence Wheelock Ayscough MacNair was noted in her own right. Born in Shanghai and educated in Boston, she wrote several books relating to Chinese poetry and society including *Chinese Women Today and Yesterday*, also published in 1937.[48] The couple married in Guernsey, Channel Islands, after the death of her first husband in 1935. Perhaps that trip provided inspiration for this house, which soon became "a gathering place" for people with a special interest in China.[49]

6.08. The small, fanciful Cotswold cottage was popular across the country during the twenties and thirties. The asymmetrical shape, small-paned windows, sloping second floor with dormers and side chimney articulate this plain structure as a takeoff of the medieval-style cottage built across southwestern England since the Middle Ages.

③ The Promontory, 1947–1949.
5530–5532 South Shore Drive. Ludwig Mies van der Rohe, PACE Associates.

By the forties, architect Mies van der Rohe was clearly famous yet had received few commissions. That changed with his collaboration with developer Herbert Greenwald, which yielded over a dozen major buildings, including Mies's first apartment building. Greenwald, then only thirty years old, wanted to build "the finest architecture using modern technology," and was told that "Mies was his man."[50] Rising twenty-two stories, the Promontory reflects the beginning of a new and widely copied style Mies developed, which reshaped American architecture.

The lakefront site was once intended to house an elaborate beach and country club; however, the plans had been abandoned twenty years earlier as improvements

6.09. The luxury of space and amenities that were trademarks of earlier apartment hotels constructed along the lakefront were simplified in this cooperative. The 120 apartments of the Promontory were small, efficient, and modestly priced.

to the lakefront began. In its place rose "a prototype of high-rise slab construction,"[51] a style that reached its pinnacle in Mies's design for 860–880 Lake Shore Drive. For Promontory Point Mies used only stock materials—reinforced concrete, aluminum window frames, and a buff brick for the inserted panels. The concrete frame recedes ever so subtly as the building rises, stepping back to indicate the logical requirement of thicker lower columns carrying a heavier load than those above. The first floor glass-walled lobby features a polished stone aggregate that extends to the exterior, where the same material was left rough. This simple concept represents a fundamental principle of Modernism, the use of materials to express beauty and use. In this example the finish of a single material makes a transition at a plate of glass.

Kenwood

④ Residence, 1936.
4812 South Greenwood Avenue. Thomas Bishop & Company.

In 1936 local developers purchased the large piece of vacant land at the southwest corner of Greenwood and 48th Street from the estate of Elizabeth Morse Genius, intending to construct six new residences on the property.[52] Elizabeth Genius, the daughter of Charles Hosmer Morse, had resided in a twenty-room mansion on the property until her sudden death in March 1928. In November 1931, the structure was torn down at the request of a presumably distraught Dr. Genius. The land lay vacant until purchased by the Greenwood Development Corporation, and construction of the homes began in 1936. Architect Thomas Bishop was hired to prepare the plans for the first house, a colonial-style residence to be constructed at a "moderate and efficient cost."[53]

Throughout the 1930s Bishop designed a number of single-family houses in

6.10. The traditional red brick house at 4812 Greenwood is efficiently planned; its 3,000 square feet are modest in comparison to the house originally on the property.

6.11. The original stone wall and wrought iron gate remain on the East 48th Street side of the old Charles Hosmer Morse estate. The Richardsonian Romanesque mansion that stood on this wooded lot was demolished in 1931.

Kenwood and apartment buildings in Hyde Park. All were traditionally detailed masonry structures following various stylistic themes and constructed for a reasonable cost. In 1938 construction began on the second residence, for developer Harry A. Zisook, who often utilized the services of Thomas Bishop on his neighborhood projects. Zisook lived at 1100 East 48th Street in a Bishop-designed house; however, after experiencing difficulties during the Depression years, he moved his family to this smaller house across the street.

For the Morse property project, in total the developers constructed only three of the intended six residences. While each of these residences is stylistically unique, they are similar in massing and represent a trend toward smaller, more efficient houses, each a variation on the traditional American foursquare design.

⑤ Toomin Residence, 1937.
4816 South Greenwood Avenue. Bertrand Goldberg.

The Greenwood Development Company awarded a contract for one of the six houses to be constructed on the old Morse estate to a rising young architect, Bertrand "Bud" Goldberg. After he organized his own firm in 1937, one of Goldberg's earliest commissions was the Kenwood home of Philip R. Toomin. A University of Chicago Law School graduate, Toomin began a private legal practice in 1938[54] and was the attorney who took title of the 254' × 207' property from the estate of Elizabeth Morse Genius.

The buff-colored brick house contained innovative amenities that we now take for granted. "A year round air conditioned ten room residence is being built for attorney Philip R. Toomin on a 50 × 153 lot," the *Chicago Tribune* announced. "An open terrace with a wading pool and two other terraces, an open sleeping porch

6.12. Philip Toomin was familiar with the neighborhood; he graduated from the University of Chicago Law School in 1927. In 1938 he opened a private practice, according to his May 23, 1993, obituary.

and a sun deck are features. It will have an all-electric kitchen, including stove, refrigerator, garbage disposal unit and complete metal built in cabinets."[55] The garage is a later addition to the structure, replacing the original den.

⑥ Katzin Residence, 1939.
4820 South Greenwood Avenue. Bertrand Goldberg.

In 1938 Frank Katzin commissioned Goldberg to design a unique gas station at Clark and Maple Streets. Goldberg's "eye-catching design" resulted in sales that soared, and he noted, "It has shown that even Standard Oil could underestimate . . . what a new building like this could do for one of its gasoline dealers."[56] Katzin then commissioned Goldberg to design his residence in Kenwood.

The Katzin residence could easily be mistaken for a typical suburban ranch house; however, the simplicity of the exterior belies the drama of the interior, and the project marked an important development in Goldberg's creative vision.[57] Goldberg used a combination of load-bearing walls and a grid of exposed steel columns to support the structure, which allowed for an open, free-flowing interior plan. He designed a series of spaces made dramatic through walls of glass, brick, rich ebony veneer, and a large expanse of unpolished limestone perpendicular to the main entry.

Traditionally, architects have placed the best face of the house toward the street. Goldberg rethought this concept, placing the sleeping areas along the street and a semicircular living area anchored on a central fireplace at the rear of the house. At the time Goldberg designed this single-story residence, he was interested in the design and use of prefabricated elements for bathrooms and kitchens. Goldberg felt the integrity of this house to be compromised when a later owner ripped out the original kitchen, and in 1988 he worked with the new owner to rejuvenate the

6.13. The typical ranch exterior of the Katzin house belies the forward-thinking interior, with sleeping areas, a maid's room, and a children's play area clustered nearest the street. The tight floor plan of this area is separated from the living-dining-kitchen, an open area that visually extends the interior into the surrounding garden.

Cushing Residence, c. 1880. Demolished 1939. 4820 South Greenwood Avenue. Architect/builder unknown.

6.14. The residence, here as photographed for *Picturesque Kenwood* around 1890, was demolished to provide the land for the Katzin house.

kitchen, including the use of overhead refrigerator units. When asked fifty years later in an Art Institute Oral History Project interview how he reacted to this house, Goldberg replied he was satisfied with the return to its initial form, now freed of "the junk that had been applied over and over to things like the natural brick and natural stone and paint over wood—the beautiful wood veneers that we had." He added, "The house has really come alive."[58]

The first residence on this site was built around 1880 for Mary and Edward T. Cushing, the secretary and treasurer of the Union Foundry Company, an enterprise that was owned by Kenwood neighbor Christopher Bouton. The two-and-a-half-story frame house survived until May 1939, when it was demolished and construction of the Katzin residence began. The site was large, 404' in depth with 100' of street frontage.

7 **Guthman Residence, 1939.**
 4949 South Ellis Avenue. Lynn C. Jones.

Although Modernism influenced American residential design, among most architects working in the neighborhood time-honored styles persisted. Leo S. Guthman contracted architect Lynn C. Jones to design a decidedly suburban and traditional two-story fieldstone residence on a very large corner lot.[59] The land was a gift from Cleo and David B. Silberman, who lived next door at 4933 Ellis, now demolished. The Silbermans were Guthman's wife Cecile's well-to-do parents.

Guthman did not come from wealth; he was the son of a stockyards cattle broker and made his own fortune in chemical coatings and the stock market. "Handsome, smart" and a "charmer," he rose in business, growing his father-in-law's paint store into a large business concern.[60] Well into his nineties, Guthman looked back on his accomplishments as a civic and business leader and acknowledged, "It's been a great run." At the time of his death, the local papers wrote that he "indulged his passions of fine art and fishing, and relaxed in the European playgrounds of Monaco and St. Moritz."[61] The quiet Kenwood residence where he lived for ten years provides little indication of such a life. Guthman's legacy was the establishment of a family foundation to support programs that use the arts as a tool for community building.[62]

8 **Gidwitz Residence, 1943.**
 4912 South Woodlawn Avenue. Ralph Rapson and John van der Meulen.

Willard and Adele Gidwitz, members of the family that owned the Helene Curtis Company, commissioned an extensive remodeling project in the midst of the Second World War after an architectural exhibit at the Art Institute piqued the young couple's interest in modernist design.[63] This was one of the few large residential projects constructed during the war years.

The challenges of the Gidwitz project were multiple, as the architects had to work within the foundation of the existing structure, a stately turn-of-the-century residence constructed for Jonathan and Mary Brooks.[64] The dark gray "rubble

6.16. Willard Gidwitz ran the day-to-day operations of Helene Curtis, a cosmetics company founded by his brother Gerald.

Brooks Residence, 1888. 4910 Woodlawn Avenue. Thomas Wing.
6.17. The original house was designed for Jonathan W. Brooks, the president of Pitkin & Brooks, a Chicago retailer of pottery, porcelain, glass, and lamps. Wing, the first draftsman hired by Burnham & Root, was the architect of the Zoopraxographical Hall at the World's Columbian Exposition where Eadweard Muybridge presented life-sized images in motion.

stone" of the recessed base and the chimney from the original house were combined with new materials that included wood panels and steel supports.[65] The glass walls, balcony on the second floor, the cantilevered steel stair, and slender support columns produced an expansive interior.

Rapson prepared plans for another starkly modern residence in Kenwood, although it was never constructed. Publisher John B. Johnson, the founder of *Jet* and *Ebony* magazines, asked Rapson to design a residence about one block to the north of the Gidwitz property on Woodlawn Avenue. In 1942 Rapson conceptualized a single-story design where rooms were clustered around several light-filled atriums.

6.18. The ceiling design of the Gidwitz house was both sculptural and practical. Rapson did the interior design work, including built-ins and custom furniture. Other furnishings included Barcelona chairs by Mies van der Rohe, and Eero Saarinen's Womb Chair.

6.19. The clutter-free kitchen demonstrated the use of new materials and appliances, and marked the progression from a servant-oriented space toward a center of family life.

According to his company website, that same year Johnson published his first issue of *Negro Digest*. He financed the magazine with $500 made by selling his mother's furniture after being refused a business loan from the banks. The issue was reportedly an instant success.[66]

When this house was being contemplated, African Americans were not welcome in the heart of Kenwood, so it is curious that Johnson and Rapson discussed the potential of a new home in this location.

Century Hotel, c. 1893. Demolished. 1435–1459 East 55th Street. Architect unknown.

7.01. Fifty-Fifth Street was a thoroughfare with a bustling, yet unsavory, character in the years prior to land clearance. The four-story Century Hotel housed kitchenette apartments on the upper levels with low-end retail on the ground floor.

CHAPTER SEVEN

Deconstruction, 1949–1978

Here we stand, black and white, shoulder to shoulder against the lower classes.

—Comedian Mike Nichols, on the neighborhood's redevelopment program, 1958[1]

The Hyde Park and Kenwood neighborhoods in the years following the Second World War were marked by turbulence and change. Like many residential communities within large cities across the United States, the community was in decline due to the influx of lower-income residents and the flight of middle-class residents to the suburbs. The university found itself surrounded by the inner city; the strain of the Depression and two world wars shifted the character of the neighborhood, where aging buildings showed clear signs of overcrowding and neglect. Muriel Beadle, the wife of university president George Beadle and an "amusing, shrewd and observant" author, was active in the larger Hyde Park community and wrote of her experiences in the neighborhood.[2] She saw first-hand that the failure to enforce building and zoning codes increased pressure on both the housing stock and community facilities. "Taverns with late night hours established themselves in location after location," she wrote, "as lower wage earners took the place of the middle class, moving into subdivided and declining structures as they escaped the expanding ghetto."[3] Sociologist at the university studying urban communities recognized that Hyde Park followed a trend: older neighborhoods grew more blighted and were bulldozed as part of slum clearance programs.[4]

As the number of Hyde Park's residents swelled, Chicago's population reached its peak in 1950 and then began to fall. Following the completion of the Congress (Eisenhower) Expressway in 1954, the Tri-State Tollway in 1956, and the Kennedy Expressway in 1960, homebuyers were enticed to suburban locations. The ease of movement and lower land costs were not unlike what had made the Hyde Park community so attractive nearly a century earlier. Innovative financing encouraged Chicagoans to purchase houses, while developers used the mass-production tech-

295

Rhythm Liquors. Demolished. 1526–1528 Hyde Park Boulevard. Architect/builder unknown.

7.02. Housed in a storefront addition surrounding an old frame residence, the tavern and liquor store at the northeast corner of 51st Street and Lake Park provided cocktails and entertainment until four o'clock in the morning. East of the Illinois Central embankment are 5000 East End, the Algonquin Apartments, and the Chicago Beach Hotel, from left to right in this photograph taken on May 31, 1960.

niques pioneered by the Levitt brothers to fill acres of land with affordable single-family houses.[5] Vast areas of farmland around the city were converted into developments, so that by 1960 practically all construction of new single-family houses was in suburban locations.[6]

At the start of this huge shift in living patterns sections of the neighborhood remained attractive; however, the housing shortage created during the war years meant hundreds of dwellings were cut up into kitchenettes. In Kenwood, the population increased 41 percent between 1940 and 1960, while new construction virtually ceased. Mansions that were once home to Chicago's elite operated as rooming houses, nursing homes, or churches, while others sat abandoned and boarded up. A mere glance at the building permits issued tells much of the story. On Drexel Boulevard six apartments were converted into twelve, twelve apartments became thirty-six. By 1950 renters, far less vested in the community, occupied nearly 90 percent of the housing units.[7]

Although Chicago was known as a city of neighborhoods, it was among the most segregated cities in the nation. The half-million African Americans who came north desperate for better wages and decent housing continued to be unwelcome in most neighborhoods. The borders of the black community that had been partially sustained through racially restrictive housing covenants proved ever more fluid as the population slid into historically white areas. However, in 1948 the boundary lines for the neighborhood were unambiguous—no significant black population lived east of Cottage Grove Avenue in Hyde Park or east of Drexel and south of 47th Street in Kenwood.

In his book *Making the Second Ghetto*, Arnold Hirsch documented the second wave of the black migration to the North during the fifteen-year period after the Second World War. He wrote that the city "witnessed a renewal of the massive black migration to Chicago and the overflowing of the black population from established areas of residence grown too small, too old, or too decayed."[8] In an attempt to address the problem, the Chicago Housing Authority erected a series of low-income high-rises on vacant land that had been cleared of slums. At the time it was a generally accepted belief that it was easier and less costly to demolish entire neighborhoods of dilapidated buildings than to renovate existing structures. The result was a massive land clearance of the area around the downtown business district that extended several miles into the South Side. The effect was to propel the African American population further south.[9]

Eight years after the Hansberry case focused on restrictive covenants in Chicago's Washington Park community, the US Supreme Court heard the case of *Shelley v. Kraemer*. The result of this St. Louis–based case was the 1948 landmark civil rights ruling that struck down the racial restrictions nationally. The movement of African Americans into Hyde Park and Kenwood was immediate and significant; the racial composition of the community changed dramatically after the ruling.[10]

Before the color lines were erased, the community remained predominantly white; the largest ethnic group in the neighborhood was composed of German Jews.[11] Politically the neighborhood had shifted from its traditional Republican constituency to a Democratic one, but more importantly, Muriel Beadle noted, "economically there was a downward shift in income and purchasing power."[12]

After the racial boundaries that had held for decades became porous, the influx of lower-income minorities created widespread concern as middle- and upper-income wage earners left. Looking at the Hyde Park community as a whole, the nonwhite population rose from 1.5 percent in 1940 to about 6 percent in 1950. However, by 1956, the nonwhite percentage exploded to 36.7 percent.[13] Between 1950 and 1956, 20,000 whites had left the Hyde Park area and 24,000 blacks had moved in.[14]

The results of a study published by the South Side Planning Board and the Hyde Park–Kenwood Community Conference in 1952 showed that the physical conditions varied significantly within the neighborhood. North of 47th Street one of every three dwelling units was in a building that should no longer be inhabited. In comparison one of ten units was in a similar condition south of 47th Street. Density varied from 72,000 people per square mile west of Cottage Grove to 30,000 in Kenwood.[15] Compounding the racial shift was the serious strain put on the neighborhood's infrastructure and housing stock by steadily increasing overcrowding. During the thirties, apartments were often shoddily constructed, and subsequent conversions did meet building codes. The study found that many buildings were badly deteriorated and portions of the area were threatened by "creeping blight."

7.03. Money was scarce for improvements and upkeep on residential streets as well as in commercial areas. The rear portion of this frame house was removed in 1950, after it caved in during a heavy rainstorm and injured seven people. Doors opened precipitously into thin air, and a solitary sink overlooked the rubbish-strewn back yard.

The 1952 study recommended that buildings should be razed, yet the population was reluctant to leave; seven of every ten families wanted to remain.[16]

Organized efforts to combat the problems first took shape on a grass-roots level. The Hyde Park–Kenwood Community Conference (HPKCC), organized in 1949, drew support from local religious institutions. Characterized as the "community's conscience," this grass-roots organization addressed the tensions of race relations, along with the issues of housing and increasing crime.[17] In contrast to previous neighborhood groups dedicated to segregation, the HPKCC imagined a future as not only a stable and prosperous community, but also one that would be integrated. Neighborhood lawyers represented the HPKCC, volunteering their services to prosecute specific zoning ordinance or building code violations. They targeted property owners who claimed that the large houses were no longer viable for single-family use and modified the structures for rooming houses.

In 1954 the Kenwood Open House Committee formed with the purpose of increasing awareness of the community's history and viability, through tours of the large, well-maintained houses that remained in South Kenwood. The neighborhood organized group opposition to changes in zoning ordinances that would permit conversions, and monitored homeowners who converted properties illegally.[18] The Kenwood Neighborhood Redevelopment Corporation capitalized by selling shares of stock—the goal was to raise funds to purchase properties in danger of becoming tenements through eminent domain, and then either improve or tear down the house and sell the property.[19] While each of these community organizations contributed to the overall effort, they lacked the necessary power and funding to combat the problems individually.

During the early fifties, the police district of which the neighborhood was part had one of the highest crime rates in the city.[20] Confronted by crime and surrounded by poverty and decline, the University of Chicago faced a "sixty-percent drop in student applications . . . and increasing difficulty in recruiting faculty."[21] After years of substantial investment in the campus, a solution to the crisis of urban decay and sweeping racial change was a matter of urgency to the institution. President Lawrence A. Kimpton and the board of trustees gave serious thought to relocating, but decided to remain. As one faculty member noted, there was not much of a "second-hand market" for a university.[22]

For the university this decision represented the culmination of decades of a guarded approach to involvement with the surrounding community. Seeking a "compatible environment"[23] for its campus, the institution had used all the tools available, from secretive land purchases to silent approval of racially restrictive covenants, to protect its property—always in a reactionary manner. Now recognizing that racial homogeneity could not be maintained, and that conservative ambition would not address the obvious physical decay, the university decided to act.

The turning point followed a sensational event—the home invasion, robbery, and kidnapping of a faculty member's wife.[24] When the "community erupted in anger and fear," a mass meeting was held in May 1952, attended by over a thousand residents who demanded the university address the growing problems.[25] Presented with the opportunity to forcefully intercede, the university made a commitment to the stabilization of the neighborhood with the foundation of the South East Chicago Commission (SECC).

The SECC, organized under the auspices of the University of Chicago and led by executive director Julian Levi, left no doubt as to the university's position. Financed by the institution, the commission took the initiative "in order to combat the forces of uncertainty and deterioration at work in the neighborhood."[26] The initial goal of the SECC was to increase police protection, enforce building codes, and promote residential stability. Under the direction of Levi, the commission pressured insurance companies to cancel policies on buildings with chronic housing violations. The SECC took legal action against slumlords and made federal financing available to homeowners for improvements.[27] But the most far-reaching project was a plan for developing the area's most seriously deteriorated areas while fighting to create a "controlled, integrated environment."[28]

The Field Foundation authorized a grant to establish and operate a planning unit to work on the Hyde Park and Kenwood communities.[29] Led by Jack Melt-

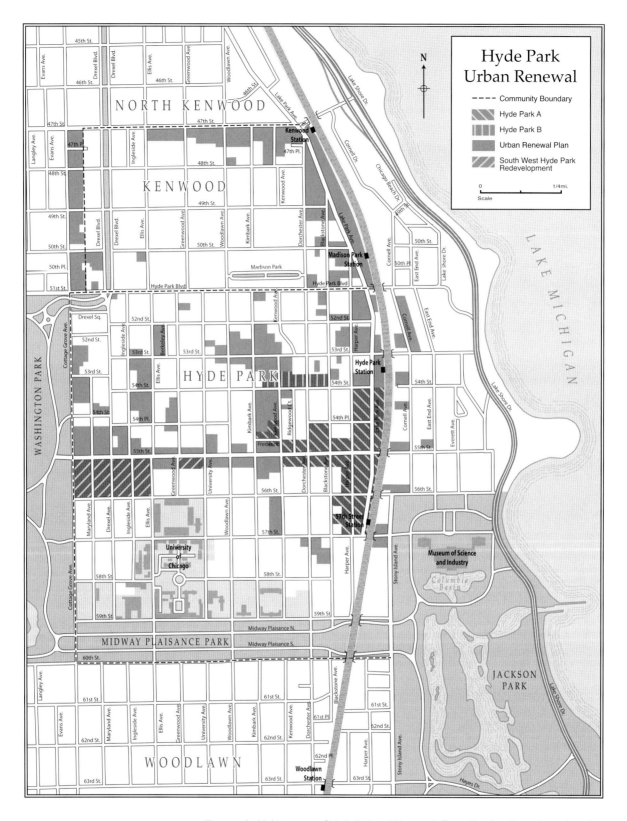

7.04. This map, highlighting areas of Hyde Park and Kenwood affected by demolition during the urban renewal years, demonstrates the deterioration prevalent on properties adjacent to East 55th Street and Lake Avenue.

zer, "the planner in the middle of the maelstrom,"[30] the university and the SECC sought to direct the city's policy "away from the destruction of slums and toward the preservation of sound but threatened neighborhoods"[31] through a targeted renewal program. At this time land clearance was the primary mechanism available to the city to deal with the problems; a program where specific demolition could save a larger community was a new idea. The Field grant had been made in the belief that this "pilot project would serve to demonstrate to other American cities" that residents have the ability to make their environments into "what they want them to be."[32] While a forceful program to find solutions for an increasingly precarious state developed, the university was hardly engaged in a "noble experiment on the viability of integrated communities." Rather, the institution was "locked in a battle for its existence."[33]

Urban renewal became "one of the most far-reaching events" in the history of Hyde Park, just as the founding of the university and the Columbian Exposition had transformed the area over a half century earlier.[34] The effort to rebuild the community went far deeper than the development of a plan and the subsequent demolition and rebuilding. According to Bruce Sagan, owner and editor of the *Hyde Park Herald* and a passionate advocate for the neighborhood, urban renewal demonstrated "a remarkable inner city neighborhood seeking to come to grips with some of the city's and the country's most difficult problems," and "central to it all" was the issue of race.[35] These were the years prior to the civil rights movement, the work of Dr. Martin Luther King Jr., the ruling of *Brown v. Board of Education*, and before the enactment of antidiscrimination laws.[36] As the *Hyde Park Herald* noted, it was legal at the time to discriminate on the basis of race.

Although the plan commonly known as "Urban Renewal" was not formally approved by the City Council until November 7, 1958, work began in May 1955 with the removal of structures that had deteriorated beyond repair. Residents were anxious about the community's problems, and the university "pushed the city hard" to ensure that this portion happened quickly.[37] This, the first of four separate initiatives, was referred to as "Hyde Park A and B" and was completed under the city agency called the Land Clearance Commission.[38] Buildings that stretched along the Illinois Central tracks from 54th to 57th Street, east on 55th from Lake Park to Kimbark, and a small section on 54th at Dorchester were demolished. The cleared acreage represented 6.5 percent of the total area of Hyde Park and contained 9 percent of the community's dwelling units. However this area contained 41 percent of the total substandard housing units within the entire Hyde Park community.[39]

After land clearance, the community's character was greatly changed. Wide expanses of open land were created by the demolition of crowded, decaying buildings on Lake Park and along 55th Street in the business district. Firetraps, slum buildings, and bars were gone; however, the heart of the neighborhood was completely altered as blocks of historic buildings were lost. Small, vacant stores, "ones with dirty windows and rotting floors; and taverns, from whose murky interiors drunks stumbled onto the streets in early morning hours," had vanished, Julia Abrahamson wrote. "But gone too were the familiar places run by pleasant people who had

7.05. To address the community's concern that something happen immediately to address the blight, a series of deteriorated mixed-use buildings were slated for demolition as part of land clearance on Lake Avenue, photographed southwest from the 55th Street Illinois Central Station. The demolition of the two blocks of buildings facing the tracks was but one portion of the "Hyde Park A and B" plans.

served Hyde Park well. The corner drug store, the hardware and cleaning establishment, the repair shop and the 55th Street Post Office had all disappeared."[40]

Within four years, construction was underway on structures on the forty-seven cleared acres of Hyde Park A and B. Buildings were erected by New York developer William Zeckendorf Sr., president of Webb & Knapp Company, and designed by I. M. Pei in collaboration with Loewenberg & Loewenberg and Weese & Associates. A series of simple buff-colored brick row houses completed in March 1959 were among several groups of town houses planned throughout the area by Pei and Weese. The two buildings of the University Apartments were designed by Pei to occupy an island in the middle of 55th Street, completely altering the urban high-density street into a thoroughfare.

Clearance of the blighted areas did remove many aging, dilapidated buildings, but did not address deterioration in the adjoining areas. Added to land clearance was the second major initiative, commonly referred to as the "Urban Renewal Plan." The boundaries of the work expanded from the land clearance area westward to Cottage Grove, north to 47th Street, and south to 59th Street. The Urban Renewal Plan encompassed an area of 856 acres, of which over 100 were targeted and cleared for new housing, parks, schools, a fire station, and a new shopping center, and improvements to streets and parking facilities.[41]

A partnership between the local and federal governments, with the support of the university, made the financial aspect of the Urban Renewal project possible. Twenty percent of the community was affected, by a process forecasted to take as long as five years, which stretched to twice that number. It cost $40 million to acquire the "slum land," which was sold for only $4 million; the majority of the $36 million loss was absorbed by the federal government, and the balance by the city.[42] To encourage renewal, the university provided $7 million to the city for the redevelopment project. Additionally, the university supported the overall effort through a planned expansion estimated to cost $50 million.[43] The institution added the final two elements of renewal, the Southwest Hyde Park Redevelopment Corporation and the South Campus, in which they added acreage south of the Midway to the university in a controversial program where owners were forced to sell deteriorated properties.[44]

Despite the size and complexity of the Urban Renewal Plan, it was carried out with a high degree of local participation. "The level of education among the citizens of the area and their strong institutional, professional, and intellectual commitments," argued historian Carl Condit, "implied that if the job could be done properly at all, it ought to achieve success in this community."[45] This is not to suggest that the urban renewal process was free of controversy; it was a "titanic struggle"[46] to define what the city would become. As variations on the large-scale plan were submitted to the public, the entire proposal came under intense scrutiny from many directions.

When the *Hyde Park Herald* came under new ownership, it began aggressively covering the community's problems.[47] Purchased by Bruce Sagan in 1953, the local paper quickly became an active participant in the renewal process. For years weekly columns listed zoning violations and building court cases, and urban renewal plans were covered in depth along with a large section of letters to the editor. The paper argued for an interracial community, angering many of its university-connected readers, and for transparency in the planning process. The *Herald* declared, "A demonstration that neighbors of all races can live in a community of peace and self-respect is worth whatever price must be paid."[48]

7.06. Throughout the central area of Hyde Park, the demolition of old multistory buildings was pervasive. This building, removed at an unknown location in the clearance area, was photographed in 1956.

Much of the participation was divisive—as the overall plan developed, it seemed to some parties that proposed solutions to the community's problems were primarily a response to "threatened racial succession."[49] The university created an "enormous controversy" by dislocating many low and moderate-income African Americans in a secretive forty-one-acre takeover of land for expansion at its southwestern border and south of the Midway.[50] In 1954 the *Defender*, Chicago's leading black-owned newspaper, and the Catholic Archdiocese of Chicago found the plan to be "elitist, selfish, and displacing low-income blacks."[51]

A bitter debate focused on how much public housing should be constructed within the community. Many argued that blight was the result of dilapidated housing, not the poor who occupied the structures and that building public housing would allow the poor to remain while improving the housing stock. Although the university was adamantly opposed,[52] it denied any attempt to create a buffer zone between the black and white communities.[53] Only thirty-four units of public housing were eventually constructed, and of those, twenty-two were reserved for the elderly.[54]

Although driven by the university, Hyde Park's political forces did not remain unspoken on the topic. Democrat and Hyde Park resident Paul H. Douglas was elected to the US Senate in 1948, serving from 1949 until 1967.[55] An economist, Douglas taught at the university before making his first foray into elected govern-

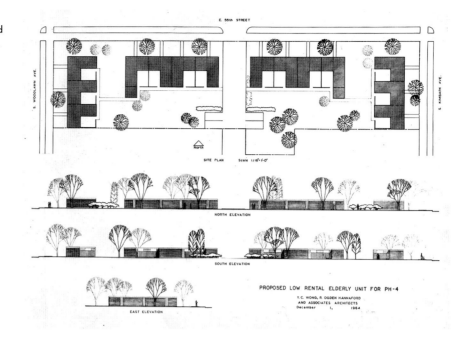

ment in 1939, when he served on the City Council. A reformer, scholar, and war hero, Douglas was an advocate of fair housing and equal rights for African Americans.[56] His views on housing were summed up in a 1949 article entitled "Democracy Can't Live in These Houses," in which he weighed in on a federal housing program to clear slum areas:

> We Americans like to think of the typical home as a vine-clad cottage, with roses growing on trellises, and trees and grass in the yard; and with all this we associate the pleasing and lively sounds of healthy children at play. It is one of the glories of America that so many of our homes are of that kind—or, at least, equally attractive. But it is one of our moral, political and economic responsibilities to do something to lift more homes at least to the minimum level for satisfactory living. The 15,000,000 or more Americans who live in the blighted areas are not inferior to the rest of us. They are only less fortunate. Imagine how you would feel if you and your family were housed as they are. Trouble does not come from men who live agreeable lives. It breeds among men who are frustrated, ashamed and envious.[57]

The story of Hyde Park's urban renewal would not be complete without a further description of one of its major participants, Julian Hirsch Levi, the executive director of the South East Chicago Commission. In the fall of 1952 Levi was hired to lead the commission, a post he held for nearly thirty years. "Brilliant and inventive,"[58] Levi drove the SECC to enlarge its program from a "law enforcement mission" into a plan to make "the kind of community in which the students and the faculty of the university will live."[59]

A life-long Hyde Parker, Levi graduated from college of the University of Chi-

cago in 1929 and received a degree from the law school two years later. His brother Edward was a faculty member and dean of the law school, then president of the university from 1968 to 1975.[60] As the Urban Renewal Plan unfolded, Levi's critics countered that the university wielded too much influence, that the process was less than democratic, and that Levi was driven by a restricted view of what the community should be like. The *Hyde Park Herald* wrote, "His penchant for deciding on his own and his aggressive approach made him the lightening rod as criticism of the renewal programs mounted both inside and outside Hyde Park."[61]

But as housing was falling apart and residents feared what had been a desirable neighborhood would become a slum, Levi became a tenacious advocate for the cause. He used the power of the university to garner political support on all levels, and with funds from local and national sources, he drove the plans into existence

7.08. The dense urban streetscape in the heart of Hyde Park was apparent in this 1955 view west from the Illinois Central railroad tracks at 55th Street and Lake Avenue, photographed prior to demolition during land clearance and urban renewal.

7.09. The same view west from the Illinois Central railroad tracks at 55th Street and Lake Park demonstrates a remarkable transformation in the center of the community by 1961.

7.10. Possessing a fate similar
to that of 55th Street, the
thriving commercial district on
Lake Avenue was obliterated.
While renewal improved
the street from cobblestone
to a paved thoroughfare, it
destroyed any vibrancy the
avenue once exhibited. One
of Hyde Park's oldest business
establishments, Bodeman's
Pharmacy, was once housed in
an old structure at 5018 Lake
Park. The establishment closed
by the time this image was taken
in 1952; however, the building
can be seen on the right in this
photograph.

with extraordinary speed; the effort eventually became one of the country's great urban success stories.

For each of the renewal areas, public hearings were held at City Hall at which residents often protested that good structures were slated to be demolished.[62] However, by 1962 nearly all the land for the urban renewal phase was acquired, and of the 856 buildings slated to be demolished, 564 had been wrecked by the summer of that year.[63] Demolition removed a number of worn buildings occupied by artists and craftsmen. First constructed for the Columbian Exposition, these one-story spaces on 57th Street, known as the Artists Colony, had provided moderately priced spaces for painters and writers for decades.[64] Unhappy at the loss of businesses that contributed to the unique character of Hyde Park, residents took action. A "shrewd businessman, patron of the arts [and] dabbler in back-room politics," Bruce Sagan is credited with an "ingenious and complicated" financial plan for the development of a not-for-profit to house the displaced artists and craftsmen.[65] Using federal financing from the Small Business Administration in combination with equity money raised from bonds sold to the community, the Harper Court Foundation supported the development of a center for the work, exhibition, and sale of the artists' work. The structures were designed by Dubin, Dubin, Black & Moutoussamy to sit around a courtyard formed by the closing of Harper Avenue. Tenants were attracted to the new facility by initial rents of no more than $100 a month.[66] The site outlived its usefulness after fifty years, was demolished in 2011 for redevelopment as a hotel, office, and commercial complex.

Two of Hyde Park's commercial streets were completely altered to become major traffic arteries. In addition to the clearance of commercial structures and the reworking of 55th Street, all but two small structures bordering the Illinois Central

right of way were removed from Lake Park Avenue. The new, wider street was relocated adjacent to the embankment, transforming the once bustling street into a sterile roadway. For many years the site at the intersection of Lake Park at 47th Street, once the "hub of the wheel" of aristocratic Kenwood, lay vacant. At the fragile boundary between the ghetto on the north and the more stable community on the south, the redevelopment of this parcel was not clearly outlined. Consequently, the lack of a plan resulted in controversy, allowing the large area of land to lie vacant, strewn with rubble.[67] It was not until 1970 that approval was given for a project on this site: the construction of a single high-rise on the corner and two- and three-story housing on 47th Street.

As the sixties ended, the effects of the Urban Renewal Plan were clearly discernible. Social class was used as the means to achieve racial integration, and the expansion of the ghetto was halted. New residences appeared in the place of blighted buildings and a large shopping center anchored the area near the former commercial district. Critics complained that the community lacked the diversity of its recent past as the poor, especially blacks, had been relocated. The stores, restaurants, and bars of the commercial district on 55th Street were all but obliterated. Equally significant was a major shift in the population, in 1960 one-half of the residents of Kenwood lived north of 47th Street, ten years later two-thirds lived to the south.[68] The economic differences between these two distinct communities increased—home values in North Kenwood averaged $30,000, while in South Kenwood the values held firm, averaging $100,000, a disparity that would affect Kenwood for years to come.[69]

An outspoken critic of renewal, Msgr. John J. Egan of the Catholic Diocese described renewal as "planned social anarchy," bringing to the forefront the "pe-

7.11. Newly relocated Lake Park Avenue, viewed here looking north from 55th Street. All structures adjacent to the Illinois Central tracks north of 53rd were removed after this image was taken. The original location of Lake Avenue is visible to the left of the Gold Crown sign.

7.12. The Bryson, once a
luxurious apartment hotel with
views of the lakefront, was
converted to furnished units for
low-income seniors.

7.13. Demonstrating the scope
of the problems that remained
on Lake Park into the seventies,
the once elegant building was
quickly vandalized after tenants
vacated their apartments in the
late spring of 1973. The Bryson
finally came down in September
of that year.

rennial question" of what happens to those displaced.[70] The estimated number of individuals displaced during the renewal process was nearly 20,000, of which about a third were to remain in the neighborhood, and the "rest relocated by the city into standard dwelling units elsewhere."[71] The relocation of families due to land clearance and demolition was tracked, although the numbers vary depending on the source. However, what is clear is that both black and white families were displaced during the renewal process. During the first project (Hyde Park A and B) the majority of the 892 families relocated (72 percent) were white, 18 percent were black, and the balance were Hispanic and Asian.[72]

Of the 531 individuals forced to relocate, 81 percent were white. The Urban Renewal Plan required displacing 3,092 families and 2,392 individuals from the neighborhood. The vast majority of the families (2,234) were black, while the majority of individuals (59 percent) were white. There was a great disparity between the movement of blacks and whites from the neighborhood and into public housing units. While only 15 white families moved into subsidized housing, 484 African American families did.[73]

The dilemma faced by Hyde Park residents when confronted with displacement continued into the seventies. For instance, the owner of the Bryson Hotel, an apartment building not included in the Urban Renewal Plan, attempted to obtain financing for much needed rehabilitation.[74] But the Department of Urban Renewal (DUR) wanted the structure torn down, and when financing fell through, residents were advised they would have to vacate. In 1971 most of the residents, elderly and on fixed incomes, wanted to remain in the hotel until good local housing could be found.[75] Although the DUR offered the tenants the first opportunity to move to nearby Lake Village, only forty units were available to tenants who met the guidelines for low and moderate income; all others would have to pay the market rate. Additionally the space would not be ready by the time of the Bryson's demolition.[76] The DUR suggested tenants move to apartments in the South Shore neighborhood, and many simply never returned to Hyde Park.

Despite the controversy, demolition, and displacement, the Hyde Park–Kenwood neighborhood after urban renewal was a far cry from the *New York Times* declaration of the area at the height of renewal as resembling "German cities just after World War II."[77] Although the neighborhood had to destroy parts of itself for the whole to survive, the plan achieved Julian Levi's goal of creating a stable community for the students and the faculty of the university. The community was more attractive, less populated, and of higher income. And safer—by 1960 the crime rate had fallen 30 percent from its peak level in 1952.[78] Looking back on the renewal years, one long-time Kenwood resident noted that while the plan certainly could have been handled with greater sensitivity, it did save the neighborhood for future generations.

A total of 3,997 dwelling units were lost during urban renewal; however, 2,100 new units were constructed.[79] Clusters of town houses rose throughout the area. In the five-year period after 1960, the city building department issued permits for over $18 million in residential construction, and nearly $6 million in residential rehabilitation within the Hyde Park–Kenwood community.[80] Added to this was the increase of permits issued to repair sidewalks, add landscaping, and improve interiors. By the midsixties residents were confident that the tide of neighborhood decay was stemmed.

New houses constructed during the sixties and seventies spurned the excessive details of earlier periods; brickwork was simple, windows were large, and roofs typically flat. Architects worked with the modern vocabulary of Mies van der Rohe in their designs, as large firms such as Skidmore, Owings and Merrill came into prominence. Interior plans were no longer based upon a central fireplace, as the television became a dominant element in living rooms. Kitchens were revolutionized by new appliances and by new materials such as plastic laminate. America's love affair with the automobile kept the garage a permanent feature of the landscape, while the widespread availability of air conditioning forever altered the American home.

Houses had traditionally been designed to take advantage of natural cooling through the placement of windows and the addition of porches where people spent hot summer days and evenings. The introduction of air conditioning shifted traditional seasonal patterns, as well as people's relationship with each other. A cool house eliminated the need for a front porch—the visiting tradition of porches had long

Webb & Knapp, Inc., Hyde Park A & B Townhouse Model C2300, rear view. I. M. Pei & Associates, Harry Weese & Associates, Associated Architects.

7.14. Two- and three-story townhomes rose on scattered sites throughout Hyde Park. In general this type of construction had not been used since the early 1900s. Autonomy and individuality had become the norm, and something as fundamental as defining ownership of a party wall had been lost. However as land costs grew to represent 20 percent of the cost of a house, the September 24, 1958, *Hyde Park Herald* noted that the reintroduction of the town house only made economic sense.

provided a sense of community, but voices were now quieted, replaced by the sound of compressors.[81] The new postwar house turned away from street life and promoted interiors that were advertised to be free of dust and dirt.

Confidence in the future of Hyde Park and Kenwood became increasingly evident in the building activity not only on renewal sites, but also throughout the neighborhood. The executive director of the Hyde Park–Kenwood Community Conference, Irving Horwitz, noted that most of the problematic buildings were gone and the rehabilitation of those that remained was extensive, yet, Horwitz added, "much more is needed."[82] A study conducted on the feasibility of rehabbing structures in Hyde Park and Kenwood highlighted a crucial stage of the neighborhood's future.

While the Urban Renewal Plan was large, it encompassed only 20 percent of the community. The future rested with the 80 percent of the structures that were not impacted by the plan. An analysis published by the Community Conservation Board of Chicago concluded that rehabilitated structures offered more square footage per dwelling unit and more amenities at a far lower cost than could be achieved under new construction.[83] Older structures in the neighborhood were modernized—a process whereby the architecture of earlier eras was erased and Victorian interiors gutted to suit a new aesthetic. "True modernization," wrote David Zisook in his analysis, "has the basic effect of extending the economic life of a building. It places the property back in a competitive position similar to the one it enjoyed when new or nearly new."[84]

Just ten years earlier, it was not clear that white, middle-income families would remain in the neighborhood and invest money. Interracial communities that might serve as a guide for the program were rare in the United States.[85] "What characterizes the investment is a judgment by bankers to invest other persons' money in the community," Julian Levi commented in 1965. "It is a commitment of 10 to 15 years or more, and such a commitment is impossible unless the investors believe in the future of the community."

Many compromises were made during urban renewal; some were unpopular and had lasting effects. Many people believed the university played too strong a role, and others found bias and error. But in the end the greatest compromise was to accept that renewal would not be a success unless the community rejected segregation and used social class to produce an integrated community.[86] Despite all of the democratic participation, investment of capital, volume of building, removal of lower-income occupied structures, and acceptance of integration, many of those who had the means deserted Hyde Park. Between 1960 and 1970, the community lost nearly 28 percent of its population.[87] Although they left for varying reasons, overall nearly 30,000 people moved from the community, lowering Hyde Park–Kenwood's population to 46,035 in 1970 from 71,689 prerenewal.[88] However, in the end the Hyde Park–Kenwood urban renewal project become one of the largest in the United States, assuring the "community's success in preventing its annexation to the black belt."[89] The neighborhood held up in the face of an enormous challenge and survived as a middle-class, racially integrated, and architecturally significant community.

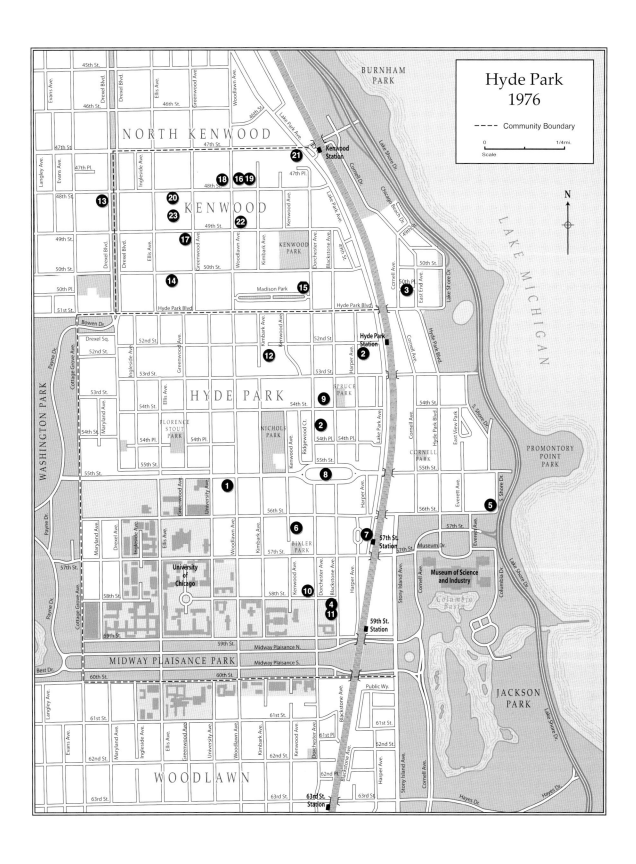

N

BURNHAM
PARK

LAKE MICHIGAN

NORTH KENWOOD

KENWOOD

KENWOOD
PARK

Madison Park

WASHINGTON PARK

HYDE PARK

FLORENCE
STOUT
Park

NICHOLS
PARK

SPRUCE
PARK

CORNELL
PARK

PROMONTORY
POINT
PARK

BIXLER
PARK

University
of
Chicago

Museum of Science
and Industry

Columbia
Basin

MIDWAY PLAISANCE PARK

JACKSON
PARK

WOODLAWN

Kenwood
Station

Hyde Park
Station

57th St.
Station

59th St.
Station

63rd St.
Station

Hyde Park

1 ## Cooperative Building, 1948.
5510–5516 South Woodlawn Avenue. Keck & Keck.

"Not all Chicago urban renewal projects were for the economically disadvantaged," wrote Keck biographer Robert Boyce, nor were they all aesthetically disappointing.[90] Some were even conceived prior to Hyde Park's formal renewal pro-

7.15. The Kecks designed the two-building cooperative on a lot where, according to a compilation of Woodlawn Avenue structures, a single-family brick residence once stood toward the rear of the property.

gram, including this twenty-unit apartment project designed for "tenant-owners," most of whom were professors at the University of Chicago. The two buildings on the site were arranged for the most effective use of the land, while providing the maximum amount of light and ventilation into the apartments.[91]

2 Pioneer Cooperative, 1949.
5427–5437 South Dorchester Avenue. Keck & Keck, with Robert Tague.

The Pioneer Cooperative was designed as a low-cost project where an owner would make an initial down payment and then pay a monthly charge that covered amortization, taxes, insurance and maintenance. Planned with associate architect Robert Tague, this multifamily building was not part of the urban renewal project but was constructed on a vacant tax-delinquent lot.[92] However, financing for the project was provided through the FHA, as private lending sources "shied away from the generally deteriorating character of the neighborhood."[93] Two buildings were conceived to house twenty-three units, planned in an L-shaped arrangement

7.16. The four-story Pioneer Cooperative features projecting balconies with a southern exposure facing the common open area.

7.17. The strong geometric shapes of the chain-link enclosed balconies are relieved by a mix of brightly painted doors in hues of red, blue, and yellow, evoking an abstract Mondrian painting.

that opened to the south and east, toward a green space and away from the parking provided along the street.

The units may have been small, but they were affordable and designed to be efficient. The project proved successful on three fronts—good housing was provided at a reasonable cost, the project was architecturally well designed, and the appearance of new construction in an area that was declining served as an example for urban renewal yet to come.[94]

③ Algonquin Apartments, 1950.
1606 East 51st Street and 1605–1606–1607–1616–1617 East 50th Street. PACE.

The Algonquin Apartments are a series of six fourteen-story concrete frame structures constructed on a portion of the Chicago Beach Hotel property.[95] Developed by Herbert Greenwald, the buildings were constructed with a simple concrete frame and yellow brick. Although the name "Algonquin" continued the Native

7.18. The Algonquin Apartments stand where the original Chicago Beach Hotel was constructed, located directly on the lakefront at the time.

American theme of the nearby buildings, the complex was completely devoid of the ornamentation of the earlier structures. PACE (Planners, Architects, and Consulting Engineers) was for a period closely associated with noted architect Ludwig Mies van der Rohe and collaborated with him on this project. He was the designer of the first phase of the FHA-financed project but removed his name when plans were altered to include first-floor apartments in place of the open lobby area.[96]

4 Helstein Residence, 1950–1951.
5806 South Blackstone Avenue. Bertrand Goldberg.

The iconic towers of Chicago's skyline, the Marina City complex by architect Bertrand Goldberg, were for a time the tallest reinforced concrete structure in the world. In a similar style he designed two other projects; the Raymond Hilliard Homes housing for the elderly in 1966, and in 1987 the River City complex, of which only the first phase was completed. All of these more famous works had their beginnings in the small residential structure that Goldberg planned for Ralph and Rachel Helstein. Designed to sit well back from the street, this was one of Goldberg's last single-family residences.

Rachel Brin came to Chicago in 1935 from Minneapolis to study comparative literature at the university. She married Ralph Helstein four years later, and he soon accepted a position as the attorney for the United Packinghouse Workers of America. They purchased a vacant lot on Blackstone near International House where Rachel had lived, and made the acquaintance of Goldberg through a family friend. According to their daughter Nina, Rachel Helstein felt Goldberg was a "kindred spirit," and enjoyed working with him as he discussed with his clients how they wanted to live with their family within the structure.

The collaboration resulted in a fascinating house that defies all convention of

7.20. Nina Helstein recalled that Bud Goldberg "always wanted to build showing the skeleton of the house." Her parents' residence once included a car park in the rear and a large, sheltered outdoor terrace that has since been enclosed. A small foyer provided access to the living space via a dramatic suspended staircase, which as a result of the addition can no longer be viewed from the street.

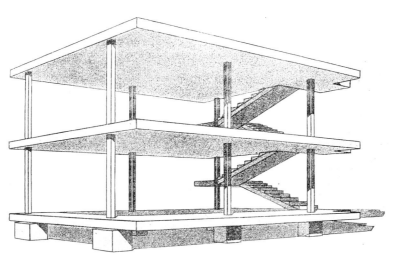

Maison Dom-ino, 1914. Unbuilt. Le Corbusier.
7.21. Goldberg mimicked the structural simplicity of the Maison Dom-ino (based on the Latin word for house, *domus*), freeing the interior of any structural constraints. Le Corbusier envisioned this as a prototype for affordable housing needed as a result of the destruction left by the First World War.

homebuilding in the neighborhood. Until this time, the wall was everything to the structure; as a midcentury modernist, Goldberg pushed the thought that the wall no longer had to perform its original function. What mattered were new and basic questions—what is the structure of the building, and how does one plan an interior freed of structural constraints?

The Helstein house was Goldberg's first use of a concrete frame, and he created an uncompromisingly modern structure. His idea is comparable to Le Corbusier's 1914 design for a basic building with freestanding pillars and rigid floors. Like Le Corbusier, Goldberg eliminated the walls of the box so the exposed

7.22. Goldberg was responsible for much of the interior of the Helstein house. He designed a number of furniture pieces, including the nesting coffee tables and a sofa that rested on a marble slab, pictured in the two-story sunlit living area.

formwork of the concrete slab floors and columns created a dramatic contrast to the glass walls.[97]

"For all its striking and modernist presence, the Helstein House was neither expensive nor extravagant," commented historian Tim Samuelson. "It was a demonstration of what common sense, ingenuity, and technology had to offer." The house retains an unexpected and forceful presence despite the alterations that have lessened some of its original intensity.[98]

Helstein was a "great intellectual in the labor movement" and spent much of his life working on "behalf of the poor and underprivileged in our society."[99] He practiced labor law in both Washington and Minnesota before joining the United Packinghouse Workers, an international union of predominantly black workers, as general counsel in 1942. Until he became the president of the UPWA in 1946, there had never been a lawyer "concerned with social justice" elected to lead a major labor organization. Helstein became a "unifying force" and developed "a democratic and honest organization," at a time when there was a split in the union. He remained as president until 1972, spearheading the union's merger with the Amalgamated Meat Cutters and Butcher Workmen in 1968 while struggling "against discrimination in all forms."[100]

Illinois Representative Charles Hayes remembered Helstein as a great supporter of the civil rights movement, and one of the "few trade union leaders who participated in marches with the Rev. Dr. Martin Luther King in the South and in Chicago."[101] However, his personal commitment to civil rights went much deeper—he was invited by Dr. King to join a relatively small group of men who met for monthly strategy meetings with Dr. King in New York.[102]

⑤ Shore Drive Motel, 1955–1956. Demolished 1988.
56th Street and South Shore Drive. A. Epstein & Sons, International, Inc.

Constructed on the site of the former Palm Grove Inn, the Shore Drive Motel opened for business in the spring of 1956. Morton's Restaurant was also housed within the complex, relocated to the hotel from its former site of twenty-three years on Lake Park Avenue when that structure was demolished during urban renewal. The motel had 150 air-conditioned rooms and an underground parking garage.[103]

The old Palm Grove Inn, which formerly stood on the site, was one of Hyde Park's classiest establishments. In 1934 Charles Morgan, the well-known modernist

7.23. Although the hotel postcard suggested the ambience of a bucolic park-like location, photographs demonstrate the reality of a gritty urban setting.

responsible for the Powhatan and Narragansett Apartments, redesigned the restaurant. The "swanky dining place" featured a sidewalk café exaggeratedly compared to those found on the expensive and fashionable avenue of Rue de la Paix in Paris.[104] In 1988, the shuttered Shore Drive Motel was razed to make way for the fourteen-story continuing-care retirement community Montgomery Place.

6 Johnson Residence, 1956.
5617 South Kenwood Avenue. Harry Weese & Associates.

Throughout his career, renowned architect Harry Weese was "an outspoken advocate for architecture that embraced the social and economic realities of urban life."[105] Credited for thinking contextually, he sought architectural harmony with the neighborhood's older buildings. Weese referred to the house of University of

7.25. The 2,000-square-foot house was built for Dr. D. Gale and Helen Johnson. According to the university, he was one of the "most eminent researchers of agricultural and development economics, who helped build the University of Chicago's Department of Economics into a global powerhouse." Johnson also served as president of the South East Chicago Commission, an organization dedicated to establishing the Hyde Park–South Kenwood neighborhood as a racially and economically integrated community.

Chicago economics professor and associate dean of the social sciences, D. Gale Johnson, as "Hyde Park contemporary."[106] Essentially it is a rework of a design Weese did for his uncle Robert P. Weese in 1939–1940 in suburban Barrington, and a predecessor of his urban renewal designs.

The two-story red brick house, detailed with Indiana limestone, is oriented toward the rear of the 50' × 180' lot. Typical of housing of this period, large picture windows allow an abundance of light into the home. Weese also designed the interiors, utilizing a slate floor in the entry and a fireplace of the same exterior brick.[107]

⑨ Hyde Park Cooperative Homes, 1958–1961.
1402-1428 East 54th Street. Harry Weese & Associates, in association with I. M. Pei.

In association with I. M. Pei, Weese & Associates worked on plans for two- and three-story townhomes on various sites. Weese's aesthetic vision for the Hyde Park Redevelopment Project included details that rendered the façade less severe, for he was concerned with suiting his buildings to the existing site conditions. In spite of their contrasting yellow brick, the plan harmoniously incorporated the new structures into the existing streetscape. The project succeeded in reintroducing the efficient town house form, which became common not only in Hyde Park, but also throughout the city. Harry Weese credited urban renewal participant Bill Zeckendorf with the very word "town house." "Row house" connoted "Baltimore slums or Philadelphia crowded districts," Weese said.[108] Brownstones were New York City—Chicago would define its own architecture.

During this time of urban renewal, Harry and Ben Weese became vital components in the struggle for the vision of a future Hyde Park. Weese & Associates were among several firms that submitted plans for the redevelopment of the area near

7.26. Clearance in this area was not yet complete when this image of the Hyde Park Cooperative Homes was taken in 1958; the apartment building on the far right of the town houses was razed as part of the Urban Renewal Plan and replaced by a park.

55th Street; however, their proposal was not accepted. Weese envisioned the street as a traditional linear element with a pedestrian bridge over 55th Street at Dorchester, as opposed to the curved roadway that was eventually built. "Harry Weese believed in democracy. He believed the public sector was a barometer of society," commented architect Jack Hartray. "He couldn't stand a world where there were great individual buildings, but the streets were out of order."[109]

⑧ University Apartments, 1960–1961.
1400–1450 and 1401–1451 East 55th Street. I. M. Pei with Loewenberg & Loewenberg.

A major force during the Hyde Park redevelopment years, renowned architect I. M. Pei designed the University Apartments complex. The twin ten-story structures on an island in 55th Street are, to a degree, representative of a concept in architecture following principles laid out by Le Corbusier. The influential Swiss architect believed that buildings such as these should be placed along transportation routes, but in park settings.[110] Pei split the typical street pattern around the complex to discourage high-speed traffic, a concept that time has proven not very successful.

For the two mid-rise structures Pei designed the supporting walls with a large,

7.27. The 540 units of the University Apartments complex promoted modern convenience, from closed-circuit TV intercom systems to clean, contemporary kitchens and baths.

number of openings, creating a lacy concrete frame that was both the buildings' façade and their supporting structure. The high cost of materials at the time was the factor behind using the frame as part of the face, which eliminated the need for an additional outside skin of metal or brick.[111] The project encountered structural and planning difficulties, and the Chicago-based firm of Loewenberg & Loewenberg was brought in to address problematic aspects of the plan without compromising the façade.

Pei used the same formula for the Kips Bay Towers project in New York City, also produced by Webb & Knapp. This new kind of bearing wall became a common engineering practice and was used on a much larger scale in the ill-fated World Trade Center buildings; there the integrity of the shell was compromised, with disastrous consequences.

⑦ University Neighborhood Homes, 1958–1961.
Lake Park Avenue between 56th and 57th Streets, Harry Weese & Associates and I. M. Pei.

Constructed of buff-color brick, the townhomes of "Hyde Park A" are repetitive and spare. The structures are pared down, constructed with uncomplicated elements and eight-foot ceilings. These geometrical façades typically feature a third-floor clerestory and stark recessed entries, and the effect is a "symphony of discipline," as described by Ben Weese.[112]

7.28. The solids and voids of the townhomes are placed around a private garden, reminiscent of Madison Park as conceived nearly a hundred years earlier. Here, the planning is rigid; the modern house resists any changes, as opposed to older houses that easily permitted expansions as families grew.

⑩ Chicago Theological Seminary Faculty Quadrangle, 1963.
58th Street and Dorchester Avenue. Edward Dart & Associates.

In 1963, the Chicago Theological Seminary commissioned Edward (Ned) Dart to design faculty housing on a site at 58th and Dorchester near the University of Chicago campus. For the past century the fundamental pattern of the urban lot had been the same. As defined by Vincent Scully, the lot was a quadrangle, the house placed in the center of it with a lawn, shrubs, and trees, a sidewalk, a thin plat along the curb, and the street.[113] This AIA Award–winning design broke that tradi-

7.29. Steeply sloped rooflines, and the relationship of buildings to one another and to the site, define Dart's project for the Chicago Theological Seminary.

tion by placing a cluster of units set on diagonals at the perimeter of the lot. The houses were arranged in a U shape around a landscaped courtyard for maximum privacy. Their steeply pitched roofs were much in fashion in the sixties.[114] The project broke all norms of common building at the time, from the placement of the structures that do not follow the line of the street to the use of common brick. While there have been issues related to construction, Dart succeeded in his task of creating a village around a central open area.

⑪ Karlin Residence, 1964–1965.
5812 South Blackstone Avenue. Keck & Keck.

The restrained contemporary design for Norman Karlin is set along a streetscape mainly composed of traditional dwellings. This parcel of land was purchased from the Helstein family, residents of the striking Bertrand Goldberg–designed house to the north. The sale of property came with the requirement that construction of this house be sited near to the street. The placement of the house on the lot also confirms the importance of the automobile in family life. Typically designers put the best face of the house toward the street, and service elements toward the rear. The utilitarian garage door was incorporated into the façade, requiring a curb cut and disturbing the traditional streetscape. Purple-black brick, white trim, and a copper mansard roof distinguish the house from its surroundings.[115]

George Fred Keck had been designing homes for forty years when his firm re-

7.30. The Karlin residence was constructed on land adjacent to Goldberg's Helstein house, but situated nearer to the street.

ceived this commission. He expressed an annoyance toward designs that "imitated past cultural styles" and felt many buyers were interested in a house as a "status symbol" and would rather spend their "money on ornaments than a fine house."[116] The composition of this and other Keck houses was often dictated by "contemporary state-of-the-art construction methods," and "by the conveniences required by an enlightened client."[117]

⑫ The Commons Townhouses, 1965–1966.
5135–5231 South Kimbark Avenue. Ezra Gordon and Jack Levin.

The Commons is a group of nineteen three- and four-bedroom town houses built on slum-clearance land on a closed-off section of Kimbark Avenue. Gordon lived in the area and was "acutely aware of the conditions of the neighborhood." He recalled that the idea to cluster the attached residences around a courtyard grew from his earlier town planning experiences, and he viewed this as a type of housing that promoted family life. Both Gordon and Levin were sensitive about the "relationship of the house to the site and the site to the community," and favored "adequate space around the house and views."[118]

The combination of "simplicity, richness of texture and color, and privacy," of these brick townhomes continued "the great tradition of Hyde Park urbanity established long ago by the university's Quadrangles."[119] The project received a number of awards, from the Chicago chapter of the American Institute of Architects and the Department of Housing and Urban Development.

7.31. Ezra Gordon lived in Madison Park for seven years and recalled that the community was "badly deteriorated" during the years prior to urban renewal. After working for Harry Weese, he bid on sites in Hyde Park independently and was awarded two. These comprised the Commons, a development conceived to exist in concert with the surrounding neighborhood.

Kenwood

13 **Drexel Boulevard Home and Gardens Houses, 1954–1955.**
4800 Drexel Boulevard. Bertrand Goldberg.

The idea behind Bertrand Goldberg's Drexel Home and Gardens project was to provide low-cost housing that did not "punish the poor for being poor."[120] Goldberg "endeavored to design attractive and integrated low-cost housing" in the Kenwood neighborhood on once-magnificent Drexel Boulevard. Working in partnership with Arthur Rubloff, he sought to develop this project privately, believing the quality would be higher. The project was marketed to an integrated buying group, with the concept of placing home ownership within reach of lower-income families. Although planned while urban renewal was just underway, this independent project was positioned as one of improvement to, rather than transformation of, an established neighborhood.

The Drexel Homes project is located on the former site of the Edward Morris estate—his three-story brick residence and coach house were demolished in April 1946. As construction began, workers hit what they believed to be the foundation of an additional house on the property. What was unearthed instead was a massive fishpond. The pond was removed, and upon completion of the project sixty-four families occupied the site of an immense and luxurious mansion constructed for but one family.

Goldberg used the idea of a simple, flat-roofed house of concrete block with little adornment. Details included simple geometric exterior patterns created with standard masonry blocks. The first floor of each town house featured large windows that extended the open plan of the main living area to patios enclosed by perforated concrete block walls. "The ceilings were beamed and the floors covered

7.32. The sixty-four units of the Drexel Boulevard Home and Gardens occupy what was formerly a single-family site.

in colorful linoleum. Each of the sixty-four three bedroom apartments featured a rear patio enclosed by screen-cut concrete block walls that created an intimate space but did not completely isolate one family from another."[121]

Other innovative ideas in urban living were a part of this project as well. For example, there was one water meter for all of the houses, forming a "water company" for the development.[122] Each owner then paid their share to the company, which not only paid the city for water, but also generated a profit intended to pay for upkeep for the amenities of the site, such as the playground and sidewalks.

Although the project won awards from Progressive Architecture and Architectural Forum, Goldberg's dream of creating affordable high-quality integrated housing was never realized. According to Goldberg, lenders would not lend to white couples who wanted to live in the predominately African American area because it was not considered a good mortgage risk.[123] Today the structures remain in a curious state—the simple geometric shapes of Goldberg's vision have been clad with faux brick and shingles. The effect is of a patchwork rather than the simple yet elegant scheme Goldberg envisioned.

14 Gleason Residence, 1954.
1025 East 50th Street. Keck & Keck.

7.33. The second level of the Gleason house, as viewed from the courtyard, was designed by architect Jonathan Beyer to accommodate a subsequent owner's growing family.

In 1948, Kenwood quietly accepted the first African American family into the neighborhood.[124] When they moved into 5009 South Ellis, Dr. Maurice Gleason was an obstetrician at nearby Provident Hospital, and his wife Eliza was a schoolteacher. Before long, the Gleasons purchased a lot on 50th Street that had once belonged to the Loeb family and was occupied by their greenhouses and a small gardener's cottage. Keck & Keck were commissioned to design a new house for the

family, and the result was a "low-slung contemporary" home that "attracted a flurry of attention" in publications of the day.[125]

The Gleasons constructed only the first level of the U-shaped structure, which was designed by the Kecks to be two stories. The small gardener's cottage was incorporated into a corner of the house. The Kecks were known for their work in solar residential architecture; here radiant heating in the green slate floors and passive solar heating provide warmth in the winter.[126] The eave line prevents sun from entering through the large floor-to-ceiling glass panes during the summer months, yet allows for an abundance of natural light from the private courtyard.[127] There were no windows that opened in the original design; fresh air was accessible through a series louvered panels.

In 1987, the current owners expanded with a second-story addition. Requiring the approval of the Landmarks Commission, the original plans were presented to document the intent of the Keck design. Architect Jonathan Beyer designed a master suite and additional bedrooms that look onto a lush private courtyard.

⑮ Atrium Houses, 1961.
1366–1380 East Madison Park. Y. C. Wong & Associates.

The windowless façades of Y. C. Wong's uncompromising Atrium Houses are located on the private grounds of Madison Park—their spartan surfaces are in complete contrast to their light-filled interiors. Each residence is oriented inward, toward a glass-walled atrium as "the house wraps around an inner garden, putting the backyard in the middle of the home."[128] This privately financed project features severe tan brick walls, beams for cornices, and simple doors. Each 2,000-square-foot unit was sold at a reasonably low cost and included two baths and three bedrooms, of which two have a sliding partition between them.[129]

During his interview for the Art Institute Oral History Project, Wong could not

7.34. The taut, unadorned surfaces of the façade exhibit no decoration. Instead, Wong used a simple concept to define the Atrium House project: stark geometric forms enclose an open space.

7.35. The interiors of each room within Wong's atrium homes are enhanced by the sunlit central court.

recall how he came up with the concept for the Atrium Homes. "At the time I designed it, I really had no preconceived idea. I was working on the project and when I found how it came out, that is, the most economical and most satisfactory, it was an atrium. I have L-shapes and rectangular—all kinds of schemes. I remember I had almost twenty-some schemes," he said. "I feel that when I get home after a day's work, I just want to be at home and I don't want to be on the street."[130]

One of the more famous occupants of the complex was the "creative and provocative promoter"[131] and owner of the Chicago White Sox, Bill Veeck, who lived at 1380 Madison Park with his wife Mary Frances. The year he bought the Sox team, they won the 1959 American League pennant, but more importantly Veeck is credited with integrating the American League.[132] Poor health (he lost part of his right leg during World War II) forced him to sell the White Sox the year these homes were constructed.[133] But he wasn't through; Veeck returned as an owner from 1975 to 1981.[134]

16 University of Chicago and Midway Properties Townhomes, 1962.
1210–1216 48th Street and 4741–4755 South Woodlawn Avenue. Keck & Keck.

The sixties "were a period of new opportunity" for George Fred and William Keck. The firm received many commissions for renovations, but also designed a number of multiunit projects, both low-rise and high-rise, in the Hyde Park–Kenwood area. Their interest in multifamily housing was provoked by the "social, political, and

economic conditions" of the time, but also by their desire to improve their neighborhood aesthetically.[135]

In addition to large-scale projects, the Kecks designed a number of town houses and duplexes. In 1962 they designed a twelve-unit, two-building complex at the corner of 48th Street and Woodlawn on an urban renewal site that had been cleared of two large old frame houses. The design of this project is consistent with their earlier work; extended walls, which indicate the individual unit, separate the flat-roofed façade. Each town house contained three to four bedrooms and one and a half baths. The design included private parking and a 20' × 30' enclosed backyard facing a large, commonly owned lawn.[136]

The residences originally built on the site were completed in the early 1890s.

(*Left*) **Marvin A. Farr Residence, c. 1890. Demolished 1961. 4737 South Woodlawn. Architect/ builder unknown.**

7.37. (*Right*) Thaddeus Dean Residence, c. 1890. Demolished 1961. 4747 South Woodlawn Avenue. Architect/builder unknown. The Woodlawn Avenue residences of Marvin and Charlotte Farr and the Thaddeus Dean family were demolished to provide the land for the town house complex.

Over time they fell into disrepair, were subdivided into rooming houses, and were finally torn down during urban renewal. The completion of the Keck & Keck project was viewed as a "major success story" of how a neighborhood could be saved from "decay and deterioration."[137]

⑰ Residences, 1965.
1044—1050 East 49th Street and 4858 South Greenwood Avenue. Keck & Keck.

Keck & Keck designed a number of multifamily projects in the area; however, the majority of their projects entailed remodeling existing residential structures. According to biographer Robert Boyce, they were "often consulted on questions of building materials, plantings and furnishings; and generally made themselves

7.38. The three Keck houses were built on the former site of Sarah and Eugene Kincaid Butler's Richardsonian Romanesque style residence at 4850 South Greenwood.

available to their neighbors in the effort to improve the aesthetics and social condition of their environment."[138]

During the midsixties, private residential projects began to rise on land that had been cleared during the action phase of urban renewal. Keck & Keck were responsible for the planning of two three-house groupings on 49th Street. The grouping nearest Greenwood and pictured here was built on the site of the twenty-two-room mansion of Mr. and Mrs. E. K. Butler. That three-story Richardsonian Romanesque-style house had faced Greenwood Avenue until cleared during renewal. The sidewalk that leads from the street to the front entry indicates the orientation of the razed house, while the coach house remains on 49th Street.

18 Hyde Park–Kenwood Townhomes, 1967.
1144–1158 East 48th Street. Y. C. Wong.

These town houses were constructed on the site of an old frame house at 4750 South Woodlawn that had been used as a nursing home for years until privately demolished in 1962. A proposal to construct a twenty-unit apartment building was abandoned for a project scaled to be more in keeping with the neighborhood.[139]

7.39. Wong continued his use of spartan, unadorned exteriors for this development on 48th Street.

7.40. The light-filled interiors of the Wong townhomes open onto private courtyards; the simplicity of the design echoes the geometric pattern of half timbering on the 1909 Tudor-style house across the street.

Here Y. C. Wong continued his use of light-toned brick with expanses of glass. The ground level of these eight townhomes is slightly recessed, and the southern exposure of the glass façades allows an abundance of light into the structures.

⑲ Barglow Residence, 1967.
1220 East 48th Street. Booth & Nagle.

Peter Barglow, an associate professor of psychiatry at the University of Chicago and clinical director of the Department of Psychology at Michael Reese Hospital,[140] purchased the property on the corner of 48th and Kimbark. The Barglows wanted to build a new three-story town house in the backyard and then sell the original residence, which had been built in the 1880s for Walter G. Coolidge.

According to the account, lead architect Larry Booth gave to the Art Institute's Oral History Project, the owners separated out a parcel for the new house that fronted 48th Street. "Basically they wanted a detached, vertical town house with four bedrooms," Booth said. "I think at the time the philosophy was to be really simple in terms of construction, because we didn't know exactly what we were doing." He recalled a modest budget and an emphasis on durability.

"If you look at the house now," Booth commented, "it looks like the day it was built because it's solid brick and stone. . . . But it was just a very simple set of building blocks . . . looking south and letting the sunlight come in. There was a wall across the front that created a private yard so that there was security and privacy."[141]

The design for the Barglows won two awards: the AIA Chicago Chapter Distinguished Building Award in 1969, and in 1970, the Record House Award from Progressive Architecture.

7.41. The Barglow house was the very first project conceived by Booth & Nagle. The architects had a "similar stylistic approach," recalled Nagle, in that they "liked hard-line architecture."

20 Morton Residence, c. 1970.

1039 East 48th Street. Edmund N. Zisook & Associates.

The son of real estate developer Harry Zisook, architect Edmund Zisook was raised in the Kenwood neighborhood. Edmund spent much of his early life in a house designed by Thomas Bishop in 1938 on the grounds of the old Charles Hosmer Morse estate. That house was one of six originally planned by the developers to be built on the site.

At the time only three houses were constructed, and many years later Edmund Zisook planned this modern single-story gray brick residence on the grounds behind his family home. Designed for Dr. Chauncey Morton, a prominent African American urologist,[142] the house is placed next to a service drive at 1031 East 48th Street. Only the remains of a sidewalk leading from the street indicate there was once a frame house on that site, the first Kenwood home of Charles Morse.

7.43. Zisook could not recall the exact year he designed this one-story house, but he was clearly familiar with the Kenwood neighborhood, having been raised just to the east of the Morton residence.

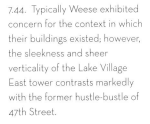

21 Lake Village East, 1971.

4700 South Lake Park Avenue. Harry Weese & Associates, with Gordon & Levin, associate architects.

During urban renewal land clearance, Lake Park Avenue was relocated to the east adjacent to the Illinois Central Railroad embankment. At the 47th Street intersection, a large parcel was determined to contain structures not worthy of rehabilitation. The property was cleared; however, its role in the redevelopment process was never exactly outlined. The area that was once the gateway to aristocratic Kenwood lay vacant and strewn with rubble for many years, becoming a tenuous boundary between the ghetto to the north and the university further south.

Various plans were proposed for the land, but none could garner community or financial support.[143] Then in the late sixties Ben Weese, with associate architects Ezra Gordon and Jack M. Levin, was hired to develop a plan for the property. The team proposed the "slim silhouette" of Lake Village East, a twenty-five-floor high-rise in the form of a polygon with thirty-eight sides. Ben Weese described the tower as using "minimum perimeter" floor planning to eliminate long corridors while providing interesting apartment layouts.[144] Additionally, the placement of the windows captured the views north to the Loop and east to Lake Michigan.[145]

In addition to the tower, a series of townhomes located west along the south side of 47th Street was included in the planning. Ezra Gordon was in charge of the design of the ten apartment buildings of Greenwood Park, which were completed in 1971. The second phase was to include an additional 100 townhouses. Designed by Weese, only fifteen were erected, near 48th Street and Kimbark. The entire project was controversial and subject to a lawsuit brought by the university because the developers, hired to produce market-rate housing, had switched to subsidized units. The university, and Julian Levi in particular, was furious at the change but lost

7.44. Typically Weese exhibited concern for the context in which their buildings existed; however, the sleekness and sheer verticality of the Lake Village East tower contrasts markedly with the former hustle-bustle of 47th Street.

the lawsuit. However, the university withdrew the right to construct the remaining townhouses on 47th Street east of Woodlawn.

Lake Village East demonstrated Ben and Harry Weese's continuing concern for the context in which their buildings exist, and their work balanced innovation with an understanding of the past. Many of their projects pay a debt to the neighborhood's history by incorporating such elements as masonry bearing walls with large plates of glass typical of the Chicago bay window.[146] This project was the recipient of a 1974 Honor Award from the American Institute of Architects.

22 Muhammad Residence, 1972.
4855 South Woodlawn Avenue. MEESI.

One of the most distinctive structures in Kenwood was constructed for the controversial leader of the Nation of Islam. After attending a lecture at the Temple of Islam in Detroit in 1931, Elijah Poole converted to Islam, became a minister and changed his name to Muhammad when promoted to the position of "Supreme Minister." Believing his mission was to teach "downtrodden and defenseless Black people" to put themselves on a path to self-independence through knowledge of God, Muhammad took leadership of the organization when he came to Chicago in 1946.[147] Preaching at the Temple of Islam No. 2, then located at 5335 Greenwood,[148] Muhammad was divisive in his role, calling for a separate state in the Union for blacks and berating whites as "devils."[149]

Muhammad (his wife Clara died the year the house was built) occupied the three-level, nineteen-room mansion, while his children and chief aides resided in the nearby complex on 1136–1158 East 49th Street. The Mediterranean-influenced houses included stained-glass windows that featured Muslim-inspired elements. On the interior of the main house, a "conversation area" next to the living room had a water fountain, a tropical garden, and a stained-glass dome featuring the Arabic word for God, Allah.[150] A very traditional red brick house with shutters with a columned entrance was torn down, not because of decay, but in order to build the main house for Muhammad. "There was a beautiful house on the property, perfectly fine," according to a long-time neighbor. "The late Mayor Daley approved the demolition permit," she continued, "and we neighbors had no knowledge prior to the teardown."[151]

7.46. The Muhammad/
Farrakhan property features
a curving driveway and tiled
fountain facing Woodlawn
Avenue. It is guarded by Nation
of Islam security and is often
photographed by curiosity
seekers.

The residences on 49th Street were constructed on vacant property, once the John Davis estate. His three-story frame and stone residence had been demolished in May 1945. The design of these four houses includes a separate back stairway for women, and a large fountain located in a two-story central court. The houses on 49th Street are now private residences.

After Muhammad's death in 1975, the Nation of Islam broke into two factions. Wallace D. Muhammad, the son of Elijah and head of the splinter group Nation of Islam of the West, built the mosque at 47th and Woodlawn in 1982. Louis Farrakhan generally retained Elijah Muhammad's ideas and practices and became the leader of the militant Black Muslim sect of the Nation of Islam. In 1986, Farrakhan purchased the property. He planned to use the house as the sect's national headquarters; however, that use was not permitted under the city's zoning ordinance. It became his residence, although not without controversy due to his inflammatory, anti-Semitic remarks.[152]

23 Mermel Residence, 1976.
1039 East 48th Street. Robert Philip Gordon.

Nestled among the trees and removed from Chicago's standard street grid is the residence designed for Irving and Anne Mermel. The property was once part of the Morse estate that had been subdivided into six sections. Morse for a time lived in a frame house fronting 48th Street, with a drive leading to the rear of the property where the Mermel house was eventually constructed.

On this sylvan setting, reminiscent of Kenwood's earliest years, is a midcentury modern residence designed for an empty-nester couple relocating to Kenwood from Texas. To celebrate their new life, Gordon designed the house with a large common space, exterior decks, and a south-facing two-story atrium that fills the home with light. In conversation, the architect recalled that he designed the house at the beginning of the "great room" living style, which combined the kitchen, dining, and living rooms into one open and informal space.[153] Following a trend that first began with Wright's Robie house and was followed decades later

7.47. The Mermel garage was placed partially below grade, so not to dominate the main entry to the house.

7.48. The dramatic light-filled atrium of the Mermel house contrasts with the neighboring turn-of-the-century residences, barely visible through the trees.

by the work of Ralph Rapson, residents delighted in open volumes after decades of houses based upon small, closeted rooms.

The Mermel house is the last residence constructed in Kenwood prior to the community's designation as a landmark district.

Morse Residence, c. 1880. Demolished. 1039 East 48th Street. Architect/builder unknown.

7.49. All that remains to indicate that this frame house once stood on the property is a concrete walk between the sidewalk and the street. Today, the drive on the left in this image leads to the secluded Mermel house.

8.01. The *Hyde Park Herald* printed an image of the scale model prepared to demonstrate the reuse of the Rosenwald property. Conceived by developer Louis Silverman, the 13,000-square-foot mansion was to be converted to three condominiums, and the coach house to a single-family home. The expansive backyard was to be occupied by twelve new town houses.

CHAPTER EIGHT

Preservation, 1979–2012

Chicago builds itself up, knocks itself down again, scrapes away the rubble and starts over. European cities destroyed in war were painstakingly restored. Chicago does not restore; it makes something wildly different. To count on stability here is madness. A Parisian can always see the Paris that was, as it has been for centuries. . . . But a Chicagoan as he wanders about the city feels like a man who has lost many teeth.

—Hyde Park resident Saul Bellow, 1983[1]

June 29, 1979, was a watershed day for the neighborhood: the Chicago City Council formally approved a major portion of Kenwood as a landmark district. The grassroots effort to preserve the historic structures that remained after urban renewal began long before the final stamp of approval was given. Local efforts accelerated as the page began to turn on the community's darker days, and they continued as restrictive covenants and enforced segregation slowly faded from memory. Many realized that as these disappeared from the common conscience, the physical history of important earlier eras was also disappearing. Others were simply glad to be rid of them.

As many of Hyde Park's buildings fell, a project began to document the moment of loss. In 1960 a project was undertaken by the Hyde Park–Kenwood Community Conference to record the changing landscape through a series of photographs and salvaged architectural pieces of historically interesting buildings slated for demolition during renewal. Members of a committee, under the guidance of project chairman Marian Despres, inspected 886 buildings and selected those to be photographed. The committee also identified "stone carvings, wooden ornaments, supports, and other details" to be salvaged fro reuse or exhibited in a proposed "architectural museum."[2]

Photographer and longtime Kenwood resident Rus Arnold worked with the team sponsored by the conference, documenting the buildings determined to no longer be an asset to the community. The goal was to continue to preserve both physically and on film the many examples of the rapidly disappearing styles of residences in the area. A report was issued recommending that forty-three structures be photographed. Exterior details such as stone carvings, wood ornament, eave supports, and interior details including tiles, fireplaces, and metalwork were salvaged from another fifteen residences. Not a single structure was recommended to be preserved.[3]

The buildings photographed were outstanding examples of how architects solved problems presented at various periods throughout the neighborhood's history. They were also representative of "the skills, taste, style of life and economic resources of their period."[4] The details from the architecture, design, and construction of the community's early days were preserved, although the houses were subsequently destroyed by urban renewal.[5] The Hyde Park–Kenwood Community Conference and the Department of Urban Renewal published the photographs in a document titled *Segments of the Past*; however, the museum was never more than a concept. More than fifty salvaged items—mantelpieces, glass windows, chandeliers, and furniture—were auctioned in 1963. Others were purchased by the Smithsonian Museum and the Museum of Science and Industry.[6]

Pictured within the booklet are examples of gracious old residences, with spacious rooms warmed by "fine old marble fireplaces" and designed with "handsome stair rails and carved woodwork."[7] Residences large and small are depicted; however, the conditions that lead to their demolition—"sagging floors, leaky plumbing, . . . hanging wires, odorous and littered halls, water filled basements and closets turned into sleeping rooms"—were not within the scope of the project.[8]

The issue of the ever-increasing loss of Chicago's architectural heritage attracted the public's attention. When Chicago's Landmarks Commission was founded in 1957, it was an organization with little power behind it. The commission hung plaques on historic buildings as architects and preservationists watched the city squander its magnificent architectural heritage. During a relatively short span of time the city lost many architectural treasures, including Adler & Sullivan's Garrick Theater, tragically demolished in 1961 to become a parking lot.[9]

In a particularly painful and repetitive episode, Frank Lloyd Wright's masterpiece of the Prairie Style, the Robie house, was nearly demolished. The house had passed through several owners until 1926, when the Chicago Theological Seminary acquired it for use as a dormitory for married students. In 1941 the seminary announced plans to demolish the house and erect a larger dormitory on the site, but a grassroots letter-writing campaign against the proposal ensued and the house was saved. Again in 1957 the iconic structure was threatened with demolition, and protecting it proved to be a difficult task. The community's determination and massive support demonstrated the importance of the structure. Poet Carl Sandburg equated the impending demolition to "Nazi book burning," and declared that there was "something sacred" about the structure.[10] The ninety-year-old architect Frank Lloyd Wright declared the house to be the finest he ever designed.

Developer William Zeckendorf, of the redevelopment firm Webb & Knapp, was persuaded to purchase the property for use as an office while constructing the University Apartments and the Hyde Park Shopping Center. Meanwhile, the university made an agreement regarding an adjacent parcel of property to the north of the Robie house for the construction of a seminary dormitory. Although the plan meant three other residences were demolished, the Robie house was saved, and in 1962 Zeckendorf donated the property to the university.[11] For the next thirty-five years the house was used as the Adlai Stevenson Institute for International Affairs, and then as university offices. Wright's dramatic formal dining table was sawn apart in order to make two conference tables, demonstrating the uneven approach to preservation, and particularly insensitive in a structure in which the architect believed in the cohesion of the interior and exterior. In 2010, after the house was designated a national landmark and one of the twelve most significant structures of the twentieth century by the AIA, a $12 million restoration program was undertaken.

Saving the Robie house gave preservationists confidence, but it was not until 1968 that a "decisive shift" in preservation policy occurred.[12] City Hall created a new Commission on Historical Landmarks, and gave it an operating staff and more authority. Appointed by the mayor and the City Council, the commissioners are responsible for recommending individual buildings, sites, objects, or entire districts to be designated Chicago landmarks, protecting them by law. In spite of the new landmark ordinance, however, the commission could not prevent the destruction of some of the city's greatest assets, including Adler & Sullivan's Stock Exchange Building.[13] In 1972 the "lush terra cotta and stone ornament" fell at the feet of the appalled preservationists trying to save the building.[14]

In Chicago and elsewhere around the country, preservationists attempted to stop urban renewal plans that clear-cut large inner-city areas. "What evolved instead was a view of cities that value incremental, rather than sweeping change; quirkiness rather than standardization; preservation rather than destruction," architecture critic Blair Kamin later explained. "The change occurred not just for sentimental reasons but because—as the urbanologist Jane Jacobs demonstrated in her 1961 book *The Life and Death of Great American Cities*—mixing old buildings with new ones helps create the social and economic diversity that makes cities hum."[15]

As demonstrated by the Robie house example, the battleground was not confined to the city center, and preservationists moved to save some of the treasures of Chicago's residential neighborhoods that had fallen into disrepair, including the house constructed for retailer and philanthropist Julius Rosenwald at 4901 South Ellis. The mansion was designed by Nimmons & Fellows and situated on 1.7 acres, one of the largest parcels in Kenwood.

In 1977 local developer Louis Silverman acquired the property. The mansion still featured all the splendors of an earlier era, including seven fireplaces, a solarium, and a wood-paneled library. However the structure had been vacant for years and was rundown and riddled with building code violations. Silverman intended to subdivide the house into three luxury condominiums and turn the coach house into a single-family residence.[16] Requiring approval from the Chicago Plan Commission, Silverman said he determined it was economically unfeasible to move forward with the plan unless he was permitted to construct town houses in the spacious backyard of the Rosenwald mansion. The commission approved his plan, but when the City Council did not, Silverman threatened to tear down the historic structure.[17]

Silverman's plan attracted significant neighborhood opposition and galvanized a local movement. The Kenwood Open House Committee fought long and hard

to prevent the zoning change necessary to carry out the plan. Others found the plan somewhat palatable if it meant saving the immense house.[18] Some thought conversion was the only way to prevent demolition, believing that unless they could find "an arab sheik, there's no one who could afford that home."[19] To further complicate matters, the majority of South Kenwood had been approved for historic status, with City Council approval pending but expected.

The neighborhood won this long zoning battle, saving the historic residence as a single-family house and marking the beginning of a new era for Kenwood with landmark designation for the entire community. The area bounded by 47th Street south to 51st and from Drexel Boulevard east to Blackstone was designated a Landmark District on June 29, 1979. The decision preserved the area; however, in the time it took, a number of structures were lost and an equal number of unremarkable structures constructed. Blair Kamin noted, "The picture has brightened since the dark days before 1968, but the battle to preserve Chicago's past is ongoing, ever-changing and more complex than ever."[20]

Hyde Park's Alderman Leon Despres had long argued for preservation, believing that while not every old building should be preserved, it was necessary to preserve "creatively and constructively." He thought protecting historic urban areas required making some sacrifices, yet was a "sign of a society's cultural maturity." And the AIA summed the issue up succinctly: "All we need is a sense of greatness and a willingness to elevate the common good above someone's hopes to make a buck."[21]

It took another fourteen years for the North Kenwood neighborhood to receive the landmark designation, and by that time significant damage to the housing stock had been done. The influence and interest of the university ended at 47th Street, and North Kenwood was left to fare on its own. The result was overwhelming poverty, in an area where vicious gangs succeeded in choking the very life out of the community. House after house was torn down, leaving Chicago's cold winds to blow through "vacant lots stripped of homes and lights and life and hope."[22] Between 1969 and 1980, not a single new structure was built in the area. During the following eight-year period, construction resumed with the completion of 246 units. Meanwhile, twice that number were demolished.[23]

The city designated North Kenwood a Historic District in 1993, centered on the masonry row houses at 45th Street and Berkeley. The district included one hundred *individual* structures, reflecting a gap-toothed approach to preservation. And in spite of all that had been lost in North Kenwood, even landmarks designation could not save the work of Prairie School architect George Maher. One of his earliest houses stood at 44th and Greenwood for over a century, until the Chicago Park District purchased the property to expand a neighborhood play lot.[24] Designed in 1888 for Stephen W. Gilman, the three-story turreted house was offered for free, in the hope that it could be preserved on another location. There were no takers, and in 1997 the neighborhood lost another treasure.[25]

There have been attempts over several decades to landmark Hyde Park, including a survey of 220 historic structures outlined in 1986 for the Chicago Landmarks Commission.[26] Additionally the Illinois Department of Conservation had proposed Kenwood and Hyde Park each be established as historic districts in 1977. While the neighborhood is listed on the National Register of Historic Places, Hyde Park's houses can be demolished for new residential and commercial structures. The structures can also be remodeled to an appearance unlike the builder or architect's original intent. The City of Chicago landmarks designation is the major tool available to broadly protect a neighborhood's architectural heritage.

Meanwhile a number of high-rises were erected in Hyde Park, including the massive Regents Park complex by Dubin, Dubin, Black, and Moutoussamy on the Chicago Beach Hotel lakefront site. Rising thirty-six stories, the two towers contain over a thousand apartments. The area witnessed the construction of a number of new single-family and town houses, utilizing modern and postmodern aesthetics, yet unlike the new larger structures, they for the most part successfully fit into the fabric of the neighborhood. However during this period, the most prevalent building activity in the neighborhood was rehab work. As a new wave of homeowners entered the community, projects ranged in scope from window replacement to the labor-intensive restoration process that returned a house to its original state. Unsightly additions and asbestos siding were scraped away and painted turrets and gleaming copper once again graced façades, while energy-efficient windows and heating systems reduced maintenance costs. Kimbark Avenue in Kenwood is one of the streets that features many residences returned to their original beauty.

Numerous multifamily structures were also renovated and converted to condominiums under a new form of ownership passed by the Illinois General Assembly in 1963.[27] The Illinois Condominium Property Act established a system in which owners of units in a condominium building pay a share of common expenses, known as assessments. Unlike cooperatives, condominiums designate the physical unit to be the property of the owner, and while a board of managers administers the building, it does not have the right of approval of a sales transfer. A study conducted in 1979 provides a picture of the impact of conversions just a decade after the act was passed. At the time, 15 percent of the housing stock within the community had been converted to condominiums, 70 percent was rental, and 15 percent private houses,

town houses, and cooperative buildings.[28] Although the conversions resulted in a
decreased number of rental units, those with a financial stake in the community increased. However there were fears within the community that the conversion process
would force those at lower income levels to relocate; purchase prices and rental rates
increased, while the number of affordable housing units decreased. Ever inventive,
some Hyde Parkers addressed the condominium conversion issue by taking matters
into their own hands. In one case, fearful of condo conversion or redevelopment of
the site, renters of the property known collectively as East View Park purchased all
ninety-nine units from the estate of the original developers.[29]

After all the turbulence of the fifties and sixties, Hyde Park and Kenwood settled into a relatively calm and stable existence during years that were a period of
adjustment for the entire city. In 1909 urban planners had focused on how to attract people to the city; now the focus shifted to how to get them to stay.[30] Daniel
Burnham's credo of "make no little plans" was revived under Richard J. Daley,
who in 1955 won the first of six consecutive terms as mayor. Three years later,
the Department of City Planning prepared the *Development Plan for the Central
Area of Chicago*, and its recommendations were extensively enacted under Daley's
administration.[31] While the plan addressed land use, public buildings, pedestrian
environments, and transportation for the city center, the improvements eventually
affected the city's neighborhoods.

By the seventies, the city's central business district began a period of revival.
Huge skyscrapers such as the John Hancock Building and Sears (now Willis) Tower
rose to dominate the skyline and reassert Chicago's architectural heritage. This
downtown office revival produced the first signs of gentrification on the city's Near

8.04. 4847 South Kimbark as it appeared after undergoing a complete renovation. Exterior work included repairing the roof, replacing windows and shingles, and reconstructing the front porch. The Chicago Commission on Landmarks honored the restoration in 2006.

North Side. By the eighties an influx of young urban professionals ("yuppies") was evident. Ethnic populations were also expanding, particularly within the Hispanic community, which brought an end to decades of declining population.

Under mayor Richard M. Daley, development of a "Central Area Plan" was underway, necessitated by the addition of over 40 million square feet of office space and 23,000 new homes between 1980 and 2002—a time during which Chicago added more downtown residents than any other American city.[32]

As people began residing close to downtown Chicago, the surrounding neighborhoods were viewed as increasingly viable and attractive options. Hyde Park and Kenwood witnessed continual incremental residential investment—it was stabilized and reflected a rich cultural heritage that many found lacking in suburban life. The broad scale of urban renewal, and the accompanying investment in modernization and improvement of the existing structures made the community an attractive option. As a result land values escalated, new residences rose on available land, and restoration and improvement projects were increasingly common throughout the community.

Demographically the neighborhood demonstrated the aftereffects of urban renewal. The population north of 47th Street decreased along with the number of housing units; in 1980 fewer than half the units of twenty years earlier still existed.[33] North Kenwood remained nearly all black, with more than a third of households with incomes below the poverty level. In contrast, for South Kenwood the 1980 census tract reflected an approximately 50-50 ratio of blacks and whites, with only 5 to 9 percent of the population below the poverty level.[34]

Although the neighborhood held up in the face of an enormous challenge and was often cited as a racially integrated community, a closer look indicates smaller areas that were not integrated, and in fact two areas remained particularly segregated. The area immediately adjacent to and east of the University of Chicago (between Stony Island and Ellis, 55th to the Midway) was nearly 86 percent white two decades after renewal (1980). In contrast, the area between Ellis and Cottage Grove, 51st Street south to 55th Street, was nearly 88 percent black.[35] Property values did increase following completion of the renewal plan—in 1980 the median value of single-family owner-occupied houses in Hyde Park was more than double the city-wide median.[36]

The university continued to be the major stabilizing factor for the adjacent community, embarking upon an aggressive period of fund-raising and expansion and continuing the program of land acquisition on several fronts, for campus expansion, student housing, and hospital expansion. To accommodate the increasing student population, the university purchased apartments and hotels for conversion. By 2011 the university owned and managed 1,800 units within the community.[37] Land use evolved for the university—Woodward Court, a dormitory designed in 1957–1958 by Eero Saarinen, was demolished to make way for the Booth School of Business. Designed by architect Rafael Vignoly, the building occupies the site across the street from the Robie house. The character of the streets adjacent to the university began to change as it acquired single-family houses for institutional purposes. The need for land continues to be an issue for the growing university; while the purchase of property has sometimes indicated improvement in neighborhood conditions, the transactions have tended to be secretive, sparking controversy.

Expansion south of the Midway was regulated by an agreement reached during urban renewal that the university would not acquire land south of 61st Street. The South Campus Residence Hall opened in 2009 and three years later the striking complex of the Logan Center for the Arts was dedicated. These projects are visually linked to the rest of the campus through the Midway Crossings project, a series of streetscape improvements at the intersections of Ellis, Woodlawn, and Dorchester. Designed by BauerLatoza Studio, the project was influenced by Frederick Law Olmsted's original concept of the Midway Plaisance as a water link between Washington and Jackson Parks, with bridges traversing the Midway. The primary design elements are a series of lighting masts that provide a modern and functional link between the two parts of the campus.

Hospital-related expansion was particularly aggressive in terms of land acquisition—the erection of the Duchossois Center for Advanced Medicine in 1996 and the Comer Children's Hospital in 2005 required demolition of blocks of residential structures in southwest Hyde Park. In 2007 the university continued with the purchase of an entire block near 5600 South Drexel for future expansion. Five of these buildings (816–822 and 838–840 East 57th, and 5601–5603, 5636, and 5654–5658 South Drexel) have façades that were certified as historic by Landmarks Illinois, a nonprofit organization founded in 1971. Under their 1976 Preservation Easement Program, the previous owners of these properties donated a façade easement to Landmark Illinois. A preservation easement is a one-time charitable federal income tax deduction equal to the appraised value of the easement. It is a legal agreement that assigns the right to review and approve alterations to a qualified organization for the

purpose of preserving the property in perpetuity.[38] The easements are an opportunity for residents of historic structures to individually aid in protecting the community's architectural heritage. However the university's position threatens the endurance of the easements over time, and the future of the structures is unclear.[39]

In the shadow of the University of Chicago's new Hospital Pavilion are several blocks of vacant six-flats. Owned by the university and likely to be demolished, one building had historic tenants for a brief period. The building on the northeast corner of 57th Street at Maryland was once the home of president Ronald Reagan. Although Reagan spent most of his childhood in western Illinois, his family occupied a first-floor apartment in Hyde Park from 1914 to 1915. Reagan warmheartedly recalled that horse-drawn fire wagons "come down the street at full gallop."[40] He remembered other, more personal, events in his 1990 autobiography *An American Life*—a beer wagon injuring his older brother, a nasty bout of pneumonia, and playing with lead soldiers belonging to a neighbor.[40] Although the university acquired the apartment building in 2004 and residents were vacated several years later, the institution has yet to publicly detail their plans for the structure.

Reagan's presence was long forgotten as the Hyde Park–Kenwood neighborhood became known as a launching point for African American politicians assembling a multiracial alliance in the race for various elected offices. The community had shed the Republican leanings that made Reagan politically successful later in his life, and although known as a liberal bastion, Hyde Park remained independent from the city's Democratic establishment.[41] Local resident Harold Washington rose to become Chicago's first black mayor, and Carol Moseley-Braun became the first African American woman elected to the US Senate.[42] Both were successful thanks to an ability to craft a position that appealed across the racial spectrum. Both used Hyde Park, with its racial diversity and accompanying historical tensions, to address a broader audience. And the community certainly relished its appearance on the larger platform, setting the stage for a gifted young politician named Barack Obama.

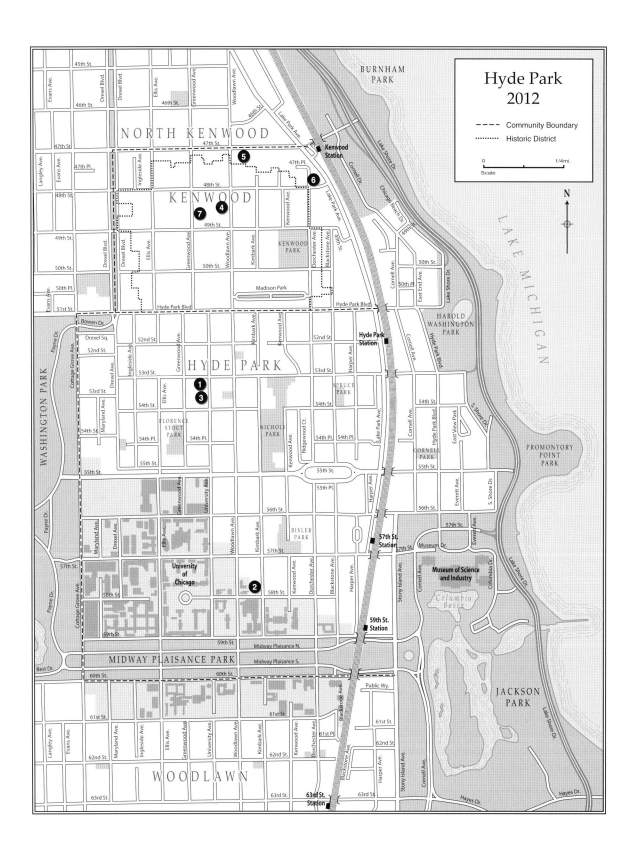

--- Community Boundary
.... Historic District

0   1/4mi.
Scale

N

BURNHAM
PARK

LAKE MICHIGAN

NORTH KENWOOD

Kenwood
Station

❺

❻

KENWOOD

❼   ❹

KENWOOD
PARK

Madison Park

HAROLD
WASHINGTON
PARK

WASHINGTON PARK

HYDE PARK

Hyde Park
Station

SPRUCE
PARK

FLORENCE
STOUT
PARK

NICHOLS
PARK

❶
❸

CORNELL
PARK

East View Park

PROMONTORY
POINT PARK

55th St.

BIXLER
PARK

57th St.
Station

Museum Dr.

University
of
Chicago

❷

Museum of Science
and Industry

Columbia
Basin

59th St.
Station

MIDWAY PLAISANCE PARK

Midway Plaisance N.
Midway Plaisance S.

JACKSON
PARK

Public Wy.

WOODLAWN

63rd St.
Station

Hyde Park

1 Speculative Town Houses, 1980.
1119–1125 East 53rd Street. David Swan.

Land for the town houses at the southwest corner of East 53rd Street and South University became available following a lawsuit pursued by residents concerned about the dilapidated apartment building on the site.[43] Citing code violations and criminal activity, they succeeded in having the structure condemned and torn down. Then, in 1978, the city offered the vacant land to bids from developers.[44] David Swan typically functioned as both architect and developer. For this project he

8.06. David Swan is both an architect and a developer and works in a variety of styles.

received the support of the community, and was also high bidder for the property. It was his second design/build project, and is one of his most uncompromising.[45] Originally conceived as an eight-unit complex, the scheme was revised to four units of approximately 4,000 square feet each. The width of the property allowed Swan to join the houses at the ends of the floor plan instead of at the sides, which permitted a minimum of shared walls and a maximum of light.

The severe northern façade of ironstone brick was designed with narrow slit windows to provide privacy. In contrast, the south side of the structure was designed with a series of setbacks, providing layers of terraces that overlook the lush garden area.

② Speculative Residences, 1985.
5748, 5752, 5756 South Kimbark Avenue. David Swan.

David Swan purchased this land from the Chicago Theological Seminary, and planned to construct four town houses on the site. To do so required a zoning variance that was denied after neighbors objected. The issue was not so much the four town houses, but that the land could be resold with a variance that would allow the construction of up to twenty-one units on the property.[46]

Without the variance, Swan altered his concept to include three "very expensive" single family homes.[47] Although the scope of his work is greatly varied, Swan's concept for these houses was not to "make a lot of architectural waves" on a Hyde

Park street he viewed as special.[48] Looking down Kimbark at a group of frame pattern-book houses, Swan wanted to achieve a similar effect. He replicated their rhythm by relying on compositions of cylinders and rectangles, instead of the shingles and porch details of the earlier structures.

③ Barr-Kane Residence, 2002.
5320 South University Avenue. Kuklinski & Rappe Architects.

Designed by architect Scott A. Rappe, this house was constructed on the site of a brick Tudor-style residence that had fallen into disrepair. The owners desired a unique residence and determined that renovation of the existing structure would not meet their needs. The older house was demolished in 2001 and plans for the new one were well underway when the tragedy of 9/11 happened. The economy ground to a halt, and this project was delayed until construction began in the spring of 2002.

Exterior elements were selected to complement the adjacent smaller-scale houses: dark iron-spot brick, substantial limestone trim, mahogany windows, and weathered zinc.

8.08. A curving window faces the street, while the rear elevation of the Barr-Kane residence is of sweeping glass.

The interior of the five-bedroom house has an open layout that permits an abundance of light into the structure. It represents an evolution in the style of interior plans that began a century earlier. The family-oriented kitchen is centrally located within the dwelling, anchoring the house emotionally and physically.

Kenwood

④ Epstein Residence, 1980.
4824 South Woodlawn Avenue. Nagle Hartray.

After landmark designation was awarded to the Kenwood community, the first major residence constructed was the Epstein residence on Woodlawn Avenue. In 1979, University of Chicago professor Richard Epstein and his wife Eileen purchased the 90' × 300' vacant parcel and hired Nagle Hartray to design a contemporary house that would be a "good neighbor" to the surrounding mansion-sized houses.[49]

A requirement of the Chicago Landmark Commission is that the members

8.09. The Epstein residence was constructed on the site of the old frame residence of Horace and Elizabeth Dupee. Their original 200' · 300' parcel had been subdivided by this time.

approve any permit issued for construction within the landmark area. Designed by Jim Nagle and although decidedly contemporary, the house received approval from the commission. As an architect not bound to tradition, Nagle was able to fit the house into the fabric of the neighborhood by combining the flavor of the surrounding houses with his own idea of a modern residence.

The formal symmetrical façade recalls the traditional styles prevalent in Kenwood. The residence maintains the existing setback, and the massing and eave line replicate that of the neighboring structures. The two shades of red brick are in keeping with the streetscape, as are the details on the façade that recall more traditional forms, such as the modified fanlight over the center door.

However as the brick wraps around the house it dramatically gives way to a sculptural rear façade. The idea of the house is a dichotomy, "front and rear, public and private, past and present."[50] This idea is carried into the interior spaces as well, divided by a serpentine wall that separates the entry and service areas from the living spaces. The master bedroom is on the main floor, offering privacy from the three bedrooms and study on the second floor.

5 Kennicott Place, 1990.
South Woodlawn Avenue and 47th Street. David Swan.

In 1990 David Swan developed Kennicott Place, a series of eighteen single-family and duplex cottage-style houses facing a private drive. Initially designed in a modern vocabulary, the plans were changed to mimic the Queen Anne frame houses

8.10. The sculptural rear elevation of the Epstein residence looks over the deep grounds typical of a Kenwood lot. This section of the neighborhood was planned without any alleys, providing complete privacy in the backyard.

8.11. Swan attempted to
replicate the ambience of a
typical Kenwood Street in this
development, through the use of
brick and wood shingled houses
stained in different colors, and
designed with distinctly styled
porches.

on Kimbark near 48th Street. Swan conceived of the development to meet the
need for affordable single-family housing in the area.[51] The project was named for
Kenwood's first settler, Dr. Jonathan Kennicott, and features traditionally styled
residences, many details originally found in pattern books of the 1880s.

⑥ Kenwood Gateway, 1986–1994.
South Dorchester and 48th Streets, David Swan.

By the time the urban renewal site for the Kenwood Gateway project was purchased from the city of Chicago, the value of the property had nearly tripled in
value since the developers first won the bid for the land. The initial market value
was three dollars per square foot; three years later the contract had not yet closed
and the fair market value had risen to eight dollars per foot. The agreement eventually moved forward, with residences offered at a new pricing structure.[52]

The property also came with a number of restrictions. The development was
required by the city to be low-density, with the maximum number of units not to
exceed fifteen. The units had to face away from heavily traveled Lake Park Avenue,
and the curb cuts disturbing the pedestrian path were kept to a minimum. Swan
designed this series of fourteen three-story single-family houses, orienting their
main entrances toward the side streets of Dorchester and 49th Streets, and addressing the parking issue with an inner court of garages.[53]

Built of brick, limestone, and textured concrete block, these masonry units
could not be built today: "In the mid-nineties," Swan commented when discussing
the project, "Chicago changed the building code in an attempt to stop overbuild-
ing on the city's gentrified North Side."[54] Three-story residences now require two
stairways, in effect limiting the height of a structure with this smaller-size footprint.

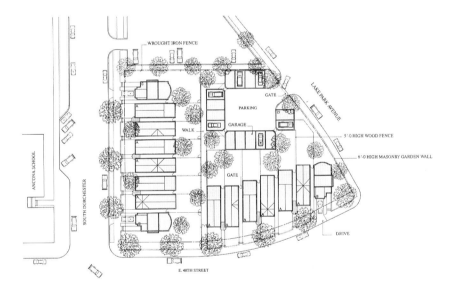

In a similar vein Swan designed his largest project, a fifty-unit development for a large parcel in northwest Hyde Park named Egandale, after the grand, nineteenth-century Egan estate at that site. Located at 54th and Ingleside, the development offered the "elegance of Hyde Park-Kenwood with an affordable price tag."[55]

⑦ Davis Residence, 2000.
4835 South Greenwood Avenue. Vinci/Hamp Architects.

In 1998 Allison and Susan Davis purchased the last parcel of land owned by the university in the Kenwood landmark area. The land was vacant; according to ur-

8.14. The spacious, light-filled interiors of the Davis residence feature high ceilings to accommodate the owner's art collection and face a dining terrace overlooking the garden.

8.15. The house was conceived with a central corridor running through the house. "It's like a street through the house," Vinci explained, "and I have rooms coming off it."

ban legend the century-old residence of Franklin Ames had been demolished in error. In the 1970s the Nation of Islam had expressed an interest in purchasing this site and the old Schaffner house adjacent on the north with the intention of constructing a series of houses similar to the complex on 1136–1158 East 49th Street. The University of Chicago was offered an option on the land and purchased both properties. The university sold the Schaffner house, but held on to a thirty-foot strip adjacent to the vacant land on which to construct faculty town houses, although nothing came of the plans.

Twenty years later, John Vinci was commissioned to design a single-family residence on the site; his background in preservation ensured sensitivity to the aesthetics of the historic neighborhood. Nonetheless the university retained the right to approve the plans for the house, and furthermore the plans required the approval of the Landmarks Commission. Vinci designed a modern structure that fit into the context of the landmark district without reliance on historic devices. Instead, Vinci specified exterior materials of richly colored Roman brick and limestone trim to mimic the materials of nearby turn-of-the-century houses. He also raised the house a half level, and designed the eave line, the overall massing, and the placement of the house on the lot to be consistent with earlier structures. However, there the similarities end; the exterior features a dramatic front stair tower, and the interior, large volumes of light-filled space.

8.16. Chimneys of a Victorian
era residence are reflected in
the windows of the stair tower
adjacent to the main entrance to
the house.

9.01. As it did in the aftermath of the great fire, Chicago's downtown business district has once again experienced a renaissance; today its architecture is renowned worldwide. The city center rises in the distance in this image taken south of Hyde Park's beloved "Point." Constructed during the thirties as an extension of Daniel Burnham's plan for lakefront improvements, the Point was landscaped by Alfred Caldwell, an architect influenced by Jens Jenson and the concepts of Frank Lloyd Wright.

Rewoven

Time goes, you say? Ah no!

Alas, time stays, *we* go.

—Austin Dobson, "The Paradox of Time"[1]

In 1978 Kenneth Jackson wrote a foreword to a book beloved by Hyde Parkers, entitled simply *Hyde Park Houses*. In a prescient manner, he noted, "Although the Hyde Park which is the subject of this volume is an Illinois Historic District and has been nominated for the national designation, it has not yet produced an American president."

Calm and cool, Barack Obama was often misunderstood during the first years of his presidency. The public gravitated to his message of unity during the historic 2008 campaign, yet labored to come to terms with the man as president. Obama struggled to present a cohesive narrative despite his major legislative achievements. As the American nation sought to better recognize the man they elected, there is perhaps no better way to understand a person than by where he chooses to be comfortable building a life and raising a family.

To understand Obama, it helps to understand the complex, often difficult history of his chosen home. The growth of Hyde Park is a history of the development of the American city and those who participated in the development of our nation. It is a local story and the nation's story, for Hyde Park and Kenwood followed a course that many urban neighborhoods took over the past century. After establishment they became sought-after locales, and their desirability increased as investment in new housing flourished . After attaining a peak of desirability, a community would stabilize for a period and then begin to deteriorate. This neighborhood's large-scale urban renewal project and the substantial investment in modernization, rehabilitation, and restoration that followed, disrupted this cycle.

Today Hyde Park is "the most racially integrated neighborhood in the nation's most racially segregated city." It has endured a tremendous shift in a relatively short period of time, and through negotiation and compromise achieved a stable racial and economic balance. A predominantly middle-class population is now interspersed between mansions of the wealthy and apartments of subsidized units.

The neighborhood was indentified as one of the most income diverse in the city in a 2008 study—just over 15 percent of the families earn more than $100,000 a year; nearly 38 percent were classified as middle income; and 46 percent as low income. Although there was wholesale change in parts of the community, during the sixty years following urban renewal the overall racial balance has not changed significantly.

Although Hyde Park was for decades surrounded by some of the worst slums in the country, crime has lessened. In the adjacent neighborhoods, one still finds littered, weed-filled abandoned lots, long-shuttered storefronts, and dilapidated residential buildings. However all this changes at the clearly defined edges of Hyde Park and Kenwood, where restored mansions and ivy-covered apartment buildings define the landscape. Largely spared of wholesale land clearance, South Kenwood displays a variety of houses constructed over its long history, yet demonstrates a cohesiveness and sense of intimacy. Tour buses meander the quiet streets today, and curious visitors admire the century-old mansions fronted by deep green lawns, flowers cascading over black iron fences, and streets shaded by stately trees. The efforts of community organizers in the fifties and the fight for preservation in the seventies proved successful. For the most part landmark designation put an end to teardowns, restricted zoning to the single-family classification, and prohibited exterior modernization.

This is not to suggest a return to a bucolic atmosphere, for a deeper look reflects the urban setting. Blue police cameras flash at the site of a homicide, and drug dealers ply their wares on busy street corners. Many houses have undergone extensive restoration, yet some remain in disrepair. And the fight to protect a single-family zoning designation is never really over, as property values continue to escalate. In contrast to the anonymity of many suburbs, the built environment, although cohesive, suggests the variety of urban life.

South of the Kenwood historic district, the spacious lawns give way to a more tightly woven urban fabric. Many of Hyde Park's original houses have been replaced by renovated apartment buildings, shading the streets into long corridors. The Gothic arches, spires, and gargoyles of one of the world's great learning institutions, the University of Chicago, continue to define the community. Naturally the university has evolved over the course of time, but it has never lost the vision William Rainey Harper defined for the institution, attracting people to the neighborhood who are open-minded, with creative and intellectual tendencies.

Rather than pulling up stakes in the prerenewal years as was contemplated, the university remained and anchors the area both economically and architecturally, combining the neo-Gothic style of its early buildings with new structures by Cesar Pelli, Harry Weese, Ricardo Legorreta, and other distinguished designers. While adjacent blocks were demolished in their entirety as the university and its hospital expanded, often in controversy, on other nearby streets apartments and houses have been refurbished or restored. However residents' concerns have not ebbed as the university continually seeks to expand its boundaries. A protracted episode occurred as the institution requested zoning variances along a three-block stretch of residential Woodlawn Avenue.

9.02. The shopping district on 53rd Street, from the northwest. Although altered during urban renewal, it was not as severely impacted as 55th Street, where 80 percent of the structures were razed.

In the half century since renewal, the institution has moved away from its historic pattern of studying, but not befriending, the community. An agreement was reached with Woodlawn Avenue homeowners whereby the university would work to prevent the demolition or disfigurement of historic residences in this area. Long focused inward, the institution is beginning to turn in a new direction, "seeking to create trust and to dissolve old boundaries." University-sponsored charter schools have opened in nearby communities, and the institution is working to keep the community is safe—the private police force now patrols well beyond the traditional boundaries of the institution. There has been considerable investment in real estate, particularly necessary in the heart of Hyde Park.

During urban renewal, the future of the surrounding neighborhood was dependant upon the center's renewal, where the varying approaches to removing blight are apparent. East 53rd Street retained a number of historic structures, while those on East 47th and 55th Streets were obliterated. When the shop window proclaimed "Everything must go!" urban planners meant it—641 business were gone. Where older structures were retained, the street exhibits a completely different vibrancy. Jane Jacobs described it best, "Cities need old buildings so badly it is probably impossible for vigorous streets and districts to grow without them." She was speaking not only of older buildings that had been completely rehabbed, but also of ordinary old buildings. Jacobs argued that if a neighborhood has only new construction, high overhead follows, and typically only chain stores, banks, and supermarkets can afford the rent for those new spaces. "Hundreds of ordinary enterprises, necessary to the public life of the streets and neighborhoods and appreciated for their convenience and personal service, do quite successfully in older buildings, but are slain by the high overhead of new construction."

As evident in Hyde Park and the surrounding neighborhoods, when the older buildings were clear-cut, it proved difficult to regain the vitality once found in these communities. Because Hyde Park's population is significantly lower than in the prerenewal years, many structures built for a larger population are no longer relevant. Several lie vacant and crumbling, making reuse more costly with each passing year. In the midst of residential blocks, institutional structures lie boarded up, vandalized, and deteriorating. The collapse of the financial markets and mortgage crisis of 2008–2009 stalled the improvement or reuse of these structures.

From a twenty-first-century vantage point, it seems that the standard urban renewal planners relied on was not urban, but based on the midcentury suburbs that drew city dwellers away. The planners then viewed the community's main assets as the major institutions, with lesser regard for the vitality of urban life. In general not much commerce remains, and it is by and large found in strip malls fronted by parking lots. One theater escaped demolition, and its future is fortunately no longer uncertain. Retail establishments are lacking in number, although Jimmy's Tap managed to endure and thrive as the local bar. Bookstores are plentiful, as one would expect in a university neighborhood, but there isn't an abundance of restaurants. People don't move to the area for the retail amenities, although that too is changing. In 2011 construction began on a massive hotel project designed by Hartshorne Plunkard Architecture on the Harper Court site at East 53rd and South Lake Park. Planned to include a restaurant, wine bar, retail stores, and fitness facility in addition to the hotel. Ironically, the twelve-story glass box is located just blocks from the former site of Paul Cornell's Hyde Park Hotel.

And on that site, a future vision of an increasingly urban Hyde Park is in the planning stages. Early in 2012, a half century after Cornell's structure came down in the name of progress, a multifamily residential project intended to "invigorate one of Hyde Park's most important gateways" was unveiled for community approval. Jeanne Gang, the architect of the City Hyde Park, as this project is known, views architecture as a tool of urban revitalization, where the structure performs a role in addition to its specific function. For this project Studio Gang designed a playfully textured midrise building above a plinth base that will feature retail amenities. Gang commented that the project's most important element is its "urbanism," as she oriented the structures toward the surrounding public spaces—articulating the street level as a friendly gathering place and creating a vibrant environment much as it was when the Hyde Park Hotel commanded the intersection.

Much has changed since Cornell erected his second hotel. The attractions of that earlier era—steam heat, call bells, and luxurious dining rooms—have been replaced by concerns for the environment, sustainability, and affordability. For the first time in history, the majority of people live in cities, fostering an ever-increasing density and requiring a heightened awareness of the impact of a structure on the once suburban neighborhood. A building's "relationship to the street, the shadow it casts on its neighbors, the air rights it occupies and the sight lines it obstructs" must all now be taken into account. Gang's concern for the context in

St. Stephen's Church, 1915. 5640 South Blackstone Avenue. Coolidge & Hodgdon.
9.03. Originally constructed as the Tenth Church of Christ, Scientist, the building has turned into a heartbreaking ruin—its majestic interior rests beneath a canopy of deteriorating plaster, broken glass, and decay. The church has been vacant for over a decade, tied up in a mix of issues including zoning laws, a lack of funding, and neighborhood concerns.

City Hyde Park, scheduled for completion 2014.
1525 East Hyde Park Boulevard.
Studio Gang Architects.

9.04. Gang remarked that architecture of Chicago's large buildings is "all about the structure," and designed this 382-unit building with a concrete frame. Although the expression of that structure provides the building's aesthetic, it is the series of balconies that create an energetic, tactile façade. The clever use of concrete panels allows the faceted bays to be column-free, while the balconies are disengaged from the slabs inside and give the building its sculptural quality.

which her building exists echoes the vision of Harry Weese a half-century earlier, and is a reflection of the deep affection Hyde Parkers hold for their neighborhood.

"I never had roots growing up," Barack Obama has said. In his book, *Dreams from My Father*, the president wrote of trying to find a permanent place for himself in world he had traveled. The twenty-three-year-old Obama moved to Chicago's South Side to become a community organizer, returning after graduating from Harvard Law School in 1991. As a single man, Obama lived in a first floor rental of a typical Hyde Park courtyard apartment building at 5429 South Harper. It was here that he dated his future wife Michelle Robinson, describing her as "a daughter of the south side, raised in one of those bungalow-style houses" that he spent hours visiting when he first arrived in Chicago. And here their children were born and attended the Lab Schools; at the university he taught constitutional law; and in Kenwood is the house bought with the royalties from the first of his best-selling books.

Today, Obama's community no longer exhibits the racial segregation that prevails in most of the country. Although the renewal program was a successful experiment, Hyde Park and Kenwood did not become a national model for integration, perhaps because its success was dependent on many requirements that are difficult to replicate. However, as Rebecca Janowitz noted in her book on Hyde Park's politics, the racial balance of the community he chose provided opportunities for progressive, independent-minded politicians, both black and white, that they otherwise might not have had. While that certainly benefited Obama, the community offered other unique attributes. His role at the university "challenged his thinking," while the mix of black and white reflected his heritage and upbringing— here Obama could move easily between those worlds. In fact some have argued that the community itself is not integrated; like Obama, it is biracial.

Marked by a history that was sometimes turbulent, Hyde Park welcomed many different people into its fold. Here lived politicians who fought against slavery and for the advancement of civil rights. Inventors and scientists, suffragettes and servants, carpenters and cattlemen have each called Hyde Park and Kenwood home. Today it is a tolerant community, resilient and hopeful. It has seen the effects of depression and war. It has endured civil strife. It has housed rich and poor. From south of the 31st Street beach where the race riots of 1919 began, to the corner where Lincoln lingered for a quiet evening before the turmoil of the Civil War; from the vacant lots of 47th Street where commerce once flourished, to shuttered churches built to serve a once flourishing population; from the restored mansions of Chicago's wealthy industrialists to wide boulevards filled with family barbeques on hot summer days—there is a complex layering to life here, richly appreciated.

From Paul Cornell's vision through Barack Obama's hope, history has the capacity to teach us humility, and to increase an awareness and appreciation of our surroundings. Saul Bellow once remarked he could not walk a block here without remembering who had lived here and who had died here. "You have to live with all these extinguished lives," he said, "and because you've encouraged your own sentimentality and nostalgia about a place, perhaps you feel it all the more." And often these lives have quite a story to tell.

A.01. Meander carefully the quiet streets of the neighborhood today, and reminders of its deep history can be found—poignant memories of a past woven into the present.

Appendix

ARCHITECTS: BIOGRAPHIES AND STRUCTURES

The appendix was assembled from an array of sources as we examined the built environment of Hyde Park and Kenwood and its transformation from bucolic suburbs to urban neighborhood. Only a limited number of residences could be selected for inclusion in the book, and it was often difficult to edit the options. This list attempts to provide the reader with an appreciation of the volume of work done by each architect and may not be inclusive of all work designed by a particular firm; it is an ever evolving document. Sources included Jean Block's compilation in *Hyde Park Houses*, articles from the *Hyde Park Herald* and *Chicago Tribune*, the Chicago Historic Resources Survey, building permits, and books on various architectural firms.

Contemporary street names are used; older street names are given here for reference:

CHICAGO BEACH DRIVE	*Lake Shore Drive 5000–5099, and South Shore Drive 5300–5699*
EVERETT AVENUE	*East View Park 5400–5450*
SOUTH HYDE PARK BOULEVARD	*East End Avenue; Park Street*
LAKE PARK AVENUE	*Hyde Park Avenue; Lake Street*
HARPER AVENUE	*Jefferson Street; Rosalie Court from 57th to 59th Street*
BLACKSTONE AVENUE	*Adams Street; Washington Street*
DORCHESTER AVENUE	*Madison Street*
KENWOOD AVENUE	*Monroe Street; Hibbard Street 5100–5499; George Place 5200–5299*
KIMBARK AVENUE	*Jackson Street*
RIDGEWOOD COURT	*Tompkins Place*
WOODLAWN AVENUE	*Van Buren Avenue 5100–5900*
ELLIS AVENUE	*Egandale Avenue 4700–5099*
UNIVERSITY AVENUE	*Lexington Avenue*
INGLESIDE AVENUE	*Wharton Avenue 5100–5499*
MARYLAND AVENUE	*Madison Avenue; Jackson Avenue*
DREXEL BOULEVARD	*Grove Parkway*
EAST 47TH STREET	*Mason Street*
EAST HYDE PARK BOULEVARD	*East 51st Street; Laurel Street*
EAST 52ND STREET	*Grove Street*
EAST 53RD STREET	*Oak Street*
EAST 54TH STREET	*Chestnut Street*
EAST 54TH PLACE	*Walnut Street*
EAST 55TH STREET	*Elm Street*

EAST 56TH STREET	*Ash Street*
EAST 57TH STREET	*Willow Street*
EAST 58TH STREET	*Cedar Street*
EAST 59TH STREET	*Washburn Street*

WALTER W. AHLSCHLAGER, AIA (1887–1965)

A graduate of the Armour Institute of Technology (now IIT), Ahlschlager was the architect of numerous traditionally designed apartment hotels. He began his career in the architectural offices of his father and uncle in 1914, and after his father's death in 1921 assumed control of the business.[1] In addition to specializing in apartment design, Ahlschlager received a number of large commercial commissions, including a twelve-story warehouse for the Chicago Cold Storage Company, buildings for the Beatrice Creamery Company, and bakeries for the Schulze Baking Company.[2]

Most notable of Ahlschlager's Chicago commissions was the 1929 onion-domed Medinah Athletic Club, which operated as an exclusive men's club for the Shriner organization until 1934. The building on North Michigan Avenue now houses the Intercontinental Hotel.

| 1924 | 5555 S. Everett Ave. | Jackson Towers |

ALFRED S. ALSCHULER, AIA (1876–1940)

Born in Chicago, Alschuler studied at the Art Institute, but graduated from the Armour Institute of Technology in 1899. He began work as a draftsman in the office of Dankmar Adler. When Adler died the following next year, Alschuler moved to the office of Samuel Treat, and by 1904 the firm became known as Treat & Alschuler. In 1907 he established an independent practice and specialized in commercial and industrial buildings—including warehouses, department stores, offices, and synagogues.[3] His factories were "direct, modern expressions of their reinforced concrete frames, while in his office and religious buildings he demonstrated a detailed knowledge of historic motifs."[4]Alschuler's best-known work was the London Guarantee and Accident Building at 360 North Michigan Avenue, for which he received the AIA Gold Medal.

Treat & Alschuler:

| 1906 | 4907 S. Greenwood Ave. | Louis A. and Irma R. Kohn |

Alfred S. Alschuler:

1907	4921 S. Ellis Ave.	Julius E. and Sarah Weil
1908	5009 S. Ellis Ave.	David and Eda Yondorf
1924	1100 E. Hyde Park Blvd.	Temple Isaiah Israel (now Kehilath Anshe Ma'ariv Temple)

ANDREWS & JACQUES
ROBERT DAY ANDREWS, FAIA (1857–1928)
HERBERT JACQUES, FAIA (1857–1916)

Andrews was educated at the Massachusetts Institute of Technology and worked as a draftsman in the office of widely admired and often imitated Boston architect Henry Hobson Richardson.[5] In 1885 he joined with fellow MIT graduate Jacques and established a practice. They were responsible for the design of public buildings, banks, offices, and residences not just in their home state but also across the country. However their most important work was found in Boston—the east and west wing additions for the Massachusetts State House.

| 1883 | 4820 S. Woodlawn Ave., demolished by 1979 | Horace M. and Elizabeth Dupee |

ARMSTRONG, FURST & TILTON
JOHN ARCHIBALD ARMSTRONG, AIA (n.d.–1969)
WILLIAM HENRY FURST, AIA (n.d.–1965)
JOHN NEAL TILTON, AIA (1891–1970)

Armstrong, Furst, & Tilton practiced together between 1927 and 1950—the firm's work was largely focused on churches, schools, and various other public buildings.[6] Their residential commissions included the sixteen-story Talbott Hotel on the city's North Side. In Hyde Park, the partnership was selected by the University of Chicago to design the 1929 Sunny Gymnasium and the 1931 Charles Hubbard Judd Hall, both for the Laboratory Schools.

John A. Armstrong:

1922	4940 S. Greenwood Ave.	John A. and Josephine McCormick

Armstrong, Furst & Tilton:

1928	1220 E. 50th St.	Albert S. and Myrna (or Mary) H. Cummins

RICHARD E. BARINGER, FAIA (1921–1980)

Dick Baringer studied painting under former Bauhaus professor László Moholy-Nagy at the Institute of Design. After receiving a master's degree from Harvard, he returned to Chicago to become the chief designer with Keck & Keck. A specialist in town planning and redevelopment, Baringer joined in the trend of remodeling the existing housing stock during the fifties. The residence of Dr. and Mrs. William H. T. Murray, situated on the private grounds of Madison Park, was one of nine houses featured for the Fifth Annual Kenwood Open House in 1958. The *Tribune* commented that the exterior of 1324 Madison Park "lies in sharp contrast to its formerly identical neighbor with which it shares a common wall."[7]

Between 1973 and 1977, Baringer collaborated with architect John van der Meulen on various college and public buildings in the US Virgin Islands. In 1980, Baringer and his wife Rachel were found strangled at their ransacked vacation home in St. Croix, a horrific crime that "sent shocks rumbling through a tourist industry."[8]

1958	1324 E. Madison Park	Murray residence, interior renovation

GEORGE BEAUMONT, FAIA (1854–1922)

Born and educated in England and a member of the Royal Institute of British Architecture, Beaumont came to Chicago in 1881. He worked with Wheelock & Clay (William Wilson Clay, 1849–1926) prior to entering into private practice in 1886. Beaumont twice served as president of the Chicago Architectural Sketch Club.[9]

1891	1500 block of E. 57th St., demolished 1962	Artists Colony
1904	4933 S. Woodlawn Ave.	Bernard F. and Ellen C. Sunny

MINARD LEFEVER BEERS, FAIA (1847–1918)

Minard Beers was the son of a builder who apparently had great plans for his offspring. Beers was named after influential architect Minard Lafever [*sic*], the author of several books on construction and architecture, ranging from his *Modern Builders Guide* of 1833 promoting the Greek Revival style, to the *Architectural Instructor* of 1856. Beers came to Chicago in 1871 and worked as a draftsman for Otis Leonard Wheelock (1816–c. 1886). He was responsible for a large number of residences in the area; however, very few examples of his "unpretentious simple family homes" remain.[10] Beers was a Hyde Park resident; Connorton's 1883 *Directory* gives his address as 5464 Frederick Place (Kenwood Ave.), a large frame home designed by him and now demolished.

1884	53rd St. near Dorchester Ave., demolished	Dr. W. H. D. Lewis
c. 1887	90 47th St. (SE corner of 47th St. and Kimbark Ave.) demolished	George R. and Ellen M. Thorne
1889	5411 S. Harper Ave.	L. A. Barstow
1889	5464 S. Harper Ave., demolished	Minard L. and Harriett M. Beers
by 1890	5410 S. Harper Ave.	C. M. Houghton
c. 1890	5318 S. Blackstone Ave.	David Quigg

BEERS, CLAY & DUTTON
MINARD BEERS (1847–1918)
WILLIAM WILSON CLAY, FAIA (n.d.–1926)
LLEWELLYN BANCROFT DUTTON, AIA (1860–1944)

Beers also worked in partnership with William Clay, between 1876 and 1886. In 1888 Llewellyn Dutton joined the firm, and they practiced together until 1894.[11] Dutton had worked with William LeBaron Jenney, Cobb & Frost, and Daniel Burnham on the Flat Iron Building in New York City, and eventually went to California in 1903 for Burnham, opening his own practice there in 1906.[12]

c. 1890	5036 S. Harper Ave., demolished	Thomas G. Butlin
1891	5247 S. University Ave.	Robert G. Smith
c. 1891	5012 S. Woodlawn Ave., demolished 1915	Jonathan J. and Louise M. Mitchell
1892	Demolished	Residences for Montgomery Ward
1892	5729, 5731 S. Blackstone Ave.	Double house for Henry V. Freeman
1892	5601, 5603 S. Dorchester Ave.	—

MIFFLIN EMLEN BELL, AIA (1846–1904)

Mifflin Bell was a government architect who practiced in Chicago after resigning as supervising architect of the US Treasury in 1887. Harsh criticism of his office had made life in the position difficult.[13] He moved to Chicago that year and was appointed the superintendent of repairs for the federal and government buildings at the 1893 Columbian Exposition, a position from which he also resigned. Bell was awarded the commission for several residences of varying scale in the Hyde Park area, which he designed using elements of the popular Richardsonian Romanesque style. However, only one frame house exists as an example of his work in the neighborhood.

1891	5554 S. Woodlawn Ave.	Theodore F. and Edith Rice
1893	4800 S. Greenwood Ave., demolished 1931	Charles H. and Martha Morse

SOLON SPENCER BEMAN, FAIA (1853–1914)

A native of Brooklyn, Solon Beman began his architectural training in the offices of New York architect Richard Upjohn. He came to Chicago in 1879 to design a company town for railroad car magnate George Mortimer Pullman, which became known as a model of urban development and planning. Designed when Beman was only twenty-six years old, the Pullman project was located on a fifty-two-acre site near Lake Calumet on the city's Far South Side. The project included more than 1,300 houses, a factory, a massive water tower, a theater, a church, a hotel, a market, and a school, all designed in Gothic and Romanesque Revival styles. Beman was a Hyde Park resident at this time; Connorton's 1883 *Directory* lists his address as 5318 Washington Street (Blackstone).

Although Pullman remained Beman's most significant commission, his other projects included the Mines and Mining Building and the Merchant Tailors' Building for the World's Columbian Exposition.[14] After the fair Beman was responsible for several institutional and ecclesiastical buildings in the neighborhood—the Blackstone Public Library; the Fifth Church of Christ, Scientist, in Kenwood; and the First Church of Christ, Scientist—each exhibiting his preferred Classic Revival style.[15]

1884	5708 S. Harper Ave.	John C. and Jannie (Jennie) B. Cook
1884	5732 S. Harper Ave.	Frederick Reynolds
1884	5759 S. Harper Ave.	Frederick Reynolds
1884	5822 S. Harper Ave.	William Riley Beman
1884	5832–5834 S. Harper Ave.	John A. Jackman Jr.
1886	SE corner of 57th St. and Harper Ave.	Rosalie Villas Clubhouse
by 1887	1030 E. 49th St., remodeled 1892	Solon and Mary Beman
1887	1035 (originally 244) E. 47th St., demolished	James R. and Agnes T. Crocker
1888	1019 E. 48th St.	David O. and Catherine Strong
1888	4935 S. Greenwood Ave.	Edward H. Turner
1892–1893	World's Columbian Exposition, demolished	Merchant Tailors' Building
1892–1893	World's Columbian Exposition, demolished	Mines and Mining Building
1897	4017 S. Drexel Blvd.	First Church of Christ, Scientist
1899	4945 S. Dorchester Ave., demolished following a fire, 1957	St. Paul's Episcopal Church
1901	4932 S. Lake Park Ave., demolished 1973	Bryson Apartments
1902	4904 S. Lake Park Ave.	Blackstone Public Library
1904	5317 S. University Ave.	Joseph S. and Alice W. Tomlinson
1904	4840 S. Dorchester Ave.	Fifth Church of Christ, Scientist

WASHINGTON IRVING BEMAN (1852–1937)

W. Irving Beman was a resident of Hyde Park; Connorton's 1883 *Directory* lists him as living with Solon Beman at 5318 Washington Street (Blackstone). He worked with his younger brother on the Pullman project and was responsible for several smaller houses in the neighborhood.

1886	5744 S. Harper Ave.	Ernest W. Heath
1889	5222 S. Kenwood Ave.	Speculative for W. Irving Beman
1889	5228 S. Kenwood Ave.	Speculative for W. Irving Beman

BEMAN & PARMENTIER

FERNAND PARMENTIER, FAIA (1868–1915)

Parmentier was born in Paris, France, and educated abroad before coming to Chicago to study architecture. He entered into a partnership with Solon Beman's brother Irving, and they practiced together between 1888 and 1893. Parmentier then partnered for a short time with Frederick Baumann, and they are credited with the design of the Hyde Park Club House, now demolished.[16] Parmentier relocated to California and later died in battle near the Dardanelles, at Gallipoli, while a volunteer for the French army.[17]

1889	5200, 5202 S. Kimbark Ave.	Atwood Vane
1890	1353, 1355, 1357, 1359 E. 50th St.	John H. Dunham
1890	1321, 1323, 1327 E. Hyde Park Blvd.	Speculative for W. Irving Beman
1891	5100 S. Hyde Park Blvd., unbuilt	Hotel for R. P. Smith & Company
1892	5000, 5002, 5004 S. Blackstone Ave.	
1892	5142 S. Blackstone Ave.	Dr. Henry C. and Selina L. Allen

HENRY BENRITTER (n.d.)

Benritter was a Hyde Park resident, living at 5510 Blackstone Avenue and later moving to the Holland Hotel at 53rd and Lake Avenue.

1897	5434, 5436, 5438 S. Cornell Ave.	Maria Bennett
1897	5530, 5532, 5534, 5536, 5538 S. Blackstone Ave.	Speculative construction for Anna Root
1897	5717 S. Blackstone Ave.	W. Starr Whiton
1897	5765, 5801, 5803, 5805, 5807 S. Blackstone Ave.	Town houses for Howard Sunderland

THOMAS BISHOP & COMPANY

THOMAS BISHOP (1869–1934)

Bishop was son of a builder and took an interest in his father's business. Although responsible for numerous speculative houses in the neighborhood, including one later purchased by President Obama in Kenwood, Bishop specialized in the design of flats and apartment buildings throughout the city. Developer Harry Zisook often worked with Bishop's firm on projects, and together they concentrated on purchasing large old properties and subdividing the lots to build smaller-scale, efficiently designed houses and walk-up apartment buildings with baroque detailing and terra-cotta roofs. Bishop's impact on the Hyde Park neighborhood is apparent when looking at his development and construction projects over a relatively short period of time. In a single year, 1911, Bishop built seven apartment buildings, and while the pace of development tempered during the war years, he was prolific well into the twenties, to be slowed only by the depression of 1929.

1902	5842–5844 S. Harper Ave.	C. D. Armstrong
1905	5641 S. Woodlawn Ave.	Charles W. Hoff
1906	5039 S. Ellis Ave.	
1906	5045 S. Ellis Ave.	
1907	5645 S. Woodlawn	Frank H. Connor
1909	5329–5337 S. Woodlawn Ave.	
1909	5431–5437 S. Woodlawn Ave.	
1909	4800–4810 S. Dorchester Ave.	Charles W. Hoff
1911	5658–5660 S. Blackstone Ave.	The Dellray
1911	5303–5311 S. Woodlawn Ave.	
1911	5118–5120 S. Greenwood Ave.	
1911	5201–5209 S. Greenwood Ave.	
1911	5142 S. Ellis Ave.	
1915	1417–1419 E. 56th St.	
1915	5517–5523 S. University Ave.	A. E. Seward
1915	5600–5608 S. Blackstone Ave.	
1915	5631–5639 S. Kenwood Ave.	
1915	5715–5725 S. Kimbark Ave.	
1921	5841–5851 S. Blackstone Ave.	
1922	4959 S. Greenwood Ave.	L. Larsen
1924	5724–5734 S. Blackstone Ave.	
1924	5130–5136 S. Dorchester, demolished	Apartments
1925	5480 S. Cornell Ave.	The Carolan Hotel
1926	5750 S. Kenwood Ave.	
1926	5218–5220 S. Kenwood Ave.	The Grosvenor, Garrard Trust
1927	1100 E. 48th St.	Harry S. and Marian Zisook
1927	5715–5719 S. Kenwood Ave.	

1928	Hyde Park Blvd. and Kimbark St., demolished	Apartments
1936	4812 S. Greenwood Ave.	Speculative residence
1936	4800 S. Greenwood Ave.	Harry S. and Marian Zisook

BOOTH & NAGLE

LAURENCE OGDEN BOOTH, FAIA (b. 1936)

JAMES LEE NAGLE, FAIA (b. 1937)

After graduating from Stanford in 1958, Larry Booth continued his education at Harvard, and received a BA in architecture from the Massachusetts Institute of Technology in 1960. Following service in the US Army, Booth began his practice as the first employee in the offices of Stanley Tigerman in 1962. Jim Nagle later joined the firm, and in the spring of 1966 they left to found the firm of Booth & Nagle.[18]

According to the Art Institute Oral History Project, "Booth chose a path that led away from large-scale corporate architecture and the dominance of modernism toward a more ecumenical appreciation of historical and vernacular forms." He joined with other "brash young architects" during the 1970s; the "Chicago Seven" challenged the dominance of Miesian architecture and sought to "encourage new approaches to architecture in Chicago" though writings and exhibitions.[19] In 1980 Booth organized a partnership with Paul Hansen. Booth is the recipient of numerous honors and awards and is active in the Chicago History Museum, Metropolitan Planning Council, Cliff Dwellers, and Commercial Club.[20] Booth Hansen continues to operate offices in Chicago and San Francisco.

| 1967 | 1220 E. 48th St. | Peter and Martha Barglow |

GEORGE HENRY BORST (1848–1917)

Born in England, George Borst moved to Chicago, where he began work as an architect by 1889. In 1895 he partnered with William E. Kleinpell and then practiced independently from 1900 to 1903. He is known to have designed a variety of buildings; however, much of his work on the city's South Side has been demolished. Borst died at his home in the Elms Hotel in Hyde Park.[21]

| 1901 | 5421 S. Hyde Park Blvd. | Emily C. Weeks |

BORST & HETHERINGTON

In 1903 Borst and John Todd Hetherington formed the architectural firm of Borst & Hetherington. The partnership was active until 1910.

1900–1904	1634 E. 53rd St., demolished	Elms Hotel
1902–1903	5450 Hyde Park Blvd.	Richard S. and Catherine Thompson
1902–1903	5659 S. Woodlawn Ave.	James A. and Katie Rankin
1907	5327 S. University Ave.	J. H. McNamara

BOUCHARD & FRANCE

LOUIS C. BOUCHARD (n.d.)

ROY F. FRANCE (n.d.)

Attributed to France:

1913	5816 S. Blackstone Ave.
1914	5756 S. Blackstone Ave.
1914	5822 S. Blackstone Ave.
1915	5511–5515 S. University Ave.

Bouchard & France:

| 1911 | 4711–4717 Ellis Ave. | Apartment for Sherman T. Cooper |

WILLIAM W. BOYINGTON, FAIA (1818–1898)

Boyington was the architect of two of Chicago's most beloved structures, the Water Tower and the Pumping Station. Located on North Michigan Avenue, they were both spared during the Chicago Fire of 1871. Trained in New York, Boyington came to Chicago in 1853 and began a prolific career as one of the city's first practicing architects. He was the architect of the original University of Chicago on Stephen Douglas's land along the lakefront and in the course of a forty-year career designed many of the burgeoning city's most prominent buildings, including many early churches, hotels, educational buildings and railroad stations.[22]

1887–1888	4600 S. Greenwood Ave.	Kenwood Evangelical Church (Kenwood United Church of Christ), with Harry B. Wheelock (1861–1934)
1889	5752 S. Harper Ave.	Charles and May K. Bonner
1893	4501 S. Drexel Blvd., demolished	Charles H. and Alice Smith

JAMES C. BROMPTON (n.d.)

Brompton had a long association with Chicago developer Samuel Eberly Gross, designing houses and apartment buildings for him. They are well known for their development of the 3800 block of Alta Vista Terrace on the city's North Side. Designed in 1904, these residences display a variety of architectural styles and detail, duplicated with slight variations at diagonally opposite ends of the block.[23] The two-story height and sympathetic façades create a unified streetscape, a concept partially echoed in the Greenwood Avenue project in Hyde Park.

1903	5200–5244 S. Greenwood Ave.	Samuel Eberly Gross

BURNHAM & ROOT

DANIEL HUDSON BURNHAM, FAIA (1846–1912)
JOHN WELLBORN ROOT, FAIA (1850–1891)

The famed partnership of Daniel Burnham and John Root was formed in 1873, a difficult year when commissions were cancelled in the midst of a widespread financial panic. They had met while employed as draftsmen in the office of Carter, Drake & Wight.[24] From humble beginnings designing small houses and barns, Burnham and Root eventually were responsible for the design of many influential commercial buildings in Chicago, beginning with their ten-story Montauk Building, constructed in 1882. Their significant contributions to Chicago's skyline went on to include the Rookery and Monadnock Buildings and the Masonic Temple.[25] Each brought unique talents to the firm. Burnham had solid business judgment and the necessary sales skills, while Root was the creative genius.

Root often followed Burnham's suggestions as to the overall scheme; however, he "perfected the spatial relations and proportions, harmonized the plan to materials and site, . . . and gave the building its ultimate architectural personality."[26] The partnership ended with Root's sudden death in 1891 during Burnham's tenure as the chief of construction for the World's Columbian Exposition.

Although born in New York, Burnham came to Chicago with his family at the age of eight. He was later sent to Massachusetts to be tutored, but he did not pass the entrance examination for Harvard. After returning to Chicago, Burnham expressed an interest in architecture and showed a "talent for drawing." He worked for William LeBaron Jenney and John Mills van Osdel prior to joining Carter Drake & Wight.[27]

Root was born in western Georgia and raised in Atlanta, but his father sent him to England during the Civil War. He returned in 1866 and received a degree in engineering from New York University, and in 1871 headed to Chicago where he found employment with Carter, Drake & Wight.

1884	152 47th St. (at the SW corner of Woodlawn Ave.), demolished	Robert and Juliet Strahorn
1884	164 47th St., demolished	Henry F. Griswold
1885–1886	4545 S. Drexel Blvd.	William E. and Mary Hale
1887	4941 S. Drexel Blvd.	John H. and Emily Nolan
1887	5035 S. Greenwood Ave., demolished 1973	Charles and Jennie Counselman
1890	4545 S. Drexel Blvd., demolished	Kenwood Astrophysical Observatory, George Ellery Hale

DANIEL H. BURNHAM & COMPANY

After Root's death, Burnham reorganized the firm as Daniel H. Burnham & Company. Building upon his experience with the vast scale of planning for the 1893 World's Columbian Exposition, Burnham became one of the early participants in the City Beautiful aesthetic. He then developed various city plans that culminated in his *Plan of Chicago* in 1909.

At the time of Burnham's death in 1912 the firm had nearly two hundred employees, making it one of the largest architectural businesses in the country.[28] Burnham's partner Ernest R. Graham and Burnham's two sons, Daniel H. Burnham Jr. and Hubert Burnham, continued the practice as Graham, Burnham & Company after his death. In addition to his professional legacy, Burnham's donation to the Art Institute of Chicago resulted in the creation of the Burnham Library of Architecture, now the Ryerson & Burnham Libraries.

| 1899 | 4935 ½ S. Greenwood Ave. | Green Coach House |

BARRY BYRNE, AIA (1883–1968)

Born in Chicago, Francis Barry Byrne sought work with Frank Lloyd Wright after viewing a display of his works. Having no formal architectural education past the ninth grade, he began work as an apprentice in Wright's Oak Park studio. Byrne left Wright in 1908 and after a very brief time with Walter Burley Griffin, departed for the West Coast. He returned to Chicago in 1914 when Griffin offered Byrne the position of manager of his Chicago office, after Griffin won a competition to design the new capital city of Canberra, Australia. After the First World War, Byrne established his own practice in Chicago, which flourished as he established a long association with the Roman Catholic Church designing churches and schools for the Archdiocese.[29]

| 1924 | 5472 S. Kimbark Ave. | St. Thomas the Apostle Church |

CHATTEN & HAMMOND

MELVILLE CLARKE CHATTEN, FAIA (1873–1957)
CHARLES HERRICK HAMMOND, FAIA (1882–1969)

Founded in 1907, the firm of Chatten & Hammond was known for the design of factories and residences in Chicago and throughout the Midwest. Hammond received his architectural education at the Armour Institute of Technology (now IIT), graduated in 1904, and received a traveling scholarship for the Chicago Architectural Club to study in Paris.[30]

Chatten attended the University of Illinois, where he received a BS in architecture in 1896. He worked in the office of Frost & Granger until 1906, when he also went to study at the École des Beaux-Arts in Paris. Upon their return a partnership was formed.[31] The firm became known as Perkins, Chatten & Hammond from 1927, when Dwight Perkins joined the partnership. In 1933 Chatten began to practice independently and Hubert Burnham joined Hammond; the firm became known as Burnham Brothers & Hammond.

| 1915 | 5620 S. Woodlawn Ave. | John P. and Mary Marsh |
| 1924 | 4608 S. Greenwood Ave. | Kenwood United Church of Christ gymnasium |

HENRY IVES COBB, FAIA (1859–1931)

Cobb was educated at the Massachusetts Institute of Technology and Harvard University. After spending a year traveling in Europe, he went to work for the firm of Peabody & Sterns in Boston. After winning a competition to design the Union League Club in Chicago, he moved to the city in 1882. Keenly aware of the many opportunities Chicago offered, Cobb remained in Chicago and formed a partnership with Charles Frost, an MIT classmate who also worked at Peabody & Sterns. The partnership continued until 1888, when Cobb was commissioned to design the Romanesque-style Newberry Library. Locally he is best known as the designer of the first buildings constructed for the University of Chicago. Although his association with the institution ended in 1901, his firm went on to design many notable buildings in the city, including the Chicago Opera House and the Chicago Athletic Club.[32]

1890	4938 S. Drexel Blvd.	John A. and Caroline McGill
1892–1893	World's Columbian Exposition, demolished	Fisheries Building
1894	5855 S. University Ave.	William R. and Ella Harper
c. 1896	5747 S. University Ave., demolished	J. L. and Mary C. Laughlin
1896	5630 S. Woodlawn Ave.	William C. and Harriet R. Wilkinson

COBB & FROST

Cobb and Charles Frost practiced together between 1882 and 1888. Their most notable residence was the elaborate mansion of Potter and Berthe Palmer at 1350 North Lake Shore Drive on the Near North Side, demolished.

c.1890	4520 Drexel Blvd., demolished	Norman Wait and Emma Gale Harris

COLE & DAHLGREN

Arthur Cole was responsible for a number of row houses and Queen Anne single-family homes in the neighborhood in partnership with Rudolph W. Dahlgren (n.d.) and later in an independent practice.[33]

1888	5201, 5203, 5205, 5207, 5209 S. Kenwood Ave.	Charles H. Root
1888	5736 and 5738 S. Blackstone Ave.	Henry H. and Anna M. Belfield
1892	5210 S. Kenwood Ave.	George W. and Flora Hoyt

ARTHUR COLE (n.d.)

Cole was a Hyde Park resident; J. W. Connorton's 1883 *Directory* lists his address as 22 Madison Park.

1898	5411 S. Greenwood Ave.	Edward E. and Rosa May Hill
1898	5413 S. Greenwood Ave.	Arthur W. and Mary W. Cole
1902	5407 S. Greenwood Ave.	A. F. Webster

CONE & DORNBUSCH

"It is interesting that you mention Charles Dornbusch," commented architect Myron Goldsmith. "He designed very modern, not moderne but modern, International style–looking houses."[34]

Charles H. Dornbusch worked for Loebl, Schlossman & Hackl, and taught at the Illinois Institute of Technology. He and his wife, an artist, had rented all but the top floor of a house on 49th Street for many years, before purchasing it in the early 1950s. The house consisted of two duplexes that had been converted into rooming houses like many others in the Kenwood area. The Dornbusches redesigned the structures into a single-family residence. Dornbusch wanted to add modern conveniences yet maintain the appearance of the 1893 house, as a "good example for others who are trying to preserve this beautiful old south side neighborhood."[35] The houses are across from Beulah Shoesmith Elementary School, which was designed by Cone & Dornbusch on a portion of the property owned by John H. Dunham.

1953	1354 E. 49th St., renovation	Charles and Magrette Dornbusch

W. CRAIG (n.d.)

1894	4827 S. Kenwood	Horace Kent Tenney

EDWARD DART & ASSOCIATES
EDWARD DUPAQUIER DART, FAIA (1922–1975)

Edward Dart, known as Ned, graduated from Yale School of Architecture, where he studied under and was influenced by Marcel Breuer, Eero Saarinen, Louis Kahn, and Paul Schweikher, among other notable architects. After graduating, Dart was hired by Schweikher until he began an independent practice.

Over the course of his career, Dart received a total of eighteen awards from the AIA and was made a fellow at the age of forty-four. He was responsible for fifty-two custom-designed houses and the "House of the Fifties" featured by *Good Housekeeping* magazine. Additionally Dart won the National Home Builders Competition in 1951 for the design of his own house, set on twelve acres west of suburban Barrington.

In 1965 Dart became a partner in the large firm of Loebl, Schlossman, Bennett & Dart. He was responsible for Augustana Lutheran Church in Hyde Park on 55th Street between University and Woodlawn. His largest project was Water Tower Place on North Michigan Avenue. Completed in 1968, the mixed-use retail, residential, and business center was under construction at the time of his death at the age of fifty-three.[36]

1957	1150 E. 55th St.	Augustana Evangelical Lutheran Church
1963	58th St. and Dorchester Ave.	Chicago Theological Seminary Faculty Quadrangle

ROBERT SEELEY DEGOLYER, FAIA (1876–1952)

Robert DeGolyer was responsible for many fashionable, upper-class apartments throughout the city. He was among a group of progressive-thinking architects and worked as the lead architect of the Lathrop homes, a public housing project on the city's North Side.[37]

1927	5000 S. East End	5000 East End Building
1928	4950 S. Chicago Beach Dr., with Charles L. Morgan	The Powhatan

LOVATT B. DIXON (n.d.)

1884	4830 S. Greenwood Ave.	John A. Lane
1886	4717 S. Kimbark Ave., demolished	Charles P. and Martha E. Parish
1886	4721 S. Kimbark Ave., demolished	Samuel C. and Flora Parish Tobin

WILLIAM J. DODD, AIA (1862–1930)

Born in Quebec, Dodd trained in the office of William LeBaron Jenney and worked as a draftsman for Solon Spencer Beman on the planning of Pullman, residing in Chicago from 1880 to 1885. Dodd left Chicago and worked predominantly in the Louisville, Kentucky, area until the end of 1912, when he relocated to Los Angeles. His portfolio extended beyond architecture to include decorative architectural glass, ceramics, furniture, appliances, and even literary illustration.[38]

1885	5425 S. Blackstone Ave.	W. I. and Iva L. Beman

DOERR & DOERR
JACOB DOERR (n.d.–1930)
JOHN DOERR (n.d.)

The Doerr brothers were builders of a copious number of apartment houses in the Hyde Park and Kenwood neighborhoods. William and Henry Morris, suppliers of doors and windows, and a third brother, William Doerr, were frequent clients. The Doerrs' Hyde Park activity began in 1890 and continued well into the twenties. Jean Block noted that the brothers built "substantial, roomy apartments in a period when much that was done was cheap and shoddy." Many of their apartment buildings are virtually indistinguishable—three stories in height and detailed with only slight variations in the façades.[39]

1900	5330 S. University Ave.	Mary A. Hearn
1901	5008–5014 S. Dorchester Ave.	William Doerr
1902	5000–5006 S. Dorchester Ave.	
1902	5216–5218 S. Dorchester Ave.	W. L. DeBeck
1902	1369–1371 E. 50th St.	
1903	4915 S. Woodlawn Ave.	William H. Morris
1903	4919 S. Woodlawn Ave.	William H. Morris
1903	5201–5209 S. Blackstone Ave.	William Doerr
1904	5213–5215 S. Dorchester Ave.	Joseph Schmidt
1905	4932 S. Kimbark Ave.	William H. Morris
1905	4936 S. Kimbark Ave.	William H. Morris
1907	5647–5649 S. Dorchester Ave.	
1907	5443–5445 S. Cornell Ave.	Henry F. Morris
1908	5463–5465 S. Hyde Park Blvd.	Harry (Henry) Morris
1908	5487–5499 S. Hyde Park Blvd.	William Doerr
1910	5427–5429 S. Hyde Park Blvd.	Henry F. Morris
1910	5478–5484 S. Everett Ave.	William Doerr
1910	5514–5522 S. Everett Ave.	William Doerr

WILLIAM P. DOERR, AIA (1870–1944)

William Doerr's influence on "modern" Hyde Park has been compared to Paul Cornell's establishment of the pioneer suburban settlement a half century earlier.[40] An architect by training, Doerr had a prominent role in transforming the Hyde Park area by building a large number of apartment buildings during the period following the Columbian Exhibition through the First World War. Born in Strasbourg, Alsace-Lorraine, he came to America in 1887 and worked for his brothers for eight years before returning to study architecture at the Stuttgart Polytechnicum.[41] His apartment hotels transformed city living for many, as they provided small, convenient kitchenette apartments as opposed to large houses with expansive grounds that required the support of a staff. While building was his principal occupation, he also invested in many large real estate transactions in Hyde Park.[42]

1918	1380 E. Hyde Park Blvd.	Madison Park Apartment Hotel
c. 1920	5326 S. Cornell	Dornell Hotel Apartments
1923	5236–5252 S. Hyde Park Blvd.	East End Park Hotel (East Park Tower)
by 1926	5237 S. Cornell, demolished	Park Beach Hotel
1928	5510 S. Cornell, demolished	Cornell Hotel

DUBIN, DUBIN, BLACK & MOUTOUSSAMY
HENRY DUBIN, AIA (1892–1963)
ARTHUR DETMERS DUBIN, AIA (1923–2011)
MARTIN DAVID DUBIN, FAIA (n.d.)
JOHN T. BLACK, AIA (n.d.–2003)
JOHN W. MOUTOUSSAMY, FAIA (n.d.–1995)

Henry Dubin was known for his award-winning 1930 Battledeck house in north suburban Highland Park. An early example of a modern structure in design and construction, the family house had a great influence on the young Arthur Dubin. Arthur was fascinated with the trains that ran near the home and became a passionate authority on the golden age of train travel.[43] He studied architecture at the University of Michigan, and although World War II cut his education short, he received a degree in 1949. That year Dubin joined his father and uncle's firm, Dubin & Dubin, and the leadership of the firm eventually passed to Arthur and his brother, Martin. Black joined the firm in 1965, and later Moutoussamy, an African American architect educated at IIT, became the managing partner.

Commissions included high-rise office and apartment buildings, college dormitories, and work for the United States Army.[44] Arthur Dubin was fortunate—able to "merge his passions," as the firm was awarded projects for both the Chicago Transit Authority and the Chicago & Northwestern Railway.[45]

| 1970–1972 | 5020–5050 S. Lake Shore Dr. | Regent's Park Complex |
| 1981 | 5656 South Stony Island | Alpha Kappa Alpha Sorority |

N. MAX DUNNING, FAIA (1873–1945)

Dunning attended the University of Wisconsin and began to practice architecture in Chicago in 1894 in the office of Joseph C. Llewellyn (1855–1932), a specialist in school design. In 1900 Dunning won the first traveling scholarship of the Chicago Architectural Club and continued his studies abroad.[46] He returned and in 1910 established a partnership with his brother, Hugh Dunning (1883–1958). Dunning's most prominent project was the huge American Furniture Mart (now residential condominiums at 680 North Lake Shore Drive), designed in collaboration with Henry Raeder and George Nimmons. During the World War I, Dunning was appointed to the US Housing Corporation. In 1933 Dunning again returned to Washington, where he held various architectural and housing posts in federal agencies and was widely regarded as an authority on housing.[47]

1910	4940 S. Kimbark Ave.	Charles and Catherine Antoine
1910	4949 S. Woodlawn Ave.	Charles Antoine
1924	5538–5552 S. Hyde Park Blvd.	The Broadview

A. EPSTEIN & SONS, INTERNATIONAL, INC.
ABRAHAM EPSTEIN, AIA (1887–1958)
RAYMOND EPSTEIN, AIA (n.d.–2007)
SIDNEY EPSTEIN, AIA (n.d.)

A 1911 University of Illinois graduate, Russian emigrant Abraham Epstein founded a small civil and structural engineering firm on the city's West Side in 1921. His sons Raymond and Sidney later joined the company, and during the fifties A. Epstein & Sons began to grow dramatically and became "pioneers in the emerging new project delivery method known as Design-Build."[48] The company continues to operate today and is one of the oldest and largest architecture, interiors, engineering, and construction firms operating worldwide.

1952	1645–1649 E. 50th St.	Twin Towers
1955–1956	56th St. and S. Shore Dr., demolished 1988	Shore Drive Motel
1965	52nd St. and Harper Ave., demolished, 2011	Harper Court

FLANDERS & ZIMMERMAN

JOHN J. FLANDERS, FAIA (1848-1914)

WILLIAM CARBYS ZIMMERMAN, FAIA (1859-1932)

A native of north suburban Chicago, John Flanders received his early training as an apprentice in various offices, including that of W. W. Boyington, a pioneer in the concept of steel-framed construction. His first partnership was with Charles Furst, whom he met while they were both employed by Burling & Adler. After the devastating fire of 1871, Flanders was one of the many architects who participated in the rebuilding of the city. His 1884–85 Mallers Building on South La Salle Street was one of the city's first masonry skyscrapers, rising twelve stories.[49] After eight years as the architect for the Chicago Board of Education, in 1898 he began a partnership with William Carbys Zimmerman, and later practiced independently.[50]

1886	5611 S. Blackstone Ave.	William C. Zimmerman
1886	5621 S. Blackstone Ave.	William C. and Emily Zimmerman
1892	4830 S. Kenwood Ave.	C. Matthews
1894	1119 E. 46th Street	Ariel Community Academy
1898	4848 S. Ellis Ave.	Gustavus F. and Anna Maria Swift

MEYER FRIDSTEIN (1883-1964)

Educated at the University of Wisconsin, Meyer Fridstein moved to Chicago to work in the offices of Richard Schmidt and Marshall & Fox. Fridstein partnered with the general contracting firm of Gustav H. Gottschalk, for which Fridstein was secretary as well as the architect of record for the Shoreland project. Gottschalk and Fridstein remained business partners until 1926, when Fridstein opened an independent operation under the name Fridstein & Company.[51] His firm was responsible for a number of hotels, theaters, and industrial buildings, including the Belden-Stratford on the city's North Side. In the Hyde Park area, his firm was the contractor for the building on the old Chicago Beach property at 5000 South Cornell.

| 1925-1926 | 5454 S. Shore Dr. | The Shoreland |

FROMMANN & JEBSEN

EMIL HENRY FROMMANN (1860-1950)

ERNST JEBSEN (1850-1917)

Frommann was the son of German immigrant and architect George N. Frommann. In 1871, the elder Frommann moved from Peoria to Chicago to participate in the reconstruction of the city. The younger Frommann apprenticed in his father's office prior to leaving to study architecture at the Massachusetts Institute of Technology in 1880. He did not complete his studies, as his father's death a year later forced Frommann to return to Chicago, where he continued his father's practice with the assistance of Ernst Jebsen. Few biographical records of Jebsen remain, but it is known that he suffered a "facial disfigurement" that prevented him from interacting with clients, requiring Frommann to be the partner responsible for business relations.[52] Frommann continued to practice architecture after Jebsen's death, with his last-known design completed in 1925.[53]

The firm designed only one building in the Hyde Park area; however, another prime example of their multifamily work can be found at 533 West Diversey Parkway on the city's North Side, a structure that features Art Nouveau inspiration and lavish ornament.

| 1907 | 5451-5455 S. Hyde Park Blvd. | 5451-5455 S. Hyde Park Blvd. Apartments |

CHARLES SUMNER FROST, FAIA (1856–1931)

A native of Maine, Frost graduated from the Massachusetts Institute of Technology in 1876, and then worked in the offices of Peabody & Stearns in Boston. Arriving in Chicago in 1882, he entered into a successful and recognized partnership with Henry Ives Cobb for the following six years.[54] They were responsible for a number of noteworthy buildings, including the Newberry Library. Frost left Cobb to practice independently and designed a number of homes in Kenwood, including two for the children of industrialist Orrin Potter.[55] His designs often mimicked the work of East Coast architects McKim Mead & White.[56] In 1898 he became partners with his brother-in-law Alfred Granger.

c. 1890	4353 S. Drexel Blvd., demolished 1963	George A. and Ellen M. Fuller
1892	4613 S. Drexel Blvd., demolished	Elijah C. and Ella Wilson
1892	47th St. and Kenwood Ave., demolished c. 1960	The Kenwood Hotel
1892	4800 S. Ellis Ave.	Edward C. and Emma Potter
1894	4810 S. Ellis Ave.	James C. and Agnes Hutchins
1895	1361 E. 47th St. with Patton & Fisher, demolished c. 1960	The Kenwood Club
1896	4857 S. Greenwood Ave.	John B. and Annie E. Lord

FROST & GRANGER

CHARLES SUMNER FROST, FAIA (1856–1931)
ALFRED HOYT GRANGER, FAIA (1867–1939)

Brothers-in-law Charles Frost and Alfred Granger became partners in 1898, several years after each married a daughter of Marvin Hughitt, the president of North Western Railway. Not surprisingly they were selected as the architects for the railroad and became prolific specialists in train station design.[57] Their partnership was responsible for the design of the North Western Terminal Building, the office building for the North Western Railway, Municipal (Navy) Pier, and the Northern Trust Bank Building.

Born in Ohio, Alfred Granger received his BA from Kenyon College, and like Frost, attended MIT, graduating in architecture in 1887. He continued his education at the École des Beaux-Arts in Paris, and after returning to the States, entered the Boston offices of Shepley, Rutan & Coolidge.[58] In 1891 the firm sent Granger to supervise the erection of two of their important commissions, the Art Institute and the Chicago Public Library.[59]

1901	4920 S. Greenwood Ave.	Enos M. and Mary Barton
1901	4801 S. Drexel Blvd.	Moses and Isabella Born
1901	4925 S. Drexel Blvd., demolished	Simon and Pauline Mandel
	4935 S. Drexel Blvd., coach house	
1902	4835 S. Greenwood Ave., demolished c. 1970	Franklin L. and Emma C. Ames
1902	4847 S. Woodlawn Ave.	William F. and Annie L. Burrows
1905	1400 E. 53rd St., demolished 1983	Hyde Park YMCA
1910	4801 S. Woodlawn Ave.	Arthur G. and Mary J. Leonard

HUGH MACKIE GORDON GARDEN, FAIA (1873–1961)

Hugh Garden was a native of Toronto, Canada, and at the age of fourteen moved to Minneapolis, Minnesota, with his widowed mother and family. Arriving in Chicago in the late 1880s, he apprenticed with several firms, including Flanders & Zimmerman and Henry Ives Cobb.[60] He was a talented draftsman and well known for his architectural renderings—preparing drawings for Howard van Doren Shaw, Louis Sullivan, and Frank Lloyd Wright. Like many of his contemporaries, Garden strove to formulate an American style of architecture freed from a reliance on classical forms.

1897	5727 S. University Ave.	William G. and Harriett S. Hale
1901	5735 S. University Ave.	Robert and Harriett Herrick
1902	4825 S. Woodlawn Ave., with Richard Schmidt	Lester E. and Anne Frankenthal

GEORGE OTIS GARNSEY (1840–1923)

A Hyde Park resident, George Garnsey began work with J. C. Rankin in 1856 as a draftsman, where he remained for five years. He worked with various small firms before opening an independent office in 1868. Garnsey was the editor of the *National Builder*, a monthly journal that was devoted to "practical building."[61]

1888	4800 S. Kimbark Ave.	George L. Miller

BERTRAND GOLDBERG, FAIA (1913–1997)

"Bud" Goldberg was born in Chicago and began his architectural education at the Cambridge School of Landscape Architecture, now a part of Harvard. In 1932 he moved to Berlin and studied under Mies van der Rohe at the Bauhaus, returning to Chicago to complete his education at the Armour Institute (now IIT). After working in the offices of Keck & Keck and Paul Schweikher, Goldberg organized his own firm in 1937.[62]

As his career progressed, Goldberg became known for his "commitment to socially progressive design in large-scale residential and institutional projects."[63] In a 1982 essay "Rich Is Right," Goldberg recalled "The box was recognized as the perfect shape to package a right angled society. The design of the perfect box kept pace with the mechanization of all types of production: with factory made clothes, with steel rolling mills, with automobiles, radios and packaged foods."[64]

Goldberg rallied against the Miesian tradition of rectilinear architecture, which he "considered to be dehumanizing."[65] His distinctive later work often "juxtaposed fluid organic shapes against rectilinear forms" popular during the post–World War II period.[66] This departure became an iconic part of the Chicago skyline with his distinctive Marina City, an innovative design that required equally innovative technology. Constructed between 1960 and 1966, Marina City was unlike any high-rise the city had seen before, and until the construction of the Hancock building and the Sears Tower, was arguably the city's most visually compelling work of contemporary design.

1937	4816 S. Greenwood Ave.	Philip R. Toomin
1939	4820 S. Greenwood Ave.	Frank Katzin
1950–1951	5806 S. Blackstone Ave.	Ralph and Rachel Helstein
1954–1955	4800 Drexel Blvd.	Drexel Boulevard Town and Garden Houses

EZRA GORDON, JACK M. LEVIN & ASSOCIATES
EZRA GORDON, FAIA (1921–2009)

Gordon received his architectural degree from the University of Illinois in 1951, although he also studied at IIT. He worked for a variety of architectural firms, including Pace Associates and Harry Weese & Associates, prior to forming a partnership with Jack Levin in 1961. It was their experience in Weese's office that led to an interest in socially responsible housing, and together the partners planned numerous residential development complexes. Gordon designed "thoroughly practical, functional buildings—no pretense," commented architect John Macsai.[67]

1965–1966	5135–5231 S. Kimbark Ave.	The Common
1967	5401 S. Hyde Park Blvd.	Apartment High-rise

ROBERT PHILIP GORDON, AIA

Bob Gordon received his architectural education at IIT, where he continued with a master of science in City and Regional Planning. He has had numerous academic appointments and is the author of several books, including *Perspective Drawing: A Designer's Method*.[68] His Mermel house was the last to be constructed in Kenwood prior to the community's designation as a landmark district.

1976	1039 E. 48th St.	Irving and Anne Mermel

GRANGER, LOWE & BOLLENBACHER
ALFRED HOYT GRANGER, FAIA (1867–1939)
ELMER CAMERON LOWE, FAIA (1876–1933)
JOHN CARLISLE BOLLENBACHER, FAIA (1884–1939)

Granger, Lowe & Bollenbacher were responsible for numerous churches and public buildings in Chicago and throughout the Midwest. Lowe studied for two years at the University of Chicago before graduating with a degree from the Massachusetts Institute of Technology in 1905. That year he became associated with fellow MIT graduate John Bollenbacher in a partnership that operated for sixteen years. In 1924, Alfred Granger joined the practice, and Granger, Lowe & Bollenbacher operated until Lowe's death in the early thirties.[69]

1911	5305 S. Greenwood Ave. (Lowe & Bollenbacher)	Frederic Bruce Johnstone
1922	E. 53rd St. and Dorchester Ave., demolished	Hyde Park YMCA Annex
1927	5801–5811 S. Dorchester Ave.	The Cloisters

GRUNSFELD SCHAEFFER ARCHITECTS
ERNEST ALTON GRUNSFELD III, FAIA (b. 1929)

Tony Grunsfeld III is the son of the prominent architect of the same name. His father, Ernest Grunsfeld Jr., had many ties to the Hyde Park area, including the Rosenwald and Adler families, and was the architect for Max Adler's Planetarium, and for the Michigan Boulevard Apartments at 47th Street and Michigan Avenue, commissioned by Julius Rosenwald.

Grunsfeld III studied under Ralph Rapson at the Institute of Design prior to attending MIT, where he received his bachelor's degree in 1952. He worked as a draftsman for Keck & Keck and entered the air force, where he designed buildings for air force bases in the Northeast. He joined with a former partner of his father, Wallace Yerkes, in a small residential practice in 1956. They established a firm specializing in residential commissions for prominent clients, many on Chicago's North Shore. Grunsfeld is "highly regarded for his sensitivity to site and landscape, architectural massing, and building materials."[70]

1964	1203 E. 50th St.	Orville Morris
1964	1207 E. 50th St.	Phil Neal

HANDY & CADY
FRANK W. HANDY (n.d.)
JEREMIAH KIERSTED CADY (1855–1924)

Born in Indianapolis, Cady received his degree in architecture from Cornell in 1876. He came to Chicago in 1883 and was first employed as a draftsman by Burnham & Root. In 1885 Cady went to Europe and on his return became the head of the drafting room for the firm. Between 1887 and 1909 he practiced with Frank W. Handy.[71]

1897	4858 S. Dorchester Ave.	Dr. Archibald and Margaret Church
1902	4842 S. Kenwood Ave.	Charles F. and Hattie H. Harding
1916	5639 S. University (Cady)	PSI Upsilon Fraternity House

JOHN TODD HETHERINGTON (1858–1936)

Hetherington designed solidly constructed brick homes, of which several examples are found near the university campus. Hetherington was born in Canada but raised in Scotland, where he received his architectural training. He practiced in Edinburgh until coming to America in the early 1880s, beginning his career in Chicago as a draftsman in the offices of Treat & Foltz.[72] Hetherington left after eight years, and except for his association with George Borst between 1903 and 1910, worked as an independent architect specializing in public, ecclesiastical, and residential work.[73]

1914	1221, 1225, 1229, 1233 E. 56th St.
1914	5600 S. Kimbark Ave.

ARTHUR HEUN, AIA (1866–1946)

Heun designed some of the most distinguished houses in Chicago and country estates in the exclusive suburb of Lake Forest on the city's North Shore. Born in Michigan, Heun came to Chicago at the age of twenty-one and worked in the office of Frank Whitehouse, Chicago's "most popular residential architect of that time."[74] He took over Whitehouse's clientele in 1893 and became a prominent architect during a period that was "noted for the splendor of home building."[75] Heun also designed the prestigious Casino Club and the original Arts Club buildings.[76]

| 1916 | 4939 S. Greenwood Ave. | Max and Sophie Adler |
| 1910 | 5017 S. Ellis Ave., demolished 1971 | Albert H. and Anna Loeb |

HOLABIRD & ROCHE
WILLIAM HOLABIRD, FAIA (1854–1923)
MARTIN ROCHE, FAIA (1853–1927)

In 1881, William Holabird and Martin Roche joined forces to establish what was to become an enduring and influential architectural firm. Pivotal in the development of early skyscrapers, especially the architectural style known as the Chicago School, they used the expression of structure as ornamentation for their buildings, which eventually led to the creation of modern commercial architecture. Holabird & Roche developed the skeleton type of building that revolutionized high-rise construction.[77]

An imposing figure at nearly six and a half feet tall with a "larger-than-life personality,"[78] Holabird was the senior member and in charge of the business side of the firm. He was considered "scrupulously honest, earning the firm a reputation for absolute reliability."[79] The *New York Times* called him "one of the great pioneer builders of Chicago," in the "foremost rank among the architects of the country."[80]

Holabird attended West Point Academy for two years and prospered as the front man for the partnership with Roche, traveling across the Midwest and obtaining most of the firm's commissions. Martin Roche was the creative director of the firm, with a very different personality. "Shy and retiring, he was a lifelong bachelor" who seemed uncomfortable in the business world.[81] Roche was brought to Chicago as a boy, studied at the Armour Institute of Technology (now IIT), and first practiced with William LeBaron Jenney. In his partnership with Holabird, Roche would have had a say in the overall plan of a structure, but his specialty was the design and detailing of the building.

Holabird & Roche's first commissions were largely residences, small flats, and minor commercial buildings, until they received the commission for the Tacoma Building (1889, demolished). They went on to design the Marquette Building (1895), Pontiac Building (1891) Chicago Building (1904–1905), and Old Colony Building (1904–1905), among others. Much of their work features the "Chicago window," a large central pane of glass with narrow, moveable sash windows on either side. By 1910, Holabird & Roche was one of the largest architectural firms in the country, employing nearly one hundred draftsmen.[82]

1886	5809 S. Blackstone Ave.	Miss Nellie D. Woods
1896	4548 S. Drexel Blvd., demolished	Arthur O. Slaughter
1904	4819 S. Greenwood Ave.	Joseph and Sarah Schaffner
1905	5540 S. Woodlawn Ave.	Ephraim F. and Lucy S. Ingals
1905	5637 S. Woodlawn Ave.	Lucius and Clara L. Teter
1910	5036 S. Ellis Ave.	Henry G. and Selma A. Hart
1922	4913 S. Kimbark Ave.	Bernard E. and Ellen C. Sunny

HOLABIRD & ROOT
JOHN AUGUR HOLABIRD, FAIA (1886–1945)
JOHN WELLBORN ROOT JR., FAIA (1887–1963)

Holabird's son John and John Wellborn Root Jr., the son of Daniel Burnham's partner,

John Wellborn Root, reorganized the firm of Holabird & Roche. Renamed in 1929, Holabird & Root was as significant as the earlier firm, and it continues operation today.

1931	1414 E. 59th St.	International House
1931	5550 S. University Ave.	Henry Crown Field House
1985	5720 S. Ellis Ave.	Kersten Physics Teaching Center

HENRY K. HOLSMAN, FAIA (1866–1963)

Henry Holsman studied architecture at Grinnell College, and although he practiced for sixty-five years, for a brief time he had an interesting diversion in the earliest days of the automobile industry. He founded the Holsman Automobile Company of Chicago, an enterprise that manufactured a carriage automobile equipped with "high solid tire buggy wheels," enabling the car to travel over rough roads. Holsman's intent was to design and manufacture a "usable, sturdy car that was inexpensive to buy and easy to maintain, so that all people, especially those of the working class, could afford one."[83] Between 1904 and 1910, the company manufactured the automobiles just south of Hyde Park, at their factory at 63rd and Washington (Blackstone) Street. But with smaller wheels for city driving, the Ford Model T became popular, and Holsman's product could not compete.

After the failure of the automobile company, Holsman returned to architecture. In Hyde Park, he designed a number of apartment buildings, many of which were designated for the junior faculty of the University of Chicago. Holsman designed attractive yet affordable dwellings, and his most important contribution may have been "creating inexpensive housing in conjunction with a mutual ownership concept."[84]

For the Disciples Divinity School of the University of Chicago, he designed the Chapel of the Holy Grail, and his wife, artist Elizabeth Tuttle Holsman, painted the religious images on the ceiling. The Holsmans were neighborhood residents, living at 5617 Madison Avenue (now Dorchester). One of their sons, Henry T. Holsman, shared his father's interest and in 1931 founded the Parker-Holsman Company, which manages and sells properties on the South Side. This firm continues to operate in Hyde Park today.

Partial listing:

1897	5128 S. Cornell Ave., with W. L. Brainerd	Arthur B. Mulvey
1897	5138–5140 S. Cornell Ave., with W. L. Brainerd	Arthur B. Mulvey
1898	5124 S. Cornell Ave.	Arthur B. Mulvey
1899	5537 S. Woodlawn Ave.	George M. and Edith Eckels
1901	5733 S. University Ave.	Carl D. and Clarinda Buck
1913	1320 E. 58th St. (Holsman & Hunt)	Charles H. and Ellen L. Judd
1923	5525–5529 S. University Ave.	
1924	1149–1159 E. 56th St.	
1925	5712 S. Kimbark Ave.	
1927	5617–5619 S. Dorchester Ave.	
1927	1157 E. 56th St.	56th and University Cooperative
1928	1156 E. 57th St.	Chapel of the Holy Grail, Disciples Divinity School of the University of Chicago
1929	1321 E. 56th St.	
1930	5810 S. Blackstone Ave. (Holsman & Holsman)	Holsman Co-op Flats
1937	5527 S. Woodlawn Ave.	Harley F. and Florence MacNair

JARVIS HUNT (1863–1941)

An avid golfer, Jarvis Hunt was educated at Harvard and MIT, and designed the Vermont Building, a Pompeian-style house, for the Columbian Exposition of 1893. Hunt's later works include the original buildings of the Great Lakes Naval Training Station, now on the National Register; railway stations in Joliet and Kansas City, the clubhouse at Chicago Golf Club, and the Lake Shore Athletic Club.[85]

| 1905 | 5017 S. Greenwood Ave., Coach House, demolished 2010 | Homer Stilwell |

MYRON HUNT, FAIA (1868–1952)

Widely known for his work Pasadena, California, Myron Hunt attended Northwestern University before studying architecture at MIT. In 1896 he returned to Chicago and worked as a draftsman in the local office of Shepley, Rutan & Coolidge before striking out on his own.[86] He completed the Drexel Square commission the year he left for the West Coast.

| 1897 | 5720 S. Woodlawn Ave. | Edwin O. and Elsie F. Jordan |
| 1903 | 823 E. Drexel Square | Arthur S. and Louisa B. Jackson |

JENNEY & OTIS

WILLIAM LEBARON JENNEY, FAIA (1832–1907)
WILLIAM A. OTIS, FAIA (1855–1929)

A native of Massachusetts, William LeBaron Jenney studied engineering prior to graduating from the École des Beaux-Arts in 1856. He came to Chicago in 1867 after serving in the army during the Civil War, and in 1871 formed the firm of Jenney, Schermerhorn & Bogart.[87] The firm achieved great success designing buildings to replace those lost by the devastation of the Chicago fire. This work led to Jenney's greatest impact—his role in the development of the steel-framed skyscraper, represented by the 1879 Leiter Building (demolished) and the 1884 Home Insurance Building (demolished). Jenney's firm provided training for many young architects, including Daniel Burnham, William Holabird, Irving Pond, Martin Roche, and Louis Sullivan.[88]

Two years after designing the Home Insurance Building, Jenney partnered with William Otis, a former draftsman who had studied at L'École des Beaux-Arts in France. The partnership between Jenney and Otis lasted only three years, after which Otis practiced independently. Jenney then partnered with William Mundie, and they worked together until 1905. Jenney retired to Los Angeles, where he died.

| 1886 | 4751 S. Kimbark Ave. | William R. and Florence Page |
| c. 1887 | 4942 S. Greenwood Ave | Frank E. and Maria Spooner |

JENNEY, MUNDIE & JENSEN

WILLIAM LEBARON JENNEY (1832–1907)
WILLIAM BRYCE MUNDIE, FAIA (1863–1939)
ELMER C. JENSEN (1870–1955)

Mundie came to Chicago in 1884 and was hired by Jenney; they became partners in 1891. After Jenney retired the firm name was changed to Jenney, Mundie & Jensen, becoming Mundie & Jensen after Jenney's death in 1907.[89]

| 1908 | 5317–5343 S. Harper Ave. | Henry Phipps |

ALVIN M. JOHNSON (n.d.)

| 1928 | 4830–4848 S. Drexel Blvd. | Tudor Gables Apartments |

JOHNSON & LEE, ARCHITECTS/PLANNERS

PHILLIP CRAIG JOHNSON, FAIA
CHRISTOPHER LEE, FAIA

Phillip Johnson and Christopher Lee founded this certified minority business enterprise (MBE) partnership in 1983. Lee received a master of architecture in urban design from

Harvard University, and a bachelor of architecture in design from the University of Illinois at Chicago. Johnson was educated at Kent State University, receiving a bachelor of architecture.[90]

| 1998 | 5019 S. Ellis Ave. | Earl and Barbara Bowles |

LYNN C. JONES (n.d.)

| 1939 | 4949 S. Ellis Ave. | Leo S. and Cecile S. Guthman |

KECK & KECK
WILLIAM KECK, FAIA (1908–1995)
GEORGE FRED KECK, AIA (1895–1980)

George Fred, known as Fred, studied at the University of Wisconsin and received his degree in architectural engineering from the University of Illinois in 1920. He came to Chicago in 1921 to work with William Pruyn, an architect specializing in residential work, primarily walk-up apartments in the Hyde Park area. Fred went on to work for D. H. Burnham, and for Schmidt, Garden & Martin, where he met R. Vale Faro, and together they established an independent office in 1926. William Keck received his degree in architecture from the University of Illinois in 1931. After graduation, he joined his older brother until both served their country during World War II.[91] The partnership of Keck & Keck was founded in 1946.

The Keck brothers were generous, donating their time to design and supervise the construction of a neighborhood project, the Hyde Park Neighborhood Club at 55th and Kenwood.[92] One of their most successful projects, according to Keck biographer Robert Boyce, is the Chicago Child Care Society building, a three-story structure of reinforced concrete and glass. The building received an Honor Award from the Chicago Chapter of the AIA in 1964.

Partial listing:

1937	5551 S. University Ave.	Keck-Gottschalk-Keck Residences
1948	5510–5516 S. Woodlawn Ave.	Cooperative Building
1949	5427–5437 S. Dorchester Ave., with Robert Tague	Pioneer Cooperative
1954	1025 E. 50th St.; second-level addition, Jonathan Beyer, 1987	Maurice F. and Eliza Atkins Gleason
1955	1400 E. 57th St.	University of Chicago Apartment Building
1960	51st Street and Cottage Grove	Drexel Square Apartment, Chicago Dwellings Association
1962	48th St. and Woodlawn Ave.	University of Chicago and Midway Properties Townhomes
1964–1965	5812 S. Blackstone Ave.	Norman and Marge Karlin
1965	1044–1050 E. 49th St. and 4858 S. Greenwood Ave.	Residences
1970	4800–4850 S. Lake Park Ave.	Amalgamated Clothing Worker's, Harper Square

MOSES LOUIS KROMAN, AIA (n.d.–1989)

| 1929 | E. 55th St. at Lake Park Ave. | Ritz 55th Garage |

ROY H. KRUSE & ASSOCIATES, LTD.

| 2006 | 1122, 1126, 1134 E. 49th St. | Speculative residences |
| 2008 | 4958 S. Woodlawn Ave. | Alan and Sophia King |

KUKLINSKI & RAPPE ARCHITECTS
SCOTT A. RAPPE, AIA
Rappe received a degree in architecture from the University of Illinois and a master's degree in business administration from the same institution. His education included a year of study in Versailles, France, and a semester in Rome before working with his father, and then Graham, Anderson, Probst & White, before starting an independent practice in 1992.[93]

2002	5320 S. University Ave.	Barr-Kane residence

PAUL C. LANTROP (n.d.)

1893	University between 52nd and 53rd Sts.	Columbian Exposition Women's Dormitory

LEBENBAUM & MARX
FRED CHARLES LEBENBAUM, AIA (1883-1917)
SAMUEL ABRAHAM MARX, FAIA (1885-1964)
Although primarily known as industrial designers, Fred Lebenbaum and Samuel Marx received several commissions in Kenwood. Born in San Francisco, Lebenbaum studied at MIT and completed his education in Paris.[94] He partnered with Marx in 1909; however, his career in Chicago was brief; he died of influenza at the age of thirty-four.[95]

Born in Natchez Mississippi, Marx attended the École des Beaux-Arts. His diverse work combines a "bon vivant's" love of the present with a "connoisseur's passion" for the past.[96]

1913	1030 E. 48th St.	Elmer Schlessinger
1916	4856–4858 Drexel Blvd.	Apartments

LEICHENKO & ESSER, WITH CHARLES L. MORGAN
PETER M. LEICHENKO (1893-1961)
CURT AUGUST ESSER, AIA (1892-1984)
CHARLES MORGAN (1890-1947)
Leichenko & Esser was founded in 1921 as an architectural and engineering firm that focused on multifamily residential buildings.[97] Many of their buildings were designed in the Art Deco style, and for the Narragansett they worked with modernist Charles Morgan for the detailing of the exterior ornamentation.

1929	1640 E. 50th St.	The Narragansett

LOEWENBERG & LOEWENBERG
ISRAEL S. LOEWENBERG, AIA (1892-1979)
MAX L. LOEWENBERG, AIA (1889-1984)
Educated at the Armour Institute, architect Israel Loewenberg and structural engineer Max Loewenberg founded the firm in 1919, and became specialists in architecture and construction.[98]

1926	5496 S. Hyde Park Blvd.	Mayfair Apartments
c. 1950	1215 E. Hyde Park Blvd.	Max Mason House Dormitories
1968	1799 E. 56th St.	1799 E. 56th Apartments

LOEWENBERG-FITCH

1990	5140 S. Hyde Park Blvd.	Hyde Park Tower

JOHN MACSAI & ASSOCIATES
JOHN MACSAI, FAIA (b. 1926)

Born in Budapest, Hungary, Macsai was sent to a work camp during World War II, where he "built airfields, cleared forests, and starved."[99] In 1945 Macsai resumed his studies at the Polytechnic University in Budapest, then transferred to Miami University in Ohio, where he received his BA in architecture. He was associated with several partners, then founded John Macsai & Associates in 1975, developing a practice that specialized in housing for the elderly and disabled. In 1991 Macsai merged his office with O'Donnell, Wicklund, Pigozzi & Peterson; he retired from the firm in 1999.

1986	5701–5719 Dorchester Ave.	University Townhomes

GEORGE WASHINGTON MAHER, FAIA (1864–1926)

Regarded as an influential Prairie School architect, George Maher sought to create an American architecture that departed from the use historical forms. After training as a draftsman, Maher worked for Joseph Lyman Silsbee, a large firm that also employed George Elmslie and Frank Lloyd Wright. Maher opened his own practice in 1888, and his work, like that of Elmslie and Wright, blended "traditional American house styles with more progressive European Arts & Crafts–style designs."[100] As a resident of Kenilworth, an elite suburb on the city's North Shore, Maher was affiliated with numerous clubs and maintained a wide list of social relationships that resulted in many residential commissions.[101] His son Philip joined him in practice in 1922; however, Maher was subject to bouts of depression throughout his life, became despondent and in 1926 took his own life.

1888	257 (1120) E. 49th St., demolished	Stephen H. and Lena Hurd
1888	4544 S. Greenwood Ave., demolished 1997	Stephen W. Gilman
1888	5518 S. Hyde Park Blvd.	William B. Conkey
1888	5522 S. Hyde Park Blvd.	N. Anderson
1889	5517, 5519 S. Cornell Ave.	Alex F. Shuman (attributed to Maher)
1889	5533, 5535, 5537 S. Cornell Ave.	Alex F. Shuman (attributed to Maher)
1891	5482 S. Hyde Park Blvd.	D. Johnston
1891	5484 S. Hyde Park Blvd.	L. P. Perry
1897	4807 S. Greenwood Ave.	J. J. Dau
1908	4930 S. Greenwood Ave.	Ernest J. and Hattie H. Magerstadt
1909	5024 S. Ellis Ave.	Frank Schoenfeld
1909	5028 S. Ellis Ave.	Joseph Bolivar DeLee

PHILIP BROOKS MAHER, FAIA (1894–1981)

Philip Maher studied architecture at the University of Michigan and was licensed as an architect in 1921. After graduation, he worked in the offices of his father, and in 1922 they became partners under the name George W. Maher & Company.[102] While many of his structures have been demolished, two that contributed to the development of North Michigan Avenue remain: the Farwell Building at 664 North Michigan (1926) and the Women's Athletic Club at 620 North Michigan (1927–1928).

1923	1220 E. 58th St.	Albert and Edna S. Michelson

MANN, MACNEILLE & LINDEBERG
HORACE B. MANN (1868-1937)
PERRY R. MACNEILLE (1872-1931)
HARRIE T. LINDEBERG (1879-1959)

New York–based architect Horace Mann was educated at Columbia University, and like other architects of the time, received a scholarship and traveled abroad for two years prior to beginning work as a draftsman.[103] His partner Perry MacNeille worked in planning for the city of New York, and their firm was responsible for the construction of business buildings, schools, churches, and residences. Local architect Argyle E. Robinson became the firm's representative here in Chicago. The firm dissolved in 1931.

1903	5603 S. Kenwood Ave.	Professors' Row Houses, Addison W. Moore; sold to Alexander Smith in 1906
1903	5607 S. Kenwood Ave.	Eliakim H. and Martha Moore
1903	5609 S. Kenwood Ave.	George L. Hendrickson
1903	5611 S. Kenwood Ave.	Kurt and Luise Laves
1903	5615 S. Kenwood Ave.	Edward T. and Margaret Lee
1903	1351 E. 56th St.	Professors' Row Houses, Edward Hutchinson
1903	1357 E. 56th St.	Charles R. Barnes
1903	1361 E. 56th St.	Theodore L. and Cora L. Neff
1904	5309 S. Greenwood Ave.	Professors' Row Houses, C. Riborg and Adrienne Mann
1904	5315 S. Greenwood Ave.	Edward Capps
1904	5317 S. Greenwood Ave.	George E. and Edith C. Shambaugh
1904	5319 S. Greenwood Ave.	Lester Bartlett
1904	1220 E. 56th St.	Professors' Row Houses, Herbert L. and Gussie Price Willett
1904	1222 E. 56th St.	Frank J. and Lida W. Miller
1904	1224 E. 56th St.	Mrs. Paul Kern
1904	1228 E. 56th St.	Francis and Harriet Blackburn
1904	1234 E. 56th St.	K. B. Miller
1904	5558 S. Kimbark Ave.	Francis W. and Cora W. Shepardson
1905	5714 S. Woodlawn Ave.	Floyd R. and Jessie C. Mechem

OLIVER W. MARBLE (n.d.)

1891	5026, 5028, 5030, 5032, 5034, 5036, and 5038 S. Blackstone Ave.	Taylor, Allen & Company
1897	5008 S. Blackstone Ave.	Hannah A. Larmine

MARSHALL & FOX
BENJAMIN H. MARSHALL, AIA (1874–1944)
CHARLES ELI FOX, AIA (1870–1926)

Born in Chicago, Marshall attended a South Side prep school, the Harvard School in Kenwood. Although he received no formal education in architecture, Marshall apprenticed with the firm of Wilson & Marble from 1893 until 1895, when he became a junior partner and the firm became known as Wilson & Marshall. He started his own firm in 1902 and established a reputation as a designer of theaters, including the "ill-fated" Iroquois Theater.[104] In 1905, Marshall formed a partnership with Charles Fox that lasted until Fox's death in 1926. A native of Pennsylvania, Fox studied civil engineering and architecture at MIT. He moved to Chicago and worked as a draftsman in the office of Holabird & Roche from 1891 to 1905.[105]

As in other successful partnerships, responsibilities were divided. Fox served as the construction specialist and project manager, and the "dashingly handsome"[106] Marshall utilized his talents to solicit commissions from Chicago's elite. The firm was known for luxury apartment buildings, attracting "wealthy tenants to these high-rise buildings by adopting the characteristics of the elegant French flat."[107] Marshall & Fox also designed several opulent hotels with elegant terra-cotta façades and lavishly appointed interiors, including the 1908 Blackstone Hotel on South Michigan Avenue and in 1919 the Drake Hotel on East Lake Shore Drive.

| 1906 | 4930 S. Woodlawn Ave. | Walden W. and Bessie K. Shaw |
| 1909 | 5825 S. Blackstone Ave. | Frederick and Esther Bode |

THOMAS MCCALL (1857–1925)

Born in Scotland, McCall worked in London before coming to Chicago in 1891. He worked on the design of hotels for the 1893 Columbian Exposition, and later erected a large number of residences and three-story apartment buildings in the neighborhood.[108]

1895	5736 S. Woodlawn Ave.	Shailer and Mary E. Mathews
1900	5704 S. Kenwood Ave.	John and Catherine M. Lally
1902	5553–5555 S. Blackstone Ave.	M. R. Porter
1903	5716–5718 S. Dorchester Ave.	George Low
1905	5525 S. Woodlawn Ave.	Ernest D. Burton
1905	5427–5433 S. Harper Ave.	John A. Carroll
1906	5541 S. University Ave.	Theodore G. and Lillian M. Soars
1906	5642 S. Kimbark Ave.	E. Washburne
1906	5046–5056 S. Blackstone Ave.	Joseph Cormack
1907	1356–1360 E. 58th St.	
1907	5413 S. Cornell Ave.	
1908	5536 S. Kimbark Ave.	Rudolph and Lena Bobb
1909	5527–5529 S. Cornell Ave.	John W. Coutts
1909	4933–4935 S. Dorchester Ave.	Henry Peterson
1909	5400–5402 S. Dorchester Ave.	
1909	5631 and 5635–5637 S. Dorchester Ave.	
1909	5557–5559 S. Blackstone Ave.	
1910	5756–5758 S. Kenwood Ave.	Frank E. and Ida F. Livengood

MEESI

Little is known of the architects; however, MEESI is presumed to have been an acronym for a consortium of business and construction enterprises.

| 1972 | 4855 S. Woodlawn Ave. | Elijah and Clara Muhammad |
| 1972 | 1136, 1144, 1150, and 1158 E. 49th St. | Nation of Islam |

LUDWIG MIES VAN DER ROHE, FAIA (1886–1969)

Celebrated architect Mies van der Rohe had humble beginnings, working on various projects with his father, a master mason who owned a small stonecutter's shop in Germany. He received his architectural training through apprenticeships with several noted German architects. After working with progressive architect Peter Behrens, Mies opened his own office in 1914 and went on to achieve international recognition as one of the leading figures of modern architecture. In 1930 Mies was named the director of the Bauhaus School, leading a faculty of progressive architects, designers, and artists, where he served until 1933, when the political pressures of Nazi Germany forced it to close.

Mies came to Chicago in 1938 from Germany to become director of the school of architecture at the Armour Institute, at the time "a relatively modest technical training school" that merged with Lewis Institute to become the Illinois Institute of Technology.[165] After his Bauhaus years, Mies developed new techniques and clearly understood the inherent qualities of the materials he used, creating an architecture that was reduced to essentials. "He combined these same materials—aluminum, glass and steel—with traditional marble, granite, travertine, bronze and even brick, to give his buildings inside and out a sensuous richness for all their austerity."[166] "Less is more" was his credo.

Mies designed many significant buildings, including, in 1951, the minimalist Farnsworth house in Plano, Illinois, and in 1954–1958, the Seagram Building on Park Avenue in New York. After twenty years as director of architecture at IIT, Mies resigned the position in 1958 at the age of seventy-two. Throughout his life, he maintained a private practice and ranks as one of the most notable and influential architects of the twentieth century. Mies "simply changed the way people do architecture."[167]

1947–1949	5530–5532 S. Shore Dr. (with Pace Associates)	The Promontory

EDGAR MILLER (1899–1993)

Edgar Miller was a key figure among the artists and writers in Hyde Park's Artists Colony during the twenties. Miller arrived in Chicago at the age of seventeen to attend the Art Institute but dropped out of the program. He worked in the studio of Alfonso Iannelli and was a part of the bohemian world of the "Chicago Renaissance," a community of writers, visual artists, and designers during the twenties.[109]

Miller's work was diverse; he is known as an architect, sculptor, woodcarver, and painter. He is best recognized for taking a decaying German neighborhood, originally a fashionable district of Victorian houses, and using all of his talents to create "Old Town," now a desirable enclave on the city's near North Side.

c. 1928	1338 E. Madison Park, remodeling
c. 1928	5132–5136 S. Blackstone Ave., remodeling

ARTHUR MYHRUM (n.d.–1973)

Myhrum, a graduate of Williams College, studied architecture at Harvard.[110] He designed the Visitor's Center at the Morton Arboretum and the Junior Museum in the Art Institute, and remodeled the president's house at the University of Chicago.[111]

1965	1126 E. 48th St., remodeling	Ben and Natalie Heineman

NAGLE, HARTRAY ARCHITECTURE
JAMES LEE NAGLE, FAIA (b. 1937)

Born in Iowa, Nagle received a BA from Stanford and a BA in architecture from the Massachusetts Institute of Technology in 1962. He continued his education, receiving an MA from the Graduate School of Design at Harvard University. Named a Fulbright Scholar, Nagle went to the Netherlands to study architecture and urbanism. Returning to Chicago, he joined the office of Stanley Tigerman in 1965, where Larry Booth was also employed. The following year, Booth and Nagle left to open their own firm that operated until 1980.[112]

In the 1970s, Nagle joined the "Chicago Seven," a group of rising architects who challenged the dominance of Miesian architecture and sought to "encourage new approaches to architecture in Chicago" though writings and exhibitions.[113] During this time Nagle contributed to the restoration of H. H. Richardson's Glessner House on Prairie Avenue and was a founding member of the Chicago Architecture Foundation.

After Booth left to found his own firm in 1980, Nagle, Hartray & Associates expanded, and the firm received awards for the design of numerous projects—from the AIA (locally and nationally), Architectural Record, Structural Engineers of Illinois, Chicago Building Congress, and the Chicago Athenaeum to name a few.[114] The firm has completed a number of projects for the University of Chicago, including the Laboratory Schools gymnasium and the warming house for the ice rink on the Midway.

1980	4824 S. Woodlawn Ave.	Richard and Eileen Epstein
1991	5550 S. Shore Dr.	Montgomery Place

HENRY NEWHOUSE (1874–1929)

Newhouse is best known as the architect of large apartment hotels and for his 1923 classically inspired design of the Kehilath Anshe Ma'ariv Temple on Drexel Boulevard, now the home of Operation PUSH. Born in Chicago, Newhouse graduated from MIT in 1894. After opening a practice in 1896, he worked in the Hyde Park neighborhood for several decades. For a time Newhouse specialized in theater design, initially specializing in small motion picture houses and nickelodeons.

1901	924 E. 50th St., demolished	Albert H. and Anna Loeb
1908	5020 S. Ellis Ave.	A. Hoefield
1908	5728–5730 S. Drexel Blvd., demolished	Emanuel and Mollie Winter
1909	5125 S. Ellis Ave.	Andrew Harper
1909	5237–5245 S. Kenwood Ave.	Collins & Morris
1910	932 E. 51st St.	Jacob and Flora Franks
1911	5337 S. University Ave.	Adolph and Ray Kramer

NEWHOUSE & BERNHAM

HENRY NEWHOUSE (1874–1929)
FELIX M. BERNHAM (n.d.)

Newhouse partnered with Bernham in 1913 and they are best known for large commercial buildings and apartment houses.

1917	4659 S. Drexel Blvd.	Cooper-Monotah (Sutherland) Hotel
1918	5307 S. Hyde Park Blvd.	Cooper-Carleton (Del Prado) Hotel
1922	930 E. 50th St.	Kehilath Anshe Ma'ariv Temple
1924	5401 E. View Park	—
1928	1631–1649 E. 55th St.	Goodfriend Store and Flat Building

GEORGE CROLL NIMMONS, FAIA (1865–1947)

Nimmons practiced for nearly fifty years, and was "prominently known" in Chicago.[115] A native of Wooster, Ohio, he graduated from the local academy and like other architects of the time, studied in Europe. In 1885 he came to Chicago to work for Burnham & Root as a draftsman, where he stayed for ten years. In 1897 Nimmons formed a partnership with William Fellows.[116] They became the architects for many Sears facilities constructed during the early 1900s.[117] The partnership dissolved in 1917, and afterward Nimmons practiced independently as George C. Nimmons & Co. until 1933, and then as Nimmons, Carr & Wright until 1945.

1898	4851–4853 S. Kenwood Ave.	E. G. Chase
1899	4820 S. Kenwood Ave.	Charles G. and Angie W. Fellows
1919	1600 E. Hyde Park Blvd., demolished 1970	Chicago Beach Hotel Annex

NIMMONS & FELLOWS

GEORGE CROLL NIMMONS (1865–1947)
WILLIAM KINNE FELLOWS, FAIA (1870–1948)

Born in Minnesota, Fellows studied architecture at Columbia University and graduated in 1894. He was awarded a fellowship and a scholarship, permitting him a year and a half of travel and study abroad. Upon his return from Europe, Fellows, like George C. Nimmons, went to work for Burnham & Root.[118] In 1898 he formed a partnership with Nimmons.

Mainly Nimmons & Fellows received industrial commissions, and were chiefly concerned with "the solution of structural and utilitarian problems."[119] One of their first large projects was a store for Sears Roebuck & Company, and following its successful completion they became the architects for many other Sears facilities constructed during the early 1900s.[120] Fellows was also an instructor at the Chicago School of Architecture, president of the Architectural Sketch Club, and a fellow of the American Academy in Rome.[121]

1899	5757, 5759 S. Blackstone Ave.	Speculative for Katherine Rush
1903	4901 S. Ellis Ave.	Julius and Augusta Rosenwald
1904	4823 Kenwood Ave.	Platt C. Gibbs

PAUL FREDERICK OLSEN (n.d.–1946)

Olsen was one of a number of architects who specialized in speculative cooperative apartment ventures during the twenties.

| 1926 | 5830–5844 S. Stony Island Ave. | Vista Homes |
| 1930 | 5200 S. Blackstone Ave. | Blackwood Apartments |

WILLIAM A. OTIS, FAIA (1855–1929)

Born in New York, Otis studied at the University of Michigan and the École des Beaux-Arts. He moved to Chicago in 1882 to work as a draftsman in the office of William LeBaron Jenney, where he became a partner in 1886. After 1889 Otis practiced independently and taught at the new School of Architecture at the Art Institute.[122] Otis continued his practice until 1914 when Edwin H. Clark joined him (Otis & Clark).[123]

1896	4917 S. Greenwood Ave.	Charles E. and Sarah Gill
1896	4923 S. Greenwood Ave.	Laurence A. and Edith Carton
1905	1219 E. 50th St.	Leroy D. and Elsie Kellogg

OTTENHEIMER, STERN & REICHERT

HENRY LEOPOLD OTTENHEIMER (1868–1919)
ISAAC S. STERN (n.d.)
WILLIAM C. REICHERT (n.d.)

Ottenheimer began his architectural training with Adler & Sullivan, drafting plans for one of their most important projects, the Auditorium, a theater, hotel, and office building complex. Ottenheimer also worked on Adler & Sullivan's Standard Club, a Romanesque building for the German Jewish elite, and on the remodeling of Temple Sinai. After leaving Adler & Sullivan, he continued his architectural education, spending three years in Paris and returning to Chicago in 1892.[124] Prior to founding Ottenheimer, Stern & Reichert, he collaborated with Henry J. Schlacks between 1892 and 1896.

Dubbed "the dainty designer of beautiful homes," Ottenheimer produced many residences with a "charming baroque exuberance," for German Jewish businessmen and exclusively on Chicago's South Side.[125] The *Tribune* noted Ottenheimer as the designer of two "handsome houses in the modern French style" for S. Guthman and M. Greenebaum on the southwest corner of Drexel Boulevard and 45th Street. They were constructed of brick and terra-cotta in the summer of 1899.[126]

Evidently Ottenheimer had more than a bit of a temper, leaving him with an unusual legacy. In 1885, When he was out for a stroll one morning, a neighborhood boy "called him a 'Polish Jew.' Henry took the small boy across the knee and whipped him," whereupon the boy's father "caught the draughtsman by the collar, laid him on the sidewalk and trod upon him." Ottenheimer was fined a sum of five dollars.[127]

In another incident Ottenheimer stabbed fellow Adler & Sullivan employee Frank Lloyd Wright in the back with a drafting knife during a disagreement. Their dislike was mutual, for Wright described Ottenheimer as "heavy-bodied, short-legged, pompadoured, and conceited." Although he never saw Ottenheimer again after the incident, Wright wrote decades later in his autobiography, "I bear the welts of Ottie's fancy work on my shoulder blades. But not because I turned my back on him."[128]

| 1904 | 4838 S. Woodlawn Ave. | Daniel N. and Maud Eisendrath |
| 1912 | 4901 S. Greenwood Ave. | August and Isabel Gatzert |

PACE
CHARLES BOOHER GENTHER, FAIA (1907–1987)

Influenced by the design of the Barcelona Pavilion, Charles "Skip" Genther came to Chicago in 1940 to study under Ludwig Mies van der Rohe at the Illinois Institute of Technology. After working at the offices of Skidmore, Owings & Merrill and Holabird & Root, Genther founded PACE Associates in 1946 and employed many who had worked or trained in the offices of Holabird & Root.[129]

PACE (Planners, Architects, and Consulting Engineers) was for a period closely associated with architect Mies van der Rohe and collaborated with him on several projects, including 860–880 Lake Shore Drive, Promontory Point, a student and faculty apartment at the IIT campus, and the Algonquin Apartments in East Hyde Park. Genther resided in Hyde Park, first in Mies's Promontory Apartments and then in one of Y. C. Wong's Atrium homes.

| 1950 | 1606 E. 51st St. and 1605, 1606, 1607, 1616, and 1617 E. 50th St. | Algonquin Apartments |

HARVEY LINDSLEY PAGE, AIA (1859–1934)

Born in Washington DC, Page attended the Emerson Institute and worked as an apprentice prior to opening his own office. He was in Chicago for only a brief period, arriving around 1896 and leaving for San Antonio, Texas, in 1900, where he spent the remainder of his life.[130]

| 1896 | 5730 S. Woodlawn Ave. | Joseph Iddings, Frank Tarbell, Ernst Freund |

CHARLES M. PALMER, AIA (n.d.–1928)

Although a lesser-known architect, Palmer was associated with real estate magnate Potter Palmer, designing several houses for him on land west of Palmer's mansion on fashionable North Lake Shore Drive, as well as the Palmer House Hotel.[131]

1895	5121 S. Dorchester Ave.	
1895	5123 S. Dorchester Ave.	
1895	5125 S. Dorchester Ave.	Arthur G. Jones
1895	5129 S. Dorchester Ave.	
1895	5131 S. Dorchester Ave.	Will H. Moore
1896	831 E. Drexel Square	

PATTON & FISHER
NORMAND SMITH PATTON, FAIA (1852–1915)
REYNOLDS FISHER, FAIA (n.d.)

A native of Connecticut, Normand Patton was educated at Amherst and MIT and, following his graduation in 1874, came to Chicago. In 1885 he formed a partnership with Reynolds Fisher and they practiced together until 1901, when Fisher moved to Seattle to join his brother's brick business.[132] They were favored among the city's Queen Anne designers and several examples of their work can still be found in Kenwood, including Fisher's own residence.

Although not in partnership for a long time, Patton and Fisher were responsible for many well-known buildings, including the 1893 administration building at the Armour Institute (now IIT) and in 1894 the Chicago Academy of Science Building, which now housing the administration of the Lincoln Park Zoo on the city's North Side.[133]

1890	4734 S. Kimbark Ave.	Reynolds and Ellen Fisher
1891	4801 S. Kimbark Ave.	Joseph H. Howard
1895	5740 S. Woodlawn Ave.	Henry H. and Julia D. Donaldson
c. 1896	5754 S. Woodlawn Ave., demolished	Jacques and Annie L. Loeb

PEI, COBB, FREED & PARTNERS ARCHITECTS LLP

I. M. PEI, FAIA (b. 1917)

Internationally known architect Ieoh Ming Pei was born in Canton, China, and came to the United States to study architecture at the age of seventeen. After receiving a bachelor of architecture from MIT in 1940, he received his master's in architecture from the Harvard in 1946. After teaching at Harvard from 1945 to 1948, Pei accepted a position as director of architecture at Webb & Knapp. This real estate development corporation had many sizeable planning and architectural ventures across the country, including the Hyde Park Redevelopment Project. Pei continued at Webb & Knapp until 1955, when he founded I. M. Pei and Associates.[134]

Pei's designs include the East Building of the National Gallery of Art in Washington DC and the John F. Kennedy Library in Boston as well as numerous churches, hospitals, municipal buildings, schools, libraries, and museums. Among Pei's skyscraper designs are the Bank of China Tower in Hong Kong and the Four Seasons Hotel in midtown Manhattan. In 1983, Pei was chosen as the Laureate of the Pritzker Architecture Prize in addition to his many other honors: doctorates from Harvard University, the University of Pennsylvania, Columbia University, New York University, Brown University, the Chinese University of Hong Kong, and the American University in of Paris. In 1979, I. M. Pei received the AIA Gold Medal, the highest architecture honor in the United States.[135] Pei continues to practice today at Pei Cobb Freed & Partners, which was founded in 1989.

1958–1961	Blackstone Ave. and 54th St. (with Weese)	Hyde Park Cooperative Homes (Hyde Park A and B)
1958–1961	S. Lake Park Ave. between 56th and 57th Sts. (with Weese)	University Neighborhood Homes (Hyde Park A and B)
1958–1961	S. Harper Ave. between 56th and 57th Sts. (with Weese)	Hyde Park A and B
1958–1961	E. Park Place between Harper and Blackstone Aves. (with Weese)	East Harper Terrace (for Hyde Park A and B)
1960–1961	1400–1450 and 1401–1451 E. 55th St.	University Apartments

DWIGHT HEALD PERKINS, FAIA (1867–1941)

A noted authority in the field of school design, Dwight Perkins came to Chicago from Memphis when he was twelve years old. His mother's longtime friend, Annie Hitchcock, later financed his education at the Massachusetts Institute of Technology. He returned to Chicago, worked briefly as a draftsman for Wheelock & Clay and for H. H. Richardson, and for Burnham & Root as John Root's principal assistant. After Root's death, and with Burnham's obligation to the Columbian Exposition, Perkins was placed in charge of their downtown office and supervised the completion of Root's Monadnock Building.[136]

When Root died, there were more than a dozen major buildings in the late stages of design in the office in addition to the Monadnock. One commission that came into their office around the time of Root's death was for a refectory building in Washington Park. Today the Washington Park Refectory is the oldest surviving original park building in the South Park System.[137]

In 1894 Perkins established his own office and received a commission from the Steinway Piano Company to design a new building. After Steinway Hall was completed, he moved his office to the eleventh floor of the building and encouraged fellow architects to share the space. It was there that the Prairie School of architecture had its beginning. Fellow MIT graduate Robert Closson Spencer was the first to arrive, followed by his friend Frank Lloyd Wright, and then Myron Hunt. Each contributed to the development of an original form of American architecture "seeking above all truthfulness in the use of materials and the beauty that comes from the utility of the structure."[138]

In 1905 Perkins was appointed the chief architect for the Board of Education, and he designed over forty schools while in that position. His established style was reflected in school buildings designed to provide for the city's children, particularly those from "lesser circumstances."[139] Perkins continued to maintain a private practice, in partnership with John Hamilton, and in 1911 William Fellows joined the firm.

1897	1120 E. 48th St.	James J. and Ada Wait
1899	4914 S. Greenwood Ave., with H. H. Waterman	Robert and Clara Vierling
1901	5711 S. Woodlawn Ave.	Russell and Ethel Wiles
1902	4741 S. Greenwood Ave., barn, demolished 1964	Annie McClure Hitchcock
1902	1009 E. 57th St.	Charles Hitchcock Men's Residence hall

FREDERICK W. PERKINS, FAIA (1866–1928)

A native of Wisconsin, Frederick Perkins attended MIT and then studied, as did architects of the time, at the École des Beaux-Arts in Paris. He came to Chicago in the late 1880s, became a prominent architect to Chicago society, and married the daughter of a client. A "bon vivant," Perkins was the owner of a Mexican coffee plantation.[140] Although he moved to Boston in 1920, Perkins practiced "intermittently" in Chicago until his death in Paris in 1928.[141]

1898	4515 S. Drexel Blvd., with Edmund Krause, demolished	John G. and Mary Shedd
1890	4921 S. Dorchester Ave.	Albert H. Trotter
1890	4832 S. Ellis Ave.	Alonzo M. and Charlotte Fuller
1891	4840 S. Ellis Ave.	Frank H. and Annie Fuller
1898	4860 S. Kimbark Ave.	Norman and Imogine Carroll
1899	4827 S. Ellis Ave., demolished	Frederick W. Jackson

POND & POND

IRVING KANE POND, FAIA (1857–1939)
ALLEN BARTLETT POND, FAIA (1858–1929)

Members of the Steinway Hall group, the Pond brothers were unique; their buildings characterize the English Arts and Crafts movement of architecture and represent the best examples of the style in the city. The Ponds' inventive designs are noteworthy for their crafted details and for an influence on modernist architecture.[142] Pond & Pond began to practice at an auspicious time in the development of the university community, and received a number of commissions from their social contacts and the university. The institution's progressive approach to building was reflected in its choice of innovative architects such as the Pond brothers.

Irving Pond received a degree in civil engineering from the University of Michigan in 1879 and came to Chicago in the summer of that year to begin his architectural training in office of William LeBaron Jenney. Within six months he joined Solon S. Beman, where he worked on the design of the company town of Pullman, gaining experience in brick detailing and craftsmanship.[143] He was one of the founders of the Cliff Dwellers and was a member of the literary club for fifty-one years. Pond possessed a lifelong interest beyond architecture—he traveled with the circus for a time and often entertained children with an array of gymnastic stunts, showing "great agility in his performances."[144]

In 1886 Irving partnered with his younger brother Allen, and they worked together for the following forty years. Many of the firm's buildings were related to social services. The brothers were closely connected with the Hull-House movement, and over the years designed and built both the Hull-House complex and Chicago Commons, studying the problems of urban settlement house buildings. They were also selected to design several buildings located near the university; the American School for Home Correspondence at 850 East 58th Street, and the Lorado Taft Studio at 6016 South Ingleside.[145]

Allen Pond also received his education at the University of Michigan. Before joining his brother, Allen acted as assistant to his father, who was a warden at a local prison. His experiences there presumably influenced his interest and work in the field of social reform.[146]

Pond & Pond never received the large commissions that many other firms of the time did. However their steadiness in combining innovation and tradition attracted progressive clients—they designed with simplicity and an inherent respect for building materials.

1885	5751 S. Harper Ave.	Irving Pond
1885	5755 S. Harper Ave.	Irving Pond
1889	4446 S. Greenwood Ave.	James and Sarah Mullen
1894	5515 S. Woodlawn Ave.	James G. Miller Apartments
1895	5117, 5119 S. Dorchester Ave.	Wheeler and Goldsmith
1897	4575 S. Oakenwald, demolished	Frederick W. and Helen Job
1898	5531 S. Woodlawn Ave.	Frederick Ives Carpenter
1899	5747 S. Blackstone Ave.	James Westfall Thompson
1900	5222 S. Hyde Park Blvd.	John S. Coonley
1901	5801 S. Kenwood Ave.	Frank R. and Frances C. Lillie
1903	5749 S. Woodlawn Ave., demolished 1958	Sigmund and Fannie B. Zeisler
1910	5625 S. Woodlawn Ave.	Charles F. Miller
1912	5621 S. Woodlawn Ave.	Fred Lorenz

JOHN E. OLDAKER PRIDMORE, AIA (1867–1940)

Born and educated in England, J. E. O. Pridmore arrived in Chicago in 1883 and practiced here for nearly fifty years. Best known for his church and theater buildings in the historic revival styles favored by many Chicagoans at this time, he was commissioned for relatively few single-family homes.[147]

1893	5722 S. Kimbark Ave.	D. H. Stapp
1895	4841 S. Greenwood Ave. (Pridmore & Stanhope)	Richard Nash
1905	1223 E. 50th St.	A. C. Barnes
1905	1225 E. 50th St.	Charles E. and Annie G. Murison
1909	1420 E. 56th St., demolished 1968	Episcopal Church of the Redeemer
1915	5550 S. Blackstone Ave.	Rectory of the Episcopal Church of the Redeemer

WILLIAM H. PRUYN JR. (n.d.)

Pruyn was the son of a building contractor and followed his father's trade, specializing in the development of speculative properties.[148]

1894	4630 S. Drexel Blvd.	Speculative, E. Iverson & Sons, Contractors
1897	5441, 5445 S. Hyde Park Blvd.	Wheeler and Goldsmith
1898	1316 E. Madison Park	Kirk Hawes
1900	5407 S. Hyde Park Blvd.	B. Witt
1900	1361–1363 E. 50th St.	George Williams

1901	1321, 1323, 1325, 1327, 1329, 1331, 1335, 1337 E. 50th St.	J. D. Hawes
1902	1310 E. Madison Park	Kirk Hawes
1902	4941 S. Kimbark Ave.	Kirk Hawes
1903	4948 S. Kimbark Ave.	D. Hawes
1905	4505 S. Greenwood Ave.	
1905	4901 S. Kimbark Ave.	Edwin A. and Josephine Graff
1906	4926 S. Kimbark Ave.	Herbert B. and Louise C. Leavitt
1910	931–949 E. 51st St.	
1911	5600–5602 S. Dorchester Ave.	

PURCELL, FEICK & ELMSLIE
GEORGE GRANT ELMSLIE, FAIA (1869–1952)

Prairie School architect George Elmslie began his career in the office of Joseph Silsbee, where Frank Lloyd Wright also worked. After Wright left to join Adler & Sullivan, he asked Elmslie to join him. In 1889 Elmslie became a draftsman and designer in Sullivan's office rendering designs and ornamentation. He worked on details for the Wainwright building in St. Louis and the Carson Pirie Scott Department store (originally Schlesinger & Mayer) in Chicago.[149] A loyal employee, Elmslie was the last to remain with Sullivan as his practice failed. He then joined Purcell and Feick in Minneapolis, where the firm was headquartered, and moved to Hyde Park to open an office on 53rd Street in 1913. Elmslie resided at 5535 South Cornell.

1913	5712 S. Dorchester Ave.	Newman, Marsh & Baskerville Flat

ROBERT RAE, JR. (n.d.)

1888	5719, 5729, 5731, 5735, 5737 and 5745 S. Harper Ave.	
1901	5710 S. Woodlawn Ave.	George Middledorf

GURDON P. RANDALL (1821–1884)

A native of Vermont, Randall moved to Boston at the age of twenty-two and began to practice architecture, specializing in the construction of churches and railroad buildings. By 1856 he was keenly aware of the advantages the growing city of Chicago offered, and moved west. He branched out into school design, preparing plans for the Theological Seminary of the Northwest in Hyde Park, which was never built.[150] *Inland Architect* described Randall as a "man of sterling worth" with an "upright character securing to him a reputation for honesty and integrity that was always beyond reproach." He was "an architect of the old school, always true to the principles of his art."[151]

1859	53rd St. at Lake Michigan, destroyed by fire, 1877	Hyde Park House

RAPP & RAPP
CORNELIUS W. RAPP (1861–1926)
GEORGE RAPP (1878–1941)

The Rapp brothers maintained that the show started on the sidewalk, and their residential architecture often follows that credo. Cornelius and George Rapp were prominent architects known for the design of a number of elaborate theaters both in Chicago and across the country. George began work for Edmund Krause, preparing plans for a vaudeville theater, the Majestic (1906) at 22 West Monroe. Then came the transformation from the nickelodeon in storefront buildings to the more modern movie houses, and the Rapp brothers began to work in that field of architecture. After their first success designing the Central Park Theater on Roosevelt Road (1917, now closed), they followed with the Tivoli (demolished), the Riviera, the Chicago, the Uptown, the Palace, and the Oriental Theaters, to name just a few. George Rapp once said their theaters were "a shrine to democracy, where the wealthy rub elbows with the poor."[152]

1900	5725 S. Woodlawn Ave.	George C. and Cora R. Howland
1901	5729 S. Woodlawn Ave.	John A. Roche, Jr.
1908	5430 S. Cornell Ave.	J. Frank and Caroline McKinley
1908	5539 S. Cornell Ave.	C. L. Anderson
1916	5490 S. Shore Dr.	Jackson Shore Apartments
1924	1642 E. 56th St.	The Windermere East
1926	1429–1451 E. Hyde Park Blvd.	Piccadilly Theater and Apartments; theater demolished 1972

RALPH EARL RAPSON, FAIA (1914–2008)

Although modernist Ralph Rapson was among the country's longest practicing architects, he never achieved international recognition. However, Rapson influenced many architecture and design students as the dean of the architecture school at the University of Minnesota. Born with a deformity in his right arm that required amputation, Rapson learned to draw skillfully with his left hand. He earned his architecture degree at the University of Michigan and received a scholarship for graduate study at the Cranbrook Academy of Art led by the Finnish architect Eliel Saarinen, in whose offices he began to practice architecture.[153]

Rapson came to Chicago in 1941 to teach under the direction of Hungarian-born artist László Moholy-Nagy at the New Bauhaus, a school based on the influential German Bauhaus and the forerunner to the 1944 Institute of Design.[154] He worked briefly for George Fred Keck where he gained experience "translating modernist principals into built form."[155] In 1954 he began a thirty-year tenure at the University of Minnesota in Minneapolis. Ralph Rapson & Associates was formed that same year.

Rapson was noted for his superb renderings and applied his modernist ideas to a wide array of household items, especially furniture, in collaboration with Knoll Associates. Like his architecture, Rapson's furniture emphasized "affordability, the utilization of new materials and advances in fabrication techniques, and the exploration of new forms to accommodate the changing needs of modern life."[156]

1942	4810 Woodlawn Ave., unbuilt	John Johnson

RALPH RAPSON AND JOHN VAN DER MEULEN
JOHN HARPER VAN DER MEULEN, FAIA (n.d.–1994)

Rapson was associated with another young modernist architect, John van der Meulen, from 1951 until 1954. Van der Meulen received a degree in architecture from the University of Michigan in 1938, and after military service, opened an independent architectural practice in Chicago. He too was an instructor at the Institute of Design under the director Moholy-Nagy. In 1958 he began an independent practice, and the majority of his work was located in the Great Lakes area.[157]

1943	4912 S. Woodlawn Ave.	Willard and Adele Gidwitz

WILLIAM C. REICHERT (n.d.)

1926	1755–1765 E. 55th St.	Parkshore Apartments
1927–1928	5500 S. Shore Dr.	Flamingo-on-the-Lake
1928	5421 S. Cornell Ave.	5421 Apartments

RIDDLE & RIDDLE
HERBERT HUGH RIDDLE, AIA (1875–1939)
LEWIS W. RIDDLE (n.d.–1877)

Herbert Riddle, an 1896 graduate of the Massachusetts Institute of Technology, practiced with his brother Lewis for twenty years. Lewis was also trained in architecture at MIT, and worked as a structural engineer before joining his brother in 1905.

They received many significant commissions in Chicago, including the Mather Tower, a slender silhouette on East Wacker Drive and a Chicago landmark where the partners had an office for several years.[158] In 1918 Lewis Riddle joined a mortgage banking enterprise. In 1928, Herbert Riddle received a large local commission, the Chicago Theological Seminary at University Avenue and 58th Street, a complex that included the Thorndike Hilton Chapel, and which was controversially purchased by the university in 2008 for the establishment of the Milton Friedman Institute.[159]

1911	5622 S. Woodlawn Ave.	Lewis W. and Elizabeth E. Riddle
1911	5626 S. Woodlawn Ave.	Herbert Riddle
1911	923 E. 50th St.	Plymouth Congregational Church Society Church (now First Baptist Church)
1924	5521–5529 S. Blackstone Ave.	
1926	5760 S. Blackstone Ave.	
1928	1163 W. 58th St.	Chicago Theological Seminary

ARGYLE EGGLESTON ROBINSON, AIA (1872–1945)

Argyle Robinson was a local; his family moved to Hyde Park in 1874.[160] Robinson graduated from Hyde Park High School and received his education at both the Armour Institute and the Massachusetts Institute of Technology. Robinson was responsible for two firehouses near the neighborhood, the 1928 structure at 4600 South Cottage Grove, on the site of the village of Hyde Park's first firehouse, and a second structure erected that same year in Woodlawn. Robinson is also responsible for the Washington Park Fireproof Warehouse, designed at 5155 South Cottage Grove in 1905.[161]

1907	1308 E. 58th St.	James P. and Evelyn Hall
1908	5757 S. Kimbark Ave.	William G. and Harriet Hale
1909	5714–5724 S. Kenwood Ave.	John B. Jackson for the Chicago Theological Seminary

JAMES GAMBLE ROGERS, FAIA (1867–1947)

Best known for his work at major American universities, James Gamble Rogers produced "a built expression of the country's elite" in the years between the two world wars.[162] Born in Kentucky, he soon came with his family to Chicago. Rogers graduated from Yale University in 1889, and after traveling in Europe returned to the city. His family's neighbor was William Bryce Mundie, partner of William LeBaron Jenney, and influential in Gamble's future. Mundie recommended Rogers to Jenney, where the young man worked for two years before moving to Burnham & Root. In 1892 Rogers left to study architecture at the École des Beaux-Arts in Paris, graduating in 1898.[163]

Rogers was a member of the team responsible for Yale's master plan and was the architect of many of the university's buildings constructed until the midthirties.[164] Rogers's use of American Collegiate Gothic forms was similar to Henry Ives Cobb's for the University of Chicago. Closer to home, he designed Blaine Hall for the University of Chicago Laboratory Schools in 1905, and the following year, the Hyde Park Union Church (Hyde Park Baptist Church) at 5600 South Woodlawn.

| 1903 | 5528 S. Woodlawn Ave. | George and Harriet Hamlin |
| 1904 | 5235 S. University Ave. | Hunter W. and Lena J. Finch |

ANDREW C. SANDEGREN (1867–1924)

Born in Sweden, Sandegren was primarily a designer of large apartment buildings for Hyde Park and Kenwood's middle- and upper-class residents. He is credited with the "pronounced bay windows" that permit an abundance of sunlight into the city apartment.[168] Sandegren came to Chicago in 1888, went east for a time, and returned to the city to open an independent office in 1892.[169]

1901	1352–1354 E. 48th St.	Frank Gustafson
1905	5227–5229 S. Dorchester Ave.	Charles F. Hallgren
1906	4816–4828 S. Dorchester Ave.	Claus Carlson
1906	5474–5480 S. Hyde Park Blvd.	The East End, Frank Gustafson
1907	4715–4721 S. Greenwood Ave.	Charles F. Hellgren
1907	1358–1364 E. 48th St.	Charles F. Hellgren
1908	1219 E. 55th St., demolished	C. A. Carlson
1909	5312–5318 S. Hyde Park Blvd.	Sherman Cooper
1909	1716–1726 E. 55th St.	C. A. Carlson
1910	5411–5413 S. Hyde Park Blvd.	M. Anderson
1910	5457–5459 S. Hyde Park Blvd.	Charles Anderson

SCHMIDT, GARDEN & MARTIN
RICHARD ERNST SCHMIDT, FAIA (1865–1958)
HUGH MACKIE GORDON GARDEN, FAIA (1873–1961)
EDGAR MARTIN (1871–1951)

Richard Schmidt and Hugh Garden began a partnership in 1895 and became prominent architects practicing during the latter years of the period referred to as the first "Chicago School" of architecture. Schmidt possessed the "business acumen and social connections," while Garden brought the "imagination, inventiveness, and sensitivity" of an inspired designer. He was responsible for the firm's progressive style and his architectural motifs were unique. The Prairie-style Humboldt Park Refectory, or boathouse, and the Madlener House on Burton Place each feature Schmidt's extraordinary detailing.[170]

When Edgar Martin joined them in 1906, the firm became known as Schmidt, Garden & Martin. An enormously skilled engineer, Martin was able to solve the technical problems related to the construction of large buildings, such as how to use new construction materials and methods. For example, the Montgomery Ward & Company Catalogue House, at 600 West Chicago Avenue, was an early building constructed of reinforced concrete.[171]

1902	4825 S. Woodlawn Ave., (Schmidt, Garden)	Lester E. Frankenthal
1912	5749–5759 S. Kenwood Ave.	Mosheim Craig Apartments
1913	1314 E. 58th St.	James Rowland Angell
1914	5744 S. Stony Island, demolished 2011	Illinois Central (Doctor's) Hospital
1916	1442 E. 59th St.	The Eleanor Club

HOWARD VAN DOREN SHAW, FAIA (1869–1926)

One of the leading architects of his era, Howard van Doren Shaw designed well over two hundred buildings and projects during his thirty-two-year career. It was Shaw's early work in the Hyde Park area that established his prominence and led to a body of work that included small city residences and adaptations of English country houses, as well as churches, collegiate structures, and municipal spaces.

Shaw was born in Chicago to a prominent couple that lived in one of the city's most fashionable districts of the time, Prairie Avenue. Educated at the Harvard School for Boys (his introduction to the Kenwood neighborhood), he was accepted at Yale University during his junior year. In 1890 Shaw entered the two-year program at MIT, during a time when students studied classical Greek and Roman architecture.[172] Returning to Chicago,

Shaw apprenticed as a draftsman for Jenney & Mundie, a firm that was known as a training ground for up-and-coming architects.

In 1894 Shaw established his own practice. He designed over twenty residences in the Hyde Park and Kenwood neighborhoods and a number of institutional spaces, including the foundation and basin for Lorado Taft's *Fountain of Time* on the Midway Plaisance. Although a contemporary of Frank Lloyd Wright and Dwight Perkins, Shaw designed using traditional, historical styles. He was successful in Hyde Park and Kenwood, attracting a wide clientele drawn from society and business. Shaw responded in kind—he imbued their houses with symbols of bounty—fruits, flowers, and grape vines.

A trustee of the Art Institute of Chicago and chair of the library committee, Shaw personally selected architecture books for the Ryerson Burnham Library and designed the stately reading room for the collection.[173] He died in 1926, the year the AIA awarded him its Gold Medal, its highest honor, and he is remembered as "the most rebellious of the conservatives and the most conservative of the rebels."[174]

1894	4833–4847 S. Lake Park Ave., demolished 1961	Shaw-Atkinson residence, "Dorencote"
1895	5533 S. Hyde Park Blvd.	Henry C. Thompson
1896	4911 S. Greenwood Ave.	Cornelia W. (Thomas G. deceased) McLaury
1897	4917 S. Blackstone Ave., demolished	Washington Ave. Townhome, Mr. Turner
1897	4919 S. Blackstone Ave.	Washington Ave. Townhome
1897	4921 S. Blackstone Ave.	Washington Ave. Townhome
1897	4923 S. Blackstone Ave.	Morton D. Hull
1897	4925 S. Blackstone Ave.	Washington Ave. Townhome
1897	5737 S. University Ave.	George Edgar Vincent
1902	4901 S. Woodlawn Ave.	Charles A. and Mary Starkweather
1902	5724 S. Kimbark Ave.	Wilbur S. Jackman
1903	4924 S. Woodlawn Ave.	Morris and Mae Rosenwald
1904	5615 S. University Ave.	James H. and Francis Breasted
1904	5715 S. Woodlawn Ave.	Arthur J. and Hattie Mason
1905	5541 S. Woodlawn Ave.	B. Albert Streich
1906	5533 S. University Ave.	Oskar and Anna Bolza
1906	5706 S. Woodlawn Ave.	Edgar and Elfreda Goodspeed
1907	5728 S. Woodlawn Ave.	Mrs. Ella (William R.) Harper
1907	5730 S. Kimbark Ave.	Mrs. Wilbur S. Jackman
1907	5744 S. Kimbark Ave.	Charles S. and Davida Eaton
1907	4830 S. Woodlawn Ave.	James H. and Inez B. Douglas
1907	4900 S. Greenwood Ave.	Henry and Darlene Veeder
1909	5615 S. Woodlawn Ave.	Bertram W. and Mabel L. Sippy
1910	4815 S. Woodlawn Ave.	Thomas E. and Elizabeth Wilson
1911	5638 S. Woodlawn Ave.	Henry H. and Charlotte Hilton
1913	4800 S. Drexel Blvd., demolished 1946	Edward and Helen Swift Morris
1919	5620 S. Kimbark Ave.	H. A. Krisohl
1921	5655 S. University Ave.	University Church, Disciples of Christ
1922	5555 S. Woodlawn Ave.	Phi Kappa Psi Fraternity
1922	1155 E. 57th St.	Quadrangle Club

SHEPLEY, RUTAN & COOLIDGE
GEORGE FOSTER SHEPLEY, FAIA (1860–1903)
CHARLES HERCULES RUTAN, FAIA (1851–1914)
CHARLES ALLERTON COOLIDGE, FAIA (1858–1936)

When influential architect Henry Hobson Richardson died in 1886, three of his employees took over the Boston-based practice. George Shepley studied architecture at MIT, graduating in 1882 and joining Richardson that year. Coolidge studied at both Harvard and MIT and joined the practice the following year. Charles Rutan began, like many other architects of the time, as an apprentice, working with Richardson when he was only eighteen years old. Predictably the firm initially designed in the Romanesque style associated with Richardson; however, they established their own reputation in the neoclassical style popularized by another East Coast firm, McKim, Mead & White.[175] In 1892 they were selected as the architects for the Chicago Public Library, and the firm was commissioned the following year to design a new building for the Art Institute of Chicago. Charles Coolidge then moved from Boston to open their Chicago office in 1893.

| 1897 | 4830 S. Drexel Blvd., demolished 1928 | Chauncey and Mary A. Blair |

After the deaths of George Shepley 1903 and Charles Rutan in 1914, Charles Coolidge reorganized the firm in Boston, taking Charles Hodgdon (1856–1953) from the Chicago office as his partner. They officially changed the firm name to Coolidge & Hodgdon in 1915, and were associated with the University of Chicago through the early 1930s, designing Swift Hall at 1025–1035 East 58th Street, Joseph Bond Chapel at 1025 East 58th Street (1926), and the Albert Merritt Billings Hospital at 950 East 59th Street (1925–1927).

| 1916 | 1212 E. 59th St. | Ida Noyes Women's Residence Hall |
| 1919 | 5640 S. Blackstone Ave. | Tenth Church of Christ, Scientist (St. Stephen's Church) |

SKIDMORE, OWINGS & MERRILL (SOM)
LOUIS SKIDMORE, FAIA (1897-1962)
NATHANIEL ALEXANDER OWINGS, FAIA (1903-1984)
JOHN OGDEN MERRILL, FAIA (1896-1975)

Louis Skidmore formed a partnership with his brother-in-law and fellow MIT graduate Nathaniel Owings in 1936; John Merrill joined the firm as partner in 1939. Renamed Skidmore, Owings & Merrill, the firm grew to become one of the largest and most successful architectural and engineering firms in the country. By the early 1940s, the firm had developed an architectural style "emphasizing clean lines and functional geometric designs."[176] The firm grew rapidly after the war ended, and by the 1970s and 80s was known for high-rise buildings that defined the skyline of cities worldwide, including Chicago's Sears (now Willis) Tower and John Hancock Center.

| 1966-1967 | 5825 S. Dorchester Ave. | Stein Building |

ROBERT CLOSSON SPENCER JR., FAIA (1864-1953)

A native of Milwaukee, Wisconsin, Robert Spencer completed a two-year program at the Massachusetts Institute of Technology and won the Rotch Traveling Scholarship for 1891–1892. After spending two years in Europe, he came to Chicago to work with Shepley, Rutan & Coolidge on the Chicago Public Library. Active in the Arts and Crafts movement, Spencer was closely associated with architects, including Dwight Perkins, Myron Hunt, and Frank Lloyd Wright. In 1897 they maintained their individual practices; however, they came together to share the expenses of a single office in Steinway Hall, believing in "the principles of cooperation rather than competition."[177] While this arrangement was financially practical, the office also "fostered a sharing of artistic ideas, and permitted criticism and encouragement."[178]

A prolific writer, in 1900 Spencer wrote many articles for the *Architectural Review*; the first highlighted the work of his office mate Frank Lloyd Wright. His articles for *Brickbuilder* and *House Beautiful* highlighted the theory and practice of domestic architecture.[179]

| 1896 | 5719, 5721, 5723 S. Blackstone Ave. | L. K. Whiton |

SPENCER & POWERS
ROVERT CLOSSON SPENCER JR., FAIA (1864–1953)
HORACE SWETT POWERS, AIA (1872–1928)

In 1905 Spencer formed a partnership with Horace Powers, a graduate of the Armour Institute of Technology, (now IIT) and the Art Institute.[180] Specializing in residential architecture, they divided the responsibilities. Spencer was the designer and Powers handled the business aspects of the firm. The firm dissolved in 1923.[181]

| 1914 | 1366–1374 E. 57th St. | Stephen T. Mather |
| 1916 | 5648–5656 S. Dorchester Ave. | |

HENRY H. SPRAGUE (n.d.)

1889	4810 S. Kenwood Ave.	John S. and Ann G. Miller
c. 1890	4828 S. Kimbark Ave.	William F. and Kate B. Parrish
c. 1891	4840 S. Kimbark Ave.	Charles Listman
c. 1892	4830 S. Kimbark Ave.	A. W. Sullivan or William Craig, builder

HENRY FLETCHER STARBUCK (1850–1935)

Born in Nantucket, Henry Starbuck apprenticed in Boston under Harvard-educated architect Abel C. Martin. He formed his first of several partnerships in the area and then moved often, first to New Brunswick, then to Chicago for several years, followed by a brief stint in Milwaukee. Starbuck's most important work in Chicago is Quinn AME Chapel at Wabash and 24th Street, designed in 1891 and the oldest church for an African American congregation in the city.[182] By 1894 he had established a practice in California, where he earned a reputation as a specialist in church architecture.[183]

| 1884 | 5810 S. Harper Ave. | William and Anna W. Waterman |

STARRETT & FULLER
THEODORE STARRETT (1864–1917)
GEORGE ALLON FULLER (1851–1900)

Theodore Starrett was not an architect by training, but a structural engineer who had worked with Burnham & Root. He partnered with architect George A. Fuller for the construction of the Hyde Park Hotel. Starrett's brother, Paul, later became president of the George A. Fuller Company, a pioneering specialist in the construction of high-rises.

Fuller came to Chicago in 1883, where his first contract was for the Chicago Opera House, designed by Cobb & Frost.[184] He began with a daring concept for the time; the floor beams were made of steel. Fuller began to use the material in greater quantities and applications; he built the Tacoma and Pontiac Buildings with Holabird & Roche, and the steel skeleton of the Rand-McNally Building with Burnham & Root. The Fuller Company "revolutionized the building industry," coordinating all aspects of construction by hiring a series of smaller subcontractors, a process known today as general contracting.[185]

The company opened a New York office during the 1890s and built several large structures in that city, including Daniel Burnham's Flatiron Building, which was known briefly as the Fuller Building because the company headquarters were there. During the 1960s the firm still employed hundreds in the Chicago area; however, it was eventually sold and the assets liquidated.[186]

| 1887–1888 | 1511 E. 51st St., demolished 1962 | Hyde Park Hotel |
| 1892 | Four-story addition, demolished 1962 | Hyde Park Hotel |

STILES & STONE

CLARENCE LUTHER STILES, FAIA (1852–n.d.)

JOHN R. STONE (n.d.)

Clarence Stiles and John Stone specialized in the design of row houses and apartment buildings.[187]

1891	5324 S. Blackstone Ave.	Dr. Walter S. Johnson
1891	5332 S. Blackstone Ave.	William S. and Emma M. Johnson
1892	5723 S. Kenwood Ave.	Walter C. Nelson
1892	5725 S. Kenwood Ave.	Walter C. Nelson
1892	5727 S. Kenwood Ave.	Walter C. Nelson
1892	5729 S. Kenwood Ave.	Walter C. Nelson
1892	5732 S. Kenwood Ave.	Nicholas and Joanna C. Hunt
1892	5735 S. Kenwood Ave.	Walter C. Nelson
1892	5737 S. Kenwood Ave.	Walter C. Nelson
1894	5742–5744 S. Kenwood Ave.	Nicholas Hunt
1894	5762 S. Harper Ave.	Emma Over

John R. Stone:

1897	5701–5707 S. Kenwood Ave.	Walter Nelson
1897	1355, 1361 E. 57th St.	Walter Nelson
1898	5626 S. Blackstone Ave.	Lucy Norton
1898	5628 S. Blackstone Ave.	Lucy Norton
1898	5630 S. Blackstone Ave.	Lucy Norton
1898	5632 S. Blackstone Ave.	Lucy Norton
1898	5634 S. Blackstone Ave.	Lucy Norton
1898	5636 S. Blackstone Ave.	Lucy Norton
1898	5638 S. Blackstone Ave.	Lucy Norton
1898	5335 S. Harper Ave.	J. M. Marshall
1905	5740 S. Kimbark Ave.	F. G. Wright
1909	941–945 E. 52nd St.	E. F. Henshaw
1910	5700–5710 S. Kimbark Ave.	
1910	1227–1229 E. 57th St.	

STUDIO/GANG/ARCHITECTS

JEANNE GANG, FAIA (b. 1964)

One of two female architects to design a major building in the Hyde Park area, Jeanne Gang graduated with a BA in architecture from the University of Illinois in 1986. She received an MA from Harvard in 1993, exactly 100 years after architect Sophia Hayden designed the Women's Building for the 1893 Columbian Exposition.

After receiving a fellowship to study in Switzerland, Gang worked with influential Dutch architect Rem Koolhaas, then returned to Chicago to form an independent practice in 1997. Influenced by Koolhaas's provocative urban thinking, her studio's work is both innovative and award-winning, with projects that confront contemporary issues including density, climate, and sustainability (www.studiogang.net.people/jeannegang). Locally her work includes a renovation of the historic Del Prado and Shoreland Hotels, and an unbuilt twenty-eight-story condominium building that was the victim of the economic downturn of 2008.

2007	1616 E. 56th St.	Solstice on the Park, unbuilt
2010	5307 S. Hyde Park Blvd.	Del Prado renovation
2012	5454 S. Shore Dr.	Shoreland renovation, scheduled for completion 2013
2013	1525 E. Hyde Park Blvd.	City Hyde Park, scheduled for completion 2014

LOUIS HENRI SULLIVAN, FAIA (1856–1924)

One of the most noted and influential architects, Louis Sullivan was born in Boston and briefly studied architecture at MIT. His first job with architect Frank Furness in Philadelphia ended during the financial panic of 1873 when he was dismissed after only six months. However, with architects in great demand in the years immediately following the fire, Sullivan came to Chicago where his parents lived and found work with William LeBaron Jenney. After a year, he left to study at L'École des Beaux-Arts in Paris. He returned to Chicago and in 1879, Sullivan was hired by Dankmar Adler, and shortly became a full partner in the firm.[188]

Adler & Sullivan were widely acclaimed—known for theaters and synagogues, residences and high-rise buildings. Adler concentrated on the business aspects of the office and Sullivan on design. Sullivan became determined to develop a "cohesive relationship" between the form and the function of a building[189] and believed one could create a new architecture freed from the traditions of the past. He emphasized the form of a building with a bold use of ornaments, incorporating them into an organic whole. One of the firm's most important works is the Auditorium Building on Michigan Avenue, a mixed-use building that included offices, a hotel, and a majestic 4,200-seat theater. This period with Adler was the most prolific of Sullivan's career, inspiring a group of young Chicago architects, including Frank Lloyd Wright.

In the early 1890s the nation experienced deep financial difficulties, and Adler & Sullivan were not exempt. They parted ways in 1895, and at first Sullivan was a success, completing the Carson Pirie Scott Building between 1899 and 1904. The remainder of Sullivan's career was a story of decline, not in the strength of his designs, but in the ability to attract clients. Although he received commissions for a number of small banks and commercial buildings, he slowly sank into depression and poverty, living through his final years in obscurity. Yet today his legacy is clear—Sullivan fought vigorously for principles that have become the precepts of modern architecture.

| 1892 | 4575 S. Lake Park Ave., demolished | Albert W. and Mary Sullivan |

DAVID SWAN, AIA (b. 1940)

David Swan's work includes custom single-family homes, theaters, high-density low-rise housing developments, and historic restoration. Swan studied at the Illinois Institute of Technology, where he received a BA in architecture and an MA in city planning. Between 1962 and 1972 he worked in a variety of offices, including the Chicago Department of City Planning, the University of Auckland School of Architecture in New Zealand, and Maki Associates in Tokyo, Japan. Locally Swan worked in the offices of Loebl, Schlossman, Bennett & Dart, and Booth & Nagle, prior to establishing an independent practice in 1973.[190] On local projects, he typically functions as both architect and developer.

1980	1119–1125 E. 53rd St.	Speculative town houses
1985	5748, 5752, 5756 S. Kimbark Ave.	Speculative residences
1986–1994	48th St. between Lake Park and Dorchester Aves.	Kenwood Gateway Development
1990	Woodlawn Ave. and 47th St.	Kennicott Place Development

TALLMADGE & WATSON
THOMAS EDDY TALLMADGE, FAIA (1876–1940)
VERNON SPENCER WATSON, AIA (1879–1950)

Thomas Tallmadge, a graduate of the Massachusetts Institute of Technology, met Vernon Watson while both were employed at D. H. Burnham & Company. In 1905 they formed a partnership, were closely associated with other Prairie School architects, and practiced together until 1936. Tallmadge was considered a "brilliant and perceptive" architectural historian and is credited with the widely used term "Chicago School."[191]

1908	5605 S. Woodlawn Ave.	Robert and Greta Millikan
1908	5609 S. Woodlawn Ave.	Andrew C. and Lois A. McLaughlin
1908	1201 E. 56th St.	Clark B. and Winifred C. Whittier
1908	1215 E. 56th St.	Andrew Allen

WILLIAM C. THAYER (n.d.)

| 1889 | 5211–5221 S. Blackstone Ave. | Row houses for Myrtella Watkins |

TREAT & FOLTZ
SAMUEL ATWATER TREAT, FAIA (1839–1910)
FREDERICK L. FOLTZ, FAIA (1843–1916)

Samuel Treat was one of the city's earliest practicing architects. After enlisting during the Civil War, Treat returned to his native New Haven. Soon he departed for Chicago, and began his career as an assistant to C. E. Randall, where he met Frederick "Fritz" Foltz. Treat joined in partnership with Foltz the year after the Chicago fire, a time when architects were in high demand. Treat functioned as the business partner and Foltz was the designer of the firm.[192]

Foltz was born and educated in Germany and came to this country in 1866, first practicing in New York. Although responsible for many types of commissions, Foltz preferred residential work. He designed private houses and apartment buildings, including the first duplex constructed in Chicago, which once stood at the southeast corner of Chicago and Michigan Avenues across from the city's main waterworks.[193]

The partners established a reputation for planning large industrial plants, apartment buildings, and lavish residences, and worked together until 1897.[194]

1887	4439 S. Greenwood Ave., demolished	Thomas S. Fauntleroy
1887	4851 S. Drexel Blvd.	Martin and Carrie Ryerson
1888	4801 S. Kenwood Ave.	H. S. Coulter
1889	5120 S. Kenwood Ave.	Charles S. and Anne S. Dennis
1889	5730 S. Kenwood Ave.	William Patterson
by 1890	4900 S. Drexel Blvd., demolished	James Bolton
1892	5022 S. Greenwood Ave.	George A. and Cora Tripp
1892	5026 S. Greenwood Ave.	William O. and Eva Goodman
1892	5416 S. Harper Ave.	Orville M. and Angie Powers
1895	5130 S. University Ave.	Elisha E. and Cornelia M. K. Chandler

LEON FRANÇOIS URBAIN, AIA (1887–n.d.)

Leon Urbain was an architecture graduate of the University of Illinois. He worked for Spencer & Powers before opening his own firm in 1912.

| 1929 | 5528 S. Hyde Park Blvd. | Poinsettia Apartments |

JOHN MILLS VAN OSDEL (1811–1891)

The city's most well-known early architect, van Osdel arrived in the city in 1836 to design a home for then mayor William B. Ogden. Legend has it that van Osdel rushed to save blueprints for his projects during the great Chicago fire of 1871, burying them in the ground. At the time, he had practiced in the city for over thirty years and clearly was an astute man—his drawings were retrieved and work was able to proceed.[195] In her book Jean Block attributes to van Osdel the house for owner I. K. Hamilton.[196] However, van Osdel's death occurred six years prior to that date, and others have attributed the house to his son, John Mills van Osdel Jr. By 1900 the house was occupied by physician Frank Montgomery.

| c. 1873 | 4960 South Drexel Blvd., demolished | Robert D. Fowler |
| 1897 | 5548 S. Woodlawn Ave. | Irenus K. Hamilton (Frank H. Montgomery) |

VINCI/HAMP
JOHN VINCI, FAIA (b.1937)

One of seven children born to immigrant parents, John Vinci fully expected to join his father's small construction company, as did two of his brothers who became bricklayers. Instead Vinci enrolled at the nearest school in the neighborhood, the Illinois Institute of Technology, and received his degree in architecture in 1960. During his time as a student Vinci developed a lifelong interest in historic preservation and restoration, and today he is a nationally recognized authority in what was then a little-known field.[197]

Vinci began his architectural career at Skidmore, Owings & Merrill (1960) and the office of Brenner, Danforth, Rockwell (1962–1969). He opened his own office in 1970 with Larry Kenny, continuing independently from 1978 to 1994, and in 1995 entered into partnership with Philip Hamp. Over and above his work in preservation, Vinci is credited with the design of many new structures, and respected for his museum and exhibition installations at the Art Institute of Chicago and other museums and galleries nationwide.

When speaking of the way his career evolved Vinci spoke in terms of problem-solving "by thinking everything is a specimen — the site is a specimen, a work of art is a specimen, a building is a specimen. I'm there to look at them and solve the problem, not to create a showpiece."[198]

| 2000 | 4835 S. Greenwood Ave. | Allison and Susan Davis |

VON HOLST & FYFE
HERMANN VON HOLST, AIA (1874–1955)
JAMES L. FYFE (n.d.–1928)

Von Holst came to the United States in 1891 with his father, Hermann Eduard von Holst, a professor of history at the University of Chicago. The younger Von Holst studied at the university before continuing his studies at MIT, where he earned a BS degree in architecture in 1896.[199] He returned and entered the Chicago office of Shepley, Rutan & Coolidge, working there until 1905 when he began an independent practice. When Frank Lloyd Wright scandalously departed for Europe with the wife of a client in 1909, he left a number of commissions in various phases of completion.[200] Von Holst agreed to take over his practice if Wright's employee, architect Marion Mahony (Griffin), an "exceptionally talented artist and draftsman," remained.[201] Von Holst established an office with Fyfe in 1910; the partnership dissolved in 1918.[202] He was the author of *Modern American Homes* (1913) and lived in Hyde Park at 5801 Kenwood (1910).

| 1910 | 5028 S. Ellis Ave., garage | Charles DeLee |
| 1912 | 5700 S. Woodlawn Ave. | H. B. Horton |

HARRY HALE WATERMAN, AIA (1869–1948)

Waterman was born in Wisconsin but soon moved with his parents to Chicago. He attended, but did not graduate from, Northwestern University. Waterman began his architectural career as a draftsman in the office of Joseph Lyman Silsbee in 1886, at a time when Frank Lloyd Wright and George Washington Maher also worked for Silsbee.

Waterman left Silsbee's firm in June 1893 and, despite working alongside the two founders of the Prairie School, apparently had "no desire to establish a style of his own, preferring instead to do work in whatever style seemed appropriate to the particular project."[203] He was a self-promoter, however, arranging to have several of his houses published in the *Scientific American Architects and Builders Edition*, a predecessor of *House and Garden*. One of these residences was Waterman's own, on Longwood Drive in the Beverly neighborhood. The house is locally known as the "honeymoon cottage," because Waterman lived there from 1893 until the death of his first wife, Louise, in 1896.[204]

| 1905 | 4849 S. Kenwood Ave. | Harry H. and Emily Waterman |
| 1912 | 5621 S. University Ave. | C. C. Buckley |

HARRY WEESE & ASSOCIATES
HARRY MOHR WEESE, FAIA (1915–1998)
BENJAMIN WEESE, FAIA (b. 1929)

"A planner, a visionary," Harry Weese was known as "Chicago's conscience."[205] Throughout his career, Weese was a frank and honest promoter of "architecture and planning that embraced the social, political, and economic realities of urban life."[206] Studying at Yale and under the Finnish architect Alvar Aalto at MIT, he received his bachelor's degree in 1938. Weese was awarded a fellowship to study city planning at the Cranbrook Academy of Art, and began his career in the Chicago office of Skidmore, Owings & Merrill in 1939. During World War II, he served in the United States Navy and afterward returned to SOM until 1947, when Harry Weese & Associates was founded.

The firm's best-known designs include the Seventeenth Church of Christ Scientist on East Wacker Drive (1968), the Time-Life Building (1969), and the William J. Campbell United States Courthouse Annex (Metropolitan Correctional Center, 1965).[207] In addition, Weese engaged in historic renovation, as the chairman of the committee for Adler & Sullivan's Auditorium, he helped to save the structure from demolition.

| 1956 | 5617 S. Kenwood Ave. | D. Gale and Helen Johnson |

Harry's younger brother was associated with him for a period of twenty years, from 1957 until 1977. Ben Weese received both a bachelor's and master's degree from Harvard University, and also studied at the École des Beaux-Arts in Fontainebleau, France. He was named a Fellow of the AIA in 1974 and received a Distinguished Service Award from the Chicago chapter in 1984. In 1977 Ben Weese formed his own firm, which operates today as Weese, Langley, Weese.[208]

1960	5514 S. University Ave.	Stanley R. Pierce Dormitory
1958–1961	Blackstone Ave. and 54th St. (with I. M. Pei)	Hyde Park Cooperative Homes (Hyde Park A and B)
1958–1961	Lake Park Ave. between 56th and 57th Sts. (with I. M. Pei)	University Neighborhood Homes (Hyde Park A and B)
1958–1961	S. Harper Ave. between 56th and 57th Sts. (with I. M. Pei)	Hyde Park A and B
1958–1961	E. Park Place between Harper and Blackstone Aves. (with I. M. Pei)	East Harper Terrace (for Hyde Park A and B)
1971	4700 S. Lake Park Ave.	Lake Village East

WILSON & MARBLE
HORATIO R. WILSON, FAIA (1857–1917)
OLIVER W. MARBLE (n.d.)

Horatio Wilson was a well-known architect in Chicago and a member of the Western Association of Architects, the association that preceded the American Institute of Architects. Following its merger with the AIA, he became a fellow. Wilson's training began in the Chicago office of Charles J. Hull, working as a draftsman when he was twenty. In 1889, Wilson entered into partnership with another of Chicago's early architects, Oliver Marble.[209]

| 1891 | 4938, 4940, 4942, 4944 S. Ellis Ave. | C. A. Marshall |

1893	4628 Drexel Blvd.	Benjamin E. and Rose Bensinger
1894	4512 Drexel Blvd.	Herman Stern
1895	4331 Drexel Blvd., demolished	William and Louise G. Best
1896	4518 Drexel Blvd.	Maximilian Morganthau
1896	4950 S. Ellis Ave.	H. M. Wilcox

WILSON & MARSHALL

When Oliver Marble retired from the partnership of Wilson & Marble, Wilson hired nineteen-year-old Benjamin Marshall as a draftsman. Within two years they became partners, and the firm Wilson & Marshall operated between 1895 and 1902.

1898	4936 S. Ellis Ave.	Horatio and Lilie C. Wilson, developer
1898	NE Corner of Hyde Park Blvd. and Blackstone Ave., demolished	Salisbury Apartment Building
1899	4900 S. Ellis Ave.	Charles Samuel Roberts
1899	4906 S. Ellis Ave.	Robert H. and Minnie Lanyon
1899	4928 S. Ellis Ave.	
1899	5001 S. Greenwood Ave.	David F. and Catherine Bremner
1899	5009 S. Greenwood Ave.	David F. and Immelda Bremner Jr.
1901	1000 E. 48th St.	William T. and Mary Fenton
1902	4845 S. Ellis Ave.	Elliott H. and Mary Phelps

H. R. WILSON & COMPANY

Following the turn of the century, Wilson established an independent office and practiced for a decade, organizing the firm of H. R. Wilson & Company with John Armstrong.

1906	4905 S. Woodlawn Ave.	Frederic A. and Lida W. Price
1906	4929 S. Woodlawn Ave.	Charles E. Scribner
1907	4900 S. Woodlawn Ave.	Albert W. and Julia Wolfe
1907	4925 S. Woodlawn Ave.	Benjamin H. and Lee Conkling
1907	4943 S. Woodlawn Ave.	George and Elizabeth Birkhoff Jr.
1908	4815 S. Ellis Ave.	Harry D. and Ida R. Oppenheimer
1908	4804 S. Woodlawn Ave.	Robert and Persis B. McDougal
1908	5100 Hyde Park Blvd.	J. P. Smith and E. Smith
1909	5324–5330 S. Hyde Park Blvd.	Sherman T. Cooper
1910	4805 S. Drexel Blvd.	George B. and Lillian E. Robbins
1910	4801 S. Ellis Ave.	James C. and Agnes Hutchins
1910	5100–5116 S. Ellis Ave.	Gustav Freund
1910	4920 S. Kimbark Ave.	F. Edson and Lillian White
1910	949–953 E. Hyde Park Blvd.	Gustav Freund
c. 1910	4923 S. Kimbark Ave.	Albert W. and Harriet Harris
1913	4907 S. Kimbark Ave.	Edwin A. and Josephine Graff
1914	5625 S. University Ave.	George E. and Edith Shambaugh, Sr.
1915	4944 S. Woodlawn Ave.	John and Janey Grassell
1915	5238 S. Harper Ave.	Harper Theater, with architects Mark D. Kalischer and Z. Erol Smith
1917	4850 S. Greenwood Ave., addition to residence, demolished	H. E. Greenebaum
1917	1725 E. 53rd St. (with John A. Armstrong)	Sisson Hotel, Harry Sisson

YAU CHUN WONG, FAIA (1921–2000)

Born in Nanjing, China, Y. C. Wong studied architecture at the National Central University of China. He was awarded a scholarship at the Illinois Institute of Technology and came to Chicago to study under Ludwig Mies van der Rohe, earning his master's degree in 1951. Wong worked in Mies's office for seven years and at Skidmore, Owings & Merrill for a year prior to opening his own office in 1959. Except for several years when Wong was in partnership with R. Ogden Hannaford, he had his own firm, named Y. C. Wong & Associates.[210]

1961	1366–1380 E. Madison Park	Atrium Homes
1964	Woodlawn Ave. and 53rd St. and Woodlawn Ave. at 55th St.	Low-rental housing for the elderly
1966	1223–1239 Madison Park	Madison Park Townhomes
1967	1144–1158 E. 48th St.	Hyde Park–Kenwood Townhomes

FRANK LLOYD WRIGHT (1867–1959)

The leader among the Prairie School architects, Frank Lloyd Wright studied civil engineering at the University of Wisconsin. He arrived in Chicago in 1887. His early work in the office of Joseph Silsbee was in the fashionable Queen Anne and Shingle styles. A skilled draftsman, Wright was then hired by Dankmar Adler and Louis Sullivan, one of Chicago's most important and influential firms. Sullivan was Wright's mentor, and the young architect absorbed Sullivan's style of ornamentation based on American themes rather than traditional or European influences—an idea that Wright was later to fully develop.[211]

While employed by Adler & Sullivan, Wright accepted private commissions for seven houses. Despite his efforts to conceal these "bootleg" jobs, he was discovered. Sullivan abruptly terminated his five-year contract.[212] In 1893 Wright established his own architectural practice.

Although he received other types of commissions, Wright's effect on residential architecture in particular is profound. He reenvisioned the traditional house, opening up the interior plan, stressing the special connections between rooms, and unifying the relationship between the interior and the strong horizontal elements of the exterior.

1892	4414 S. Greenwood Ave., demolished 1963	Dr. Allison W. and Eliza M. Harlan
1892	4852 S. Kenwood Ave.	Warren and Minnie McArthur
1892	4858 S. Kenwood Ave.	George and Carrie Blossom
1892–1893	Transportation Building, demolished	World's Columbian Exposition
1897	5132 S. Woodlawn Ave.	Isidore H. and Ida Heller
1907	1332 E. 49th St.	Blossom Coach House
1909	5757 S. Woodlawn Ave.	Frederick and Lora Robie

WILLIAM CARBYS ZIMMERMAN, FAIA (1859–1932)

Born in Wisconsin, Zimmerman studied at MIT, graduated in 1880, and then worked for Burling & Adler, among others, eventually opening a private practice. He partnered with John Flanders between 1898 and 1908, after which he practiced independently at an office in Steinway Hall. He was appointed the Illinois state architect in 1905, a post Zimmerman held for nine years.[213]

1898	5544 S. Woodlawn Ave.	
1902	4840 S. Greenwood Ave.	Charles Adams Goodyear
1906	4841 S. Woodlawn Ave.	Frank K. and Effie Hoover
1908	5001 S. Ellis Ave.	William M. and Louise Crilly
1908	4940 S. Woodlawn Ave.	Frank B. and Carrie Stone
1909	5633 S. Woodlawn Ave.	Roy O. and Louisa McWilliams West

| 1909 | 5707 S. Woodlawn Ave. | W. B. and Eda R. Wolff |
| 1910 | 4906 S. Greenwood Ave. | William O. and Lois Cook Johnson |

EDMUND N. ZISOOK & ASSOCIATES

EDMUND NEWTON ZISOOK, AIA

The son of real estate developer Harry Zisook, architect Edmund Zisook received both his undergraduate and master's degree at the Illinois Institute of Technology.

| c. 1970 | 1039 E. 48th St. | Dr. Chauncey Morton |

Notes

CHAPTER ONE

1. According to the *Illinois Public Domain Land Tract Sales Database*, on May 13, 1835, Obadiah Hooper purchased the west half of the Northeast corner, Section 14, Township 38 North, Range 14 East. The eighty acres were sold at a cost of $1.25 per acre for a total purchase price of $100, http://www.ilsos.gov/GenealogyMWeb/PublicLandSalesNameServlet.

2. Watson's tavern was a simple structure, a cabin with a lean-to shed attached and surrounded by a stand of trees. There was a single fireplace with a window placed directly opposite, according to an unpublished 1938 Writer's Project by Lucretia Harper; Chicago History Museum.

3. "101 Facts about Hyde Park," *Hyde Park Herald*, March 17, 1933.

4. This property was located from Cornell west to Jefferson (Blackstone) Street, and Chestnut Street (52nd) south to Walnut Street (53rd). According to a "History of 5438 South Cornell" manuscript by Carolyn Osiek, an unknown owner lost this piece of land in 1841, and the sheriff sold the land for back taxes to Alexander Brand in 1842. The deed references "premises," indicating that the property was improved with at least one building. Brand sold the property to John S. Wheeler on December 2, 1844. John and Clarissa Wheeler then sold the 75.4 acres for $377 to Nathan W. Watson on December 21, 1844.

5. In 1951 Nelson Algren published an essay entitled *Chicago: City on the Make*, portraying Chicago's rich 120-year history as a mix of the downtrodden, of gangsters, and of corrupt politicians that represented the city as a whole.

6. Chicago's characteristics changed dramatically as the early settlers disappeared and the importance of the fur trade declined. In 1840 Joseph Balestier, a land speculator and lawyer, proclaimed, "Capacious warehouses and commodious dwellings have taken the place of the 'log and bark houses, low, filthy, and disgusting'—'The miserable race of men' have been superseded by a population distinguished for its intelligence and enterprise; and all the comforts of our Eastern homes are gathered around us." Jacqueline Peterson, "Goodbye Madore Beaubien: The Americanization of Early Chicago Society" *Chicago History* 9, no. 2 (Summer 1980): 111.

7. Douglas Cox and Michael Conzen, "1848," *Encyclopedia of Chicago* (Chicago: University of Chicago Press, 2004), B26.

8. For a further discussion of the importance of the year 1848 in the city's history see Michael P. Conzen, Douglas Knox, and Dennis H. Cremin, *1848 Turning Point for Chicago, Turning Point for the Region* (Chicago: Newberry Library, 1998).

9. John M. Scott, *The Bench and Bar of Chicago: Biographical Sketches* (Chicago: American Biographical Publishing Co.), 593.

10. Ibid., 592.

11. Josiah S. Currey, *Chicago: Its History and Its Builders; A Century of Marvelous Growth*, vol. 5 (Chicago: S. J. Clarke, 1912), 135.

12. Letter sent by Paul Cornell to his uncle Heman K. Hopkins in Glen Falls, New York,

dated May 21, 1848. Paul Cornell Collection (manuscript) c. 1853–1893, Chicago History Museum.

13. Stephen Douglas was the Democratic opponent of Abraham Lincoln in the presidential election of 1860. At the time, the issue of slavery was a major concern in the city. Lincoln was viewed as opposed to the expansion of slavery, while Douglas was thought to be open to expansion. While many Chicagoans did not believe in the equality of the races, most were opposed to the institution of slavery. Douglas recognized that Chicagoans at the time typically supported Republican candidates, and did not put forth much effort there during the election. In Chicago 10,697 votes were cast for Abraham Lincoln and 8,094 for Douglas. Robert E. Bailey and Elaine Shemoney Evans, *Early Chicago, 1833–1871: A Selection of City Council Proceedings Files* (Springfield: Illinois State Archives, 1986), available at http://www.cyberdriveillinois.com/departments/archives/early_chicago/home.html.

Douglas developed his property; he established two residential parks and donated land for the establishment of Chicago University, the precursor of the University of Chicago. In 1856 Douglas constructed a residence at 34 East 35th Street. Olivia Mahoney, "The Past and the Promise," *Chicago History* 24, no. 1 (Spring 1995): 21.

14. "Gallery of Celebrities," *Chicago Tribune*, March 25, 1900.

15. William Bross, Charles Cleaver, Joseph Jefferson, and Alfred Andreas, *Reminiscences of Chicago during the Forties and Fifties* (Chicago: Lakeside Press, 1913), 59.

16. Charles Cleaver, *Early Chicago Reminiscences* (Chicago: Fergus Printing, 1882), 42–43.

17. "How Chicago's Suburbs Were Planned and Named," *Chicago Tribune*, March 4, 1900.

18. The Boyd survey map has been the subject of searches by various parties interested in the Hyde Park community; however no record of it has been located to date.

19. This section of the Watson property was sold to Thomas Webb on May 26, 1854. Webb purchased 63.67 acres of their original tract. The Watsons had earlier sold 6.55 acres to the Illinois Central Railroad for $5,000. Thomas and Josephine Webb sold half of it on May 26, 1855, for $11,750 to Paul Cornell. The other half of the Webbs' property they sold to James L. Crane, except for ten acres on the north end sold to John Borden. Paul and Helen G. Cornell took out a mortgage from James L. Crane to buy the other half on May 15, 1856.

20. Cornell and James L. Crane purchased eighty acres to the west of the Garnsey land from the Trustees of the Illinois & Michigan Canal on August 6, 1855. The Hyde Park Land Company began improvements in 1856. *Twenty-Fifth Anniversary of the First Presbyterian Church, Hyde Park, Illinois* (April 1885): 8.

21. Paul Stanford, "Electric Commuting and a Cleaner Hyde Park," *Hyde Park History* 1 (Chicago: Hyde Park Historical Society, 1980), 14–16.

22. Carleton J. Corliss, *Main Line of Mid-America: The Story of the Illinois Central* (New York: Creative Age Press, 1950), 346.

23. According to Andreas's *History of Cook County*, initially three trains were scheduled to run in each direction, but only as far south as 56th Street; A. T. Andreas, *History of Cook County, Illinois: From the Earliest Period to the Present Time* (Chicago: A. T. Andreas, 1884).

24. According to a paper read to the Chicago Historical Society on February 20, 1883, William K. Ackerman recollected several nonrevenue riders on the initial trip: conductor H. L. Robinson, a friend of Abraham Lincoln, ex-mayor Thomas Dyer, Hon. William T. Barron, ex-probate judge, Charles Cleaver, founder of Cleaverville, Perkins Bass, Junius Mulvey, and Paul Cornell.

25. Joseph Kirkland, *The Story of Chicago*, vol. 1 (Chicago: Dibble Publishing, 1892), 222.

26. The "Hyde Park Special" schedule initially offered four round trips daily; however, by September, ridership was low and the train leaving Central Station at 6:00 a.m. and Hyde Park at 6:30 a.m. was discontinued. Corliss, *Main Line of Mid-America*, 347–49.

27. Lewis Mumford, *The City in History: Its Origins, Its Transformations, and Its Prospects* (Harcourt, 1989), 484–85.

28. Ibid., 490.

29. Lewis Mumford, *The City in History: Its Origins, Its Transformations, and Its Prospects* (Harcourt, 1989), 485.

30. According to Andreas, *History of Cook County*, 531, Paul Cornell stipulated that all purchasers of his lots situate their houses twenty feet from the front edge of the lot. He may

have accomplished this through the use of deed restrictions, although no actual documents representing or confirming this have been uncovered.

31. Jean Block, *Hyde Park Houses* (Chicago: University of Chicago Press, 1977), 4.

32. In 1910 on the twenty-fifth anniversary of the Hyde Park Presbyterian Church, Mrs. Hibbard recalled the neighborhood's earliest days: "Fifty years ago Hyde Park was a cluster of scattered houses, less than a score, dropped down among the oak trees. There was no store, no post office, no market, and a single passenger car on the Illinois Central, three times a day, was the only connection with the city except Purcell's ox-cart, which served as an express to bring from the city barrels of flour and groceries. The one sidewalk, a board-walk on Lake Avenue, was fringed with ferns and violets, wild flowers and strawberries", http://www.archive.org/details/fiftiethanniversoounit.

33. Eliza Denison Jameson recalled first coming to Hyde Park in 1856, at a time when there was nothing but "sand hills, prairie, trees, and wild flowers." The following year her husband, Judge Jameson, built their home on the incorrect lot and sold it, erecting one in the proper position. By the spring of 1858 they finally settled at the corner of Cornell and 53rd Street. She remembered only seven other families living in Hyde Park: those of Warren S. Bogue, Chauncey Stickney, Paul Cornell, Dr. A. B. Newkirk, Charles Spring Sr., Charles Spring Jr., and Dr. Kennicott. Andreas, *History of Cook County*, 532.

34. Ann Durkin Keating, *Building Chicago: Suburban Developers and the Creation of a Divided Metropolis* (Columbus: Ohio State University Press, 1988), 30.

35. Paul Cornell accomplished this by purchasing a tract of six hundred acres near the intersection of the Illinois Central and Lake Shore & Michigan Central railroads from William B. Ogden in 1854. He predicted this site south of his Hyde Park holdings would become valuable as a location for factories and industry.

36. Hassan Hopkins operated the small grocery store in a small space "about ten feet square." At the time it opened, Hopkins recalled, there were only two residents nearby, Michael Purcell and Dan (possibly John) Hogan, squatters on the Illinois Central land. Andreas, *History of Chicago*, 531.

37. Julia Abrahamson. *A Neighborhood Finds Itself* (New York: Biblo and Tannen, 1971), 4.

38. Annie McClure Hitchcock, "Reminiscences," manuscript, Chicago History Museum.

39. "Visit to Hyde Park: A New Summer Resort," *Chicago Tribune*, July 20, 1859.

40. "Environs of Chicago: Hyde Park," *Chicago Tribune*, April 28, 1859.

41. From a letter written by Paul Cornell, dated January 3, 1861, to Hon. Wm. H. Osborn. Illinois Central Railroad Archives, ICH N1.5, Box 201, Folder 155, Newberry Library.

42. In 1848, Illinois townships were established as units of state government under the 2nd Illinois Constitution. In a township form of government, board members were popularly elected from districts based on towns, and were directly responsible for conducting business necessary to maintain their communities. "TOI History," Township Officials of Illinois, http://www.toi.org/About/History.aspx.

43. The election was held to fill the positions of supervisor, town clerk, collector, three commissioners of highways, two constables, two justice of the peace and one pound master. The supervisor was responsible for all taxes collected in the town except for those related to highways and bridges.

44. "Kenwood Named for Pioneer's Home by General McClellan," *Chicago Tribune*, March 2, 1930.

45. Dr. Kennicott came to Chicago via Milwaukee, arriving in 1853. According to Andreas' *History of Cook County*, his most valuable contribution to dentistry was to cap exposed nerves of teeth, as opposed to "the barbarous practice of killing them."

46. "Mabel Kennicott Gleason, First White Child Born in Hyde Park, Is Spending Summer Here," *Hyde Park Herald*, September 6, 1929.

47. The Kennicott house was substantially built of a solid oak frame and heavy stone. When it was torn down in 1908 to make way for a three-story apartment building, it took workmen an entire month to dismantle the structure, and the cellar had to be removed with dynamite. Ibid. An image of the house is available: Paul Gilbert and Charles Bryson, *Chicago and Its Makers* (Chicago: Felix Mendelsohn, 1929), 500.

48. Remmer and Waters both lived on Lake Park Avenue (then Hyde Park Avenue or Lake Street) between 48th and 49th Streets.

49. Corliss, *Main Line of Mid-America*, 349–50.

50. Sherman came to Chicago from New York; a specialist in civil law, he had "few peers." Scott, *The Bench and Bar of Chicago*, 604–5.

51. John Dickinson Sherman was not born in this house in 1859, but in that of his great uncle, Mayor James H. Woodworth. He graduated from Hyde Park High School in 1876, and after college became a correspondent for the *Chicago Tribune*, working his way up to city editor. Sherman and his wife Mary Belle King lived at 4433 Lake Avenue. *A History of the City of Chicago: Its Men and Institutions; Biographical Sketches of Leading Citizens*, 325, http://fkdocs.sesp.northwestern.edu/nodes/show/57202.

52. "All Gone Now, Even the Village," *Hyde Park Herald*, May 15, 1892.

53. Currey, *Chicago*, 5:340.

54. A native of Massachusetts and a teacher and composer of music, George Frederick Root (1820–1895) helped establish the New York Normal Institute, an institution dedicated to training music teachers. His brother, Ebenezer Root, founded the musical publishing firm Root & Cady in Chicago in 1858, and George moved to Chicago to join him the following year. With the outbreak of the Civil War, Root composed more than thirty inspirational war songs. Root later moved, J. W. Connorton's *1883 Directory* lists his address as 5320 Jefferson (Harper).

55. In 1826 the Illinois General Assembly petitioned the US Congress to request a grant of public land, for the construction of a proposed canal. The following year Congress gave Illinois part of the public domain that was to be used for the construction of the waterway. In addition to the area set aside for the Illinois & Michigan Canal, Congress gave to the state alternate sections of land five miles on either side of the proposed route to be sold to finance construction. The governor appointed three canal commissioners who were responsible for the establishment of a canal route and to oversee sales of lands. For further information on the canal see: Michael P. Conzen and Kay J. Carr, eds., *The Illinois & Michigan Canal National Heritage Corridor: A Guide to Its History and Sources* (DeKalb: Northern Illinois University Press, 1988).

56. Mrs. B. F. Ayer, "Old Hyde Park," in *Chicago Yesterdays: A Sheaf of Reminiscences*, ed. Caroline Kirkland (Chicago: Daughaday, 1919), 179.

57. Ibid., 180.

58. "Egandale," *Chicago Tribune*, May 28, 1859.

59. "Hon. William B. Egan," *Chicago Tribune*, October 29, 1860.

60. James B. Runnion, *Out of Town* (Chicago: Western News Co., 1869), 7.

61. Scott, *The Bench and Bar of Chicago*, 595.

62. "Hyde Park Politics, 1861–1919," *Hyde Park History* 2 (Chicago: Hyde Park Historical Society, 1980), 8.

63. The estimated cost of purchasing the land for the South Parks was $1,865,750. However it was soon determined that the actual cost would greatly exceed the estimate, and by June 1871 the amount was nearly doubled, rising to $3,320,000. Andreas, *History of Chicago*, 167.

64. Out of thirty-three entries Olmstead and Vaux won the competition to design New York City's Central Park in 1858. They are considered to be the "founders of the profession of landscape architecture in America," and their "Greensward Plan" became one of the most significant works in the history of American landscape architecture. "The History of Central Park," Central Park Conservancy, http://www.centralparknyc.org/visit/history/.

65. Runnion, *Out of Town*, 8.

66. Ibid.

67. Lewis Mumford, *The City in History: Its Origins, Its Transformations, and Its Prospects* (Harcourt, 1989), 440.

68. Early in 1831 Chicago's population hovered around five hundred, and the town was comprised of 175 buildings. It was estimated that by the summer of that same year 160 frame houses were quickly built to accommodate newcomers. The population swelled to 3,265 by the fall of 1835. In a letter Caroline Clark described the growing city. "The buildings are now mostly small and look as though they have been put up as quickly as possible, many of them are what they call here balloon houses, that is built of boards entirely—not a stick of timber in them except for the sills." Mabel R. Skjelver, "The Balloon Frame: The Housing System of the Common Man," *Journal of Interior Design Education and Research* 7.2: 28.

69. "Balloon Frames Launch World-Class Architecture," *Chicago Tribune*, January 30, 1983.

70. "Thieving at Hyde Park," *Chicago Tribune*, June 28, 1860.

71. "Saturday's Fires," *Chicago Tribune*, August 16, 1868.

72. According to Carolyn Osiek's history of the property at 5438 South Cornell, on April 29, 1864, Sophia Sachse, wife of physician and surgeon Dr. Theodore Sachse, purchased lots 6, 7, and 8 of Block 38 for $2,800. The Sachse home would have stood north of 55th Street on the west side of Cornell. The year after the fire, lots 6–9 were sold to John Johnson Jr. on April 21, 1869, for $14,690.

73. Paul T. Gilbert, *Chicago and Its Makers* (Chicago: F. Mendelsohn, 1929), 637. In July 1856 Cornell wed Helen M. Gray, and the following year they settled in Hyde Park. Her family was from Bowdoinham, Massachusetts, and her sisters also married prominent Chicago men. Margaret married John Evans, the founder of Evanston, Illinois, and later governor of the territory of Colorado; Cornelia married Orrington Lunt, a founder of Northwestern University; and Elizabeth married George Masten Kimbark, Hyde Park's early settler and the developer of the Riverside, Illinois, community.

74. Scott, *The Bench and Bar of Chicago*, 596.

75. "Stephen A. Douglas Inspired Paul Cornell to Found Hyde Park: John E. Cornell Tells Lions of Illustrious Father," *Hyde Park Herald*, October 2, 1931.

76. "History," United Church of Hyde Park, http://uchpeace.org/?page_id=10.

77. "The Hyde Park House," *Chicago Tribune*, March 13, 1866.

78. Although Hyde Park House was less expensive than the downtown hotels, it remains curious that Mrs. Lincoln would choose it as a place of refuge. Mary Lincoln's circle of friends had dwindled as she "continued to graft partisanship onto her private affairs." Her relationship with Julia Jayne Trumbull, the wife of Hyde Park Township resident Senator Lyman Trumbull, ended because Mary believed Julia should have influenced her husband's politics. Mary dismissed her once-intimate friend as "ungainly," "unpopular," and "cold." Jean H. Baker, *Mary Todd Lincoln: A Biography* (New York: W. W. Norton 1987), 150.

During that "hot, disease-ridden summer" of 1865 Mrs. Lincoln spent her days "contemplating the waves of Lake Michigan," returning correspondence, and walking through the nearby park. She saw almost no one, for she did not have "sufficient courage, to receive but very few of her friends" (255).

79. Jim Stronks, "Mary Todd Lincoln's Sad Summer in Hyde Park," *Hyde Park History* 20 (Chicago: Hyde Park Historical Society, 1988).

80. Charles Lachman, *The Last Lincolns, Rise and Fall of a Great American Family* (New York: Sterling Publishing, 2008), 77.

81. "Father of Hyde Park Was Young Lawyer," *Chicago Tribune*, April 20, 1961.

82. Maria Bockée Flint, *The Bockée Family (Bocquet) 1641–1897* (Poughkeepsie, NY, 1897), 76.

83. Jacob Bockée enlisted as an assistant surgeon on February 19, 1862, and was commissioned in Company S of the 13th Regiment. He was promoted to a full surgeon a month and a half later. Bockée mustered out on March 1, 1866. Historical Data Systems, comp., American Civil War Soldiers website (Provo, UT: Ancestry.com Operations, 1999), http://search.ancestry.com/search/db.aspx?dbid=3737.

84. "Hyde Park Home Built in 1857 Is Occupied by 23," *Chicago Tribune*, November 8, 1942.

85. Gerald Foster, *American Houses: A Field Guide to the Architecture of the Home* (Boston: Houghton Mifflin, 2004), 242.

86. "S. Shore Group Tries to Blend Past, Present," *Chicago Tribune*, November 7, 1978.

87. Wilbert Hasbrouck, "Field-Pullman-Heyworth House: Architectural and Historical Assessment" (April 1980). Prepared for the South Shore Historical Society, Calumet City Library.

88. Sarah Downey, "Old Glory," *Chicago Magazine*, April 2006.

89. "Have You a Ewe?" *Chicago Tribune*, August 26, 1917.

90. Wilbert Hasborouck, "Field-Pullman Heyworth House, Architectural and Historical Assessment" (April 1980).

91. "Civil War Composer's Home Becomes Landmark," *Hyde Park Herald*, May 23, 1990.

92. John Drury, *Old Chicago Houses* (Chicago: University of Chicago Press, 1941), 250–53.

93. "Civil War Composer's Home Becomes Landmark," *Hyde Park Herald*, May 23, 1990.

94. Ibid.

95. Ibid.

96. Bridges was commissioned as an officer in Company G of the 18th Illinois Infantry on July 30, 1861. He was promoted to a full captain the following January and full major in December 1864. Historical Data Systems, American Civil War Soldiers.

97. *Chicago Census Report and Statistical Review: Embracing a Complete Directory of the City* (Chicago: Richard Edwards Directory Publisher, 1871).

98. William P. Blake, ed., *Reports of the United States Commissioners to the Paris Universal Exposition, 1867* (Washington; Government Printing Office, 1870), 253, 257.

99. Michael O'Brien, "Aesthetic and Production Theories as Enablers of Prefabricated Housing," *Without a Hitch: New Directions in Prefabricated Architecture* (Amherst: University of Massachusetts, 2008): 256.

100. "Obituary," *San Francisco Chronicle*, April 12, 1919.

101. Samuel M. Fassett, salt print of Abraham Lincoln taken October 4, 1859, Smithsonian Institution, http://www.civilwar.si.edu/lincoln_byfassett.html.

102. Harriett Taylor Upton, *History of the Western Reserve*, vol. 1 (Lewis Publishing Company, 1910), 582.

103. Drury, *Old Chicago Houses*, 256.

104. Ibid., 258.

105. Jean Block, *Hyde Park Houses* (Chicago: University of Chicago Press, 1978), 43.

106. Ibid., 14.

107. Joseph C. Bigott, *From Cottage to Bungalow: Housing the Working Class in Metropolitan Chicago* (Chicago: University of Chicago Press, 2001), 22.

108. Drury, *Old Chicago Houses*, 260.

109. John I. Bennett, "Memorial," *Hyde Park Herald*, August 22, 1885.

110. "Marched with Sherman," *Reading Eagle*, November 9, 1926.

111. *The Beginnings of True Railway Mail Service* (Lakeside Press, 1906), 23.

112. "Mrs. Martha H. Ten Eyck," obituary, *Chicago Tribune*, March 12, 1917.

113. "5704 Dorchester," *Hyde Park Herald*, June 9, 1965.

114. John W. Reps, "Horace William Shaler Cleveland," *Urban Planning, 1794–1918: An International Anthology of Articles, Conference Papers and Reports* (Cornell University, updated 2002), http://www.library.cornell.edu?Reps/DOCS/hwscleve.htm.

115. Daniel Joseph Nadenicek, *Nature and Ideology: Natural Garden Design in the Twentieth Century* (Washington, DC: Dumbarton Oaks Research Library, 1997), 79, available at http://www.doaks.org/publications/doaks_online_publications/Nature/natur005.pdf.

116. Horace William Shaler Cleveland, *Landscape Architecture, as Applied to the Wants of The West; With an Essay on Forest Planting on the Great Plains* (Chicago: Jansen, McClurg, 1873), 37–38.

117. Ibid., 33–34.

118. Charles Lachman, *The Last Lincolns, the Rise and Fall of a Great American Family* (New York: Sterling Publishing, 2008). 77.

119. "J. Young Scammon Gone," *Chicago Tribune*, March 18, 1890.

120. Ibid.

121. "Mrs. J. Y. Scammon Dies Two Days after Big Gift," *Chicago Tribune*, May 6, 1901.

122. David Allen Robertson, *The University of Chicago: An Official Guide* (Chicago: Chicago University Press, 1919), 118.

123. Reps, "Horace William Shaler Cleveland."

124. By the 1870s Kenwood earned the moniker "Lake Forest of the South Side," comparing the community's wealthy attributes with Chicago's premiere north shore suburb. "Kenwood," in *The Encyclopedia of Chicago*, ed. James R. Grossman et al. (Chicago: University of Chicago Press, 2004), 445.

125. "Laborer" James Liston and his wife Mary appear in the 1860 US Census. Although they were born in Ireland, their two-year old son was born in Illinois.

126. The 1860 US Census lists "Legman" Bailey, a thirty-year old teamster, his wife Catherine, and a one-year-old child. The child was born in Illinois and the parents in Ireland. There were two common laborers, also Irish, residing with them. And even in these modest quarters, a seventeen-year-old domestic servant is recorded.

127. "'Peggy' Sheehan, the Squatter, Dies," *Chicago Tribune*, May 5, 1897.

128. "Hon. Norman B. Judd," *Chicago Tribune*, November 12, 1878.

129. Annie McClure Hitchcock, "Reminiscences," manuscript, Chicago History Museum.

130. Andreas, *History of Chicago*, 19.

131. "History," United Church of Hyde Park, http://uchpeace.org/?page_id=10.

132. Frances F. Browne, *The Everyday Life of Abraham Lincoln*, 2nd ed. (Chicago: Brown & Howell, 1913), 73.

133. "Letter from Mary Todd Lincoln to David Davis, January 17, 1861," Justin G. Turner and Linda Levitt Turner, editor, *Mary Todd Lincoln: Her Life and Letters*, 71.

134. "Hon. Norman B. Judd," *Chicago Tribune*, November 12, 1878.

135. Ibid.

136. "Many Honor Memory of Mrs. Charles Hitchcock," *Chicago Tribune*, July 4, 1922.

137. Hitchcock, "Reminiscences."

138. Ibid.

139. Ibid.

140. Ibid.

141. Ibid.

142. "Fearful Railroad Accident," *Chicago Tribune*, January 9, 1862.

143. Hitchcock, "Reminiscences."

144. Ibid.

145. Ibid.

146. Ayer, "Old Hyde Park," 185.

147. Hitchcock, "Reminiscences."

148. What remained of the Hitchcock estate was sold to Richard M. O'Brien, who lived in the house for nearly thirty years. In 1950 the house was sold to Tom Floyd and graced Greenwood Avenue at least until 1964. The Hitchcock house stood for over one hundred years and was for a time the oldest in Kenwood. A developer purchased the property in the late sixties, intending to construct five houses. A gray brick bi-level was the only one completed on the property prior to landmark status of the Kenwood neighborhood.

149. "A Pleasant Kenwood Musicale," *Chicago Tribune*, February 22, 1891.

150. A native of Massachusetts, Charles Hitchcock came to Chicago in 1854. He established a "large and lucrative" practice and ventured briefly in politics, holding two public offices. After his marriage he spent his time in "the beautiful home in Kenwood," which they made a "place for their domestic affections and a center of refined and generous hospitality." Scott, *The Bench and Bar of Chicago*, 408.

151. Brandon L. Johnson, "Annie Hitchcock," in *Building for a Long Future: The University of Chicago and Its Donors, 1889–1930* (Chicago: University of Chicago Library, 2001), www.lib.uchicago.edu/e/spcl/excat/donorsint.html.

152. "Hitchcock Gift Is Presented," *Chicago Tribune*, February 20, 1900.

153. Jean Block, *The Uses of Gothic* (Chicago: University of Chicago, 1983), 115.

154. Ibid., 115.

155. "News of Society World," *Chicago Tribune*, August 10, 1902.

156. "620 Acre Tract Brings $100,000," *Chicago Tribune*, July 23, 1916.

157. Daughter Mary E. Remmer occupied the home at 4827 South Lake Street for many years, and donated several images of the two Remmer houses to the History Museum.

158. "Ezra Leander Brainerd," in The Genealogy of the Brainerd-Brainard Family in America, 1649–1908, http://www.ebooksread.com/authors-eng/lucy-abigail-brainard/the-genealogy-of-the-brainerd-brainard-family-in-america-1649–1908-iar/page-41-the-genealogy-of-the-brainerd-brainard-family-in-america-1649–1908-iar.shtml.

159. Runnion, *Out of Town*, 10.

160. The 1880 US Census lists lawyer Ezra L. Brainerd, his wife Harriett, and four sons residing on Woodlawn Avenue, near the house of Christopher Bouton.

161. *Encyclopedia of Biography of Illinois*, vol. 1. (Chicago: Century Publishing and Engraving, 1892), 43.

162. At the time they incorporated the firm, the Bouton brothers did not live in Kenwood. The 1871 *Chicago City Directory* lists Christopher Bouton as residing at 1131 Indiana Avenue. Nathaniel had also not yet moved to Kenwood, his address is listed as 590 Wabash.

163. Currey, *Chicago*, 5:225–27.

164. James Boughton, *Bouton-Boughton Family* (Albany: Joel Munsell's Sons 1890), 112.

165. Runnion, *Out of Town*, 7.

166. "The History of the Pacific Garden Mission," Pacific Garden Mission website, http://www.pgm.org/abt_history1.html.

167. "Chicago Victims of the Fire," *New York Times*, March 21, 1899; "Windsor Hotel Lies in Ashes," *New York Times*, March 18, 1899.

168. "Warren F. Leland Dead," *New York Times*, April 5, 1899.

169. "Wreck Leland Home to Make Way for Hotel," *Chicago Tribune*, August 3, 1917.

170. A mile north of the Kenwood, the small town of Cleaverville was laid out by Charles Cleaver. He had purchased a small soap and candle making company in 1835, originally located in a log barn at the north branch of the Chicago River at Kinzie Street. According to Andreas's *History of Chicago*, Cleaver purchased twenty acres from Samuel Ellis in 1851, and although many thought him foolish for moving his factory so far out of the city, before long the Illinois Central Railroad passed nearby.

In 1853 he and his wife Mary Brooks built a house at what would now be 3938 South Ellis. It was called Oakwood Hall and became the nucleus of the little settlement, which eventually gave its name to Oakwood Boulevard and the entire area. Cleaver erected numerous houses in his development; however, the great drawback to the area was that the mosquitoes were bad. His hopes were that by draining the low-lying land, the pests would disappear. Cleaver's development did not fare well. In April 1889 the *Chicago Tribune* wrote that he went from "well-to-do to comparatively poor." Cleaver died in his son's residence at 4741 Kenwood Avenue. "Old Resident Dies," *Chicago Tribune*, October 29, 1893.

171. Allan G. Bogue, *The Earnest Men: Republicans of the Civil War Senate* (Ithaca: Cornell University Press, 2009), 41.

172. Paul Gilbert and Charles Lee Bryson, *Chicago and Its Makers* (Felix Mendelsohn, 1929), 641.

173. Harry E. Pratt, ed., *Concerning Mr. Lincoln: Lincoln as He Appeared to Letter writers of His Time* (Springfield: Abraham Lincoln Association, 1944), 75.

174. Mark M. Krug, *Lyman Trumbull: Conservative Radical* (New York: A. S. Barnes & Co., 1965), 170.

175. Abraham Lincoln and Mary Todd were married in the home of Ninian and Elizabeth Edwards in Springfield, Illinois, on November 4, 1842. Julia Jayne lived near Mary Todd's sister and brother-in-law. When Julia married Trumbull on June 21, 1843 Norman Judd was his groomsman. Horace White, *The Life of Lyman Trumbull* (Boston: Houghton Mifflin, 1913), 15.

176. William Lee Miller, *Lincoln's Virtues* (Alfred A. Knopf, 2002), 312.

177. Ralph J. Roske, *His Own Counsel: The Life and Times of Lyman Trumbull* (Reno: University of Nevada Press, 1979), 114.

178. Drury, *Old Chicago Houses*, 267.

179. "Proceedings of the Illinois State Bar Association" (Springfield, 1889), 28.

180. "Lyman Trumbull," *New York Times*, July 6, 1872.

181. George Trumbull to William C. Ackerman, October 26, 1876, Newberry Library, Illinois Central Archives, ICII N1.5, Box 202, Folder 458.

CHAPTER TWO

1. Karen Sawislak, *Smoldering City: Chicagoans and the Great Fire, 1871–1874* (Chicago: University of Chicago Press), 25–27.

2. Harold M. Mayer, *Chicago: Growth of a Metropolis* (Chicago: University of Chicago Press, 1969), 106.

3. "Fire of 1871," in *The Encyclopedia of Chicago*, ed. James R. Grossman et al. (Chicago: University of Chicago Press, 2004), 297.

4. "Early Chicago, 1833–1871: A Selection of Documents from the Illinois State Archives", http://www.cyberdriveillinois.com/departments/archives/teaching_packages/early_chicago/home.html

5. Mayer, *Chicago*, 120.

6. Donald L. Miller, *City of the Century: The Epic of Chicago and the Making of America* (New York: Simon & Schuster, 1996), 275.

7. Sawislak, *Smoldering City*, 13.

8. Christine Meisner Rosen, *Limits of Power: Great Fires and the Process of City Growth in America* (Cambridge: Cambridge University Press, 1986), 140.

9. "South Parks System 1869–1900," The City in a Garden: A Photographic History of Chicago's Parks website, http://www.chicagoparkdistrict.com/history/city-in-a-garden/south-park-system/

10. Therese O'Malley and Marc Treib, eds., *Regional Garden Design in the United Sates*, vol. 15 (Washington: Dumbarton Oaks for Harvard University, 1995), 82.

11. "Gallery of Local Celebrities: Paul Cornell," *Chicago Tribune*, March 25, 1900.

12. Block, *Hyde Park Houses* (Chicago: University of Chicago Press, 1978), 22.

13. Figures for the August 10, 1872, election were taken from "A History of Hyde Park: A Study in Local Government," written by University of Chicago student Laura Willard in 1896, and available at the Chicago History Museum.

14. For one example of a suburb near Chicago with a similar form of government, see Village Governmental Structure, Village of Palatine, http://www.palatine.il.us/government/default.aspx.

15. Block, *Hyde Park Houses*, 23.

16. "Our Special Improvement System," *Hyde Park Herald*, January 30, 1886.

17. Block, *Hyde Park Houses*, 19.

18. *Chicago Herald*, November 3, 1887.

19. Block, *Hyde Park Houses*, 20.

20. Ibid.

21. In 1874, one publication dealing with Chicago suburbs stated, "Kenwood is the Lake Forest of the south, without the exclusiveness of its northern rival." "Kenwood," in *The Encyclopedia of Chicago*, ed. James R. Grossman et al. (Chicago: University of Chicago Press, 2004), 445.

22. Dan Rottenberg, *The Man Who Made Wall Street: Anthony J. Drexel and the Rise of Modern Finance* (New York: University of Pennsylvania, 2006), 203.

23. For a general discussion of the development of *boulevard*, see Jan Cigliano and Sarah Bradford Landau, *Grand American Avenue 1850-1920* (San Francisco; Pomegranate Artbooks, 1994.)

24. "Real Estate," *Chicago Tribune*, November 1, 1885.

25. Gwendolyn Wright, *Moralism and the Model Home: Domestic Architecture and Cultural Conflict in Chicago, 1873–1913* (Chicago: University of Chicago Press, 1985), 98–99.

26. Catherine Esther Beecher was an early leader in the field of home economics and the author of *Woman Suffrage and Woman's Profession* (Hartford: Brown & Gross, 1871).

27. "History of the American Institute of Architects," American Institute of Architects website, http://www.aia.org/about/history/AIAB028819.

28. James D. McCabe, *The Illustrated History of the Centennial Exhibition* (Philadelphia: National, 1876), 609.

29. Wright, *Moralism and the Model Home*, 97.

30. Block, *Hyde Park Houses*, 37.

31. Ibid., 95.

32. *Annual Reports of the President and Village Officers of the Village of Hyde Park* (Chicago: S. D. Childs & Co., 1887)

33. Wright, *Moralism and the Model Home*, 75.

34. Block, *Hyde Park Houses*, 34.

35. "Hyde Park," *Chicago Tribune*, June 2, 1878.

36. Mrs. B. F. Ayer, "Old Hyde Park," in *Chicago Yesterdays: A Sheaf of Remembrances*, ed. Caroline Kirkland (Chicago: Daughaday, 1919), 182–83.

37. In 1883 a group of prominent Chicagoans formed the Washington Park Jockey Club, purchasing land to establish an exclusive venue for horse racing that opened the following year. Located at 61st and Cottage Grove, the prestigious club operated until 1905 when a ban on gambling was enacted. Steven A. Riess, "Horse Racing," Encyclopedia of Chicago website, http://www.encyclopedia.chicagohistory.org/pages/601.html.

38. The Chicago Public Library took over the books of the public, but noncirculating, Hyde Park Lyceum. In 1904 these books became part of the T. B. Blackstone Branch of the city library, housed in a building designed by Solon Beman and named for Timothy Blackstone, a noted businessman, developer, and philanthropist. Curiously the Blackstones were not Hyde Park residents. "A Treasure in our Midst," Hyde Park Kenwood Community Conference, http://www.hydepark.org/communityorganizations/culture/blackstone.htm.

39. Block, *Hyde Park Houses*, 22.

40. "Real Estate," *Hyde Park Herald*, May 10, 1884.

41. "The Inadequacy of Our Village Government," *Hyde Park Herald*, February 4, 1887.

42. "Big Land Deals in Hyde Park," *Hyde Park Herald*, January 18, 1889.

43. Paul Markun, "Village Problems and City Solutions: A Divided Hyde Park Chooses Chicago," Hyde Park Historical Society, no. 1, 1980.

44. Josiah S. Currey, *Chicago: Its History and Its Builders; A Century of Marvelous Growth*, vol. 5 (Chicago: S. J. Clarke, 1912), 335.

45. "All Gone Now, Even the Village," *Chicago Tribune*, May 15, 1892.

46. "Village of Hyde Park," *Hyde Park Herald*, September 5, 1885.

47. "Death in Hotel Helene Fire," *Chicago Tribune*, May 16, 1900.

48. "Hotel Helene Set Afire," *Chicago Tribune*, June 3, 1900.

49. "Fredricks, Porter of Burned Hotel Helene, Arrested in New York," *Chicago Tribune*, June 13, 1900.

50. "Hotel Helene Set Afire," *Chicago Tribune*, June 3, 1900.

51. The boundaries of the Ayer property were 52nd Street south to 53rd Street, Drexel east to Wharton (University).

52. Ayer, "Old Hyde Park," 181.

53. Currey, *Chicago*, 5:425.

54. Samuel Agnew Schreiner, *The Trials of Mrs. Lincoln* (Bison Books, 1987), 43.

55. "An Insanity Episode," *New York Times*, June 4, 2010.

56. John M Scott, The Bench and Bar of Chicago: Biographical Sketches website, 552, http://www.archive.org/stream/benchbarofchicagoochic/benchbarofchicagoochic_djvu.txt.

57. Letter from William K. Ackerman to H. Osborn Esq., October 31, 1876. Illinois Central Railroad Archives, Newberry Library, ICIIN1.5, Box 202, Folder 478.

58. "Hyde Park Real Estate," *Hyde Park Herald*, October 24, 1885.

59. "Conflagrations," *Chicago Tribune*, January 15, 1884.

60. Ibid.

61. "Rising From Its Ashes," *Hyde Park Herald*, January 26, 1884.

62. Ayer, "Old Hyde Park," 181.

63. "Old Hutch," as Benjamin P. Hutchinson was familiarly known, came to Chicago in 1856. With a "limited education," Hutchinson worked in the pork packinghouse business with the firm of Burt, Hutchinson & Snow. When the firm dissolved, he organized the Chicago Packing and Provision Company, and was known for eliminating brokers and doing business directly. Hutchinson became a grain speculator and founded the Corn Exchange Bank, opening an office in the Board of Trade in 1888 at the height of his success. However within three years he found himself on the wrong side of a deal, and was "financially crushed." "B. P. Hutchison Dead," *New York Times*, March 17, 1899.

64. John Drury, *Old Chicago Houses* (Chicago: University of Chicago Press, 1941), 281–83.

65. "People & Events: Charles Lawrence Hutchinson (1854–1924) and the Art Institute of Chicago," American Experience: Chicago City of the Century website, http://www.pbs.org/wgbh/amex/chicago/peopleevents/p_hutchinson.html.

66. Ibid.

67. A twentieth-century art historian, Vincent Scully, coined the term "Stick Style." For further reading see Vincent Joseph Scully, *The Shingle Style and the Stick Style: Architectural Theory and Design from Richardson to the origins of Wright* (New Haven, CT: Yale University Press, 1955).

68. Gerald L. Foster, *American Houses: A Field Guide to the Architecture of the Home* (Boston: Houghton Mifflin, 2004), 266.

69. "A Line o Type or Two," *Chicago Tribune*, June 25, 1959.

70. Ibid.

71. Henry Cleaveland, William Backus, and Samuel D. Backus, *Village and Farm Cottages: The Requirements of American Village Homes* (New York: D. Appleton, 1856), 157. "Cleaveland" is more commonly spelled "Cleveland."

72. "Victory," *Hyde Park Herald*, April 1, 1887.

73. "Wedding Bells," *Hyde Park Herald*, June 14, 1884.

74. In 1882 Bennett constructed 5436, 5438, 5440, and 5442 South Dorchester in addition to 5437, 5439, 5441, 5443, 5405, 5411, 5413, 5419, 5423, 5427, 5429, 5443, 5445, 5447, 5455, 5456, 5458, 5465, 5467, 5470, 5475, 5476, 5477, and 5481 Ridgewood Court. Block, *Hyde*

Park Houses, 116, 122. The *Hyde Park Herald* notes construction began on eight homes for Bennett on Madison Avenue and Tompkins Place in 1885. "Hyde Park Real Estate," *Hyde Park Herald*, October 24, 1885.

75. "Mrs. Ott, Pioneer of Hyde Park, Dies at 93," *Hyde Park Herald*, May 19, 1933.

76. "Hyde Park Hotel Is Purchased for about $500,000," *Chicago Tribune*, December 14, 1947.

77. "Just Outside the City," *Chicago Tribune*, January 13, 1889.

78. "Once Proud Hyde Park Hotel Will Be Torn Down for Progress," *Chicago Tribune*, December 2, 1962.

79. "Hyde Park Hotel Is Purchased for about $500,000," *Chicago Tribune*, December 14, 1947.

80. "Rescuing a Small But Sweet Piece of Local History," *Hyde Park Herald*, July 21, 2004.

81. "Sidewalks of Hyde Park," *Hyde Park Herald*, July 11, 1930.

82. "Rosalie Music Hall," *Hyde Park Herald*, June 6, 1885.

83. Ibid.

84. "Real Estate: Rosalie Villas; A Contemplated Improvement at South Park," *Hyde Park Herald*, January 19, 1884.

85. *Chicago Legal News* 20:7 (April 1858): 259.

86. Scott, *The Bench and Bar of Chicago*, 582–84.

87. "History," United Church of Hyde Park website, http://uchpeace.org/?page_id=10.

88. According to the Illinois State Archives Marriage Index, Higgins married Elizabeth S. Alexander in 1847. According to Andreas' *History of Cook County*, they moved to Kenwood in 1866. Elizabeth died in 1882, and the following year Higgins remarried, to Lena M. Morse.

89. Transcript of a letter from Martha Freeman Esmond to her friend Julia Boyd of New York, April 29, 1893. Herma Clark, "When Chicago Was Young," *Chicago Tribune*, April 20, 1941.

90. "Hyde Park's Fence War," *Chicago Tribune*, August 21, 1891.

91. Al Chase, "Boul Mich Residence Last to Go," *Chicago Tribune*, July 30, 1929.

92. "Hyde Park's Fence War," *Chicago Tribune*, August 21, 1891.

93. Ibid.

94. Ibid.

95. "Twelve More One-Story Cottages," *Chicago Tribune*, July 31, 1890.

96. "Mr. Dunham's Big Fence," *Chicago Tribune*, August 20, 1891.

97. "Hyde Park's Fence War," *Chicago Tribune*, August 21, 1891.

98. Al Chase, "Boul Mich Residence Last to Go," *Chicago Tribune*, July 30, 1929.

99. "Dunham-Higgins Feud is Recalled," *Chicago Tribune*, June 7, 1896.

100. Ibid.

101. Virginia was Dunham's daughter and his last surviving heir; she passed away in 1928 at nearly eighty years of age.

102. Drury, *Old Chicago Houses*, 264.

103. Ibid., 266.

104. Terry Heller, "A Sketch of the Lives of Henry Jewett Furber, Sr. and Jr.," June 2008, http://www.public.coe.edu/~theller/soj/unc/tame-indians/furber-fam.html.

105. "Gorham History," Gorham 1831 website, www.gorham1831.com.

106. The Furbers' Victorian silver service is now housed at the Rhode Island School of Design. The Gorham Company purchased the silver from Furber's son in 1927 and donated it to the school in 1991. The serving pieces and hollowware depict images of nymphs and cherubs, and the flatware is decorated with cranes, cherry blossoms, and parasols. "School Acquires Large Silver Collection," *New York Times*, December 19, 1991.

107. "North America Life's Troubles," *New York Times*, February 28, 1887.

108. "Real Estate: A General Review of the Market during the Week," *Hyde Park Herald*, March 1, 1884.

109. Scott, *The Bench and Bar of Chicago*, 509–10.

110. "Silver Settings Reflect the Past," *New York Times*, May 5, 1960.

111. *Important Americana: Furniture, Folk Art, Silver, Porcelain, Prints, and Carpets* (New York: Sotheby's, 2012), lot 87, "An American Parcel-Gilt Silver Wine Cooler circa 1875." http://www.sothebys.com/en/catalogues/ecatalogue.html/2012/americana-n08823#/r=/en/

ecat.fhtml.No8823.html+r.m=/en/ecat.lot.No8823.html/87/+r.o=/en/ecat.notes.No8823.
html/87/.

112. Terry Heller, "A Sketch of the Lives of Henry Furber, Sr. and Jr.," June 2008; www.
public.coe.edu/~theller/soj/unc/tame-indians/furber-fam.html.

113. "Chicago Real Estate," *Chicago Tribune*, March 10, 1889.

114. Although awarded to Chicago, the location for the Olympic games was moved to
St. Louis, Missouri. George Matthews and Sandra Marshall, *St. Louis Olympics* (Chicago:
Arcadia Publishing, 2003), 7.

115. "Mr. Strahorn's Idaho Investment," *Hyde Park Herald*, January 18, 1889.

116. "Real Estate: General Review of the Market during the Week Just Passed," *Hyde Park
Herald*, May 10, 1884.

117. "Real Estate: General Review of the Market During the Week Ending Thursday
Night," *Hyde Park Herald*, March 29, 1884.

118. *The Economist: A Weekly Financial, Commercial and Real-Estate Newspaper* 27
(June 28, 1902), 838.

119. "Biographical Note," in "Guide to the Wallace Heckman Papers, 1871–1926," University of Chicago Library, Special Collections Research Center, http://www.lib.uchicago.
edu/e/scrc/findingaids/view.php?eadid=ICU.SPCL.WHECKMAN.

120. Thomas Wakefield Goodspeed, *A History of the University of Chicago: The First
Quarter Century* (Chicago: University of Chicago Press, 1916), 337.

121. Drury, *Old Illinois Houses*, 204.

122. "Lowden State Park," Illinois Department of Natural Resources website, http://dnr.
state.il.us/lands/landmgt/parks/r1/lowdensp.htm.

123. "Biographical Note," in "Guide to the Wallace Heckman Papers," University of Chicago Library, Special Collections Research Center, http://ead.lib.uchicago.edu.

124. "The Curious Case of Dr. Adamson B. Newkirk," *Hyde Park History* 12, nos. 1 and 2
(Chicago: Hyde Park Historical Society, 1990).

125. A. T. Andreas, *History of Cook County, Illinois: From the Earliest Period to the Present Time* (Chicago: A. T. Andreas, 1884), 539.

126. *Maryland Historical Magazine*, 1.8, Maryland Historical Society, Baltimore, 1913,
p.331.

127. "Hail Stars and Stripes," *Chicago Tribune*, November 1, 1896.

128. "Real Estate," *Hyde Park Herald*, June 7, 1884.

129. "Flag Dedication Put Off," *Chicago Tribune*, June 19, 1898.

130. *Album of Genealogy and Biography, Cook County, Illinois with Portraits*, 4th rev. ed.
(Chicago: Calumet Book & Engraving, 1896), 16.

131. Ibid.

132. "Horace M. Dupee," A. T. Andreas, *History of Cook County* (Chicago: A. T. Andreas, 1884), 15.

133. "Kenwood," *Hyde Park Herald*, November 9, 1888.

134. "Real Estate," *Hyde Park Herald*, January 12, 1884.

135. "Real Estate," *Hyde Park Herald*, April 12, 1884.

136. Oakwood Boulevard was constructed as part of the South Parks Plan. It extends for
half a mile, connecting Grand Boulevard (now Martin Luther King Jr. Drive) with Drexel
Boulevard at Cottage Grove.

137. "Real Estate," *Hyde Park Herald*, June 7, 1884.

138. Mitchell C. Harrison, *Prominent and Progressive Americans: An Encyclopedia of
Contemporaneous Biography*, vol. 1 (New York: New York Tribune, 1902), 73.

139. "Death List of a Day," *New York Times*, March 21, 1904.

140. "Ward Residence Sale One of the Year's Biggest," *Chicago Tribune*, January 1, 1921.

141. "KAM-Isaiah Israel addition will soon be completed," *Hyde Park Herald*, July 25,
1973.

142. Linda E. Smeins, *Building an American Identity: Pattern Book Houses and Communities, 1870–1900* (Walnut Creek; AltaMira Press,1999) 267.

143. Alice Sinkevitch, *AIA Guide to Chicago*, 2nd ed. (Chicago: Mariner Books, 2004),
426.

144. Walter J. Karcheski, Jr., "George F. Harding Jr. and His 'Castle,'" *Arms and Armor:
Highlights of the Permanent Collection*, Art Institute of Chicago.

145. Drury, *Old Chicago Houses*, 288.

146. "Shaw-Wells Family Papers, 1792-1977, Descriptive Inventory," Chicago History Museum, http://chsmedia.org/media/fa/fa/M-S/Shaw-Wells-inv.htm

147. "Wherein George F. Harding Guides Tour of Famous Art Museum in Lake Pk. Home," *Hyde Park Herald*, May 10, 1929.

148. "Harding Museum Fighting Condemnation by the City," *Hyde Park Herald*, October 30, 1963.

149. Karcheski, Jr., "George F. Harding Jr. and His 'Castle.'"

150. Susan S. Benjamin and Stuart Earl Cohen, *Great Houses of Chicago, 1871–1921* (New York: Acanthus, 2008), 31.

151. "Alonzo Fuller, Pioneer Wholesale Grocer, Dead," *Chicago Tribune*, May 25, 1928.

152. "Real Estate," *Hyde Park Herald*, May 10, 1884.

153. Thomas S. Hines, *Burnham of Chicago: Architect and Planner* (Chicago: University of Chicago Press, 2009), 31.

154. Ibid., 29.

155. Miller, *City of the Century*, 311.

156. Walter S. Adams, "Biographical Memoir of George Ellery Hale," *National Academy of Sciences* 21 (1939), 12.

157. "George Ellery Hale," University of Chicago Faculty, University of Chicago Centennial Catalogues, http://www.lib.uchicago.edu/e/spcl/centcat/fac/facch04_01.html.

158. Alice Sinkevitch, "John H. Nolan House," in *AIA Guide to Chicago* (San Diego: Harcourt Brace, 1993), 406.

159. Benjamin and Cohen, *Great Houses of Chicago*, 33.

160. Thomas S. Hines, *Burnham of Chicago: Architect and Planner* (Chicago: University of Chicago Press, 2009), 36.

161. Currey, *Chicago*, 5:66.

162. Block, *Hyde Park Houses*, 32.

163. Patrice Cunningham, *Reforming Women's Fashion 1850–1920: Politics, Health, and Art* (Kent, OH: Kent State University Press, 2003), 164.

164. Ibid.

165. Mr. and Mrs. Martin Ryerson Collection, Art Institute of Chicago, www.artic.edu/artaccess/AA_American/pages/Amer_Ryerson.html.

166. "The Ryerson Home," Chicago Chapter, Society of Architectural Historians Tour, June 26, 2010.

167. John W. Boyer, "Martin Ryerson," *in Building for a Long Future: The University of Chicago and Its Donors, 1889–1930* (Chicago: University of Chicago Library, 2001), http://www.lib.uchicago.edu/e/spcl/excat/donors1.html#b.

168. By the middle of the nineteenth century, manufacturing these elixirs was a "major industry in America." Remedies were sold to the public claiming to cure or prevent nearly every known ailment. The remedies' ingredients were seldom disclosed and the language used to promote the product was less than realistic. In 1906, Congress, paving the way for action against "unlabeled or unsafe ingredients, [and] misleading advertising," passed the Pure Food and Drug Act. "History of Patent Medicine," Hagley Museum and Library, Wilmington, DE, http://www.hagley.org/library/exhibits/patentmed/history/history.html.

169. For further information on McGill and the Chateauesque style see: "McGill House, Preliminary Landmarks Recommendation Report," City of Chicago website, May 4, 2005, http://www.cityofchicago.org/content/dam/city/depts/zlup/Historic_Preservation/Publications/McGill_House.pdf.

CHAPTER THREE

1. Erik Larson, *The Devil in the White City: Murder Magic and Madness at the Fair That Changed America* (New York: Crown Publishers, 2003), 13.

2. Jean Block, *The Uses of Gothic* (Chicago: University of Chicago Press, 1983), 5.

3. For a complete history of the old University of Chicago, including images of the buildings, see Thomas Wakefield Goodspeed, *A History of the University of Chicago: The First Quarter Century* (Chicago: University of Chicago Press, 1916), 1–19.

4. Ibid., 10.

5. William Rainey Harper and other leaders of American universities recognized the potential impact of urbanization on the future of higher education. "A university which

shall adapt itself to urban influence, which will undertake to serve as an expression of urban civilization, and which is compelled to meet the demands of an urban environment," commented Harper in a 1902 speech at Columbia University, will "gradually take on new characteristics both outward and inward, and it will ultimately form a new type of university." "The University and the City," *Chicago History* (Spring-Summer 1992): 38.

6. Goodspeed, *A History of the University of Chicago*, 83.

7. The site proposed for the university consisted of three blocks of six and two-thirds acres each, and was between 56th and 59th Streets, Ellis to Greenwood. The north half was a gift of Marshall Field; the south half was purchased from him for $132,000. Ibid., 476.

8. David Allen Robertson, *The University of Chicago: An Official Guide* (Chicago: Chicago University Press, 1919), 2–3.

9. Muriel Beadle, *The Hyde Park–Kenwood Urban Renewal Years: A History to Date* (Chicago: N.p., 1964), 2.

10. "A Brief History of the University of Chicago," The University of Chicago News Office, http://www-news.uchicago.edu/resources/brief-history.html.

11. In 1856 the Presbyterian Theological Seminary of the Northwest selected a site on the lakeshore between 53rd and 54th Street for their college. Paul Cornell conveyed eighteen acres to the seminary, fenced in the land, and planted shade trees according to Andreas's *History of Cook County* (Chicago: A. T. Andreas, 1884), 529. G. P. Randall designed plans for the college building to be constructed at a cost of $180,000. Cyrus McCormick donated $100,000 for an institution; however, his gift required that the location be north of the Chicago River. The land was conveyed back to Cornell and the Hyde Park House was subsequently constructed on a portion of the site.

12. Three of six firms responded to an invitation by the board of trustees to submit sketches for the university's first buildings. On June 6, 1891, the board decided to erect three buildings, a divinity-school dormitory, a university dormitory, and a "recitation building." Henry Ives Cobb was selected as the architect. Goodspeed, A *History of the University of Chicago*, 219.

13. "History of the University," University of Chicago, www.uchicago.edu/about/history.shtml.

14. Robertson, *The University of Chicago*, 9.

15. After eight ballots, Congress approved Chicago as the site of the 1893 exposition on February 24, 1890.

16. The board of directors created a construction department that included Burnham & Root, engineer Abram Gottleib, and Olmsted & Co. as landscape architects. Harlow Niles Higinbotham, *Report of the President to the Board of Directors of the World's Columbian Exposition, 1892–93* (Chicago: Rand McNally, 1898), 28.

17. The initial site recommended for the fair was in the central business district, on "a strip of vacant ground" between Michigan Avenue and the Illinois Central Railroad tracks, from Randolph south to 12th Street. Extensive landfill would be required to provide two hundred acres for the exposition. The "most important features of the Exposition" were proposed to be located here, and the remainder placed in Jackson Park. While many favored this idea for the benefits it would bring to the heart of the city, in the end a split location was not acceptable. After extensive consideration and much negotiation, on November 25, 1890, the World's Columbian Commission adopted the general plan for a site within Jackson Park and the Midway. Harlow Niles Higinbotham, *Report of the President to the Board of Directors of the World's Columbian Exposition, 1892–93* (Chicago: Rand McNally, 1898), 19–28.

18. Carl W. Condit, *The Rise of the Skyscraper* (Chicago: University of Chicago Press, 1952), 209.

19. According to the *New York Times*, "News of the World's Fair," April 15, 1892, George Pullman donated the site, and the Women's Dormitory Association was organized with a capitol stock of $125,000. Furnished rooms were offered at thirty cents a day.

20. Moses P. Handy, *The Official Directory of the World's Columbian Exposition . . . A Reference Book of Exhibitors and Exhibits, of the Officers and Members . . . and General Information concerning the Fair* (Chicago: W. B. Conkey, 1893), 205.

21. "Quarters for Women," *Chicago Tribune*, September 17, 1892.

22. Robin Faith Bachin, *Building the South Side: Urban Space and Civic Culture in Chicago, 1890–1919* (Chicago: University of Chicago Press, 2008), 39.

23. Ibid., 42.

24. On May 1, 1893, the opening day of the exposition, the Illinois Central put its world's fair cars into use for the first time. The bench seats, which each held five people, were arranged crosswise within the car. The exits were at either end of the car, enabling travelers to step off quickly when the train came to a stop. Canvas curtains covered the openings for protection against the rain. Higinbotham, *Report of the President*, 209–10.

25. Ibid., 306.

26. Wilbert R. Hasbrouck, *The Chicago Architectural Club: Prelude to the Modern* (New York: Monacelli, 2005), 129.

27. Higinbotham, *Report of the President*, 29.

28. The Venetian Village was to be a structure placed at the end of a large pier extending into the lake from the Court of Honor. The plan was later withdrawn. Higinbotham, *Report of the President*, 29–31.

29. Hasbrouck, *The Chicago Architectural Club*, 131.

30. Burnham was observed by Nellie Mitchell in the hours after his partner's death. She later recounted this version of Burnham's despair to her niece. Thomas Hines, *Burnham of Chicago: Architect and Planner*, 2nd ed. (Chicago: University of Chicago Press, 2009), 82.

31. "John Wellborn Root," *The National Cyclopaedia of American Biography*, vol. 7 (New York: James T. White & Co., 1898), 114.

32. Lynn Becker, "An Odd Way to Honor Burnham," *Chicago Reader*, July 16, 2009.

33. "Photographs Recall the Glories of Chicago's Columbian Exposition," *New York Times*, April 9, 1978.

34. Thomas Eddy Tallmadge, *The Story of Architecture in America* (New York: W. W. Norton, 1936), 207.

35. Herbert K. Russell, *Edgar Lee Masters: A Biography* (Urbana: University of Illinois Press, 2001), 36.

36. Bruce Craig, "Expositions Inspire Host of Inventions," *Chicago Tribune*, July 16, 1997.

37. Electricity and its various applications were a main focus of the fair, demonstrated by the Edison, Westinghouse, and Western Electric companies. The miniature electric house focused on potential uses of electricity: a push-button doorbell, the convenience of electrical light switches, the warmth of electric heat, and cooling breezes of electric fans. There were telephones and telegraph instruments, a portable phonograph and electrical music boxes, and electric stoves and dishwashers to make everyday life easier. "Exhibit of Electricity," *Chicago Tribune*, April 12, 1891.

38. "World Columbian Exposition (1893)," *Chicago Tribune*, http://www.chicago-tribune.com/topic/science-technology/technology/world-columbian-exposition-(1893)-EVHST000087.topic.

39. Hyde Park was at the forefront of the progressive movement, and by one estimate between 1892 and 1919, 32 percent of the leading reformers in Chicago lived within the borders of 40th and 60th Streets, from Drexel Boulevard to the lake. Andrew Yox, "Hyde Park Politics, 1861–1919," *Hyde Park History* 2 (Chicago: Hyde Park Historical Society, 1980), 23.

40. Founded by Jane Addams and Ellen Starr Gates in 1889, Hull House provided support to the disadvantaged citizens of Chicago's Near West Side neighborhood. According to the *Jane Addams Hull House Association* website, the mission of Hull-House was to "Provide a center for a higher social and civic life, to institute and maintain educational and philanthropic enterprises and to investigate and improve the condition in the industrial districts of Chicago."

41. Jane Adams Hull-House Museum, http://www.uic.edu/jaddams/hull/_learn/_about-jane/aboutjane.html.

42. Horace White, *The Life of Lyman Trumbull* (Boston; Houghton Mifflin Company, 1913), 413-414.

43. Andrew E. Kersten, *Clarence Darrow,: American Iconoclast* (New York: Hill and Wang, 2011), 74-77.

44. Olmsted's firm remained true to their original concept for the park, and the new design of Jackson Park included an interconnected series of serene lagoons with lushly planted shores. The plan also incorporated an elongated meadow for lawn tennis and the first public golf course in the Midwest, and an eighteen-hole course that still exists today.

45. "Village Items," *Hyde Park Herald*, May 24, 1884.

46. Ibid.

47. "Fruit Stand's Gone," *Chicago Tribune*, May 10, 1896.

48. Local property owners began to purchase all available lots in order to keep away commercial enterprises and apartment buildings. Upon learning of a proposed butcher shop at the northwest corner of Woodlawn and 47th Street, Eugene S. Kimball (4706 South Woodlawn) purchased the 100' × 150' lot in order to protect the value of his nearby property. "Stores and Flats Barred," *Chicago Tribune*, August 11, 1901.

49. "To Fight Lake Avenue Boulevard," *Chicago Tribune*, April 19, 1897.

50. Masters married Helen Jenkins, the daughter of affluent lawyer and president of the Metropolitan Elevated Railroad Robert Jenkins. The Jenkins family resided at 4200 Drexel, where the newlyweds occupied the third floor. Herbert K. Russell, *Edgar Lee Masters: A Biography* (Urbana: University of Illinois Press, 2001), 41–44.

51. "Lorado Taft, Art," University of Chicago Centennial Catalogues, http://www.lib.uchicago.edu/e/spcl/centcat/fac/facch19_01.html.

52. The full text is available in Bruce Brooks Pfeiffer, ed., *Frank Lloyd Wright Collected Writings*, vol. 1, *1894–1930* (New York: Rizzoli, 1992).

53. John Ruskin and William Morris were leaders of the British Arts and Crafts movement. They stressed the integrity of materials, the beauty of natural finishes, and simple design. When American architects incorporated elements of the movement, they took the concept a step further, stressing the relationship of a structure to the natural environment of the surroundings.

54. Bachin, *Building the South Side*, 53.

55. "The University and the City," *Chicago History* (Spring and Summer 1992).

56. Bachin, *Building the South Side*, 53.

57. "Thirty Per Cent Living in Flats," *Chicago Tribune*, April 21, 1901.

58. Al Chase, "Stony Island's Old Art Center Property Sold," *Chicago Tribune*, December 8, 1946.

59. Walter Bates Rideout, *Sherwood Anderson: A Writer in America*, vol. 1 (Madison: University of Wisconsin Press, 2006), 169.

60. Al Chase, "Stony Island's Old Art Center Property Sold," *Chicago Tribune*, December 8, 1946.

61. Robert Grimm, "Art Colony Folds its Easels, But Not Quietly," *Chicago Tribune*, May 20, 1962.

62. Block, *The Uses of Gothic*, 190.

63. Ibid., 53.

64. "Among Architects and Builders," *Chicago Tribune*, August 14, 1892.

65. "Chicago Beach Hotel Is Sued," *Chicago Tribune*, April 3, 1910.

66. Ibid.

67. "Warren F. Leland Dead," *New York Times*, April 5, 1899.

68. "At Hyde Park," *Chicago Tribune*, October 7, 1892.

69. William R. Host and Brooke A. Portmann, *Early Chicago Hotels* (Charleston, SC: Arcadia, 2006), 103.

70. Ibid.

71. "Chicago Beach Hotel Is Sued," *Chicago Tribune*, April 3, 1910.

72. "Citizens Ask Demolition of Ancient Hotel," *Chicago Tribune*, April 14, 1957.

73. William R. Host and Brooke Anne Portman, *Early Chicago Hotels* (Charleston, SC: Arcadia, 2006), 114–15.

74. "Edna Ferber, 1885–1968," Chicago Tribute Markers of Distinction, http://www.chicagotribune.org/Markers/Ferber.htm.

75. Edna Ferber, *The Girls* (New York: Doubleday, Page, 1921), 176.

76. "Fire in Fair Hotel," *Chicago Tribune*, October 30, 1893.

77. "Pond & Pond," Chicago Landmarks, City of Chicago website, http://webapps.cityofchicago.org/landmarksweb/web/architectdetails.htm?arcId=12.

78. Frances Wells Shaw, *Concerning Howard Shaw in His Home*, 1926, comp. Evelyn Shaw McCutcheon (1977) (N.p.: Howard van Doren Shaw Society, 1997), available at http://www.marktown.org/pdf/concerning_howard_van_doren_shaw.pdf.

79. Virginia Greene, "Howard van Doren Shaw (Chicago: Chicago Review Press, 1998), 45.

80. Obituary Notices, George E. Vincent (1864–1941), 273–74.

81. J. P. Lichtenberger, "George E. Vincent 1864–1941," *American Sociological Review* (1941): 273–75, available at http://www2.asanet.org/governance/vincentobit.html.

82. John Heyl Vincent, *The Chautauqua Movement* (Boston: Chautauqua Press, 1886), 2.

83. Jean F. Block, *Hyde Park Houses* (Chicago: University of Chicago Press, 1978), 85.

84. "Biographical Note," in "Guide to the William Gardner Hale Papers, circa 1880–1928," University of Chicago Library, Special Collections Research Center, http://www.lib.uchicago.edu/e/scrc/findingaids/view.php?eadid=ICU.SPCL.HALEWG

85. Ibid.

86. John M. Manly, "Frederick Ives Carpenter: November 29, 1861–January 28, 1925," *Modern Philology* 122, no. 4 (May 1925): 421.

87. "Biographical Note," in "Guide to the Frederick Ives Carpenter Papers, 1885–1925," University of Chicago Library, Special Collections Research Center, http://www.lib.uchicago.edu/e/scrc/findingaids/view.php?eadid=ICU.SPCL.CARPENTER.

88. James Cate Lea, ed., *Medieval and Historiographical Essays: In Honor of James Westfall Thompson* (Chicago: University of Chicago Press, 1938), vii.

89. "James Thompson, Educator, 72, Dies," *New York Times*, October 1, 1941.

90. US Department of the Interior, National Park Service, *National Register of Historic Places: Nomination Form*, 49.

91. For the complete story of the American Dodd family in Berlin see Erik Larsen, *In the Garden of Beasts* (New York: Crown, 2011).

92. "Guide to the Virginia Eckels Malone Family Papers, 1854–1974," the University of Chicago Library, Special Collections Research Center, http://www.lib.uchicago.edu/e/scrc/findingaids/view.php?eadid=ICU.SPCL.ECKELSMALONEV&q=cromwell%20collection.

93. "The Nobel Prize in Physics 1938, Enrico Fermi," Nobel Prize website, http://www.nobelprize.org/nobel_prizes/physics/laureates/1938/fermi-bio.html.

94. "The Quiet Man Who Helped to Build the Atom Bomb," *Hyde Park Herald*, September 21, 1983.

95. "Mayors Make Gold Mine for New Booklet: Facts on City's Chiefs Listed," *Chicago Tribune*, December 30, 1947.

96. "Before Jane Byrne, There Were 40," *Chicago Tribune*, May 20, 1979.

97. "G. C. Howland Dies: On First Staff at U. of C.," *Chicago Tribune*, June 6, 1954.

98. Tim Samuelson, "Hyde Park and Kenwood Issue: Beyond the Robie House," *Chicago Reader*, March 4, 2010.

99. Ibid.

100. B. H. Willier, "Frank Rattray Lillie, 1870–1947: A Biographical Memoir," (Washington, DC: National Academy of Sciences, 1957), 183.

101. "Frank R. and Frances Crane Lillie," in *Building for the Long Future: the University of Chicago and Its Donors, 1889–1930* (Chicago: University of Chicago Library, 2001), available at http://www.lib.uchicago.edu/e/spcl/excat/donors4.html.

102. "Rich Woman Now Socialist," *New York Times*, December 8, 1915.

103. Samuelson, "Hyde Park & Kenwood Issue."

104. Ibid.

105. "Robert Herrick: Rhetoric," in *The University of Chicago Faculty: A Centennial View*, University of Chicago Centennial Catalogues (Chicago: University of Chicago Library, 1992), www.lib.uchicago.edu/e/spcl/centcat/fac/facch11_01.html.

106. Robert Herrick, *The Common Lot* (New York: MacMillan, 1904), 155.

107. *City of Chicago Social Service Directory, 1915* (Chicago: Department of Public Welfare, 1915), 191.

108. Alistair Cooke, *The American Home Front 1941–42* (New York: Grove Press, 2006), 2.

109. Frank L. Kluckhohn, "Japan Wars on U.S. and Britain; Makes Sudden Attack on Hawaii; Heavy Sea Fighting Reported," *New York Times*, December 8, 1941.

110. Block, *Hyde Park Houses*, 101.

111. Paul Avrich, *The Haymarket Tragedy* (Princeton, Princeton University Press, 1984), 207.

112. Ibid.

113. "Biography of Sigmund Zeisler," *Inventory of the Fannie Bloomfield-Zeisler and Sigmund Zeisler Papers, 1869–1981*, Newberry Library, available at http://www.newberry.org/collections/findingaids/zeisler/zeisler.html.

114. "Biography of Fannie Bloomfield-Zeisler," *Inventory of the Fannie Bloomfield-Zeisler and Sigmund Zeisler Papers, 1869–1981*, Newberry Library, available at http://www.newberry.org/collections/findingaids/zeisler/zeisler.html.

115. James Terry White, Raymond D. McGill, and I. A. Harvey, *National Cyclopedia of American Biography*, vol. 14 (New York: James T. White & Co., 1910), 192–93.

116. "Fannie Bloomfield Zeisler, Artist, Pianist, Dead," *Hyde Park Herald*, August 26, 1927.

117. "Probate Wills of Late Sigmund Zeisler and Dr. Albert Michelson," *Hyde Park Herald*, July 17, 1931.

118. Donald L. Miller, *City of the Century: The Epic of Chicago and the Making of America* (New York: Simon & Schuster, 1996), 279.

119. "Alta Vista Terrace Historic District," US National Register of Historic Places website, http://www.waymarking.com/waymarks/WM6GZ6_Alta_Vista_Terrace_Historic_District_Chicago_IL.

120. Emily Clark, "Samuel Eberly Gross' Subdivisions," Encyclopedia of Chicago website, http://www.encyclopedia.chicagohistory.org/pages/2449.html.

121. Perry R. Duis, *Challenging Chicago: Coping with Everyday Life, 1837–1920* (Urbana: University of Illinois, 1998), 370.

122. "Real Estate Transaction 4," *Chicago Tribune*, November 15, 1903.

123. Sinkevitch, *AIA Guide to Chicago*, 458.

124. "Excavating Apparatus," US Patent Office, May 26, 1903.

125. "Edgar J. Goodspeed Collection," University of Chicago Library website, http://www.lib.uchicago.edu/e/spcl/goodspeed.html.

126. "Edgar J. Goodspeed, 90, Is Dead; A Biblical Scholar and Author," *New York Times*, January 14, 1962.

127. For example, see Mrs. W. S. Jackman, *Proceedings of the Second National Peace Congress*, Chicago, May 2–5, 1909, http://www.ebooksread.com/authors-eng/ill-american-peace-congress-2nd--1909--chicago/proceedings-of-the-second-national-peace-congress—chicago-may-2-to-5-1909-rem/page-43-proceedings-of-the-second-national-peace-congress—chicago-may-2-to-5-1909-rem.shtml.

128. Virginia A. Greene, *The Architecture of Howard van Doren Shaw* (Chicago: Chicago Review Press, 1998), 50.

129. Nathaniel Butler, "Wilbur Samuel Jackman: A Personal Appreciation," in *The Elementary School Teacher*, vol. 4 (Chicago: University of Chicago Press, 1907), 439–42.

130. "Ephraim Fletcher Ingals Papers (1881–1964)," Rush University Medical Center Archives, http://www.rushu.rush.edu/servlet/Satellite?blobcol=urlfile&blobheader=application%2Fpdf&blobkey=id&blobnocache=true&blobtable=document&blobwhere=1254085341190&ssbinary=true.

131. "The Nobel Prize in Physics 1923, Robert A. Millikan," Nobel Prize website, http://www.nobelprize.org/nobel_prizes/physics/laureates/1923/millikan-bio.html.

132. Leslie Hudson, "The Washington Park Fireproof Warehouse and Its Architect Argyle E. Robinson," *Hyde Park History* 27, no. 3 (Chicago: Hyde Park Historical Society, 2005).

133. "Julie and J. Parker Hall III," Alumni & Friends: The University of Chicago Online Community, University of Chicago, alumniandfriends.uchicago.edu/site/c.mjJXJ7MLIsE/b.5110571/k.66BE/Julie__J_Parker_Hall_III.htm.

134. Block, *Hyde Park Houses*, 94.

135. Al Chase, "Kenwood Hotel Sold: Landmark of World Fair," *Chicago Tribune*, July 2, 1936.

136. History of the Yellow Cab Manufacturing Company," http://www.coachbuilt.com/bui/y/yellow_cab/yellow_cab.htm.

137. "Albert W. Sullivan House," *Historic American Buildings Survey* (Philadelphia: National Park Service, 1963), available at http://lcweb2.10c.gov/cgi-bin/ampage.

138. David A. Hanks, *The Decorative Designs of Frank Lloyd Wright* (Mineola NY: Dover Publications, 1979), 9–10.

139. According to David Hanks, the letter regarding the site of the fair was written on February 16, 1882.

140. Marjory Harlan Sgroi, "Frank Lloyd Wright's Lost Harlan House," Harlan Family website, http://www.harlanfamily.org/record/record29.htm#Frank.

141. *Frank Lloyd Wright*, 78.

142. Frank Lloyd Wright, *An Autobiography* (Petaluma; Pomegranate Communications, 2005), 110.

143. Houghton D. Wetherald, "E. E. Boynton House," Historic American Building Survey, February 1973.

144. Wright called these "textile blocks" based on the thought that they could be woven, like a basket, to provide additional strength. McArthur's name is on the building permit for the Biltmore, a building that Wright claimed to have designed. William Allen Storrer, *The Architecture of Frank Lloyd Wright: A Complete Catalogue*, 3rd ed. (Chicago: University of Chicago Press, 2002), 226–27.

145. "Warren M'Arthur, Design Engineer, 76," *New York Times*, December 18, 1961.

146. George W. Hotchkiss, *Industrial Chicago: the Lumber Interests*, vol. 6 (Chicago: Goodspeed Publishing Co., 1894), 406.

147. Nancy Ethiel, "A History of the Elizabeth Morse Charitable Trust," *The Elizabeth Morse Charitable Trust*, www.morsetrust.org/historyofthetrust.html.

148. Ibid.

149. Ibid.

150. "F. C. Wright Takes Reporter for Ride in Dear Old Kenwood," *Hyde Park Herald*, November 6, 1931.

151. "Fashionable Wedding in Chicago," *New York Times*, September 3, 1884.

152. US Department of the Interior, National Park Service, National Register of Historic Places Inventory: Nomination Form, http://gis.hpa.state.il.us/hargis/PDFs/200151.pdf.

153. "Q. W. Potter Coming East," *New York Times*, March 27, 1901.

154. Alfred Hoyt Granger married Belle Hughitt on 10/4/1893. Charles S. Frost married Mary Hughitt on 1/7/1885; *State of Illinois Marriage Index*, www.ilsos.gov.

155. "Van Doren Village," *Hyde Park Herald*, February 3, 1954.

156. "Stone Is Laid Plumb," *Chicago Tribune*, March 24, 1895.

157. "Home of Kenwood Club," *Chicago Tribune*, November 3, 1895.

158. Ibid.

159. Al Chase, "Hotel Man Buys Kenwood Club's Home, Landmark," *Chicago Tribune*, August 20, 1922.

160. "John B. Lord," *New York Times*, January 21, 1933.

161. "Edward E. Ayer House: Photographs, Written Historical and Descriptive Data," (Washington, DC: Historic American Buildings Survey, National Park Service, 1964), 5.

162. Alice Sinkevitch, *AIA Guide to Chicago* (San Diego: Harcourt Brace &, 1993), 407.

163. "Risk Much to Rob," *Chicago Tribune*, September 25, 1903.

164. "Gustavus F. Swift Dead," *New York Times*, March 30, 1903.

165. US Department of the Interior, National Park Service, *National Register of Historic Places: Nomination Form*.

166. Helen Louise Swift, *My Father and My Mother* (Chicago: Lakeside Press, 1937), 122–24.

167. "Gustavus F. Swift Dead," *New York Times*, March 30, 1903.

168. "George W. Maher," *City of Chicago, Chicago Landmarks* website, www.cityofchicago.org/Landmarks/Architects/Maher.html.

169. "Houses Designed by George W. Maher," *House Beautiful* 14, no. 6 (November 1908): 131–32.

170. John W. Leonard and Albert N. Marquis, eds., *The Book of Chicagoans: A Biographical Dictionary of Leading Living Men of the City of Chicago* (Chicago: A. N. Marquis, 1905), 175.

171. "Reid Murdoch Building," Chicago: A National Register of Historic Places Travel Itinerary, National Park Service, http://www.cr.nps.gov/nr/travel/chicago/c6.htm.

172. "Heller, Isidore, House," National Register of Historic Places Nomination Form, United States Department of the Interior, http://pdfhost.focus.nps.gov/docs/NHLS/Text/72000450.pdf.

173. Leonard and Marquis, *The Book of Chicagoans*, 589.

174. "Dan Aucunas for the Restoration of the Robert Vierling House, *Hyde Park Historical Society*, www.hydepark.org/historicpres/athistsoc.htm.

175. Ibid.

176. "Adolphus W. Green Dies at the Plaza," *New York Times*, March 9, 1917.

177. Nat Brandt, *Chicago Death Trap: The Iroquois Fire* (Carbondale: Southern Illinois University Press, 2003), 12.

178. "Chicago Banker, 73: A Suicide in Lake," *New York Times*, March 31, 1922.

179. Herbert Newton Casson, *The History of the Telephone* (Chicago: A. C. McClurg, 1910), 164.

180. "Enos M. Barton Dies," *New York Times*, May 5, 1916.

181. *The National Cyclopaedia of American Biography* (New York: James T. White & Co.), 111–12.

182. Peter Max Ascoli, *Julius Rosenwald: The Man Who Built Sears, Roebuck and Advanced the Cause of Black Education in the South* (Bloomington: Indiana University Press, 2006), 7–9.

183. Peter M. Ascoli, "Julius Rosenwald: Chicago Businessman and Philanthropist," Encyclopedia of Chicago website, http://www.encyclopedia.chicagohistory.org/pages/2413.html.

184. Ascoli, *Julius Rosenwald*, 62.

185. Evidently Jens Jenson was responsible for the design of a number of gardens in and around Kenwood. In addition to the 1913 plans for Morris Rosenwald, the Bentley Historical Library at the University of Michigan holds the following architectural drawings: a sketch for a new roadway for Jacob Franks (1911), planting plans for Albert Loeb (1911), and plantings for the arbors and gardens of Julius Rosenwald's grounds (1911), among others, http://bentley.umich.edu/research/guides/jensen/.

186. "Morris Rosenwald Near Death," *New York Times*, March 26, 1924.

187. "Business: Hart Schaffner, Marx & Hilman," *Time*, April 19, 1937.

188. Henry Simonhoff, *American Jewry, 1865–1914: Links of an Endless Chain* (New York: Arco Publishing Co., 1959), 342.

189. Ibid., 343.

190. "Business: Hart Schaffner, Marx & Hilman," *Time*, April 19, 1937.

191. Josiah S. Currey, *Chicago: Its History and Its Builders; A Century of Marvelous Growth*, vol. 5 (Chicago: S. J. Clarke, 1912), 56.

192. "Obama to Shuttle: How's My Lawn?" *Chicago Tribune*, May 21, 2009.

193. Exact quote found at "Obama calls Astronauts aboard Shuttle Atlantis," May 21, 2009, www.physorg.com/news162108523.html.

194. "For Sale," *Chicago Tribune*, April 24, 1910.

195. "Chicagoans Die as Yacht Burns in Georgian Bay," *Chicago Tribune*, July 8, 1927.

196. Charles B. Bernstein and Stuart L. Cohen, "The Jewish History of Barack Obama's House," *Chicago Jewish News Online*, November 28, 2008, http://www.chicagojewishnews.com/story.htm?sid=1&id=252515.

197. Ibid.

198. "Hyde Park 'Live-In' Seeks End to Black-White Hatred," *Chicago Tribune*, July 9, 1970.

199. "Firebombs Damage Hyde Park Church," *Chicago Tribune*, June 21, 1971.

200. "George W. Maher," *City of Chicago, Chicago Landmarks* website, www.cityofchicago.org/Landmarks/Architects/Maher.html.

201. Mark R. Wilson, "Fuller (George A.) Co.," *Encyclopedia of Chicago*, http://www.encyclopedia.chicagohistory.org/pages/2678.html.

202. "George A. Fuller Dead," *New York Times*, December 15, 1900.

203. Carol Bradford, "Historic Drexel Boulevard," *Hyde Park History* (Chicago: Hyde Park Historical Society, 2009), 15.

204. Ibid.

205. Richard C. Lindberg, *The Gambler King of Clark Street: Michael C. McDonald and the Rise of Chicago's Democratic Machine* (Carbondale: Southern Illinois University Press, 2009), 206–7.

206. "Charles Head Smith," *New York Times*, October 4, 1938.

207. Lindberg, *The Gambler King of Clark Street*, 207.

208. "Mrs. C.J. Blair Dies: An Art Collector," *New York Times*, August 5, 1940.

209. "Business: Shedd," *Time Magazine*, November 1, 1926, http://www.time.com/time/magazine/article/0,9171,722684-1,00.html. "Remembering John G. Shedd," Shedd Aquarium, July 20, 2010, http://interactive.sheddaquarium.org/2010/07/remembering-john-g-shedd-on-his-birthday.html.

210. "Martha Washington Home Aids Children," *Hyde Park Herald*, May 3, 1950.

211. Leonard and Marquis, *The Book of Chicagoans*, 73–74.

212. Lynn Becker, "Decline and Fall," *Architecture Chicago Plus*, December 2, 2008, http://www.arcchicago.blogspot.com/2008/12/decline-and-fall.html.

213. Bob Breunnig, "Remembering Great American Department Stores," http://www.dshistory.com/stores/mandel_brothers_chicago/.

214. Andreas, *History of Chicago*, 718.

CHAPTER FOUR

1. The population of the city of Chicago was 2,185,283 by 1910.

2. The *1909 Plan of Chicago* noted the conditions of the city at the time. Carl Smith, *The Plan of Chicago* (Chicago: University of Chicago Press, 2006), 36.

3. Carl Smith, *The Plan of Chicago Daniel Burnham and the Remaking of the American City* (Chicago: University of Chicago Press, 2006), 38.

4. A list of the Commercial Club of Chicago Members from H. B. Stevens, *A Trip to Panama* (St. Louis, 1907) 244–48.

5. Ibid., 103.

6. Chicago's central business district became known as the Loop, for the elevated transit line built in 1897 that encircles the area.

7. "Wreck Leland Home to Make Way for Hotel," *Chicago Tribune*, August 3, 1917.

8. "Prefer Bad Road to Autos," *Chicago Tribune*, November 11, 1908.

9. "Seipp Buys $250,000 Lots," *Chicago Tribune*, May 5, 1909.

10. These properties would typify the continually changing character of the boulevard. Blair's residence became the office of the United Bakers Corporation during the twenties before being demolished to make way for another apartment building. And the building at 4856–4858 Drexel, which he had worked hard to prevent, would be subdivided to accommodate thirty-six small apartments during the forties.

11. The Kenwood Country Club formed in 1894 and used Marshall Field's land for an outdoor sports facility. Goldwin Starrett designed the clubhouse, where members watched tennis tournaments from the large-roofed verandah in the summer and enjoyed a 125' × 600' skating rink during the winter. The club even considered building a toboggan slide, a popular diversion of the time. Immediately following the sale by Field's estate, the wide-open vistas provided by the club were replaced by a series of three-and-a-half-story apartment buildings, completely altering the landscape. "Big Sale by Field Ousts Kenwood Country Club," *Chicago Tribune*, May 14, 1914.

12. "$40,000 Is Paid for High Grade Kenwood Home," *Chicago Tribune*, April 30, 1919.

13. "John J. Mitchell Home Site Sold; Flats Planned," *Chicago Tribune*, February 12, 1916.

14. Nancy F. Cott, *No Small Courage: A History of Women* (Oxford: Oxford University Press, 2005), 365.

15. "Flat Building Replaces Homes in Hyde Park," *Chicago Tribune*, February 10, 1918.

16. Ann Durkin Keating, *Building Chicago* (Chicago: University of Illinois Press, 2002), 38.

17. US Department of the Interior, National Park Service, *National Register of Historic Places Inventory: Nomination Form*, 3, http://gis.hpa.state.il.us/hargis/PDFs/200151.pdf.

18. The 1910 US Census lists both blue- and white-collar workers living in the area. Professions included stenographers, pipe welders, and railroad baggage markers.

19. Robin Faith Bachin, *Building the South Side: Urban Space and Civic Culture in Chicago, 1890–1919* (Chicago: University of Chicago Press, 2004), 60.

20. Christopher Manning, "African Americans," in *The Encyclopedia of Chicago*, ed. James R. Grossman et al. (Chicago: University of Chicago Press, 2004), 5–7.

21. Chicago Commission on Race Relations, *The Negro in Chicago: A Study of Race Relations and a Race Riot* (Chicago: University of Chicago Press, 1922), 118.

22. "A Crowd of Howling Negroes: The *Chicago Daily Tribune* Reports the Chicago Race Riot, 1919," History Matters website, http://historymatters.gmu.edu/d/4975/.

23. "Home Owners Again Roused by Negro Flood," *Chicago Tribune*, July 14, 1917.

24. Bachin, *Building the South Side*, 58.

25. Chicago Commission on Race Relations, *The Negro in Chicago*, 119.

26. Ibid., 121.

27. Bachin, *Building the South Side*, 251–52.

28. In 1913 an African American purchased the building at 5230 South Maryland Avenue through a white-owned real estate firm. S. P. Motley and his wife resided peacefully in the location for four years, until a bomb exploded in the vestibule of their house in July 1917. No arrests were made as a result of the incident. When it was rumored that Motley intended to purchase the house next door two years later, the front of that house was destroyed by dynamite. Again, no arrests were made. *The Negro in Chicago: A Study of Race Relations and a Race Riot*, 2nd ed. (Chicago: University of Chicago Press, 1923), 144.

29. For a complete discussion of race in Chicago after the war see William M. Tuttle Jr., *Race Riot Chicago in the Red Summer* (Champaign; University of Illinois Press, 1970).

30. Bachin, *Building the South Side*, 248.

31. "Hyde Park Politics, 1861–1919," *Hyde Park History* 2 (Chicago: Hyde Park Historical Society, 1980), 24.

32. Thompson's legacy as mayor included the early development of the patronage system, by the Democratic Party as a "machine," which shaped the future political atmosphere of Chicago.

Roger Biles, "Machine Politics," *Encyclopedia of Chicago*, http://www.encyclopedia.chicagohistory.org/pages/774.html.

33. "Charles E. Merriam: Political Science," in *The University of Chicago Faculty: A Centennial View*, University of Chicago Centennial Catalogues (Chicago: University of Chicago Library, 1992), http://www.lib.uchicago.edu.

34. Douglas Bukowski, *Big Bill Thompson, Chicago and the Politics of Image* (Urbana: University of Illinois Press, 1998), 76–78.

35. "William Rainey Harper's Index," *University of Chicago Magazine*, September-October 2010, 17.

36. Robert C. Wombly ed., *Frank Lloyd Wright: Essential Texts* (New York: W. W. Norton & Co., 2009), 128.

37. *Turn of the Century Home* (Chicago: Renaissance Society at the University of Chicago, 1994), 10.

38. Sigfried Giedion, *Space, Time and Architecture* (Cambridge, MA: Harvard University Press, 1941), 405.

39. Irving M. Modlin and George Sachs, *Acid Related Diseases: Biology and Treatment*, 2nd ed. (Philadelphia: Lippincott Williams & Wilkins, 2004), 131.

40. Greene, *The Architecture of Howard van Doren Shaw*, 53.

41. *Illinois: A Descriptive and Historical Guide* (Chicago: A. C. McClurg & Co., 1939), 281.

42. Elizabeth Blackwell, "Think Tank," *Chicago Magazine*, October 2005.

43. Alice Sinkevitch, *AIA Guide to Chicago* (San Diego: Harcourt Brace, 1993), 443.

44. C. W. Tolman, "Angell, James R. (1869–1949)," in *Encyclopedia of Psychology* (New York: APA & Oxford University Press, 2000), accessed at http://www.igs.net/~pballan/Angell.htm.

45. W. S. Hunter, *James Rowland Angell, 1869–1949: A Biographical Memoir* (Washington, DC: National Academy of Sciences, 1951), 6–7.

46. Charles Lane, "Heartbreak Hotel," *Chicago Magazine*, August 2006.

47. Ibid.

48. "Armed Men Invade Home of Indicted Insurance Man in Search of 'Millions,'" *New York Times*, February 15, 1933.

49. "R. W. Stevens Dies from a Pistol Shot," *New York Times*, March 23, 1933.

50. E. J. Stevens Found Guilty of Theft," *New York Times*, October 15, 1933.

51. Supreme Court of the United States, no. 00-949, George W. Bush, et al., Petitioners *v.* Albert Gore, Jr., et al., On Writ of Certiorari to the Florida Supreme Court, Justice Stevens, dissenting, December 12, 2000.

52. George A. Larson and Jay Pridmore, *Chicago Architecture and Design* (New York: H. N. Abrams, 1993), 105.

53. "Purcell & Elmslie Accounting Materials, Annual Report for 1912 [B4b5.2]," and "Purcell & Elmslie Accounting Materials, Annual Report for 1913 [B4b5.3]," William Gray Purcell Papers, Northwest Architectural Archives, University of Minnesota Libraries.

54. Reverend John Henry Hopkins, "The Life of Marie Moulton Graves Hopkins," 1934, http://anglicanhistory.org/women/mmghopkins/11.html.

55. Ibid.

56. "Church Closes after Acts of Vandalism," *Chicago Tribune*, June 23, 1968.

57. Letter to the Reverend Gerald Francis Burrill from the Rector, June 4, 1968, Courtesy of St. Paul and the Redeemer, Chicago, IL.

58. "Home is a Manse," *Hyde Park Herald*, March 27, 1985.

59. Jeanne Catherine Lawrence, "Chicago's Eleanor Clubs: Housing Working Women in the Early Twentieth Century," *Perspectives in Vernacular Architecture*, vol. 8, *People, Power, Places* (Knoxville: University of Tennessee Press, 2000), 219.

60. "Eleanor Club Sold to U of C," *Hyde Park Herald*, March 8, 1967.

61. For a complete discussion on the history of the Doctor's Hospital (Illinois Central Hospital) and its fate see the Hyde Park–Kenwood Community Conference website: http://www.hydepark.org/hpkccnews/DrsHospHotel.htm.

62. Neil Harris, *Chicago Apartments* (New York: Acanthus, 2004), 82.

63. "The Sisson Hotel Apartments," *Hotel Monthly* 26 (1918).

64. Ibid.

65. "Klansmen Should Stop at the Sisson Hotel," *Imperial Nighthawk*, June 23, 1923, accessed at http://history.hanover.edu/courses/excerpts/227kkknews.html.

66. Cheryl Corley, "The Legacy of Chicago's Harold Washington," NPR radio broadcast, May 8, 2012. available at http://www.npr.org/templates/story/story.php?storyId=16579146.

67. "Hotel Del Prado," National Register of Historic Places, National Park Service website, http://www.nps.gov/nr/travel/chicago/c23.htm.

68. "Chicago Beach Hotel Is Sued," *Chicago Tribune*, April 3, 1910.

69. "Chicago Beach Hotel Surrenders Shore Rights," *Hyde Park Herald*, June 18, 1926.

70. "New Hotel to Cost $2,000,000," *Chicago Tribune*, June 11, 1919.

71. In a "remarkable opinion," Judge Landis imposed a fine of nearly $30 million dollars on Standard Oil, saying the defendants were no better than "Counterfeiters or thieves of the mail." His opinion was later overturned.
"Oil Trust Fine is $29,240,000," New York Times, August 4, 1907.

72. Shayna M. Sigman, "The Jurisprudence of Judge Kenesaw Mountain Landis," *Marquette Sports Law Review* 15 (2): 284.

73. "Chicago Beach Hotel Taken for Army Hospital," *Chicago Tribune*, September 23, 1942.

74. US Department of the Interior, National Park Service, *National Register of Historic Places Inventory: Nomination Form*, 29.

75. Constance D. Leupp and Marguerite Tracy, "Medicine: Childbirth; Nature v. Drugs," *Time*, May 25, 1936.

76. "Chicago Lying-In Hospital," Department of Obstetrics and Gynecology, University of Chicago, http://www.jewellgems.com/portfolio/obgyn/clihistory.htm.

77. Jean F. Block, *Hyde Park Houses* (Chicago: University of Chicago Press, 1978), 80.

78. Gerald Foster, *American Houses: A Field Guide to the Architecture of the Home* (Boston: Houghton Mifflin, 2004), 348.

79. *American Artisan and Hardware Record*, March 11, 1916, 20.

80. John W. Leonard and Albert N. Marquis, eds., *The Book of Chicagoans: A Biographical Dictionary of Leading Living Men of the City of Chicago* (Chicago: A. N. Marquis, 1905), 691.

81. "Antoine's Kenwood Home Is Purchased," *Chicago Tribune*, August 27, 1916.

82. "A History of 4815 Woodlawn, August, 2008," supplied by the owners.

83. Ibid.

84. Virginia A. Greene, *The Architecture of Howard van Doren Shaw* (Chicago: Chicago Review Press, 1998), 54.

85. Josiah Seymour Currey, *Chicago: Its History and Its Builders, A Century of Marvelous Growth*, vol. 4 (Chicago: S. J. Clarke Publishing Co., 1912), 624.

86. "Albert Loeb, Father of Franks's Slayer, Dies in Home Where Crime Was Planned," *New York Times*, October 28, 1924.

87. "Reminders of 'Bobby's' Fate Cause Sale of Franks Home," *New York Times*, September 1, 1924.

88. "Big Tract Changes Owners," *Chicago Tribune*, August 27, 1908.

89. Charles Henry Taylor, ed., *History of the Board of Trade of the City of Chicago*, vol. 3, pt. 1 (Chicago: Robert O. Law Co., 1917), 218.

90. Ibid., 130.

91. City of Chicago Building Permit 15870, August 7, 1913.

92. "Acres Southwest in Demand," *Economist* 55, no. 20 (May 13, 1916).

93. Rochelle Berger Elstein, "The Jews of Houghton-Hancock and Their Synagogue," *Michigan Jewish History* 38 (November 1998): 5. Herman Eliassof, "The Jews of Illinois," *Reform Advocate* (May 4, 1901): 28. "Hyde Park and Kenwood Issue: Beyond Robie House," *Chicago Reader*, March 4, 2010.

94. "Max Adler, Donor of Planetarium, 86," *New York Times*, November 6, 1952.

95. Leonard and Marquis, *The Book of Chicagoans*, 491.

96. "Realty Record Is Good," *Chicago Tribune*, September 11, 1904.

97. "Ed. Morris Dead; Left $40,000,000," *New York Times*, November 3, 1913

98. Susan Benjamin and Stuart Cohen, *Great Houses of Chicago, 1871–1921* (New York: Acanthus Press, 2008), 259–61.

99. "Mrs. Morris Weds British Statesman," *New York Times*, September 6, 1917.

100. Betty J. Blum, "Oral History of Bertrand Goldberg," *Chicago Architects Oral History Project* (Chicago: Art Institute of Chicago, 1992), 155, http://www.artic.edu/research/archival-collections.

101. Robert B. Osgood, "A Survey of the Orthopaedic Services in the U.S. Army Hospitals, General, Base, and Debarkation," *Journal of Bone & Joint Surgery* (1919): 374, http://www.ejbjs.org/cgi/reprint/1/6/359.pdf.

102. "Spotlight on Chicago's Legendary South Side," *Chicago Tribune*, October 7, 2001.

103. "Etta James," *Musician Biographies*, http://www.musicianguide.com/biographies/1608004513/Etta-James.html.

CHAPTER FIVE

1. In 1912 the South Park Board took steps to fulfill Daniel Burnham's plan for the lakefront. Condemnation proceedings began against all lakefront property owners to compel them to release their riparian rights. The Illinois Central controlled the land from 12th Street to East 50th Street, marked by a fisherman's shack that the railroad took over after the owner's death. The stretch from 51st to 53rd had been given to the city by Paul Cornell to be used in perpetuity for a public park; 53rd Street to 54th Street was owned by Harry W. Sisson & Associates and was occupied by the apartment hotel of the same name. T. A. Collins owned 600' south of 54th, and Fanny Bregh owned the remaining footage. H. R. Shedd owned from 55th to 56th. All released their rights to the lakefront. However the Chicago Beach Hotel property between 50th and 51st Streets was in litigation, and a solution was not reached until 1926. "An Historical Sketch of the Rubbish Pile," *Hyde Park Herald*, April 23, 1926.

2. "Burnham Park Timeline," Hyde Park–Kenwood Community Conference. Data based on "Park History" in Julia Sniderman Bachrach and Timothy N. Wittman, *2000 Burnham Park Framework Plan* (Chicago: Chicago Park District, 1999), available at http://www.hydepark.org/parks/burnham/burnhamtimeline.htm.

3. It was not until 1929 that sod and other landscaping features were added to the south lakefront parks. The Promontory Point was not completed until the late 1930s, funded by the Works Progress Administration. Architect Alfred Caldwell created the plans; architect E. V. Buchsbaum designed the field house. Gary Ossewaarde, "Promontory Point Park and Promontory Annex in Burnham Park, Chicago, Illinois," Hyde Park Kenwood Community Conference website, http://www.hydepark.org/parks/point.html.

4. Aviator Amelia Earhart visited Chicago on July 19, 1928, shortly after she became the first woman to fly across the Atlantic and came into the national spotlight. Hyde Parkers proudly welcomed the one-time Hyde Park High School student with a reception at their former school, a parade, and a banquet at the Shoreland. "Hyde Park Prepares for 'Our Amelia,'" *Hyde Park Herald*, July 13, 1928.

5. "Gilded Palaces of the Silver Screen," *Chicago Sun-Times*, December 8, 1968.

6. In 1907 the Illinois General Assembly passed a "local option bill" sponsored by the Anti-Saloon League; the sale of alcohol was prohibited in two-thirds of Chicago's precincts by 1909. In 1919 Illinois lawmakers ratified the Eighteenth Amendment to the Constitution, making the manufacture, sale, and transport of alcohol illegal in the state. Rachel E. Bohlmann, "Prohibition and Temperance," in *The Encyclopedia of Chicago*, ed. James R. Grossman et al. (Chicago: University of Chicago Press, 2004), 649–50.

7. "Where to Quench Thirst Now?" *Hyde Park Herald*, July 19, 1929.

8. Ibid.

9. The Annan apartment was at 811–833 East 46th Street between Drexel Boulevard and Cottage Grove; the building is still there today, bearing no trace of its notorious history. "Woman Plays Jazz as Victim Dies," *Chicago Tribune*, April 4, 1924.

10. Kathleen McLaughlin, "Beulah Annan, Chicago's Jazz Killer is Dead," *Chicago Tribune*, March 14, 1928.

11. Maurine Watkins, "Beulah Annan Sobs Regret for Life She Took," *Chicago Tribune*, April 6, 1924.

12. Maurine Watkins, "Jury Finds Beulah Annan Is 'Not Guilty,'" *Chicago Tribune*, May 25, 1924.

13. "Research Resources on Chicago, Jazz and the Great Migration," University of Chicago Library, Special Collections Research Center, http://www.lib.uchicago.edu/e/su/cja/greatmigration.html.

14. Timothy Samuelson, "Excerpts from the Black Metropolis Thematic Nomination," US Department of the Interior, National Park Service, National Register of Historic Places: Nomination Form, http://www.nps.gov/history/nr/twhp/wwwlps/lessons/53black/53factsr.htm.

15. St. Clair Drake and Horace Cayton, *Black Metropolis: A Study of Negro Life in a Northern City* (New York: Harcourt, Brace, 1945), 78.

16. Ibid., 79.

17. The turreted, gabled house designed for dry goods merchant George W. Hoyt and his wife Flora was situated on a pleasant stretch of the only curved street within Hyde Park's rectangular city grid. Designed by Cole & Dahlgren about 1892, the house became famous as the residence of Chicago newspaperman Ben Hecht.

Edgar Lee Masters was a Kenwood resident. He lived in a double house at 4853 Kenwood designed by George Nimmons in 1898.

18. "A One-Man Storm Centre," *Sydney Herald*, August 1, 1954, http://trove.nla.gov.au/ndp/del/page/1079853?zoomLevel=1.

19. "1,000 Room Addition to Take Place of Old Chicago Beach," *Chicago Tribune*, September 4, 1921.

20. Ibid.

21. Chicagoans were proud of the new roadway, and none perhaps more than banker and builder John A. Carroll, who declared two major achievements, the electrification of the Illinois Central and the completion of the outer drive, as "beginning to rival the achievements of the builders of Rome." Scarcely had the celebrations ended, however, when a blizzard began and the road was made impassable by the "fury of the lake's waves and the blinding snow." "Predict New Outer Drive Will Pay for Itself during 1930," *Chicago Tribune*, December 20, 1929.

22. "Chicago's Finest Transportation, the Illinois Central Electric," *Hyde Park History* (Chicago: Hyde Park Historical Society, 2006), accessed at www.hydeparkhistory.org/newsletter/Summer06.pdf.

23. "Will Rival old 'Deestrict' of Cap Streeter," *Chicago Tribune*, November 7, 1926.

24. Jennifer Ames, "Understanding Coop Apartments in Chicago," *Live and Play in Chicago*, http://www.liveandplayinchicago.com/index.php/understanding-coop-apartments-in-chicago/.

25. Chicago Commission on Landmarks, "Shoreland Hotel," *Landmarks Designation Report*, July 1, 2010, 13, http://www.cityofchicago.org/content/dam/city/depts/zlup/Historic_Preservation/Publications/Shoreland_Hotel.pdf.

26. Streeterville is the name given to a large tract of land east of Michigan Avenue and north of the Chicago River. After sand and silt accumulated north of a pier built at the mouth of the river, squatters claimed the land as their own. In 1886 Captain George Wellington Streeter maintained that his grounded ship, the *Reutan*, created even more land, and it was outside jurisdiction of the State of Illinois. (Not unlike James Morgan and his Hyde Park acreage.) Confrontations and court fights ensued until as late as 1918. Today some of the city's most expensive property occupies the once contested site on the city's "Gold Coast." "Streeter's Odd Land Fight Continues after 39 Years," *New York Times*, June 8, 1924. "Chicago Claimant Dead," *New York Times*, January 25, 1921.

27. "Chicago Beach Hotel Surrenders Shore Rights," *Hyde Park Herald*, June 18, 1926.

28. Philip Hamspon, "American Architecture and Design Features of New Co-op," *Chicago Tribune*, September 25, 1927.

29. Block, *The Uses of Gothic*, 225–27.

30. Paul Stanford, "Electric Commuting & a Cleaner Hyde Park," *Hyde Park History* (Chicago: Hyde Park Historical Society, 1980), 22.

31. Ibid., 22–24.

32. Irving Cutler, *The Jews of Chicago from Shtetl to Suburb* (Urbana, IL: University of Illinois Press, 1996), 199.

33. Amanda I. Seligman, *Block by Block: Neighborhoods and Public Policy on Chicago's West Side* (Chicago: University of Chicago Press, 2005), 5.

34. "Kenwood's Best Known Home Is Sold," *Chicago Tribune*, July 21, 1920.

35. "Landmark Status on Track for Classical Revival Style Hyde Park Bank," *Hyde Park Herald*, July 23, 2008.

36. "Valuable Corner Still Vacant," *Hyde Park Herald*, March 29, 1929.

37. "Shoreland Hotel Landmark Designation Report," Commission on Chicago Landmarks, July 1, 2010, http://www.cityofchicago.org/content/dam/city/depts/zlup/Historic_Preservation/Publications/Shoreland_Hotel.pdf.

38. "Electric Consumer Appliances Proliferate, 1920" A Science Odyssey: People and Discoveries, PBS Online, http://www.pbs.org/wgbh/aso/databank/entries/dt20ap.html.

39. "United Action Keeps Negroes Out of 57 Homes," *Chicago Tribune*, January 10, 1920.

40. Arnold R. Hirsch, "Restrictive Covenants," in *The Encyclopedia of Chicago*, ed. James R. Grossman et al. (Chicago: University of Chicago Press, 2004), 702–3.

41. William M. Tuttle, *Race Riot: Chicago in the Red Summer of 1919* (Urbana: University of Illinois Press, 1996), 173.

42. Hirsch, "Restrictive Covenants," 702–3.

43. Edna Ferber, *The Girls* (New York: Doubleday, Page & Co., 1921), 69.

44. "Citizens Hire Own Police Protection," *Hyde Park Herald*, April 28, 1933.

45. "Indict Boy Slayers for Double Crime; Confession Is Out," *New York Times*, June 6, 1924.

46. "Rich Men's Sons Bare the Crime; Solve Mystery," *Chicago Tribune*, May 31, 1924.

47. "Indict Boy Slayers for Double Crime: Confession Is Out," *New York Times*, June 6, 1924.

48. Clarence Darrow was known for his role in cases that "addressed the rights of labor unions, the abuses of child labor, the importance of freedom of expression, and the ineffectiveness of capital punishment." He first achieved prominence for his role as a labor lawyer, defending labor organizer Eugene Debs and the American Railway Union following the Pullman strike of 1894. After the 1924 Leopold and Loeb court case came his last trial: he defended John Scopes, a Tennessee schoolteacher accused of teaching the theory of evolution in the classroom, in a case known as the Scopes "Monkey Trial." "Clarence Darrow, 1857–1938," Chicago Tribute Markers of Distinction, http://chicagotribute.org/Markers/Darrow.htm.

49. "Indict Boy Slayers for Double Crime: Confession Is Out," *New York Times*, June 6, 1924.

50. Simon Batz, "Leopold and Loeb's Criminal Minds," *Smithsonian Magazine*, August 2008, http://www.smithsonianmag.com/.

51. The coach house where the car was cleaned of evidence is now hidden behind an apartment building and several smaller houses. However early maps indicate the Leopold coach house may have been nearer to 48th Street and the existing coach house may have belonged with the property at 4734 Greenwood.

52. "Clarence Darrow," Chicago Tribute Markers of Distinction, http://chicagotribute.org/index.html.

53. "Michelson House," Hyde Park Walking Tour, Frank Lloyd Wright Preservation Trust website. http://gowright.org/MoodleWright/mod/book/print.php?id=59&chapterid=28

54. "The Bichl House: Significant Structures," Village of Wilmette Historic Preservation Commission, http://68.72.75.214/details/110chestnut.htm.

55. "Hyde Park to Have $2,000,000 Hotel-Theater," *Chicago Tribune*, March 14, 1920.

56. "Piccadilly Theater," Cinema Treasures Website, http://cinematreasures.org/theaters/2512.

57. Ibid.

58. Neil Harris, *Chicago Apartments* (New York: Acanthus, 2004), 74.

59. "Work Begins on New Windermere: Already Talk of Duplicate," *Chicago Tribune*, June 4, 1922.

60. Harris, *Chicago Apartments*, 74.

61. "The Work of Walter W. Ahlschlager," *American Builder Magazine*, 1921, http://www.compassrose.org/downloads/Ahlschlager.pdf.

62. "19 Story South Side Apartment Building Is Sold," *Chicago Tribune*, October 12, 1947.

63. "Comiskey Takes Apartment at Jackson Towers," *Chicago Tribune*, May 24, 1931.

64. The success of the National League Chicago White Stockings baseball team under Albert Goodwill Spalding attracted many competitors. In 1894, Charles A. Comiskey, the son of an early Chicago alderman, became involved in the founding of a new Western League. Despite intense opposition from the White Stockings, Comiskey moved his franchise to the grounds of the old Chicago Cricket Club at 39th and Princeton Streets. When the White Stockings changed their name to the Cubs in 1901, Comiskey decided to use their old name. That year the Western League became the American League, and baseball became enormously popular, drawing large crowds. The Cubs eventually moved to the North Side of the city, and Comiskey purchased property at 35th Street and Shields in 1908 for construction of a baseball field, named Comiskey Park. Although Comiskey's original baseball park was demolished in 1990, the rivalry between these two early baseball teams is ever present today. Perry Duis, "Whose City? Public and Private Places in Nineteenth-Century Chicago," *Chicago History* (Spring 1983): 23–24.

65. *Chicago Tribune*, April 13, 1940.

66. Harris, *Chicago Apartments*, 78.

67. "Shoreland Hotel," Landmark Designation Report, Commission on Chicago Landmarks, July 1, 2010, http://www.cityofchicago.org/content/dam/city/depts/zlup/Historic_Preservation/Publications/Shoreland_Hotel.pdf.

68. "Once Grand, Fading Hotel Going Condo," *Chicago Sun-Times*, August 29, 2004.

69. "Deco in Chicago," *Chicago Tribune*, June 11, 1978.

70. Hamspon, "American Architecture and Design Features of New Co-Op," *Chicago Tribune*, September 25, 1927.

71. National Register of Historic Places plaque, 5528 S. Hyde Park Boulevard.

72. "New Apartment Buildings Rising on Local Streets," *Hyde Park Herald*, December 28, 1928.

73. By the 1880s house moving was so common that the City Council was forced to revise the building code to address problems caused by moving hundreds of houses each year. Anyone desiring to move a house was "required to take out a license, post a ten thousand-dollar bond, and pay a five-dollar permit fee for each move." Additionally, no building worth less than half its original value could be moved. According to Perry Duis, the number of permits issued for house moving rose from 726 in 1884 to a record high of 1,710 in 1890. Perry Duis, *Challenging Chicago: Coping with Everyday Life, 1837–1920* (Urbana: University of Illinois, 1998), 91–92.

74. Sunny Gymnasium, at 5823 South Kenwood, was designed by Armstrong, Furst & Tilton and completed in 1929.

75. "Chicago Beach Hotel Surrenders Shore Rights," *Hyde Park Herald*, June 18, 1926.

76. "4900 Blackstone New Addition to Successful Zisook Hotel System," *Hyde Park Herald*, February 15, 1929.

77. "Six Servant Home," *Chicago Tribune*, June 18, 1961.

78. Alan G. Artner, "Old Town Founder Edgar Miller, 93," *Chicago Tribune*, June 4, 1993.

79. Richard Cahan and Michael Williams, *Edgar Miller and the Hand-Made Home: Chicago's Forgotten Renaissance Man* (Chicago: CityFiles Press, 2009), 58.

CHAPTER SIX

1. Carl W. Condit, *Chicago, 1930–70: Building, Planning and Urban Technology* (Chicago: University of Chicago Press, 1974), 3–4.

2. Robert W. Rydell, "The Century of Progress," in *The Encyclopedia of Chicago*, ed. James R. Grossman et al. (Chicago: University of Chicago Press, 2004), 124–26.

3. Lisa D. Schrenk, *Building a Century of Progress: The Architecture of Chicago's 1933–34 World's Fair* (Minneapolis: University of Minnesota Press, 2007).

4. Ibid.

5. Rydell, "The Century of Progress," 124–26.

6. *House of Tomorrow: America's First Glass House* (Chicago: B. R. Graham, 1933), University of Chicago Library Special Collections Research Center, http://century.lib.uchicago.edu/images/century0094.pdf.

7. Rydell, "The Century of Progress," 124–26.

8. "The University and the City," *The University of Chicago Centennial Catalogues*, http://www.lib.uchicago.edu/e/spcl/centcat/.

9. Kenneth Jackson argued that these policies "accelerated suburbanization at the expense of urban areas." Amy E. Hillier. "Redlining and the Home Owners' Loan Corporation (Pennsylvania)," University of Pennsylvania, Electronic Dissertations (2001): 394–96. D. Bradford Hunt, "Redlining," in *The Encyclopedia of Chicago*, ed. James R. Grossman et al. (Chicago: University of Chicago Press, 2004), 863.

10. "Chicago Beach Hotel Taken for Army Hospital," *Chicago Tribune*, September 23, 1942.

11. Damon Darlin, "Hyde Park versus the Tavern," *Hyde Park History* 1, no. 1 (Chicago: Hyde Park Historical Society, 1980), 44.

12. Although Drexel Boulevard was about to undergo a steep decline, at the beginning of the thirties apartments on the southern end of the avenue were occupied by white middle-class families, including the Skakel family, residents of 5019 South Drexel in 1931. Their daughter Ethel was baptized at St. Ambrose Church on 47th Street and married Sen. Robert F. Kennedy in June 1950.

13. Gladys Priddy, "Fact Finding Book Gives Detailed Hyde Park Report," *Chicago Tribune*, January 31, 1954.

14. In but one example, the three-story brick house at 4758 South Lake Park was originally built as a single-family residence. It was remodeled into six kitchenette apartments on the upper floors, with a five-room apartment on the first floor for the owner. "Hotel Man Buys Furnished Apartment Building," *Hyde Park Herald*, March 21, 1946.

15. "Unwelcome Neighbors," *Chicago History* (Spring and Summer 1992): 56–57.

16. Ibid., 59. At the request of McKay & Pogue Realtors, the university financed a lawsuit filed by the Woodlawn Property Owners Association. To enforce the restrictions, signatures of 95 percent of the property owners were required. The WPOA had obtained only 54 percent of the signatures, yet maintained that it was sufficient to enforce the covenants.

17. Social Justice Movements, Hansberry v. Lee, http://socialjustice.ccnmtl.columbia.edu/index.php/Hansberry_v._Lee.

18. In 1940 the implications of the *Hansberry* v. *Lee* case were explained to the readers of the *Hyde Park Herald*. Under the terms of a restrictive agreement, the property owners "agree among themselves, for a term of years, not to permit their property to be sold to, occupied by or used by negroes." "Haylett Explains the Facts," *Hyde Park Herald*, December 5, 1940.

19. *Chicago Defender*, November 16, 1940.

20. Perry Duis, *Challenging Chicago: Coping with Everyday Life, 1837–1920* (Urbana: University of Illinois, 1998), 353.

21. "Chicago: Destination for the Great Migration," The African-American Mosaic, Library of Congress, http://www.loc.gov/exhibits/african/afam011.html.

22. Rebecca Janowitz, *Culture of Opportunity* (Chicago: Ivan R. Dee, 2010), 120.

23. "Unwelcome Neighbors," *Chicago History* (Spring and Summer 1992): 63.

24. Ibid.

25. "Biographical Note," Guide to the Allison Davis Papers 1932–1984, University of Chicago Library, Special Collections Research Center, http://www.lib.uchicago.edu/e/scrc/findingaids/view.php?eadid=ICU.SPCL.DAVISA&q=Anthropology.

26. "Enrico (1901–1954) and Laura (1907–1977) Fermi," Chicago Tribute Markers of Distinction, http://chicagotribute.org/index.html.

27. Arnold R. Hirsch, "Democratic Party," in *The Encyclopedia of Chicago*, ed. James R. Grossman et al. (Chicago: University of Chicago Press, 2004), www.encyclopedia.chicagohistory.org/pages/371.html.

28. Roger Biles, "Machine Politics," in *The Encyclopedia of Chicago*, ed. James R. Grossman et al. (Chicago: University of Chicago Press, 2004), http://www.encyclopedia.chicagohistory.org/pages/774.html.

29. Dominick A. Pisano, "The Airplane and Streamlined Design," Smithsonian National Air and Space Museum, October 25, 2010, http://blog.nasm.si.edu/tag/streamline/.

30. Eric Larrabee and Massimo Vignelli, *Knoll Design* (New York: H. N. Abrams, 1981), 9.

31. Ibid.

32. Frédéric Edelmann and Ante Glibota, *Chicago: 150 Ans d'architecture, 1833–1983* [*Chicago, 150 Years of Architecture, 1833–1983*] (Paris: Paris Art Center, 1985), 183.

33. "In Levittown, Old Myths Meet Hard Reality," *New York Times*, November 19, 2008.

34. Condit, *Chicago, 1930–70*, 79.

35. Mardges Bacon, *Le Corbusier in America: Travels in the Land of the Timid* (Cambridge, MA: MIT Press, 2001), 117.

36. Le Corbusier and Francis Edwin Hyslop, *When the Cathedrals Were White, a Journey to the Country of Timid People* (New York: Reynal & Hitchcock, 1947), 85.

37. Bacon, *Le Corbusier in America*, 117.

38. Andrew Abbott, *Department & Discipline: Chicago at One Hundred* (Chicago: University of Chicago Press, 1999), 197.

39. Chicago in the 1920s and 1930s: the View from the Chicago School," Social Science Research Committee Maps, University of Chicago Library, http://www.lib.uchicago.edu/e/su/maps/ssrc/.

40. Chicago in the 1920s and 1930s: The View from the Chicago School," Social Science Research Committee Maps, University of Chicago Library, http://www.lib.uchicago.edu/e/su/maps/ssrc/.

41. "Funeral Held for Kenwood's Big Willow Tree," *Chicago Tribune*, August 1, 1932.

42. Ibid.

43. Ibid.

44. Betty J. Blum, "Oral History of William Keck," *Chicago Architects Oral History Project* (Chicago: Art Institute of Chicago, 1991), 110–11, http://www.artic.edu/research/archival-collections.

45. Robert Boyce, *Keck & Keck* (New York: Princeton Architectural Press, 1993), 66.

46. Ibid., 117.

47. Maurice T. Price, "Harley Farnsworth MacNair," *Far Eastern Quarterly* 8, no. 1 (November 1948): 45.

48. David Shavit, *The United States in Asia: A Historical Dictionary* (Westport CT: Greenwood Press, 1990), 328.

49. Harley Farnsworth MacNair and Florence Wheelock Ayscough Diaries: Guide, Houghton Library, Harvard College Library, http://oasis.lib.harvard.edu/oasis/deliver/~hou01886.

50. "A Two-Day Tour of Mies' Legacy," *New York Times*, June 6, 1968.

51. Harris, *Chicago Apartments*, 86.

52. "Six New Homes Will Be Built on Morse Site," *Chicago Tribune*, June 9, 1936. The land was purchased for $30,000, which would equate to approximately $475,000 in 2010 dollars, a comparatively astute purchase.

53. " Kenwood Air Conditioned Home," *Chicago Tribune*, December 27, 1936.

54. Andrew Gottesman, "Attorney Philip R. Toomin," *Chicago Tribune*, May 24, 1993.

55. " Kenwood Air Conditioned Home," *Chicago Tribune*, December 27, 1936.

56. "Clark-Maple Gas Station," Bertrand Goldberg website, http://bertrandgoldberg.org/projects/clark-maple-gas-station/.

57. Studio Blue, *The Catalogue: Bertrand Goldberg; Architecture of Invention* (New Haven: Yale University Press, 2011).

58. "Bertrand Goldberg," *Chicago Architects Oral History Project* (Chicago: Art Institute of Chicago, 1992, Revised 2001), 143, http://www.artic.edu/research/archival-collections.

59. "Building Permit," *Hyde Park Herald*, November 30, 1939.

60. Interview with Lynne Rosenthal, September 23, 2012.

61. Andrew Herrmann, "Leo S. Guthman, Businessman, Art Collector," *Chicago Sun-Times*, May 28, 2003.

62. The Leo S. Guthman Fund website, http://www.lsgfchicago.org/homeo.aspx.

63. Jane King Hession, Pip Rapson, and Bruce N. Wright, *Ralph Rapson: Sixty Years of Modern Design* (Afton, MN: Afton Historical Society Press, 1999), 56.

64. "Central Real Estate in Demand: Several Large Transactions Are Closed," *Chicago Tribune*, September 19, 1909.

65. Hession et al., *Ralph Rapson*, 56.

66. "John H. Johnson," Johnson Publishing Company website, http://www.johnsonpublishing.com/assembled/about_johnson_biography.html.

CHAPTER SEVEN

1. Bruce Sagan, "The Last Word," *Hyde Park Herald*, September 17, 1958.

2. Muriel Beadle, "Free-lance Writer, Author," *Chicago Tribune*, February 22, 1994.

3. Muriel Beadle, *The Hyde Park–Kenwood Urban Renewal Years: A History to Date* (Chicago: N.p., 1964), 4.

4. In writing about Chicago's public housing, William Mullen ("The Road to Hell," *Chicago Tribune*, March 31, 1985) noted that by 1951 Chicago was already a leader among the nation's cities in razing slum neighborhoods. In an effort to revitalize city-center economies, the Federal Housing Act of 1949 established a federally subsidized program to help cities clear areas of existing buildings for redevelopment and rehabilitate deteriorating structures.

5. Amanda I. Seligman, *Block by Block: Neighborhoods and Public Policy on Chicago's West Side* (Chicago: University of Chicago Press, 2005): 210–11.

6. Alice Sinkevitch, *AIA Guide to Chicago* (San Diego: Harcourt Brace & Co., 1993), 20.

7. Of the 12,771 housing units in Kenwood, 11,159 were renter-occupied in 1950. Of those renters fewer than 10 percent were nonwhite. By 1960 there were 15,428 units, of which 13,148 were rental units occupied by 11,081 nonwhites. "CA 39—Kenwood," *Local Community Fact Book: Chicago Metropolitan Area* (Chicago: Chicago Review Press, 1984), 933.

8. Arnold R. Hirsch, *Making the Second Ghetto: Race and Housing in Chicago, 1940–1960* (Cambridge: Cambridge University Press, 1983), 5.

9. Ibid., 136.

10. For example, the 1930 census for Kenwood shows a total population of 26,942 residents of whom 99.2 percent were white. By 1960 the population swelled to 41,533; however, the demographics were reversed, as the population was then 83.9 percent black. Will Hogan, "Kenwood," *Local Community Fact Book: Chicago Metropolitan Area Based on the 1970 and 1980 Censuses* (Chicago: University of Illinois at Chicago, 1985), 107.

11. Forty percent of the community's 72,000 residents were of the Jewish faith. Julia Abrahamson, *A Neighborhood Finds Itself* (New York: Biblo and Tannen, 1971), 7.

12. Beadle, *The Hyde Park–Kenwood Urban Renewal Years*, 4.

13. Peter H. Rossi and Robert A. Dentler, *The Politics of Urban Renewal: The Chicago Findings* (New York: Free Press of Glencoe, 1961), 72.

14. Beadle, *The Hyde Park–Kenwood Urban Renewal Years*, 19.

15. Richard Philbrick, "Housing Survey Tells Needs of South Side Area," *Chicago Tribune*, October 23, 1952.

16. Ibid.

17. Hirsch, *Making the Second Ghetto*, 137.

18. In 1952 the most problematic conversion in Kenwood was the three-story brick mansion at 4954 South Ellis. Flagrant zoning violations allowed the conversion of the home into a residence for twelve families. Gladys Priddy, "Tell Reasons Kenwood Fights to Keep Up Area," *Chicago Tribune*, January 10, 1952.

19. "Kenwood Joins Fight to Save Neighborhood," *Chicago Tribune*, February 21, 1954.

20. Julian Levi, *The Neighborhood Program of the University of Chicago* ([Chicago?]: J. Levi, 1961), 4.

21. "The University and the City," *A Centennial View of the University of Chicago*, http://www.lib.uchicago.edu/e/spcl/excat/city2.html.

22. Beadle, *The Hyde Park–Kenwood Urban Renewal Years*, 13.

23. Hirsch, *Making the Second Ghetto*, 137.

24. In May 1952 police were searching for a "thin-faced Negro gunman," who allegedly terrorized a University of Chicago atomic scientist and his wife in their home at 5321 South University. Samuel and Joan Untermeyer were robbed of over $7,000 in jewelry and a small amount of cash. The most terrifying aspect of the incident followed, when the gunman abducted Mrs. Untermeyer from her second floor bedroom. Dressed in pajamas, she was driven to a parking lot and assaulted by the intruder, who left her in the car. "Negro Robs Atomic Scientist, Kidnaps Wife," *Jet* 2, no. 4 (May 22, 1952): 51.

25. "Looking Back at Urban Renewal," *Hyde Park Herald*, July 21, 2004.

26. Levi, *Neighborhood Program of the University of Chicago*, 7.

27. Robert Boyce, *Keck & Keck* (New York: Princeton Architectural, 1993), 139.

28. Hirsch, *Making the Second Ghetto*, 137.

29. Levi, *Neighborhood Program of the University of Chicago*, 13.

30. Jack Meltzer stayed in Hyde Park after earning his master's degree in political science. He was appointed to the South East Chicago Commission in 1954, where he remained until 1963, and was a calm participant during a difficult planning process. "Jack Meltzer, 88." *Hyde Park Herald*, May 19, 2010.

31. Hirsch, *Making the Second Ghetto*, 136.

32. Levi, *Neighborhood Program of the University of Chicago*, 13.

33. Hirsch, *Making the Second Ghetto*, 137.

34. Max Grinnell, "Hyde Park," in *The Encyclopedia of Chicago*, ed. James R. Grossman et al. (Chicago: University of Chicago Press, 2004): 404–5.

35. Bruce Sagan, "The Major Story of the Last 50 Years: Urban Renewal," *Hyde Park Herald*, July 21, 2004.

36. Ibid.

37. "Looking Back at Urban Renewal," *Hyde Park Herald*, July 21, 2004.

38. Hyde Park A and B consisted of the clearance of 47 (or 48 depending on the source) blighted acres to be demolished and the construction of 540 apartment units, 250 town houses and a shopping center, according to the "Hyde Park Urban Renewal Plan as of December 1960," Hyde Park–Kenwood Community Conference website, http:/www.hydepark.org/historicpres/urbanrenp160.htm.

39. Levi, *Neighborhood Program of the University of Chicago*, 13.

40. Abrahamson, *A Neighborhood Finds Itself*, 315.

41. Of the 100 acres cleared, 43 were slated for new housing, 8.1 for commercial reuse, 17.2 for institutional use, and 8.6 for private parking. Twenty-eight acres were allotted for public agencies, with the largest portion going to the Board of Education.

42. Ronald Kotulak, "Hyde Park Story—It's Just the Beginning," *Chicago Tribune*, February 14, 1960.

43. Sagan, "The Major Story of the Last 50 Years," *Hyde Park Herald*, July 21, 2004.

44. "The Urban Renewal Period in Hyde Park," Hyde Park–Kenwood Community Conference website, http://www.hydepark.org/historicpres/urbanrenewal.htm#planning.

45. Carl Condit, *Chicago: Building, Planning and Urban Technology, 1930-70* (/Chicago: University of Chicago Press, 1974), 212.

46. Ben Weese, at the Mid-Century Modern Architects Panel, Landmarks Illinois, AIA Chicago, on June 14, 2007.

47. "Looking Back at Urban Renewal," *Hyde Park Herald*, July 21, 2004.

48. "Timeline of Hyde Park Urban Renewal and beyond, related Hyde Park development, Part I, 1930s–1964," Hyde Park–Kenwood Community Conference website, http://www.hydepark.org/historicpres/urbanrentimeline.htm.

49. Hirsch, *Making the Second Ghetto*, 136.

50. Recommendations were made as early as the spring of 1949 regarding the area south of the Midway Plaisance. A report found the area too deteriorated to stabilize and beyond the capability of the university to improve the existing buildings. The recommendation was that the property between the Midway and 61st Street be acquired to serve as a "buffer" between the university and the Woodlawn community. Hirsch, *Making the Second Ghetto*, 148.

51. Quoted in "Timeline of Hyde Park Urban Renewal," Hyde Park–Kenwood Community Conference website, http://www.hydepark.org/historicpres/urbanrentimeline.htm.

52. Adam Cohen and Elizabeth Taylor, *American Pharaoh* (Boston: Back Bay Books, 2001), 210.

53. "Renewal Project Dividing Chicago," *New York Times*, September 27, 1958.

54. The low-income housing units were designed by architect Y. C. Wong at two locations: at the southwest corner of 53rd Street and Woodlawn Avenue, and at the southeast corner of 55th Street and Woodlawn. The single-story L-shape modules were constructed of dark gray brick with no ornamentation. The windowless façades provided security and privacy, while light entered the 850-square-foot units through glass at the rear.

55. Douglas resided at 5658 South Blackstone Avenue for much of his life. "Neighbors Who Visited Together on Sunday," *Hyde Park Herald*, October 12, 1966.

56. "Douglas, Paul Howard (1892–1976)," *Biographical Dictionary of the United States Congress*, http://bioguide.congress.gov/scripts/biodisplay.pl?index=d000456.

57. Paul Douglas, "Democracy Can't Live in These Houses," *Collier's*, July 9. 1949, 22, 50.

58. Sagan, "The Major Story of the Last 50 Years," *Hyde Park Herald*, July 21, 2004.

59. Ibid.

60. "Julian H. Levi, 87, Influential Advocate of Urban Renewal," *New York Times*, October 19, 1998.

61. "Looking Back at Urban Renewal," *Hyde Park Herald*, July 21, 2004.

62. Erwin Bach, "Assail Kenwood Renewal Plan," *Chicago Tribune*, February 28, 1957.

63. "9 Million Permit Gives Hyde Pk. Building Spurt," *Chicago Tribune*, July 29, 1962.

64. Al Chase, "Stony Island's Old Art Center Property Sold," *Chicago Tribune*, December 8, 1946.

65. "Harper Court: It Takes Determination and $100 bonds," *Hyde Park Herald*, July 21, 2004.

66. Condit, *Chicago, 1930–1970*, 212.

67. Ibid., 214.

68. Hogan, "Kenwood," 107.

69. Ibid.

70. Austin C. Wehrwein, "Catholic Assails Urban Renewal," *New York Times*, September 24, 1961.

71. Ronald Kotulak, "Hyde Park Story—Its Just Beginning," *Chicago Tribune*, February 14, 1960.

72. These numbers were given in a survey conducted by the National Opinion Research Center in May 1954. Abrahamson, *A Neighborhood Finds Itself*, 203.

73. Rebecca Janowitz, *Culture of Opportunity* (Chicago: Ivan R. Dee, 2010), 123–24.

74. "Bryson Owner Still Trying to Rehab," *Hyde Park Herald*, January 29, 1969.

75. "So Far No Evictions at Bryson Hotel," *Hyde Park Herald*, August 2, 1972.

76. Tom Connors, "Bryson Tenants Will Get Lake Village Apartments," *Hyde Park Herald*, October 11, 1972.

77. Austin C. Wehrwein, "Chicago U. Spurs Renewal Project; 900 Acres Being Cleared in 5-Year Plan to Eliminate Slums and Crime," *New York Times*, November 1, 1959.

78. Kotulak, "Hyde Park Story—Its Just the Beginning," *Chicago Tribune*, February 14, 1960.

79. Abrahamson, *A Neighborhood Finds Itself*, 210.

80. Bruce Ingersoll, "Private Boom Aids Renewal: Hyde Park Builds a Future," *Chicago Tribune*, October 31, 1965.

81. "Stay Cool! Air Conditioning America," National Building Museum Exhibition, May1999–January 2000, http://www.eweek.org/site/news/Features/staycool.shtml.

82. "9 Million Permit Gives Hyde Pk. Building Spurt," *Chicago Tribune*, July 29, 1962.

83. David Zisook, "Analysis of the Feasibility of Rehabilitation of Residential Structures in the Hyde Park–Kenwood Renewal Area," Community Conservation Board of Chicago, n.d., 43.

84. Ibid.

85. Ingersoll, "Private Boom Aids Renewal: Hyde Park Builds a Future," *Chicago Tribune*, October 31, 1965.

86. Beadle, *The Hyde Park–Kenwood Urban Renewal Years*, 17.

87. Condit, *Chicago, 1930–1970*, 214.

88. Sagan, "The Major Story of the Last 50 Years," *Hyde Park Herald*, July 21, 2004.

89. Hirsch, *Making the Second Ghetto*,136.

90. Boyce, *Keck & Keck*, 136.

91. "Tenants Will Build 20 Unit Apartment," *Chicago Tribune*, May 2, 1948.

92. Boyce, *Keck & Keck*, 136.

93. "Chicago: A Wide Variety of Apartment Sizes," *Architectural Record*, June 1954, 176–178.

94. Ibid.

95. "Eight New Area Skyscrapers to Be Home to 950 Families," *Hyde Park Herald*, November 1, 1950.

96. Alice Sinkevitch and Laurie McGovern. Petersen, *AIA Guide to Chicago* (Orlando: Harcourt, 2004): 427.

97. "Helstein House," Bertrand Goldberg Archive, http://bertrandgoldberg.org/projects/helstein-house/.

98. Tim Samuelson, "Hyde Park & Kenwood Issue: Beyond Robie House," *Chicago Reader*, March 4, 2010.

99. "Ralph Helstein, 76 is Dead; Headed Packinghouse Union," *New York Times*, February 15, 1985.

100. Cyril Robinson, *Marching with Dr. King: Ralph Helstein and the United Packinghouse Workers* (Santa Barbara: Praeger, 2011), 70.

101. "Ralph Helstein, 76 is Dead; Headed Packinghouse Union," *New York Times*, February 15, 1985.

102. Conversation with Nina Helstein, December 5, 2011.

103. "Morton's Relocates to Lake Front Site," *Hyde Park Herald*, December 7, 1955.

104. "Hyde Park to Have Its Own Parisian Sidewalk Cafe—Palm Grove Inn," *Hyde Park Herald*, May 4, 1934.

105. "Harry Weese (1915–1998),"*Chicago Architects Oral History Project* (Chicago: Art Institute of Chicago, 1988), http://www.artic.edu/research/archival-collections.

106. "The Home of the Week," *Chicago Tribune*, December 14, 1957.

107. Ibid.

108. Betty J. Blum, "Oral History of Harry Mohr Weese," *Chicago Architects Oral History Project* (Chicago: Art Institute of Chicago, 1991), 112, http://www.artic.edu/research/archival-collections.

109. Blair Kamin, "Harry Weese, Visionary Architect," *Chicago Tribune*, November 1, 1998.

110. Mike Stevens, "University Park Towers Gets Preservation Nod," *Hyde Park Herald*, September 8, 2004.

111. "Hyde Park's Project's Architecture Unusual," *Chicago Tribune*, July 24, 1960.

112. Interview with Ben Weese, June, 2010.

113. Vincent Scully, *Architecture* (New York: St. Martin's Press, 1991), 340.

114. Condit, *Chicago, 1930–70*, 80.

115. Boyce, *Keck & Keck*, 143.

116. "Architect Specializes in Design of Homes," *Chicago Tribune*, April 7, 1968.

117. Boyce, *Keck & Keck*, 150.

118. Annemarie van Roessel, "Ezra Gordon," *Chicago Architects Oral History Project* (Chicago: Art Institute of Chicago, 2002), 82, http://www.artic.edu/research/archival-collections.

119. Condit, *Chicago, 1930–70*, 212.

120. Bertrand Goldberg Archive, website. www.bertrandgoldberg.org/works/drexel_home.html.

121. Ibid.

122. Betty J. Blum, "Bertrand Goldberg," *Chicago Architects Oral History Project* (Chicago: Art Institute of Chicago, 2000),150, http://www.artic.edu/research/archival-collections.

123. Ibid.

124. "Death," *Hyde Park Herald*, April 29, 1998.

125. Elinor Richey, "Kenwood Foils the Blockbusters," *Harper's Magazine* (August 1963): 42–47.

126. "2 brothers here designing solar buildings 40 years," *Chicago Tribune*, November 4, 1979.

127. "Maurice Gleason Home: A Look Ahead—." *Hyde Park Herald*, February 10, 1954.

128. "Plan 8 'Inner Directed' Homes," *Chicago Tribune*, March 3, 1960.

129. Ibid.

130. Betty J. Blum, "Yau Chun Wong," *Chicago Architects Oral History Project* (Chicago: Art Institute of Chicago, 1995): 25–26, http://www.artic.edu/research/archival-collections.

131. Joseph Durso, "Bill Veeck, Baseball Innovator, Dies," *New York Times*, January 3, 1986.

132. "Bill Veeck, 1914–1986," Chicago Tribute Markers of Distinction, http://chicagotribute.org/Markers/Veeck.htm.

133. "Veeck: A Man for Any Season," Chicago Stories, WTTW, http://www.wttw.com/main.taf?p=1,7,1,1,54.

134. "Bill Veeck Was Kenwood's Loveable Winner," *Hyde Park Herald*, January 8, 1986.

135. Boyce, *Keck & Keck*, 135.

136. Ibid., 141.

137. "Showplace for Urban Renewal, *Chicago Tribune*, March 1, 1964.

138. Boyce, *Keck & Keck*, 142.

139. "5617 Blackstone, 4750 Woodlawn," *Hyde Park Herald*, July 25, 1962.

140. 142. Brian E. Vaughn, Gretchen B. Lefever, Ronald Seifer, and Peter Barglow, *Child Development* 60, no. 3 (June 1989).

141. Annemarie van Roessel, "Laurence Booth," *Chicago Architects Oral History Project* (Chicago: Art Institute of Chicago, 2000): 39–40, http://www.artic.edu/research/archival-collections.

142. "Chicago Medic Arrested for Beating Wife," *Jet*, August 15, 1954.

143. Carl W. Condit, *Chicago, 1930–70: Building, Planning and Urban Technology* (Chicago: University of Chicago Press, 1974), 214.

144. Devereux Bowley, *The Poorhouse: Subsidized Housing in Chicago*, 2nd ed. (Carbondale: Southern Illinois University Press, 2012), 151.

145. Alice Sinkevitch and Laurie McGovern Petersen, *AIA Guide to Chicago* (Orlando: Harcourt, 2004), 425.

146. Frank A. Randall and John D. Randall, *History of the Development of Building Construction in Chicago* (Urbana: University of Illinois, 1999), 41.

147. "A Brief History of the origin of the Nation of Islam in America," Nation of Islam website, http://www.noi.org/.

148. Advertised in the *Hyde Park Herald*, January 1, 1958.

149. "Farrakhan Buys Kenwood Mansion for Headquarters," *Hyde Park Herald*, June 25, 1986.

150. "Farrakhan's New Home May Violate Zoning Law," *Hyde Park Herald*, October 22, 1986.

151. Interview with Kenwood resident Ruth Horwich, April 2007.

152. "Farrakhan Buys Kenwood Mansion for Headquarters," *Hyde Park Herald*, June 25, 1986.

153. Telephone conversations and e-mails with Gordon, October 2011.

CHAPTER EIGHT

1. From an 1983 article for *Life* magazine, quoted in "Bellow on His and Our City," *Chicago Tribune*, April 6, 2005.

2. "Photo Display Depicts Home Architecture," *Chicago Tribune*, May 3, 1962.

3. Hyde Park–Kenwood Community Conference and the Department of Urban Renewal, *Segments of the Past* (Chicago: HPKCC and DUR, 1962).

4. Ibid.

5. Joseph Boyle, "Photos Protect Hyde Park Legacy," *Chicago Tribune*, September 25, 1966.

6. "Hyde Park 'Links to Past' Up for Auction," *Chicago Tribune*, November 24, 1963.

7. HPKCC and DUR, *Segments of the Past*.

8. Ibid.

9. Blair Kamin, "Preserving at a Pace, Protecting History Proves an Endless Race," *Chicago Tribune*, May 4, 2008.

10. "Likens Seminary 'Murder' to German Book-Burning," *Hyde Park Herald*, August 28, 1957.

11. "The Surprising Savior of Wright's Robie House," *Hyde Park Herald*, July 21, 2004.

12. Kamin, "Preserving at a Pace," *Chicago Tribune*, May 4, 2008.

13. Ibid.

14. Richard Cahan, Michael Williams, and Richard Nickel, *Richard Nickel's Chicago: Photographs of a Lost City* (Chicago: CityFiles, 2006), 10.

15. Kamin, "Preserving at a Pace," *Chicago Tribune*, May 4, 2008.

16. "Developer Reveals Plans for Historic Mansion—Condos and 12 Townhouses," *Hyde Park Herald*, April 20, 1977.

17. Michele Gasper, "Committees Rally to Save Old Homes," *Chicago Tribune*, April 5, 1979.

18. Cheryl Fries, "A House Divided—Community Split on Mansion Fate," *Hyde Park Herald*, May 1, 1977.

19. Gasper, "Committees Rally to Save Old Homes," *Chicago Tribune*, April 5, 1979.

20. Kamin, "Preserving at a Pace," *Chicago Tribune*, May 4, 2008.

21. "5th Ward Ald. Leon M. Despres, Alderman Reports Preserving our Architectural Landmarks," *Hyde Park Herald*, February 2, 1966.

22. Ron Grossman and Charles Leroux, "The Unmaking of a Ghetto," *Chicago Tribune Magazine*, January 29, 2006.

23. Ibid.

24. An image of the early Maher-designed house can be seen in "Free House Has Big Price Tag," *Hyde Park Herald*, February 19, 1997.

25. Caitlin Devitt, "Park District Looking for 3-Way Land Swap," *Hyde Park Herald*, December 23, 1998.

26. Mike Stevens, "Hyde Park Landmarked?" *Hyde Park Herald*, October 27, 2004.

27. "Condominium Property Act," Illinois General Assembly, http://www.ilga.gov/legislation/ilcs/ilcs3.asp?ActID=2200&ChapterID=62.

28. "New Study Shows Condos at 15% in Area," *Hyde Park Herald*, June 13, 1979.

29. The four-acre site of East View Park developed over a period of time. Contractor Thomas A. Collins constructed the first apartment building in 1913 adjacent to the lake. In 1924 Collins and a partner, A. G. Mahoney, constructed an additional forty-six units. The buildings were all of a similar design, three stories in height, and the street was closed to permit only local traffic, creating an enclave not unlike Madison Park. "Do-It-Yourself Condo Conversion Pays Off," *Hyde Park Herald*, September 21, 1977.

30. Carl Smith, *The Plan of Chicago* (Chicago: University of Chicago Press, 2006), 159.

31. Ibid., 159–62.

32. "Great Plans for a Great City," Chicago Central Area Plan, July 2003, http://www.cityofchicago.org/dam/city/depts/zlup/Planning_and_Policy/Publications/Central_Area_Plan_DRAFT/02_Central_Area_Plan_Chapter1.pdf.

33. Will Hogan, "Kenwood," *Local Community Fact Book: Chicago Metropolitan Area Based on the 1970 and 1980 Censuses* (Chicago: University of Illinois at Chicago, 1985), 108.

34. "Community Area 39," *Local Community Fact Book: Chicago Metropolitan Area Based on the 1970 and 1980 Censuses* (Chicago: University of Illinois at Chicago, 1985), 113.

35. Hogan, "Kenwood," *Local Community Fact Book*, 113.

36. Ibid.

37. University of Chicago Residential Services website, http://rs.uchicago.edu/about_reo/index.shtml.

38. "Preservation Easement Program," Landmarks Illinois website, www.landmarks.org/easement.

39. "University Balks at Easement Protection," *Hyde Park Herald*, August 29, 2007.

40. "Is Ronald Reagan's Chicago Boyhood Home Doomed?" *Chicago Sun-Times*, February 6, 2011.

41. Don Terry and Dan Mihalopoulos, "Hyde Park–Style Politics Are Evident in Preckwinkle Victory," *New York Times*, February 5, 2010.

42. Harold Washington was twice elected to the US House of Representatives for the 1st Congressional District, in 1980 and in 1982. He resigned his seat in 1983, after running a successful campaign for mayor by building a broad coalition of voters. "Washington, Harold (1922–1978)," Biographical Directory of the United States Congress, http://bioguide.congress.gov/scripts/biodisplay.pl?index=W000180.

A University of Chicago Law School graduate, Carol Moseley Braun rose through the state's political system and was first elected to the Illinois House of Representatives in 1978. After four years as recorder of deeds for Cook County, she ran for the US Senate in 1992, the first African American woman ever to be elected. She lost her bid for a second term in 1998. "Moseley Braun, Carol (1947–)," Biographical Directory of the United States Congress, http://bioguide.congress.gov/scripts/biodisplay.pl?index=m001025.

43. "They Are Looking for New Neighbors," *Hyde Park Herald*, August 29, 1979.

44. "Record High Bid Made for 53rd and University," *Hyde Park Herald*, July 12, 1978.

45. At the time, Swan was building seven townhouses at 54th and Kenwood on an urban renewal site. Ibid.

46. "Deny Zoning Change," *Hyde Park Herald*, October 27, 1982.

47. Ibid.

48. "Sleek Modern," *Hyde Park Herald*, March 27, 1985.

49. "Architecture: James L. Nagle," *Architectural Digest*, April 1982.

50. "Hyde Park House on Woodlawn Avenue," *GA Houses* 8 (1981): 38–41.

51. "Swan to Make 47th St. Housing Proposal," *Hyde Park Herald*, February 15, 1989.

52. "Developers Get Month for New 48th St. Plan," *Hyde Park Herald*, September 27, 1989.

53. "Turn of the Century Home," *The Renaissance Society Catalogue* (1994): 84.

54. Personal conversations with Swan, Hyde Park, May 2010.

55. "Construction to Begin for Egandale Rowhouse Development," *Hyde Park Herald*, April 4, 1990.

EPILOGUE

1. The couplet from "The Paradox of Time," by Austin Dobson, was the inspiration for Lorado Taft's *Fountain of Time* sculpture on the Midway Plaisance in Washington Park.

2. Andrew Ferguson, "Mr. Obama's Hyde Park," *Weekly Standard* 13:38 (June 2008), 2, http://staging.weeklystandard.com/Content/Public/Articles/000/000/015/197wxqsf.asp. Of living in an area of diversity and intellect, John Rogers, founder of Ariel Investments, suggested that the neighborhood offers "a measure of a man." Rogers offered, "What better way to define what you're all about than where you choose to live and bring up a family?" Deanna Belandi, "Obama's Neighborhood Rich in Diversity," *USA Today*, July 23, 2007, http://www.usatoday.com/news/topstories/2007-07-23-2766958871_x.htm.

3. David Zisook, *Analysis of the Feasibility of Rehabilitation of Residential Structures in the Hyde Park–Kenwood Renewal Area*, Community Conservation Board of Chicago (No date): 43.

4. Andrew Ferguson, "Mr. Obama's Hyde Park," 2.

5. Lauren Fischer and Joseph P. Schwieterman, *A Kaleidoscope of Culture: Measuring the Diversity of Chicago's Neighborhoods* (Chicago: DePaul University 2008), 8; http://las.depaul.edu/chaddick/docs/Docs/Chaddick%2520Policy%2520Study%2520-%2520Neighbor.pdf.

6. In 1960 the population of Hyde Park and Kenwood was 47 percent black. The 2000 US census showed the population to be 46 percent black, 37 percent white, almost 10 percent Asian, 4 percent Hispanic and the balance as multiracial.

7. Ron Grossman and Charles Leroux, "The Unmaking of a Ghetto," *Chicago Tribune Magazine*, January 29, 2006.

8. Danielle S. Allen, *Talking to Strangers: Anxieties of Citizenship since Brown v. Board of Education* (Chicago: University of Chicago Press, 2004), 180.

9. Brian J. L. Berry, Sandra J. Parsons, and Rutherford H. Platt, *The Impact of Urban Renewal on Small Business*, The Hyde Park–Kenwood Case (Chicago: University of Chicago Center for Urban Studies, 1968), 23.

10. Jane Jacobs, *The Life and Death of Great American Cities* (New York: Random House, 1961), 244–45.

11. Ibid.

12. Rebecca Janowitz, *Culture of Opportunity* (Chicago: Ivan R. Dee, 2000), 120.

13. Sandra Guy, "130-Room Hotel Slated for Hyde Park," *Sun-Times*, March 4, 2011.

14. "SGA Releases Design for City Hyde Park," Studio /Gang/Architects, February 2, 2012; www.studiogang.net/news/updates/2012/02/cityhydepark.

15. "Building: Inside Studio Gang Architects," Art Institute of Chicago, September 2012–February 2013.

16. Ferguson, "Mr. Obama's Hyde Park," 3.

17. Barack Obama, *Dreams from My Father* (New York: Three Rivers Press, 2004), 439.

18. Ferguson, "Mr. Obama's Hyde Park," 1.

19. Janowitz, *Culture of Opportunity*, 137.

20. Ibid., 223.

21. Allen, *Talking to Strangers*, 180.

22. Margaret MacMillan, *Dangerous Games: The Uses and Abuses of History* (New York: Modern Library, 2008), 169.

23. Patrick T. Reardon, "Bellow on His and Our City," *Chicago Tribune*, April 6, 2005, quoting a 1994 *Tribune* interview, after Bellow's move to Boston.

APPENDIX

1. Paul Gilbert and Charles Lee Bryson, *Chicago and Its Makers* (Chicago: F. Mendelsohn, 1929), 869.

2. "Walter W. Ahlschlager," *Lewis Annual* (Alumni Addition, 1926), Chicago Architect's Biographies Pamphlet File, Ryerson Burnham Libraries, Art Institute of Chicago.

3. "Alschuler, Alfred," *Armour Engineer*, Oct.–Nov. 1985, Chicago Architect's Biographies Pamphlet File, Ryerson Burnham Libraries, Art Institute of Chicago.

4. "Alfred S. Alschuler," *Serving, Saving & Saluting the South Loop*, Columbia College Library, http://www.lib.colum.edu/archhistory/alschuler.htm.

5. Henry F. Withey and Elsie Rathburn Withey, *Biographical Dictionary of American Architects (Deceased)* (Detroit, MI: Omnigraphics, 1956).

6. "Guide to the Armstrong Furst & Tilton Records, ca. 1927–1955." Division of Rare and Manuscript Collections, Cornell University Library, http://rmc.library.cornell.edu/ead/htmldocs/RMM02243.html.

7. "Charming Homes Minutes from Loop," *Chicago Tribune*, May 4, 1958.

8. Diana Pearson, "Three St. Croix Residents Murdered," *Virgin Islands Daily News*, January 29, 1980."

9. H. B. Wheelock, "Obituary, George Beaumont, F.A.I.A.," *Journal of the American Institute of Architects* 10, no. 1 (January 1922).

10. Jean F. Block, *Hyde Park Houses* (Chicago: University of Chicago Press, 1977), 90.

11. John W. Leonard, ed., *The Book of Chicagoans: A Biographical Dictionary of Leading Living Men of the City of Chicago* (Chicago: A. N. Marquis, 1905), 140.

12. Don Hibbard, Glenn Mason, and Karen Weitze, *Hart Wood Architectural Regionalism in Hawaii* (Honolulu: University of Hawaii Press, 2010), 257.

13. Antoinette Josephine Lee, *Architects to the Nation: The Rise and Decline of the Supervising Architect* (Oxford: Oxford University Press, 2000), 142.

14. Withey and Withey, *Biographical Dictionary of American Architects (Deceased)* (Detroit, MI: Omnigraphics, 1996), 49.

15. Three years after Solon Beman's work for the Columbian Exposition of 1893, Mary Baker Eddy, founder of the First Church of Christ, Scientist, selected a site on the north end of Drexel Boulevard for the construction of a church. Twelve leading architects submitted plans, including Beman, whose wife had been "healed" through Christian Science treatment. His concept was a departure from the Romanesque styles that had been popular for ecclesiastic architecture in Chicago and echoed his classical work at the world's fair. It was unanimously selected and established Beman as the premier architect for the Christian Science Church.

Paul McClelland Angle, *Chicago History* 23.3 (Summer 1994), 25.

16. "Fernand Parmentier," *Press Reference Library, Southwest Edition, Notables of the Southwest* (Los Angeles: Los Angeles Examiner, 1912), 286.

17. *American Architects' Biographies*, Society of Architectural Historians, http://www.sah.org.

18. Booth Hansen Firm profile, http://www.boothhansen.com.

19. Annemarie van Roessel, "Laurence Booth," *Chicago Architects Oral History Project* (Chicago: Art Institute of Chicago, 2000), iv, http://www.artic.edu/research/archival-collections.

20. Booth Hansen Firm profile, http://www.boothhansen.com.

21. Douglas Kaarre, "John D. Caldwell House, Oak Park Historic Landmark Nomination Report" (Oak Park Historic Preservation Commission, 2011), 10–11.

www.oak-park.us/public/pdfs/Historic%20Preservation/landmarks/East_130_S.pdf.

22. *Biographical Sketches of the Leading Men of Chicago* (Chicago: Wilson & St. Clair, 1868), 215–22.

23. *AIA Guide to Chicago*, 2nd ed. (Orlando: Harcourt, 2004), 222.

24. Withey and Withey, *Biographical Dictionary of American Architects (Deceased)*, 1996 ed., 97.

25. "Burnham & Root," in *The Encyclopedia of Chicago*, http://www.encyclopedia.chicagohistory.org/pages/2581.html.

26. Thomas S. Hines, *Burnham of Chicago: Architect and Planner* (Chicago: University of Chicago, 2009), 25.

27. Withey and Withey, *Biographical Dictionary of American Architects (Deceased)*, 1996 ed., 97.

28. "Burnham & Root," in *The Encyclopedia of Chicago*, http://www.encyclopedia.chicagohistory.org/pages/2581.html.

29. "Barry Byrne," The Architects, the Artisans, and the Styles of the Prairie School of Architecture, http://www.prairiestyles.com/byrne.htm.

30. Kim Coventry, Daniel Meyer, Arthur H. Miller, *Classic Country Estates of Lake Forest* (W. W. Norton, 2003).

31. "Kenwood United Church of Christ," *Landmark Designation Report* (City of Chicago, 2011), 27.

32. Withey and Withey, *Biographical Dictionary of American Architects (Deceased)*, 1956 ed., 128–29.

33. Block, *Hyde Park Houses*, 93.

34. "Myron Goldsmith," *Chicago Architects Oral History Project*, Art Institute of Chicago (1986), 12, http://www.artic.edu/research/archival-collections.

35. "Architect Draws on His Own 'Good Neighbor' Policy," *Chicago Tribune*, August 16, 1953.

36. Joe Kunkel, "Edward Dart, Architect," Chicago Bauhaus and Beyond, 2006, http://www.chicagobauhausbeyond.org/cbb/mission/edart.htm.

37. Designed by DeGolyer in 1938, the Julia Lathrop Homes are considered to be among the better public housing projects developed in the city. Hugh Garden and Tallmadge & Watson also worked on the project, as did noted landscape designer Jens Jensen; http://www.preservationchicago.org/userfiles/file/lathrop.pdf.

38. "Building," *Louisville Courier-Journal*, March 13, 1897, sec. 2, p. 8, http://en.wikipedia.org/wiki/William_J._Dodd.

39. Block, *Hyde Park Houses*, 94.

40. Gilbert and Bryson, *Chicago and Its Makers*, 967.

41. Ibid.

42. Ibid.

43. Dennis Hevesi, "Arthur Dubin, Historian of Railroads Golden Era, Dies at 88," *New York Times*, October 13, 2011.

44. "Arthur B. Dubin," Biographical Summary, *Chicago Architects Oral History Project*, 2003, Art Institute of Chicago, http://www.artic.edu/research/archival-collections.

45. Hevesi, "Arthur Dubin," *New York Times*, October 13, 2011.

46. Withey and Withey, *Biographical Dictionary of American Architects (Deceased)*, 1996 ed., 184–85.

47. "N. Max Dunning, 72, Obituary," *New York Times*, April 20, 1945.

48. Epstein, Company Profile, http://www.epsteinglobal.com/comp_profile.html.

49. Carl W. Conditt, *The Chicago School of Architecture* (Chicago: University of Chicago Press, 1964), 59.

50. Withey and Withey, *Biographical Dictionary of American Architects (Deceased)*, 1996 ed., 213.

51. "Shoreland Hotel," Landmark Designation Report (Commission on Chicago Landmarks, 2010), 10.

52. Susan Perry, *Landmark Designation Report, Humboldt Park Receptory Building and Stable* (Chicago: City of Chicago Department of Zoning and Land Use Planning, 2007), 11.

53. Matt Crawford, *Landmark Designation Report, Brewery-Tied Houses* (Chicago: City of Chicago Department of Zoning and Land Use Planning, 2010), 32.

54. Withey and Withey, *Biographical Dictionary of American Architects (Deceased)*, 1996 ed., 224.

55. The former president of the North Chicago Rolling Mill Company, Orrin Potter later became president of the Illinois Steel Company. He became successful by integrating the company's various plants through a network of railways, permitting the buildup of the steel industry in Chicago.

56. *AIA Guide to Chicago*, 2nd ed. (Orlando: Harcourt, 2004), 421.

57. Http://www.ilsos.gov.

58. "Alfred Hoyt Granger," Gilbert and Bryson, *Chicago and Its Makers*, 866.

59. Withey and Withey, *Biographical Dictionary of American Architects (Deceased)*, 1996 ed., 247.

60. "Hugh Garden, Prairie Styles: The Architects, the Artisans and the Styles of the Prairie School," http://www.prairiestyles.com/garden.htm.

61. Linda E. Smeins, *Building an American Identity: Pattern Book Homes and Communities, 1870–1900* (Walnut Creek, CA: Altamira, 1999), 284.

62. "Bertrand Goldberg" Biographical Summary, *Chicago Architects Oral History Project*, Art Institute of Chicago, 1992, http://www.artic.edu/research/archival-collections.

63. "Architecture for Urbanism: Selections from the Bertrand Goldberg Archive, Art Institute of Chicago, Library Exhibitions, http://www.artic.edu/aic/collections/exhibitions/Ryerson/Goldberg.

64. Bertrand Goldberg, "Rich Is Right," Museum of Science & Industry, Chicago (March 1986), http://bertrandgoldberg.org/writings/rich-is-right/.

65. David W. Dunlap, "Bertrand Goldberg Dies at 84; Architect Reshaped Chicago," *New York Times*, October 10, 1997.

66. Bertrand Goldberg Archive, Art Institute of Chicago, Ryerson Burnham Library, http://www.artic.edu/aic/libraries/research/specialcollections/goldberg/.

67. Blair Kamin, "Ezra Gordon, 1921–2009: Socially-Conscious Architect and Educator," *Chicago Tribune*, June 30, 2009,

68. Robert Philip Gordon Architect: Architecture/Planning/Design, http://www.robert-gordonarchitect.com/RGA/Bio.html.

69. Withey and Withey, *Biographical Dictionary of American Architects (Deceased)*, 1996 ed., 381.

70. "Tony Grunsfeld III," Biographical Summary, *Chicago Architects Oral History Project*, 2004, Art Institute of Chicago, http://www.artic.edu/research/archival-collections.

71. Leonard and Marquis, *The Book of Chicagoans*, 112.

72. Withey and Withey, *Biographical Dictionary of American Architects (Deceased)*, 1996 ed., 280.

73. "Hold John Todd Hetherington Rites Tomorrow," *Chicago Tribune*, December 28, 1936.

74. "Arthur Heun, 79, Noted Designer of Homes, Dead," *Chicago Tribune*, June 21, 1946.

75. Ibid.

76. Withey and Withey, *Biographical Dictionary of American Architects (Deceased)*, 1996 ed., 281.

77. "William Holabird Dead," *New York Times*, July 19, 1923.

78. Robert Bruegmann, *The Architects and the City: Holabird & Roche of Chicago, 1880–1918* (Chicago: University of Chicago, 1997), 18.

79. Ibid., 19.

80. "William Holabird Dead," *New York Times*, July 19, 1923.

81. Bruegmann, *The Architects and the City*, 21.

82. Mark R. Wilson, "Holabird & Root," *Encyclopedia of Chicago*, http://encyclopedia.chicagohistory.org/pages/2704.html.

83. "Henry K. Holsman and the Holsman Automobile," http://www.holsmanautomobile.com/history.

84. Historical Notes on 56th & University Cooperative, http://www.56thuniversitycoop.com/history-of-building.html.

85. "Jarvis Hunt," DuPage County Historical Society, http://www.dupagehistory.org/hunt.html.

86. "Hunt, Myron," Pacific Coast Architecture Database, https://digital.lib.washington.edu/architect/architects/197/.

87. Withey and Withey, *Biographical Dictionary of American Architects (Deceased)*, 1956 ed., 324.

88. "William LeBaron Jenney," City of Chicago, Chicago Landmarks website, http://www.cityofchicago.org/Landmarks/Architects/Jenney.html.

89. Jensen & Halstead Ltd. website, http://www.jensenandhalstead.com/firm/Publicity/Mundie.html.

90. Johnson & Lee website, http://www.jlarch.net/.

91. "William Keck," Biographical Summary, *Chicago Architects Oral History Project*, 1990, Art Institute of Chicago, http://www.artic.edu/research/archival-collections.

92. Robert Boyce, *Keck & Keck* (New York: Princeton Architectural Press, 1993), 143.

93. Kuklinski & Rappe Architects website, http://www.kplusr.com.

94. Withey and Withey, *Biographical Dictionary of American Architects (Deceased)*, 1996 ed., 365–66.

95. *The Technology Review*, vol. 21 (Cambridge: MIT Alumni Association, 1919), 262.

96. Douglas Brenner, "Marxism," *New York Times*, October 7, 2007.

97. "History of the Morris B. Sachs Building," http://peoplingplaces.wordpress.com/2010/03/30/history-of-the-morris-b-sachs-building-part-i/.

98. Loewenberg Architects website, http://www.loewenberg.com/.

99. "John Macsai," Biographical Summary, *Chicago Architects Oral History Project*, Art Institute of Chicago, http://www.artic.edu/research/archival-collections.

100. "George W. Maher," Chicago Landmarks, City of Chicago, http://webapps.cityof-chicago.org/landmarksweb/web/architectdetails.htm?arcId=11.

101. Ibid.

102. "News of the Architects," *Chicago Tribune*, March 5, 1922.

103. Withey and Withey, *Biographical Dictionary of American Architects (Deceased)*, 1996 ed., 389–90.

104. Ibid., 392.

105. Ibid., 217.

106. Blair Kamin, "Hooray for Benjamin Marshall," *Chicago Tribune*, January 16, 2001.

107. "Marshall & Fox," *AIA Historical Directory of American Architects*, http://communities.aia.org/sites/hdoaa/wiki/Wiki%20Pages/ahd4006038.aspx.

108. Block, *Hyde Park Houses*, 97.

109. Carlo Rotella, "Chicago Literary Renaissance," in *The Encyclopedia of Chicago*, ed. James R. Grossman et al. (Chicago: University of Chicago Press, 2004), 143–44.

110. "Miss Margaret Young Wed to A. R. Myhrum," *Chicago Tribune*, June 10, 1946.

111. "Arthur Myhrum," *Chicago Tribune*, April 5, 1973.

112. Nagle Hartray Architecture Firm Profile, http://www.naglehartray.com/firm-profile/talent/james-l-nagle-faia.htm.

113. Biographical Summary, "Laurence Booth," *Chicago Architects Oral History Project*, Art Institute of Chicago (2000), http://www.artic.edu/research/archival-collections.

114. Nagle Hartray Architecture Firm Profile, http://www.nhdkmp.com.

115. Withey and Withey, *Biographical Dictionary of American Architects (Deceased)*, 1996 ed., 442.

116. Albert N. Marquis, ed., *The Book of Chicagoans* (Chicago: A. N. Marquis, 1911), 507.

117. Withey and Withey, *Biographical Dictionary of American Architects (Deceased)*, 1996 ed., 442.

118. Ibid.

119. Block, *Hyde Park Houses*, 100.

120. Withey and Withey, *Biographical Dictionary of American Architects (Deceased)*, 1996 ed., 442.

121. "Fall in Chicago Home Kills W. K. Fellows," *New York Times*, August 9, 1848.

122. Wilbert R. Hasbrouck, *The Chicago Architectural Club: Prelude to the Modern* (New York: Monacelli, 2005), 92.

123. Block, *Hyde Park Houses*, 100.

124. Rochelle Berger Elstein, "The Jews of Houghton-Hancock and Their Synagogue," *Michigan Jewish History* 38 (November 1998): 5, http://www.michjewishhistory.org/pdfs/vol38.pdf.

125. Ibid., 5.

126. "Looking Backward," *Chicago Tribune*, August 4, 1929.

127. "His Father to the Rescue," *New York Times*, August 22, 1885.

128. Frank Lloyd Wright, *Frank Lloyd Wright: an Autobiography* (Petaluma, CA: Pomegranate, 2005), 101, 102.

129. "Charles Booher Genther," Biographical Summary, *Chicago Architects Oral History Project*, Art Institute of Chicago, 1983, http://www.artic.edu/research/archival-collections.

130. "Page, Harvey Lindsley (1859–1934)," obituary, http://boards.ancestry.com/topics.obits/63825/mb.ashx.

131. "Palmer, Charles," American Architects Biographies, Society of Architectural Historians, http://www.sah.org/index.php?src=gendocs&ref=BiographiesArchitectsP&category=Resources.

132. Withey and Withey, *Biographical Dictionary of American Architects (Deceased)*, 1996 ed., 460.

133. "Hotel Dana," Chicago's Seven Most Threatened Buildings, Preservation Chicago, http://www.preservationchicago.org/chicago7/2005/hoteldana.pdf.

134. "I. M. Pei, Founder," Pei Cobb Freed & Partners Architects LLP, http://www.pcf-p.com/a/f/fme/imp/b/b.html.

135. Pei Cobb Freed & Partners Architects LLP, http://www.pcfandp.com/.

136. "Dwight Perkins," Prairie Styles, http://www.prairiestyles.com/perkins.htm.

137. Hasbrouck, *The Chicago Architectural Club,* 119.

138. Block, *Hyde Park Houses,* 101.

139. Ibid.

140. "Her Wedding a Romance, Miss Vandeveer Marries Frederick W. Perkins, Architect of Her Father's Home," *New York Times,* November 8, 1911.

141. Withey and Withey, *Biographical Dictionary of American Architects (Deceased),* 1996 ed., 469.

142. "Pond & Pond," Chicago Landmarks, City of Chicago, http://webapps.cityofchicago.org/landmarksweb/web/architectdetails.htm?arcId=12.

143. Withey and Withey, *Biographical Dictionary of American Architects (Deceased),* 1996 ed., 479.

144. American Circus Collection 1891–1939, Newberry Library, http://mms.newberry.org/html/AmericanCircus.html.

145. Block, *Hyde Park Houses,* 102.

146. Withey and Withey, *Biographical Dictionary of American Architects (Deceased),* 1996 ed., 478.

147. Ibid., 490.

148. Block, *Hyde Park Houses,* 101.

149. Mark Hammons, Biographical Essay, *Guide to the William Gray Purcell Papers,* 1985, http://www.prairiestyles.com/purcell.htm.

150. John Carbutt, *Biographical Sketches of Leading Men of Chicago* (Chicago: Wilson & St. Clair, 1868), 327–30.

151. Frank Alfred Randall and John D. Randall, *The Development of Building Construction in Chicago,* 2nd ed. (Chicago: University of Illinois Board of Trustees, 1999), 33.

152. Heidi Emery, "Returning the Grandeur to the Historic American Theatre," http://www.conradschmitt.com/getstarted/articles/?articleid=24.

153. Robin Pogrebin, "Ralph Rapson, Modernist Architect, Is Dead at 93," *New York Times,* April 3, 2008.

154. Moholy-Nagy was a painter, sculptor, photographer, filmmaker, and teacher who fled the political turmoil of 1919 Budapest for Berlin, where he joined the faculty of the Bauhaus in 1923. In 1937 he came to Chicago to become the director of the New Bauhaus and the following year established the School of Design with other faculty members. The school became the Institute of Design in 1944 and eleven years later part of the Illinois Institute of Technology. "The New Bauhaus/Institute of Design—A Legacy for Chicago," Chicago Bauhaus and Beyond, http://www.chicagobauhausbeyond.org/cbb/mission/newBauhaus.htm.

155. Jane King Hession, Rip Rapson, and Bruce N. Wright, *Ralph Rapson: Sixty Years of Modern Design* (Afton, MN: Afton Historical Society, 1999), xvi.

156. Ibid., 91.

157. Kenan Heise, "Architect, Musician John van der Meulen," *Chicago Tribune,* September 19, 1994.

158. Withey and Withey, *Biographical Dictionary of American Architects (Deceased),* 1996 ed., 512.

159. "Save the Glass: Preservationists Fear Fate of CTS Art Glass," *Hyde Park Herald,* June 9, 2010.

160. Argyle Robinson and his first wife Elizabeth lived at 5406 Harper and later at 5227.

161. Leslie Hudson, "The Washington Park Fireproof Warehouse and Its Architect, Argyle E. Robinson," *Hyde Park History* 27, no. 3 (Fall 2005).

162. Aaron Betsky, *James Gamble Rogers and the Architecture of Pragmatism* (New York: Architectural History Foundation, 1994), mitpress.mit.edu/catalog/item/default.asp?ttype=2&tid=7810.

163. "James Gamble Rogers: Architect of Laurel Court," Laurel Court website, http://www.laurelcourt.com/about.html.

164. Cooper, Robertson & Partners, "A Framework for Campus Planning," Yale University, April 2000, 17–19.

165. "Mies van der Rohe," Illinois Institute of Technology, http://www.iit.edu/arch/about/history/mies.shtml.

166. "A Two-Day Tour of Mies' Legacy," *New York Times,* June 6, 1968.

167. Quote attributed to developer Bernard Weissbourd, in ibid.

168. Lauren Hunter-Thomas, "Sunrooms in the Off-Season," *Chicago Weekly,* March 1, 2012, http://chicagoweekly.net/2012/03/01/sunrooms-in-the-off-season/.

169. "Architect Sandegren Is Dead," *Svenska Tribune Nyheter,* January 30, 1924, http://www.conradschmitt.com/getstarted/articles/?articleid=24.

170. "Schmidt, Garden & Martin," Chicago Landmarks, City of Chicago website, http://egov.cityofchicago.org/Landmarks/Architects/Schmidt.html.

171. Ibid.

172. Virginia A. Greene, *The Architecture of Howard van Doren Shaw* (Chicago: Chicago Review Press, 1998), 3.

173. Ibid., 34.

174. Thomas E. Tallmadge, "Howard van Doren Shaw," *Architectural Record,* July 1926.

175. Susan S. Benjamin and Stuart Earl Cohen, *Great Houses of Chicago, 1871–1921* (New York: Acanthus Press, 2008), 314.

176. "Skidmore Owings & Merrill LLP, Company History," http://www.fundinguniverse.com/company-histories/Skidmore-Owings-amp;-Merrill-LLP-company-History.html.

177. Ibid., 213.

178. Hasbrouck, *The Chicago Architectural Club,* 158.

179. Block, *Hyde Park Houses,* 105.

180. "Horace Powers Funeral Will Be Held Tomorrow," *Chicago Tribune,* September 4, 1928.

181. "Robert C. Spencer, Jr.," From Louis Sullivan to SOM, Massachusetts Institute of Technology, 1996, http://web.mit.edu/museum/chicago/chicago.html.

182. Quinn Chapel AME Church History, http://www.restorequinnchicago.org/History_of_Quinn.html.

183. John Powell, "Henry F. Starbuck," *Guide to Historic Architecture in Fresno, California,* http://historicfresno.org/bio/starbuc1.htm.

184. Bruegmann, *The Architects and the City,* 484.

185. "George A. Fuller Dead," *New York Times,* December 14, 1900.

186. Mark R. Wilson, "Fuller (George A.) Co.," in *The Encyclopedia of Chicago,* ed. James R. Grossman et al. (Chicago: University of Chicago Press, 2004), http://www.encyclopedia.chicagohistory.org/pages/2678.html.

187. Block, *Hyde Park Houses,* 105.

188. "Louis Sullivan at 150," Biography, Chicago History Museum, http://www.chicagohistory.org/sullivan150/about/bio.php.

189. Richard Nickel and Aaron Siskind, *The Complete Architecture of Adler & Sullivan* (Chicago: Richard Nickel Committee, 2010), 18.

190. David Swan Architect website, http://www.davidswanarchitect.com.

191. Block, *Hyde Park Houses,* 106.

192. Withey and Withey, *Biographical Dictionary of American Architects (Deceased),* 1996 ed., 406–7.

193. Ibid., 213.

194. *Quarterly Bulletin of the American Institute of Architects* 11–12 (1910): 120.

195. John Mills van Osdel, *Chicago Tribute Markers of Distinction,* http://www.chicagotribute.org/Markers/Osdel.htm.

196. Block, *Hyde Park Houses,* 123.

197. "John Vinci," Biographical Summary, *Chicago Architects Oral History Project,* Art Institute of Chicago, 2002, http://www.artic.edu/research/archival-collections.

198. Betty J. Blum, "John Vinci," *Chicago Architects Oral History Project,* Art Institute of Chicago (2002), 165, http://www.artic.edu/research/archival-collections.

199. Leonard and Marquis, *The Book of Chicagoans,* 691.

200. "Marion Mahony," *The Griffins,* PBS website, http://www.pbs.org/wbgriffin/griffins.htm.

201. "Herman von Holst," *From Louis Sullivan to SOM,* Massachusetts Institute of Technology, http://web.mit.edu/museum/chicago/vonholst.html.

202. "Personal," *American Architect* 13, no. 2211 (May 8, 1918): 572.

203. Harold T. Wolff, "Giving Drama to a Simple House," Ridge Historical Society, http://www.ridgehistoricalsociety.org.

204. "H. H. Waterman House," Historic Home Tour, Beverly Area Planning Association, http://www.bapa.org/content.asp?contentid=1.

205. Blair Kamin, "Harry Weese, Visionary Architect Known as Chicago's Conscience," *Chicago Tribune*, November 1, 1998.

206. "Harry Weese," *Chicago Architects Oral History Project*, Art Institute of Chicago, Biographical Summary, http://www.artic.edu/research/archival-collections.

207. Ibid.

208. "Benjamin Horace Weese," Biographical Summary, *Chicago Architects Oral History Project*, Art Institute of Chicago, 1998, http://www.artic.edu/research/archival-collections.

209. Withey and Withey, *Biographical Dictionary of American Architects (Deceased)*, 1996 ed., 663.

210. "Yau Chun Wong," Biographical Summary, *Chicago Architects Oral History Project*, Art Institute of Chicago, 1983, http://www.artic.edu/research/archival-collections.

211. "A Brief Biography," Frank Lloyd Wright Foundation, http://www.franklloydwright.org/fllwf_web_091104/Biography.html.

212. Wright, *Frank Lloyd Wright*, 110.

213. "W. C. Zimmerman," *New York Times*, April 12, 1932.

Figure Credits

The Art Institute of Chicago, Ryerson and Burnham Archives, Archival Image Collection, Digital File 75857, **2.28**

The Art Institute of Chicago, Ryerson and Burnham Archives, Chicago Architectural Sketch Club Collection, Digital File casc.1898_009, **3.92**

The Art Institute of Chicago, Ryerson and Burnham Archives, Historic Architecture and Landscape Image Collection:

> Architecture Lantern Slide Collection, Digital File 18373, **4.11**
>
> Architecture Photograph Collection, photograph by C. Allgeiere, Digital File M524943, **2.57**
>
> Architecture Photograph Collection, photograph by Rus Arnold, Digital File 75854, **1.11**; Digital File 75854, **2.15**
>
> Architecture Postcard Collection, photograph by Charles R. Childs Company, photographers, Digital File 44745, **3.47**
>
> Architecture Photograph Collection, photograph by Henry Fuermann, Digital File 17860, **4.07**
>
> Architecture Photograph Collection, photograph by Kaufmann & Fabry Co., photographers, Digital File 51257, **6.02**
>
> Architecture Photograph Collection, Digital File 70713, **3.52**; Digital File 24455, **5.21**

The Art Institute of Chicago, Ryerson and Burnham Archives, *Inland Architect*:

> 12:5, Digital File IA1205_0246, **2.46**
>
> 15:6, Digital File IA1506_0557, **2.51**
>
> 10:9, Digital File IA1009_0125, **2.54**
>
> 20, Digital File IA2001_cob21, **2.59**
>
> 41:1, Digital File IA4101_3652, **3.27**
>
> 39, Digital File IA3901_3415, **3.28**
>
> 27:2, Digital File IA2702_2017, **3.62**
>
> 24:6, Digital File IA2406_1726b, **3.63**
>
> 26:4, Digital File IA2604_1934, **3.64**
>
> 39, Digital File IA3906_3506, **3.79**
>
> 21:3, Digital File IA2103_1220, **3.90**
>
> 41:3, Digital File IA4103_3694, **3.94**; Digital File IA4103_3696, **3.95**
>
> 40, Digital File IA4004_3589, **7.12**

The Art Institute of Chicago, Ryerson and Burnham Archives, Pond & Pond Collection, Digital File 200101.090515-34, **3.22**; Digital File 200101.080818-07, **3.30**

The Art Institute of Chicago, Ryerson and Burnham Libraries Book Collection, Archival Image Collection, Digital File 000000.090421-34, **2.60**

The Charles Hosmer Morse Museum of American Art, Winter Park, FL © The Charles Hosmer Morse Foundation: **3.57**, **3.59**, **3.60**, **7.49**

The Chicago History Museum: ICHI36660, **1.01**; ICHI65011, **1.05**; ICHI62325, **1.08**; ICHI65013, **1.22**; ICHI65018, **1.26**; ICHI65014, **1.27**; ICHI65026, **2.12**; ICHI65022, **2.37**; ICHI61477, **4.01**; ICHI65020, **5.01**, **5.24**

The Chicago History Museum

    Photograph by H. A. Atwell: ICHI65009, **5.12**

    Photograph by W. T. Barnum: ICHI65066, **3.14**

    Photographs by Hedrich Blessing: HB-04872A, **5.13**; HB-04872B, **5.14**;
        HB-03803N, **5.18**; HB 03923, **6.06**; HB-18341-A, **7.15**; HB15588A,
        7.20; HB15588J, **7.22**; HB-22339, **7.25**; HB 24243, **7.27**; HB-24243-B,
        7.28; HB-28403, **7.35**; HB-28403, **7.40**; HB-38308-D, **7.44**

    Photograph by Lil and Al Bloom: ICHI65025, **7.23**

    Photograph by the *Chicago Daily News*: DN-0075197, **4.03**; DN-0007275, **4.21**;
        DN-0061400, **4.42**; DN-0092530, **5.07**; DN-0077059, **5.08**; DN-075190, **6.05**

    Photograph by Copelin: ICHI65017, **3.91**

    Photograph by Charles T. Glanzer: ICHI65028, **5.03**

    Photograph by Larry Hemingway: ICHI65065, **3.10**

    Photograph by Betty Henderson Hulett: ICHI65016, **3.93**; ICHI35936, **6.09**

    Photograph by Kaufman & Fabry: ICHI65024, **4.27**

    Photograph by Mildred Mead: ICHI65010, **5.05**; ICHI65019, **6.04**; ICHI65021, **7.01**

    Photograph by J. Sherwin Murphy: ICHI25393, **4.32**; ICHI64985,
        7.02; ICHI65012, **7.10**; ICHI39003, **7.45**

    Photograph by Richard Nickel: ICHI65023, **3.50**

The Chicago History Museum and the Hyde Park Historical Society, photograph by Nancy
    Campbell Hayes: **1.21**

Chicago Tribune, September 30, 1908: **3.86**

Henry W. Cleaveland and William Samuel D. Backus, *Village and Farm Cottages: The Re-
    quirements of American Village Homes Considered and Suggested; With Designs for Such
    Houses of Moderate Cost* (New York: D. Appleton, 1856): **1.10**

Leslie Coburn: **2.58**, **3.13**, **4.24**, **4.25**, **4.28**, **7.24**

Susan Davis: **1.07**, **2.42**, **2.45**, **2.49**, **3.16**, **3.45**, **3.67**, **4.29**, **4.36**, **5.20**, **5.23**, **5.31**, **6.10**, **6.11–13**,
    7.18, **7.19**, **7.30**, **7.31**, **7.36**, **7.38**, **7.41**, **7.43**, **7.46**, **8.02**, **8.03**, **8.06**, **8.07**, **8.09**, **8.12**, **9.01**, **A.01**

Susan and Allison Davis, photographs by Hedrich Blessing: **8.14–16**

John Drury, *Old Chicago Houses* (Chicago, University of Chicago Press, 1941): **1.06**

Kevin Eatinger: **1.09**, **1.12–17**, **1.24**, **1.25**, **2.09**, **2.16**, **2.18**, **2.20**, **2.21**, **2.23**, **2.29–32**, **2.43**, **2.47**,
    2.48, **2.50**, **2.52**, **2.53**, **2.56**, **3.15**, **3.17–21**, **3.23–26**, **3.29**, **3.31–34**, **3.36**, **3.37**, **3.39–44**, **3.46**,
    3.48, **3.53–56**, **3.58**, **3.61**, **3.65**, **3.66**, **3.68–72**, **3.75–78**, **3.80–85**, **3.87–89**, **3.96**, **4.04**, **4.05**,
    4.08, **4.09**, **4.12**, **4.13**, **4.15–17**, **4.20**, **4.22**, **4.23**, **4.26**, **4.30**, **4.31**, **4.33–35**, **4.37–41**, **4.43**, **4.44**,
    5.09, **5.10**, **5.15–17**, **5.19**, **5.22**, **5.25**, **5.26**, **5.28–30**, **6.07**, **6.08**, **6.15**, **6.16**, **7.16**, **7.17**, **7.29**,
    7.32–34, **7.39**, **8.04**, **8.05**, **8.10**, **8.11**, **9.02**, **9.03**

Robert Philip Gordon, photographs by Ron Gordon: **7.47**, **7.48**

Bruce and Nancy Halbeck, Plan by Pond & Pond: **4.14**

Isaac H. Hobbs and Son, Philadelphia, *Hobb's Architecture, Containing Designs and Ground
    Plans for Villas, Cottages, and Other Edifices, Both Suburban and Rural Adapted to the
    United States. With Rules for Criticism, and Introduction* (Philadelphia: J. B. Lippincott
    & Co., 1873): **2.17**

Hyde Park Herald: **7.07**, **8.01**; photograph by Hedrich Blessing: **7.13**; photograph by Tony
    Griffin: **7.14**, **8.13**

Illinois Institute of Technology, The Paul V. Galvin Library: **3.09**

Inland Architect and News Record 6, no. 6 (December 1885): **2.22**; 8, no. 1 (January 1887): **2.24**

Charles D. Lakey, *Lakey's Village and Country Houses, or Cheap Homes for All Classes* (New
    York: American Builder Pub. 1875): **1.23**

The Library of Congress, Prints and Photographs Division, Historic American Buildings Sur-
    vey or Historic American Engineering Record, photograph by Cervin Robinson: **3.51**, **3.73**

J. B. McClure, *Stories and Sketches: Chicago* (Chicago: Rhodes & McClure, 1840): **2.04**

*New Cottage Homes and Details, Containing Nearly Two Hundred & Fifty New & Original
    Designs in All the Modern Popular Styles* (New York: Palliser & Co., c. 1887): **2.01**

Richard Nickel Committee, photograph by Richard Nickel, Chicago, Illinois: **3.74**

J. S. Ogilvie, *Ogilvie's House Plans; Or, How to Build a House* (Chicago: J. S. Ogilvie, 1885): **2.07**, **2.19**

The Pullman State Historic Site, Image 9554: **3.49**

Rapson Architects, photographs by Hedrich Blessing: **6.18**, **6.19**

Clemens and Judy Roothaan, from *Brickbuilder* 16, no. 2: **3.35**

Doug Snower Photography: **8.08**

Studio Gang Architects: **9.04**

University of Chicago Library: Map Collection: **3.06**; Special Collections Research Center: **1.18–20**, **2.02**, **2.03**, **2.05**, **2.06**, **2.08**, **2.10**, **2.11**, **2.13**, **2.14**, **2.25–27**, **2.33**, **2.34**, **2.36**, **2.38–41**, **2.44**, **2.55**, **3.01–05**, **3.07**, **3.08**, **3.11**, **3.12**, **3.38**, **4.02**, **4.06**, **4.10**, **5.04**, **5.11**, **6.01**, **6.03**, **6.14**, **6.17**, **7.03**, **7.05**, **7.06**, **7.08**, **7.09**, **7.11**, **7.26**, **7.37**, **7.42**

University of Melbourne Faculty of Architecture: **2.35**

University of Minnesota Libraries, Northwest Architectural Archives: American Terra Cotta Company Records: **5.06**, **5.27**; William Gray Purcell Papers: **4.18**, **4.19**

Tom Willcockson, Mapcraft.com: Sand ridges based on J. Harlen Bretz, *Chicago Area Geologic Maps*, State Geological Survey Division, 1930–1932, sheet 12: **1.02**; map based on St. Clair Drake and Horace Cayton, *Black Metropolis: A Study of Negro Life in a Northern City* (New York: Harcourt, Brace, 1945): **5.02**; **7.04**; maps for **1870** (p. 12), **1891** (p. 62), **1908** (p. 120), **1919** (p. 208), **1929** (p. 254), **1848** (p. 282), **1976** (p. 312), **2012** (p. 350)

Geo. E. Woodward and Edward G. Thompson, *Woodward's National Architect: Containing 1000 Original Designs, Plans and Details, to Working Scale, for the Practical Construction of Dwelling Houses for the Country, Suburb and Village. With Full and Complete Sets of Specifications and an Estimate of the Cost of Each Design* (New York: G. E. Woodward, 1869): **1.03**

Index of Addresses

Subject Index

Beman, Mary, 153–154, 373
Beman, Solon, 58, 59, 60, 75–77, 92, 111, 113,
    153–154, 177, 308, 372, 373, 379, 399, 425n38,
    453n15
Beman, W. Irving, 69–70, 373, 379
Beman, W. Riley, 76, 373
Bennett, Anna, 68
Bennett, Edward, 197, 198
Bennett, Frank, 68–69, 426n74
Bennett, John, 68
Benritter, Henry, 374
Berlin & Swern, 103
Bernham, Felix, 395
Berry, Jonathan, 14
Beyer, Jonathan, 328, 329
Bigott, Joseph, 23
Bishop, Alexander, 81–83
Bishop, Carrie, 81–83
Bishop, Thomas, 186, 269, 287–288, 335, 374
Black Belt, 205, 206, 243, 244, 250, 251, 275, 277,
    278
Black Hawk, 1, 87
black migration, 205, 243, 274, 277
Black, John, 381
Blackstone Library, 169
Blackstone, Timothy, 425n38
Blair, Chauncey, 191–192, 200, 238, 270, 275, 406,
    437n10
Blair, Mary, 191–192, 406
Block, Jean, xv, 6, 39, 105, 147, 227
Bloom, Allan, 256
Blossom, Carrie, 157, 414
Blossom, George, 157, 414
board and batten, 23, 214
Board of Trade, 2, 66, 79, 91, 190, 232, 233,
    426n63
Bock, Richard, 36, 173
Bockee, Catherine, 16–17
Bockee, Jacob, 16–17, 276, 421n83
Bogue & Hoyt, 24
Bogue, Hamilton, 183
Bogue, Warren, 183, 419n33
Bollenbacher, John, 385
Booth & Nagle, 334–335, 375, 409
Booth, John Wilkes, 88
Booth, Larry, 334, 375, 394
Born, Isabella, 194
Born, Moses, 194, 383
Borst & Hetherington, 375
Botsford, Charles, 21–22
Bouchard & France, 375
Bouton, Christopher, 40–41, 232, 290, 423n160,
    423n162
Bouton, Ellen, 40
Bouton, Nathaniel, 40, 423n162
Bouton, Nellie (Eleanora), 40–41, 232
Bouton, Persis, 41, 232
Boyce, Robert, 313, 332, 389
Boyd, John, 3, 418n18

Boyington, William W., 376, 382
Bradley, Mr., 67–68
Brainerd, Ezra Leander, 39, 423n160
Brainerd, Harriett (Hattie) Moorehouse, 39,
    423n160
Braun, Carol Moseley, 349, 451n42
Bremmer, Albert, 180
Brenner, Danforth, Rockwell, 411
Breuer, Marcel, 379
Bridges, Lyman, 20–21, 422n96
Brompton, James C., 143–144, 376
Brooks, Jonathan, 291–292
Brooks, Mary, 291–292
Bryan, William Jennings, 43
Brydges, E. Norman, 98
Bryson Hotel, 169, 307, 308, 373
Buchsbaum, E. V., 440n3
Bungalow style, 227, 249, 366
Burling & Adler, 415
Burnham Brothers & Hammond, 377
Burnham, Daniel Hudson, 84, 92, 111, 177, 178,
    241, 245, 346, 360, 431n30; in appendix, 372,
    377, 386, 388, 389, 409
Burnham & Root, 19, 53, 84, 91, 92, 97, 99, 100,
    108, 109, 115, 173, 249, 292; in appendix, 376,
    385, 395, 398, 403, 407
Burling & Adler, 382
Bush, George, 216
Busse, George, 73
Butler, Eugene, 332–333
Butler, Sarah, 332–333
Byrne, Barry, 139, 140, 248, 271, 377

Cady, Jeremiah, 385
Caldwell, Alfred, 360, 440n3
Calvert House, 140
Campbell, William, 25, 26
Capon, Al, 263
Carpenter, Frederick, 131–132, 400
Carpenter Gothic style, 20
Carroll, John A., 441n21
Carter, Drake & Wight, 376
Carton, Edith, 168, 395
Carton, Laurence, 168, 395
Century of Progress, 267, 273, 274; House of
    Tomorrow, 274, 284
Cermak, Anton, 278
Chateauesque style, 102, 192, 193
Chatten & Hammond, 377
Chautauqua, 130
Chicago Beach Hotel, 42, 124–125, 152, 204, 224,
    240, 245, 246, 247, 268, 275, 296, 315, 345,
    440n1
Chicago Beach Hotel Annex, 224–225, 395
Chicago Beach Towers, 225
Chicago Commission on Historical Landmarks,
    155, 329, 342, 343, 345, 347, 354, 355, 358
Chicago Housing Authority, 297
Chicago Lying-In Hospital, 226, 227

Chicago Plan Commission, 343
Chicago Public Library, 35, 425n38
Chicago Renaissance, 243, 271, 394
Chicago School of Sociology, 280
Chicago School style, 111, 148, 404
Chicago Theological Seminary, 14, 342, 352, 403;
    Faculty Quadrangle, 324–325, 379
Christian Science Church, 153, 453n15
Christy, Edwin, 20
Church, Archibald, 253, 385
churches: Augustana Evangelical Lutheran, 379;
    Episcopal Church of the Redeemer and Rec-
    tory, 218–219, 400; First Unitarian, 272; Hyde
    Park Lutheran, 186; Kenwood Evangelical,
    163, 376; St. John Episcopal, 59; St. Paul, 219;
    St. Stephen's (Tenth Church of Christ Sci-
    entist), 364–365; St. Thomas the Apostle, 110,
    139, 248, 377; University Church, Disciples
    of Christ, 405
City Hyde Park, 364, 366, 408
Civil War, 6, 16, 20, 24, 25, 39, 42, 44, 45, 47, 100
Clark & Fuller, 190
Clark & Trainor, 186
Clark, C. Everett, 190
Clark, Edwin, 395
Clarke, Col. George, 41–42, 239
Clarke, Sarah Dunne, 41–42
Classical Revival style, 249
Clay, William W., 372
Cleaveland, Henry, 20
Cleaver, Charles, 418n24, 424n170
Cleaver, Mary Brooks, 424n170
Cleaverville, 7, 42–45, 61, 281, 424n170
Cleveland, Horace W. S., 27–30, 48, 53, 55
Cloisters, 256, 385
clubs: Chicago Athletic, 185; Chicago Women's,
    36, 100; Cliff Dwellers, 142; Commercial, 185,
    192; Eleanor Club, 220, 404; Fortnightly, 36;
    Kenwood Barge, 59; Kenwood, 30, 33, 59, 60,
    117, 165–167, 185, 232, 337; Kenwood Country,
    89, 232, 437n11; Mendelssohn, 59, 88; Mid-
    Day, 185; Midlothian, 185; Quadrangle,
    117, 130, 247, 278, 405; Rosalie, 60, 373;
    Shakespeare, 59; Society for the Promotion
    of Physical Culture and Correct Dress, 100;
    South Park, 60; South Shore Country, 19,
    185; Washington Park, 59, 190, 425n37
Cobb, Henry Ives, 53, 102, 103, 104, 106, 107, 111,
    123, 378, 383, 403, 430n12
Cobb & Frost, 372, 378, 407
Cole, Arthur, 378
Cole & Dahlgren, 378, 441n17
Colonial style, 287
Columbian Exposition. *See* World's Columbian
    Exposition
Comiskey, Charles A., 261, 443n64
Comiskey, Grace, 261
commercial areas, 6, 58, 59, 63, 64, 73, 74, 75,
    110, 117, 196, 200, 203, 204, 242, 249, 306, 363

commons, 326, 384
Condit, Carl, 109, 280, 303
condominiums, 246
Cone & Dornbusch, 378
construction methods: balloon frame, 10,
    420n68; bearing wall, 323; iron frame, 72;
    post and beam, 10; reinforced concrete, 287,
    316–318, 366; steel frame, 90, 177, 274
conversions, 276
Cook, John, 77, 373
Coolidge & Hodgdon, 365
Coolidge, Charles, 405–406
Coolidge, Walter G., 53, 334–335
Cooper, James Fenimore, 223
Cooper-Carleton Hotel, 143, 223–224, 395
Cooper-Monotah Hotel, 239, 395
cooperatives, 246, 260, 263, 283, 313, 314, 321
Cornell, Eliza Hopkins, 14
Cornell, Helen Gray, 14–15, 421n73
Cornell, Hiram King, 14
Cornell, John, 14
Cornell, Paul: arrival in city, 2; establishment
    of Hyde Park, 5, 6, 7, 105, 107, 367, 418n19,
    418n20, 418n30, 430n11; fence war, 79, 80;
    Grand Crossing, 14, 419n135; hotels, 6, 15, 16,
    18, 29, 72, 73, 222; Illinois Central, 3, 5, 6,
    418n24; letter to Heman Hopkins, 2; parks, 9,
    10, 440n11; residence, 6, 14–15, 61, 69, 419n133
Cornell, Thomas, 14
Corwin, Cecil, 158
Cottage Grove Balloon Park, 59
Counselman, Charles, 91–92, 144, 248, 249, 377
Counselman Building, 91
Craig, Mosheim, 214–215, 404
Craig, W., 379
Crane, Richard, 138
crime, 11, 216, 242, 243, 251–253, 298, 299, 309,
    362, 446n24
Crosby's Opera House, 35
Cummins, Albert, 270–271, 371
Cummins, Myrna, 270–271, 371
Cushing, Edward, 290
Cushing, Mary, 290

Dahlgren, Rudolph, 378
Daley, Richard J., 337, 346
Daley, Richard M., 347
Danforth, Douglas, 13
Darrow, Clarence, 116, 252, 253, 442n48
Dart, Edward, 324–325, 379
Dau, J. J., 172–173, 187, 198, 391
Davis, Allison, 357–359, 411
Davis, Andrew Jackson, 17
Davis, David, 32
Davis, John, 338
Davis, Miles, 239
Davis, Susan, 357–359, 411
Davol, James, 42
Dean, Thaddeus, 332

Foursquare style, 288
Fox, Charles, 392
France, Roy, 375
Franks, Bobby, 229, 230–231, 251–253
Franks, Jacob, 230–231, 395, 437n185
French Provincial style, 256
French Renaissance style, 258
Fridstein, Meyer, 261–263, 382
Friedrich, Charles, 58
Frommann & Jebsen, 151, 382
Frothingham, Clara, 17
Frothingham, Herbert, 17
Frost & Granger, 172, 179, 180, 194, 195, 201, 383
Frost, Charles S., 152, 163, 165, 166, 167, 189, 190, 378, 383, 435n154
Fuller, Alonzo, 96, 97, 399
Fuller, Charlotte, 96–97, 399
Fuller, Emily Channing, 189–190
Fuller, Frank, 96–97, 399
Fuller, George A., 18, 72, 189–190, 383, 407, 407
Furber, Elvira, 83–84
Furber, Henry, 83–84
Furness, Frank, 409
Furst, Charles, 382
Fyfe, James, 227, 411

Gang, Jeanne, 364–365, 408
Gapp, Paul, 11
Garden, Hugh, 119, 130, 139, 140, 151, 383, 404, 454n37
Garnsey, Chester, 3
Garnsey, Electa Watson, 3
Garnsey, George, 13, 93, 384
Garrick Theater, 342
Gates, Ellen S., 431n40
Gatzert, August, 234, 397
Gatzert, Isabel, 234, 397
Gaye, Marvin, 239
Genius, Richard, 163, 287
Genius, Elizabeth Morse, 162, 163, 287, 288
Genther, Charles (Skip), 397
Georgian style, 147, 213
Gibbs, Frederick, 122
Gidwitz, Adele, 291–293, 402
Gidwitz, Gerald, 292
Gidwitz, Willard, 291–293, 402
Giedion, Sigfried, 211
Gill, Charles, 168
Gilman, Stephen, 345, 391
Gleason, Maurice, 328–329, 389
Gleason, Eliza, 328–329, 389
Goes, Arthur, 228
Goldberg, Bertrand, 41, 238, 280, 288–289, 289–290, 316–319, 325, 327–328; projects outside Hyde Park, 316
Goldsmith, Myron, 378
Goldstine, Ethel, 186
Goldstine, Max, 92, 186
Goodfriend, H. H., 250, 395

Goodhue, Bertram, 247, 248, 269
Goodman, Eva, 159, 410
Goodman, Kenneth, 159, 243
Goodman, William, 159, 276, 410
Goodspeed, Edgar, 147, 405
Gordon, Ezra, 326, 336–337
Gordon, Levin & Associates, 336–337, 384
Gordon, Robert, 338–339, 384
Gore, Albert, 216
Gorham Silver Co., 84, 427n106
Gothic/Gothic Revival style, 10, 17, 36, 106, 107, 137, 212, 247, 267, 285
Gottschalk, Gustav, 221, 261, 382
Gottschalk, Louis, 283–285, 389
Graff, Edwin, 232–233, 413
Graff, Josephine, 232–233, 413
Graham, Anderson, Probst & White, 390
Granger, Alfred H., 164, 383, 385, 435n154
Granger, Lowe & Bollenbacher, 256, 385
Grant, Ulysses, 35, 43
Grassell, Janey, 234, 413
Grassell, John, 233, 234, 413
Great Chicago Fire (1873), 29, 30, 35, 47, 48, 59, 81, 89, 161, 180, 194
Greek Revival style, 37, 38
Green, Adolphus, 92, 177–178, 377
Green, Esther, 177–178
Green, John, 13
Greenwald, Herbert, 315
Greenwood Park, 336
Greenwood row houses, 144
Griffin, Marion Mahony, 411
Griffin, Walter Burley, 377
Grimsley, Elizabeth, 43
Griswold, Henry, 85, 377
Gropius, Walter, 279
Gross, Samuel E., 143–144, 376
Grove Parkway, 52
Grunsfeld Schaeffer Architects, 385
Guard, Sam, 265
Guimard, Hector, 214
Guthman, Cecile Silberman, 291, 389
Guthman, Leo, 291, 389

Hale, George, 97
Hale, George Ellery, 99, 150, 377
Hale, Harriett, 130–131, 383
Hale, William E., 97–99, 100, 124, 377
Hale, William G., 124, 130–131, 150–151, 383
Hall, James P., 151, 403
Hammond, Charles, 377
Hampton House, 222
Hancock Building, 346
Handy & Cady, 253, 385
Hannaford, R. Ogden, 304, 414
Hansberry, Carl, 277, 297
Harding, George, 93–94
Harlan, Allison, 156, 414
Harper Court, 306, 364, 381

Harper, William Rainey, 36, 107, 123–124, 130, 147, 151, 362, 378, 405, 429n5

Harris, Albert, 81, 268, 269, 281, 413

Hartray, Jack, 322

Hartshorne Plunkard Architecture, 364

Hawes, Kirk, 81, 401

Hayden, Sophia, 408

Haymarket, 142

Hays, Charles, 319

Hecht, Ben, 241, 242, 243, 245, 441n17

Heckman, Tillie, 86–87

Heckman, Wallace, 86–87

Heller, Ida, 173–175, 414

Heller, Isidore, 173–175, 414

Helstein, Nina, 316, 317

Helstein, Rachel Brin, 316–319, 384

Helstein, Ralph, 316–319, 325, 384

Herrick, Harriett, 139–140, 383

Herrick, Robert, 118, 139–140, 204, 383

Hertz, John, 154, 235, 236

Hetherington, John Todd, 375, 385

Heun, Arthur, 229–230, 235–236, 386

Heyworth Building, 19

Heyworth, Cecile Young, 18

Heyworth, Lawrence, 17–19, 69

Heyworth, Marguerite, 17–19

Hibbard, Mrs. Homer, 419n32

Higgins & Furber, 84

Higgins, Elisabeth Alexander, 78, 427n88

Higgins, Van, 78–81, 84, 233, 234, 427n88

Higgins, Lena Morse, 427n88

Hilton, Charlotte, 212, 405

Hilton, Henry, 212, 213, 405

Hilton, Thorndike, 213

Hirsch, Arnold, 297

Hitchcock, Annie McClure, 1, 30, 33–37, 175, 269, 399, 423n148

Hitchcock, Charles, 33–37, 61, 423n150

Hodgdon, Charles, 406

Hodgkins, William, 186

Hoffa, Jimmy, 263

Holabird & Roche, 107, 148, 149, 183, 268–269; in appendix, 386, 392, 407

Holabird & Root, 99, 126, 269; in appendix, 386–387, 397

Holabird, John, 386

Holabird, William, 386, 388

Holden, Martha, 154

Holsman, Elizabeth, 387

Holsman, Henry, 134, 285, 387

Home Owners Loan Corporation, 275

Hook, Weller van, 134

Hooper, Obadiah, 1, 5, 417n1

Hopkins, Hassan, 5, 6, 7, 25, 216, 419n36

Hopkins, Heman, 2

Hopkins, John, 218

Hopkins, Sarah, 5

Horwitz, Irving, 311

hotels: Arizona Biltmore, 158, 435n144; Barry, 127; Beatrice, 108; Bryson, 169, 307, 308, 373; Century, 294; Chicago Beach, 42, 124–125, 152, 204, 224, 240, 245, 246, 247, 268, 275, 296, 315, 345, 440n11; Chicago Beach Annex, 224–225, 395; Cooper-Carleton, 143, 223–224, 395; Cooper-Monotah, 239, 395; Del Prado, 109, 126–127, 152, 204, 223; Elms, 375; Hotel Helene, 63–64; Hotel Marquette, 256; Hyde Park House, 6, 10, 15–16, 29, 72, 204, 222, 401, 430n11; Hyde Park, 18, 72–74, 109, 152, 204, 256, 364, 407, 421n78; Kenwood, 152–153, 245, 383; Lake House, 2; Leland, 42; Raymond & Whitcomb Grand, 112, 113, 126; Ritz, 245; Shore Drive Motel, 319–320, 381; Sisson, 222–223, 413; South Park, 8; Stevens (Chicago Hilton and Towers), 215–216; Sutherland, 239; Windermere, 109, 125–126, 240, 258–259; Windsor, 42

house moving, 17, 130, 267, 268, 443n73

Howland, Cora, 136, 402

Howland, George, 136, 402

Hoyt, Eleanora (Nellie), 40

Hoyt, Emily, 183

Hoyt, George W., 441n17

Hoyt, Mary Betteley, 25, 40

Hoyt, William, 8, 24–26, 40, 41, 97, 183

Hughitt, Belle, 435n154

Hughitt, Marvin, 164

Hughitt, Mary, 435n154

Hull-House, 116, 138, 139, 431n40

Hull, Charles, 412

Hull, Cordell, 140

Hull, Denison B., 272

Hunt, Jarvis, 185, 387

Hunt, Myron, 119, 388, 399, 406

Hunt, Richard, 111

Hutchins, Agnes, 163–164, 383, 413

Hutchins, James, 163–164, 383, 413

Hutchins, Robert Maynard, 123, 277

Hutchinson, Benjamin P., 66–67, 426n63

Hutchinson, Charles, 66–67

Hutchinson, Frances, 66

Hutchinson, Sarah, 67

Huxtable, Ada Louise, 111

Hyde Park: early descriptions, 419n32, 419n33; improvements, 6, 51, 80; map of village, 5; township government, 6, 7, 50, 419n42; village government, 49, 50, 60, 425n14

Hyde Park Bank, 64, 249, 273

Hyde Park Herald, 50, 59, 60, 70, 75, 85, 251, 340

Hyde Park Hotel, 18, 72–74, 109, 152, 204, 256, 364, 407, 421n78

Hyde Park House, 6, 10, 15–16, 29, 72, 204, 222, 401, 430n11

Hyde Park–Kenwood Community Conference, 74, 297, 298, 311, 341, 342

Hyde Park–Kenwood Townhomes, 333, 414

Hyde Park Lyceum, 35, 59, 425n38

Hyde Park YMCA, 117, 383, 385

Iannelli, Alfonso, 139, 207, 249, 271, 394

Illinois & Michigan Canal, 2, 418n20, 420n155

Illinois Central Hospital, 220, 404

Illinois Central Railroad, 34, 58, 117, 124, 241, 242, 248, 296, 301, 336; 1863 accident, 35, 37; demolition along, 306, 307; electrification, 245, 441n21; elevation of rail bed, 77, 109, 110; employees, 7, 32, 37, 38, 44, 45, 65; ridership, 5, 6, 418n26; stations, 4, 7, 49, 110; survey, charter, and initial route, xvi, 3, 5

Illinois Institute of Technology, 279

Ingals, Ephraim, 148–149, 386

Ingals, Lucy, 148–149, 386

interior images, 26, 95, 101, 103, 133, 145, 171, 175, 188, 211, 218, 231, 236, 262, 265, 293, 318, 330, 333, 339, 358

interiors, 21, 24, 25, 56, 57, 72, 90, 101, 109, 124, 145, 162, 166, 172, 211, 214, 228, 229, 231, 258, 260, 261, 264, 265, 279, 289, 338, 339, 343, 354

International style, 284, 285

Isaiah Israel Synagogue, 92, 248, 370

Italian Renaissance Revival style, 191

Italianate style, 10, 11, 14, 21, 23, 25, 26, 40, 55, 56, 78

Italianate Villa style, 78

Jackman, John, 75, 373

Jackman, Mrs. Wilbur, 147–148, 405

Jackman, Wilbur, 147–148, 405

Jackson Shore Apartments, 204, 221, 261, 402

Jackson Towers, 240, 260–261, 370

Jackson, Kenneth, 361, 444n9

Jacobs, Jane, 343, 363

James, Etta, 239

Jameson, Eliza, 419n33

Janowitz, Rebecca, 366

Jayne, Julia, 43, 44, 421n78, 424n175

Jenkins, Robert, 432n50

Jenney & Mundie, 111, 405

Jenney, Mundie & Jensen, 388

Jenney & Otis, 90–91, 268, 388

Jenney, William LeBaron, 90–91, 168, 372, 376, 379, 386, 388, 395, 399, 403, 409; Home Insurance Building, 48, 90, 388; Leiter Building, 90, 388

Jensen, Elmer, 388

Jensen, Jens, 182, 360, 437n185, 454n37

Johnson & Lee, 388

Johnson, Alvin, 192, 270, 388

Johnson, Davis, 13

Johnson, D. Gale, 320–321, 412

Johnson, Helen, 320–321, 412

Johnson, John, 292–293, 402

Johnson, Lydia, 90

Johnson, Phillip C., 388

Jones, Lynn C., 291, 389

Judd, Adeline, 31–33

Judd, Norman, 29, 31–33, 35, 53, 54, 91, 165, 166, 335, 424n175

Kahn, Louis, 379

Kalstedt, Harry, 243

Kamin, Blair, 343, 344

Kane, Scott, 353–354, 390

Karlin, Norman, 325–326, 389

Katzin, Frank, 289–290, 384

Keck & Keck, 55, 274, 280, 283–285, 313–314, 314–315, 325–326, 328–329, 330–332, 332–333; in appendix, 384, 385, 389

Kehilath Anshe Ma'ariv Synagogue (KAM), 91, 92, 249, 370, 395

Kelly, Edward, 278, 279

Kennedy, Ethel Skakel, 444n12

Kennedy, Robert F., 444n12

Kennicott Place, 355–356, 409

Kennicott, Jonathan, 7, 34, 356, 419n33, 419n45, 419n47; naming "Kenwood," 7

Kennicott, Marie Antoinette Fiske, 7, 59

Kenny, Larry, 411

Kenwood Astrophysical Observatory, 99, 377

Kenwood Club, 30, 33, 59, 60, 117, 165–167, 185, 232, 337

Kenwood Country Club, 89, 232, 437n11

Kenwood Gateway, 356–357, 409

Kenwood Hotel, 152–153, 245, 383

Kenwood Neighborhood Redevelopment Corporation, 299

Kenwood Open House Committee, 271, 298, 343

Kenwood Park/Farmer's Field, 81, 281

Kilbourn, Mrs. Frederick, 67–68

Kilburn, Edward, 80

Kimball, Eugene, 86, 432n48

Kimbark, Elizabeth Gray, 421n73

Kimbark, George M., 5, 9, 421n73

King, Martin Luther Jr., 301, 319

kitchenettes, 73, 276

Kleinpell, William, 375

Knoll Associates, 402

Koolhaas, Rem, 408

Krause, Edmund, 192–193, 401

Kroman, M. Louis, 73, 249, 389

Kruse, Roy H. & Associates, 389

Ku Klux Klan, 222

Kuklinski & Rappe, 353–354, 390

Kurusu, Alice, 140

Kurusu, Saburo, 140

labor unions: Amalgamated Clothing Workers, 183; Amalgamated Meat Cutters, 319; Pullman, 116, 442n48; United Packinghouse Workers, 319

Lake Calumet, 3

Lake Park Avenue, 83, 94, 118, 196, 200, 242, 245, 249, 300, 306, 336, 356, 357

Lake Township, 6

Lake Village East, 309, 336–337, 412

Mitchell, Robert, 278
Modernism, 139, 184, 273, 279, 280, 285, 286, 287, 290
Moderne style, 247, 249
Mohammed Ali, 234
Moholy-Nagy, Lazlo, 402, 457n154
Monadnock Building, 18, 177, 398
Monroe, Harriett, 122
Montgomery Place, 320, 394
Moore, Henry, 134, 278
Morgan, Charles, 263–265, 319, 390
Morgan, James, 17, 124, 224, 225, 246, 441n26
Morgan, Rebecca, 17
Morgan, Thomas, 1
Morris, Edward, 116, 237–238, 327, 405
Morris, Helen Swift, 237–238, 405
Morris, Nelson, 237
Morris, William, 432n53
Morse, Charles H., 160–163, 287, 288, 335, 339, 372
Morse, Martha, 160–163, 372
Morse Museum of American Art, 163
Morton, Chauncey, 335, 415
Morton's Restaurant, 319
Moutoussamy, John, 381
moving of houses, 17, 130, 267, 268, 443n73
Muhammad, Elijah Poole, 337–338, 393
Muhammad, Wallace, 338
Mumford, Lewis, 5, 10
Mundie, William, 388, 403
Museum of Science and Industry, 115, 182, 259, 342
Muybridge, Eadweard, 292
Myhrum, Arthur, 394

Nagle Hartray, 354–355, 394
Nagle, James, 334, 355, 375, 394
Narragansett, 240, 247, 320, 390
Nation of Islam, 337, 338, 358
National Register of Historic Places, 36, 138, 173, 223, 266, 345
Native Americans: Potawatomie, 1; themes, 223, 224, 263, 264, 315, 316
Neemes, John, 81
Neilson, Francis, 238
Nelson, Claudius, 20
Nelson, Walter, 20
Newhouse & Bernham, 223–224, 239, 395
Newhouse, Henry, 230–231, 248, 267, 395
Newman, Marsh and Baskerville Flat, 217–218
Nichols, Mike, 295
Nimmons, George, 173, 224–225, 245, 381, 395, 441n7
Nimmons & Fellows, 134, 135, 181, 182, 245, 246, 343, 395
Nobel Prize, 134, 149, 255, 256, 352
Nolan, Emily, 100, 377
Nolan, John, 100, 377
Nomura, Kichisaburo, 140
North Kenwood, 83, 86, 87, 154, 156, 198, 307, 344, 345, 347

Norton, Charles, 8

O'Donnell, Wicklund, Pigozzi & Peterson, 391
O'Leary, Catherine, 47
O'Leary, Patrick, 47
Oak Woods, 7, 15
Obama, Barack, xiii, 186, 187, 349, 361, 365, 366, 367, 374
Obama, Michelle Robinson, 366
Ogilvie, John Stuart, 54
Olmsted & Vaux, 48, 420n64
Olmsted, Frederick, 9, 10, 52, 108, 111, 117, 348, 431n44
Olsen, Paul Frederick, 395
Olympics, 1904, 84, 428n114
Operation PUSH, 248
Osborne, William, 6
Otis, William, 91, 168, 388, 395
Ottenheimer, Henry, 234
Ottenheimer, Stern & Reichert, 234, 396

PACE, 286–287, 315–316, 384, 397
Pacific (Beer) Garden Mission, 42
Page, Florence, 90–91, 388
Page, Harvey L., 397
Page, William, 90–91, 388
Palladian style, 157, 172, 223
Palm Grove Inn, 319
Palmer, Charles M., 397
Parker, Francis, 148
Parmentier, Fernand, 373
patent medicine, 102, 429n168
pattern books, 11, 17, 20, 38, 46, 54, 68, 69, 93, 353, 356
Patton & Fisher, 95, 165, 166, 397–398
Patton, Norman, 95, 397–398
Peabody & Sterns, 111, 189, 378, 383
Pearce, J. Irving, 16
Pei Cobb Freed & Partners Architects LLP, 398
Pei, I. M., 302, 310, 321, 322, 323, 398
Pelli, Cesar, 362
Perkins, Chatten & Hammond, 377
Perkins, Dwight, 36, 107, 119, 129, 141, 175–176, 176–177, 184, 398–399, 405, 406
Perkins, Frederick, 56, 96–97, 192–193, 209, 399
Perkins, Marian Heald, 33, 36
Perkins, Marland Leslie, 33
Piano, Renzo, 159
Piccadilly Theater and Apartments, 256–258, 402
Picturesque Kenwood, 31, 54, 55, 65, 73, 78, 79, 82, 83, 85, 86, 89, 199, 290, 292, 332, 335
Pioneer Cooperative, 314
Plan of Chicago, 192, 197, 198
Poinsettia Apartments, 266–267, 410
Pond & Pond, 87, 119, 127, 129, 131–133, 138, 142, 201, 399–400
Pond, Allen, 198, 205, 399–400
Pond, Irving, 388, 399–400

population: Chicago, 2, 47, 197, 295, 420n68, 437n11; Hyde Park, 49, 59, 247, 297, 364, 446n10, 452n6; Kenwood, 296, 307, 311, 452n6; North Kenwood, 347

Post, George, 111

postmodern style, 352

Potter, Agnes, 163–164

Potter, Delonas, 86

Potter, Edward, 164, 167, 198, 383

Potter, Orrin, 163, 383, 454n55

Powers, Horace Swett, 407

Powhatan, 240, 247, 263–265, 320, 379

Prairie Avenue, 18, 66, 119

Prairie School style, 36, 119, 141, 149, 150, 151, 157, 172, 205, 209–211, 213, 217, 226, 342

Presbyterian Theological Seminary of the Northwest, 4, 17, 107, 430n11

Prescott, W. B., 13

Pridmore, John E. Oldaker, 218–219, 400

Prohibition, 242, 440n6

Promontory Apartments, 279, 286–287, 394

Promontory Point, 221, 241, 360, 440n3

property owners' associations, 250; Hyde Park–Kenwood Property Owners Association, 206, 251; Hyde Park Protective Club, 206; Woodlawn Property Owners Association, 277, 444n16

Pruyn, William, 233, 389, 400–401

public housing, 303, 304, 336, 446n4, 447n54, 454n37

Pullman Car Co., 38, 40, 75, 76, 116, 153

Pullman, Florence, 151

Pullman, George M., 17, 58, 69, 151

Pullman strike, 116, 442n48

Purcell, Feick & Elmslie, 217–218, 401

Purcell, Michael, 419n32, 419n36

Quadrangle Club, 117, 130, 247, 278, 405

Queen Anne style, 56, 57, 71, 95, 161, 355

racial boundaries, 206, 207, 243–244, 275, 277, 296, 297, 438n28

Rae, Robert Jr., 401

Raeder, Henry, 381

Randall, C. E., 410

Randall, Gurdon P., 6, 15, 401, 430n11

Rankin, J. C., 384

Rapp & Rapp, 136–138, 204, 221, 256–258, 258–259, 401–402

Rapp, Cornelius, 401–402

Rapp, George, 242, 401–402

Rappe, Scott, 353–354, 389

Rapson, Ralph, 280, 291–293, 339, 385, 402

Raymond & Whitcomb Grand Hotel, 112, 113, 126

Reagan, Jack, 349

Reagan, Nellie, 349

Reagan, Ronald, 349

redlining, 275

Regent's Park, 225, 345, 381

rehabilitation/renovation, 330; modernization/remodeling, 311, 332; restoration, 346, 347

Reichert, William C., 396, 402

Remmer, Elizabeth, 37–38

Remmer, John, 7, 37–38, 419n48

Remmer, Mary, 423n157

Republican Party, 13, 32, 43, 44, 61, 79, 105, 136, 207, 278, 349, 418n13

restrictive covenants, 187, 251, 275, 277, 278, 296, 444n18

Reynolds, Frederick, 77, 373

Rhythm Liquors, 296

Rice, Edith, 161, 372

Rice, Theodore, 161, 372

Richardson, Henry H., 56, 87, 93, 97, 162, 190, 191, 370, 394, 398, 406; design of Marshall Field & Co., 48

Richardson, William, 14

Riddle & Riddle, 213–214, 403

Riddle, Elizabeth, 213–214

Riddle, Herbert, 213–214, 403

Riddle, Lewis, 213–214, 403

riparian rights, 124, 125, 224, 225, 241, 268, 269, 440n1

Ritz 55th Garage, 249, 389

Robie House, 205, 209–211, 255, 256, 342, 343, 348, 414

Robie, Frederick, 209–211, 414

Robie, Lora, 209–211, 414

Robinson, Argyle, 131, 146, 150, 392, 403

Roche, John, 136

Roche, John Jr., 136–137, 402

Roche, Martin, 386, 388

Rockefeller Chapel, 247, 248

Rockefeller, John D., 104, 105, 107

Rogers, James Gamble, 107, 144–145, 198, 403

Rogers, John, 542n2

Romanesque Revival style, 56, 87, 92, 97, 101, 165, 194, 288, 332, 333

Rookery, 18, 48

Roosevelt, Eleanor, 140

Roosevelt, Franklin D., 134, 140

Root, Ebenezer, 420n54

Root, George F., 8, 420n54

Root, John Wellborn, 56, 84, 92, 100, 111, 387, 398, 431n30

Root, John Wellborn Jr., 386

Rosalie Club, 60, 373

Rosalie Music Hall, 59, 76

Rosalie Villas, 58, 59, 75–77, 92

Rosenwald, Julius, 115, 181–182, 234, 235, 340, 343, 385, 395, 437n185

Rosenwald, Mae, 182, 405

Rosenwald, Morris, 181, 182, 234, 405, 437n185

Rostand, Edmund, 143

Rubloff, Arthur, 327

Runnion, James, 9, 10, 32, 39, 41, 42

Rush Medical College, 7

Rush, Katherine, 134, 135, 395

Ruskin, John, 432n53
Russell, Lillian, 84
Rutan, Charles, 405–406
Ryerson, Martin, 101–102, 107, 116, 410

Saarinen, Eero, 293, 348, 379
Saarinen, Eliel, 402
Sachse, Sophia, 421n72
Sachse (Saxchi), Theodore, 13, 421n72
Sagan, Bruce, 75, 301, 303
Sampson, Guy, 20
Samuelson, Tim, 138, 139, 234, 318
Sandburg, Carl, 122, 342
Sandegren, Andrew C., 404
Scammon Garden at the Laboratory Schools,
     29, 215
Scammon, Jonathan Young, 9, 15, 27–30, 138
Scammon, Maria Sheldon Wright, 27–30
Schaffner, Joseph, 183, 358, 386
Schaffner, Sarah, 183, 386
Schlacks, Henry, 396
Schmidt, Garden & Martin, 194, 214, 215, 220,
     389, 404
Schmidt, Richard, 220, 382, 383, 404
Schoenfeld, Frank, 226
Schoenstadt, Herman, 256, 257
schools: Akiba Schechter, 186; Chicago Normal
     School of Physical Education, 159, 276; Elm-
     wood Home, 85; Faulkner School for Girls,
     82; Harvard School for Boys, 41, 164, 251; St.
     George's for Girls, 164; Starrett for Girls, 193
Schuyler, Benjamin, 16
Schweikher, Paul, 379, 384
Schweppe, Laura, 193
Scully, Vincent, 324, 426n67
Sears (Willis) Tower, 346
Sears, Roebuck & Co., 135, 181, 235
Second Chicago School style, 279
Segments of the Past, 342
Selfridge, Harry, 75, 198
Shaw, Frances Wells, 94, 128, 165, 405
Shaw, Howard van Doren, 94, 128, 129–130,
     146–147, 147–148, 159, 165, 169, 182, 201, 212,
     228–229, 237–238, 267; in appendix, 383,
     404–405
Shaw, Weldon, 154
Shedd, John Graves, 192–193, 399
Shedd, Mary, 192–193, 399
Sheehan, Peggy, 30–31
Sheehan, Thomas, 30–31
Shelley v. Kraemer, 297
Shepley, Georges, 405–406
Shepley, Rutan & Coolidge, 36, 191, 200, 383,
     388, 405–406, 411
Sherman, John D., 8, 420n51
Sherman, Mary Belle, 420n51
Sherman, Pennoyer, 7, 8, 33
Sherman, William Tecumseh, 25
Sherman, William Watts, 93

Shingle style, 71
Sholes, Clarence, 25, 26
Shore Drive Motel, 319–320, 381
Shoreland, 221, 261–263, 382, 408, 440n4
Short, Albert, 257
Silberman, Cleo, 291
Silberman, David, 291
Silsbee, Joseph, 391, 401, 411, 414
Silverman, Louis, 340, 343
Sippy, Bertram, 212, 405
Sisson, Harry, 222, 413, 440n1
Sisson Hotel, 222–223, 413
Skakel, Ethel, 444n12
Skidmore, Owings & Merrill, 309, 397, 406, 411,
     412, 414
Skinner & Hoyne, 2
Skinner, Mark, 2
Smith, Alice, 190, 376
Smith, Charles, 190, 376
Smith, George, 9
South East Chicago Commission, 299, 301, 304,
     320
South Park, 75–77, 110
South Park System: as boundaries, 51, 119, 207;
     board, 268, 440n1; commission, 9, 49, 65,
     198; creation/plans, 9, 10, 27, 35, 48, 420n63;
     Grove Parkway, 52; Jackson (Lake) Park, 48,
     49, 51, 108, 109, 431n44; Midway Plaisance,
     48; Shore Drive, 241, 242, 441n21; South
     Shore development, 240, 241, 245, 440n13;
     Washington (South) Park, 48, 49, 51
South Shore Country Club, 19, 185
South Shore neighborhood, 17, 19, 281, 309
Spalding, Albert, 79, 80, 443n64
Spalding, Josephine, 79
Spanish Colonial style, 266, 269
Spellman, Amelia, 143
Spencer & Powers, 406–407, 410
Spencer, Robert Closson, 129, 399, 406–407
Spooner, Frank, 267, 268, 388
Spooner, Maria, 267, 268, 388
Sprague, Henry H., 407
St. Thomas the Apostle, 110, 139, 248, 377
Starbuck, Henry F., 407
Starr, Ellen Gates, 139
Starrett & Fuller, 72, 124, 407–408
Starrett, Goldwin, 437n11
Starrett, Paul, 72, 407
Starrett, Theodore, 72, 407–408
Steinway Hall, 119, 129, 141, 185, 399, 406
Stephen, James, 66
Stern, Isaac, 396
Stevens, Ernest, 215–216
Stevens, John Paul, 215–216
Stevens, Raymond, 216
Stick style, 66, 67
Stickley, Gustav, 36
Stiles & Stone, 408
Stilwell, Homer, 185, 198

urban renewal and redevelopment, 295, 299, 311, 313, 315, 321, 326, 327, 332, 333, 356; displacement and relocation, 308, 309; financing, 302; Hyde Park A and B, 301, 302, 308, 310, 447n38; *Hyde Park Herald*, 301, 303, 305; land clearance, 294, 297, 301, 362; South Campus, 303; Southwest Hyde Park Redevelopment Corporation, 302

Urban Renewal Plan, 74, 301, 302, 303, 305, 306, 307, 308, 311

Van Brunt & Howe, 111
Van der Meulen, 291–293, 402
Van Hook, Weller, 134
Van Inwegan, Mrs., 22
Van Osdel, John Mills, 376, 410
Vaux, Calvert, 9, 10, 55
Veeck, Bill, 330
Veeck, Mary Frances, 330
veteran's housing, 276
Vierling, Clara, 176–177, 399
Vierling, Robert, 176–177, 209, 399
Vignoly, Raphael, 348
village government, 49, 60, 425n14
Vincent, George, 129–130, 405
Vinci, John, ix–xi, 358, 411
Vinci/Hamp, 265, 357–359, 411
Vitzhum & Co., 249
Von Holst & Fyfe, 227, 411

Wadsworth, Henry, 27
Wait, Ada, 175–176, 399
Wait, James, 175–176, 399
Walker, George, 42
Ward, Montgomery, 53
Washington, Harold, 17, 222, 349, 451n42
Washington Park Club, 59, 190, 425n37
Washington Park subdivision, 277, 278, 297
Waterman, H. H., 176–177, 184–185, 411
Waters, William, 7, 419n48
Watkins, Maurine, 243
Watson, Electa, 3
Watson, J. B., 17
Watson, Mary, 17
Watson, Nathan, 1, 2, 3, 417n4, 418n19; tavern of, xvi, 3, 4, 5, 417n2
Watson, Vernon, 410
Webb & Knapp, 302, 310, 323, 342
Weese & Associates, 302, 310, 320–321, 321–322, 323, 336, 337, 384, 412
Weese, Ben, 321, 323, 337, 412
Weese, Harry, 321, 322, 326, 337, 362, 365, 412
Weese, Robert, 321
Weil, Julius, 181, 234, 370
Wells, Brenton, 94
Wells, Moses, 94, 165
Western Association of Architects, 55
Western Engineering Company, 202
Wheeler, Harry, 144

Wheelock & Clay, 398
Wheelock, Otis, 20, 371
Windermere East, 258–259, 402
Whitehouse, Fran, 386
Whiton, L. K., 129
Wiles, Ethel, 141, 399
Wiles, Russell, 141, 176, 399
Willard, Mary, 37
Williams, Alice, 190
Williams, Eugene, 207
Williams, John, 190
Williamson, George, 88, 89
Williamson, Josephine, 89
Williamson, Samuel, 88
Wilson & Freer, 2
Wilson, Horatio R. & Company, 178, 222, 232, 233, 267, 278, 413
Wilson & Marble, 392, 412
Wilson & Marshall, 178, 392, 413
Wilson, Thomas, 228–229
Windermere, 109, 125–126, 240, 258–259
Wing, Thomas, 292
Wolf Lake, 252
women's roles, 54, 55, 250
Wong, Y. C., 304, 329–330, 333–334, 414, 447n54
Woodpile (Woodville, South Park), 7, 8, 21, 22, 40, 52, 61, 75
Woods, Nellie, 148, 386
Work, Henry, 19–20
Work, Sarah, 19–20
World's Columbian Exposition, 108–115; accommodations, 72, 108, 109, 110, 124, 125, 126, 127, 152; architects, 111, 273; buildings and villages, 109, 111, 113, 114, 115, 127, 154, 181–181, 292, 373, 378, 390, 414, 431n28; hotels constructed for, 105, 109, 124, 125, 126, 127, 152; site, 105, 108, 109, 112, 430n17; transportation, 77, 109, 110
Wright, Catherine Tobin, 157
Wright, Frank Lloyd, 118, 119, 129, 217, 234, 256, 338, 360, 435n44; in appendix, 377, 383, 391, 396–397, 399, 401, 405, 406, 407, 409, 411, 414; "bootleg" houses, 156–158; Heller house, 173–175; Midway Gardens, 139, 207; Robie House, 205, 209–211, 255, 256, 342, 343, 348
Wright, John, 9

Yerkes, Walter, 385
Young, Otto, 18

Zeckendorf, William, 302, 321, 342, 343
Zeisler, Fannie Bloomfield, 142–143, 400
Zeisler, Sigmund, 142–143, 400
Zimmerman, Emily, 71
Zimmerman, William Carbys, 71, 382, 415
Zisook, David, 311
Zisook, Edmund, 335, 415
Zisook, Harry, 269, 335, 374, 375, 415
Zisook, Marian, 269, 374, 375
zoning violations, 446n18